13th IADIS International Conference on Cognition and Exploratory Learning in Digital Age (CELDA 2016)

Mannheim, Germany
28 - 30 October 2016

ISBN: 978-1-5108-3210-7

Printed from e-media with permission by:

Curran Associates, Inc.
57 Morehouse Lane
Red Hook, NY 12571

CURRAN ASSOCIATES INC. proceedings.com

Some format issues inherent in the e-media version may also appear in this print version.

Printed by Curran Associates, Inc. (2016)

For permission requests, please contact
the International Association for Development of the Information Society (IADIS)
at the address below.

International Association for Development of the Information Society (IADIS)
Rua Sao Sebastiao Da Pedreira
No. 100, 30, 1050-209
Lisbon, Portugal

Phone: 351 21 3151373
Fax: 351 21 3151244

secretariat@iadis.org

Additional copies of this publication are available from:

Curran Associates, Inc.
57 Morehouse Lane
Red Hook, NY 12571 USA
Phone: 845-758-0400
Fax: 845-758-2633
Email: curran@proceedings.com
Web: www.proceedings.com

TABLE OF CONTENTS

FULL PAPERS

SHORT PAPERS

REFLECTION PAPERS

Full Papers

A SERVICE-LEARNING PROJECT USING CROWDFUNDING STRATEGY: STUDENTS' EXPERIENCE AND REFLECTION

Jessnor Elmy Mat-jizat and Khalizul Khalid
Universiti Pendidikan Sultan Idris

ABSTRACT

The aim of this study was to explore students' experience and reflection in doing a Service Learning project as part of their course work. The Service Learning project allows the students to practice their knowledge of raising capital through crowdfunding, and at the same time situates them in an environment where they could learn from the community and provide services to them. After the students had completed their project, they were given a set of questionnaire that asked them about their experience and reflection. The findings showed that the students were able to understand their civic responsibility better and at the same time they were willing to self-learn and be creative when they were given an interesting task which they were passionate about, and the task was an authentic, real-life situation which was familiar to them. The researchers hope that more courses in Universities and schools in Malaysia would integrate Service Learning into their courses with a hope that it could enhance civic responsibility and increase moral values among Malaysians.

KEYWORDS

Service learning, crowdfunding, authentic learning, Malaysia

1. INTRODUCTION

Service Learning had been identified as a teaching strategy that offers students opportunities to learn both in the classroom and in the wider world (Levesque-Bristol, Knapp & Fisher 2010). This pedagogical tool can provide students with chances to directly interact with local agencies and effect change in the community. However, most universities were too focused on improving students' professional skills and knowledge, rather than emphasising the importance of service within the community and civic responsibility (Bringle & Hatcher 1996). By participating in a Service Learning activity, previous studies had shown a significant positive effects on students' academic performance, values, leadership and professional development (Astin et al. 2000; Mahasneh et al. 2012). Service Learning could also increased students' awareness of the world, sense of responsibility and increase their personal values.

Lately, there were an increasing number of reported cases been highlighted in the news regarding bullies, gangsterism and robberies involving teenagers in Malaysia. Few researchers suggested that the declining moral values were caused by unfiltered media exposure via television and the Internet (Buerah et al. 2012; Wan Norina et al. 2013). Others blame the current educational system (Mohamad Khairi & Asmawati 2010; Muhamad Suhaimi et al. 2011), and the failing of family institutions (Adeline Annet, Mohd Mahzan & Abdul Razaq 2015). Based on the findings of previous researchers, it was anticipated that by incorporating Service Learning as part of students' academic requirement, it could help to increase students' civic responsibility and at the same time improve students' discipline and moral values.

2. SERVICE LEARNING IN EDUCATION

Bringle and Hatcher (1996) defines Service Learning as "a credit-bearing, educational experience in which students participate in an organised service activity that meets identified community needs and reflect on the service activity in such a way as to gain further understanding of the course content, a broader appreciation of the discipline, and an enhanced sense of civic responsibility" (p. 222). Service Learning offers effective pedagogical strategies, promotes a scholarship of engagement among students and institutions, fosters a more active citizenry, and enhances student development through active learning and participation, engagement in the community, critical thinking, and information on real-life conflictual situations (Bringle & Hatcher 1996; Butin 2010).

In Malaysia, Service Learning is still in its infancy. There were a few private and public universities as well as schools that attempted to implement the concept of Service Learning in their institutions. However, the numbers were still too small. Service Learning had only been explored in Malaysia around the year 2005, while in developed countries Service Learning had been researched and integrated into the academic curriculum a decade earlier.

Though it has many similarities with charity and community service, Service Learning emphasised more on the 'learning' rather than 'service'. The focus of Service Learning was to promote both academic knowledge and civic skills of students. Students would go to the community, try to understand their needs, and then try to apply their knowledge and skills in a real situation to help solve community problems (Hamdan et al. 2015; Lemieux & Allen 2007). The process of Service Learning was described as the acquisition, discovery and reflection of skills and knowledge through experience (Reinke 2003). Aside from developing civic propensities, Service Learning could also enhance academic learning and higher thinking skills among students (Howard 2003).

3. CROWDFUNDING STRATEGY

Crowdfunding is a new alternative of raising enough business capital from a large number of people to start a new business (Profatilov, Bykova & Olkhovskaya 2015). Previously, to start a small business, business owner tend to rely on their own savings, family and friends.

Currently, there are many crowdfunding platforms had been developed such as Indiegogo, Kickstarter, FundMe and PitchIN. The platform provides opportunities for new business to pitch their business ideas to anyone with Internet access and raise enough money to realise their business plan. Currently, the crowdfunding platforms were not limited to business fund only, but also includes campaigns for educational support, new film/album creation, new technology creation and community services.

To start a crowdfunding campaign, business owners will need to create a creative business pitch video which will be uploaded to the crowdfunding platform. They will also need to decide on the total targeted fund that they wanted to achieve and how long the campaign would last. Each successful campaign will need to pay around 5% campaign fees to the crowdfunding platform. However, some crowdfunding platform allows 0% campaign fees if the campaign is for a charity cause (example: Indiegogo).

4. RESEARCH OBJECTIVES

This study explores the experience and reflections of a group of Malaysian University students' in relation to a service learning project conducted for their classes. A recent technology-based strategy which is crowdfunding was introduced as the strategy that the students' employed to help selected non-government organisations (NGO).

The objectives of this study were to explore:

i. students' experience after the Service Learning project; and
ii. students' reflection on the Service Learning project.

5. THE SERVICE LEARNING PROJECT

At the beginning of the semester (end of February 2016), 98 students from the Faculty of Business and Management, Sultan Idris Education University registered for the E-Commerce class, which runs for 14 weeks. The students were given an assignment sheet that contains the instruction for their class project, which was a Service Learning project. To tie in with the E-Commerce class requirement and objectives, the students were required to create a crowdfunding video to help Non-government Organisation (NGO) to raise money for their needs. Crowdfunding was one of the options for raising business capital discussed during lecture. The aim of this project was to allow the students to practice their knowledge of raising capital through crowdfunding, and at the same time situate them in an authentic environment where they could learn from the community and provide services to them.

The class project was a four to five members group project and was divided into three main phases which were pre-production, video production and post-production activities. Figure 1 showed the three main phases and the activities in each phase:

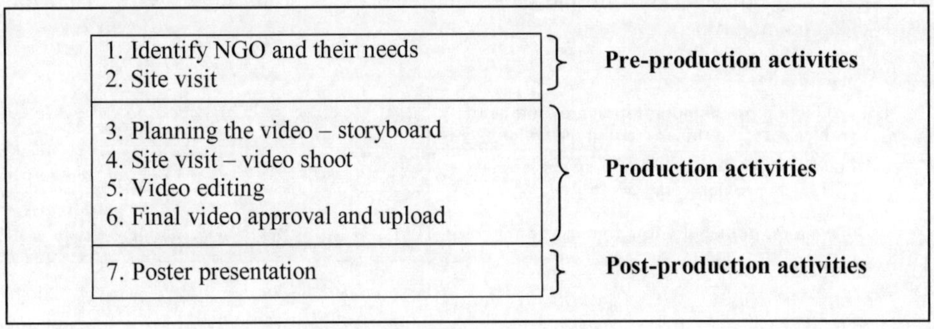

Figure 1. Project development phases

For the first three weeks of their class, the students need to complete the pre-production activities. Each group was required to submit a brief introduction of their selected NGO to their lecturers for approval. Upon approval, the students had eight weeks to plan, complete and uploaded their crowdfunding video either to a crowdfunding website (such as Indiegogo, GoFundMe or PitchIN) or a social networking sites (such as Facebook or Youtube). By week-13, each group had to do a poster presentation of their Social Learning project experience, and their presentations were evaluated based on:

i. the ability of each group to properly introduce their NGO and the purpose of the needed fund;
ii. the explanation on how they create their crowdfunding video;
iii. the impact made by their crowdfunding video (either monetary or an increase of awareness); and
iv. their creativity in creating the video and conveying the correct message.

6. METHODOLOGY

A questionnaire was developed based on the Student Service Learning Survey questionnaire developed by the American Association of Community Colleges (2004) through its Community Colleges Broadening Horizons through Service Learning project.

The questionnaire was divided into three sections. Section A was for demographic information: gender, semester, course and the name of their selected NGO. Section B consisted of 15 questions that describe the students' experience after they completed the Service Learning project. The students need to indicate their beliefs and attitudes towards each of the issues raised by the question on a numerical interval marked between 4 for Strongly Agree to 1 for Strongly Disagree. Finally, for Section C, the students were required to write their reflections based on their experience in doing the Service Learning project.

The questionnaires were distributed to the students after they had completed their final phase, which was the poster presentation. All 98 questionnaires were returned and analysed.

7. DATA ANALYSIS AND DISCUSSION

The NGOs selected by the students consists of institutions that provide services for the orphanage, old folks homes, old folks transit center, homeless, stray cats, and *pondok* (private religious school) education. Section B of the questionnaire describes the students' experience in completing the Service Learning project. The questionnaire was consisting of 15 items which were divided into three constructs: 1) student awareness (3 items); 2) integration of Service Learning into University courses (6 items); and 3) impact of Service Learning (6 items).

For student awareness (Figure 1), mean analysis showed that all students had a positively high awareness on the needs and problem faced by the community and the students were aware of their responsibility towards their community.

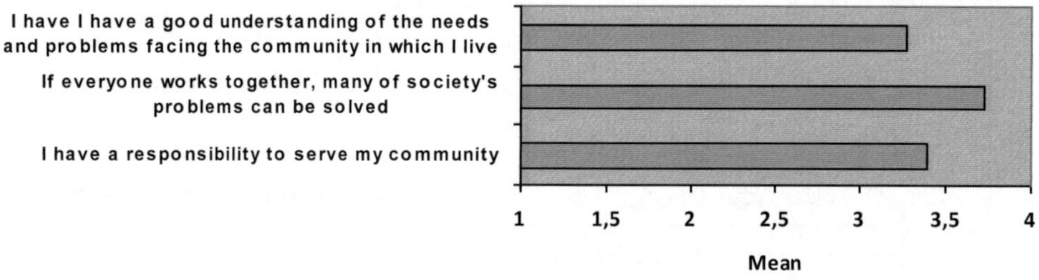

Figure 2. Mean values for student awareness

Most of the student understands that to improve the well-being of the community is a team effort (mean = 3.725). Everyone must work together, no matter how small the contribution; it does make a difference to the community.

For integration of Service Learning into university courses (Figure 2), most of the students agree that there should be more courses that include Service Learning into the course work. However, the students were in-between when asked whether they would continue volunteering or participating in the community after the end of the course (mean = 1.898). Some students were not certain when asked about their own biases and prejudice. They somewhat agree that the Service Learning project made them realise of their own biases and prejudices (mean = 3.061).

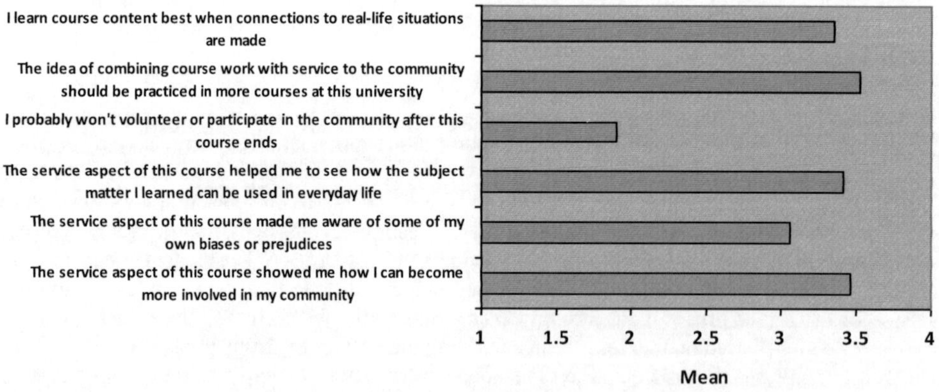

Figure 3. Mean values for integration of service learning into university courses

Figure 3 showed the mean values for the third construct which was the impact of the Service Learning project. The students were not sure whether the Service Learning project for this class was beneficial for the community (mean = 1.950). This could probably cause by either the explanation about the project were not clearly presented, or the students were not able to understand their role in this project as this was the first time a Service Learning project was introduced as part of their course work requirement.

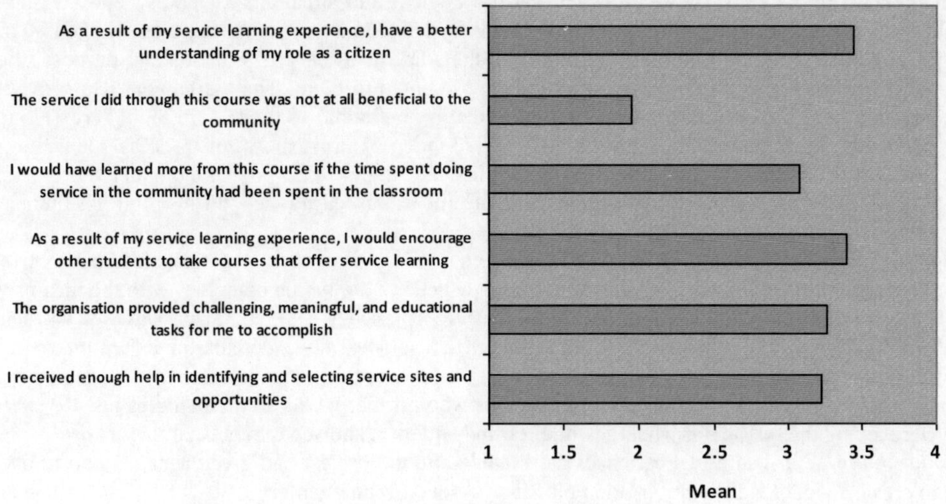

Figure 4. Mean values for impact of service learning

Section C of the questionnaire, the students was asked to write a reflection based on their Service Learning experience. All students reflected that we need to be thankful for what we had. Some students described that the Service Learning project had changed their perspective and they learn to be more empathetic towards others. One student quote:

> This project had opened my eyes and I feel excited and a sense of responsibility to help more people who are unfortunate. Before this I never really cared about others, but now I know that not everybody is as fortunate as I am and seeing their smile made me feel happy.

Another student felt that the Service Learning project had made him realised that he actually had the ability to help other people.

> What I learned from this project is that I actually had the ability to help and find ways to help those who were unfortunate.

Some students expressed that the project helped them to be confident in public. They were initially unsure how they were going to approach the people in their selected institution. One student described that she is usually shy and quiet. However, this project had taught them to be more organised, more confident and opportunity for them to practice their communication skills.

Two students wrote that this project had shown them an alternative way of raising money for the unfortunate using technology. Not only that but they also realised that there were procedures to be followed if you wanted to raise money for charity causes.

> I learn how to correctly use crowdfunding to help others raise money. There are procedures that I need to follow. Not as easy as I thought.

> I learn how to raise money following the correct procedure, as to ensure that there will be no misappropriate used of the money that we raised.

8. OBSERVED UNIQUE STUDENT EXPERIENCE

Lately, educators in Malaysia were highly encouraged to adapt a different style of student learning where students would apply their knowledge in a real-life context and situations as it was believed that students would learn and understand more by applying their knowledge in an authentic situation (Hursen 2016). Based on this current study, it showed that by immersing the students a real-life situation and purpose, the student could and will find their ways in solving problems presented to them. The assignment had proved that not only students were able to work and learn independently, but some of them were highly creative in editing and producing a high quality short documentary-styled video. During the whole process, the lecturer did not interfere with the students' idea and creativity, but instead support them to make the idea more manageable. The aim was not to 'spoon-feed' the students with our ideas, but letting the students think for themselves and be creative.

Through this assignment, it also showed that when a student is excited or passionate about a certain thing, they do not mind the extra works (and study) that they need to do, which coincides with the idea proposed in the Theory of Reasoned Actions and the Technology Acceptance Model (Bagozzi, Davis & Warshaw 1992; Fishbein & Ajzen 1975). The students even willing to do self-learning / collaborative learning on topics that the do not understand (e.g.: how to use video creation software). To the researcher, this was an interesting finding. This was a group of undergraduate students who normally will do their studies just for exams. Now they were telling the researcher what they had learned and even showed others what they know.

One student described her experiences as valuable and the project had given her the opportunity to learn how to create a video, video editing, and uploading a video to the Internet.

> Before this I am not very good in using computer technology and the Internet. However, as the editor of the video that our group had created, I had learned how to create a video, how to edit the video, how to include subtitle to the video, how to add voice over etc. This project had shown me that I can do many things. Never say 'I do not know'.

However, the lecturer must play an active role at the beginning of the assignment to promote the idea for example by showing them examples of a crowdfunding video, crowdfunding success stories, etc. Most of the students were not sure of their own ability, especially when it involved computer-based technology. By trying to put the assignment in a positive light, it gives the student the little push to try harder and be confident.

9. CONCLUSION

This study explores the experience and reflections of a group of Malaysian University students' in relation to a service learning project conducted for their classes. Crowdfunding strategy for raising business capital was used as the medium which the students will use to raise money for their selected NGOs. The findings showed that the students had a positive experience in doing the Service Learning project. They understand their role as a citizen better and it enhanced their civic responsibilities. The study also showed that by incorporating the element of 'fun' and technology in a task can be the key to promoting active-learning, creative and innovative thinking among the Gen-Y students. This new generation can easily relate themselves with technology, as long as enough guidance was provided along the way. Hopefully, Service Learning would be implemented in more courses, not only in Universities, but also in schools. By learning about others, it is hopeful that Malaysians will be a more sympathetic and empathetic community and hopefully could help to increase moral values among teenagers.

REFERENCES

American Association of Community Colleges 2004, 'Faculty Service Learning Survey', <http://www.aacc.nche.edu/Resources/aaccprograms/horizons/Documents/faculty_survey.pdf>.

Astin, AW, Vogelgesang, LJ, Ikeda, EK & Yee, JA 2000, *How Service Learning Affects Students*, DigitalCommons@UNO, University of Nebraska Omaha.

Bagozzi, RP, Davis, FD & Warshaw, PR 1992, 'Development and Test of a Theory of Technological Learning and Usage', *Human Relations*, vol. 45, no. 7, pp. 659-86.

Bringle, RG & Hatcher, JA 1996, 'Implementing Service Learning in Higher Education', *Journal of Higher Education*, vol. 67, no. 2, pp. 221-39.

Butin, DW 2010, *Service Learning in Theory and Practice*, Palgrave Macmillan, New York.

Fishbein, M & Ajzen, I 1975, *Belief, Attitude, Intention, and Behavior: An Introduction to Theory and Research*, Addison-Wesley, Reading, MA.

Hamdan, S, Iqbal, A, Zainudin, H & Zubaidah, A 2015, 'Service Learning as Critical Pedagogy: Implications for Student Community Awareness and Citizenship Development', *Mediterranean Journal of Social Sciences*, vol. 6, no. 2, pp. 471-8.

Howard, J 2003, 'Service-learning research: Foundational issues', in SH Billig & AS Waterman (eds), *Studying service-learning: Innovations in education research methodology*, Erlbaum, Mahwah, NJ, pp. 1-12.

Hursen, C 2016, 'The impact of curriculum developed in line with authentic learning on the teacher candidates' success, attitude and self-directed learning skills', *Asia Pacific Education Review*, vol. 17, no. 1, pp. 73-86.

Lemieux, CM & Allen, PD 2007, 'Service learning in social work education: The state of knowledge, pedagogical practicalities, and practice conundrums ', *Journal of Social Work Education*, vol. 43, no. 2, pp. 309-26.

Mahasneh, R, Tawalbeh, A, Al-Smadi, R, Ghaith, S & Dajani, R 2012, 'Integrating service learning in Jordanian higher education', *Innovations in Education and Teaching International*, vol. 49, no. 4, pp. 415-25.

Profatilov, DA, Bykova, ON & Olkhovskaya, MO 2015, 'Crowdfunding: Online charity or a modern tool for innovative projects implementation?', *Asian Social Science*, vol. 11, no. 3, pp. 146-51.

Reinke, SJ 2003, 'Making a difference: Does service-learning promote civic engagement in MPA students?', *Journal of Public Affairs Education*, vol. 9, no. 2, pp. 129-38.

TOWARDS A THEORY-BASED DESIGN FRAMEWORK FOR AN EFFECTIVE E-LEARNING COMPUTER PROGRAMMING COURSE

Ian S. McGowan
University of Technology, Jamaica

ABSTRACT

Built on Dabbagh (2005), this paper presents a four component theory-based design framework for an e-learning session in introductory computer programming. The framework, driven by a body of exemplars component, emphasizes the transformative interaction between the knowledge building community (KBC) pedagogical model, a mixed instructional strategy of student collaboration and scaffolding, and learning technologies that supports the community. The foundation knowledge perspective of situated cognition derived the KBC model. Specific examples of how to apply this framework over computer programming sessions in e-learning context are provided.

KEYWORDS

e-Learning; Pedagogy; Learning theories; Computer Programming and Algorithm

1. INTRODUCTION

Computer Programming (CP) is a very useful skill and can be a rewarding career. In recent years, the demand for programmers and student interest in the area have grown rapidly. Introductory CP courses at the university level have become increasingly popular as a result. Learning to program is hard however. Student programmers suffer from a wide range of difficulties and deficits. These courses are generally regarded as difficult, and often have the highest dropout rates (Robins et al 2003). CP seems to demand complex cognitive skills such as procedural and conditional reasoning, planning, and analogical reasoning (Kurland et al, 1986). Instructors in the subject, generally agree that CP is a difficult matter, because it's more of an art than a body of knowledge (Hadjerrout, 2008). Knuth (1974) says preparing a computer program to solve a problem, feels like composing poetry or music. Hence Knuth further emphasized that in crafting a computer program, there is no "best" style in approach; everyone has his or her own preference of style, and it's a mistake to try to force learners of CP into an unnatural mold in this regard.

Pedagogical approaches, which take advantage of learning theories and information technology, have been proposed in the research literature to tackle the learning problems associated with CP. However, there are very few evidence-based research, and the difficulties of learning CP remain to be researched (Bank et al, 2006).

Research on the instructional uses of technology, however, has revealed that instructors in higher education often lack the knowledge to successfully integrate technology in their teaching and their attempts tend to be limited in scope, depth and variety (Kochler, 2013).

With recent advances in internet and web-based technologies that have redefined the boundaries and pedagogies of distance learning by stretching it scope and interconnectedness (Dabbagh, 2005), computer science departments now have the ability to explore an additional delivery environment for CP in the form of e-learning.

Generally a grand unifying theory of e-learning remains elusive and e-learning practitioners continue to operate largely on the basis of trial and error (Chin et al, 2006). E-learning thus, like all instructional delivery environments, must be rooted in epistemological frameworks to be effective for teaching and learning (Dabbagh, 2005). In other words, describing learning of and designing instructions for e-learning CP, must include appropriate e-learning instructional systems and the use of suitable learning technologies or tools to facilitate student learning.

Building on Dabbagh (2005)'s three component theory-based framework (Figure 1) for designing an e-learning course, this paper aims to present a four-component theory-based framework (Figure 2) for designing an e-learning CP session delivery that capitalizes on a pedagogical model, a body of examplars, instructional strategies and learning technologies to facilitate meaningful learning of proper CP practices and knowledge building. Dabbagh (2005) framework is based on Coleman et al's (1997) work on specifications of pedagogical models and strategies resulting from situated cognition and constructivist views of learning, and Hannafin (1992)'s work on tasking the learner with constructing representations of individual meaning.

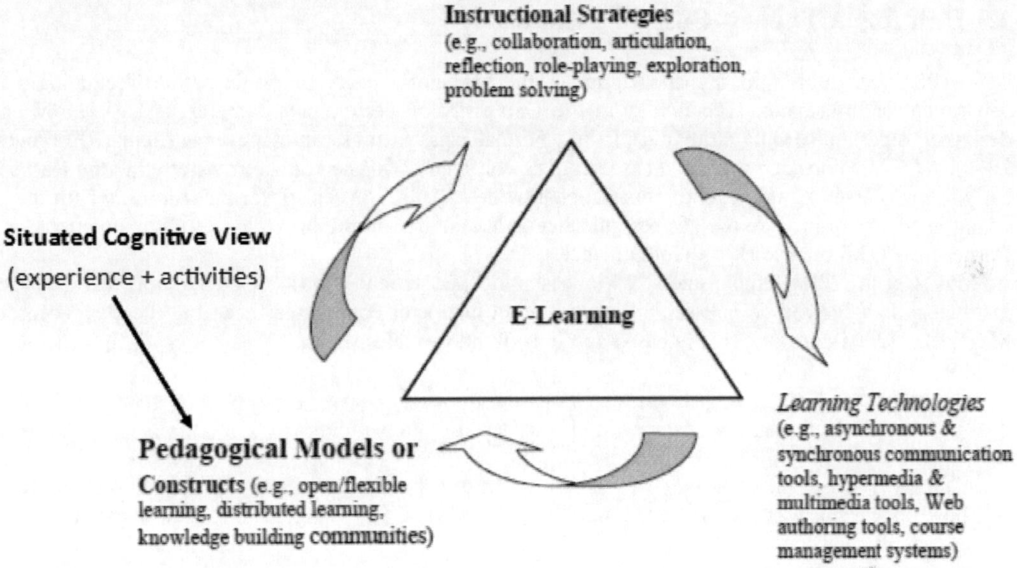

Figure 1. Theory-Based Design Pedagogical Framework for an E-Learning course (Dabbagh, 2005)

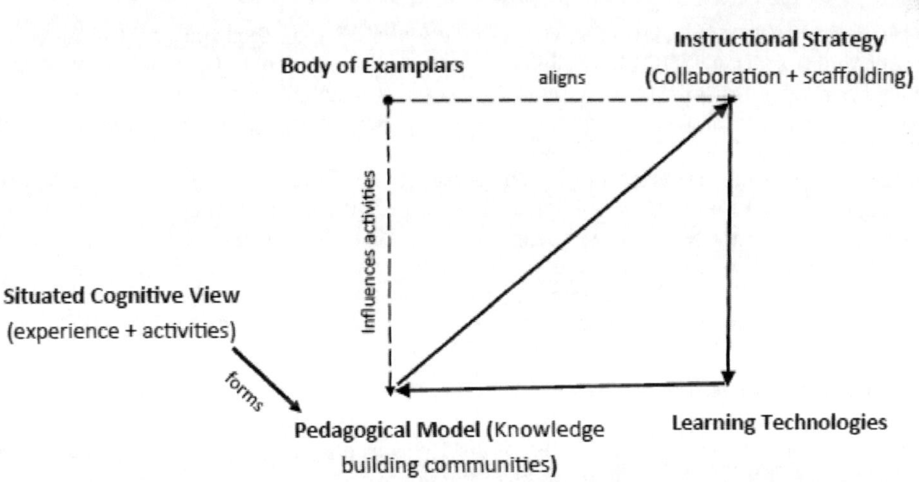

Figure 2. Proposed four-component Theory-Based Design Pedagogical Framework for E-Learning CP course (Built on Dabbagh, 2005)

This paper is a reflection of some of my observations into the current teaching practices, and learning habits of first-year students in relation to the subject of CP in recent years at a higher education institute in the Caribbean where I work as a CP instructor. With failure rates in excess of sixty-five percent year after year in first year, the subject, and by extension, the academic department, have been receiving negative attention consistently from the school's academic administration. As the institution begins to consider an e-learning route for CP and investing large sums of money on this e-learning initiative as a possible reaction to this crisis in the department, this review is aimed at generating a fresh pedagogical framework on which CP instructors could consider and build on to improve on the student learning outcome.

2. GROUNDING ASSUMPTIONS FOR AN E-LEARNING COMPUTER PROGRAMMING COURSE

2.1 Defining a Theory-Based Framework

CP, a first year subject in the curriculum of the bachelor's degree in Information Technology, in the department of Information Technology at the University of Technology, Jamaica, is basic knowledge of designing algorithms. Only studying CP in a normal class is most times never sufficient (Rodmunkong, 2015). As CP is more of a practiced based course, confidence will need to be transferred to the learner from early in the course. A high level of confidence provides a sense of security for the learner in both the ability of the instructor to provide the correct guidance as is required in the providing of CP instructions, and the learner's own ability to work without guidance.

Mayes et al (2005) emphasizes that in designing instructions for the learner, knowing why you (the instructor) do what you do is essential in generating instructor confidence. Learning theories, according to Mayes et al (2005), are empirically based accounts of the variables which:

- influence the learning process
- lend coherence and consistency in instructional design planning

A theory-based framework thus uses one or a mix of learning theories to explain views about cognition and how knowledge was constructed. These views then form the pedagogical model or the starting of the pedagogical framework.

2.2 Pedagogical Framework

A well understood pedagogical framework is essential for a good pedagogical design in higher education/further education (HE/FE) contexts (Mayes, 2013; Biggs, 1999). Pedagogical frameworks describe the broad principles through which theory is applied to learning and teaching practice. Narrowing Mayes's definition to include technology, Hadjerrouit (2008) explains a pedagogical framework to an understanding of the relationships among learning theory, information technology, educational practice, and more specifically to an academic subject. Ivala (2013) argues that a pedagogical framework offers instructional designers an effective means of embedding a subject's pedagogical model into the e-learning environment. Dabbagh (2005) appears best to have strengthened Ivala's definition, in that the relationships among the pedagogical components are iterative (Fig 1). An iterative relationship embedded in a pedagogical framework would be more adaptive in an e-learning environment as learning technologies become ubiquitous, and continue to evolve school year to school year in any computer science department in a HE/FE.

2.3 Situated Cognition Views

Situated cognition (SC) emerged at the end of the 1980s as a new way of theorizing human performance. Roth et al (2013) describe the central aspect of the SC hypothesis is that intelligent behavior (perceiving, remembering, reasoning and problem solving), arise from the dynamic coupling between intelligent subject and its environment, rather than only from the agent's mind (brain and control system) itself.

Roth argued that the shift to SC hypothesis in cognitive science, adopted to the perspective that information does not exist prior, but emerges from, and is a function of the organism-environment relation (coupling). Environments include physical and social (communities, social networks and society). Roth explained further, that the cognition in a subject is enacted, and that human behavior is characterized by relations of reference to the surrounding world. For example, from the SC hypothesis, the rules in a spoken language are not considered formal symbolic relations stored in the mind that a subject use to generate a phase. Spoken language is learned by participating in societal relations.

Wilson (2002) uses a different terminology than that of Roth in the push to understand the mind in the context if its relationship to the physical body that interacts with the world: *embodied cognition.* Wilson agrees with Roth that cognition inherently involves perception and action, and takes place in the real world environment. Wilson went on further to argue that because human cognitive work is limited, it off-loads the work on to the environment. We make the environment hold or even manipulate information for us. We then harvest the information only on a need-to-know basis. Wilson's definition of SC narrows the content to task related. That is, cognition that takes place in the context of task-relevant inputs and outputs. While a cognitive process is being carried out, perceptual information continues to come in that affects processing. Motor activities are then executed that affects the environment in task-relevant ways. For example walking down an isle in a supermarket, holding a conversation with a neighbor, and moving around a used-car lot as you imagine how you would look in that car as you pass it, are all cognitive activities that are situated in this sense. With this definition, any cognitive activity that takes place in the absence of task relevant input and output or "off-line", is not *situated.* Examples include planning, remembering, and day-dreaming.

Dabbagh's (2005) situated cognitive view is consistent with the epistemological assumptions of constructivism, which stipulate that meaning is a function of how the individual creates meaning from his or her experiences and actions.

CP is markedly distinct of other disciplines because proficiency in other areas does not predict success. Evidence suggests however, that deliberate practice is a key element in the acquisition of programming competencies (Scott et al, 2013). Learning activities encourages deliberate practice. Deliberate practice generates experience as Dabbogh (2005)'s SC view highlights. A body of examplars thus would help to direct independent learning activities.

2.4 Body of Examplars

In my experience teaching CP, I have found that worked examples or problem statements serving as reference points relating to a particular topic, are invaluable to learning outcome, and designing of instructions.

For example:

#1 Problem statement (topic Iterations or looping): *Write an algorithm that displays the total of all numbers from 10 to 20 inclusive.*

Model solution:

```
t = 0
for c = 10 to 20 step 1
   t = t + c
display t
```

#2 Problem statement: *Write an algorithm that asks the user to enter 5 numbers, then displays the largest number after the input. For example, if the numbers entered are 89, 45, 9, 91 and 90, then the output should be 91.*

Model solution:

```
input num
largest = num
for c = 1 to 4
   input num
```

```
    if num > largest
        largest = num
display largest
```

Made available in sufficient numbers before, during and after topic, learners that make use of the provided examplars, tend to fall in line with course expectations at the minimum, much faster, and independently.

Should another problem statement (for example: *Write an algorithm that displays the total of all even numbers from 30 to 39*), be challenged to the learners, then some reference point for guidance may be available.

A body of examplars, forming the first component of the theory-based design framework, is a database of worked examples made available by course designers for both the learners and instructors. For the learners, this database would serve to influence independent learning activities and experience gathering. For instructors, the database would guide the designing and aligning of instructions to topic.

2.5 Pedagogical Models: Knowledge Building Communities (KBCs)

A pedagogical model, the second component of the theory-based design framework, is a cognitive model or theoretical construct derived from knowledge acquisition models or views about cognition and knowledge, which form the basis for learning theory (Dabbagh, 2005). In this paper for example (as Figure 2 and 3 show), from the situated cognition view knowledge acquisition model, the focused *KBC* model was derived. In other words, theory to practice was linked using a pedagogical model.

Some of the other noted pedagogical models available include *open learning*, *distributed learning*, *learning communities* and *communities of practice*.

A common goal of KBCs, is to advance and share knowledge of the collective (Dabbagh, 2005). In knowledge building, discourse, ideas, theories, hypothesis, and other similar intellectual artifacts, are objects of enquiry. These objects are scrutinized, improved, and put to new use as participants progressive discourse analogous to the enquiry processes of research communities (Gan et al, 2007). Driven or helped by the body of examplars, ideas and discourse about algorithm design for given problem statements would normally then be at the minimum level required for the course.

In initiating a CP KBC session for example, the instructor could present a problem statement such as:

Write an algorithm that asks the user for 6 pairs of first names and ages, then displays the name of the youngest person at the end of the input. For example, if the pairs entered are "Paul", 16; "Dianna", 14; "Tuvak", 16; "Dwayne", 23; "Kayeem", 21 and "Allison", 23, then the output should be "Dianna".

to generate (a) an initial idea or solution from one of the groups possibly in reference to or guided by the body of examplars, and (b) recursive discourse evidenced by debugging results from the same and other groups, until a final solution agreed by the collective, is arrived at or until KBC session times out.

In my own experience in learning and teaching CP at the university level, the art is best learnt in peers, with regular feedback from instructors, referencing the body of examplars for possible similar challenges, examining what others have done for similar projects (and most times copying a prior approach), and deliberate practice.

Phillips (2007) describe learning in a KBC classroom as a by-product of creation of a new knowledge, but the focus of classroom work is the continual improvement of ideas. In the case of CP problem statements, members of the group would be encouraged to use the body of exemplars as a starting point on which to build new design ideas.

2.6 Instructional Strategies: Promoting Collaboration + Providing Scaffolding

Lead by the pedagogical model and guided by the body of exemplars, the specifications of the instructional strategies form the third component of the theory-based design framework. Instructional strategies are what instructors do to facilitate student learning (Dabbagh, 2005). Dabbagh presented other noted instructional strategies in *articulation, reflection, role-playing, exploration* and *problem solving*.

2.6.1 Promoting Collaboration

In collaborative learning, information sharing is not enough – students are expected to learn to work together so that the deliverables are from group effort (Lazarva, 2015).

From a constructivist or situated cognition perspective however, Dabbagh (2005) defined collaborative learning with the emphasis of encouraging students, in their respective work groups, to engage in joint negotiation of alternatives through argumentation and debate. Therefore Dabbagh viewed social negotiation as an integral component of collaborative learning.

In a small group of CP students for example, we can often find varying levels of cognitive and experience strengths among the members. One or few maybe stronger in analyzing problem statements, another maybe stronger in visualizing user experience, and another maybe stronger in flowcharting. For a CP project, these strengths will need to be maximized and shared among the members for the end product to be at the minimum required level for the course. Social negotiation allows for members of a group to share workload with minimum conflict and promotes peer tutorial (Dabbagh, 2005; Duffy & Cunningham, 1996).

In E-learning contexts, collaborative learning and social negotiation over a student CP project can be enacted using:

- Online group discussion (for problem statements)
- Share ideas online
- Using an online database for recoding designing, flowcharting and coding ideas
- Virtual chat and video conferencing (brainstorming, debating, group sharing of ideas)

2.6.2 Providing Scaffolding

Scaffolding, a short-term strategy as intended, is used to help students through a learning task that is just outside their level competency (Ontario, 1992).

The concept of instructional scaffolding has its origins in the work psychologist Vygotsky (Foley, 1994). For a positive learning outcome, an appropriate social interactional framework must be provided (Foley, 1994; Bruner, 1978). Foley explains that scaffolding is viewed as a gradual process of internalization by the learner of routines and procedures. As the learner's competence grows, the scaffolding is gradually reduced until the learner is able to function autonomously in the given task and generalize to similar circumstances.

Scaffolding is no longer restricted to interactions between individuals as Foley describes. Puntambeker et al (2005) argues that with an increase in project-based and design-based environments for teaching engineering, science and mathematics in the context of a classroom, the notion of scaffolding is now increasingly being used to describe the prompts and hints in tools to support learning. Artifacts, resources and environments themselves are being used as scaffolds.

Dabbagh (2005) recommends a different approach from that of Foley. As novice students and students who already have a significant knowledge base require different levels of task support to push them to perform at their potential development zone, Dabbagh suggests a layered structure to scaffolding. In a group setting, the required support level of each member could vary. This layered approach would help to prevent weaker members from slowing down the stronger members.

For example – at the design stage of a CP group project, the instructor, aided by the body of examplars, could (1) develop a set of flowchart exercises at increasing levels of difficulties leading to minimum level required for the project, and (2) provide a one-to-one out of class and/or emailing mentoring sessions with students in need.

3. CONCLUSION

The main objective of this paper has been to contribute to the advancement of introductory computer programming education at the university level through the additional delivery mode option of E-Learning. The paper presented a proposed four-component theory-based design framework built on Dabbagh (2005)'s three-component framework. Dabbagh's framework emphasizes the systematic and transformative interaction between the knowledge building community pedagogical model driven by situated cognition and constructivist views of learning, instructional strategies that support group work on computer programming learning projects while managing guaranteed conflicts, and online learning technologies that could sufficiently allow students to record, debate, discuss and share their coding and design specifications on a CP course. A forth, but initial component in that of a body of examplars would serve to "level the playing field" going into a CP session or topic, depict the course topic expectations early, reduce the stress levels of and conflicts among learners in a KBC environment, and provide that crucial guidance needed by both the learners and instructors in an e-learning CP environment especially in the general absence of a sufficient body of knowledge usually associated with CP courses.

Armed with this new understanding of learning from a distance and the theory-into-practice framework that characterizes the instructional implications of situated cognition, computer programming instructors have the knowledge and tools to carefully craft e-learning programs with strategic interactions to promote proper computer programming practice and meaningful learning.

ACKNOWLEDGMENT

This research was undertaken as part of the PhD in E-research and Technology Enhanced Learning in the Department of Educational Research at Lancaster University. I am pleased to acknowledge the contribution of tutors and peers in supporting the development of this study and its report as an assignment paper.

REFERENCES

Biggs, J. & Tang, C. (1999). Teaching for Quality Learning at University 3rd Ed. *The Society for Research into Higher Education*

Bruner, J. (1978). The Child's Concept of Language. New York *Springer-Verlag*

Carr, N. (2008). Knowledge Building Communities & Authentic Pedagogies In Pre-service Teacher Education. *ascilite Melbourne 2008*

Chin, S. T., Williams, J. B. (2006). A Theoretical Framework for Effective Online Course Design. *MERLOT Journal of Online Learning and Teaching*

Coleman, S. D., Perry, J. D., & Schwen, T. M. (1997). Constructivist instructional development: Reflecting on practice from an alternative paradigm. *Instructional Development Paradigms*

Dabbagh, N. (2005). Pedagogical models for E-Learning: A theory-based design framework. *International Journal of Technology in Teaching and Learning*

Foley, J (1994). Scaffolding ETL Journal

Gan, Y., & Zhu, Z. (2007). A Learning Framework for Knowledge Building and Collective Wisdom Advancement in Virtual Learning Communities. *Educational Technology & Society*

Hadjerrouit, S. (2008). Towards a Blended Learning Model for Teaching and Learning Computer

Programming: A Case Study. *Informatics in Education*

Hannafin, M. J. (1992). Emerging technologies, ISD, and learning environments: Critical perspectives. *Educational Technology Research & Development*

Ivala, E., Gachago, D., Condy, J. & Chigona, A. (2013). Enhancing student engagement with their studies: A digital storytelling approach. *Scientific Research Online*

Koehler, M. J., Mishra, P., Kereluik, K., Shin, T. S., and Graham, C. R (2013). The Technological Pedagogical Content Knowledge Framework. *Handbook of Research on Educational Communications and Technology*

Lazareva, A. (2015). Promoting Collaborative Interactions in a Learning Management System. *2015 International Conference on Interactive Collaborative Learning (ICL)*

Mayes, T., de Freitas, S. (2013). Review of e-learning theories, frameworks and models. *JISC e-Learning Models Desk Study*

Ontario Government (1992). Professional learning guide. *Connecting Practice and Research in Mathematics Education*

Phillip, D (2007). The Knowledge Building Paradigm: A Model of Learning for Net Generation Students Innovate

Puntambeker, S., Kolodner, J. L. (2005). Distributed Scaffolding: Helping Students Learn Science from Design

Robins, A., Rountree, J., Rountree, N. (2003). Learning and Teaching Programming: A Review Computer Science Education

Roth, W. M. & Jornet, A. G. (2013). Situated Cognition. *WIREs Cognitive Science*

Scott, M. J., Ghinea, G. (2013). Educating programmers: A reflection on barriers to deliberate practice.*The Higher Education Academy*

Wilson, M (2002). Theoretic and Review Articles. Six views of embodied cognition. *Psychonomic Bulletin & Review*

AN ONTOLOGY FOR LEARNING SERVICES ON THE SHOP FLOOR

Carsten Ullrich
Educational Technology Lab, DFKI GmbH
DFKI Projektbüro Berlin, Alt-Moabit 91c, 10559 Berlin, Germany

ABSTRACT

An ontology expresses a common understanding of a domain that serves as a basis of communication between people or systems, and enables knowledge sharing, reuse of domain knowledge, reasoning and thus problem solving. In Technology-Enhanced Learning, especially in Intelligent Tutoring Systems and Adaptive Learning Environments, ontologies serve as the basis of adaptivity and personalization. For mathematics learning and similarly structured domains, ontologies and their usage for adaptive learning are well understood and established. This contribution presents an ontology for the industrial shop floor (the area of a factory where operatives assemble products) and illustrates its usage in several learning services.

KEYWORDS

Adaptivity, Domain Model, Workplace Learning

1. INTRODUCTION

An ontology expresses a common understanding of a domain that serves as a basis of communication between people or systems. It enables knowledge sharing, reuse of domain knowledge, reasoning and thus problem solving (Chandrasekaran, 1999). In Technology-Enhanced Learning, especially in Intelligent Tutoring Systems and Adaptive Learning Environments, ontologies serve as the basis of the domain model, which is the basis for adaptivity and personalization. In highly structured domains such as mathematics, physics and computer science, ontologies with the aim of supporting learning are well understood and several examples exist. This has enabled a large body of research. For instance, ActiveMath (Melis, et al., 2001) is a web-based learning environment for Mathematics that creates on the learners' demand courseware adapted with respect to their knowledge state and learning goals. Similarly, the physic tutor Andes generates problems specifically targeted to the individual learner in order to achieve the best possible learning gain (VanLehn, et al., 2005). Without a domain ontology, such advanced adaptive features would not be possible.

In the domain of the shop floor (the area of a factory where operatives assemble products) no such ontology exists, despite the high relevance of technology-supported learning for industry. Today's workplace on the shop floor is highly demanding (Mavrikios, Papakostas, Mourtzis, & Chryssolouris, 2013). The employee is under constant pressure to solve problems occurring on the shop floor as fast as possible, and simultaneously to improve his work-related knowledge, skills, and capabilities. Yet, research on the potential of adaptive learning on the shop floor is rare. Given the progress in other domains, we suspect that one reason is that the groundwork, in the form of descriptions of the central concepts of the domain to be learned, and how they are interrelated, is still missing. This paper addresses this short-coming by describing an ontology that represents entities on the shop floor relevant from a pedagogical perspective. The following section describes related work in this area, followed by an account of the central concepts and their relations (Section 3) and an illustration of its benefits by examples of adaptive services that make use of it (Section 4). The conclusion (Section 5) discusses the problem of scalable application of the proposed ontology and suggest a possible solution.

2. RELATED WORK

The relevance of educational technology in supporting workers in manufacturing (Mavrikios, Papakostas, Mourtzis, & Chryssolouris, 2013) as well the potential of smart and adaptive environment for workplace-based learning (Koper, 2014) have been clearly recognized. However, most existing work has focused on very specific areas, such as assembly, in order to increase process quality (Stoessel, Wiesbeck, Stork, Zaeh, & Schuboe, 2008) (Stork, Stößel, & Schubö, 2008), collaboration between machine and operator (Sebanz, Bekkering, & Knoblich, 2006) (Lenz, et al., 2008), control (Bannat, et al., 2009) or monitoring (Stork genannt Wersborg, Borgwardt, & Diepold, 2009). Recent work investigated how to use data from factory-wide sensor networks to control information flow so that cognitive overload of employees can be avoided (Lindblom & Thorvald, 2014) or how to display the data in a way that workers' satisfaction is increased (Arena & Perdikakis, 2015).

Research in the Semantic Web has led to formalizations that enable distributed ontologies, easily linked and reused (Allemang & Hendler, 2008). In the area of manufacturing, prior work has investigated informal classifications of universal, shop-level, and machine-level knowledge (Shah & Mäntylä, 1995) and ontologies for very restricted areas such as toolpath planning (Xu, Wang, & Rong, 2006) or fixture design (Ameri & Summers, 2008). The SemProM project has taken wider approach, representing all information collected during the lifespan of a product (Wahlster, 2013). In contrast to the limited work on ontologies stands a plethora of standards and specifications. The technical committee ISO/TC 184 for instance, has published more than 800 ISO standards that describe different aspects of automation systems and integration. These, however, have a very technical focus, and none we have seen is on the required level of abstraction for learning on the shop floor. What is required is a focused domain description, which focuses on the learning needs of the operators. The potential of such descriptions has been shown for generating assembling instructions automatically from product lifecycle data (Stoessel, Wiesbeck, Stork, Zaeh, & Schuboe, 2008), for supporting the transfer of practical knowledge (Blümling & Reithinger, 2015), as well as for providing manufacturing assembly assistance (Alm, Aehnelt, & Urban, 2015). However, none of this work has described the employed ontologies in sufficient detail to judge their general applicability nor to enable reuse.

3. DESCRIPTION OF THE ONTOLOGY

The ontology serves as a blueprint to describe the general concepts (also called types, in the following highlighted in bold font) relevant for teaching and learning on the shop floor. Figure 1 gives an overview of the type hierarchy of the ontology.

The highest level of the ontology distinguishes between the types **state**, **organizational unit**, **production item**, **function**, and **process model entity**.

The **state** describes the state of a domain entity. It distinguishes between **machine state**, which describes the state of a **production machine** (defined below), and **software state**, which describes the state of a software. Both types of states have a priority, indicating their severity (10, highly critical, to 1, not critical) and can be further divided into specific sub-states (adapted from (Kasikci, 2010)):

- **Up state** is the state of a machine characterized by the fact that it can perform a required function, with the specializations **operating state**, which describes when a machine is performing as required, and **idle state**, which describes a machine which is in an up-state and non-operating, during non-required time.
- **Disabled state** is the state of a machine characterized by its inability to perform a required function, for any reason. It has the specializations **external disabled state**, for describing a machine in an up-state, but lacking required external resources or is disabled due to planned actions other than maintenance, and **internal disabled state**, the state of a machine characterized by an inability to perform a required function.

The type **organizational unit** and its specializations allows to describe the structure of a company, from the top-most unit **organization**, to **location**, **department**, **department unit**, **workplace unit**, **workplace**, down to **employee**.

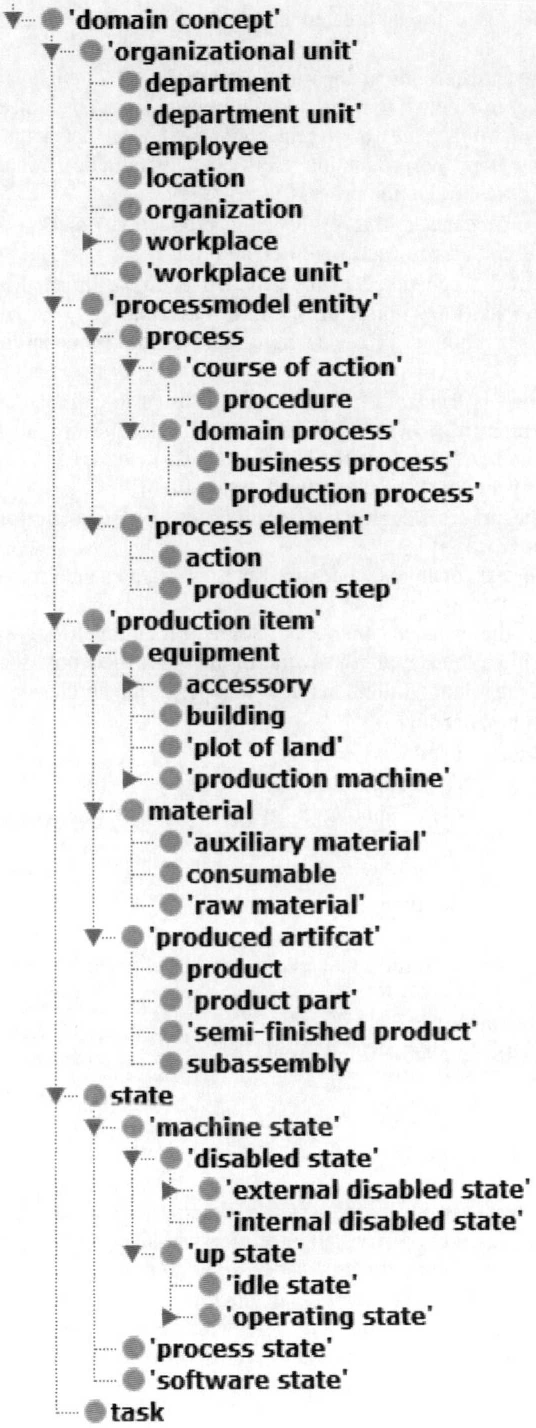

Figure 1. Overview of the Type Hierarchy of the Ontology

The type **production item** describes entities used for or created during the production of goods. Its specializations are:

- **Equipment**: Equipment includes the entire technical apparatus used during production as well as property (plot of land), buildings, etc. In contrast to materials, equipment is not consumed. It has the specializations **building**, **plot of land**, **accessory** (a mechanical device that supports the production process, but does not perform the production itself.), and **production machine** (a stationary device directly involved in the production process.).
- **Produced artifact**: The marketed object that is the result of the production process, with the specializations **subassembly**, **semi-finished product**, **product**, and **part.**
- **Material**: Materials are physical entities consumed in the production of the finished product, with the specializations **consumable**, **auxiliary material**, and **raw material**.

The type **processmodel entity** represents types required for describing processes that occur in the target domain. Its subtypes are

- **Process**: A sequence of states, which is triggered by an event and leads to a final state. The ontology distinguishes between **domain process** (overarching process performed for the realization of the product, such as the **production process** and **business process**) and **course of action** (a process that is performed by a human, such as a work **procedure**).
- **Process element:** The states of the process, such as an **action** (for **course of action)** or a **production step** (for the production process).

The final type is **task**, which describes the task of human operator such as maintenance, repair, and operations or management.

Relations (also called properties) specify how the instances interrelate. Some of the properties only apply to specific types (written in bold font below), while others apply to several of the types (non-bold font). The following list describes the intended meaning of the relation (all nouns refer to types of the ontology):

- **requires: a machine state requires a procedure.**
- **produces: a production step produces a produced artifact**
- **executes: a production machine executes a production step**
- **has part:** expresses that some entity is part of another entity. This relation can be applied to many of the types.
- **has task: an employee has tasks**
- **has step: a process 'has the step' process element**
- **has state: a production machine has a machine state**
- **has procedure: a task has a procedure** (meaning that a task can be achieved by following a series of actions).
- **is part of**: the inverse relation of **has part**
- **realizes**: **a production machine realizes a production process.**

4. USAGE OF THE ONTOLOGY

This section illustrates how the ontology is used by several software services to support workplace-integrated learning. The services have been implemented in the APPsist architecture, which consists of mobile, context-sensitive and intelligent-adaptive assistance systems for knowledge and action support on the shop floor (Ullrich, et al., 2015). APPsist provides assistance to the human operator in solving problem by guidance through step-by-step instructions and provision of relevant documents. It also suggests content (learning materials, user manuals, other documents) relevant for medium- and long-term development goals to the operator.

4.1 Domain Modeling

The foremost usage of the ontology is to build up a domain model, i.e., a formal representation of the shop floor at a specific site of a company. This requires to specify instances (in the following highlighted in bold font) of the types. For example, if we were to say that Lenovo in its production department P1 in Guandong produces the laptop X, then we had to create the instance **Lenovo** of the concept **organization**, the instance **Guandong** of **location**, the instance **P1** of **department**, and the instance **X** of **product**. Using the property **produces**, one can specify that **X** is produced in **P1**.

In APPsist, the ontology was used to define the domain models representing three different companies, ranging from small- over medium- to large-sized: The small-sized company produces complex customer-specific tools and devices for car manufacturers and their suppliers. The APPsist pilot learning scenario focuses on installation and use of devices (milling machines). The medium-sized company produces customer-specific welding and assembly lines for car manufacturers. The pilot scenario focuses on error diagnosis and correction in the customer-specific machines. The large-sized company produces pneumatic and electric controllers for the automation of assembly-lines, which are used in customer-specific products as well as in their own production. The pilot scenario focuses on maintenance and repair, in particular outages (replacement of adhesives).

If a domain model is stored in a database, then it can be queried to retrieve information. In APPsist, the ontology and its instantiation are stored in a semantic database that allows queries involving reasoning. For instance, by follow the appropriate relations, a query might return all produced products in a given location, even if that information is not specified directly. This functionality is a prerequisite of several of the following services.

4.2 Content Metadata

The types and instantiations of the ontology can be used to describe available content, such as learning materials, documentation (user manuals, programming handbooks), and order-related information (parts lists, wiring diagrams). Specifically, it allows to specify the production items a piece of content refers to, the target-audience, etc. Other services, as described below, will use this information to perform information retrieval tasks in different contexts.

4.3 Machine Information

The machines on the shop floor use a multitude of sensors for managing the production process. Some of the sensor values are relevant for triggering actions of the human operators, especially in case of machine states that result in stopping the production process. However, the low-level senor data is too specific to be interpreted by support software. In APPsist, a machine information service translates the sensor data into instances of the type **machine state** and propagates the instances to the supporting services. This way, the learning supporting services can be set up to react to high-level, abstract machine states and thus can be more easily reused with new machines.

4.4 Content and Procedure Selection

If available content and the situation of the shop floor are described using the terms specified in the ontology, then that information can be used to select content suited for both assistance and knowledge building processes. For instance, the content selector service in APPsist uses a set of rules that are applied when a production machine gives an error state. The rules inspect the **organizational units** to determine which **employees** are assigned to the **production machine**, and uses information specified about the relevant **production items** to find content relevant for the **employee** in the specific situation. Analogous to the content selection, the procedure selection service recommends work **procedures** to be performed by the **employee** based on the current situation on the shop floor.

The rules used by the two services are abstract in the sense that they perform their reasoning on the ontology and do not encode information about the specific company in which they are used (the instances of the domain). Thus, they are transferable between companies. They thereby implement knowledge analogous to what a trainer or instructor possesses: given a specific set of circumstances, a trainer knows how to help the learner. Figure 2 contains a screenshot in which the APPsist system shows a selection of content relevant to the current context and user. The top row contains the main menu showing the available tabs, with the currently opened tab ("Vertiefung" meaning "consolidating content") being highlighted. The main screen below shows two work content items the system determined to be relevant to the employee in the current situation (“Montageprozess in der Roboterzelle” meaning “assembling process of the roboter station” and “MPS Station Roboter - Sicherheitshinweise” meaning “MPS station robot – security notes”). If the employees selects one of the work procedures, she will see the corresponding item. The other relevant tab is the first from the right (“Assistance” meaning “assistance”), which provides access to work procedures relevant to the current situation.

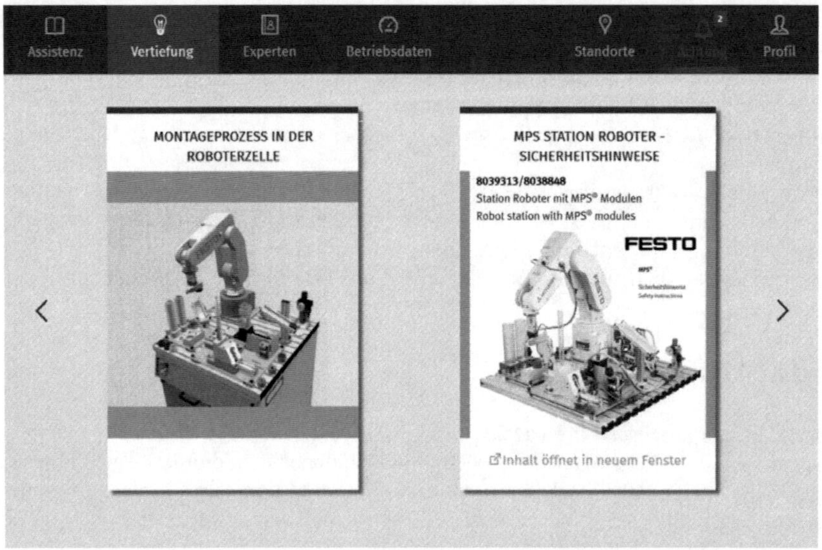

Figure 2. Screenshot showing recommended content

5. CONCLUSION

The contribution of this paper is an ontology that captures the entities and their interrelationships relevant for describing and reasoning about the shop floor from an educational perspective. The ontology is of general value as illustrated by its usage a) to represent the shop floor of three different companies and b) as a basis for a number of learning services, i.e., functionally highly specialized software applications that aim at supporting problem solving and learning of human operators. By referring to the terms defined in the ontology, these services become reusable, i.e., applicable in other companies than the three they were originally developed for.

It is a lightweight ontology, meaning that it does not use features such as axioms that would allow even more advanced reasoning but which come with the cost of higher complexity and difficulty of understanding.

The ontology was designed to focus on the production items, states, and processes. Still unclear is a generally applicable structure of the **tasks** of human operators for the shop floor. Currently, each of the industry partners has its own set of tasks, e.g., **installation**, **commissioning**, **maintenance**, **repair**, **operations**, or **assembly**. Due to the very different, company-specific views on the relevant tasks, we were not yet able to devise a suitable abstract representation.

Highly relevant is the problem of scalability. Architectures supporting problem solving and knowledge acquisition will only find widespread application if the cost of applying them to a new setting is reasonably low. Currently, integrating new content, processes and production machines into APPsist, requires manual input of the metadata, machine instances, etc., resulting in significant costs. Here, methods of information extraction that analyze existing documents might allow automating the ontology creation, instance creation and metadata annotation, and thus enabling low-cost, scalable support of human operators.

ACKNOWLEDGEMENT

This publication is a result of work performed in the context of the project "APPsist – Intelligente Wissensdienste für die Smart Production", funded under the initiative "Autonomics for INDUSTRY 4.0" at the German Federal Ministry for Economic Affairs and Energy (BMWi), number 01MA13004C and supervised by the DLR. The authors are solely responsible for its content.

REFERENCES

Allemang, D., & Hendler, J. (2008). *Semantic Web for the Working Ontologist: Effective Modeling in RDFS and OWL.* San Francisco, CA, USA: Morgan Kaufmann Publishers Inc.

Alm, R., Aehnelt, M., & Urban, B. (2015). Processing Manufacturing Knowledge with Ontology-based Annotations and Cognitive Architectures. *Proceedings of the 15th International Conference on Knowledge Technologies and Data-driven Business* (pp. 25:1-25:6). New York, NY, USA: ACM.

Ameri, F., & Summers, J. D. (2008). An Ontology for Representation of Fixture Design Knowledge. *Computer-Aided Design and Applications, 5*(5), 601-611.

Arena, D. N., & Perdikakis, A. (2015). *DELIVERABLE D2.2 Knowledge model for human resource optimization.* Tech. rep., SatisFactory project.

Bannat, A., Gast, J., Rehrl, T., Rösel, W., Rigoll, G., & Wallhoff, F. (2009). A Multimodal Human-Robot-Interaction Scenario: Working Together with an Industrial Robot. In J. Jacko (Ed.), *Human-Computer Interaction. Novel Interaction Methods and Techniques. 5611*, pp. 303-311. Springer Berlin Heidelberg.

Blümling, S., & Reithinger, N. (2015). Aufbereitung und Speicherung von Erfahrungswissen im PLuTO-Projekt. *8. AAL-Kongress.* Frankfurt/Main: VDE Verlag.

Chandrasekaran, B., Josephson, J. R., & Benjamins, V. R. (1999). What Are Ontologies, and Why Do We Need Them? IEEE Intelligent Systems, 14(1), 20-26.

Gruber, T. R. (1995). Toward principles for the design of ontologies used for knowledge sharing. *International Journal of Human-Computer Studies, 43*(5-6), 907-928.

Henze, N., & W.Nejdl. Knowledge Modeling for Open Adaptive Hypermedia. In *Adaptive Hypermedia and Adaptive Web-Based Systems: Second International Conference,* pp. 174-183. Springer Berlin Heidelberg.

Kasikci, I. (2010). *DIN EN 13306 (2010-12): Instandhaltung - Begriffe der Instandhaltung.* Tech. rep., Beuth Verlag.

Koper, R. (2014). Conditions for effective smart learning environments. *Smart Learning Environments, 1*(1), 5.

Lenz, C., Nair, S., Rickert, M., Knoll, A., Rosel, W., Gast, J., . . . Wallhoff, F. (2008). Joint-action for humans and industrial robots for assembly tasks. *Robot and Human Interactive Communication, 2008. RO-MAN 2008. The 17th IEEE International Symposium on*, (pp. 130-135).

Lindblom, J., & Thorvald, P. (2014). Towards a framework for reducing cognitive load in manufacturing personnel. In K. Stanney, & K. S. Hale (Ed.), *Advances in Cognitive Engineering and Neuroergonomics* (pp. 233-244). AHFE Conference.

Mavrikios, D., Papakostas, N., Mourtzis, D., & Chryssolouris, G. (2013, 06). On industrial learning and training for the factories of the future: a conceptual, cognitive and technology framework. *Journal of Intelligent Manufacturing, 24.*

Melis, E., Andrès, E., Büdenbender, J., Frischauf, A., Goguadze, G., Libbrecht, P., . . . Ullrich, C. (2001). ActiveMath: A Generic and Adaptive Web-Based Learning Environment. *International Journal of Artificial Intelligence in Education, 12*(4), 385-407.

Melis, E., Büdenbender, J., Goguadze, G., Libbrecht, P., Pollet, M., & Ullrich, C. (2003). Knowledge Representation and Management in ActiveMath. *Annals of Mathematics and Artificial Intelligence, Special Issue on Management of Mathematical Knowledge, 38*(1-3), 47-64.

Sebanz, N., Bekkering, H., & Knoblich, G. (2006). Joint action: bodies and minds moving together . *Trends in Cognitive Sciences , 10*(2), 70-76.

Shah, J. J., & Mäntylä, M. (1995). *Parametric and Feature-Based CAD/CAM: Concepts, Techniques, and Applications.* John Wiley and Sons, Inc.

Stoessel, C., Wiesbeck, M., Stork, S., Zaeh, M., & Schuboe, A. (2008). Towards Optimal Worker Assistance: Investigating Cognitive Processes in Manual Assembly. In M. Mitsuishi, K. Ueda, & F. Kimura (Ed.), *Manufacturing Systems and Technologies for the New Frontier* (pp. 245-250). Springer London.

Stork genannt Wersborg, I., Borgwardt, F., & Diepold, K. (2009). Real-time cognitive technical systems, a learning material processing system, social and future aspects. In IEEE (Ed.), *Advanced Robotics and its Social Impacts.*

Stork, A., Sevilmis, N., Weber, D., Gorecky, D., Stahl, C., Loskyll, M., & Michel, F. (2012, Sept). Enabling virtual assembly training in and beyond the automotive industry. *Virtual Systems and Multimedia (VSMM), 2012 18th International Conference on*, (pp. 347-352).

Stork, S., Stößel, C., & Schubö, A. (2008). The Influence of Instruction Mode on Reaching Movements during Manual Assembly. In A. Holzinger (Ed.), *HCI and Usability for Education and Work. Proceedings of the 4th Symposium of the Workgroup Human-Computer Interaction and Usability Engineering of the Austrian Computer Society, USAB 2008. 5298*, pp. 161-172. Springer Berlin Heidelberg.

Ullrich, C., Aust, M., Blach, R., Dietrich, M., Igel, C., Kreggenfeld, N., . . . Schwantzer, S. (2015). Assistance- and Knowledge-Services for Smart Production. In S. N. Lindstaedt, T. Ley, & H. Sack (Ed.), *Proceedings of the 15th International Conference on Knowledge Technologies and Data-driven Business* (pp. 40:1-40:4). ACM.

VanLehn, K., Lynch, C., Schulze, K. G., Shapiro, J. A., Shelby, R., Taylor, L., . . . Wintersgill, M. (2005). The Andes Physics Tutoring System: Lessons Learned. *I. J. Artificial Intelligence in Education, 15*(3), 147-204.

Wahlster, W. (Ed.). (2013). *SemProM: Foundations of Semantic Product Memories for the Internet of Things.* Springer.

Xu, X., Wang, L., & Rong, Y. (2006). STEP-NC and function blocks for interoperable manufacturing. *Automation Science and Engineering, IEEE Transactions on, 3*(3), 297-308.

THE IMPACT OF TECHNOLOGY INTEGRATION UPON COLLEGIATE PEDAGOGY FROM THE LENS OF MULTIPLE DISCIPLINES

Joan Ann Swanson
Skidmore College, Saratoga Springs, NY, USA

ABSTRACT

Technology integration on college campuses has become both a reality and necessity to meet the demands for function and flow in an ever advancing world of learning. This study qualitatively reviewed how a multi-disciplinary sample of collegiate instructors viewed technology and how they incorporated it into their pedagogy. Results indicated a range of technology use largely dependent upon personal faculty self-efficacy with technological tools, and additionally their philosophical and pedagogical beliefs rather than disciplinary alignment. However, significant impact was reported on technology enhancing all discipline-related information, tools, and methods of study.

KEYWORDS

Collegiate pedagogy, technology, teaching philosophies

1. INTRODUCTION

Technology integration on college campuses is no longer a question for the future, but rather a reality for today. It is central to the function and flow of everyday business for colleges. There isn't a realm of collegiate operation that has not been touched and influenced in some way by technological advances and innovations; this invites inquiry into the impact of the integration of technology into collegiate pedagogy. Technology provides faculty opportunities to modify teaching approaches beyond the traditional lecture within four walls (Renes & Strange, 2011). All academic divisions and disciplines on college campuses have experienced encouragement to integrate and infuse technology into their pedagogy and disciplinary practices. It has been clearly heralded that success for the future is to involve technology. Even the United States Department of Education claims that technology is an impetus for improving learning, productivity and performance (Georgian & Olson, 2008).

Trends to increase the use of technology have led educators to think in new and innovative ways to face the challenges for education today. In 2010, a report predicted that the key technologies that in the next five years would surface in the collegiate realm: mobile computing, open content, electronic books, augmented reality, gesture-based computing and visual data analysis (Johnson, et al., 2010). As each of these innovations has and is taking a foothold in collegiate education, it is not clear which have become more discipline specific and which are being effectively integrated, and additionally, for what purposes.

For the purpose of this study, technology is defined as tools, innovations and advancements designed to improve conditions or states of being. According to *Merriam Webster*, technology is "a manner of accomplishing a task especially using technical processes, methods, or knowledge" (http://www.merriam-webster.com/dictionary/technology). Educational technology accomplishes the task of promoting educative experiences, often using software and hardware. Additionally, emerging technologies for education are interdisciplinary. For the purposes of this study, technology used for instruction was defined as technology that was used beyond the perfunctory role of classroom management, and includes uses such as presentation applications, collaboration tools, interactive software applications, multimedia adaptive diagnostic tools and learning management systems (Paver, Walker, and Hung, 2014). The use of learning technologies is often described as technology-enhanced learning; and includes innovations such as computer-based learning, computerized tools and applications which provide multimedia options, animations, virtual environments, games and simulations, mobile learning, digital portfolios, wikis, blogs and more (Graesser, Chipman, & King, 2008; Ragupathi & Hubball, 2015).

The theoretical lens used in this study centered on the work done by Bernauer and Tomei (2015) in which they purport that the integration of pedagogy and technology must center on the pillars of teaching and learning: content (what), implications (how), philosophy (why), and the teacher-learner relationship. The following research questions then became the framework from which the researcher examined the higher education technology integration:

1) What do faculty members report as the impact that technology has had on their discipline, their pedagogy, and their research?

2) How is their teaching philosophy evident in their technology implementation?

3) What does faculty's technological implementation reveal about the teacher-learner relationships in the case study?

2. LITERATURE REVIEW

Most higher education institutions have invested in equipment and infrastructure, enabling them to have technology enhanced classrooms, learning management systems, and online administrative functioning. In the collegiate setting students complete online admissions applications, utilize online registration, communicate primarily through email, and now even have options for online and blended learning courses. Modern technological structures have also changed how higher education institutions function administratively. The demand for increased technology in the collegiate setting has resulted in an environment where knowledge is convenient and accessible which impacts instruction both in content and delivery (Chaudhry & Malik, 2014). Literature is now surfacing which investigates how technology is being integrated into education and has enhanced learning, specifically, the impact of technology on pedagogy and student learning outcomes. Kirkwood and Price (2013) argue that "technology itself is not the agent of change: it is the teacher." Despite all the innovative implementations of technology into collegiate life and study, the most effective uses appear to be in concert with student learning style preferences and adaptations that align most to the cultural and epistemological uniqueness of academic disciplines (Arenas, 2015). The actual characteristics of particular disciplines need to be taken into consideration as well as the teacher's pedagogical stance and the student's learning style. Additionally, technologies also embody philosophies and ideologies in themselves (Siemens & Tittenberger, 2009) so the philosophical and ideological components of the technology used should be considered within the alignment and integration into the course content and delivery.

2.1 Faculty

According to current studies, faculty typically approach technology according to their conceptions about learning and their teaching style (teacher-centered or learner-centered) and either have the perspective that technology use should be "strategic (i.e. general approach)" or "tactical (i.e. particular applications)" (Kirkwood & Price, 2013, p.328). These beliefs about teaching are intricately tied to their pedagogical development and what role and influence technology will play. One of the largest barriers to new technology use in collegiate situations is reported is a lack of relevance for using technology in a particular situation (Greener & Wakefield, 2015). Literature reviews of technology use in higher education have revealed more of an emphasis on the implementation of technology, creating and using new innovations in higher education, and less about the actual process of teaching and learning (Kirkwood & Price, 2013). Essentially, these findings serve to challenge faculty to be sure their technology use is aligned with their pedagogy, rather than the technology driving the teaching methods.

Newer faculty, especially those beginning their tenure-track journey, tend to seek appropriate and applicable selections of technologies compatible with their discipline and desired learning outcomes (Ragupathi & Hubball, 2015). Many colleges are encouraging increased use of technology for educational purposes by creating support systems through faculty learning groups, and developing teaching and learning centers which offer workshops, seminars and one-on-one support (Ragupathi & Hubball, 2015). Information technology and media services are growing as a result of the need to service technical support for teaching and learning. Professional development for technology integration is on the rise and needs to continue as the rapid rate of advancements in technology are very difficult for individual faculty to keep abreast of on their own. This is especially true for early career faculty who very much need the support of a professional learning community (Ragupathi & Hubball, 2015). However, Georgian and Olson (2007) found that only half of faculty offered trainings about technology integration actually utilize that resource. They stress that when training does occur, faculty need to go beyond learning how the technology works; they need to assess if it is appropriate for their circumstances, and if it can be integrated appropriately into their discipline. Other researchers also stress that departmental cultures differ and should have unique trainings geared toward integration that fits that discipline (Brown, 2003, Ertmer, 2005). Additionally, "Broadening technological and pedagogical horizons may include re-visioning our ideas, practices, and training schemes in order to impart our pedagogical messages" (Georgian & Olson, 2007, p. 8).

Some institutions have begun to provide incentives such as funding to faculty for experimenting with innovative technological pedagogies (Greener & Wakefield, 2015; Ragupathi & Hubball, 2015). However, some spheres of faculty are hesitant about, and even resistant to incorporating technology into their repertoire of instructional strategies. Although collegiate administrations attempt to persuade faculty use of technology through examples of peer success, professional development, and support, Paver, Walker, and Hung (2014) found that intention and attitude significantly predicted the successful integration of technology for instruction by community college faculty. Other research also supports increased success when peers are used for technology integration training, especially when the training is discipline specific (Brown, 2003, Ertmer, 2005, Georgian & Olson, 2008). Naturally, an educator's self-efficacy for using the technology will increase as technology application and integration become transferable to their discipline. One key mentioned by Paver, Walker and Hung (2014) was for faculty to understand such integration could occur within already existing teaching styles.

Changes occur as new generations, with new perspectives, replace leadership. Faculty need to be aware that the students of today, who are becoming leaders, are entering college campuses with the experience of always having technology as a part of their lives. They were born post the invention of the world wide web. These students don't know a world where technology is not integral in their daily functioning. "No generation has ever had to wait so little time for so much information" (Renard, 2005, p. 44). Today's students are often called "digital natives", having grown up around technology and are instructed by "digital immigrants" , professors who often struggle to adapt teaching to available technological resources and formats (Prensky, 2010). Using technology is not foreign to these students. However, even digital natives sometime struggle with the rate of change in technology and how to appropriately incorporate that into educational experiences (Li, Worch, Ahou & Aguiton, 2015), especially since they view specific technology as compartmentalized only for specific purposes (Swanson & Walker, 2015).

2.2 Disciplines

Faculty members are typically well trained in discipline specific content and research methodology. With the introduction of new technologies, a new struggle has emerged in which these faculty members are now challenged to make pedagogical adaptations to accommodate the technological advances. Considering these disciplines may have unique and tailored perspectives on how they approach instruction, then their nature may impact how they potentially incorporate technology. Biglan (1973) classifies the nature of academic disciplines according into four groups: hard-pure, hard-applied, soft-pure and soft-applied. There seems to be a lack of research to date that explores the different manners in which these disciplines integrate technology. It is essential for institutions to know how to support academic and professional development while taking into consideration technological advances and multidisciplinary applications of technology.

Serious considerations need to be made as to how and when technology should be used on college campuses for pedagogical purposes. Research is being done to determine the impact on learning when specific components of technology are integrated into teaching and learning situations. Churcher, Downs, and Tewksbury (2014) who researched using social media and web 2.0 technologies in collegiate courses purport more deliberative consideration needs to be given about using theoretical implications of supplementing higher education experiences with technology. "Content, context, and pedagogy must be equal partners with technology" when there is technology integration in collegiate courses (Renes & Strange, 2011; Harris,

Mishra, & Koehler, 2009). Each technological component has implications specific to that medium and to the discipline in which it is being integrated.

"As in all moments of major technological change, people, companies, and institutions feel the depth of the change, but they are often overwhelmed by it, out of sheer ignorance of its effects" (Castells, p.10). To better understand the process and impact in which technology integration is happening at the collegiate level, this study provides an interdisciplinary analysis as to how faculty at one institution have incorporated technology. The study sought to reveal patterns and purposes for technology integration and to determine factors upon which that technology use was dependent. Lastly, the study sought to analyze disciplinary perspectives on the impact of technology integration on their particular pedagogy.

3. METHODS

This study is a descriptive comparative, qualitative analysis conducted in the form of a case study which focused upon the technological integration experiences of faculty in one private liberal arts intuition in north eastern United States. The study examines how the use of technology intersected with pedagogical approaches across a sample of disciplines.

3.1 Sample/Participants

The populations for this study consisted of a cross sectional sample of higher education faculty in a liberal arts institution in northeastern United States (N=16). Data for this research study was gathered via interviews and lectures presented by these faculty who were specifically asked to address technology integration into their discipline. Each of the faculty members who were interviewed or presented their perspectives on technology integration in their discipline were described as either un-tenured, tenure-track or tenured faculty. Their range of experience in their discipline spanned three years to nearly thirty years in higher education. The disciplinary fields represented were distributed broadly across academic programs and departments (see Appendix A).

Additional data was gathered from a student survey where they indicated their coursework they had taken that year and the ways technology was being used in those courses. Those students additionally represented a range of programs and majors, thus having had courses in a variety of disciplines.

3.2 Procedure

Faculty members from across disciplines were asked to present to a freshman seminar about the impact of technology upon their discipline, their pedagogical approach, and their research. They were allowed to present in any manner that they desired and in any location on campus. The instructions were general in effort keep researcher bias from tainting faculty participants' concepts of technology as they shared with their audience. Notes were taken during the faculty presentations which were then coded for indications of technological impact on the faculty's particular discipline and on their personal pedagogical approach and use. Additionally, the researcher noted the faculty's choice of whether to use technology in their presentation and coded what type of innovation was accessed.

4. RESULTS

4.1 What do Faculty Members Report as the Impact that Technology has had on their Discipline, their Pedagogy, and their Research?

An analysis displaying how technology was utilized by faculty and their self-report of how technology impacted their different disciplines is displayed in Appendix A. A total of 16 faculty presented to a group of students about the impact of technology. Each instructor represented a different discipline or program including the following: Information Technology - GIS, Library Science, Chemistry, Geology, Physics, Psychology, Management and Business, World Language and Literature (Spanish), Information Technology – Media Services, Classics, Anthropology, Music, Dance, Art – Visual Design, and Performing Arts - Lighting and Sound.

The overwhelming consensus for technological impact centered in how these faculty were able access and present information. They shared about new content but also about the processes of getting that data. Some of the content knowledge they teach about was not even in existence or available prior to recent technological advancements. One example of such advancement was clearly evident when the psychology professor demonstrated how her technological equipment allowed for measurement and analysis of rapid eye movement during reading. Another example of change and impact was noted by the Information technologist who used GIS (Geographic Information System) mapping to gather data on a local tree census, which was then used by local environmentalist and government for community decision making. Additionally, the Management and Business professor explained how technology helps industries gather consumer preference information which businesses and her students use.

There was no significant difference in types of technology used when compared by faculty gender. There was, however, a difference in using technological advancements when it came to faculty status. Most of the early career faculty members were more inclined to incorporate presentation software. Most faculty in the case study also revealed that advancements in technology have significantly impacted their research endeavors. The archeology professor demonstrated this by explaining how instead of having to carry a tremendous amount of equipment, she was able to easily and effectively use digital equipment for capturing images deep in caves, and the recent use of multispectral imaging and lasers to gather data.

4.2 How is their Teaching Philosophy Evident in their Technology Implementation?

Technology doesn't take the place of the teacher, it should enable the educator to more deeply explore and express their beliefs and understandings about pedagogy for their particular discipline. In each of the presentations and interviews with the faculty in the case study, it became evident that they have developed their own style and comfort level with how they used technology. The technology use varied more by teaching philosophy than by discipline. This was evident when the classics professor demonstrated the use of required pre-class homework involving online lectures exploring ancient images in order to utilize class time for discussion and interaction. Contrastingly, the language instructor mentioned student's having access to many online tools but little to no technology was required in or out of class. Both classes involved pedagogy based upon discussion format but their philosophy of teaching varied when it came to how technology could be incorporated.

4.3 What Does Faculty's Technological Implementation Reveal about the Teacher-Learner Relationships in the Case Study?

Two of the faculty admitted they personally do not frequently use technology in their lectures and presentations; rather they encourage students to practice and apply materials using simulations and online activities outside of class as a means of enrichment. This process gives students autonomy and responsibility for deeper learning. In contrast, some instructors require technologically based assignments inside and/or outside of class, or within labs. The physics professor demonstrated lab projects involving technology (computer simulations, robotic equipment, etc.) he would require using technology which then would supplement his lectures and reading. Both perspectives, required or not required, understood that the technology use could serve to motivate and provide deeper learning.

Several faculty members commented on how technology has assisted in collaborative research with students. Projects were able to be expanded because of the skills students brought to the situation, or developed as a result of the collaboration. Technology played a major role in these cases, exemplified when a classics student discovered ways to enhance ancient script to a readable level.

5. CONCLUSION AND DISCUSSION

One major implication from this study is the importance of encouragement for effective implementation and integration of technology via peer collaboration and demonstration of possibilities for technology use. Faculty shared they had participated in workshops to strengthen their technological skills and several mentioned having met with peers to share about their pedagogical practices. These were the individuals most readily taking advantage of technological innovations. The workshops and peer collaborations described were primarily interdisciplinary and highly productive.

Even when the instructor themselves did not have the necessary skills to implement and produce technology enriched pedagogy, it was noted many encouraged student projects which utilized the students' technological skills and knowledge. One implication from the study reinforces the concept of empowering students education related technological advancements. Regardless of the discipline, instructors play a role in assisting learners in transferring and applying their knowledge, which often is often expressed with or uses technological innovations. As evidenced in this study, effective technology use can be in addition to or utilized outside regular class time.

Changes in higher education will always include technology. The impact of technology integration rests heavily upon faculty's personal approach to the process and their theoretical belief about teaching and learning. Faculty in this study who were successfully using technology, regardless of their discipline were motivated by enhancing their students' learning. Numerous opportunities exist for professional development and peer collaboration. Faculty taking advantage of those opportunities show greater self-efficacy for technology integration and increase potential for student learning.

REFERENCES

Arenas, E., 2015. Affordances of learning technologies in higher education multicultural environments. *Electronic Journal of e-Learning*, Vol. 13, No. 4, pp. 217-227.

Bernauer, J. A. & Tomei, L. A. (2015). *Integrating pedagogy and technology*. New York, NY: Rowman & Littlefield.

Biglan, A., 1973. The characteristics of subject matter in different academic areas. *Journal of Applied Psychology*, Vol. 57, No. 2, pp. 195-203.

Brown, A. H., 2003. Fitting workshops into faculty mores. In D. G. Brown (ED.), *Developing faculty to use technology: Programs and strategies to choices and challenges*, Madison. WI: Atwood Publishing.

Castells, M., 2014. The impact of the internet on society: A global perspective. *OpenMind*, BBVA. Retrieved from: https://www.bbvaopenmind.com/wp-content/uploads/2014/03/BBVA-OpenMind-Internet-Manuel-Castells-The-Impact-of-the-Internet-on-Society-A-Global-Perspective.pdf

Chaudhry, M. Y., & Malik, A., 2014. Intersection of pedagogy and emerging technologies to enhance student-centered learning in higher education. *Pakistan Journal of Social Science*, Vol. 34, No.2, pp. 397-407.

Churcher, K. M. A., Downs, E., & Tewksbury, D., 2014. "Friending" Vygotsky: A social constructivist pedagogy of knowledge building through classroom social media use. *The Journal of Effective Teaching*, Vol. 14, No.1, pp. 33-50.

Ertmer, P., 2005. Teacher pedagogical beliefs: The final frontier in our quest for technology integration? *Educational Technology, Research and Development*, Vol. 53, No.4, pp. 25-39.

Georgiana, D. A. & Olson, M. R., 2008. Integration of technology in higher education: A review of faculty self-perceptions. *The Internet and Higher Education*, Vol. 11, No. 1, pp. 1-8.

Graesser, A. C., Chipman, P. & King, B. G., 2008. Computer-mediated technologies. In J. M. Spector, et al. (Eds.), *Handbook of Research on Educational Communications and Technology (3rd Edition),* New York, NY: Erlbaum p. 211-224.

Greener, S. L. & Wakefield, C., 2015. Developing confidence in the use of digital tools in teaching. *Electronic Journal of e-Learning*, Vol. 13, No. 4, pp. 206-267.

Harris, J., Mishra, P., & Koehler, M., 2009. Teachers' technological pedagogical content knowledge and learning activity types: Curriculum-based technology integration reframed. *Journal of Research on Technology in Education*, Vol. 41, No. 4, pp. 393–416.

Johnson, L. F., Levine, A., Smith, R. S., & Haywood, K., 2010. Key emerging technologies for postsecondary education. *Education Digest: Essential Readings Condensed for Quick Review*, retrieved from www.eddigest.com.

Kirkwood, A., & Price, L., 2013. Missing: evidence of a scholarly approach to teaching and learning with technology in higher education. *Teaching in Higher Education*, Vol. 18, No. 3, pp. 327-337.

Li, L., Worch, E., Zhou, Y., & Aguiton, R., 2015. How and why digital generation teachers use technology in the classroom: An explanatory sequential mixed methods study. *International Journal for the Scholarship of Teaching and Learning*, Vol. 9, No. 2, pp. 1-9.

Paver, J., Walker, D. A., & Hung, W., 2014. Factors that predict the integration of technology for instruction by community college adjunct faculty. *Community College Journal of Research and Practice*, Vol. 38, No.1, pp. 68-85.

Prensky, M., 2010. *Teaching digital natives: Partnering for real learning*. Thousand Oaks, CA: Corwin.

Ragupathi, K & Hubball, H., 2015. Scholarly approaches to learning technology integration in a research-intensive university context: Impact of a new faculty initiative. *Transformative Dialogues: Teaching & Learning Journal*, Vol. 8, No. 1, pp. 1-16.

Renard, L., 2005. Teaching the DIG generation. *Educational Leadership*, Vol. 62, No. 7, pp. 44-47.

Renes, S. L., & Strange, A. T., 2011. Using technology to enhance higher education. *Innovations in Higher Education*, Vol. 36, pp. 203-213.

Siemens, G. & Tittenberger, P., 2009. *Handbook of emerging technologies for learning – emerging technologies for learning*. Retrieved from http://ltc.umanitoba.ca/wikis/etl/index.php/Handbook_of_Emerging_Technologies_for_ Learning.

Swanson, J. A. & Walker, E., 2015. Academic versus non-academic emerging adult college student technology use. *Technology Knowledge and Learning*, Vol. 20, No.2, pp. 147-158.

Veletsianos, G., 2010. A Definition of Emerging Technologies for Education. In G. Veletsianos (Ed.), *Emerging Technologies in Distance Education* (pp. 3-22). Edmonton, AB: Athabasca University Press. - See more at: http://www.veletsianos.com/2008/11/18/a-definition-of-emerging-technologies-for-education/#sthash.DtieszikK.dpuf.

Weld, J. & Trainer, J., 2007. A faculty interdisciplinary institute as liberator from stifling disciplinary mythology. *College Teaching*, Vol. 55, No. 4, pp. 157-163.

Appendix A – Sample of technological use and impact on disciplines

Faculty/ Discipline	Gender	Impact on medium/tools used	Impact on discipline	Impact on pedagogy
Information Technology GIS instructor	male	computers/ projection *Fulcrum* software Mobile Devices/ smart phones	core content	presentation mode digital mapping enables research, use of satellites, rapid changes
Library Science	female	computer/ projection, web-based databases new resources	changed access to information revolutionized use of library space & tools	communication presentation, research, all modes changed
Science – Chemistry	female	computer/projection, Interactive software lab tools, visuals	advanced analysis software & tools access to information	use of interactive software, simulations,
Science – Geology	female	projected visuals	access to information software & tool advances	changed modes of displaying information
Information Technology	female	computer/projection software applications	rapid changes	constant professional development needed
Music	male	computer, synthesizers, soundboard, recording equipment, instruments	production time and modes changed, performance changed	instant playback, visuals and other new tools available
Dance	female	large screen projection	enhanced productions performance critiques	recording used for access to examples

A LEARNING SUPPORT SYSTEM REGARDING MOTION TRIGGER FOR REPETITIVE MOTION HAVING AN OPERATING INSTRUMENT

Hiroshi Toyooka[1], Kenji Matsuura[2] and Naka Gotoda[3]
[1]*Graduate School of Advanced Technology and Sciences, Tokushima University, Japan*
[2]*Center for Administration of Information Technology, Tokushima University, Japan*
[3]*Information Technology Center, Kagawa University, Japan*

ABSTRACT

In the learning support for repetitive motions having an operating instrument, it is necessary for learners to control not only their own body motions but also an instrument corresponding to the body. This study focuses on the repetitive motion learning using single operation instrument without the movement in space; i.e. jump-rope and hula-hoop. The proposed system makes it possible for learners to strengthen their ability of perceiving the motion timing depending on the instrument state in time.

KEYWORDS

Repetitive motion, Learning support, Skill development, Motor control

1. INTRODUCTION

In the science of physical sports, it is often used the term skill. (Magill 1998) stated that skills have meant the task with the specific goal to be achieved. For example, the batting skill in baseball has a goal to hit back a ball to a certain direction aiming at accurate timing. Therefore, players require spontaneous body motions. This study deals with motor skills in such a context. In addition to movements such as batting, piano and dance, they need a kind of motor control. On the other hand, movements that respond quickly to opponents and kicking accurate shot to avoid the keeper's saving in soccer games need perceptual skill. Further deeper sensing of foreseeing a step ahead and instructing next play are developed on cognitive skill. In these skills, it is mentioned that accuracy of time, position, and force are factors of the success. This study regards target fields focused on human nervous system, the musculoskeletal system, the body, and the behavior to enable these skills as motor control. Additionally, this study touches upon fields focused on learning process and promotion of acquisition as motor learning.

Tracing a body movement as digital data has become easier with the rapid progress of wearable devices and sensor technologies. A lot of studies on learning support are proposed using information processing techniques. According to (Soga et al. 2004), learning support systems for physical skill development require major three functionalities. The first one is to observe skills of a human, whereas the second one is a function to evaluate a motion using an observed data. The third one is a function to provide the feedback to the learner based on an evaluation result. In repetitive motion, the accuracy of the motion timing is significantly effective. It should be adjusted dynamically through these processes. Therefore, we need to take into account of what good timing of a motion is in order to evaluate and to provide the feedback.

This study supports human development of the repetitive motion with an instrument such in playing hula-hoop and jump-rope. Motor control depends on the ability of parallel processing for both controlling the body motion and the instrument thereof. Namely, learners need appropriate motion in accordance with the movement of an instrument. Therefore, this paper tries to design the learning support system that estimates an instrument trajectory and a presented body motion for controlling it.

2. FEEDBACK FOR MOTOR SKILL DEVELOPMENT

2.1 Repetitive Motions

A kind of continuous skill includes the repetitive motion. As the feature of continuous motion, there is no end assuming ideal condition to repeat periodically same/similar motion divided by segmentation criteria. For example, a swimmer repeats normally same motion paddling water by the arms and legs as long as possible. In swimming neither devices nor instruments are used for experts. Running or swimming without any instruments are controlled by only own body motions. In other words, these movements do not operate anything but their body. Just imagine consider rope skipping and performing hula-hoop. Figure 1 illustrates relationship between human's motion and an instrument's motion. From Figure 1, the success or failure with an instrument in continuing are influenced by not only player's own body motion but also the instrument motion.

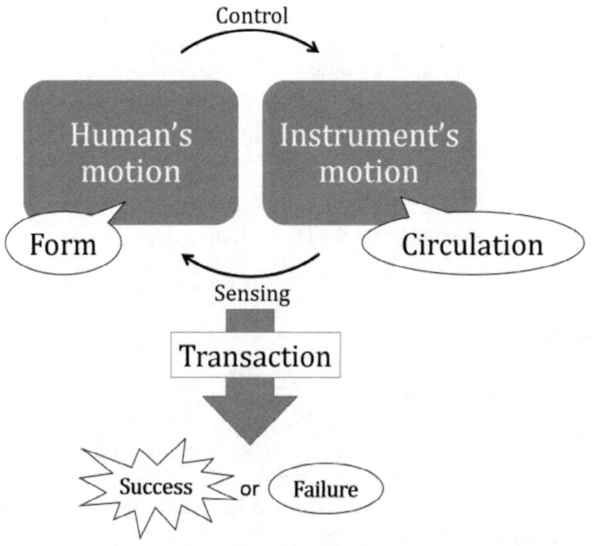

Figure 1. Relationship Human's Motion and Instrument's Motion

2.2 Feedback Timing

A system provides generally a feedback to learners in learning support of motor skills. The feedback information for learners is presented aiming at improving performance. It is significantly necessary to apply the feedback information to learners at effective timing. The feedback timing is available in three cases which are clearly distinguished by relative order. The first one is a case of where the system supplies it before exercise, as a preparatory phase. The second one is a case of where the system supplies after exercise, as a recalling phase. These two types work on asynchronous timing. In contrast, the last one is a case of where the system supplies during exercise. This type works on synchronous timing.

2.3 Purpose

Repetitive motions tend to take a long time. Therefore, when the repetitive motion is supplied with the feedback to learners at asynchronous timing, an influence to them is small, because a consciousness about the body motion during exercise fades as time goes by. In contrast, when the repetitive motion is supplied with the feedback to learners at synchronous timing, they can immediately remind the feedback information and reflect to the motion because they can aware the movement form of their body motion during exercise.

Synchronous timing is more appropriate in applying the feedback information. Therefore, this study tries to design and develop the learning support system to provide the appropriate feedback at synchronous timing. In this study, the proposed system supports repetitive motions with an instrument, where its concrete target is hula-hoop. Furthermore, this study focuses on a timing to control body motions.

3. METHODOLOGY

3.1 Timing of Hula-Hoop

Hula-hoop exercise has a circle instrument called a hoop. To keep a rotation of the hoop as long as possible by a waist motion back and forth becomes a hula-hoop skill. In addition, a hula-hoop player must control both player's body motion and the hoop. Therefore, s/he needs to give appropriate vibrations to keep a rotation of the hoop. Although this exercise is a continuous skill, there is actual end of exercise by failing. In order not to fail, the hula-hoop player should acquire the timing to give appropriate vibrations. In other words, the player needs to learn the motion timing of the waist for restoring the hoop, which is falling down, to a stable position during this exercise. This study focuses on the timing as one of a factor for stabilizing an instrument motion and proposes a supporting method of the motion timing for controlling the hoop.

3.2 Concrete Motion Image

Figure 2 illustrates the bird's eye view of simple forward and backward movement of the waist and the hoop in time series. Z-axis is front and back direction of the player and X-axis is right and left direction of the player. From the Figure 2, when the player performs a hula-hoop, the position of the hoop is always changing. Therefore, the player needs to apply vibration in line with the position of the hoop. This study focuses on positional relationship between player's waist and the hoop in front and back direction of the player. When the hoop is positioned in front of the player, the player's waist should be controlled backward. When the hoop is positioned behind the player, the player's waist should be operated forward. The player adjusts the hoop height along with the movement of the waist. However, the timing of the implication dominantly depends on each learner's movement from the frequency view point.

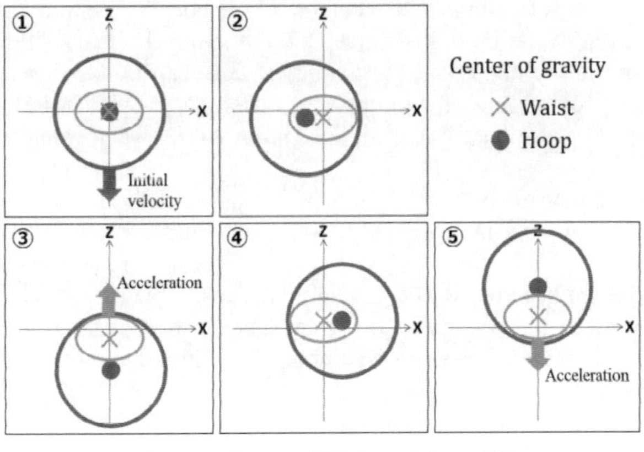

Figure 2. Concrete Image of Waist and Hoop Movements

3.3 Monitoring System

In this study, the system monitors hula-hoop using a motion capture system. Especially, we use the optical type being applicable for a quick movement. The optical type uses plural infrared cameras and markers. At first, a total of ten infrared cameras are placed in a room to eliminate blind spot. We set player's left and right directions as each plus and minus of X-axis, upper and lower direction as each plus and minus of Y-axis, and front and back direction as plus and minus of Z-axis in the three-dimensional coordinate.

Markers are reflected infrared light to acquire motion data, and attached several positions of the object where we want to acquire the motion data. We place markers to attach the waist of hula-hoop players and the hoop. Four markers are placed to the waist and the hoop respectively so that they can organize a space consisting of these markers. A motion capture system can calculate the center of gravity of these 4-points as a rigid body, and acquire data every 10 milliseconds.

3.4 Analysis System

3.4.1 Feature Extraction

The system detects the hoop state positioned in foremost and rearmost, because motion direction of the waist and hoop changes at these points in time. When the system plots the monitoring data in time series, we can observe the waveform expressing the feature of the repetitive motion. The horizontal axis is indicates passed time, and the vertical axis is the amplitude of the waist and the hoop. Figure 3 shows the hula-hoop data as an example. Large waveform shows the time shift of the waist, and small waveform shows the time shift of the hoop. From Figure 3, the hoop state positioned in foremost is expressed the local maximum point in the waveform. Similarly, its state positioned in rearmost is also expressed the local minimum point in the waveform. The system compares the current data and the latest data, and it judges the large/small relation of Z-values. In the case of the current data is larger than the latest one, when the current data changes smaller than the latest one, the system detects the local maximum point. Similarly, in the case of the current data is smaller than the latest one, when the current data changes larger than the latest one, it detects the local minimum point.

From these points, the system extracts some features. We call a cycle of waist from that the waist is operated foremost to that next motion is operated. We call similarly a cycle of hoop from that the hoop is operated foremost to that next motion is operated. In these cycles, we call a phase that an index showing a position in the cycle. The phase that between the waist and the hoop may have a gap of phase. We regard this gap as phase difference. Therefore, the local maximum/minimum point between the waist and the hoop may have a gap in time perspective. We define this gap as time difference. Further, we express these features above in the waveform. Figure 3 also expresses the hoop cycle and the time difference. This study regards intervals from a local maximum point to a next local maximum point as the hoop cycle, and regards gaps between the local maximum point of the waist and that of the hoop as the time difference. Then, it defines the phase difference as a ratio of the time difference to the hoop cycle. From Figure 3, the hoop cycle can be confirmed to the waist and the hoop, and the time difference can be confirmed between the waist and the hoop. Namely, the hula-hoop performed with the time difference by which the hoop state is delayed than the waist state. Therefore, we try to identify the motion timing of the waist using the phase difference from the hoop phase.

Furthermore, the system observes the hoop height and phase difference at time course. Figure 4 expresses one of these observations in five male subjects. Solid polylines are the hoop height relative to the waist height, and broken polylines are the phase difference. From Figure 4, the phase difference tends to be increased as the hoop height becomes lower. In addition, Table 1 reads a correlation between the hoop height and each feature value based on those subjects. From Table 1, there is larger negatively correlation between the hoop height and the phase difference in common. From this relationship, the system predicts the phase difference in future, and identifies the timing.

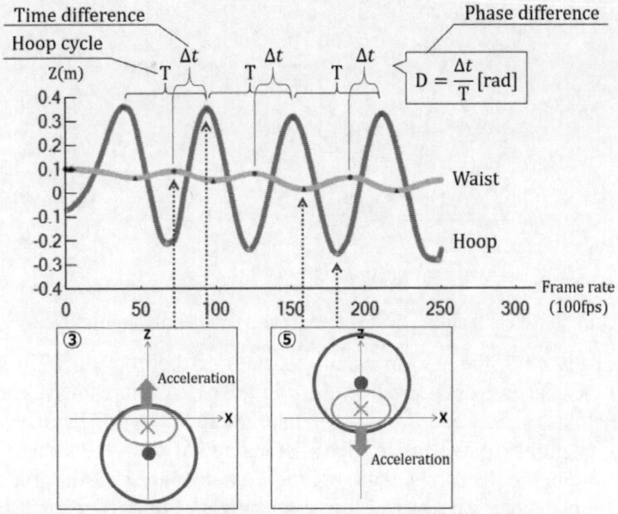

Figure 3. Motion Timing and Phase Difference in Waveform

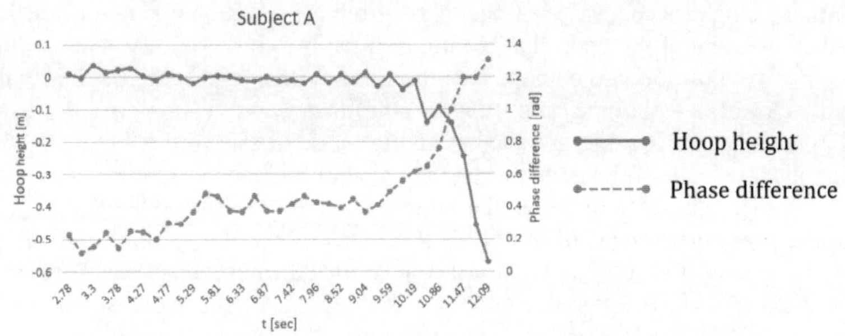

Figure 4. Hoop Height and Phase Difference at Time Course (Subject A)

Table 1. Correlation Coefficient between Hoop Height and Each Feature Value

Subjects	Phase difference	Hoop cycle	Hoop amplitude
A	**-0.88**	-0.62	0.10
B	**-0.88**	-0.60	0.51
C	**-0.92**	0.09	0.43
D	**-0.86**	0.75	0.82
E	**-0.97**	-0.10	0.33

3.4.2 Timing Prediction

The system identifies the hoop phase during hula-hoop. For this proposal, we need to estimate the hoop cycle, because the hoop phase can't be identified without the hoop cycle. Figure 5 illustrates a reason to estimate the hoop cycle. From Figure 5, the system can identify the hoop phase during hula-hoop, and estimate the hoop phase that should operate the waist. Therefore, it identifies the hoop phase from the estimated hoop cycle and provides the timing of the waist motion that is mentioned in previous section as feedback to the learner.

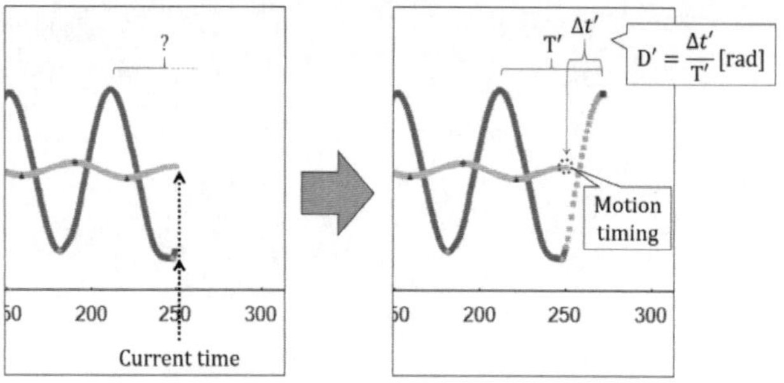

Figure 5. No estimation of Next Cycle (Left) and Estimation of Next Cycle (Right)

In addition, from Figure 5, the system calculates the next hoop cycle from value of the time difference and the phase difference. Therefore, it predicts them in the next cycle using regression analysis. At that time, this study uses a relationship between the hoop height and the phase difference. Value of the hoop height is applied to the hoop height being relative to the waist height. At first, the system acquires a two-dimensional regression formula from the learner's data by regression analysis. An objective variable is the phase difference, and an explanatory variable is the hoop height. Figure 6 expresses an example on result of regression analysis. 'R2' is a coefficient determination. It is accuracy index of approximation and good model that is nearer to a value of one. From Figure 6, the system observes the coefficient determination of a regression formula being near to a value of one. Next, from the result, the system can calculate the next hoop cycle and predict the cycle of the hoop that is falling. It tends to be relatively short in higher position of the hoop and long in lower position of the hoop. Therefore, the system predicts to be shorter the hoop cycle when the hoop height is lower. At that time, this study assumes that players can control most stable the hoop when a value of the hoop height is same as a value of the waist height. From Figure 5, the calculated phase difference is an ideal value for the learner when the value of the hoop height is zero. The system detects the hoop height lower than the waist height as the falling hoop, and estimates the hoop cycle calculable by the ideal value of the phase difference. At this time, it estimates excessively small the value of the hoop cycle while the hoop height is better to be low. At last, it identifies the hoop phase to operate the waist in the next cycle using the predicted phase difference and the estimated the hoop cycle based on the hoop height. Then, when the hoop phase during hula-hoop has arrived the identified hoop phase, it implies to move the waist to learners.

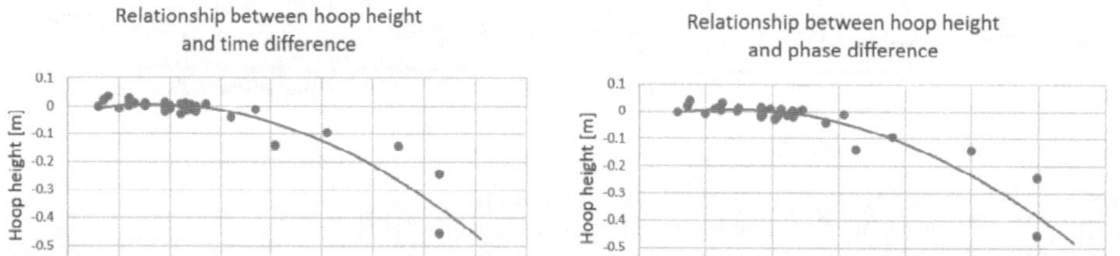

$y_1 = -3.31x^2 - 2.88x + 0.19$ R2 = 0.88

$y_2 = -4.68x^2 - 4.23x + 0.35$ R2 = 0.87

Figure 6. An Example on Result of Regression Analysis (Subject A)

3.5 Feedback System

In this study, the system supports the waist motion of front and back direction. The feedback is desired simple contents so that learners can also understand intuitively during hula-hoop. Figure 7 illustrates a user interface under development. From Figure 7, the left side shows the feedback to be move the waist from front to back and the right side shows the feedback to be move the waist from back to front. The feedback system displays the square in right edge of a screen. The square moves until green line with the lapse of time. When it arrives on green line, it is changed to a triangle. Display position of the square shows an arrival state until the hoop phase to operate the waist. In addition, the system displays two color of the square into red color and blue color. The former shows an operation to backward of the waist, the triangle moves downward. The letter shows an operation to forward of the waist, the triangle moves upward. Therefore, learners operate the waist in accordance with the movement of triangles while watching squares. Thereby, the system can induce learners to predict the motion timing of the waist.

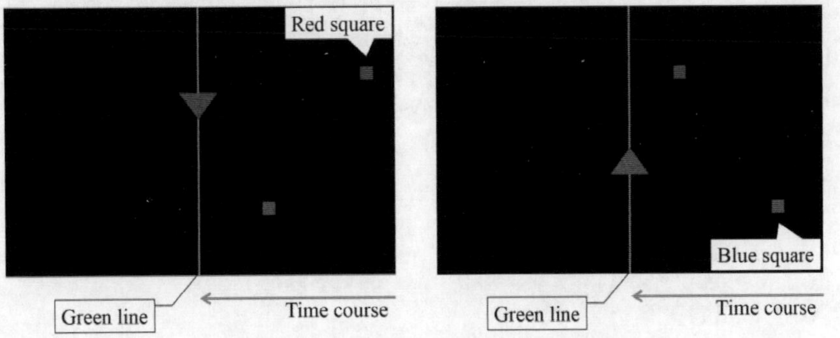

Figure 7. User Interface Under Development

4. SUPPORTING METHOD

4.1 Supporting Scenario

This section describes a supporting scenario. This study aims at acquisition of the timing of body motion for stable hula-hoop exercise by the synchronous learning support. There are a pre-trial phase, a main trial phase, and a post-trial phase in the learning support by this study so that the system needs several accumulated data to create the feedback. Therefore, learners of supporting target in this study is not a novice that can't rotate the hoop but an intermediate-level learner that can rotate the hoop a little. At first, in pre-trial phase, the system observes the learner's hula-hoop and creates a model for the learner from the observation. Next, in main trial, the system provides the feedback to the learner using the model during exercise. The learner acquires a sense of an appropriate operation interval corresponding to the hoop height through the feedback. After then, in post-trial, the learner performs the hula-hoop without the feedback. Therefore, the learner gradually acquires the timing of the hula-hoop by iteration of the main trial and the post-trial.

4.2 System Flow

In this section, this paper describes a system configuration. Figure 8 illustrates our supporting flow in the system. At first, in monitoring system, the system acquires the learner's motion data using motion capture system. Next, in analysis system, it performs the regression analysis from the inputted time series data of the hoop height and the phase difference when it is inputted the monitoring data, and created the learner's model. At this time, if it already creates that, it predicts the phase difference in next cycle corresponding to the hoop height using the time when it detects the local maximum point or the local minimum point. It calculates the next hoop cycle and estimates the hoop cycle required to restore the hoop height when the hoop height is lower than the waist height. Then, it identifies the hoop phase to operate the waist from the predicted phase difference and the estimated hoop cycle. At last, in the feedback system, it displays the feedback animation on screen. Therefore, it repeats these flow and provides the synchronous learning support.

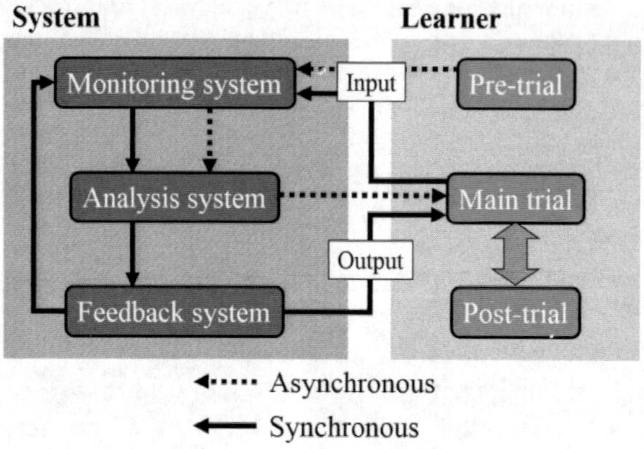

Figure 8. Supporting Flow

5. CONCLUSION

This paper proposed a learning support method based on the timing in repetitive motion using an instrument. Especially for hula-hoop, this study tried to give the feedback to learners during motion in real-time support. Hula-hoop was observed using the motion capture system and motion data was acquired. We focused on the time difference between the waist and the hoop, and estimated the motion timing to adjust the hoop height. In addition, we developed the system for improving.

The system in this paper only implements a supporting function of the timing. We plan to design the total supporting system to combine functions of the spacing and the grading. Further, the system needs to adjust the feedback timing for each learner in terms of synchronous support. Therefore, to implement the adjustment of the feedback timing is made as an issue to be addressed in the future.

ACKNOWLEDGEMENT

This work was supported by JSPS KAKENHI Grant Number JP15K01072.

REFERENCES

Book

Magill, E. R., 1998.: *Motor learning*: *Concepts and Application*, McGraw-Hill, USA.

Fitts, P. M. & Possner, M. I., 1967.: *Human Performance*. Brooks and Cole, Oxford, England.

Hurukawa, K. et al, 2009.: *Introduction to skill science*, Ohmsha, Japan.

Journal

Soga, M. et al., 2005. Skill of Learning Support and Learning Support Environment. *Journal of the Japanese Society for Artificial Intelligence*, Vol. 20, No. 5, pp. 533-540.

Conference paper or contributed volume

Hamagami, K. et al., 2013. A Consideration on Supporting Stabilization in Learning od repetitive Motions. *Workshop Proceedings of the 38th Annual Conference of JSiSE*, Kanazawa, Japan, pp. 315-316.

Yamada, K. & Matsuura, K., 2014. Design of an Environment for Motor-skill Development Based on Real-time Feedback. *Workshop Proceedings of the International Conference on Computers in Education*, Nara, Japan, pp. 799-804.

Toyooka, H. & Matsuura, K., 2015. Development of a system to imply well-timed action in a drill practice of motor actions. *Procceding of 11th International Conference on Knowledge Management*, Osaka, Japan, pp. 321-328.

TASK-BASED ASSESSMENT OF STUDENTS' COMPUTATIONAL THINKING SKILLS DEVELOPED THROUGH VISUAL PROGRAMMING OR TANGIBLE CODING ENVIRONMENTS

Takam Djambong and Viktor Freiman
Université de Moncton
Moncton, NB, Canada

ABSTRACT

While today's schools in several countries, like Canada, are about to bring back programming to their curricula, a new conceptual angle, namely one of computational thinking, draws attention of researchers. In order to understand the articulation between computational thinking tasks in one side, student's targeted skills, and the types of problems they aim to solve, we conducted a small-scale pilot case-study with two groups of students for the elementary (grade 6) and middle (grade 9) grades. While the students were working on 5-week-long curricular units in technology using robotics-based and computer-programming environments, we assessed their computational thinking abilities with 23 tasks given as pre- and post-test. Aiming to validate the tasks, namely, to see in what way it allows measuring computational things, we found a disparity between the types of the skills assessed, the easiness of the tasks, and the age groups, which makes difficult to arrive to some stable conclusion. We stated then a need for a longer and more sophisticated assessment as a subsequent research perspective to establish a stronger empirical evidence of possible relationships between related variables.

KEYWORDS

Computational thinking skills, Problem solving tasks, Technology-rich learning environment

1. INTRODUCTION: ISSUES AND PROBLEM STATEMENT

The world in which we live today, is already and will continue to be characterized by (1) increasing ubiquity of digital and computer technologies, (2) an extremely rapid changes in society and in the labor market in respect to the access to technology-rich environments,(3) increasing complexity of problems people will need to solve and challenges associated with this complexity, (4) the emergence of a networked communities marked by a strong trend towards connectivity combined to social and professional collaboration. The citizens of the 21st century are called to show great resilience capabilities and to develop specific skills, in order to adequately adapt to the constraints of an increasingly digital, complex and interconnected society.

How does today's society through teaching and learning system, prepare young citizens to adapt to these changes? For example, results of a recent survey[1] conducted in 2012, revealed that a number of Canadians, even those who belong to so-called 'born digital' generations showed the lowest levels of competence in problem solving in technology-rich environments (PS-TRE)[2]. Hence, in addition to traditionally known types of digital divides related to the access to technology and Internet and to its meaningful usage, other kinds of divide may emerge, among them the ability to use technology more productively and effectively in a larger variety of technology-rich contexts and tasks.

[1]Programme for International Assessment of Adult Competencies (PIAAC)
[2]Statistics Canada, 2013, p.13.

One of possible explanations of these new types of divides could be that many everyday activities young people naturally conduct using technology do not automatically enable them to make appropriate use of ICT in more formal (academic) contexts, especially in solving complex tasks. This somehow justifies the recommendations that UNESCO has made in its recent policy framework[3] for a sustainable development goals (SDG) putting a greater emphasis on the acquisition of high level skills, both cognitive and non-cognitive, such as critical thinking, problem-solving, decision making and teamwork. These skills are necessary to facilitate technology transfer to other contexts and the adaptation of young people to the current constraints of a (technology-richer) labor market in constant mutation.

How can we develop these skills and the abilities of transfer, remains an unsolved psychological and techno-pedagogical issue. The problem of "*how to teach effectively*" in order to enhance students to "*make learning in depth*" in the era of digital technologies, with its multiple Web-based resources and Mobile Apps must be analyzed in terms of learning environments that build on the principles of deep learning. The later require combination of (1) the ability to transfer skills from one context to another, (2) a more thoughtful understanding of academic content, and (3) the development of a variety of high-level skills. The deep learning requires exemplary teaching practices using the project-based approach and assignment of students to group tasks (Beaudoin et al., 2014, p.18-19).From this pedagogic perspective, as already mentioned in some previous research (Weintrop et al., 2015), the thoughtful use of computational tools and skillsets can deepen learning of disciplines like science, technology, engineering and mathematics (STEM).

In this respect, programming and coding has been recognized as one of the important competencies that require students to effectively use computational tools and devices, in order to solve complex real-problem today(Chao, 2016, p.202). The construct of computational thinking (CT), while not yet well defined, is often related to programming and coding while being considered as particular type of analytical thinking that employs mathematical and engineering thinking along with the abilities to understand and to solve complex problems within the constraints of the real world (Voskoglou& Buckley, 2012, p.32). The study of learning situations which are likely to favor the development of computational thinking in students through the use of programming and coding environments may therefore be an interesting line of inquiry in order to identify the most appropriate teaching practices to achieve this goal. But before we identify such practices, we need to determine key aspects of computational thinking and the set of tasks or activities that contribute to its development.

2. THE RESEARCH STUDY

2.1 The Context

The present study arose from the initiative launched in Canada in 2011 by the Council for Research in Social Sciences (SSHRC), calling for identification of new ways of learning that Canadians will need to succeed in society and the labor market of tomorrow (Beaudoin et al. 2014, p.40). It is in this context, the ICT Competences Network in Atlantic (CompéTICA, Compétences en TIC en Atlantique), a partnership development team, presently conducts several case studies oriented toward the identification and measurement of the acquisition and transfer of digital literacy to transition points between the family and school, between primary and secondary, between school and post-secondary institutions, and finally, between educational institutions and the labor market. This research-and-practice-based partnership aims among others axis of research, identify best teaching practices of different educational environment and life, from the perspective of the life-long continuum of digital competences. At the first stage of the project, several aspects related to digital competences development were identified by our partners as important to develop in all citizens, starting from the young age, and among them computational thinking related to the computer programming (Gauvin et al., 2015). At the second stage, we conducted preliminary observations on how development of computational thinking occurs during programming and coding activities among students of from the elementary (Grade 6) and middle school (Grade 9) in New Brunswick, Canada. More precisely, we aimed to investigate whether it is possible to establish a link between problem-solving tasks in a computer

[3] Education 2030 framework for action (SDG4), p.17

programming and robotics-based environments and second, the targeted skills related to computational thinking. At this preliminary stage of our data analysis, we focus on validating assessment tasks, namely to see, based on the results of the pre- and post-tests, a variation according to the estimated difficulty of the task, evolution of results from the pre- to the post-tests for particular types of tasks, and what are the tasks that could be more helpful in capturing the development of computational thinking.

2.2 The Conceptual Framework

2.2.1 Computational Thinking (CT)

First postulated by Seymour Papert in 1980s and 90s through the use of LOGO programming language and the development of cognitive abilities in solving a variety of computer-based problems, computational thinking (CT) emerged as core concept being popularized by Jeannette Wing (2006), who defines it as a set of attitudes and skills that all universally applicable, not just IT professionals should learn and master. Since then, CT is considered both as: (i) an essential component of 21st century skills, (ii) a computational approach of problem-solving process, (iii) a complex construct enabling STEM[4] disciplines skills acquisition, and (iv) the fundamental aspect of digital and computer science literacy. The CT then might well be regarded as a cognitive and intellectual tool, that would most effectively foster the implementation of the problem-solving process, through the use of technology-rich environments, and this, in a both socio-constructivist and socio-cultural perspective of situated and distributed cognition. CT could then be viewed as a type of analytical thinking that employs mathematical and engineering thinking to understand and solve complex problems within the constraints of the real world (Voskoglou & Buckley, 2012).

The educational intervention conducted in the context of our study was to develop among target students some skills[5] related to computational thinking such as: (i) capture different angles of approach to a problem and its solution (abstraction) (ii) reflect on the tasks to be performed by considering a series of steps (algorithmic thinking), (iii) assess the opportunity after assessing the complexity of a given problem, whether to break it down into several simple problems (decomposition), (iv) be able to link a specific problem to other problems of the same type that has already been solved (pattern recognition) and (v) realize that the solution to a given problem, can be the basis of the resolution of a wide range of similar problems (generalization). These targeted skills justify the choice of the different solving tasks proposed to students during the pretest and posttest of our study and rely despite the lack of a consensus definition of the construct of computational thinking, on the one proposed by the Computer Science Teachers Association (CSTA) as follows: "formulating problems in a way that enable us to use a computer and other tools to help solved them; logically organizing and analyzing data; representing data through abstractions such as models and simulations; automating solutions through algorithmic thinking (a series of ordered steps); identifying, analyzing and implementing possible solutions with the goal of achieving the most efficient and effective combination of steps and resources; and generalizing and transferring this problem solving process to a wide variety of problems". (Barr, Harrison & Conery, 2011).It is also noted that this study is justified by the fact that the construct of in computer thinking remains unclear in its definition, as well as in its practical implementation and its conceptualization as learning object in the school system, both in primary, secondary and postsecondary level, because of the lack of a disciplinary field that is her own despite her almost natural connection to the field of computer science.

2.2.2 Technology-Rich Learning Environments (TRE)

Digital literacy is today considered as one of the key skills of the 21st century[6]. Because we live in an increasingly digital world, the use of learning environments with high technological component will be further promoted and sought. Technology-rich learning environments can be defined as educational environments that rely heavily on digital resources and have massively invested in their technology infrastructure[7].As part of this study, we are particularly focused on environments that promote the

[4]Science, Technology, Engineering and Mathematics

[5] Skills identified through the operational definition of CT released by CSTA in collaboration with The International Society for Technology in Education (ISTE) in 2011

[6]OECD, 2011

[7]OECD, 2014, p.60.

implementation of problem-solving activities to the development of skills related to computational thinking. Literature (Allan et al., 2014; National Research Council, 2011; Grover & Pea, 2013) identifies several types of environments associated with the implementation of learning for the development of computational thinking. These environments can be classified into three main categories: (i) simulation and modeling environments (Wilensky, 2014, Basawapatna et al., 2014), (ii) the games design environments (Repenning et al., 2014), (iii) programming (both visual and tangible) environments (Lye & Koh, 2014; Kalelioglu & Gülgahar, 2014; Berland & Wilensky, 2015; Bers et al., 2013; Chao, 2016; Leonard et al., 2016).Through the literature it appears a strong relationship between firstly, programming and computational thinking, and secondly between programming and STEM education. A recent study[8] conducted in Australia on the conceptions of teachers on computational thinking, revealed that a majority of these teachers perceived programming environments (visual and robotics) as the most appropriate to foster the development of computational thinking in their students. However, the criteria for choosing the most appropriate learning environment to support a specific learning activity for the development of these skills are not always clearly documented. However, programming could better expose students to computational thinking which involves problem-solving tasks using computer science concepts like abstraction, algorithmic thinking and decomposition (Lye & Koh, 2014, p.51). The choice of technology-rich learning environments (Scratch and EV3 Robotics kit) made in our study to support computational thinking skills acquisition taking place in a context of technology course, based on this assumption found throughout the literature, needs more strong empirical evidence through more classroom-based interventions studies. One can postulate that this choice may depend on the subject taught, the type of learning activity considered, targeted skills, the complexity of the problem (ill-defined or well-defined) that students face during the educational intervention, the nature of the problem solving tasks given to students, etc. Because intervention takes place in the context of a particular technology-rich learning environment, the ability of student may depend upon the level of complexity of problem solving tasks performed during the intervention so that there might be some relationship with their ability to perform task-based assessment during the different tests.

2.2.3 Problem Solving Tasks

Perhaps, the most important cognitive goal of education both formal and informal in every educational context is problem solving (Jonassen, 2010). The ability to solve problems is probably one of the most important manifestation of human thinking process and a critical component of intelligence, but its actual assessment is far to be obvious, especially in connection with computational thinking, a construct yet being conceptualized. Then an important question would be how to choose the most appropriate tasks to measure the ability to solve problems in connection with the development of skills associated with computational thinking? Some studies have already addressed the issue, and here are some computational thinking test assessments that have been reported in the literature: (1) tests based on standardized exercises as a collection tool (Dee Miller et al., 2012), (2) tests based on the traces of activities in an IT environment as collection tool (Koh et al. 2014), (3) assessments based on already classical cognitive validated test (Ambrosio et al. (2014), Bebras international challenge on informatics and computational thinking (Dagienė & Stupurienė, 2015; Dolgopolovas et al., 2015), (4) the Google for Education Exploring CT problems[9] and (5) Computer Science Unplugged[10] tests activities. Our study was globally based on the test proposed by the Bebras[11] contests which consist of a set of tasks in a form of short questions or quizz. Each Bebras task can demonstrate an aspect of computer science (CS) and test the aspects of CT of the participant (Dolgopolovas, Jevsikova, Savulionienė & Dagienė, 2015). Additionnaly, each Bebras task has at least some component of CT: abstraction (AB), decomposition (DE), algorithmic thinking (AL), pattern recognition (PR), or generalization (GE). In order to solved these tasks, students have to mobilize abilities related to CS, discrete strutures, computation, data processing, data visualisation, algorithmic and programming operations (Diagene & Stupuriene, 2014). Some criteria for good Bebras taks are presented in table 1 below:

[8] Bower et al., 2015
[9] https://www.google.com/edu/resources/programs/exploring-computational-thinking/
[10] http://tabs.chalifour.fr/la-science-informatique-a-lecole/cs-unplugged/
[11] http://www.bebras.org/

Table 1. Criteria of good Bebras tasks (Diagene & Futschek, 2008, p.22; Diagene &Stupuriené, 2015, p.22-27)

Good tasks	Explanation
Are related to computer science and computational thinking	Bebras contest is a competition on CS and CT
Student could achieve 18 to 24 tasks within 45 55 minutes	Three minutes is approximately the average time to solve a task
Have three levels of difficulty	*Level A* (easy): all pupils of target group should be able to solved *Level B* (medium or intermediate): challenging tasks need some thinking to solve *Level C* (hard): only the best pupils can solved these tasks
Are adequate for the age of participants	Bebras contest has five age groups: Little beaver (grade 3-4; age 8-10) Benjamin (grade 5-6; age 11-12) Cadet (grade 7-8; age 13-14) Junior (grade 9-10 age 15-16) Senior (grade (11-12; age 17-19)
Are independent from any curriculum	The International Bebras contest cannot support all curricula of a large number of countries

2.3 Methodology

Our exploratory study was conducted during 2015-2016 school year through three stages. We began meeting with our partners in October to set up a research procedure. The first stage consisted in the literature review on computational thinking, its definition, development and assessment (November – January). The results of this work were communicated elsewhere (Djambong, 2016). Then, at the second stage, we started building up a questionnaire while making the first selection of tasks, their validation first by the partners, then in one Grade 10 classroom (February – April). Finally, due to the time restriction by the end of the school year, we opted for a small pilot study over 6 weeks (May-June) in which we conducted pre- and post- tests using selected tasks from the Stage 2 along with in-class observations and interviews with the teacher and students. While the data analysis is still underway, we present in this paper preliminary data from the pre- and post- tests. We mainly seek to investigate two research questions:

1) How do the scores vary according to the estimated difficulty of the task between the pre- and the post-test?
2) How do the scores vary according to the elements (or their combination) of computational thinking of each task?

2.3.1 Participants and Context

This pilot study took place in one school (with approximately 310 students enrolled in grades 6 through 12) in New-Brunswick, Canada. Two groups of students (one from Grade 6 and one from Grade 9, for a total of 24 students, 15 females and 9 males) took part in the study. Each group has achieved a variety of programming activities over a period of five weeks (the pre-test was given during the week 0, and the post-test and interviews during the week 6). Grade 6 students (n=10) were working mainly with the Scratch programming environment on a weekly basis (on hour per week) whereas Grade 9 students were doing activities with LEGO EV3 Robotics Kit, a tangible programming environment on a daily basis (1 hour per day). The choice of the programming environment was not prescribed by the curriculum and was made by the teacher.

2.3.2 Data Collection Instruments and Procedure

The preparation of the questionnaire consisted of several steps:

First, 19 Bebras multiple-choice tasks were selected from available online materials which were combined with 11 tasks designed by team researchers were selected. The main selection criteria were:

- The presence of at least one well-expressed CT concept in the task;

- The focus on algorithmic thinking because, intervention activities were base on programming and coding through visual or tangible environments.

The second step included analysis of selected tasks by one classroom teacher and her students from Grade 10. After this validation phase, 14 Bebras tasks and 9 tasks designed by the research team were finally selected to form the final 23 paper-pencil tasks-based assessment test.

After their parents have completed consent forms as required by the Ethics Committee, we have submitted participating students to a series of coding tasks using a questionnaire before the beginning of classroom learning activities (pre-test) and after five weeks of learning (post-test).We have also made observations (including video-recording) during 5-weeks long learning period .Just to remind, in this particular paper, we aim to investigate the tasks using only pre- and post-test results. Other data will be presented later upon the completion of their analysis.

2.3.3 Data Analysis

During this pilot case study, we use descriptive quantitative methods to analyze the data collected during the pre-test and the posttest. Because of a very small sample, we were not able to conduct more sophisticated analysis which we hope to be able to do next year, when we plan to extend our sample and observation period.

2.4 Results

We recall that our first research question was to investigate in what way the set of tasks (the same for Grade 6 and Grade 9) reflect (the changes in) computational thinking while comparing the results before the classroom learning activity and after five week of programming classes.

2.4.1 Question 1: Global Performance on the Pre- and Post-Tests

We begin with presenting general score on the pre- and post-tests for both Grades (6 and 9) (Table 2).

Table 2. Average Scores of Solving Computational Tasks by Grade

Grade	Average score	
	Pre-test	Post-test
Grade 9 (n=14)	44.9%	48.2%
Grade 6 (n=10)	29.6%	33.0%

As we notice, for the Grade 9, the global results from the pre-test to the post-test have only slightly increased (from 44.9% on the pre-test to the 48.2%) whereas for Grade 6, the increase was slightly at the same extent (from 29.6% to 33.0%). We also observed that the results in Grade 9 are significantly higher than in Grade 6.

While presenting the results according to the difficulty level of the task (as being attributed by the Bebras team for the Bebras tasks and by our research tem for other tasks, Table 3), we take into account that the difficulty level was not the same for Grade 9 and Grade 6, there is why, we mentioned the number of problems for each Grade.

Table 3. Average Scores of Solving Computational Tasks by Level of Task Difficulty

Level of task difficulty				Average score Grade-6		Average score Grade-9	
		K-6	K-9	Pre-test	Post-test	Pre-test	Post-test
Easy	(A)	2*	9*	40.0%	55.0%	46.7%	48.4%
Medium	(B)	8*	8*	25.0%	28.7%	44.2%	41.1%
Hard	(C)	13*	6*	26.9%	32.3%	36.7%	34.5%

(*): *number of tasks by level of difficulty in each grade*

We observed that, for the Grade 6, the highest score was obtained for the Easy task (39.4% for the pre-test and 55.0% for the post-test). For this Grade and difficulty level (Grade 6, level Easy), we also have the (significantly) highest increase from the pre-test to the post-test. For the problems of the difficulty levels Medium and Hard, the scores are significantly lower, 25.0% and 28.7% for Medium and 26.9% and 32.3% for High. We also noticed that for both levels, Medium and High, the increase between the scores for the pre-test and the post-test is much smaller than for the level Easy. Also, we can see that the hardest problems were solved slightly with a better score than those for the Medium level. As for the Grade 9, the highest score was also obtained for the Easy level, although the difference between pre- and post-test scores is lower (46.7% vs 48.4%. Yet, we see that the Medium problems were solved with only slightly smaller score (44.2% and 41.1%). For the hard problems, it the scores are significantly lower (36.7% and 34.5%). We also notice that for this Grade (9), there was actually a slight decrease in scores from the pre- to the post-test.

Table 4. Average scores of solving computational tasks by type of computational thinking skill involved

Type of CT skill involved	(*)	Average score Grade-6		Average score Grade-9	
		Pre-test	Post-test	Pre-test	Post-test
AB[12]	(1)	20.0%	50.0%	86.7%	71.4%
AL[13]	(3)	40.0%	36.7%	55.6%	42.9%
PR[14]	(1)	90.0%	100%	73.3%	85.7%
AB+DE[15]	(1)	60.0%	80.0%	86.7%	71.4%
AB+PR	(4)	25.0%	20.0%	23.3%	21.4%
AL+DE	(1)	60.0%	70.0%	93.3%	71.4%
AL+PR	(2)	10.0%	10.0%	13.3%	25.0%
AB+AL+DE	(5)	14.0%	24.0%	38.7%	27.2%
AB+DE+PR	(1)	10.0%	30.0%	60.0%	71.4%
AL+DE+PR	(1)	40.0%	10.0%	20.0%	42.9%
AB+AL+DE+PR	(3)	33.3%	30.0%	44.4%	52.4%

(*):*Number of tasks for each type*

The best average scores in grade 6(90.0% for the pre-test and 100% for the posttest) were obtained for the only task involving PR as the only CT skill to be assessed, while in grade 9, best average scores were obtained in pre-test (93.3%) for the task involving a combination of AB and De CT Skills, and in post-test (85.7%) for the only task involving PR as the only CT skill to be assessed. The lowest average score were obtained for four tasks involving AL and PR as CT skills taken together (10.0% for the pre-test and 10.0% for the posttest in grade 6; and 13.3% in the pre-test and 25.0% for the post-test in grade 9). Interestingly, all types of tasks which included AL skills seemed to produce lower results with some scored having actually decreased on the post-test compared to the pre-test (like in both Grades for isolated AL tasks). In this respect we also noticed that the only combination of skills that did not have this component (AB+DE+PR) has produced and increase for both Grades whereas Grade 9 students have outperformed their Grade 6 peers for this same combination.

[12] Abstraction
[13] Algorithmic thinking
[14] Pattern recognition
[15] Decomposition

2.4.2 Question 2: Scores for Each of Proposed Tasks

Table 5. Average scores of solving computational tasks per each proposed task

Task N°	CT skill involved	Level of difficulty		Average score Grade-6		Average score Grade-9	
		Grade 6	Grade 9	Pre-test	Post-test	Pre-test	Post-test
Task 1	PR	A	A	90.0%	100%	73.3%	85.7%
Task 2	AL	C	B	80.0%	80.0%	73.3%	64.3%
Task 3	AL+DE	B	A	60.0%	70.0%	93.3%	71.4%
Task 4	AB+PR	C	B	70.0%	30.0%	33.3%	21.4%
Task 5	AB	C	B	20.0%	50.0%	86.7%	71.4%
Task 6	AB+AL+DE+PR	B	A	50.0%	40.0%	60.0%	64.3%
Task 7	AB+DE	C	C	60.0%	80.0%	86.7%	71.4%
Task 8	AL+PR	B	A	20.0%	10.0%	26.7%	42.9%
Task 9	AL+PR	C	C	0.0%	10.0%	0.0%	7.1%
Task 10	AB+PR	C	B	0.0%	10.0%	6.7%	7.1%
Task 11	AB+AL+DE+PR	C	C	10.0%	10.0%	13.3%	35.7%
Task 12	AB+PR	B	A	10.0%	10.0%	46.7%	35.7%
Task 13	AB+DE+PR	B	B	10.0%	30.0%	60.0%	71.4%
Task 14	AL+DE+PR	C	B	40.0%	10.0%	20.0%	42.9%
Task 15	AB+AL+DE+PR	C	C	40.0%	40.0%	60.0%	57.1%
Task 16	AL	B	A	20.0%	10.0%	46.7%	28.6%
Task 17	AL	B	A	20.0%	20.0%	46.7%	35.7%
Task 18	AB+AL+DE	C	B	10.0%	10.0%	46.7%	28.6%
Task 19	AB+AL+DE	B	A	10.0%	40.0%	26.7%	42.9%
Task 20	AB+AL+DE	A	A	30.0%	10.0%	60.0%	28.6%
Task 21	AB+PR	C	B	10.0%	30.0%	6.7%	21.4%
Task 22	AB+AL+DE	C	C	20.0%	40.0%	33.3%	21.4%
Task 23	AB+AL+DE	C	C	0.0%	20.0%	26.7%	14.3%

We note that the best average scores were obtained for the tasks 1(90.0% for the pre-test and 100% for the post-test in grade 6; 73.3% for the pre-test and 85.7% for the post-test in grade 9), 2(80.0% for the pre-test and 80.0% for the post-test in grade 6; 73.3% for the pre-test and 64.3% for the post-test in grade 9) ,3 (60.0% for the pre-test and 70% for the post-test in grade 6; 93.3% for the pre-test and 71.4% for the post-test in grade 9) , 5 (86.6% for the pre-test and 71.4% for the post-test in grade 9)and 7 (60.0% for the pre-test and 80.0% for the post-test in grade 6; 86.6% for the pre-test and 71.4% for the post-test in grade 9) while the lowest ones were obtained for the task 9 (0.0% for the pre-test and 10.0% for the post-test in grade 6; 0.0% for the pre-test and 7.1% for the post-test in grade 9)and 10(0.0% for the pre-test and 10.0% for the post-test in grade 6; 6.7% for the pre-test and 7.1% for the post-test in grade 9). While more detailed and sophisticated analysis of this table is yet to be conducted, we can notice that that the task 7 labeled as difficult (Level C) for both Grades, 6 and 9, the results are quite good whereas for the task 9 (also Level C) they near 0% of success for both Grades. We also observe from the table that generally for the tasks that require a combination of abilities, the results of Grade 9 students are generally higher than for Grade 6 students. We also see the biggest increase from the pre- to the post-test for the tasks 19 and 21 whereas for the tasks 4 and 20, the score have rather dropped for both Grades.

2.5 Discussion

The results displayed in the above table suggest that: (i) the type of programming environment in which the students worked during the intervention phase may have some influence in their ability to solve tasks; (ii) the type of problems solving activities, in terms of complexity[16] and structuredness[17] the students faced during

[16] Complexity is more concerned with how many components are represented implicitly or explicitly in the problem and how much they interact and how much the students understand those components (*J.M. Spector et al., 2014)*

[17] In general, ill-defined problems tend to be more complex then well-defined problems (*Ibid.*)

the intervention phase may have some influence in their ability to solve tasks; (iii) generally, we can observe that, the more difficult is a task, the lowest are the average scores. It then appears that, the ability to correctly solve a task seems to decrease with the level of difficulty of the task. But this observation needs more strong empirical evidence; (iv) these results suggest that, the CT competence involved in a task may have some influence on the average score obtained during the assessment; (v) it seems to appear no clear or apparent relationship between task competence composition and average scores obtained.

The Bebras International Contest is considered as homogenous test for evaluating students' implicit ability of computational thinking in the context of the process of solving tasks which implicitly involve cognitive procedure of CT and problem solving (Dolgopolovas, Jevsikova, Savulionienė & Dagienė, 2015).The development of computational thinking skills then, suggests the implementation of a more or less complex problem-solving strategy involving several mental processes as stated in its operational definition. Student results obtained during pre-test and post-test, assuming that they are valid performance indicators, do they allow the effective implementation of such a strategy? We can just see that the average scores obtained by students in 6th Grade and 9th Grade at both pre-test, post-test, does not allow to obtain an objective picture of the evolution of students mental representations and schemes in tasks problem solving process during the test and during the learning activities in class between two tests. This finding could justify the need to develop measurement tools that have not only the characteristics of a classical psychometric test, but are also able to allow the capture of changes in implementation of thinking processes through a problem-solving activity for the development of cognitive and non-cognitive skills related to computational thinking. It therefore seems difficult to affirm that the set of tasks we used is a valid instrument for evaluating or measuring computational thinking as stated in recent study (Ibid.). It would be wise to achieve this end, to undertake further studies combining the tasks from our set with additional and eventually more appropriate data collection tools, such as in-depth interviews and analysis of students' 'thinking-aloud' discourse.

The results at both pretest at post-test, highlight a certain balance between the average scores obtained by task, with the difficulty level predicted by designers for each proposed task. This complies with the claim of the validity of the prediction criterion of Bebras tasks, which stipulates that the success rate for a particular task can be used to describe the difficulty level of that task (Vegt, 2013, p.133). However, one cannot ignore the case of some tasks for which, the average scores have not reflected the difficulty levels predicted by the designers. What seems to be in agreement with the findings of previous studies[18] indicating that, the prediction of the level of difficulty of a task is an inexact science, because its estimation is the result of task designer intuition, which can be mistaken, hence the need to properly conduct the validation process tasks for large-scale studies.

The tasks proposed in this study, differ from one another both by type (AB, AL, DE or PR) of skills related to computational thinking involved, their number per task (which can be 1, 2, 3 or 4), the level of difficulty (easy, medium or hard) of the task, and the nature of the task to be solved (checking or performing a procedure). The complexity of a task generally is the result of a joint of several parameters among which we can mention: (i) the breadth of knowledge required to solve the task, (ii) the level of prior knowledge, (iii) the intricacy for the problem-solutions procedures, and (iv) the number of relations that need to be processed in parallel during the problem solving process (Jonassen, 2010, p.3).

In our study, the level of complexity of the proposed tasks, could therefore combine parameters mentioned above. However, taking into account only those parameters as complexity indicators, it would be difficult to establish and clearly define a scale comparison of the complexity of the tasks proposed in the quiz, in the light of the difference in average scores observed for certain tasks (tasks 11 and 15, for example, which appear to have the same complexity indicators). It is therefore possible that other intervening factors such as complexity indicators and not highlighted in our study are likely to better explain the results.

The results obtained in our study need to be further supported by empirical evidence, given the following limits: (1) the small sample size does not allow analysis that could lead to a generalization of observations; (2) the choice of participants who has not subject to random assignment was able to influence and bias the results. Other limitations are inherent to the format of the tests: paper-and-pencil and multiple-choice. For instance, the teacher mentioned to us that the fact of switching from working at computers during the class hours to filling-in paper forms could be demotivating for some students. Moreover, the multiple-choice does not allow to get a track of the work done by the students leading her or him to the selection of an answer; which could also be done randomly in some cases. As we said before, it would be important to conduct

[18] Ibid. p.134

interviews with students to learn how they arrive to the answer; we also think of constructing a virtual form of this test. Our final remark concerns that period of the post-test – only few weeks before summer vacations – this could be also a factor of certain decrease in some post-test scores. However, our results point that this is not the case for all tasks, hence, our observations at this stage indicate of possibility of tasks to discriminate CT abilities and tasks-complexity levels.

3. CONCLUSION

In conclusion, this study shows that there could be a link between the students' ability to solve the tasks proposed, the type of targeted skills related to computational thinking, and the degree of difficulty or complexity of the proposed tasks. The influence of the programming environment to which the students were exposed in the context of problem solving tasks during the intervention, is difficult to demonstrate given the limitations associated with the experiment (small size of sample, non-randomized sample, lack of a control group). However, this study justifies the need for further studies to establish the validation of the proposed tasks based on more solid empirical evidence. It could thus be useful to look at the effect that the nature of the pedagogical intervention in programming environments (visual versus tangible) could have on the validation of the proposed set of tasks. For this purpose, more subtle research design for the study and instruction design for the problem-solving tasks are needed.

ACKNOWLEDGEMENT

This ongoing study is being conducted with the help of the Canadian Social Sciences and Humanities Research Council (Partnership Development Grant #890-2013-0062), New Brunswick Innovation Foundation (2016 Research Assistantship Program) and le Secrétariat aux Affaires Intergouvernementales Canadiennes du Québec (Programme de soutien à la Francophonie Canadienne). CRSH (Social Sciences and Humanities Research Council of Canada).

REFERENCES

Book

Beaudoin, J. et al, 2014. *Usages du numérique dans les écoles québécoises. L'apport des technologies et des ressources numériques à l'enseignement et à l'apprentissage. Recension des écrits*. Centre de Recherche et d'intervention sur la réussite scolaire, Montréal, Québec.

Committee for the Workshops on Computational Thinking; National Research Council, 2010. *Report of a workshop on the scope and nature of computational thinking*. The National Academies Press, Washington, USA

Dagiene, V., Futschek, G., 2008. Bebras Intetnational Contest on Informatics and Computer Literacy: Criteria for Good Tasks. *In Informatics Education-Supporting Computational Thinking*, Springer Berlin Heidelberg pp. 19-30

Godefroid, J., 2008. *Psychologie : Science humaine et science cognitive*. De Boeck, Bruxelles, Belgique, pp 420-425

Jonassen, D., 2014. Assessing Problem Solving in Spector, J.M. et al, (Eds.) *Handbook of Research on Educational Communications and Technology*, Springer Science + Business Media, New York, USA

OCDE, 2014. *Environnements pédagogiques et pratiques novatrices, La recherche et l'innovation dans l'enseignement*, Éditions OCDE

Journal

Barr, D., et al, 2011. Computational Thinking: A Digital Age Skill for Everyone. *In Learning & Leading with Technology*, Vol. 38, No 6, pp. 20-23

Berland, M., Wilenski, U., 2015. Comparing Virtual and Physical Robotics Environments for Supporting Complex Systems and Computational Thinking. *In Journal of. Science Education and Technology*, (2015) 24, pp. 628-647

Bers, M.U., et al., 2014. Computattional thinking and thinkering : Exploration of an early chilhood robotics curriculum. *In Computer & Education*, 72 (2014) pp. 145-157

Chao, P., 2016. Exploring Students' computational practice, design and performance of problem-solving through a visual programming environment. *In Computer & Education*, 95 (2016) pp. 202-2015

Dagiene, V., Stupurienė, G., 2015. Bebras – a Sustainable Community Building Model for the Concept Based Learning of Informatics and Computational Thinking. *In Informatics in Education*, Vol. 15, No. 1, pp. 25-44

Dolgopolovas, V., et al, 2016. Exploration of Computational Thinking of Software Engineering Novice Students Based on Solving Computer Science Tasks. *In International Journal of Engineering Education*, Vol. 32, No. 3(A), pp. 1-10

Grover, S., Pea, R., 2013. Computational Thinking in K-12: A Review of the State of the Field. In Educational Researcher, Vol. 42, No. 1, pp. 38-43

Kalelioglu, F., Gülbahar, Y., 2014. The Effects of Teaching Programming via Scratch on Problem Solving Skills : A Discussion from Learner's Perspective. *In Informatics in Education*, 2014, Vol. 13, No. 1, pp. 33-50

Lee, I., et al., 2011. Computational Thiking for Youth in Practice. *In ACM Inroads*, Vol. 2, No. 1, pp. 32-37

Leonard, J. et al., 2016. Using Robotics and Game Design to Enhance Children's Self-Efficacy, STEM Attitudes, and Computational Thinking Skills. *In Journal of. Science Education and Technology*, (2016). Doi:10.1007/s10956-016-9628-2

Lye, S., Koh, J., 2014. Review on teaching and learning of computational thinking through programming: What is next for K-12. *In Computers in Human Behavior*, Vol. 4, No. 41, pp. 51-61

Repenning, A., et al, 2014. Scalable Game Design: A Strategy to Bring Systemic Computer Science Education to Schools through Game Design and Simulation Creation. *In ACM Transactions on Computing Education*, Vol. 15(2), No. 11, pp. 1-34

Vegt, W., 2013. Predicting the Difficulty Level of a Bebras Tasks. In Olympiads in Informatics, Vol. 7, pp 132-139

Voskoglou, M., Buckley, S., 2012. Problem Solving and Computers in a Learning Environment. In Egyptian Computer Science Journal ECS, Vol. 36, No. 4 pp. 28-37

Weintrop, D. et al., 2015. Defining Computational Thinking for Mathematics and Science Classrooms. *In Journal of. Science Education and Technology*, Vol. 2016, No. 25, pp. 127-147

Wing, J. M., 2006. Computational Thinking. *In Communications of the ACM*, Vol. 49, No. 3, pp. 33-35

Wing, J. M., 2008. Computational thinking and thinking about computing. *In Philosophical Transactions of the Royal Society a: Mathematical, Physical and Engineering Sciences*, Vol. 366, No. 1881, pp. 3117-3725

Conference paper or contributed volume

Ambrosio, A.P., et al, 2014. Exploring Core Cognitive Skills of Computational Thinking. Proceedings of PPIG, University of Sussex, Sussex, England

Basawapatna, A., et al, 2014. The Consume-Create Spectrum: Balancing Convenience and Computational Thinking in STEM Learning. *Proceedings of SIGCSE'14 Conference*, Atlanta, USA, pp. 658-664

Djambong, T., 2016. Computational Thinking in Connection with the Acquisition of Key Skills for the 21st Century: Reflection from Literature Review. *Proceedings of 8th International Conference on Education and New Learning Technologies*. Barcelona, Spain, pp.500-509

Dolgopolovas, V., et al, 2015. On Evaluation of Computational Thinking of Software Engineering Novice Students. *Proceedings* of IFIP *TC3 Working Conference "A New Culture of Learning: Computing and next Generations*, Vilnius, Lithuania

Gauvin, S., et al, 2015. Vizwik – visual data flow programming and its educational implications. In S. Carliner, C. Fulford & N. Ostashewski (Eds.), *Proceedings of EdMedia: World Conference on Educational Media and Technology* Montréal, Canada, pp. 1602-1608

Jonassen, D.H., 2010. Research Issues in Problem Solving. Proceedings of the 11th International Conference on Educational Research, New Educational Paradigm for Learning and Instruction, pp. 1-15

Koh, K.H., et al, 2014. Early Validation of Computational Thinking Pattern Analysis. *Proceedings of ITIGSE14*, Uppsala, Sweden

Miller, L.D., et al, 2014. Integrating Computational and Creative Thinking to Improve Learning and Performance in CS1. *Proceedings of SIGCSE'14*, Atlanta, Georgia, USA

FRAMEWORK FOR INTELLIGENT TEACHING AND TRAINING SYSTEMS – A STUDY OF SYSTEMS

M.Sc. Nikolaj Troels Graf von Malotky and Prof. Dr.-Ing. Alke Martens
University of Rostock, Institute of Computer Science
Albert-Einstein-Str. 22, D-18059 Rostock, Germany

ABSTRACT

Intelligent Tutoring System are state of the art in eLearning since the late 1980s. The earliest system have been developed in teams of psychologists and computer scientists, with the goal to investigate learning processes and, later on with the goal to intelligently support teaching and training with computers. Over the years, the eLearning hype appeared and vanished, and returned in a slightly different shape. However, Intelligent Tutoring Systems, as one of the most adaptive system types, remained in the focus of interest. Due to this, it is surprising that there exists no ITS architecture, no guideline how to implement these systems, and no structured, software engineered approach, which helps to develop comparable systems. In this paper, we will show the first steps toward such a system: a broad analysis of ITS over several years of research, with the resulting structured architecture.

KEYWORDS

Intelligent Tutoring System, Architecture, Framework

1. INTRODUCTION

Intelligent Tutoring systems (ITSs) are a special type of eLearning or teaching and training systems. The history of ITSs can be traced back to the early 1980s. One of the first ITSs is based on the medical expert system MYCIN, which has been developed between 1972 and 1980. The resulting ITS has been called GUDION (Clancey 1987). Expert systems were the main part of ITS. They integrated the idea of explicating the experts' knowledge, for example based on facts and rules, and sometimes extended by methods of artificial intelligence (AI), for example Bayes' Networks, in the system core. The expert knowledge was used as reference for the learner's learning progress and as basis for correcting the learner's actions. Using MYCIN and the early versions of GUIDON in medical education, it quickly became clear, that these systems can only support learning of finding the correct diagnosis, but not training of the diagnostic reasoning process. In the process of developing GUIDON, the pure expert knowledge base was extended by so-called pedagogical knowledge. This pedagogical knowledge should optimally add a teacher's knowledge regarding instructional design and supporting the learner to the existing expert knowledge. A bit later, as computer technology became quicker and storage became cheaper, learner models have been added (Lelouche 1999). Learner models allowed to generate an appropriate analysis of individual progress and recording of learner's activities. From the ITS architecture's perspective, a new component was added. Some extra ways have been investigated, for example working with bug libraries in BUGGY in the 1981, simulation in SOPHIE 1982 (an overview is given in (Nwana, 1990)). In the 1989, the growing of the commercial internet starts. The ITS quickly became web-based applications. Architectures in ITS started with client-server designs, and then moved to web-based applications, with online teaching and training material. From the system developers' and the content developers' perspective, the internet-based approach facilitates update of teaching and training material. In the years after the advent of the internet, ITS became mobile, interactive, game-based and ubiquitous pervasive.

All of these aspects have been reflected in changes of the ITS architecture in one way or the other. Whereas in the first years, the ITS architecture has been extended by integrating new components (e.g. from GUIDON to GUIDON2 (Clancey, 1988)), or completely redesigned based on a new trend (e.g. agent-based design), in the last years, the core architecture of ITS has not really been part of investigations. This is contrasted by the idea of software engineering, which itself has a long history in computer science. Starting in the 1960, and becoming a traceable branch of research in the 1980s, software engineering came with the claim that computer software design shall be an engineering task and not "art" (Gamme et.al., 2015). Due to this perspective, several authors have tried to analyze and construct the ITS architecture. However, up to date, most of the ITS developments start off from scratch. Even if ITSs are one of the oldest systems in the field of E-Learning, there exists no still valid framework, which is domain independent, and independent of the programming language.

Thus, our idea was to analyze existing ITSs, to investigate published frameworks and architecture for ITS development, and based on the insights of these steps to develop a generic framework for ITS design. The paper is structured as follows: in the next section, we will show some aspects of our analysis, first from the perspective of existing systems, second from the perspective of architectures and existing frameworks. In the third section, we will sketch our resulting approach for generic E-Learning Software design. The paper closes with a conclusion and outlook.

2. ITS ARCHITECTURE

The main perspective of the ITS architecture development has been the definition of interacting components. Over the years, the set of components has been extended. The name of the components vary, as can be seen in table 1, but the main functionality remains the same. As postulated in different papers, e.g. in (Harrer et.al., 2007) (Ruddeck et.al., 2010), the core architecture of ITSs consists of the following components:

- The expert knowledge base, which is the oldest component. This component is based on the idea that the mediated knowledge is (at least a part of) the knowledge of an expert of the application domain, e.g. medicine. The modeling of the domain knowledge is usually taking place in a combination of facts and rules, sometimes extended by AI approaches like Bayes' Networks. The main effort in developing an ITS is usually the modeling of the domain knowledge.
- The pedagogical knowledge model is the component, which is the most blurry in the set of components. Sometimes, e.g. in case-based training, the pedagogical knowledge consists of the case structure and the context dependent knowledge in contrast to the overall knowledge of the domain experts. Sometimes, the pedagogical knowledge model is realized as instructional facts and rules.
- The learner model is one of the younger components in the set. Nonetheless, the learner model reached an importance that has led to a whole branch of research, called user modeling. The components abilities range from simple recording and tracking of activities up to complicated guidance and help structures.
- The user interfaces also is related to an own branch of research, which is based in Human Computer Interaction (HCI). Moreover, we have found that the functionality of the user interface ranges from steering of the whole adaptation process up to pure showing of next possible activities.

One of the first descriptions of the architecture has been developed by Clancey (1984, 1987), who has defined the above mentioned components as part of an ITS. However, even if he has described the components, he has neither focused on the role and functionality of the components, nor on the components interaction. Thus, up to date, no reliable description of interaction of components, of tasks and of role and functionality is available. Literature review has revealed, that the above mentioned components can be treated as the common denominator in ITS (an extract of the analysis is shown in table 1). This insight has for example been formulated in form of an architecture by Lelouche (1999).

Table 1. Table of naming parts of the ITS (Martens,Harrer, 2006)

Reference	Expert Knowledge	Pedagogical Knowledge	Learner Element	User Interface
(Corbett et, all, 1997)	Domain Knowledge	Peagogical Module	Student Module	Poblem Solving Environment
(Lelouche, 1999)	Domain Expert Module	Tutorial Module (Pedagogy Expert)	User Model	User Interface
(Alpert et.al., 1999)	Expert Solver	Tutorial Module	Student Module	User Interface
(Melis et.al., 2004)	MBase (Course Generator)	Pedagogical Rules (Course Generator)	Student Model	Presentation Engine

However, one drawback has been found in the component based design: whereas the basic functionality and the structure of the components were more or less clear, the communication between the components and the role and functionality of the combined components were not. This can be seen in the following figure 1.

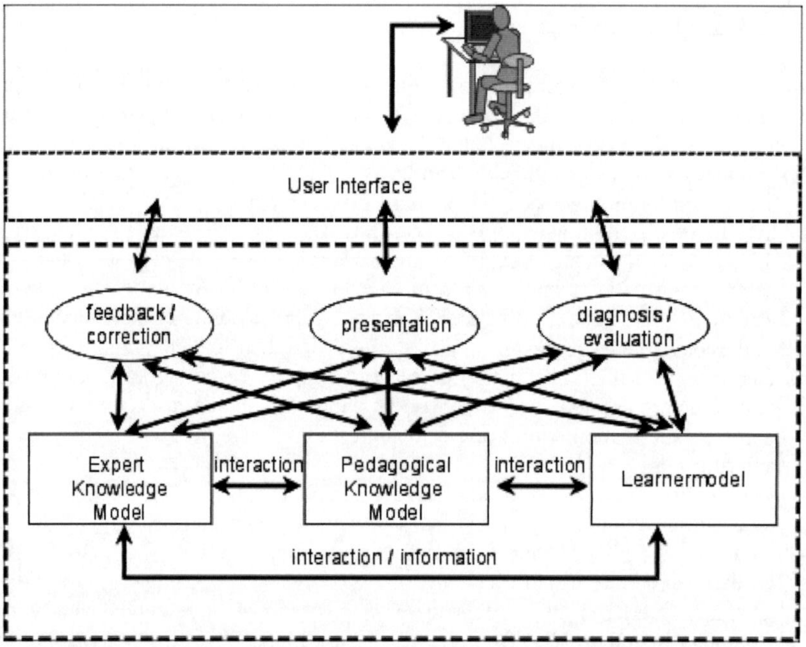

Figure 1. Abstract scheme of the classical IST architecture (Martens, 2003)

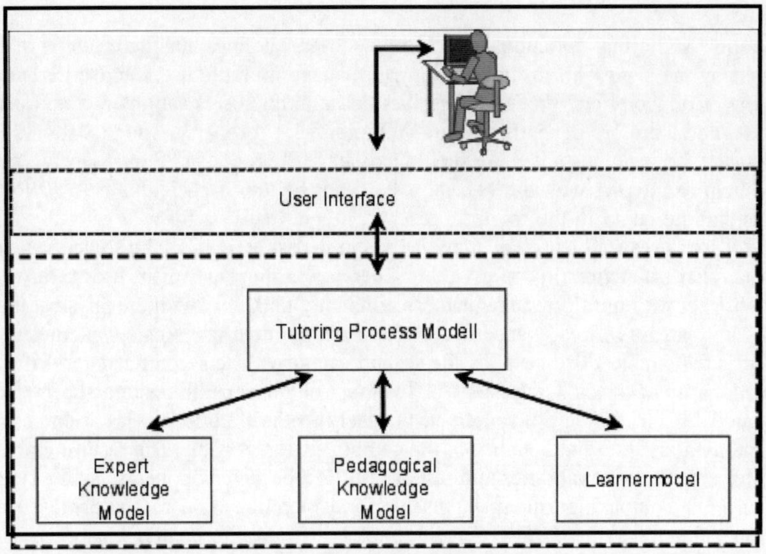

Figure 2. Architecture of ITS (Martens, 2003)

Thus, Martens et. al. chose to focus on the communication between the components. This has led to a design, where a central process steering component, the tutoring process model, takes over the adaptation functionality, whereas the tasks of the other components have been reduced to mere database functionality. This is sketched in figure 2. Harrer and Martens (2006) developed a pattern catalogue for ITS, based on the idea of centralized or externalized tutoring processes, where the role and functionality is described in detail. This pattern catalogue helped to develop ITS from scratch, however, even this approach did not help to design the communication between the components, which became clear, when we started with the effort to use our first framework as basis for implementation in 2001. So our next step in the last two years has been a deep analysis of system types, coming from the perspective of the ITS, but after all including all types of eLearning systems. We have learned, that we should better start with interaction scenarios. So we used task analysis and focused on the different modi of usage and interaction. The result has led to the framework, which we sketch in the following section.

3. ITS FRAMEWORK

As a first step, we analyzed the combinations in which students, teachers, experts, authors could interact with an ITS. The ITS has to be the only teacher in the knowledge transfer of the expert knowledge to the student. The suitable combinations showed us that there are multiple use cases for ITS aside from their capabilities as a teacher. The properties of the cases could then be split in two categories, these properties do sometimes have dependent other properties (sketched in figure 3).

The first category are properties which are the same for many learning programs and are more general: “Authoring” with the ability of automatic content creation, “Online connection” with the ability to send usage statistics, “Multiple users” and the ability to allow collaboration between them and at last a human “Supervisor” and the ability of live interaction with the student(s). “Online connection” is the property that the ITS or components of it can be accessed through the internet, which can be more up to date as a local one. Since one of the aims of the generic ITS framework is their evaluation and comparison, its usage should be accessible without help from the student itself, in a non-research environment. This is called “Send statistics” and can be met through sending the usage data over the internet back to the people which need it for scientific research or for review of the teaching content and is dependent on online connection functionality. “Authoring” means that there are authoring tools available to make it easier to experts and teachers to change and manage the teaching content, so that authoring is possible without knowledge of the internals of the ITS. Because of the always improving artificial intelligence automatic content generation is possible for selected domains and this will expand in the future, this is named “Content generation” which is dependent on the “Authoring” functionality. “Multiple Users” defines that there can be more than one student who are taught by the same ITS instance, so it can manage multiple users and differentiate them and their progresses. The “Collaboration” property describes that multiple users can interact and learn with each other through the ITS and therefore depends on the “Multiple Users” property. The ITS should teach, so if there is need for a human who is not a student, he should only have the role of a “Supervisor”, a person to control the situation and help to interact with the ITS, he would not be the teacher, this could allow him to supervise more students than he could in the role of a teacher, it could be in a form of a forum or “Live” interaction through chats or live stream. Even if the supervisor is in the same room as the students, it could be sensible to still implement such a functionality to give the supervisor a more powerful user role, which in turn would allow him to interact with multiple students more efficiently than only with the physical presence.

Since the first category already specified if there are multiple users or an internet connection, we only need to consider the simplest use case for the second category. The second category of properties describes the inner functionality of a local, single user ITS without online capabilities or a supervisor. The components would be a good fit, but they are not defined precisely in the traditional ITS architecture. In research the usage of the naming and the functionality of the components is varying. The resulting architectures from the created ITSs have different capabilities and responsibilities for the components. So the resulting architectures descriptions are not compatible among themselves and therefore hard to compare. To analyze what does specify the inner functionality of the ITS we did not split it up into components of the general ITS system architecture, but extracted which functions the components fulfill. After analyzing the functionality of the components of the ITS architectures, we could find seven main functionalities which ITSs use, it is the core of the ITS. Two of them are obligatory to create a minimal tutoring system: “Deliver” and “Evaluate”. Expert information is not saved in a way which is easily understandable for the student. “Deliver” will construct an easily to access and view content unit from a given query, either from passive lectures or interactive exercises. “Evaluate” is a correctness check of the student's answer which saves the judgement into the student's progress. The ITS can then answer with the “Feedback” functionality to react accordingly to the student's answer and give appropriate response, adaptive to the student. This intelligence can also be used as a guidance for proactive or user activated hints, but since the functionality is different and not dependent from exercises it is excluded in the “Help” functionality. “Estimate” generates a profile from the student's collected activities, which can be saved or used immediately. Like in the case of the functionality “Propose”, it will return content matching the knowledge of the student. At last is “Summarize” as a functionality for completely analyzing the behavior of the student, to show the strengths and weaknesses for different categories, like day of week, knowledge subdomain and so on.

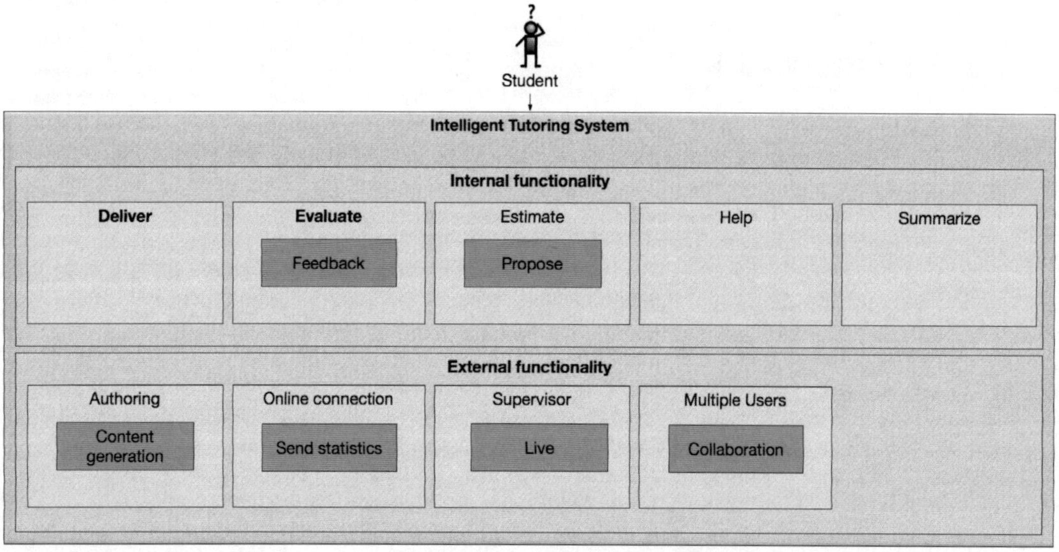

Figure 3. Suggested Architecture of ITS

After we have identified the tasks an ITS can and has to do, we could define the possible combinations of functional components for the internal and external functionalities. This allowed us to list all types of ITS and parameterize and therefore categorize an ITS (see figure 4). The system architecture uses five layers to split the business logic from database and user interface responsibilities. The business logic is what the core ITS functionality is, all the internal functionality is there. The databases have to be created accordingly to the functionality that was defined earlier, but instead of defining the concrete database, we instead use delegates to easily access information matching to one responsibility. The expert domain knowledge is what has to be transferred to the student and is split up into the passive and interactive content, named "Lectures" and "Training content", but also rules in the "Domain rule base" from the domain, formatted in a way so that the ITS can apply them. The "Student's progress" contains all the relevant steps the student did, so that the ITS can track what the student did relevant to learning. The ITS has to react to the students interactions with the learning content, to do that, errors should be easily recognized and the "Bug analysis" helps with that. Not all these database controls are necessary to create an ITS, you can for example just have "Lectures", "Reaction of Tutor" and "Student's progess", but it for a feature rich ITS it is mostly recommended to add all of them. These annotated categories are the 4 components often used in ITS: User interface, Learner model, Pedagogical knowledge and Expert knowledge. The user interface can vary drastic from one ITS to another. Still there are some separations of the user interface which makes sense in many cases. Given here is the example separation into a Statistics, Select Lecture, Learn and Train scene.

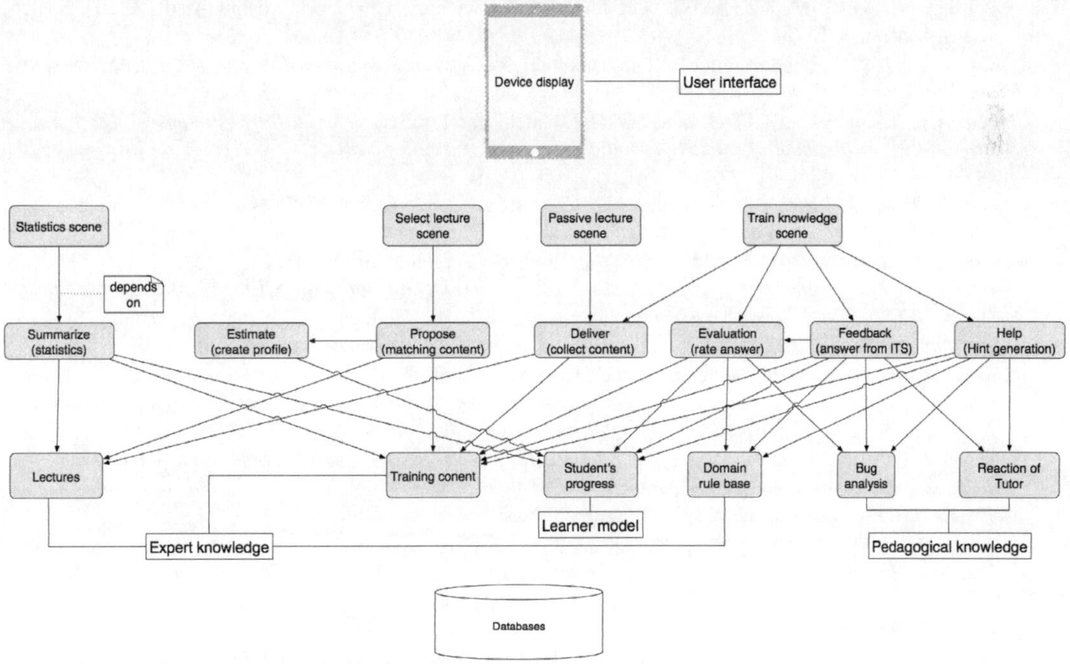

Figure 4. Dependencies of the functionalities

So these are the different components of an ITS and they are dependent from each other as shown. Instead of allowing any communication between them, the components can only communicate if they have a dependency relationship, the different parts of functionality are then eventually connected through the user interface.

4. CONCLUSION AND OUTLOOK

In our way to develop a framework of ITS, we started several years ago with a classical, component based approach. Over the years of research, we must learn that this approach was not deep enough to help in designing modern approaches in ITS. Thus, we focused on another aspect of ITS in particular, and eLearning in general, which is the role and functionality of the system in the interaction process with the learner. As a result, we developed a completely different approach to system design, which allows on the system kernel to realized the de facto existing portfolio of functionality. To cross-check our ideas, we developed a matrix of use-case scenarios, which has led us to the insight that our approach is flexible enough to allow the modeling and design of a plethora of different system types. Thus, as a next step, we go one step further and make a prototypical implementation of the concepts, and try to use this for a set of different ITS prototypes.

REFERENCES

Alpert, S.R., Singley, M.K., Fairweather, P.G. 1999 Deploying Intelligent Tutors on the Web: An Architecture and an Example. *International Journal of Artificial Intelligence,* 10 (2), pp 183- 197

Clancey, W. J., 1984, Methodology for Building an Intelligent Tutoring System. In: Kintsch, W., Miller, J.R., and Polson, P.G. (eds.): Methods and Tactics in Cognitive Sciences, Lawrence Erlbaum Associates, Hillsdale, New Jersey, London, pp 51- 84

Clancey, W. J., 1987, Methodology for Building an Intelligent Tutoring System. *In: Kearsley (ed.): Artificial Intelligence and Instruction. Addison Wesley, MA.*

Corbett, A.T., Koedinger, K.R., Anderson, J.R. 1997, Intelligent Tutoring Systems. *In: M. Helander, T.K. Landauer, P. Prabuh (Eds.): Handbook of Human-Computer Interaction. Elsevier Science B.V., 2nd completely revised edition. Pp 849—874*

Gamma, E., Helm, R,, Johnson, R, Vlissides, J. 2015, Design Patterns. Elements of Resuable Obejct Oriented Software. *Pearson Education, US. 2nd revised edition.*

Harrer, A., Martens, A., 2007, An Integrative Approach for Teaching/Tutoring Process Models Using Meta-Models. *International Conference on Cognition and Exploratory Learning in Digital Age, CELDA 2007, Algarve, Portugal.*

Harrer, A., Martens, A., 2006. Towards a Pattern Language for Intelligent Teaching and Training Systems. *8th International Conference on Intelligent Tutoring Systems, ITS 2006, Chungli, Taiwan.*

Harrer, A., Martens, A. 2010, A heterogeneous pattern language for collaborative learning systems and intelligent tutoring systems. *in: P. Goodyear, S. Retalis (eds.)Technology enhanced learning: Design Patterns and Pattern Languages, pp. 153 –166, chap. 9, Sense Publishers, Rotterdam (ISBN: 978-94-6091-060-9).*

Lelouche, R. 1999, Intelligent Tutoring Systems from Birth to Now. *In: KI-Künstliche Intelligenz,* 4 ,pp 5-11.

Martens, A., 2003, Centralize the Tutoring Process in Intelligent Tutoring Systems. *5th International Conference on New Educational Environments, ICNEE 2003 Luzern, Schweiz.*

Melis, E., Siekmann, J. , 2004. Activemath: An Intelligent Tutoring System for Mathematics. In R. Tadeusiewicz, L.A. Zadeh, L. Rutkowski, J. Siekmann, (Eds.). *7th International Conference 'Artificial Intelligence and Soft Computing' (ICAISC) Lecture Notes in AI LNAI 3070. Springer-Verlag pp 91- 101*

Nwana, H.S. 1990, Intelligent Tutoring Systems: an overview, *Artificial Intelligence Review, 4, pp 251-277.*

Ruddeck, G., Martens, A., Maciuszek, D., Weicht, M. , 2011 Communication Patterns in Component-Based Intelligent Tutoring Systems. in: *The European Journal for Informatics Professional, Special Issue on "Engineering in eLearning Systems".*

MOBILE DEVICE USAGE IN HIGHER EDUCATION

Jan Delcker[1], Andrea Honal[2] and Dirk Ifenthaler[1]
[1]*University of Mannheim, L4, 1 68161 Mannheim, Germany*
[2]*Baden-Wuerttemberg Cooperative State University Mannheim*
Käfertaler Straße 258, 68167 Mannheim, Germany

ABSTRACT

This paper focuses on mobile device usage of students in higher education. While more and more students embrace mobile devices in their daily life, institutions attempt to profit from those devices for educational purposes. It is therefore crucial for institutional development to identify students' needs and how mobile devices may facilitate these needs. This longitudinal study with $N = 172$ students compares the use of e-Readers and tablets for learning at a higher education institution. While e-Readers offer inexpensive solutions for reading texts, tablets provide a much wider range of applications, such as communicating with other students, accessing learning management systems, or conducting research online. Findings indicate that students evaluate tablets as a more useful device for learning. Interestingly, students using tablets also start to include more and more mobile learning technologies into their learning strategies.

KEYWORDS

Mobile device usage; e-Reader; tablet; mobile learning technology

1. INTRODUCTION

The use of mobile devices of higher education students has been on the rise for years. As more and more people integrate mobile devices into their personal life (Dahlstrom, Brooks et al. 2015, Poll 2015) educational institutions are including new technologies into their teaching systems to benefit from the distribution of mobile devices. This includes advanced infrastructure such as computer rooms accessible for students, digitalisation of library systems, as well as the development and implementation of learning management systems with the goal to maximize the use of mobile devices while maintaining the purpose of education (Al-Emran, Elsherif et al. 2016). Aligning students' needs with institutional offers is one of the current challenges. Gikas and Grant (2013) state that students are unlikely to involve a certain mobile device into their learning behaviour, if they do not benefit from it. Simply distributing devices to students will not facilitate educational success of an institution. To distinguish useful devices from less useful ones, it is therefore important to have a closer look at actual students' needs and compare them with the features a mobile device can offer. In 2015, researchers at the University of Mannheim and the Baden-Wuerttemberg Cooperative State University Mannheim (DHBW Mannheim) conducted a longitudinal study focusing on the use of e-Readers for students in higher education. E-Readers were characterized as inexpensive tools able to widen an institution's range of utilised media devices. Although e-Readers proved to be useful for the students' task of reading texts, additional important features were missing: students mentioned the ability to make annotations in a piece of text, search the internet for further information or use the learning management system of the institution as important for their learning needs. As a result, a follow-up study comparing tablet-computers with e-Readers was conducted. The paper consists of three parts. In the first part, relevant theoretical considerations are being made with respect to current literature and empirical work. Six hypotheses have been constructed as a result of the literature review. The second part outlines the survey methodology and the results of the survey. In the final part, the results of the survey are being interpreted and connected with the preliminary considerations.

2. LITERATURE REVIEW

2.1 Students' Tasks in Higher Education

The tasks of students at higher education institutions are manifold. Each category requires a variety of skills, competences, and tools allowing students to be successful learners in higher education. Fundamental tasks are information literacy and academic learning skills including (1) attending classes (including preparation and post processing), (2) preparing for / taking exams, (3) handing in written papers (or comparable assignments) (Stagg and Kimmins 2014). In the following chapter, the three categories will be explained in greater detail. However, several skills, competences, and tools cannot be assigned to a single category and not all of the challenges students face in higher education are included (Fook and Sidhu 2015). A comprehensive review would exceeds the boundary of the paper. Therefore, this review focuses on the tasks that can be supported through mobile devices.

Attending classes refers to the actual presence time at the respective institution. This includes taking part in mandatory lectures and tutorial groups as well as student workgroups. Students have to provide themselves with the course material, such as lecture notes and literature, to effectively handle the task of attending classes. In addition, students are securing important information in the classes by taking notes or creating audio-recordings. Securing important information helps students to follow and post process the current class and to prepare the upcoming class. This often includes performing further research (e.g., searching for information online) (Cohen, Kim et al. 2013).

Scripts, notes, literature, and the ability to conduct further research can be used in the process of preparing for exams. Time management is a necessary skill enabling students to effectively handle the workload in the stressful time in the pre-exam period. It is also needed to organize group work, which is a learning strategy often and successfully used by students (LaBossiere, Dell et al. 2016). In regard to this popular learning strategy, an important factor is the ability to communicate aspects of organization (meeting date and place, agenda) and content related topics (distribute helpful literature in a workgroup).

When working on written papers or other non-exam reviews, students not only rely on literature and information provided by lecturers. They have to search for additional information in online databases, libraries, and the Internet. This includes the ability to work with different texts and file formats. Apart from text files, information can sometimes be found in the form of video and audio files. These media files require further technology to be included in the student's learning process (Gosper, Malfroy et al. 2011, Rashid and Asghar 2016).

2.2 Mobile Learning – e-Readers and Tablets in Comparison

Gikas and Grant (2013) define mobile learning as a combination of three aspects. (1) Mobile learning as more than just learning delivered on a mobile computing device, (2) learning as both formal and informal, as well as (3) context aware and authentic for the learner. For the presented study, points (2) and (3) are especially important, because the curriculum of the DHBW Mannheim is based on the interaction of theory and practice. Students are spending half of the semester with theoretical studies at university and the other half of the semester doing practical work at companies. Mobile devices do not only allow students to have access to learning material while they are away from university, they can also include them in their practice time at work and for authentic learning situations (Gikas and Grant, 2013). Although a multitude of mobile devices for mobile learning have been developed over the last decade, students are mostly using laptops and smartphones, owned by over 90% of all students (Dahlstrom, Brooks et al. 2015). Additionally, a lot of students own e-Readers or tablets and include them in their daily learning (Dahlstrom, Brooks et al. 2015).

The basic function of e-Readers is the display of text files, such as specific e-book-formats or PDF-files. They are equipped with a special display, which was developed to optimize the readability of text documents. E-Readers are lightweight, offer a wide viewing angle and only consume a small amount of energy, therefore combining mobility and readability (Lin, Wu et al. 2013). Pollock (2012) observes e-Readers as not being capable of fulfilling the demands of educational environments, such as displaying multiple columns, detailed illustrations, and mathematical equations or symbols. Further, they often do not support activities related to research-oriented active reading as well as note-taking and highlighting. Technical reports, maps, and charts are difficult to read because of graphics quality (Clark 2008). Improvements seem to be necessary to strengthen e-Readers role in an educational context, for example the ability of browsing the internet (Hahto 2012), printing important parts of content (Miltenoff 2012), and improvements toward processing and performance speed (Shurtz, Gonzalez et al. 2012). The shortcomings of e-Readers may be reasons students do not see them as supportive for their study practices (Mallett (2010)). Nevertheless, e-Readers are characterized as "great for reading novels" (Mannonen, Nieminen et al. 2011), especially because of the eye-friendliness of the screen, weight and size of the device, as well as power of battery (Marmarelli 2010).

The most common e-Readers types are the Kindle (Amazon), the Kobo, Nook (Barnes and Noble), and the Sony Reader (Rainie, Zickuhr et al. 2012) with cost from 50€ up to 250€. Another notable product is the Tolino, a coalition of big bookstore companies, designed especially for the European market.

In comparison to e-Readers, tablets (e.g. Apple iPad) offer a much wider range of functions, while at the same time providing a similar mobility. Tablets can be described as a mixture of smartphones and laptop computers, equipped with technology to use mobile data, such as Bluetooth, Wi-Fi and LTE, but with a much bigger screen than the typical smartphone. Additional features such as microphones and cameras and the ability to install software in the form of apps are paired with intuitive usability (Ifenthaler and Schweinbenz 2013). The investigated problems of e-Readers in educational context can mostly be approached with tablets, because they allow access to the Internet (e.g. for researching further learning content). With the display keyboard, notes can easily be added to existing documents. Tablets can show 3D-models and complex simulations because of their advanced computing power. In terms of media files, video and audio files can also be rendered on tablets. Furthermore, technical features allow students to access learning management systems or use social media to connect with other learners. Students can install additional programs or applications on a tablet to structure and frame their personal learning process.

Tablets cost from 30€ to 1800€, with a wide variety of manufacturers and operating systems. Apple iPad, Samsung Galaxy Tab and Microsoft Surface are the most commonly used tablets with specific operations systems iOS (Apple), Android (Samsung) and Microsoft Surface.

A difference in fields of application for the mobile devices can be determined based on their technical characteristics and limitations. While e-Readers seem to provide as a good tool for reading text files, tablets offer a much wider set of functions. Table 1 compares e-Readers and tablets with regard to the tasks of students.

Table 1. Features of e-Readers and Tablets

Task	e-Reader	Tablet
Reading text files	Possible	Possible
Taking notes	Complicated/not possible	Possible
Browsing the internet	Not possible	Possible
Library research	Not possible	Possible
Accessing LMS	Not possible	Possible
Communication	Not possible	Possible
Additional media	Not possible	Possible

2.3 The Present Study

While the tablet looks superior in theory, it is questionable if or to what extend students are integrating the mobile device into their learning and how they rate the usefulness of the device. Multiple hypotheses for a comparative study were created, based on the theoretical assumptions of the previous chapters.

We assume that students are using tablets more often then e-Readers (Hypothesis 1). Students working with a tablet more often utilize technologies and features for learning (Hypothesis 2a). The difference between tablet and e-Reader users in this regard is getting bigger over time (Hypothesis 2b). When rating the usability of tablets for the personal learning process, tablets are rated better in comparison to e-Readers (Hypothesis 3a). The difference between tablet and e-Reader rating are getting bigger in the course of time (Hypothesis 3b). The technical feature of the tablets are rated higher than the technical features of e-Readers (Hypothesis 4).

3. METHOD

3.1 Design

This study compares the use of e-Readers and tablets at the Baden-Wuerttemberg Cooperative State University Mannheim (DHBW). The main goal was to investigate in which ways bachelor students integrate the mobile devices into their learning behavior and if there are significant differences between different mobile devices. Out of a group of 172 students two groups were chosen randomly and provided with an e-Reader or a tablet. Data was collected through an online survey at three different measurement points (start of semester, mid-semester and end of semester). At the first measurement point, students received their devices. They were asked to provide their email-address, which was later used to invite them to the online survey using the LimeSurvey tool.

3.2 Participants

In total, $N = 172$ students from 3 different classes (real-estate management, mechanical engineering, and business informatics) took part in the survey. 72.7% were male and 27.3% were female students, with an average age of 20.23 years ($SD = 2.21$). 26% of the students attended the real-estate management class, 35% studied mechanical engineering and 39% were business informatics students.

3.3 Instrument

At three measurement points (t1, t2, t3), slightly different questionnaires were used, consisting of 31 (t1), 19 (t2) and 41 (t3) items. In most cases, a seven-point Likert scale (7 = I totally agree; 6= I agree; 5 = I agree partially; 4 = I don't know; 3 = I disagree partially; 2 = I disagree; 1= I totally disagree) was used to evaluate the students' opinions and perception towards the devices. Moreover, open questions were used to collect information about positive and negative aspects of the devices. The factors have been successfully tested for reliability with Cronbach's alpha $.775 \leq r \leq .904$.

3.4 Data Analysis

The collected data was anonymized, exported and analyzed using SPSS V.23. Initial data checks showed that the distributions of ratings and scores satisfied the assumptions underlying the analysis procedures. Out of the initial 172 students, 127 datasets could be used for analysis. All effects were assessed at the .05 level.

4. RESULTS

4.1 Hypothesis 1: Frequency of Mobile Device Use

Students were asked at measurement three (t3) to provide the frequency they used the mobile device on a scale from 1 to 7 (1 = multiple times a day, 2 = daily, 3 = multiple times a week, 4 = once a week, 5 = multiple times a month, 6 = once a month, 7 = less than once a month). An independent-samples t-test was used to compare the amount of time students spent using the mobile devices. The t-test showed a significant difference between the time spent on using the mobile device between students with e-Readers ($M = 6.40$, $SD = 1.24$) and students with tablets ($M = 2.58$, $SD = 1.73$), $t(127) = 14.48$, $p < .01$. The results suggest, that there is a difference between the amount of time students spend on using e-Readers and tablets. Specifically, the results suggest that tablets are used a lot more often than e-Readers. E-Readers are approximately used once a month, while the tablets are used multiple times a week.

4.2 Hypothesis 2a: Use of Technologies and Features for Learning

Students were asked which technologies and features they use as part of their learning on a seven-point Likert scale (1 = no use; 7 = very high usage intensity). 13 different features and technologies were chosen, e.g.. online research, online library, online database, communication application, video platforms, social media platforms, and learning management systems (LMS). For analysis, a variable was created, grouping the specific intensity variables together into a single intensity variable for each measurement point. A high value represents a high use of technologies and features while a low value represents a low use of technologies and features. An independent-samples t-test was conducted to compare the use of technologies and features between the two mobile device groups at measurement points t1 and t3. There was no significant difference between e-Readers ($M = 42.58$, $SD = 12.12$) and tablets ($M = 41.64$, $SD = 11.31$) at measurement point t1, $t(127) = .0457$, $p = 0.648$. Similar, no significant difference between e-Readers ($M = 43.68$, $SD = 13.25$) and tablets ($M = 47.09$, $SD = 11.34$) was found at measurement point t3, $t(127) = - 1.57$, $p = .118$. thus, hypothesis 2a has to be rejected. The results suggest that students using tablets and e-Readers do not vary in the intensity of technologies and features used for their personal learning behavior.

4.3 Hypothesis 2b: Increased Difference over Time

Although we could not find a significant difference in the intensity of used technologies and features between e-Readers and tablets, a change in intensity over time might be observable. A paired-samples t-test was used to compare the usage intensity of technologies and features in the course of time within the two device groups. For the tablets, there was a significant difference between t1 ($M = 41.64$, $SD = 11.31$) and t3 ($M = 47.09$, $SD = 11.34$), $t(63) = -3.76$, $p < .01$. For the e-Readers there was no significant difference between t1 ($M = 42.58$, $SD = 12.12$) and t3 ($M = 43.68$, $SD = 13.25$), $t(64) = -.582$, $p = .56$. The results suggest, that while there is no significant change in the intensity of used technologies and features for e-Reader users over time, the tablet group uses technologies and features more frequently after working with the devices for some time.

4.4 Hypothesis 3a: Rating the Usability for Learning

Students were asked to rate the usefulness of the device they were equipped with. Four items were used to determine the perceived usefulness ("Using the device for learning is a good idea", "Using the device for learning makes learning more interesting", "Using the device for learning is fun" and "I like working with the device") on a seven-point Likert scale (7 = I totally agree; 6= I agree; 5 = I agree partially; 4 = I don't know; 3 = I disagree partially; 2 = I disagree; 1= I totally disagree). Those four items were computed into a group variable for further analysis. An independent t-test was conducted to compare the perceived usefulness for personal learning between the two devices. There was no significant difference between the rating of e-Readers ($M - 20.52$, $SD = 5.18$) and tablets ($M = 21.64$, $SD = 3.74$) at t1, $t(127) = -1.401$, $p = .164$. The results suggest, that the use of e-Readers and tablets was not perceived different at the beginning of the study. At the end of the study, there was a significant difference between the rating of e-Readers ($M = 15.00$, $SD = 7.23$) and tablets ($M = 21.00$, $SD = 5.23$); $t(127) = -5.392$, $p < .01$. The results show that there is a difference between the perceived usefulness between e-Readers and tablets at the end of the term. More specifically, e-Readers are perceived as less useful in contrast to tablets.

4.5 Hypothesis 3b: Increased Difference over Time

While there was not a significant difference between the perceived usefulness between e-Readers and tablets at the beginning of the study (hypothesis 3a), there was a significant difference at the end of the study. Because of the observed values from the statistical tests, we assume that the usefulness of tablets is not changing much from t1 to t2. In comparison, the perceived usefulness of e-Readers differs significantly between t1 ($M = 20.52$, $SD = 5.18$) and t3 ($M = 15.00$, $SD = 7.23$), $t(64) = 6.54$, $p < .01$. The results suggest that e-Readers are perceived much less useful after working with them for a term.

4.6 Hypothesis 4: Technical Features of Tablets

Students were asked to evaluate the technical features the devices provide, namely "access to the Internet", "access to a literature platform", "good readability", "long lasting battery", "access to additional lecture material", "flexibility to use content on multiple devices", "costs of books and lecture material", "adding notes to documents", "adding bookmarks", "lecture coverage with the provided scripts and books". On a seven-point Likert scale the students could rate the features from 1 = "totally not relevant" to 7 = "totally relevant". The items were grouped into a new variable to measure the frequency of ratings. 22% of the students rated the total features as relevant and 56.6% as very relevant. The majority (79%) of students evaluated the features of the tablet as relevant for their learning strategies.

5. CONCLUSION

The findings of this study identified differences between e-Readers and tablets. This underlines the importance of a planned mobile device usage for mobile learning at higher education institutions. The amount of time spend with a device is suggesting the usefulness of the mobile device. Literature clearly identified limitations of e-Readers (Clark 2008, Hahto 2012, Mallett 2010, Miltenhoff 2012, Shurtz, Gonzalez et al. 2012). The limited applications and sole purpose as a reading device for non-coloured, pure text files does not make it a very attractive mobile device for students. In hypothesis 4 the technical features of tablets could be identified as very relevant to students learning process. In reverse, a lack of those features can be described as not supportive for the students' learning strategies in higher education (Gosper, Malfroy et al. 2011).

Hypothesis 2a and 2b suggest an important feature of tablets: The integration of technologies and features such as online research, library access or accessing the learning management system facilitate learning at higher education institutions. Tablet users tend to utilize the available technologies significantly more often after working with the mobile devices for some time, while the e-Reader users do not change their behavior significantly. It might be possible that the further use of tablets leads to an observable significant difference between the two mobile devices. This could mean that the tablets do enable and motivate students to use more of the available mobile learning features. As a result, tablets can be interpreted as catalyst for further engaging with mobile learning. It is important to note that the feature and technologies students rated in the survey might not be used because they don't fit into the needs of the student. In the theoretical part we already hinted at the fact that students don't use technology that isn't useful for them (Gikas and Grant 2013). As an example, students might not use the learning management system because they don't profit from it, be it through the lack of content or usability. Such a phenomenon could blur the measurement of students' technology and feature usage, because in return, a learning management system that is perceived as effective by students would have a bigger impact on the rating.

The attitudes of students towards technology and features at the beginning of the term (the first measurement point) are indications for the quality of the sample. No bias between the two groups can be found at the start of the survey. The same assumption can be made with regards to hypothesis 3a, where no differences between the groups could be found. This can be interpreted as both groups having the same overall attitude towards the devices and especially trying to integrate devices into their learning strategy at the start of the survey (Al-Emran, Elsherif et al. 2016). The statements made by the students at a later point in time were therefore mainly influenced by the use of the mobile devices.

One of the most interesting aspects of the data analysis is the fact that tablets don't achieve higher ratings after the usage. The difference between the devices is based on a decreased rating of the e-Readers. This can probably be caused by a disappointing user experience with the e-Reader. At the start of the survey, the participants were most likely happy and excited about the opportunity to work with a new mobile device without having to worry about financial issues or if they would really need to have the device. The limits of the device have been mentioned in previous parts of the paper (Clark 2008, Hahto 2012, Mallett 2010, Miltenhoff 2012, Shurtz, Gonzalez et al. 2012). It is very likely that students were disappointed by the e-Readers because of its limited features and usability. The disappointment could have been enhanced by the fact that the other group of students got a 'superior' mobile device.

The assumptions derived from the data analysis can be transferred to students from other higher educational institutions offering similar features and technologies that can be accessed with a mobile device. The observed differences between the mobile devices will most likely become more apparent at institutions providing more and better features of mobile learning, such as well-engineered learning management systems or when lectures include mobile learning into their classes. It is important to notice that lecturers didn't use more special content (e.g. more online materials, higher use of audio or video files) during the survey. This probably has a big impact of the perceived usefulness of the mobile devices. The survey presented in this paper will be extended for another term to collect data towards this assumption. More materials and more features being accessed via tablets will be implemented at the DHBW Mannheim soon. This will increase the amount of data available for analysis, which is especially interesting for the assumptions made towards hypothesis 3. It will be interesting to see if the assumed catalyst effect will lead to a measurable significant difference between the two devices.

As a limiting factor, the high costs of effective tablets must be seen. It is rather difficult to provide a bigger group of students with those devices. If institutions of higher education want to include mobile devices into their media portfolio, they will most like have to equip research teams with additional funding to purchase those devices (Gikas and Grant 2013). Although 127 participants offer a good basis for the quantitative research for this paper, further research must be conducted to enhance the view on mobile devices in the context of mobile learning. Apart from the aspects already mentioned, it would be interesting to see if there are differences between advanced students and freshmen. Tablets could help freshmen overcome the gap that is often mentioned when changing from high school to university. On the one hand tablets could enable them to cope with the new challenges higher education institutions posses, e.g. finding effective learning strategies and getting easy access to course material. On the other hand, advanced students might use other aspects of the mobile device more frequently, including research work or the organization of work groups.

REFERENCES

Al-Emran, M., H. M. Elsherif and K. Shaalan (2016). "Investigating attitudes towards the use of mobile learning in higher education." Computers in Human Behavior 56: 93-102.

Clark, D. T. G., Susan P.; Samuelson, Todd; Coker, Catherine (2008). "A qualitative assessment of the Kindle e-book reader: results from initial focus groups." Performance Measurement & Metrics 9(2): 118-129.

Cohen, D., E. Kim, J. Tan and M.-A. Winkelmes (2013). "A Note-Restructuring Intervention Increases Students' Exam Scores." College Teaching 61(3): 95-99.

Dahlstrom, E., C. Brooks, S. Grajek and J. Reeves (2015). ECAR Study of Students and Information Technology 2015. Louisville, CO, ECAR: 47.

Fook, C. Y. and G. K. Sidhu (2015). "Investigating Learning Challenges Faced by Students in Higher Education." Procedia - Social and Behavioral Sciences 186: 604-612.

Gikas, J. and M. M. Grant (2013). "Mobile computing devices in higher education: Student perspectives on learning with cellphones, smartphones & social media." The Internet and Higher Education 19: 18-26.

Gosper, M., J. Malfroy, J. McKenzie and L. Rankine (2011). Students' engagement with technologies : implications for university practice.

Hahto, J. (2012). "The e-Reader -- an Educational or an Entertainment Tool? e-Readers in an Academic Setting." Liber Quarterly: The Journal of European Research Libraries 21(2): 249-261.

Ifenthaler, D. and V. Schweinbenz (2013). "The acceptance of Tablet-PCs in classroom instruction: The teachers' perspectives." Computers in Human Behavior 29(3): 525–534.

LaBossiere, M. D., K. A. Dell, K. Sunjic and G. A. Wantuch (2016). "Student perceptions of group examinations as a method of exam review in pharmacotherapeutics." Currents in Pharmacy Teaching and Learning 8(3): 375-379.

Lin, H., F.-G. Wu and Y.-Y. Cheng (2013). "Legibility and visual fatigue affected by text direction, screen size and character size on color LCD e-Reader." Displays 34(1): 49-58.

Mallett, E. (2010). "A screen too far? Findings from an e-book reader pilot." Serials 23(2): 140-144.

Mannonen, P., S. Nieminen and M. Nieminen (2011). "Usability and compatibility of e-book readers in an academic environment: A collaborative study." IFLA Journal 37(1): 16-27.

Marmarelli, T. R., Martin (2010). "Ereaders in academic libraries -- a literature review." Australian Library Journal 59(4): 180-186.

Miltenoff, P. (2012). "Challenges to E-Reader Adoption in Academic Libraries." Reference Librarian 53(3): 270-283.

Poll, H. (2015). Pearson Student Mobile Device Survey 2015 National Report: College Students: 52.

Rainie, L., K. Zickuhr, K. Purcel, M. Madden and J. Brenner (2012). The rise of e-reading. Washington, D.C., Pew Research Center's Internet & American Life Project: 68.

Rashid, T. and H. M. Asghar (2016). "Technology use, self-directed learning, student engagement and academic performance: Examining the interrelations." Computers in Human Behavior 63: 604-612.

Shurtz, S., A. Gonzalez and D. Clark (2012). "Assessing an e-Reader lending program: from pilot to mainstream service." Library Review 61(1): 8-17.

Stagg, A. and L. Kimmins (2014). "First Year in Higher Education (FYHE) and the Coursework Post-Graduate Student." The Journal of Academic Librarianship 40(2): 142-151.

FEATURES STUDENTS REALLY EXPECT FROM LEARNING ANALYTICS

Clara Schumacher[1] and Dirk Ifenthaler[2]
[1]University of Mannheim
[2]University of Mannheim and Curtin University
L4, 1, 68131 Mannheim, Germany

ABSTRACT

In higher education settings more and more learning is facilitated through online learning environments. To support and understand students' learning processes better, learning analytics offers a promising approach. The purpose of this study was to investigate students' expectations toward features of learning analytics systems. In a first qualitative exploratory study a total of 20 university students participated. They were interviewed about their expectations of learning analytics features. The findings of the qualitative study were validated in a second quantitative study in which 216 students took part. Findings show that students expect learning analytics features to support their planning and organization of learning processes, provide self-assessments, deliver adaptive recommendations, and produce personalized analyses of their learning activities.

KEYWORDS

Learning analytics; higher education; students' expectations; self-regulated learning

1. INTRODUCTION

Higher education institutions develop and implement learning analytics systems to support student learning. Therefore, it is relevant to consider students' expectations of such systems in terms of learning. Learners directly interact with the user interface of the learning analytics system, which offers different features such as visualizations, learning recommendations, prompts, rating possibilities, and self-assessments. Further, learning analytics systems aim to offer highly adaptable and personalized learning environments (Ifenthaler & Widanapathirana, 2014). Personalized learning environments can help to foster students' skills to manage, monitor, and reflect their own learning (McLoughlin & Lee, 2010). To be able to design, develop, and implement personalized learning analytics systems, it is necessary to investigate what learners expect from these systems. Otherwise the implementation of learning analytics systems as a means to support learning could fail as it might even hinder self-regulated learning for example if students feel demotivated because of their performance in comparison to their peers. Conole, Creanor, Irving, and Paluch (2007) showed in their study on e-learning that it is necessary to recognize a full range of students' perceptions as otherwise institutions might fail to meet learners' needs.

Still, empirical research regarding students' expectations on learning analytics to facilitate learning is scarce. Therefore, the purpose of this mixed-methods study was to investigate which features of learning analytics systems students expect. To validate the findings of a first exploratory qualitative study, a follow-up quantitative study was conducted to investigate how students rate learning analytics features in terms of learning and their potential implementation.

2. LEARNING ANALYTICS FEATURES

2.1 Learning Analytics

Learning analytics use static and dynamic information about learners and learning environments, assessing, eliciting and analyzing them, for real-time modeling, prediction, and optimization of learning processes, learning environments, and educational decision-making (Ifenthaler, 2015).

Learning analytics provide benefits for all levels of higher education stakeholders: mega-level (governance), macro-level (institution), meso-level (curriculum, teacher/tutor) and micro-level (learner) (Ifenthaler & Widanapathirana, 2014). The micro-level of learning analytics focusses on supporting individual and collaborative learning activities. Benefits can be divided in three perspectives and for the micro-level as follows (Ifenthaler & Widanapathirana, 2014): (a) summative: understand learning habits, compare learning paths, analyze learning outcomes, track progress towards goals; (b) real-time: receive automated interventions and scaffolds, take assessments including just-in-time feedback, support collaboration; (c) predictive: optimize learning paths, adapt to recommendations, increase engagement, increase success rates.

2.2 Learning Analytics Features

Learning analytics features include functions a learning analytics system could provide to the user (e.g., learners, tutors, administrators, etc.). Thus learning analytics features include dashboard elements, for example visualizations of activity analyses in the learning management system. Further, features include recommendations about further readings, self-assessment-questionnaires, or additional links to related video tutorials. Features focusing on learners' behavior include time spent online, analyses and forecasts of academic performance, adaptive learning recommendations, and personalized prompts with questions about the learners' dispositions.

Learning analytics features rely on analyses of various data (Ifenthaler & Widanapathirana, 2014): (a) Learner characteristics including prior knowledge, psychometric tests about learning strategies and competencies, socio-demographic data, or prior academic performance. (b) External data such as searches in the library catalogue, geo-data or information from social media. (c) Traces generated by using the online learning environment, for example online-frequency and -time, activities in discussions and other online interaction, results of self-assessment-questionnaires, up- and download of resources, as well as ratings of content. Furthermore, (d) curricular information are integrated into the analyses, for instance exemplar study paths and expected learning outcomes.

Many dashboard applications in learning analytics systems focus on visualizations of descriptive data, such as time spent online, the progress towards the completion of a course, or comparisons with other students' performance. More elaborated systems include results of self-assessments (Verbert et al., 2014). Findings of a comparative study of three learning analytics systems have shown that students prefer more detailed learning analytics systems with elaborated analyses and personalized recommendations for their learning (Ifenthaler & Schumacher, 2015).

Learning analytics systems showing descriptive summative information about past learning activities such as time spent online, login frequency, and performance results already help students to monitor their current state and increase student success rates.. However, to plan upcoming learning activities or to adapt current learning strategies, further personalized and adaptive features of the learning analytics system are needed.

2.3 Purpose of the Studies

Currently, learning analytics features are investigated in terms of visualizations and dashboard elements or their technical possibilities (Verbert, Duval, Klerkx, Govaerts, & Santos, 2013; Verbert et al., 2014). Most studies about learning analytics dashboards were conducted in controlled settings.

To better understand students' needs, this study used a mixed-methods approach combining an exploratory qualitative interview study followed by a quantitative survey study. The two studies are reported in the following sections.

3. STUDY 1

The purposes of the qualitative exploratory study were (1) to investigate which features of learning analytics students expect and (2) to deduce further research needs.

3.1 Method

3.1.1 Participants and Design

The study was designed as a qualitative exploratory study with oral interviews. Interviews were conducted in May 2016. After removing one incomplete response, the responses of 20 graduate students (14 female, 6 male) have been considered for further analyses. The average age of the participants was 24.55 years (*SD* = 2.21). Participants received one credit hour for participating in the study.

3.1.2 Materials

Introduction to Learning Analytics

A short lecture (approximately 5 minutes) including presentation slides introduced the basic concepts of learning analytics and provided an overview about various types of data used for learning analytics. The session concluded with a possibility to clarify comprehension questions.

Learning Analytics Features

Students were confronted with three guiding questions regarding learning analytics features, which they were asked to answer in oral form or by using a whiteboard or paper to illustrate. (1) Please reflect about possible features or dashboard elements, which you would like to have as an application in a learning analytics system. (2) Please explain which function these elements have. (3) Please indicate how you think these features or dashboard elements can support learning.

Technology Usage for Learning

The Technology Usage for Learning (TUL; 10 items) inventory includes items investigating students' usage and attitude towards technology for learning purposes and the potential use of learning analytics systems.

Demographic information

Demographic information included age, gender, Internet usage for learning and social media, years of study, study major, and course load.

3.1.3 Procedure

Over a period of two weeks in May 2016, students were invited to participate in the qualitative interview study, which included three parts. In the first part, participants received a general introduction into learning analytics (approx. 5 minutes). Secondly, they reported about learning analytics features, they would expect from learning analytics systems and how these features could support learning (8 up to 80 minutes). In the third part, participants completed the technology usage for learning inventory and reported their demographic information (10 minutes).

3.1.4 Data Analysis

The audio recordings of all interviews were transcribed in single text documents. Using f4anaylsis (www.audiotranskription.de), a software for qualitative data analysis, the transcribed interviews were analyzed in terms of learning analytics features and critical statements the students mentioned. Afterwards the collected features were parsed again to find out which features tended to be more relevant for the respondents but following the qualitative research approach also single statements were considered.

3.2 Results

For the majority of the students a learning analytics system would help in terms of planning their learning activities and higher education studies. The students' demands ranged from basic reminder functions for deadlines, for example to submit assignments towards automated to-do lists and agendas. Two interviewees (4, 21) would also allow the system to have access to their own calendar and recommend appropriate tasks and plans matching their personal schedule.

The majority of the participants mentioned that the system should offer self-assessments corresponding to their learning fields. The assessment conditions should be the same as during exams regarding working time and task difficulty. Ideally after completion they want to receive direct and valid feedback. The feedback should be divided into subject areas enabling students to assess their need for improvement. To initiate further learning activities, the system should provide corresponding learning recommendations such as further material. In general, they expect further learning material presenting the same content with different media such as videos, lecture recordings and short summaries or beyond that on-topic links to current news, practical examples, further literature or learning materials of previous courses to recapitulate.

An overview about their current state of knowledge, their activities in the system as well as their progress towards own or set learning objectives seems to be relevant to the students. They asked for analyses of their working progress towards learning objectives, time spent for learning, preferred daytime for learning, performance and progress over different periods as well as performance evaluations of former and current grades and also forecasts.

Students disagreed in terms of receiving analyses comparing their own performance or learning activities with those of their peers. Some perceive such comparisons as motivating others would not. To avoid demotivation and to meet all learners' needs it was suggested to have a high degree of personalization regarding the system's visualizations or that they should only be shown on request.

Personalization options were also requested regarding the layout of the learning environment in terms of colors and disposal of elements.

Interaction with fellow students but also direct contact to the lecturer via the system was essential for the students. Discussion forums and chats for communication as well as videoconferencing and online-teamwork function with the possibility to share documents were mentioned features. Additionally, two interviewees (1, 11) wanted the system to suggest learning partners, which are either close by, are dealing with the same learning subject or have complementary knowledge to create synergies.

Statements from only few or single students uttered the possibility to click on keywords in all provided materials, which would lead to definitions or further learning material concerning these keywords. Further it was argued that the system needs a feature to enter learning activities occurring offline. This aspect becomes even more relevant as the additional questionnaire revealed that all interviewed students prefer to read printed texts for their studies, only one student additionally reads texts on a screen.

Students' statements also indicated that they expect a highly evolved system, containing several programs, such as text processing, a literature management program being fed by the library, or a PDF annotation program. The students stated that they do not want to switch between programs but would prefer a holistic solution.

Two students (4, 20) would like the system to guide their breaks by analyzing their productivity and suggesting when it is time for a break. Further the system might give advices which kind of break would be reasonable, for example eating, drinking, or doing distracting activities (watching a video or doing a workout).

Most interviewees had a positive attitude regarding the application of learning analytics systems and would like to use such a system. Only two respondents indicated in the questionnaire that they do not want to use learning analytics, due to privacy concerns, the risk of too much surveillance of learning activities and a reduction of autonomous learning (9). However, also the students who agreed to use learning analytics had critical thoughts as for instance demotivating consequences due to visualization of poor performances or comparisons with fellow students or the distractive character of using media and technology for learning. One interviewee feared that even stronger as yet not acquiring knowledge but figures such as good grades are the only purpose of learning.

4. STUDY 2

Based on the findings of the qualitative study, a follow-up quantitative study was conducted. The first assumption was that the learning analytics features presented to the students were rated differently in terms of students' willingness to use the feature for their learning (Hypothesis 1). Second, it was assumed that students' evaluation of the presented features in terms of learning differed significantly (Hypothesis 2). Finally, it was assumed that students are more willing to use a certain learning analytics feature for their studies when rating the feature high in terms of learning (Hypothesis 3a), do not perceive that the feature is invasive (Hypothesis 3b), and do not think that the feature is complicated to use (Hypothesis 3c) or not useful for them (Hypothesis 3d).

4.1 Method

4.1.1 Participants and Design

The second study was designed as a quantitative online study conducted in May and June 2016. The average age of the participants was 23.83 years (SD = 2.99). The dataset included N = 216 responses (142 female (66% valid) and 73 males (34% valid) [1 missing]). More than half of the participants studied in the Bachelors program (54,6%) and 45,4% students studied in the Masters program. The average course load in the current semester was 5.42 courses (SD = 1.91). Almost half of the students (46%) indicated that they prefer reading texts for university on a display whereas 54% preferred reading printed texts. 88% of the interviewed students want to use learning analytics for their studies, whereas 12% did not want to use learning analytics. Participants received one credit hour for participating in the study.

4.1.2 Instruments

Learning Analytics Features (LAF)

The participants were confronted with 15 different learning analytics features, some of them deduced from the qualitative exploratory study: (1) time spent online; (2) suggestion of learning partners; (3) learning recommendations for successful course completion; (4) rating scales for provided learning material; (5) timeline showing current status and goal; (6) time needed to complete a task or read a text; (7) prompts for self-assessments; (8) further learning recommendations; (9) comparison with fellow students; (10) considering the students personal calendar for appropriate learning recommendations; (11) newsfeed with relevant news matching the learning content; (12) revision of former learning content; (13) feedback for assignments; (14) reminder for deadlines; (15) term scheduler, recommending relevant courses.

The students were asked to rate these 15 features in terms of learning, acceptance, and privacy aspects. All items were answered on a 5-point Likert scale (1 = strongly disagree; 2 = disagree; 3 = neither agree or disagree; 4 = agree; 5 = strongly agree; LAF; 20 items; Cronbach's α = .93).

Learning Analytics Benefits (LAB)

The learning analytics benefits scale (LAB) focuses on benefits, learning analytics could offer (Ifenthaler & Widanapathirana, 2014). The students were asked to rate the 36 items on a 5-point Likert scale (1 = strongly disagree; 2 = disagree; 3 = neither agree or disagree; 4 = agree; 5 = strongly agree) (LAB; 36 items; Cronbach's α = .94).

Privacy for Learning Analytics (LAP)

In the privacy for learning analytics questionnaire (LAP) the students were asked to state their willingness to share personal data for learning analytics systems, for example tracking of their online paths, educational history, course of studies etc. All items were answered on a Thurstone scale (1 = Agree; 2 = Do not agree; LAP; 23 items, Cronbach's α = .84).

Self-Regulated Learning Scale (SRLS)

To assess students' capability to self-regulate their learning the adapted version of the "Inventory of Learning strategies" (Boerner, Seeber, Keller, & Beinborn, 2005; Wild & Schiefele, 1994) was used and adjusted. The final scale (SRLS) included 14 subscales: effort (8 items, Cronbach's α = .76); concentration (6 items,

Cronbach's α = .91); critical thinking (8 items, Cronbach's α = .82); learning environment (6 items, Cronbach's α = .73); metacognitive awareness (7 items, Cronbach's α = .65); organization (9 items, Cronbach's α = .81); regulation (8 items, Cronbach's α = .72), help & resources (10 items, Cronbach's α = .7); self-efficacy (4 items, Cronbach's α = .64); self-assessment (7 items, Cronbach's α = .67); revision (7 items, Cronbach's α = .72); time management (4 items, Cronbach's α = .82); goal setting (7 items, Cronbach's α = .71); coherence (8 items, Cronbach's α = .69). All items were answered on a 5-point Likert scale (1 = strongly disagree; 2 = disagree; 3 = neither agree or disagree; 4 = agree; 5 = strongly agree; SRLS; 99 items, Cronbach's α = .93)

Technology use for Learning Scale (TUL)

The technology use for learning scale focuses on how often students use certain technologies and media (e.g., laptop, tablet, blogs, podcasts) for learning (TUL1; 11 items, Cronbach's α = .65). And which technologies and media they would like to use more often for learning purposes (TUL2; 11 items, Cronbach's α = .74).

Demographic Information

Finally, students stated demographic information such as age, gender, course load, Internet use, current academic performance (20 items).

4.1.3 Procedure

In May and June 2016 over a period of three weeks, students could participate in an online study, implemented on the university's server and consisting of five parts. In the first part, students received a general introduction into learning analytics (approx. 5 minutes). The second part focused on learning analytics: The students rated the 15 learning analytics features, each by answering 20 items (LAF; 30 minutes). Then, they completed the learning analytics benefits scale (LAB; 36 items, 15 minutes). And finally, they participated in the privacy for learning analytics questionnaire (LAP, 23 items, 10 minutes). In the third part, the students were confronted with the self-regulated learning scale (SRLS; 99 items, 25 minutes). Afterwards, students reported which technologies they use and would like to use more for learning (TUL; 22 items; 10 minutes). Finally, participants reported their demographic information (20 items, 7 minutes).

4.2 Results

4.2.1 Acceptance to use Learning Analytics Features

Students' rating, if they would like to use the presented learning analytics features for their studies differed significantly, $F(14,3225) = 48.069$, $p<.001$, $\eta^2 = .173$. Games Howell post-hoc comparisons between the different learning analytics features revealed that the reminder function ($M = 4.2$, 95% CI [4.06, 4.34] was evaluated significantly higher than the newsfeed providing current learning content relevant news ($M = 3.42$, 95% CI [3.24, 3.61], $p < .001$ (see Table 1).

The learning analytics function to repeat former learning content ($M = 4.12$, 95% CI [3.99, 4.25]) was rated significantly higher than the feature showing the time, which is necessary to complete a task or reading a text ($M = 2.32$, 95% CI [2.14, 2.51]), $p < .001$. Getting automated feedback for assignments ($M = 4.07$, 95% CI [3.91, 4.22]) was rated significantly higher than the function that the system considers the learner's personal schedule and gives matching learning recommendations ($M = 3.5$, 95% CI [3.33, 3.68]) $p < .001$. The rating of the features regarding the willingness to use a certain feature differed significantly, accordingly Hypothesis 1 is accepted.

Table 1. Post-hoc comparisons for item "would I like to use for my studies" by learning analytics features

Feature	Statistic		1	2	3	4	5	6	7	8	9	10	11	12	13	14	15
1 Time online	Mean	3.125	-														
	Variance	1.422															
	SD	1.1923															
2 Learning partner	Mean	3.301	.1759	-													
	Variance	1.272															
	SD	1.1277															
3 Learning recommendation for course completion	Mean	3.981	.8565***	.6806***	-												
	Variance	1.023															
	SD	1.0114															
4 Ratingscales for learning material	Mean	3.306	.1806	.0046	-.6759***	-											
	Variance	1.813															
	SD	1.3465															
5 Timeline for achievement of objectives	Mean	3.778	.6528***	.4769***	-.2037	.4722**	-										
	Variance	1.392															
	SD	1.1799															
6 Time for reading and task completion	Mean	2.324	-.8009***	-.9769***	-1.6574***	-.9815***	-1.4537***	-									
	Variance	1.848															
	SD	1.3594															
7 Prompts for self-assessment	Mean	4.074	.9491***	.7731***	.0926	.7685***	.2963	1.7500***	-								
	Variance	.999															
	SD	.9996															
8 Further learning recommendations	Mean	3.685	.5602***	.3843*	-.2963	.3796	-.0926	1.3611***	-.3889*	-							
	Variance	1.352															
	SD	1.1626															
9 Comparison with fellow students	Mean	2.491	-,6343***	-.8102***	-1.4907***	-0.8148***	-1.287***	.1667	-1.5833***	-1.1944***	-						
	Variance	1.739															
	SD	1.3189															
10 Integration of personal schedule	Mean	3.5	.375	.1991	-.4815**	.1944	-.2778	1.1759***	-.5741***	-.1852	1.0093***	-					
	Variance	1.693															
	SD	1.3012															
11 Newsfeed	Mean	3.421	.2963	.1204	-.5602***	.1157	-.3565	1.0972***	-.6528***	-.2639	.9306***	-.0787	-				
	Variance	1.938															
	SD	1.3921															
12 Repetition of learning content	Mean	4.12	.9954***	.8194***	.1389	.8148***	.3426	1.7963***	.0463	.4352**	1.6296***	.6204***	.6991***	-			
	Variance	.878															
	SD	.9373															
13 Feedback for assignments	Mean	4.069	.9444***	.7685***	.088	.7639***	.2917	1.7454***	-.0046	.3843*	1.5787***	.5694***	.6481***	-.0509	-		
	Variance	1.386															
	SD	1.1772															
14 Reminder	Mean	4.199	1.0741***	.8981***	.2176	.8935***	.4213**	1.875***	.125	.5139***	1.7083***	.6991***	.7778***	.0787	.1296	-	
	Variance	1.137															
	SD	1.0663															
15 Term scheduler	Mean	3.667	.5417***	.3657	-.3148	.3611	-.1111	1.3426***	-.4074*	-.0185	1.1759***	.1667	.2454	-.4537**	-.4028	-.5324***	-
	Variance	1.795															
	SD	1.3399															

Note: *** p<.001; ** p<.01; * p<.05

4.2.2 Learning Analytics Features Rated for Learning

After building a learning scale (14 items, Cronbach's $\alpha = .94$) and computing ANOVA it could be shown that the rating of the features in terms of learning differed significantly, $F(14,3225) = 56.49$, $p <.001$, $\eta^2 = .197$. Games-Howell post-hoc comparisons (see Table 2) indicated that students evaluated prompts for self-assessments (M = 3.73, 95% CI [3.64, 3.82] significantly higher than feedback on assignments (M = 3.39, 95% CI [3.27, 2.51]). Learning recommendations to complete the course (M = 3.7, 95% CI [3.61, 3.77]) were rated significantly higher than suggested learning partners (M = 3.13, 95% CI [3.03, 3.23]). Students evaluated a feature showing a timeline with their status quo towards their objectives (M = 3.63, 95% CI [3.53, 3.73]) significantly higher than information about their time spent online (M = 2.99, 95% CI [2.88, 3.1]). Hence, students' evaluation of the presented features concerning learning differed significantly, accordingly Hypothesis 2 is accepted.

Table 2. Post-hoc comparisons for learning scale by features

Feature	Statistic		1	2	3	4	5	6	7	8	9	10	11	12	13	14	15
1 Time online	Mean	2.9897	-														
	Variance	.641															
	SD	.80049															
2 Learning partner	Mean	3.1273	.13757	-													
	Variance	.569															
	SD	.75453															
3 Learning recommendation for course completion	Mean	3.6964	.70668***	.56911***	-												
	Variance	.45															
	SD	.67053															
4 Ratingscales for learning material	Mean	2.7913	-.19841	-.33598**	-.90509***	-											
	Variance	.823															
	SD	.90699															
5 Timeline for achievement of objectives	Mean	3.6283	.63856***	.50099***	-.06812	.83697***	-										
	Variance	.577															
	SD	.75945															
6 Time for reading and task completion	Mean	2.4005	-.58929***	-.72685***	-1.29597***	-.39087***	-1.22784***	-									
	Variance	.891															
	SD	.94404															
7 Prompts for self-assessment	Mean	3.7288	.73909***	.60152***	.03241	.93750***	.10053	1.32837***	-								
	Variance	.485															
	SD	.69613															
8 Further learning recommendations	Mean	3.4848	.49504***	.35747**	-.21164	.69345***	-.14352	1.08433***	-.24405	-							
	Variance	.544															
	SD	.7374															
9 Comparison with fellow students	Mean	2.6042	-.38558***	-.52315***	-1.09226***	-.18717	-1.02414***	.2037	-1.12467***	-.88062***	-						
	Variance	.799															
	SD	.89386															
10 Integration of personal schedule	Mean	3.2272	.23743	.09987	-.46925***	.43585***	-.40112***	.82672***	-.50165***	-.25761	.62302***	-					
	Variance	.717															
	SD	.8465															
11 Newsfeed	Mean	2.7973	-.19246	-.33003**	-.89914***	.00595	-.83102***	.39683***	-.93155***	-.68750***	.19312	-.42989***	-				
	Variance	.813															
	SD	.90176															
12 Repetition of learning content	Mean	3.5737	.58399***	.44643***	-.12269	.78241***	-.05456	1.17328***	-.15509	.08896	.96958***	.34656**	.77646***	-			
	Variance	.498															
	SD	.70591															
13 Feedback for assignments	Mean	3.3919	.40212***	.26455	-.30456*	.60053***	-.23644	.99140***	-.33697**	-.09292	.78770***	.16468	.59458***	-.18188	-		
	Variance	.766															
	SD	.87541															
14 Reminder	Mean	3.0883	.09854	-.03902	-.60813***	.29696*	-.54001***	.68783***	-.64054***	-.39649***	.48413***	-.13889	.29101*	-.48545***	-.30357*	-	
	Variance	.776															
	SD	.88097															
15 Term scheduler	Mean	2.788	-.20172	-.33929**	-.90840***	-.00331	-.84028***	.38757***	-.94081***	-.69676***	.18386	-.43915***	-.00926	-.78571***	-.60384***	-.30026*	-
	Variance	.86															
	SD	.92716															

Note: *** p<.001; ** p<.01; * p<.05

A hierarchical regression analysis was conducted to determine if students' evaluation of the features in terms of learning, privacy, difficulty, and usefulness are significant predictors if students would like to use a certain learning analytics feature. The final regression model (see Table 3) explained a statistically significant amount of variance in willingness to use a certain learning analytics feature, $\Delta R^2 = .652$, $F(7, 3235) = 1518.77$, $p < 001$. Results of the hierarchical regression analysis show that all four variables positively predict the willingness to use a certain learning analytics feature. Especially, students' rating in terms of learning and usefulness of a certain learning analytics feature positively predict students' willingness to use it. Accordingly, Hypotheses 3a, 3b, 3c, and 3d are accepted.

Table 3. Regression analysis predicting willingness to use learning analytics features on learning, privacy, difficulty, and usefulness

	R^2	ΔR^2	B	$SE\ B$	β
Step 1	.496	.495			
learning			1.011	.018	.704***
Step 2	.561	.560			
learning			.942	.017	.656***
privacy			.276	.013	.259***
Step 3	.577	.577			
learning			.918	.017	.639***
privacy			.205	.014	.193***
difficulty			.170	.015	.147***
Step 4	.653	.652			
learning			.676	.018	.471***
privacy			.096	.013	.091***
difficulty			.037	.015	.032*
usefulness			.392	.015	.392***

Note. *** $p < .001$, ** $p < .01$, * $p < .05$

5. DISCUSSION

As real-time feedback was mentioned from almost all students in the qualitative study, it has presumably high relevance for learning, as already postulated by Hattie (2009). Concerning this, learning analytics could offer an appropriate approach as the system can provide real-time feedback to each individual learner in much more detail than one single teacher could.

The qualitative results showed that the students prefer learning with printed material and a function to document learning activities occurring offline was discussed. This leads to the need to investigate how learning offline or conscious informal learning could ideally be entered into a learning analytics system, so that invalid analyses due to incomplete data could be decreased and students will not be demotivated only because the system did not consider all their learning efforts. As long as most learning takes place outside the online learning environment, learning analytics systems can only be considered as an additional service. Likewise, the study of Verbert et al. (2014) revealed that learners rated the usefulness of learning analytics dashboards low, when many relevant activities happened outside the tracked learning environment.

Students' expectations of a learning analytics system, combining several programs and functions would allow to tracking their learning behavior in an easier way. Using a PDF annotation program, highlighted content and their added thoughts would become more obvious to analyses as well as their paths through different programs. By tracking text processing, the emergence of artifacts could be analyzed by the system in terms of which further resources might help the student to proceed.

In the qualitative study students had ambivalent voices in terms of comparisons with fellow students, which was also revealed in the quantitative study, as this feature was rated significantly lower in terms of willingness to use it than almost all other features (see Table 1).

As the regression analysis showed, students' evaluation of a learning analytics feature in terms of learning positively predicts their willingness to use. Three of the five features, students are the most willing to use, are strongly related to support learning and are also evaluated to support learning by the students: repetition of learning content, prompts for self-assessment, and further learning recommendations to complete a course.

The present study shows limitations, as the interviewed students have mainly no experience in using learning analytics features, thus it seemed to be difficult to imagine the potential possibilities of big data analysis for learning purposes. To control order effects the sequence of the presented learning analytics features should be randomized. To consider the dependency of the students' rating on each feature a bigger sample size would be necessary.

Still there are many open questions in terms of how learning analytics could support learning processes and new rose especially from the qualitative study. As some students already mentioned they were concerned, if too much support from a learning analytics system might reduce autonomy of learning processes, which is related to the components of self-regulated learning. Hence, further research regarding the cohesion of learning analytics features and self-regulated learning needs to be initiated to find out if learning analytics systems are capable to foster self-regulated learning or if they even hinder it by taking over too much of the learners' responsibility and autonomy (Boekaerts, 1999; Gašević, Dawson, & Siemens, 2015). In this respect personalization of learning analytics systems will be of high relevance.

Within this study the expectations of students were considered, further research needs to take into account other stakeholders' voices and how learning analytics can support self-regulated learning in online learning environments by considering learning theoretical assumptions.

6. CONCLUSION

From a learning science perspective, the focus of learning analytics should be on understanding and supporting learning processes. As learning is a multifaceted and complex process the coherence of learning analytics features and learning, especially self-regulated learning needs to be in the focus of educational research. The design of valid learning analytics features needs to be based on (self-regulated) learning theories and results from qualitative as well as quantitative research.

However, students expect highly developed learning analytics systems, combining the functions of various programs, allowing personalization, showing the results of diverse analyses and giving recommendations for further learning. Fortunately, the prerequisite that students are interested and willing to use learning analytics seems to be given as both studies revealed similar results. To meet all stakeholders' expectations and to increase the acceptance and perceived usefulness of learning analytics systems, their voices need to be considered beforehand system-wide implementation.

REFERENCES

Boekaerts, M. (1999). Self-regulated learning: where we are today. *International Journal of Educational Research, 31*(6), 445-457.

Boerner, S., Seeber, G., Keller, H., & Beinborn, P. (2005). Lernstrategien und Lernerfolg im Studium: Zur Validierung des LIST bei berufstätigen Studierenden. [Learning strategies and learning success at university: Validation of LIST inventory for students with employment]. *Zeitschrift für Entwicklungspsychologie und Pädagogische Psychologie, 37*(1), 17-26.

Conole, G., Creanor, L., Irving, A., & Paluch, S. (2007). *In Their Own Words. Exploring the learner's perspective on e-learning.* Retrieved from http://www.webarchive.org.uk/wayback/archive/20140615220212/http://www.jisc.ac.uk/media/documents/programmes/elearningpedagogy/iowfinal.pdf

Gašević, D., Dawson, S., & Siemens, G. (2015). Let's not forget: Learning analytics are about learning. *TechTrends, 59*(1), 64-71. doi:10.1007/s11528-014-0822-x

Goetz, T., Nett, U. E., & Hall, N. C. (2013). Self-Regulated Learning. In N. C. Hall & T. Goetz (Eds.), *Emotion, Motivation, and Self-regulation: A Handbook for Teachers* (pp. 123-166). Bingley, UK: Emerald.

Hattie, J. A. C. (2009). *Visible learning: a synthesis of over 800 meta-analyses relating to achievement.* New York: Routledge.

Ifenthaler, D. (2015). Learning Analytics. In J. M. Spector (Ed.), *The Sage Encyclopedia of Educational Technology* (Vol. 2, pp. 447-451). Los Angeles, California: Sage Publications.

Ifenthaler, D., & Schumacher, C. (2015). *Divulging Personal Information within Learning Analytics Systems.* Paper presented at the Cognition and Exploratory Learning in the Digital Age (CELDA 2015), Maynooth, Ireland.

Ifenthaler, D., & Widanapathirana, C. (2014). Development and Validation of a Learning Analytics Framework: Two Case Studies Using Support Vector Machines. *Technology, Knowledge and Learning, 19*(1-2), 221-240. doi:10.1007/s10758-014-9226-4

McLoughlin, C., & Lee, M. J. W. (2010). Personalised and self regulated learning in the Web 2.0 era: International exemplars of innovative pedagogy using social software. *Astralasian Journal of Educational Technology, 26*(1), 28-43.

Nicol, D. J., & Macfarlane-Dick, D. (2006). Formative assessment and self-regulated learning: a model and seven principles of good feedback practice. *Studies in Higher Education, 31*(2), 199-218.

Park, Y., & Il-Hyun, J. (2015). Development of Learning Analytics Dashboard to Support Students' Learning Performance. *Journal of Universal Computer Science, 21*(1), 110-133.

Schmitz, B. (2001). Self-Monitoring zur Unterstützung des Transfers einer Schulung in Selbstregulation für Studierende. *Zeitschrift für Pädagogische Psychologie, 15*(3-4), 181-197.

Verbert, K., Duval, E., Klerkx, J., Govaerts, S., & Santos, J. L. (2013). Learning Analytics Dashboard Applications. *American Behavioral Scientist, 57*(10), 1500-1509.

Verbert, K., Govaerts, S., Duval, E., Santos, J. L., Van Assche, F., Parra, G., & Klerkx, J. (2014). Learning Dashboards: an overview and future research opportunities. *Personal and Ubiquitous Computing, 18*(6), 1499-1514.

Wild, K.-P., & Schiefele, U. (1994). Lernstrategien im Studium: Ergebnisse zur Faktorenstruktur und Reliabilität eines neuen Fragebogens. [Learning strategies of university students: Factor structure and reliability of a new questionnaire]. *Zeitschrift für Differentielle und Diagnostische Psychologie, 15*(4), 185-200.

Zimmerman, B. J. (2002). Becoming a Self-Regulated Learner: An Overview. *Theory into Practice, 41*(2), 64-70.

MUSIC TECHNOLOGY COMPETENCIES FOR EDUCATION: A PROPOSAL FOR A PEDAGOGICAL ARCHITECTURE FOR DISTANCE LEARNING

Fátima Weber Rosas, Leticia Rocha Machado and Patricia Alejandra Behar
Federal University of Rio Grande do Sul/Brazil
Paulo Gama Avenue, 110 - 12105 building - 4rd floor room 401, 90040-060 - Porto Alegre (RS) – Brazil

ABSTRACT

This article proposes a pedagogical architecture (PA) focused on the development of competencies for music technology in education. This PA used free Web 3.0 technologies, mainly those related to production and musical composition. The pedagogical architecture is geared for teachers and those pursing a teaching degree, working in distance education. The methodology used was a case study with a qualitative approach. XX teachers participated in the study. This article presents as a result a PA focused on the development of competencies for teachers and students in music technology in the educational context.

KEYWORDS

Pedagogical architecture, competencies, technological and musical context.

1. INTRODUCTION

Social and cultural changes arising from technological changes are directly reflected in educational activities. One of the biggest changes was the Internet, which makes it possible to carry out collective work, communicate through the network, and become an author of one's own material. Today teachers must be vigilant and constantly learning new information in order to keep up with their students, many of whom belong to the net generation. It is therefore important to understand the technological changes to reflect on new pedagogical practices.

As Palfrey and Gasser (2011) argue, the Internet with the properties that characterize the second and third generations, presents opportunities for digital natives to learn to create, express, and enjoy new works of art. Among these attributes of the Internet, tools that are dedicated to musical composition will be the focus of this study. Studies of English youth by Hargreaves (2005) argues that popular music strongly influences the lifestyle of adolescents who identify with certain styles, resulting in the construction of musical identities. In an investigation of the composition and recording of music with adolescents in public school, Lorenzi (2008) reports that the technological advances of recent decades have changed the relationship of young people with this art form. These changes are reflected in the educational context, especially in schools.

Given these assumptions, it is understood that in the current educational landscape, a large proportion of young people are familiar with technology. In the proposal presented here, the focus is on musical composition activities through free Web 3.0 technologies. They have the interactive features of Web 2.0 with cloud computing. As pointed out by Behar et al. (2013b) and Rosas (2013), composition performed by the computer associated with tools with these characteristics, can also assist in developing competencies for music technology in the educational context.

In light of this reality, it is important to reflect on musical composition in Distance Learning (DL), mainly the construction of pedagogical architectures that facilitate the improvement and/or development of competencies in this area.

It is first necessary to define pedagogical architecture (PA). In this approach, a PA is the combination and interaction of strategies and different elements that make up a teaching practice. Thus, there are possible ways to organize educational planning. There are four key aspects: organizational, content, methodological, and technological (Behar, 2009).

Hence, the construction of a PA for the music technology context is focused on the development of certain specific competencies and requires the teacher to review teaching practices. As Behar et al. (2013a) argue, a process of teaching and learning which focuses on the development of competencies is an alternative to the integral formation of the student and has a closer relationship between theory and practice.

In this article competencies are understood as a set of elements (knowledge, skills, and attitudes) that are mobilized to meet the needs arising from a particular situation or context (Behar et al, 2013a; Zabala & Arnau, 2010; Perrenoud, Thurler, 2002; Gaspar, 2004). Thus, this theme will be presented in the following sections.

2. PEDAGOGICAL ARCHITECTURE AND MUSIC TECHNOLOGY COMPETENCIES IN THE EDUCATIONAL CONTEXT

There is diversity in the combination of online courses offered. Distance education models also vary according to the institutions that offer them as well as combinations that specific teachers use.

Many courses available in this type of education use diverse materials such as videos, texts, animation, learning objects, and also benefit from the use of virtual learning environments to develop course activities.

Therefore, it is important to have a plan that encompasses these specific needs and characteristics of DL. In fact, the development of a pedagogical architecture to be used throughout the entire course is critical.

Behar et al. (2009) describes a pedagogical architecture as one of the constituent elements of a pedagogical model, along with strategies for it to be implemented. Bernardi (2011), in accordance with Franciosi (2005), defines PA as "the construction of pedagogical strategies based on a certain theory and its assumptions in order to assist in the effectiveness of learning with the help of technology resources such as Virtual Learning Environments (VLEs) and/or videoconference" (Bernardi, 2011, p.56).

A PA is structured by (1) organizational aspects, (2) content, (3) methodological aspects, and (4) technological aspects. Below is a list of each constituent element of a PA (Behar, 2009):

a) Organizational aspects: Refer to the pedagogical planning. Beginning with the definition of objectives, organization of time and space, definition of the duties of each participant in the process (student, teacher, etc.) and the competencies that will be developed;

b) Content: These are the materials and components that will be used during the course. The content should be created to meet the demands of a virtual course, making it possible to develop the competencies of these students. The content of a PA may be any type of material used for the purpose of appropriating knowledge (BEHAR et al., 2009). When selecting materials, it is necessary to take into account whether they are graphic, pedagogical, interactive, and motivational (or not) for the student. Bernardi (2011), agreeing with Behar (2009), maintains that the content may be in the form of learning objects (LO). As Behar et al. (2009) explain, learning objects are any material or digital resources such as videos, images, text, audio, web pages, etc. that have an educational purpose. Bernardi (2011) adds "[...] these are therefore materials focused on the development of learning situations in the VLE mode, semi or fully in person" (Bernardi 2011, p.60). This author also points out the importance of the LO as a theoretical and pedagogical support in a PA;

c) Methodological Aspects: Although only referring to the "how" will be addressed in the course content, it can be considered the forms of connection, associations of technological resources, and procedures adopted, taking into consideration the objectives defined in the pedagogical planning;

d) Technological Aspects: The definition of a VLE and what tools will be used, as well as other technological resources, is essential in distance learning. In fact, it is especially crucial when considering what is best suited to the proposal of the course and students.

Therefore, reflecting on the constituent aspects of a PA one can see that the development and/or improvement of competencies in virtual courses is present in all the elements of an architecture. Thus, it is necessary to define selected competencies and primarily focus on music technology in education, which is the topic of this article.

2.1 Competencies for the Music Technology in the Educational Context

As Perrenoud and Thurler (2002) have argued, competence is the ability to deal effectively with a number of problematic situations. Perrenoud (1999) uses the genetic epistemology of Jean Piaget, whose paradigm is interactional, as the theoretical basis. Thus, he argues that competency includes the mobilization of multiple cognitive resources, knowledge, and skills, in an increasingly rapid, relevant, and creative way. He further argues that an educational practice should be focused on the development of core competencies for an individual's integral formation. Behar et al. (2013a), in accordance with Zabala and Arnau (2010) and Perrenoud and Thurler (2002), believe that competence is the mobilization of three elements which together form the acronym KSA. They are: knowledge (K), skills (S) and attitudes (A). These three elements are deployed in a "[...] given context in order to solve a problem, deal with a new situation" (Behar, et al., 2013a, p.23). Knowledge refers to knowledge, skills to know-how, and attitudes are learning to be. For this author, the term competencies is used in the plural, because there is no single competency, but a group of them that have developed or develop simultaneously. Education from this perspective sees the student as a whole, in their multiple dimensions, educating them for real situations throughout their life.

Rosas (2013) points out the importance of music composition in the development of musical competencies. In the opinion of this author, competencies for the music technology in the educational context imply the mobilization of knowledge and skills in these areas and attitudes towards technology and content. Such competencies can be developed by both musicians and lay people.

Music technology in the educational context in this proposal is the use of digital technologies dedicated to music involving composition and appreciation activities in the classroom or distance learning environment. Although Swanwick (2003) holds that activities involving literature and execution are also of equal importance to that of composition and appreciation, because the target audience will have lay people in music, we emphasized practices aimed at musical composition using a computer. Thus, in the educational arena, teachers and lay students can produce music using digital technologies provided they receive adequate training, like the courses mentioned in this article.

According to Behar et al. (2013b), the computer functions as a musical instrument and an amateur studio. Thus, the active participants in DL can create their own music for their videos or other digital educational materials. They just need to have a computer with Internet access.

Hargreaves (2000) supports the definition of musical competence proposed by Stefani (2007). These authors argue that the concept means "[...] the ability to produce meaning by or through 'music' in the broad sense, that is, in all that vast and heterogeneous mass of collective practices and individual experiences involving sound [. ..]" (Stefani, 2007, p.01).

Rosas (2013) understands musical competence as the ability to mobilize knowledge, skills, and attitudes for the production and musical composition in music technology in the educational context. For this author, training courses for the development of competencies for the music technology in the educational context are also essential for subjects to act effectively in this area. Because of the proposal of digital musical composition includes lay people, instrumental performance is not addressed, although it is of equal importance to the development of competencies in specialized musicians.

Webster and Hickey (2009) are also in favor of the practice of composition in music education. The authors mention that in countries like Australia, the United Kingdom, and the United States "[...] the interest in improvisation and its role in the musical development and compositional thinking have grown as a strategy for teaching music[...]" (Webster; Hickey, 2009, p.379). Given this statement and as Rosas (2013) confirms, activities involving composition can promote musical knowledge, a fundamental element for the development of competencies.

Based on these definitions of pedagogical architecture and competencies, it was possible to build a PA to help in the development and/or improvement of competencies, as described in the methodology which follows.

3. METHODOLOGY

A qualitative approach in education is adopted regarding the methodological aspects. A study of multiple cases in two blended extension courses. The methodology was composed of four recursive and summative stages. Stage 1: The construction of a Pedagogical Architecture (Organizational, Methodological, Content, and Technological Aspects). Stage 2: Development of research tools: An online questionnaire (entitled 1) to diagnose the subjects' previous music technology experiences and a second online questionnaire (entitled 2) to assess the skills developed during the extension course and the learning object Digital Music composition (CompMUS) (Stage 3). Both instruments were built with the Google Docs tool. This step also included the development and clarification of informed consent forms to be completed by study participants in Stage 3. Stage 3: Completion of two blended model extension courses. The first had a workload of 20 hours and the second 30 hours. These courses were designed for teachers and students pursing teaching, music, other teacher qualification degrees and public school teachers. The total number of participants in the two courses were 18 students, with 8 in the first edition and 11 in the second. In Stage 3 the instruments constructed in Stage 2 (questionnaires and signing and clarification of informed consent forms). Stage 4: Analysis of data collected during the previous stages.

To address the ethical issues of this research an informed consent form was prepared and participants of the courses agreed to participate in the research.

The following instruments were used for data collection:

1- Musical productions and compositions performed by students using online digital tools and posted in the virtual learning environment (VLE) ROODA.

2 - Questionnaire applied before the course (questionnaire1).

3 - Questionnaire containing the evaluation of courses, the LO CompMUS and AP (questionnaire 2).

4- Records written in VLE ROODA: Forums, Diary, comments in the Webfolio.

5 - InterROODA functionality to check student attendance in this environment.

The productions made using digital tools and records in ROODA features were analyzed qualitatively. Musical compositions performed using digital tools and posted on the ROODA Webfolio, were analyzed, verifying what knowledge, skills, and attitudes subjects developed or improved. Questionnaires were applied and compared in order to examine what musical and technological competencies in education were developed during the extension courses. In the following section, we present this mapping which reveals the competencies that subjects developed/improved.

4. RESULTS

At the end of the study, it was shown that the PA built along with the course entitled "Digital Music Composition for Education" helped develop competencies for music technology in the educational context.

Some adjustments were necessary in the pedagogical architecture to meet the needs and develop/enhance competencies satisfactorily. From the data that has been collected and analyzed, it is possible to present a PA proposal. Therefore, the PA is presented below:

- Organizational aspects: The objectives proposed for the course were adequate and the workload of 30 hours was satisfactory. The competencies that will be developed and/or improved in the course should always be considered, especially those related to the music technology in the educational context.
- Content aspects: The use of a learning object makes all the difference in this kind of course. The use of CompMUS helped over the past two editions of the course, including the development of competencies, three in particular: Music technology fluency, cooperation, and autonomy.
- Methodological aspects: The blended model of the course for in-state students and fully distance for students from outside the state and with difficulty participating in regular classes was suitable for the characteristics and needs of target audience. The virtual diary feature was found to be important so that students could express their feelings during the course. The students used this tool to write about their difficulties, how they overcame them, and to give words of encouragement when they completed an activity. Moreover, students could post their productions and receive feedback from the teacher through comments made in the Webfolio feature.
- Technological Aspects: The ROODA features that was used proved to be adequate, with some adjustments, such as in the case of ROODAPLayer. This was rarely used and students could have used it

more. There were a sufficient amount of forums. Digital composition resources proved complex and restricted because they were free and in English.

It is clear that few adjustments to the first PA presented were necessary. It should be noted that it is advisable not to reapply the same PA, but instead to adapt it according to the social and cultural setting in which the course/subject is inserted.

Another important result was the mapping of skills that are presented in summary form in Table 1:

Table 1. Competencies in music technology in the educational context and their elements

Competence	**Music Technology fluency**
Description	This refers to the use, creation, and production of music through digital technologies.
Knowledge (K)	Learning various audio formats; learning effects to treat audio; learning the basic assumptions of electroacoustic music; notions of form and musical structure; read, interpret, and critically reflect virtual and multimedia messages.
Skills	Producing and composing music using digital technologies; converting audio formats; configuring the sound board according to the operating system; using mainly free online tools for writing, producing, editing, and mixing audio; installing and uninstalling musical software.
Attitudes (A)	Openness to new sounds originating from digital technologies.
Competence	**Cooperation**
Description	Cooperation includes social interaction where the subject learns not only in relationship with themselves and with the environment, but also with others. Knowledge is built on the relationships based on collaboration, cooperation, and communication.
Knowledge (K)	Learning digital composition tools that enable collective work.
Skills (S)	Collectively producing and composing music using digital technologies; using (ICT) for social exchanges.
Attitudes (A)	Being proactive, ability to control the structure and content of a musical composition; having the flexibility to change; being responsible in the use of ICT; openness to different musical languages, such as popular, classical and contemporary.
Competency	**Autonomy**
Description	Establishing favorable conditions for social relationships, maintaining self-motivation and motivating others. Ability to deal with their own and others' difficulties.
Knowledge (K)	Self-awareness and awareness of the other.
Skills (S)	Analyzing, discerning, and facing obstacles.
Attitudes (A)	Self-confidence; being able to motivate themselves and others.

The elements of competencies presented in the table are:

Competence: MUSIC TECHNOLOGY FLUENCY

Knowledge (K): Learning various audio formats: In order to send or download audio files on the Internet, it is essential that the subjects know about compressed digital audio formats such as MPEG Audio Layer-3, whose acronym is mp3 or similar formats like as ogg Vorbis and digital players where these formats are played. Learning effects to treat audio: This element refers to the knowledge of different audio processing functions, like audio effects such as fade in, fade out, normalize the volume, etc. Notions of form and musical structure: These are important, however, depending on the tool that is used, these notions are not necessary to write in the aforementioned context. In fact, these concepts may refine the compositions according to the skills and knowledge level of the subject. Understanding of chords according to the Western tonal system to create accompaniments in tools like JamStudio: This element refers to learning to compose a musical accompaniment or play a chord using digital tools that have this language in their interface, like the JamStudio. Learning the basic assumptions of electroacoustic music: This knowledge relates to the historical assumptions of electroacoustic music composition and the new sounds of contemporary music, such as the soundscapes; Read, interpret, and critically reflect virtual and multimedia messages: This element implies the understanding of the contents presented in digital multimedia, in addition to the technical skills to access them.

Skills (A): Producing and composing music using digital technologies: This refers to musical composition and production using a computer with digital, primarily free, tools. Converting audio formats that can be transmitted via Internet: This skill is essential for the subject to exchange and share audio files and their own compositions on social networks, websites, emails, etc. Using mainly free online tools for writing, producing, editing, and mixing audio: In music technology in the educational context, it is understood that the subject needs to know and be able to use editing software to treat and transform digital audio. We must emphasize that free tools are more accessible, given the reality of Brazilian education. Installing and uninstalling music software: This skill is not necessary to make compositions or edit using online audio tools. However, there is not always a good Internet connection, depending on the location. Therefore, this skill is basic to function in the context in question. Using mostly free software and online tools for music composition: Since this is a proposal for education, the ability to use mostly free Web 3.0 tools is key. Thus, musicians and laypeople can engage in music technology in the educational context, both in the classroom as well as fully distance learners. Configuring the sound board as the operating system: Certain software dedicated to music requires the configuration of the sound board according to the operating system. However, this skill is not required for all programs.

Attitudes (A): Openness to new sounds originating from digital technology: An open attitude is understood as one which is favorable to sounds that have undergone digital processing, and is essential to act in this context.

Competence: COOPERATION

Knowledge (K): Learning digital composition tools that enable collective work: Knowledge of the possibilities offered by digital tools is paramount to collective musical composition. When dealing with aspects of young people's socialization from the music, Setton (2009) understands this form of art as a language with strong socializing potential. For the author, analyzing the social dimension of music can clarify the relationships of meaning between it and its possible influence on individual actions (Setton, 2009, p.15).

Skills (S): Collectively/collaboratively composing and producing music: According to Behar et al. (2013a), digital fluency emphasizes the importance of collaboration between subjects and the construction of collective works to generate knowledge. Silva (2012) agrees and mentions teamwork as one of the competencies of a Distance Learning student. This context includes the two modes of teaching and therefore a collective/collaborative composition is paramount. Using (ICT) for social exchanges: Behar et al. (2013a) support the use of ICT for interpersonal communication. It is a basic skill for the subjects to perform collective and collaborative work in the intended context.

Attitudes (A): Being proactive and having the ability to control the structure and content of a Digital Music Composition (CDM): Being proactive requires anticipating problems, needs, or changes as well as having initiative. In education, a proactive attitude requires autonomy and an active role in carrying out tasks. In music technology in the educational context, the subject is proactive when they are able to control the structure and content (sound combinations such as pitch, duration, timbre, instrumentation, etc.) while composing music. Having the flexibility to change: For Silva (2012) flexibility requires dealing with different situations and looking for possible actions. It implies changes in opinion and attitudes. Flexibility is very important for individuals who use online resources and tools. Often a website that is being used starts having problems or is even taken off the Internet. Or due to technical problems, files posted on a particular site may not open or there may be a connection failure. Faced with unusual situations, flexibility is an essential attitude. Being responsible in the use of ICT: Coll and Illera (2010) suggest the use of ICT in a responsible manner as one of the basic skills in the basic competencies of adults. To be responsible is to be ethical when communicating and when downloading and publishing files on the Internet. It also involves being critical when faced with all of the available information. Openness to different musical languages, such as popular, classical and contemporary: Having an open, ethical, and respectful attitude when listening to music from different cultures, eras, styles, and genres, from classical music to popular is critical for subjects to engage with music technology in the educational context. In contemporary times, sounds which in earlier times were considered non-musical such as nature or urban environments are now considered musical, as long as the composer intends to include them in the work.

Autonomy: Knowing how to work autonomously means being active in the process of teaching and learning and having self-discipline. As Silva (2012) argues, this attitude is part of personal initiative and is vital for the development of socialization and teamwork. Autonomy is essential for the subjects faced with digital music technologies in the educational context.

Competence: AUTONOMY

Knowledge (K): Self-awareness and awareness of the other: Getting to know yourself and trying to get to know others to establish social relations is fundamental to perceiving and making distinctions regarding the mood, motivations, and feelings of others.

Skills (S): Analyzing, discerning and facing obstacles: Refers to the analysis and understanding of intra and interpersonal actions to strategize and articulate communication with the subjects. Facing difficulties is also essential so that there is motivation.

Attitudes (A): Self-confidence: Hargreaves (2005) argues that self-confidence is essential to the development of musical skills. Dorge (2010) argues that it is a personal competence. Silva (2012) states that it is an attitude concerning the competence of self-motivation. Self-confidence leads to positive dispositions such as willingness, courage, hope, satisfaction, and is interrelated with the ability to motivate yourself and others. Being able to motivate yourself and motivate others: Motivation is fundamental for the subject to deal with the challenges faced with digital technologies in the educational context, that are often new for digital immigrant teachers. Also in DL, in conjunction with the use of ICT, teachers should be motivated to help students and give them challenging situations. The ability to motivate others is of paramount importance for a teacher's practice, whether in the physical classroom or distance learning.

The majority of the subjects participating in the course stated that they were beginners in terms of using musical technology, both musicians and non-musicians. According to the answers they gave on the questionnaire, the subjects are seeking to deepen their technological and musical knowledge to work in this context.

In addition to the skills developed that are presented in Table 1, as the strengths of the implementation of the PA, from the analysis of postings of students in AVA, the use of digital technologies dedicated to music were attractive for both non-musicians as well as musicians who have had no experience with online music technologies. One student said before he did not know it was possible to compose using the computer and that he would soon present some work at his school.

On the negative side, some students had problems with one of the pieces of software which was operated online. One student said they made a composition and days later it was no longer visible. Another drawback is that when using free tools, they tend to become paid in time or disappear. Thus the teacher has to always be aware and keep updated on the tools chosen for the course. This means that, in order to apply a particular PA again, all of its elements must be reviewed and adapted, from organizational issues to technology, where software and digital tools updates should be made.

Finally, the concluding remarks will be presented in the following section.

5. CONCLUSION

This research demonstrates the importance of a Pedagogical Architecture (PA) that foresees the use of digital technologies such as the computer, Web 3.0 tools dedicated to music and learning objects (LO) used in an integrated manner for virtual learning environments (VLE) in DL, primarily focused on competencies. The PA presented in this study proved to have great potential to contribute to the development of music technology competencies in the educational context. Learning objects, such as CompMUS, can aid in the improvement of competencies if they fit with the teacher and target audience's proposal and provide consistent content. In addition to the integration of the LO and online digital tools described in this example, the use of a VLE is relevant to assist the interactions between subjects.

Due to the shortage of music teachers working in public elementary schools in Brazil, it is understood that all primary teachers can work with music education. The use of digital technologies described in this work do not require the ability to play traditional musical instruments and therefore can be used by lay subjects in music. Yet, in order to use such technologies requires adequate training, both musical and technological. One way to educate is through training courses that use a PA such as the model proposed here, focused on the development of competencies.

Furthermore, it concludes that the LO, such as CompMUS and musical composition activities, contribute to the construction of knowledge in the area through consistent content. In addition, through musical and multimedia examples with detailed explanations to handle Web 3.0 tools and proposed activities, they provided challenging situations for the target audience.

It is understood that there are other elements and competencies. This study presented those that were based on the PA developed, the technologies described, and according to the profile of the target audience. Therefore, the mapping of the competencies presented provides new perspectives for future studies with other architectures, technologies, and varied public.

REFERENCES

Amante, L; Morgado, L. 2001. Metodologia de concepção e desenvolvimento de aplicações educativas: o caso dos materiais hipermídia. *Discursos.* Lisboa, Portugal. [III Série, número especial]: 27-44, junho.

Behar, P. A. (Org). 2013a. *Competências para a Educação a Distância.* Porto Alegre, Editora Penso.

Behar, P. A.; Rosas, F. W.; Longhi, M. T.; Bernardi, M. 2013b. Competências para o contexto tecnológico-musical na educação a distância. In.: Behar, P. A. (Org.). Competências para a Educação a Distância. Porto Alegre: Editora Penso.

Behar, P. A. 2009. Modelos Pedagógicos em Educação a Distância. Porto Alegre, Artmed.

Bottentuit Junior, J.B.; Lisboa E.S.; Coutinho, C.P. 2009. *Podcast e Vodcast: o potencial da ferramenta VoiceThread.* In.: Actas do Encontro sobre Podcasts. Braga: CIEd. 2009.

Bernardi, M. 2011. *Prática Pedagógica em EAD: uma proposta de Arquitetura Pedagógica para formação continuada de professores.* Tese (Doutorado em Educação) – Programa de Pós-Graduação em Educação, Faculdade de Educação, Universidade Federal do Rio Grande do Sul, Porto Alegre.

Cazella, Sc; Nunes, Mas.N.; Reategui, E. 2010. *Estado da arte em Sistemas de Recomendação.*

Coll, C.; Illera, J.L. R. 2010. Alfabetização, novas alfabetizações e alfabetização digital: as TIC no currículo escolar. In.: Coll, C. (org), *Psicologia da Educação Virtual: aprender e Ensinar com as Tecnologias da Informação e da Comunicação.* Porto Alegre: Artmed.

Coll, C.; Monereo, C. 2010. Educação e aprendizagem no século XXI: novas ferramentas, novos cenários, novas finalidades. In: Coll, C. (org), *Psicologia da Educação Virtual: aprender e Ensinar com as Tecnologias da Informação e da Comunicação.* Porto Alegre: Artmed.

Dörge, C. 2010. Competencies and Skills: Filling Old Skins with New Wine. In: Reynolds, N.; Turcsányi-Szabó, M. Key *Competencies in the Knowledge Society (proceedings).* Brisbane, Australia.

Ferreira, B.H. 2004. *Novo dicionário Aurélio da língua portuguesa.* 3ª Ed. Curitiba: Positivo.

Franciosi, BRT. 2005. *Interação Mediada por Computador.* In.: Anais do Congresso Internacional de Qualidade em EAD: desafios para a transformação social (CIQUEAD). São Leopoldo.Disponível em: <http://www.ricesu.com.br/ciqead2005/trabalhos/apresentacoes/beatriz.pps>

Friesen, N.T. 2004. *Three objections to learning objects. Online education using learning objects.* London: Routledge, Disponível em <http://www.learningspaces.org/n/papers/objections.html>.

Fritsch, E. 2008. *Música eletrônica: uma introdução ilustrada.* Porto Alegre: Editora da UFRGS.

Gyara, F.; Sachdev, T. 2008. *Win in the flat world.* White paper - Infosys Technologies.

Disponível em: <http://www.infosys.com/offerings/it-services/informationmanagement/

white-papers/documents/personalizing-portals.pdf>.

Hargreaves, D. 2005. Within you without you: música, aprendizagem e identidade. *Revista eletrônica de musicologia.* Volume IX, p.1-12.

IEEE – Learning Technology Standards Committee. 2003. *WG12: Learning Object Metadata*. Disponível em: <http://ltsc.ieee.org/wg12/>.

Johnson, L.F. 2003. *Elusive Vison: Challenges Impeding the Learning Objects Economy*. Micromedia, jun 2003. Disponível em: <http://www.nmc.org/pdf/Elusive_Vision.pdf>.

lorenzi, G. 2008. *Educação musical e o uso da tecnologia: adolescentes gravando as próprias músicas*. In: Anais do XVII Encontro Nacional da ABEM. Disponível em: < http://www.abemeducacaomusical.org.br/Masters/anais2008/052%20Graciano%20Lorenzi.pdf >

martinez, Marina. 2010 Computação em nuvem. *Revista Infoescola [online].* Disponível em: <http://www.infoescola.com/informatica/computacao-em-nuvem/>

miletto, E. M. et al. 2004. *Minicurso: Introdução à Computação Musical*. In: IV CBCOMP - Congresso Brasileiro de Computação, Itajaí, SC. Anais. Itajaí, SC: [s.n.], p.883-902.

Módolo, M. 200.9 O que é inteligência artificial? Onde ela é aplicada? *Revista Nova Escola,* [online] Editora Abril, Disponível em: <http://revistaescola.abril.com.br/ciencias/fundamentos/inteligencia-artificial-onde-ela-aplicada-476528.shtml>

Palfrey, J; Gasser, U. 2011.Nascidos na era digital: entendendo a primeira geração de nativos digitais. Tradução de Magda França Lopes. Porto Alegre: Artmed.

Perrenoud, P. 1999. *Construir as competências desde a escola*. Porto Alegre: Artmed.

Perrenoud, P.; Thurler, M. G. As competências para ensinar no século XXI: a formação dos professores e o desafio da avaliação. Trad.:Cláudia Schilling; Fátima Murad. Porto Alegre: Artmed, 2002.176p.

Piaget, Jean. Epistemologia Genética. 3ª ed. São Paulo: Martins Fontes, 2007.

_______. Estudos Sociológicos. Rio de Janeiro: Forense, 1973.

Prensky, Marc. Digital Natives, Digital Immigrants. In: On the Horizon. NCB University Press, No. 5, Vol. 9. Oxford: University Press: 2001.

Rosas, Fátima Weber.; Behar, Patricia Alejandra. CompMUS: um objeto de aprendizagem para auxiliar no desenvolvimento de competências para o contexto tecnológico-musical. In.: Revista Novas Tecnologias na Educação (RENOTE), vol.10, número 1, julho de 2012. Disponível em: <http://seer.ufrgs.br/renote/article/view/30883/19236> Acesso em 03 jul. 2013.

Rosas, Fátima Weber. Competências para o contexto tecnológico-musical: um foco nas tecnologias digitais online para a educação. UFRGS, 2012, p212. Dissertação (Mestrado em Educação) – Programa de Pós-Graduação em Educação, Faculdade de Educação, Universidade Federal do Rio Grande do Sul, Porto Alegre, 2013.

Setton, Maria da Graça J. Reflexões sobre a dimensão social da música entre os jovens. In.: Revista Comunicação e Educação. USP. Ano XVI, nº 1. Jan/abr 2009. p.15-22.

Swanwick, Keith. Ensinando música musicalmente. São Paulo: Moderna, 2003.

Silva, Ketia. K. A. Mapeamento de competências: um foco no aluno da Educação a Distância. UFRGS, 2012, p.184. Dissertação (Mestrado em Educação) - Programa de Pós-Graduação em Educação. Universidade Federal do Rio Grande do Sul, Porto Alegre, 2012.

Tarouco, L.M.R.; Konrath, M.L.P.; Carvalho, M.J.S.; Avila, B.G. Formação de professores para produção e uso de objetos de aprendizagem. Rev. Novas Tecnologias na Educação, v. 4 nº 1 2006. Disponível em: <http://www.cinted.ufrgs.br/renote/jul2006/artigosrenote/a20_21173.pdf>. Acesso em: 20 março 2011.

Tarouco, L.M.R. Objetos de aprendizagem e a EAD. In: Litto, F.; Formiga, M. (Org.) Educação a distância: o estado da arte. São Paulo: Pearson, 2012.

Webster, Peter R.; Hickey, Maud. Computers and technology. In.: Mcpherson, Gary E. (org). The child as musician: a handbook of musical development. Oxford University Press, 2009. p.374-396.

Zabala, Antoni.; Arnau, Laia. Como aprender e ensinar competências. Tradução de Carlos Henrique Lucas Lima. Porto Alegre: Artmed, 2010, 197p.

INCREASING STUDENTS' SCIENCE WRITING SKILLS THROUGH A PBL SIMULATION

Scott W. Brown[1], Kimberly A. Lawless[2], Christopher Rhoads[1], Sarah D. Newton[1] and Lisa Lynn[2]
[1]*University of Connecticut, USA*
[2]*University of Illinois at Chicago, USA*

ABSTRACT

Problem-based learning (PBL) is an instructional design approach for promoting student learning, in context-rich settings. GlobalEd 2 (GE2) is PBL intervention that combines face-to-face and online environments into a 12-week simulation of international negotiations of science advisors on global water resource issues. The GE2 environment is described examining the impact it has had on middle school students' written scientific argumentation during the intervention. Analyses using HLM on treatment and comparison groups demonstrated a significant positive impact on the written scientific argumentation scores of 1818 middle-grade students from two states with an effect size of 0.257 ($p<.001$).

KEYWORDS

Problem-based Learning; Simulation; Writing Skills

1. INTRODUCTION

It has been broadly contended, that to develop a scientifically literate citizenry who can make local and global decisions about science related-topics, that science education needs to be grounded in meaningful socio-scientific contexts related to the world in which current students inhabit (Anderson, 2002; Sadler, 2009). Socio-scientific issues are both complex and ill-structured by nature, often not having a single clear-cut solution for all the parties involved. Such contextual issues confront students with situations in which they have to engage in formulating their own opinions based on data, their own experiences, attitudes and values, and collaborative decision-making. Further, they also require students to communicate these issues to other in a clear and precise manner.

Socio-scientific issues are regarded as real-world problems that afford students the opportunity to participate in the negotiation and development of meaning through scientific argumentation (Chinn & Malhotra, 2002; Osborne, et al., 2004; Schwarz, et al., 2003). Argumentation includes any dialog that addresses "the coordination of evidence and theory to support or refute an explanatory conclusion, model, or prediction" (Osborne, et al., 2004, p. 995). Research has demonstrated that when students engage in meaningful scientific argumentation, they not only learn to develop valid arguments but also learn science concepts associated with the topic while they are arguing (e.g., Osborne, et al, 2001; Jiménez & Pereiro-Muńos, 2002;Schwarz, et al., 2003; Erduran, et al, 2004).

Unfortunately, all too often inquiry-based approaches to teaching and learning about science that involve socio-scientific issues are not employed within typical classrooms (Chinn & Malhotra, 2002; Driver, et al., 1996; Taber, 2008; Turner, 2008). This lack of socio-scientific inquiry tasks in science classrooms likely results from fact that there has been a national and state shift in the science standards towards scientific literacy and related pedagogical reform set forth without commensurate alteration of the curricular space devoted to the teaching of science in American schools (Sadler, et al., 2007). Inquiry-based curricula, especially programs that immerse learners in active investigations of contemporary issues, can consume significant chunks of class time. Additionally, the standardized test-driven culture of today's American educational system, the allocation of limited instructional time and resources, are a major concern for both teachers and school administrators (Sadler, et al., 2006). Furthermore, research on science teachers has found that they report feeling under-prepared and often lack the efficacy necessary to implement and manage socio-scientific inquiry within their science class (Alozie, et al., 2010; Bartholomew, et al., 2004; Bennett, et al., 2005; Levinson, & Turner, 2001). So, while it appears that we know what to do in order to develop a scientifically literate citizenry and address dwindling science interest and participation among our students in STEM, we are simply not doing it as much as we should or could.

Rather than compete for the already overburdened curricular space devoted to science instruction, the GlobalEd 2 Project (GE2) expands the curricular space afforded to the teaching of science by building upon the interdisciplinary nature of social studies classes. As problem-based learning (PBL) researchers have illustrated, leveraging interdisciplinary contexts, like social studies, as a venue to engage in real world problem solving can have a profound and positive impact by deepening students' understanding, flexibility in application and transfer of knowledge (Jonassen, 2009; Koschmann, et al., 1996; Mergendoller, et al., 2000; Strobel & van Barneveld, 2009). Because PBL consists of a presentation of authentic problems as a starting point for learning, it can increase student motivation and their integration of knowledge (Bednar, et al., 1992). When working cooperatively in groups within a PBL environment, students learn how to plan and determine what they need to solve problems, pose questions, and decide where they can get these answers as they make sense of the world around them (Brown, et al., 2008; Lawless & Brown, 2015).

There can be no doubt that recent USA policy initiatives across local, state and national levels have placed increased pressure on schools to improve student performance in the domains of literacy, mathematics and science. PBL researchers have illustrated for decades that leveraging interdisciplinary contexts as a venue to engage in real world problem solving can deepen students' understanding, flexibility in application and transfer of knowledge (Bereiter & Scardamalia, 1987; Hayes, 2000; Jonassen, 2009; Koschmann, et al., 1996). Recognizing this, GE2 was created as an educational multi-team simulation that employs educational technologies currently available in most schools to build upon the interdisciplinary nature of social studies as an expanded curricular application aimed at increasing instructional time devoted to science and persuasive writing in a virtual environment (Hayes, 2000) while simultaneously enhancing the social studies curriculum.

2. GLOBALED 2 AS A SIMULATION: HOW IT WORKS

The current GE2 simulation operates within a middle school social studies class, focusing on an international science crisis created by the simulation staff. GE2 capitalizes on the interdisciplinary nature of social studies in order to expand the curricular space for additional opportunities to learn about science on a global scale and the use of educational technology, without sacrificing the curricular goals of the social studies curriculum, to address the crisis. It works as a simulation environment in which classrooms of students work across teams with the goal of reaching an agreement on a critical global science issue, while representing their specific assigned country, over a period of 12 weeks.

The GE2 simulation is implemented by trained teachers within middle-school social studies classes, focusing on a specific international science-based crisis. It works as a 12-week, interactive multiplayer simulation environment in which classrooms play the role of a specific country with the goal of reaching an agreement on a critical global science issue with at least one other of the country teams in the simulation. The scenario developed for the current simulation focused on Global Water Resources (other science-based GE2 scenarios include Global Climate Change; International Food Resources and Alternative Energy Sources). There are three phases of the 12-week GE2 Simulation: Research, Interactive and Debriefing. The simulation is coordinated across multiple classrooms, as each country-team experiences the activities associated with each of the three phases (see Lawless and Brown, 2015 for further descriptions of the GE2 phases) (see figure 1).

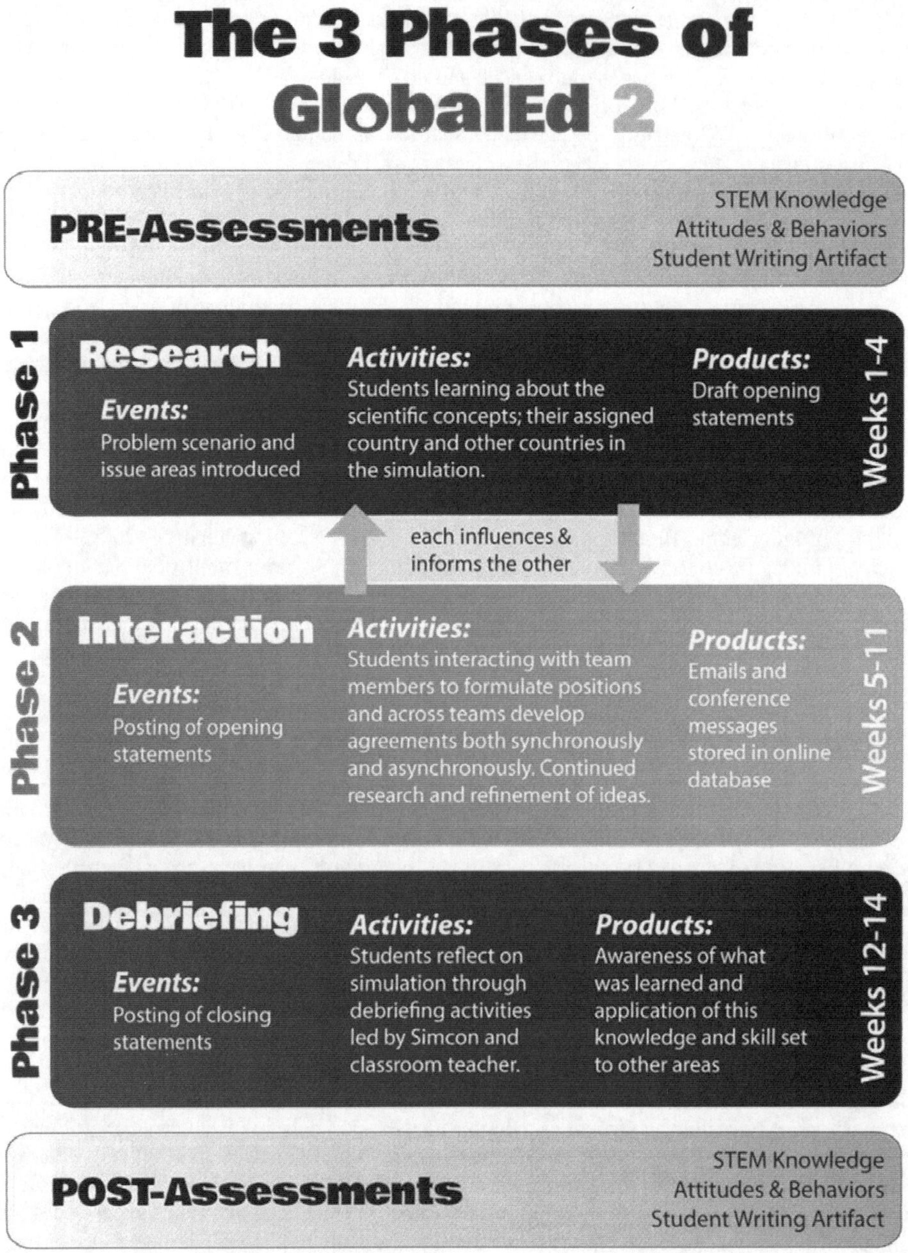

Figure 1. The Three Phases of the GlobalEd 2 Simulation

In the Research Phase, within each classroom-team, classrooms are randomly assigned to a country from our list of countries across the globe, representing diversity of region, development, size, and resource availability (Note: the USA is not randomly assigned to a class and is discussed further in the section below). Once the classes are assigned their countries, they are provided with the problem scenario, breaking into smaller issue area groups, and work on concrete analytical tasks related to four broad topical issue areas (i.e., Human Rights, International Economics, Global Health and The Environment; see figure 2). Students must use their research skills and GE2 provided resources to learn about the history, values and customs of their respective countries, as well as the other countries in the simulation, so that they are prepared to make appropriate "in character" posts as their assigned country during the negotiations in the Interactive Phase.

In the Interactive Phase, interactions between classrooms/countries are facilitated through the use of a secure, proprietary web-based platform that enables both asynchronous and synchronous written communication. Students are told that their country has to "stay in character" (e.g., remain consistent with the policy positions and core national and cultural value systems of their assigned country), while attempting to develop comprehensive policy responses to particular problems within the issue areas. The electronic interactions (asynchronous and synchronous) among the delegates are moderated by a Simulation Controller (Simcon), who is trained and knowledgeable of both international affairs and environmental science. The role of Simcon is to support/encourage and moderate the interactions so that delegates stay in character, use appropriate diplomatic language, and work towards agreements with other country-teams. During this phase there are also interactions within the classroom as delegates from the four issue areas discuss strategies of developing an agreement on water resources across the four issue areas. It is important to note that within each team the same four issue area groups exist and they must coordinate their negotiations such that one issue area group does not ignore the importance of another in trying to reach an agreement with another team. This is moderated by Simcon.

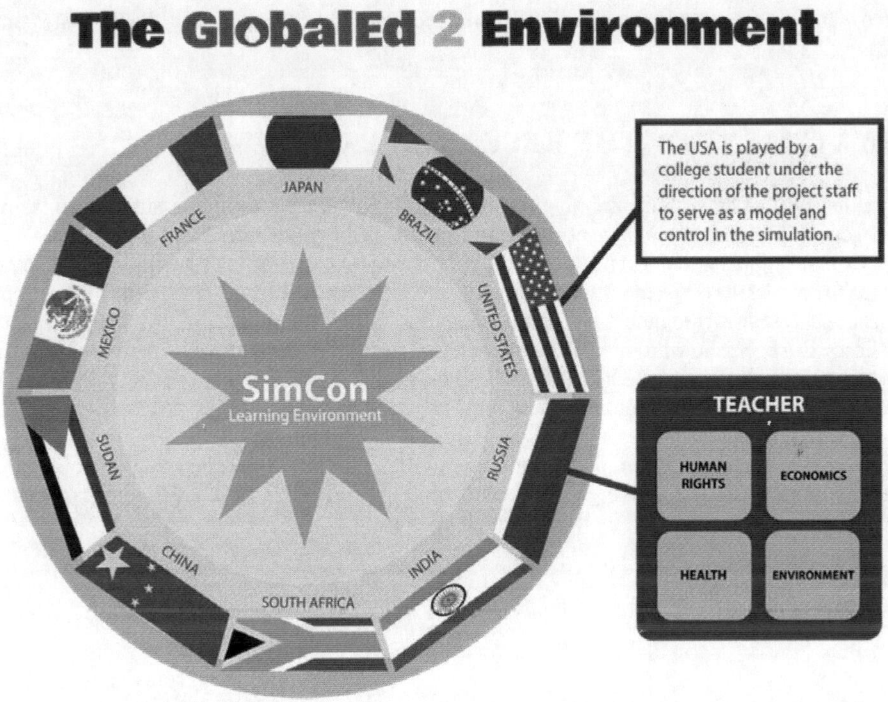

Figure 2. The GlobalEd 2 Simulation Environment

The USA team consists of two undergraduate students in the role of the USA, and is unknown by the teachers or GE2 student delegates. The role of the USA is to present a model for negotiations, through their diplomatic messages. Additionally, the USA can initiate international problems (e.g., calling for debt repayments, sending military to specific parts of the globe, or major policy changes that may affect participating countries differently) when the negotiations are unrealistically shallow or lack complexity. The USA enables the GE2 staff and Simcon to serve as a model or be disruptive, depending on the needs of the simulation during the Interactive Phase.

In the third phase, Debriefing, classrooms are led by their teachers within the class and Simcon virtually, through a series of activities and discussions to reflect on their learning. Students also think about creating opportunities for the transfer of new knowledge and skills to other global issues facing the world today, as well as local science literacy topics. The goal of the debriefing is to bring the metacognitive skills gained through the simulation to the surface so that students can explore settings in which these new skills may be employed within formal and informal learning contexts.

In summary, GE2 places a pronounced emphasis on the development of students' understanding of science topics, interest in science pursuits, science self-efficacy, and most importantly, written argumentation on science topics. For more specific information about GE2 and how the larger context of the simulation operates across the three phases of implementation: Research, Interaction and Debriefing see Lawless and Brown (2015).

The core of GE2 is the problem scenario and the interactions across teams that occurs through a web-based system enabling email and real-time conferencing in a secure environment. Classrooms of students are assigned their country and provided a briefing on the scientific crisis 4-6 weeks prior to the launch of the simulation. Students are given analytical tasks related to broad topical issue areas (human rights, economics, environment, health) common to all country-teams, and presented in the scenario. Students are instructed that their country must "stay in character" (e.g., remain consistent in policy positions and value systems of their assigned country), while attempting to develop responses to problems within the four issue areas. The scenario developed for the current simulation reported here, focused on Global Water Resources. Students did not know the name, race, sex or location of the students on other teams, only the name of the country, issue area and student's initials; there were 17-18 countries in each of the four simulations that are reported here. Country-teams in the simulation reported here spanned two different states and across one time zone.

3. STATEMENT OF THE RESEARCH PROBLEM

GE2's extensive use of written communications creates an invaluable venue for students to learn and practice written scientific argumentation in a real world context and to a large and authentic audience. Research illustrates that both instruction and authentic opportunities to write have been shown in the literature to improve writing skill (Pajares, 1996; Midgette, et al., 2008). In addition, with more opportunities to experience success in writing there is a greater chance to positively impact their writing self-efficacy. Writing self-efficacy has been shown to mediate academic performance in writing within the GE2 simulation (Brown & Lawless, 2014). As such, GE2 has the potential to impact the quality of students' written work negotiating in the STEM field within the simulation, and may also have an impact on longer term performance.

The research question addressed here was, is there a significant increase in the quality of students' written scientific argumentation based on participating in a GE2 simulation? The dependent variable examined here was the writing quality score of the students in both the GE2 and NEP classes from the pre-and post- assessment of the students' written argumentation skills.

4. METHODS

A total of 1818 middle grade students (from grade 7 & 8) participated in the study conducted during the fall of 2014 (in either the GE2 simulation or the comparison group – Normal Educational Practice with no GE2 – NEP). The student sample was 50.9% female, and 46.3% male (2.8% missing gender information); with a nearly equal split between 7th and 8th graders. The students in the sample reported their race/ethnicity as: 44.8% White, 13.4% Black, 26.3% Latino/a, 5.6% Asian/PI, and 7.7% *Other*, with the remaining not reporting race/ethnicity. A total of 51.8% were from urban settings and the remaining 48.2% were from suburban settings. There was a nearly equal split between the GE2 and NEP conditions.

Prior to the class assignment, each teacher received three days of online professional development (PD) on the purpose and implementation of the GE2 curriculum. Furthermore, the teachers also received weekly PD support and resource support for their students during the implementation of GE2 in the fall of 2014.

Each of the 51 teachers provided two "approximately" equivalent classrooms. The comparison class received the NEP curriculum that the teacher would provide as part of the school or district curriculum. An independent consultant blind to class characteristics and teacher/school identity, randomly assigned classrooms to either the GE2 or NEP condition. All students in each class participated in the educational activities, but only those who had both parental permission and student assent participated (IRB) in the data collection/research components of the study. In this way, each teacher taught both a treatment (GE2) and NEP class.

In order to obtain a measure of implementation fidelity in each classroom, observers were trained to record the teaching activities of each teacher in each condition weekly for the 12-weeks of the simulation process. Observers used the GE2 Teacher Observation Protocol to collect data on actual implementation of the GE2 curriculum and if there was any contamination, or spread of PBL into the NEP class. Initial results demonstrated that while there were different implementation practices across teachers, GE2 was implemented as a PBL environment in all the GE2 classrooms.

All consented/assented students completed the battery of pre-test assessments prior to treatment assignment; GE2 classes received their country assignments, as well as the GE2 curriculum and resources. Within this battery was an open-ended essay prompt – *Is the world running out of fresh water? Agree or disagree and defend your position.* Students had a total of 30 minutes to complete the essay prompt each time (pre- and post-). The GE2 assessment battery was administered in a pre-post format to both the GE2 and NEP students for comparison purposes. All students completed the battery across multiple classes and using paper and pencil, so as not to advantage better resourced students. For the purposes of this discussion, only one part of the battery will be presented – Written Argumentation. A rubric developed and field tested prior to implementation was applied to the essays of all participating students. Each essay was read and scored focusing on Claim – Evidence – Reasoning, adapted from the model discussed by McNeill and Krajcik (2008), by two independent raters, who maintained over .89% inter-rater agreement. Discrepancies were resolved by a third rater. Raters scored essays blind to the pre-post and group of the student (GE2 or NEP).

5. RESULTS

After collating the data for IRB compliance and removing students with missing data, a final sample of 1818 students were subjected to HLM analyses examining the impact of the GE2 intervention compared to their NEP counterparts with a total of 51 teachers.

Reporting the results in effect sizes (Cohen's d) using the standard convention indicated that there was a significant effect of the GE2 treatment on the scores of written scientific argumentation (pre- to post) compared to the NEP students ($d=0.257$; $p<.001$) and further, that there was positive impact for both females and males. Further details of the treatment effects are presented in tables 1a-1c (AIC=6779.6; Deviance=6773.6).

Table 1a. GE2 vs. NEP HLM Results Using a Fixed Effects Model

						95% CI	
Parameter	**Estimate**	**S.E.**	**df**	**t**	**Sig.**	**Lower**	**Upper**
Intercept	4.544	.090	33.251	50.444	.000	4.361	4.727
Treatment	.445	.102	46.341	4.333	.000	.238	.651
cc_writepre	.256	.023	1712.838	10.750	.000	.210	.303
tc_cm_writepre	.674	.153	56.041	4.384	.000	.366	.982
gc_tm_writepre	.461	.207	17.631	2.223	.040	.024	.898

Table 1b. HLM Estimates of Covariance Parameters for GE2 vs. NEP Using a Random Effects Model

Parameter		Estimate	S.E.	Wald Z	Sig.	95% CI Lower	95% CI Upper
Residual		2.347	.080	29.255	.000	2.195	2.510
Intercept [subject = TID]	.062084	.070	.878	.380	.006	.578	57.790
CID [subject = TID]	.119491	.053	2.240	.025	.049	.286	.297

Table 1c. HLM Estimates of Covariance Parameters for GE2 vs. NEP Using an Unconditional Model

Parameter		Estimate	S.E.	Wald Z	Sig.	95% CI Lower	95% CI Upper
Residual		2.502	.085	29.270	.000	2.340	2.676062
Intercept [subject = TID]	.277523	.094	2.923	.003	.141	.542	.539721
CID [subject = TID]	.189243	.068	2.770	.006	.093	.383	.388718

6. CONCLUSIONS

The results presented here speak to the potential of PBL simulations such as GE2 to provide a meaningful learning context within which students can develop their knowledge of socio-scientific concepts as they enhance their skills in writing about scientific topics for an authentic audience. GE2 students showed a significant increase in their writing argumentation skills compared to the NEP students while participating in a PBL focused social studies class. We were also very pleased to see the positive impact for both females and males, as they develop the written argumentation skills on science related topics and no significant differences in impact based on race/ethnicity or location setting (urban and suburban) once pre-test scores were accounted for. We believe that these outcomes may be related to the ability of students to be anonymous in their identity as they negotiate online – a specific design feature of GE2. Further, the large audience to which students are writing their international proposal to, in order to reach an agreement, may have motivated students to engage in the educational activities.

The data gathered on this sample of student includes additional pre- and post- scales focusing on science knowledge, self-efficacy related to technology, science and writing, as well as the message data shared during the interactive phase of the negotiations, enabling the research team to track the quantity and quality of messages sent, as well as the date/time and recipient information. Further analyses are underway examining the student data across urban and suburban settings, the sex of the student and the teacher implementation fidelity. These results will include an examination of sex, race/ethnicity, and school setting, as we examine potential differential effects of the GE2 intervention for various types of student groups.

These results must be interpreted with some caution because only one scenario was used in this study (Water Resources). Additional studies have been conducted since these data were analyzed enabling us to examine the impact of other scenario topics. Further, optimal treatment duration, technology access and utilization, teacher training and support, and distal impact are important foci for additional studies to better assess both proximal and distal impacts of PBL environments.

While we believe we still have much to learn about why this intervention produces these significant and positive effects for students, we can see that GE2 may afford students the opportunity to develop further scientific literacy through PBL simulations (Brown, Lawless & Boyer, 2015; Jonassen, 2009). Further analyses of this data set with the other dimensions of the assessment battery and additional data collection will enable a fuller investigation of the curricular implications regarding the utilization of interdisciplinary PBL educational simulations approaches, like GE2, in promoting STEM literacy among middle school students.

ACKNOWLEDGEMENT

This work was supported by the United States Department of Education's Institute for Education Science grant numbers Award # R305A080622 and R305A130195. The opinions and findings presented are those of the authors and do not necessarily reflect the opinion or position of the United States Department of Education.

REFERENCES

Alozie, N., Moje, E. B., & Kracik, J. S. (2010). An analysis of the supports and constraints for scientific discussion among high school project-based science. *Science Education, 94,* 395-427.

Anderson, R. D. (2002). Reforming science teaching: What research says about inquiry. *Journal of Science Teacher Education, 13*, 1-12.

Bartholomew, H., Osborne, J. F. & Ratcliffe, M. (2004). Teaching students 'Ideas-About-Science': Five dimensions of effective practice. *Science Education, 88*, 655-682.

Bednar, A.K., Cunningham, D; Duffy, T.M., & Perry, J.D. (1995). Theory into practice: How do we link? In T.M. Duffy and D.H. Jonassen (Eds.), *Constructivism and the technology of instruction: A conversation* (pp. 17-34). Hillsdale, NJ: Lawrence Erlbaum Associates.

Bennett, J., Lubben, F., Hogarth, S., & Campbell, B. (2005). Systematic review of research in science education: Rigour or rigidity. *International Journal of Science Education, 27*(4), 387-406.

Brown, S.W. & Lawless, K.A. (2014). Promoting students' writing skills in science through an educational simulation: The GlobalEd 2 project. In P. Zaphiris (Ed.) *Human-Computer interaction, Part I, HCII 2014*, LNCS 8523, pp. 371-379. Springer International Publishing: Switzerland.

Brown, S.W., Lawless, K.A., & Boyer, M.A. (2008-2012). *Expanding the Science and Literacy Curricular Space: The GlobalEd II Project.* US Department of Education: The Institute of Education Sciences, IES. # R305A080622.

Brown, S.W., Lawless, K.A., & Boyer, M.A. (2015). The GlobalEd 2 simulations: Promoting positive academic dispositions in middle school students in a web-based PBL environment (p. 147-159). In A. Walker, H. Leary, C. Hmelo-Silver & P. Ertmer (Eds.). *Essential readings in problem-based learning.* Purdue University Press: West Lafayette, IN.

Chinn, C.A., & Malhotra, B.A (2002). Epistemologically authentic inquiry in schools: A theoretical framework for evaluating inquiry tasks. Science Education, 86(2), 175-218.

Erduran, S., Simon, S., & Osborne, J. (2004). TAPping into argumentation: Developments in the application of Toulmin's argument pattern for studying science discourse. *Science Education*, *88*, 915-933.

Driver, R., Leach, J., Millar, R. & Scott, P. (1996). *Young people's images of science*. Philadelphia: Open University Press.

Hayes, J. R. (2000). A new framework for understanding cognition and affect in writing. In R. Indrisano & J.R. Squire (Eds.), *Perspectives on writing: Research, theory and practice* (p. 6-44), Newark, DE: International Reading Association.

Jiménez, A.M.P., & Pereiro-Muńos, C. (2002). Knowledge producers or knowledge consumers? Argumentation and decision-making about environmental management. *International Journal of Science Education*, *24*, 1171-1190.

Jonassen, D. H. (2009). Assembling and analyzing the building blocks of problem-based learning environments. In K. H. Silber & W. R. Foshay (Eds.), *Handbook of Improving Performance in the Workplace, Volume One: Instructional Design and Training Delivery*, Hoboken, NJ: John Wiley & Sons, Inc.

Koschmann, T.D., Kelson, A.C., Feltovich, P. J., & Barrows, H.S. (1996). Computer-supported problem-based learning: A principled approach to the use of computers in collaborative learning. In T. Koschmann (Ed.), *CSCL: Theory and Practice of an Emerging Paradigm* (p. 83-124), Mahwah, NJ: Lawrence Erlbaum.

Lawless, K.A., & Brown, S.W. (2015). Developing scientific literacy skills through interdisciplinary, technology-based Global simulations: GlobalEd 2. *The Curriculum Journal 1, p.1-22. DOI: 10.1080/09585176.2015.1009133*

Levinson, R. & Turner, S. (Eds.). (2001). *The teaching of social and ethical issues in the school curriculum, arising from developments in biomedical research: A research study of teachers.* London: Institute of Education.

McNeill, K. L. & Krajcik, J. (2008). Scientific explanations: Characterizing and evaluating the effects of teachers' instructional practices on student learning. *Journal of Research in Science Teaching, 45*(1), 53-78.

Midgette, E., Haria, P., & MacArthur, C. (2008). The effects of content and audience awareness goals for revision on the persuasive essays of fifth- and eighth-grade students. *Reading and Writing, 21*(1-2), 131-151.

Mergendoller, J. R., Bellisimo, Y., & Maxwell, N. L. (2000). Comparing problem-based learning and traditional instruction in high school economics. *Journal of Educational Research, 93*(6), 374-383.

Osborne, J. F., Erduran, S., & Simon, S. (2004). Ideas, Evidence and Argument in Science. In-service Training Pack, Resource Pack and Video. London: Nuffield Foundation.

Osborne, J. F., Erduran, S., Simon, S., & Monk, M. (2001). Enhancing the quality of argument in school science. *School Science Review, 82*(301), 63-70.

Pajares, F. (1996). Self-efficacy beliefs in academic settings. *Review of Educational Research, 56*, 543-578

Sadler, T. D. (2009). Situated learning in science education: Socio-scientific issues as contexts for practice. *Studies in Science Education, 45*, 1-42.

Sadler, T. D., Barab, S. & Scott, B. (2007). What do students gain by engaging in socioscientific inquiry? *Research in Science Education, 37*(4), 371-91.

Sadler, T. D., Amirshokoohi, A., Kazempour, M. & Allspaw, K. M. (2006). Socioscience and ethics in science classrooms: Teacher perspectives and strategies. *Journal of Research in Science Teaching. 43*(4), 353-376.

Schwarz, B. B., Neuman, Y., Gil, J., & Ilya, M. (2003). Construction of collective and individual knowledge in argumentative activity: An empirical study. The Journal of the Learning Sciences, 12(2), 221-258.

Taber, K. S. (2008). Towards a curricular model of the nature of science. *Science and Education, 17*(2-3), 179-218.

Turner, S. (2008). School science and its controversies; or, whatever happened to scientific literacy? *Public Understanding of Science, 17*(1), 55-72.

THE EFFECT OF CHOOSING VERSUS RECEIVING FEEDBACK ON COLLEGE STUDENTS' PERFORMANCE

Maria Cutumisu[1] and Daniel L. Schwartz[2]
[1]*Department of Educational Psychology, 6-102 Education North*
University of Alberta, Edmonton, AB, T6G 2G5, Canada
[2]*Stanford Graduate School of Education*
485 Lasuen Mall, Stanford, CA 94305-3096, USA

ABSTRACT

This study examines the effect of choosing versus receiving feedback on the learning performance of n = 98 post-secondary students from California on a digital poster design task. The study employs a yoked experimental design where college students are randomly assigned to play a choice-based assessment game, Posterlet, in one of two conditions, Choose or Receive. In the Choose condition, students choose confirmatory (i.e., positive) or critical (i.e., negative) feedback about their posters. In the Receive condition, students are assigned the same feedback valence that students in the Choose condition chose. Results show that 1) critical feedback and revision are positively associated with learning performance when students choose their feedback, but critical feedback is negatively associated with learning performance when students receive their feedback; 2) there is no significant effect of feedback choice between conditions; and 3) students enjoy and spend time designing posters significantly more when they choose rather than receive their feedback. Implications for designing feedback-rich environments are discussed.

KEYWORDS

Feedback, Choice, Assessment, Game, Learning, Performance

1. INTRODUCTION

Feedback plays a major role in educational performance, but it yields mixed results within the educational literature (Hattie and Timperley, 2007). Several meta-analyses found that, although feedback improved performance in general, it had no effect or it hindered performance in a third of the studies examined (Alfieri et al., 2011; Bangert-Drowns et al., 1991; Kluger and DeNisi, 1998). Moreover, the role of feedback valence (i.e., confirmatory or critical) on performance is still a matter of debate (Fishbach et al., 2010; Gregory and Levy, 2015). Furthermore, most research focuses on feedback being assigned to the learner. In contrast, in previous research, the impact of feedback choice on performance in an educational setting was investigated and results indicated that choosing critical feedback was positively associated with learning and performance (Cutumisu et al., 2015). Additionally, in the current study, the effect of feedback agency (i.e., choosing versus receiving feedback) on college students' performance is examined for the first time. This topic has wide applicability. For example, in medical research, patients who had control over their level of pain medication chose lower doses than those prescribed by medical staff (Haydon et al., 2011). In educational research, an open research question of relevance for designing feedback environments is whether students who have control over their feedback valence choose more critical feedback and learn more than students who receive (i.e., are assigned) feedback. Therefore, this paper starts tackling this question by focusing on two orthogonal dimensions of feedback: choice (feedback is chosen or assigned) and valence (feedback is confirmatory or critical).

Specifically, this research aims to examine the effect of feedback agency (i.e., choosing versus receiving feedback) on the performance of college students, by comparing learning outcomes between participants who choose feedback and those who are assigned the same amount, valence, and order of feedback. In addition to performance and time on task, students' reported enjoyment of designing posters is assessed. An experimental study was designed to address the following research questions:

1) Does critical feedback correlate with performance outcomes by condition?
2) Are there outcome differences between choosing and receiving feedback?
3) Are there enjoyment differences between choosing and receiving feedback?

The remainder of the paper reviews the related literature, then it describes the experimental study and the methods, it presents evidence of the impact of choosing *versus* receiving feedback on learning outcomes, and it concludes with a discussion and implications of this research.

2. LITERATURE REVIEW

There are many factors that influence the effectiveness of feedback for performance. For example, recent research findings point to factors that include feedback message construction, delivery of critical feedback, credibility of the source, specificity and relevance, and feedback orientation (i.e., an individual's positive affect, interest, and engagement with feedback; Anseel et al., 2015; Ashford et al., 2016; De Stobbeleir et al., 2011; Gregory and Levy, 2015; Landis-Lewis et al., 2015; Porath et al., 2015).

Critical feedback. Moreover, critical feedback seems to aid performance in some situations (Kluger and DeNisi, 1998), with individual factors, such as mindset, affecting engagement with critical feedback (Mangels et al., 2006). Although choosing critical feedback is positively associated with learning (Cutumisu et al., 2015), it is still not known whether it is the choice over feedback or the actual amount of critical feedback that impacts the performance of college students. This suggests that both feedback agency and valence are worth exploring for this population in relation with learning and performance.

Choice-based assessments. A game-based dynamic assessment, Posterlet, was employed to examine the impact of students' choices to seek critical feedback on performance and learning. In addition to confirmatory and critical feedback choices, Posterlet offers players opportunities to learn graphic design principles while designing a digital poster (Cutumisu et al., 2015). The design of Posterlet draws on constructivist, choice-based assessments (Schwartz et al., 2009; Schwartz and Arena, 2013) that emphasize learning during the assessment and that shift the assessment focus from the learning outcomes to the learning processes (e.g., choosing critical feedback) involved in solving a challenge (e.g., designing a poster). Specifically, in Posterlet, players take on the role of designing posters for booths at a fair. They choose a booth of interest (e.g., basketball toss) and they design a poster using a graphical user interface provided by the game. Posterlet measures two choices that a player makes upon completing a poster: 1) choose either confirmatory or critical feedback from three virtual characters about the poster and 2) choose to revise the poster after reading all three pieces of feedback. A variation of the Posterlet game was specifically designed to enable a performance outcome comparison between college students who choose and those who receive (i.e., are assigned) feedback. In this new version, feedback is assigned to the player in a principled way that mirrors the feedback chosen by a corresponding player of the original Posterlet version.

3. METHODS

3.1 Participants and Procedure

Participants are n = 98 (55 female) students aged 18 to 52, M_{age} = 22.71 years (SD = 5.59) from a college in California. Both versions of the Posterlet game and a post-test were employed to collect data between Spring 2014 and Spring 2015. All participants provided consent and were randomly assigned to one of two conditions, Choose (n = 49 students aged 18 to 52, M_{age} = 22.53 years, SD_{age} = 5.96, 32 female) and Receive (n = 49 students aged 18 to 38, M_{age} = 22.90 years, SD_{age} = 5.26, 23 female), according to a yoked study design described in a related study (Cutumisu and Schwartz, 2016). These conditions correspond to two different game versions. In the Choose game version, students choose their feedback valence, as illustrated in **Figure** 1a, by selecting either critical or confirmatory feedback from each virtual character. In the Receive game version, students are assigned their feedback valence, as illustrated in **Figure** 1b. After designing posters in two rounds of the game for M_{Choose} = 8.72 minutes (SD = 3.28) and $M_{Receive}$ = 7.54 minutes

(SD = 3.84), all participants completed the same online post-test that measured their knowledge of graphic design principles and enjoyment of designing posters. The time students spent on the post-test in each condition was M_{Choose} = 6.56 minutes (SD = 1.44) and $M_{Receive}$ = 7.58 minutes (SD = 5.49), respectively.

a b

Figure 1. In the Choose condition (a), the player chose critical feedback from the lion and then confirmatory feedback from the elephant. In the Receive condition (b), the player first received critical feedback from the elephant and then confirmatory feedback from the ostrich

3.2 Measures and Data Sources

Students completed one of two versions of the game, with the primary difference being whether 1) they chose between critical and confirmatory feedback or 2) they were assigned a schedule of critical and confirmatory feedback (Cutumisu and Schwartz, 2016). Posterlet measured students' behaviors and performance in the game. A post-test following the game measured students' knowledge of graphic design principles acquired through playing Posterlet.

Measures of student choices. *Critical Feedback* measures the number of times that the student chose or received critical (i.e., *I don't like*) feedback, ranging from 0 (students chose/received only confirmatory feedback across the game) to 6 (students chose/received only critical feedback across the game). *Revision* measures the number of times that the student chose to revise a poster, ranging from 0 (the student did not revise any posters) to 2 (the student revised both posters). All students had a choice to revise their posters, even though students in the Receive condition did not have a choice regarding the valence of their feedback.

Measures of student performance. *Poster Quality* measures the poster performance (i.e., the quality of the posters created by the student in Posterlet). The game evaluates each poster against a set of 21 graphic design rules provided by a graphic artist. For each poster, the game evaluates each rule with 1, if the rule is always used correctly on that poster; 0, if the rule is not applicable on that poster; and -1, if the rule is used incorrectly on that poster. The score of any individual poster created by a student represents the sum of all 21 rule scores, ranging from -21 to 21. Thus, Poster Quality represents the score sum across the game of the last individual poster on each round, ranging from -42 to 42.

Measures of time on task. *Design Duration* measures the amount of time (in minutes) students spent designing all posters, including revisions. Specifically, the game starts measuring the time a student spends from choosing a poster theme (e.g., basketball) until submitting the first poster draft. If the student chooses to revise the poster after reading the feedback, then this measure includes the additional time that the student spends updating that poster.

Measures of student learning. *Poster Ranking* measures a student's knowledge of design principles on a post-test independent of the game. After completing the game, the student is directed to an online post-test to assess four sets of posters. Each set contains two versions of a poster, featuring a design principle used correctly on one poster and incorrectly on the other poster. For each set, the student is shown in a five-second succession the first poster, a pattern image, and a modified version of the first poster, as illustrated in **Figure 2**. Then, the student decides whether the second poster is the same, better, or worse than the first poster. Each answer is scored with 1, if it is correct and 0, if it is incorrect. Thus, Poster Ranking ranges from 0 to 4.

Measures of Enjoyment. *Enjoyment* measures the enjoyment of designing posters on a 1-5 Likert-type response scale, where 1 = *none* and 5 = *a huge amount*. Students answered this question after completing the game and the post-test.

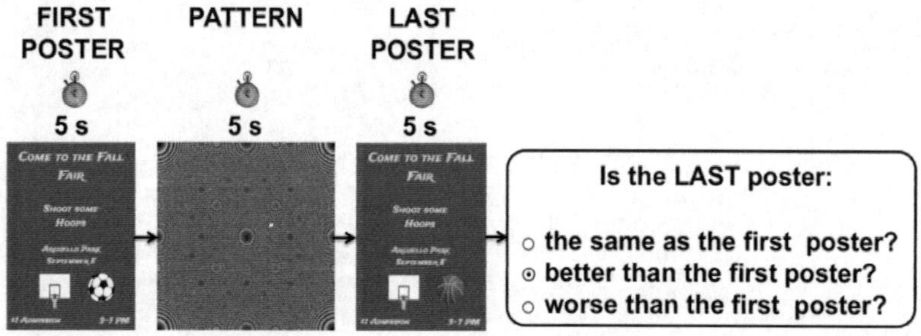

Figure 2. One of the four post-test items measuring students' knowledge of graphic design principles. This item's target feature is the relevance of graphics (a basket ball instead of a soccer ball) for the poster's theme (basketball)

4. RESULTS

4.1 Does Critical Feedback Correlate with Performance Outcomes by Condition?

Spearman's rank correlation coefficient (*rho*) is reported in all the analyses included in this section, because the variables measured were not normally distributed. In the Choose condition, Critical Feedback correlates with performance on the posters measured by Poster Quality and strongly with Revision, as shown in Table 1. The in-game poster performance (Poster Quality) can be considered to be a learning measure, because students improved their performance from the first to the second game round. Poster 1 is considered to be the pretest, being the first poster designed by the player in the Posterlet game, before revision. Poster 2 is the last poster designed by the student in the Posterlet game, after a potential revision. A repeated measures ANOVA analysis reveals that the poster quality of the students in the Choose condition increased significantly from Poster 1 (M = 9.59, SD = 5.69) to Poster 2 (M = 13.04, SD = 3.96); $F(1, 48) = 24.67$, $p < .001$, partial eta squared = .34. As well, in the Receive condition, poster quality increased significantly from Poster 1 (M = 9.33, SD = 6.93) to Poster 2 (M = 12.63, SD = 4.37); $F(1, 48) = 14.72$, $p < .001$, partial eta squared = .23. Critical Feedback also correlates positively with Poster Ranking, although not statistically significantly.

Table 1. Correlations between choices and performance outcomes (in-game and post-test) in the Choose condition

Measures (n = 49)	Revision	Poster Quality	Poster Ranking
Critical Feedback	**.64****	**.28***	.22
Revision	--	.27	.14
Poster Quality	--	--	.18
	** $p < .01$	* $p < .05$	

In the Receive condition, Critical Feedback correlates strongly with Revision and inversely with poster quality, as shown in Table 2. Although not statistically significantly, Critical Feedback also inversely correlates with performance on the graphic design principles measured by Poster Ranking in this condition.

Table 2. Correlations between behaviors and performance outcomes (in-game and post-test) in the Receive condition

Measures (n = 49)	Revision	Poster Quality	Poster Ranking
Critical Feedback	**.44****	-.16	**-.34***
Revision	--	.09	.10
Poster Quality	--	--	.23
	** $p < .01$	* $p < .05$	

Taken together, these results imply that critical feedback correlates positively with learning outcomes only when students exercise a feedback choice, not when they are assigned their feedback. In support of this conclusion, results show that the relation between critical feedback and the measures of learning differs statistically significantly between the two conditions. Specifically, a t-test analysis comparing the correlation coefficients of Critical Feedback and Poster Quality between the Choose and Receive conditions indicated that the two correlation coefficients were statistically significantly different from each other (*z-score* = 2.15, $p = .03$; Fisher, 1921; Soper, 2016). A comparison of the Critical Feedback and Poster Ranking correlation coefficients between conditions yielded similar results (*z-score* = 2.77, $p < .01$).

4.2 Are there Outcome Differences between Choosing and Receiving Feedback?

Revision. An independent-samples t-test was conducted to compare Revision between students in the two conditions. There were no significant differences in Revision between students in the Choose (M = .76, SD = .83) and Receive condition (M = .53, SD = .62); $t(88.56) = 1.52$, $p = .13$. **Figure** 3a shows the mean Revision plotted by number of Critical Feedbacks (0-6) for each of the two conditions.

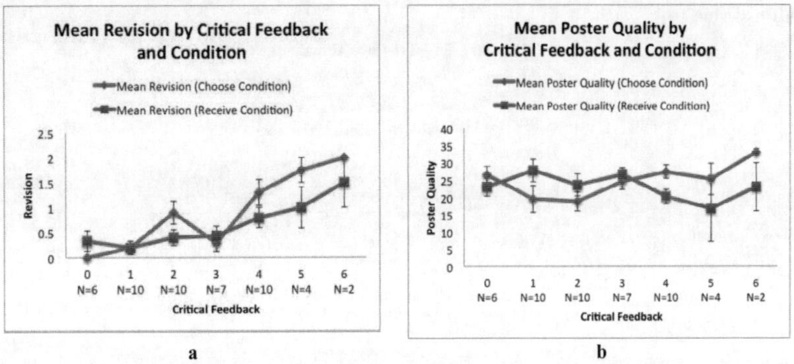

Figure 3. Mean Revision (a) and mean Poster Quality (b) by critical feedback and condition

Poster Quality. An independent-samples t-test was conducted to compare Poster Quality between conditions. There were no significant differences in Poster Quality between students in the Choose (M = 23.57, SD = 8.85) and Receive condition (M = 23.51, SD = 9.48); $t(96) = .03$, $p = .97$. **Figure 3**b shows the mean Poster Quality plotted by Critical Feedback for each of the two conditions. Another independent-samples t-test was conducted to compare the quality of the Pretest (the first poster before revisions) between students in both conditions. There were no significant differences in Pretest between students in the Choose (M = 9.59, SD = 5.69) and Receive condition (M = 9.33, SD = 6.93); $t(96) = .21$, $p = .84$.

Poster Ranking. An independent-samples t-test was conducted to compare Poster Ranking between students in the two conditions. There were no significant differences in Poster Ranking between students in the Choose (M = 1.71, SD = 1.02) and Receive condition (M = 1.63, SD = 1.07); $t(96) = .39$, $p = .70$. **Figure** 4a shows the mean Poster Ranking plotted by Critical Feedback for each of the two conditions.

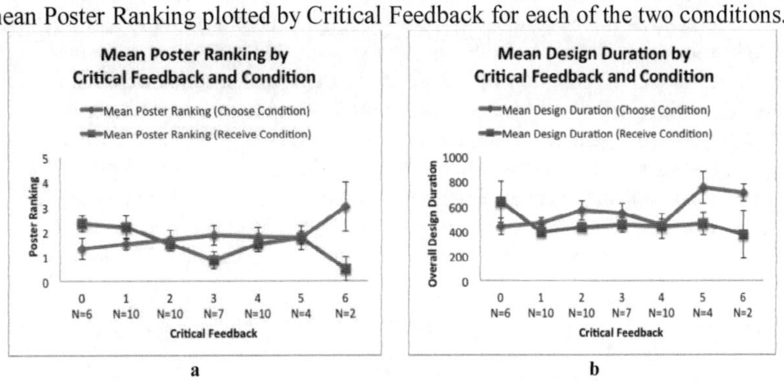

Figure 4. Mean Poster Ranking (a) and mean Design Duration (b) by critical feedback and condition

Design Duration. An independent-samples t-test was conducted to compare Design Duration between conditions. There were no significant differences in Design Duration between students in the Choose (M = 8.72 minutes, SD = 3.28) and students in the Receive condition (M = 7.54 minutes, SD = 3.84); $t(96) = 1.63$, $p = .11$. **Figure 4**b shows the mean Design Duration plotted by Critical Feedback.

4.3 Are there Enjoyment Differences between Choosing and Receiving Feedback?

An independent-samples t-test was conducted to compare Enjoyment between conditions. Results show that students in the Choose condition (M = 4.03, SD = .80) enjoyed designing posters significantly more than students in the Receive condition (M = 3.45, SD = .91); $t(81) = 2.99$, $p < .01$. **Figure 5** shows the mean Enjoyment plotted by critical feedback for each condition, indicating that enjoyment is hardly affected by the amount of critical feedback, except at the high end. These results suggest that the effect on enjoyment could be simply the existence of choice, rather than the actual valence of the choice. In the Choose condition, 76% of the students reported 4 and 5 levels of enjoyment, as opposed to only 51% of the students in the Receive condition. Moreover, Enjoyment is positively associated with Design Duration (*rho* = .37, $p = .03$) only in the Choose condition.

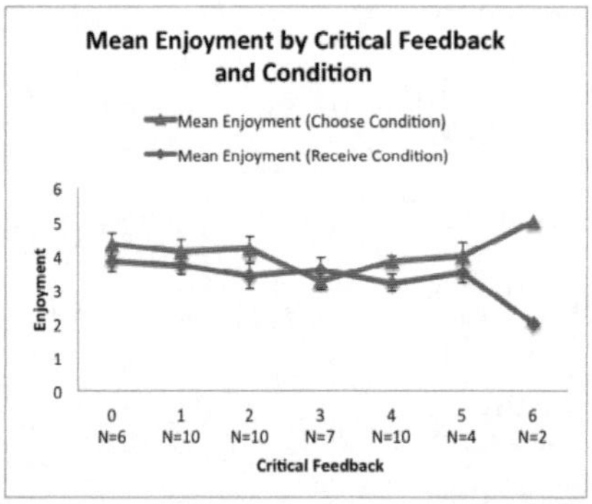

Figure 5. Mean Enjoyment by critical feedback and condition

5. DISCUSSION AND IMPLICATIONS

Critical feedback and performance outcomes. Critical Feedback and Revision were strongly correlated and students improved their poster design performance as they played the game. The more the students chose critical feedback and revised, the better they performed on the poster design task. This is consistent with research reporting that giving children a choice led to better information-seeking performance in a text search task (Reynolds and Symons, 2001). Concomitantly, the more the students were assigned critical feedback, the worse they performed on the post-test. However, the graphical representation of poster ranking by critical feedback per condition suggests that critical feedback could aid performance depending on the amount of critical feedback assigned. A limitation of this study is the reduced amount of data points for each critical feedback value. More data will be collected to better understand how students' performance relates to critical feedback. Overall, critical feedback is associated with better performance when students choose their feedback valence, but with worse performance when they are assigned their feedback valence. One possible explanation for this outcome is that choice can be a source of motivation, which may lead students to engage more with their learning. For example, high-school students who chose which of their homework assignments to complete outperformed their peers who had no choice available (Patall et al., 2010).

Outcome differences between choosing and receiving feedback. This research hypothesized that students who chose feedback performed better than students who were assigned feedback. However, results revealed no effect of feedback choice, consistent with a related prior study examining Mechanical Turk adults (Cutumisu and Schwartz, 2016). There were no differences between conditions in the choice to revise, performance on the posters and on the post-test, and time spent designing posters. This indicates that no underlying variable (e.g., mindset) drives the effect of critical feedback, since assigning the same amount of feedback leads to the same results as other factors that may cause students to choose critical feedback. A limitation of this study could serve as an explanation for this outcome: both game versions consisted of two rounds and five minutes for poster design. Future research will include one more round in each condition and provide more time per round to assess students' performance in both conditions and perhaps note differences.

Enjoyment differences between choosing and receiving feedback. Students in the Choose condition enjoyed designing posters significantly more than those in the Receive condition. Choices can promote a sense of autonomy that could be highly motivating for the students (Deci and Ryan, 1985). Although greater perceived autonomy is associated with higher levels of enjoyment and intrinsic motivation (Reeve et al., 1999), choice is not always a motivator (Katz and Assor, 2007). The finding that enjoyment correlates with the time the students took to design the posters only in the Choose condition supports this motivational hypothesis and is consistent with prior research involving a sample of Mechanical Turk adults (Cutumisu and Schwartz, 2016). The majority of the students reported high levels of enjoyment, which is encouraging for a game that is ultimately an assessment. Thus, games such as Posterlet could be enjoyable assessment environments for college students, especially when they provide feedback valence choices.

Educational implications. One lesson that can be taken away from this study is that choice of feedback seems to play an important role for performance, revision, time on task, and enjoyment for college students. Thus, feedback choice in general, and feedback choice between confirmatory and critical feedback in particular, should be considered as an important feature in instructional environments for this population to maximize feedback's effectiveness in impacting performance and learning. A feedback choice-rich learning and assessment environment could also lead to student enjoyment and more time spent on task. For example, in a physical activity intervention drawing on self-determination theory (Deci and Ryan, 1985), students who were taught by autonomy-supportive teachers participated more frequently in leisure-time physical activities than students who were taught by less autonomy-supportive teachers (Chatzisarantis and Hagger, 2009). Even though no significant differences in outcomes were found between choosing and receiving feedback, engaging with a certain threshold of critical feedback may make a difference for learning. Thus, existing assessment environments that do not provide choices could integrate dynamic ways of adjusting the amount of critical feedback available to students and evaluate their performance in each case.

6. CONCLUSION

The study presented a preliminary comparison between the impact of choosing and receiving feedback on college students' performance. Critical feedback and performance are associated positively when students choose their feedback, but negatively when they are assigned their feedback. The choice to revise is positively associated with performance, but only when students choose their feedback. Students who choose their feedback enjoy designing posters significantly more than students who receive their feedback. Moreover, students who have a choice regarding their feedback also spend significantly more time designing posters than students who are assigned their feedback. Future research in this area needs to address the theoretical underpinnings of feedback valence and choice, and further examine the impact of motivation, enjoyment, and critical feedback on students' performance and learning.

ACKNOWLEDGEMENT

We are grateful to the participants and to the Gordon and Betty Moore Foundation for their generous support.

REFERENCES

Alfieri, L. et al., 2011. Does discovery-based instruction enhance learning? *Journal of Educational Psychology*, Vol. 103, 1–18.

Anseel, F. et al., 2015. How are we doing after 30 years? A meta-analytic review of the antecedents and outcomes of feedback-seeking behavior. *Journal of Management*, Vol. 41, No. 1, 318-348.

Ashford, S. J. et al., 2016. To seek or not to seek: Is that the only question? Recent developments in feedback-seeking literature. *Annual Review of Organizational Psychology and Organizational Behavior*, Vol. 3, 213-239.

Bangert-Drowns, R. L. et al., 1991. The instructional effect of feedback in test-like events. *Review of Educational Research*, Vol. 61, 213–238.

Chatzisarantis, N. L. and Hagger, M. S., 2009. Effects of an intervention based on self-determination theory on self-reported leisure-time physical activity participation. *Psychology and Health*, Vol. 24, No. 1, 29-48.

Cutumisu, M. et al., 2015. Posterlet: A game-based assessment of children's choices to seek feedback and to revise. *Journal of Learning Analytics*, Vol. 2, No. 1, 49-71.

Cutumisu, M. and Schwartz, D., 2016. Choosing versus receiving feedback: The impact of feedback valence on learning in an assessment game. In *Proceedings of the 9th International Conference on Educational Data Mining* (EDM), 341-346, June 29 - July 2, Raleigh, NC, USA.

De Stobbeleir, K. E. et al., 2011. Self-regulation of creativity at work: The role of feedback-seeking behavior in creative performance. *Academy of Management Journal*, Vol. 54, No. 4, 811-831.

Deci, E. L. and Ryan, R. M., 1985. *Intrinsic motivation and self-determination in human behavior*. New York, NY: Plenum.

Fishbach, A. et al., 2010. How positive and negative feedback motivate goal pursuit. *Social and Personality Psychology Compass*, Vol. 4, No. 8, 517-530.

Fisher, R. A., 1921. On the probable error of a coefficient of correlation deduced from a small sample. *Metron*, 1, 3-32.

Gregory, J. B. and Levy, P. E., 2015. *Using feedback in organizational consulting*. Washington, DC: American Psychological Association.

Hattie, J. and Timperley, H., 2007. The power of feedback. *Review of Educational Research*, Vol. 77, No. 1, pp. 81–112.

Haydon, M. L. et al., 2011. Obstetric outcomes and maternal satisfaction in nulliparous women using patient-controlled epidural analgesia. *American Journal of Obstetrics and Gynecology*, *205*(3), 271-e1.

Katz, I. and Assor, A., 2007. When choice motivates and when it does not. *Educational Psychology Review*, Vol. 19, No. 4, 429-442.

Kluger, A. N. and DeNisi, A., 1998. Feedback interventions: toward the understanding of a double-edged sword. *Current Directions in Psychological Science*, Vol. 7, No. 3, pp. 67–72.

Landis-Lewis, Z. et al., 2015. Computer-supported feedback message tailoring: Theory-informed adaptation of clinical audit and feedback for learning and behaviour change. *Implementation Science*, Vol. 10, No. 12.

Mangels, J. et al., 2006. Why do beliefs about intelligence influence learning success? A social cognitive neuroscience model. *Social Cognitive and Affective neuroscience*, Vol. 1, No. 2.

Patall, E. A. et al., 2010. The effectiveness and relative importance of choice in the classroom. *Journal of Educational Psychology*, Vol. 102, No. 4, p. 896.

Porath, C. L. and Bateman, T. S., 2006. Self-regulation: from goal orientation to job performance. *Journal of Applied Psychology*, Vol. 91, No. 1, 185.

Reeve, J. et al., 1999. Autonomy-supportive teachers: How they teach and motivate students. *Journal of Educational Psychology*, Vol. 91, 537-548

Reynolds, P. L. and Symons, S., 2001. Motivational variables and children's text search. *Journal of Educational Psychology*, Vol. 93, 14–22.

Schwartz, D. L. and Arena, D., 2013. *Measuring what matters most: Choice-based assessments for the digital age*. MIT Press, Cambridge, MA, USA.

Schwartz, D.L. et al., 2009. Constructivism in an age of non-constructivist assessments. *Constructivist Instruction*, 34-61.

Soper, D. S., 2016. Significance of the Difference between Two Correlations Calculator [Software]. Retrieved from: http://www.danielsoper.com/statcalc.

THE IMPACT OF MIDDLE-SCHOOL STUDENTS' FEEDBACK CHOICES AND PERFORMANCE ON THEIR FEEDBACK MEMORY

Maria Cutumisu[1] and Daniel L. Schwartz[2]
[1]*Department of Educational Psychology, 5-145 Education North, University of Alberta, Edmonton, AB, T6G 2G5, Canada*
[2]*Stanford Graduate School of Education, 485 Lasuen Mall, Stanford, CA 94305-3096, USA*

ABSTRACT

This paper presents a novel examination of the impact of students' feedback choices and performance on their feedback memory. An empirical study was designed to collect the choices to seek critical feedback from a hundred and six Grade 8 middle-school students via Posterlet, a digital assessment game in which students design posters. Upon completing the game, students filled a survey asking them to recall the feedback phrases they encountered in Posterlet. Results show that choosing critical feedback correlated with the critical feedback students remembered. Additionally, choosing critical feedback and poster performance inversely correlated with the confirmatory feedback students remembered. A closer examination of the informational value of feedback revealed that choosing critical feedback correlated with both types (i.e., informative and uninformative) of critical feedback remembered and it inversely correlated with both types of confirmatory feedback remembered. Finally, poster performance correlated with the critical uninformative feedback remembered and inversely correlated with the confirmatory uninformative feedback remembered. Ramifications for students' learning performance are discussed.

KEYWORDS

Feedback, Memory, Assessment, Game, Revision, Learning Performance

1. INTRODUCTION

In educational settings, feedback generally improves performance (Hattie and Timperley, 2007). However, a meta-analysis found that feedback hindered performance in a third of the studies examined (Kluger and DeNisi, 1998). There are many reasons for this discrepancy. For example, task-directed feedback seems to be more helpful than person-directed feedback, such as praise or punishment unrelated to the task (Black and William, 1998; Hattie and Timperley, 2007). Moreover, although the quality of the learners' engagement with feedback is believed to be a determinant factor of feedback effectiveness (Winstone et al., 2016), few studies examine this aspect of feedback (Bounds et al., 2013). Instead of focusing on feedback that is assigned to the learner, this paper examines the mechanisms that unfold when students engage proactively with feedback by choosing between confirmatory (positive) and critical (negative) feedback. There is a paucity of research examining the effectiveness of feedback seeking (Evans, 2013) and the impact of feedback on students' memory, especially when students choose the valence of their feedback. This paper focuses for the first time on the lasting impact of choices between confirmatory and critical feedback on students' memory for feedback. It also examines the role that learning performance plays in the context of feedback choices and memory. Building on research that validated choices as predictors of learning performance (Cutumisu et al., 2015), this paper aims to gain an insight into the mechanisms of feedback processing by focusing on choices as predictors of students' memory for feedback and it hypothesizes that students' learning choices and performance reveal important insights into students' critical feedback remembered from the game. The current study employs Posterlet, an assessment game, together with a free-recall task administered immediately after the game, to examine the impact of feedback choices and performance on students' memory for feedback and it poses the following research questions:

1. Do in-game measures correlate with students' memory for critical feedback?

2. Do in-game measures correlate with students' memory for critical informative feedback?

3. Does in-school performance correlate with students' memory for critical informative feedback?

First, the paper reviews the literature relevant to this study. Second, it describes a) the Posterlet assessment instrument, a game that collects students' feedback choices while students design posters, and b) the feedback memory survey that collects students' feedback phrases recalled after playing the Posterlet game. Third, it presents empirical evidence addressing the research questions. Finally, it concludes with a discussion of the implications, limitations, and future research directions.

2. LITERATURE REVIEW

This section relates the study to the relevant literature on choice-based assessments, feedback memory, and the relation between performance and feedback memory.

Choice-based assessments. Educators aim to support learners in developing 21st-century skills that will prepare them to tackle complex problems (e.g., rapidly-spreading diseases). In 2012, the *Programme for International Student Assessment* (PISA) introduced items that collected information about students' attitudes towards problem solving for the first time since it started administering tests in 2000 (OECD, 2016). This trend is due in part to the focus of traditional assessments on outcome accuracy, rather than on the preparedness of students to perform well on new tasks. In contrast, choice-based assessments focus on the learning processes in which students engage when solving a new challenge (Schwartz and Arena, 2013). These types of novel assessments offer a glimpse into how prepared students are to learn on their own. Examining feedback choices that enable students to play an active role in their learning is also important from the perspective of self-regulated learning. Butler and Winne (1995) emphasized that, by engaging proactively with their feedback, learners can develop effective self-assessment skills that enable them to better appraise their own performance (McDonnell and Curtis, 2014; Wakefield et al., 2014). In this study, Posterlet is employed to collect and measure students' proactive choices to seek feedback and to revise as a way to capture their preparedness to learn on their own.

Feedback memory. Students adopt many strategies to cope with self-threatening feedback that accurately highlights their weaknesses. For instance, they display an inferior recall for such feedback compared to other types of feedback (e.g., self-affirming feedback that highlights one's strengths). The theory of mnemic neglect posits that such an effect is attenuated, triggering self-improvement motivation (Dauenheimer et al., 2002; Green et al., 2005; Roese and Olson, 2007; Sedikides et al., 2016), when feedback is perceived as referring to modifiable traits. In this research, critical feedback is constructive and not punishing, and students exercise a choice regarding their feedback valence. Thus, the paper hypothesizes that students will remember, and not suppress, the critical feedback they chose.

Feedback memory and performance. Research on the neural correlates of learning provides evidence that neural responses to feedback can predict future performance. Specifically, the brain responses to feedback are predictive of whether university students will repeat mistakes or will learn from their mistakes (van der Helden et al., 2010). In contrast, this paper explores the relation between students' performance and their subsequent memory for critical feedback and it examines a different population (i.e., middle-school students).

3. THE ASSESSMENT GAME AND THE MEMORY SURVEY

This section presents 1) Posterlet, the assessment instrument that collects students' choices to seek critical feedback and to revise and 2) the feedback memory survey devised to collect the feedback phrases students recall after playing the game.

3.1 Posterlet

The Posterlet game enables students to design a poster on each of the game's three rounds and to perform two main choices at the end of each poster design task. Upon completing each poster, students choose either confirmatory (e.g., *It's good you told them what day the fair is.*) or critical (e.g., *People need to be able to read it. Some of your words are too small.)* feedback from three animal characters, as shown in Figure **1**. After reading the feedback, students choose whether to revise that poster. Posterlet, described in detail in previous work (Cutumisu et al., 2015), tracks these two choices (seeking critical feedback and revising) and computes a poster score per poster round, as well as a cumulative poster score per game.

Figure 1. In the Posterlet game, the students design posters and choose either confirmatory or critical feedback

3.2 Memory Survey

Immediately following the game, students were automatically directed to an online survey, where they were asked to recall as many feedback comments as they remembered from the Posterlet game, out of a maximum of nine (i.e., there are three opportunities to choose feedback for each of the three game rounds). Students were provided with the following prompt and a screenshot from the game, as illustrated below: *If you played the Posterlet game in which you designed posters for a funfair, please list below as many **comments** as you can remember that you received from the animal characters in the game.*

Figure 2. The memory survey asking students to recall their feedback after playing Posterlet

Feedback alternated between informative and uninformative phrases exemplified in *Section 4.2.4* to avoid cognitive load for younger participants. The example presented in Table 1 of a student's survey answers and scores shows that, of the seven feedback phrases the student remembered, four were critical (two informative and two uninformative), while three were confirmatory (all informative).

Table 1. A sample of a student's answers and scoring for the memory survey. The student did not provide answers for items 8 and 9, so these answers were scored with zero. Note: Crit. = Critical, Inf. = Informative, Uninf. = Uninformative

Order	Feedback Remembered	Crit. Inf.	Crit. Uninf.	Conf. Inf.	Conf. Uninf.	Crit. Total	Conf. Total	Total
1	I don't like fairs	0	1	0	0	1	0	1
2	I like that the text does not cut off the page	0	0	1	0	0	1	1
3	I don't really go to fairs	0	1	0	0	1	0	1
4	I don't like that the text is too close together	1	0	0	0	1	0	1
5	I don't like that it doesn't have the admissions price	1	0	0	0	1	0	1
6	I like that is has the date and time	0	0	1	0	0	1	1
7	I like that it has the location	0	0	1	0	0	1	1
8	-	0	0	0	0	0	0	0
9	-	0	0	0	0	0	0	0
Total		**2**	**2**	**3**	**0**	**4**	**3**	**7**

4. METHODS

4.1 Participants and Procedure

Participants were n=106 (60 females) Grade 8 students, aged 13-14, from a public middle school in California. All students played Posterlet and n=86 of them filled an online memory survey immediately after playing the game in May 2015. Students designed three posters (M=14.76 minutes, SD=4.07) individually, as one of several assessments administered that day. Due to time constraints, a post-test to measure students' learning of graphic design principles was not administered. Upon completing the game, students filled a feedback memory survey. Students who did not provide consent (n=9) or did not complete all posters (n=8) were excluded from analyses. Thus, the analyses comprise n=89 students (50 females). Some of the students did not complete the survey due to time constraints, some parents did not provide consent for sharing their children's standardized test scores, so students were removed from the analyses as needed.

4.2 Measures

4.2.1 Choices

Critical Feedback measures the total amount of critical (*I don't like...*) feedback a student chose, ranging from zero (i.e., the student chose confirmatory feedback throughout the game) to nine (i.e., the student chose critical feedback across the game). Revision measures the total number of posters a student chose to revise, ranging from zero (i.e., the student did not revise any poster) to three (i.e., the student revised all posters).

4.2.2 In-Game Performance

As mentioned before, Posterlet computes a Poster Quality score based on 21 design principles reflecting a student's performance across the game. The quality of each poster is the sum of the scores for each of the 21 features: 1 if a feature is always used correctly on a poster, 0 if a feature is not included on the poster, and -1 if a feature is used incorrectly on a poster. Poster Quality sums the poster quality of all three posters.

4.2.3 In-School Performance

STAR (Standardized Testing and Reporting) scores indicating students' achievement outside the game were obtained from the school for a subset of students. They included scores in English Language Arts (ELA-CST) and Mathematics (Math-CST) recorded two years prior to conducting this study, when students were in Grade 6. These were the last available standardized tests before the transition to the Common Core tests.

4.2.4 Memory Survey Measures

Critical Feedback Remembered measures the number of critical feedback phrases a student recalled. Further, *Critical Informative Feedback Remembered* measures the amount of informative critical feedback phrases (e.g., *People need to be able to read it. Some of your words are too small.*) that the student recalled, while *Critical Uninformative Feedback Remembered* measures the amount of uninformative critical feedback phrases (e.g., *I don't like fairs*) that the student recalled. *Critical Feedback Remembered* constitutes the sum of these two measures. Similar measures were used for confirmatory feedback. *Total Feedback Remembered* constitutes the sum of *Critical Feedback Remembered* and *Confirmatory Feedback Remembered.*

5. DATA ANALYSES AND RESULTS

5.1 Do In-Game Measures Correlate with Students' Memory for Critical Feedback?

These analyses tested the hypothesis that students' choices and performance correlated with students' memory for critical, rather than confirmatory, feedback choices. The impact of students' choices and performance on feedback memory was investigated using Spearman rank correlations (*rho*), because these measures were not normally distributed. Thus, correlations were conducted between students' in-game measures (choices measured by Critical Feedback and Revision, and poster performance measured by Poster Quality) and survey measures (the feedback that the students remembered, such as critical, confirmatory, and total). Results presented in Table 2 show that Critical Feedback strongly correlated with the critical, and inversely with the confirmatory, feedback that the students remembered. Results show a similar pattern for Revision, but with moderate correlations. Finally, poster performance inversely correlated with the confirmatory feedback remembered. Thus, critical feedback remembered correlated significantly with both in-game choices and non-significantly with in-game performance.

Table 2. Spearman correlations between choices and measures of memory for feedback ($^{**}p < .01$, $^{*}p < .05$)

Measures (n = 73)	Critical Feedback Remembered	Confirmatory Feedback Remembered	Total Feedback Remembered
Critical Feedback	**.58****	**-.58****	.11
Revision	**.26***	**-.29***	-.05
Poster Quality	.16	**-.24***	-.09

Next, two linear standard regressions examined whether the strongly correlated (*rho* = .40, $p < .01$) choices (Negative Feedback and Revision) were independent predictors of each of the types of feedback remembered, to determine which choice is more important for feedback memory. A regression analysis was not conducted for Total Feedback Remembered, because it was not associated with any of the choices. Choices were entered as predictors of Critical Feedback Remembered and Confirmatory Feedback Remembered, respectively. Results showed that the model predicting Critical Feedback Remembered was significant [$F(2, 70) = 14.45$, $p < .001$, R Square = .29, Adjusted R Square = .27] and Critical Feedback was a significant predictor [$t(72) = 4.87$, $p < .001$], but Revision was not [$t(72) = .37$, $p = .71$]. The same pattern of results emerged for the model predicting Confirmatory Feedback Remembered [$F(2, 70) = 17.67$, $p < .001$, R Square = .34, Adjusted R Square = .32]: Critical Feedback was a predictor [$t(72) = -4.96$, $p < .001$], but Revision was not [$t(72) = -1.27$, $p = .21$]. Thus, the choice to seek critical feedback is more important for feedback memory than the choice to revise.

5.2 Do In-Game Measures Correlate With Students' Memory for Critical Informative Feedback?

These analyses tested the hypothesis that students' choices and performance correlated with their memory for critical informative feedback. Thus, the impact of the informational value of feedback on feedback memory was examined by conducting Spearman correlations between in-game measures (choices to seek critical feedback and to revise, as well as performance) and feedback memory. The latter was measured on two orthogonal dimensions: valence (i.e., critical or confirmatory) and informational value (i.e., informative and uninformative). Findings shown in Table 3 indicate that the more the students chose critical feedback, the more they remembered both types of critical feedback (informative and uninformative) and the less they remembered both types of confirmatory feedback (informative and uninformative). Results for Revision are similar but weaker, with only the correlation with confirmatory informative feedback reaching statistical significance. Finally, the better the students performed, the more they remembered the critical uninformative feedback and the less they remembered the confirmatory uninformative feedback encountered in the game. Thus, critical informative feedback remembered correlated significantly with the choice to seek critical feedback, non-significantly with the choice to revise, and inversely and non-significantly with performance.

Table 3. Correlations between game measures and feedback memory measures by feedback type ($^{**}p < .01$, $^{*}p < .05$)

Measures (n = 73)	Critical Inf. Remembered	Critical Uninf. Remembered	Confirmatory Inf. Remembered	Confirmatory Uninf. Remembered
Critical Feedback	**.46****	**.31****	**-.36****	**-.52****
Revision	.17	.19	**-.28***	-.15
Poster Quality	-.01	**.25***	-.12	**-.37****

5.3 Does In-School Performance Correlate with Students' Memory for Critical Informative Feedback?

These analyses tested the hypothesis that students' in-school performance correlated with students' memory for critical informative feedback. Results of the Spearman correlations between students' in-school performance measures and their memory for feedback are shown in Table 4. Findings revealed that ELA-CST correlated with the critical informative feedback remembered and with the overall critical feedback remembered (*rho* = .28, $p < .05$). Also, Math-CST inversely correlated with the confirmatory informative feedback remembered and with the overall confirmatory feedback remembered (*rho* = -.33, $p < .01$). Thus, both school performance measures seem to be important for students' memory for informative feedback.

Table 4. Correlations between school performance and feedback memory by feedback type ($^{**}p < .01$, $^{*}p < .05$)

Measures (n = 65)	Critical Inf. Remembered	Critical Uninf. Remembered	Confirmatory Inf. Remembered	Confirmatory Uninf. Remembered
ELA-CST	**.25***	.13	-.15	.01
Math-CST	.05	-.01	**-.29***	-.11

6. DISCUSSION, LIMITATIONS, AND FUTURE WORK

In-game measures and feedback memory. Results showed that the critical feedback remembered correlated significantly with both in-game choices to seek critical feedback and to revise, and non-significantly with in-game performance. First, the more the students choose to seek critical feedback, the more critical, and the less confirmatory, feedback they remember. This seems to support the hypothesis that choosing critical feedback has a lasting impact on students' memory for critical feedback. Although not statistically significantly, the more the students choose critical feedback, the more feedback they remember in general. One limitation of the study is a lack of a tutorial round. Instead, students used the first round of the game to explore and understand the game mechanics. Thus, the measures on the first game round were not as consistent as the measures on subsequent levels. In future analyses, only the last two rounds of the game will be considered and the correlation between choosing critical feedback and the overall feedback remembered will be reexamined. Second, a similar pattern of results emerged for the choice to revise, supporting the hypothesis that the more the students chose to revise, the more they remembered their critical feedback. One possible explanation is that students mainly choose to revise when they engage with critical feedback, a result consistent with all Posterlet studies. Consequently, during the revision process, students may fill their knowledge gaps by translating the critical feedback they had chosen into action and, thus, remembering this feedback better as a result. The next research question will test whether this result is due to the informative or uninformative value of critical feedback. However, between the two choices, results showed that seeking critical feedback is more important than revising for feedback memory, because only the choice to seek critical feedback significantly predicted the amount of critical and confirmatory feedback remembered. Third, performance showed a similar pattern of results as both choices, with the exception that the correlation between performance and memory for critical feedback did not reach statistical significance. This result contradicts the hypothesis that performance is positively associated with the critical feedback remembered. A future study will reexamine this correlation when only the last two rounds of the game are considered.

In-game measures and the informational value of feedback. Results showed that students' memory for critical informative feedback correlated significantly with their choice to seek critical feedback, non-significantly with their choice to revise, and inversely, non-significantly with their poster performance. First, the more the students choose critical feedback, the more critical (informative and uninformative) feedback and the less confirmatory (informative and uninformative) feedback they remember. This result supports the hypothesis that choosing critical feedback correlates with students' memory for critical informative feedback. Second, a similar pattern of results emerged for the choice to revise, but only the inverse correlation with the confirmatory informative feedback reached statistical significance. A possible explanation for this result is that students already know the information presented in the confirmatory informative feedback, so they do not need to attend to it nor to revise the graphic design principles included in the feedback, hence, they may not remember it as well. Third, results showed that the better the students performed on the poster design task, the better they remembered the critical uninformative feedback and the worse they remembered the confirmatory uninformative feedback. This counterintuitive result contradicts the initial hypothesis that performance is positively associated with students' memory for critical informative feedback and it points to a motivational aspect of feedback that requires further exploration. Follow-up analyses that consider only the last two rounds of the game will be conducted. A limitation of this study is that students could potentially receive more uninformative than informative feedback, because the feedback system alternates between informative and uninformative feedback of the same valence. Moreover, if no informative feedback can be generated (e.g., critical feedback is sought on a poster with no mistakes), then an uninformative feedback message of the same valence is generated. A future study will be designed to explore this aspect. Finally, an alternative explanation for these results is that individual differences might impact students' engagement with feedback more than the actual content of the feedback (Orsmond and Merry, 2013).

In-school performance measures and feedback memory. Results showed that both school performance measures seemed to be important for students' memory for informative feedback. First, students' standardized English Language Arts scores correlated with both the critical and the critical informative feedback remembered, supporting this study's hypothesis. Second, students' Mathematics scores inversely correlated with both the confirmatory and the confirmatory informative feedback remembered. One explanation for these results could be that students who perform well in arts are more open and accustomed to interacting with critical feedback and, hence, they remember it better, while students who perform well in mathematics are more inclined to filter out the information they already know.

Taken together, these results indicate that the learning environment is important for performance and feedback retention. Thus, when students have a choice regarding the valence of their feedback, the more they choose critical feedback, the more they remember critical (informative and uninformative) feedback and the less they remember confirmatory (informative and uninformative) feedback. In subsequent studies, the timing of the memory survey administration will be varied to gain an insight into how it affects students' memory for different types of feedback. Future research will also explore whether students remember critical and confirmatory feedback differentially when they are assigned feedback rather than in the current situation when they choose their feedback. Finally, future studies will examine the impact of other variables (e.g., mindset) on the valence and on the informational value of the feedback that students remember.

7. CONCLUSION

This research examined the impact of students' feedback choices and learning performance on their feedback memory. An empirical study was designed to collect students' learning choices via an assessment game, Posterlet, and their memory for feedback via a follow-up survey. Results provide evidence that choosing critical feedback is associated with better memory for critical feedback and worse memory for confirmatory feedback. Also, the better the students perform in Posterlet and on Mathematics standardized tests, the less confirmatory feedback they remember. Finally, the better the students perform on English Language Arts standardized tests, the more they remember critical informative feedback. This research has implications for the design of assessments and instructional materials. Students may benefit from learning environments where they can engage proactively with feedback to improve their performance and their memory for the feedback content. Instructors may benefit from assessment environments that integrate the measurement of students' learning choices (e.g., willingness to seek critical feedback and to revise) and learning outcomes, so that they can evaluate programs of instruction. These findings could help explain why some forms of feedback are more effective than others and, thus, they may also aid researchers in gaining insights into the mechanisms of feedback processing and recall, and in comparing different feedback interventions.

ACKNOWLEDGEMENT

We are grateful to the participants, the Gordon and Betty Moore Foundation, and the NSF (Grant # 1228831) for their generous support.

REFERENCES

Black, P. and Wiliam, D., 1998. Assessment and classroom learning. *Assessment in Education: Principles, Policy & Practice,* Vol. 5, pp. 7-74.

Bounds, R. et al., 2013. Emergency medicine residents' self-assessments play a critical role when receiving feedback. *Academic Emergency Medicine*, Vol. 20, pp. 1055-1061.

Cutumisu, M. et al., 2015. Posterlet: A game-based assessment of children's choices to seek feedback and to revise. *Journal of Learning Analytics*, Vol. 2, No. 1, pp. 49-71.

Dauenheimer, D. G. et al., 2002. Self-enhancement, self-assessment, or self-verification? The intricate role of trait modifiability in the self-evaluation process, *Revue Internationale De Psychologie Sociale*, Vol. 15, pp. 89–112.

Evans, C., 2013. Making sense of assessment feedback in higher education. *Review of Educational Research*, Vol. 83, pp. 70–120.

Green, J. D. et al., 2005. Mnemic neglect and self-threat: Trait modifiability moderates self protection, *European Journal of Social Psychology,* Vol. 35, pp. 225–235.

Hattie, J. and Timperley, H., 2007. The power of feedback. *Review of Educational Research*, Vol. 77, No. 1, pp. 81–112.

Kluger, A. N. and DeNisi, A., 1998. Feedback interventions: toward the understanding of a double-edged sword. *Current Directions in Psychological Science*, Vol. 7, No. 3, pp. 67–72.

McDonnell, J. and Curtis, W., 2014. Making space for democracy through assessment and feedback in higher education: Thoughts from an action research project in education studies. *Assessment & Evaluation in Higher Education*, Vol. 39, pp. 932–948.

OECD, 2016. *PISA 2012 assessment and analytical framework: Mathematics, reading, science, problem solving and financial literacy*, OECD Publishing, Paris.

Orsmond, P. and Merry, S., 2013. The importance of self-assessment in students' use of tutors' feedback: A qualitative study of high and non-high achieving biology undergraduates. *Assessment & Evaluation in Higher Education*, Vol. 38, pp. 737–753.

Roese, N. J. and Olson, J. M., 2007. Better, stronger, faster: Self-serving judgment, affect regulation, and the optimal vigilance hypothesis. *Perspectives on Psychological Science*, Vol. 2, pp. 124–141.

Schwartz, D. L. and Arena, D., 2013. *Measuring what matters most: Choice-based assessments for the digital age*. Cambridge, Massachusetts: MIT Press.

Sedikides, C. et al., 2016. Mnemic neglect: Selective amnesia of one's faults, *European Review of Social Psychology*, Vol. 27, No. 1, pp. 1-62.

van der Helden, J. et al., 2010. The importance of failure: feedback-related negativity predicts motor learning efficiency, *Cerebral Cortex*, Vol. 20, No. 7, pp. 1596-1603.

Wakefield, C. et al., 2014. Feeding forward from summative assessment: The Essay Feedback Checklist as a learning tool. *Assessment & Evaluation in Higher Education*, Vol. 39, pp. 253–262.

Winstone, N. E. et al., 2016. Supporting learners' agentic engagement with feedback: A systematic review and a taxonomy of recipience processes, *Educational Psychologist*. In Press.

NUMERICAL ACUITY ENHANCEMENT IN KINDERGARTEN: HOW MUCH DOES MATERIAL PRESENTATION FORM MEAN?

Maria Lidia Mascia[1], Maria Chiara Fastame[1], Mirian Agus[1], Daniela Lucangeli[2] and Maria Pietronilla Penna[1]

[1]*Department of Pedagogy, Psychology, Philosophy, University of Cagliari, Italy*
[2]*Department of Developmental Psychology and Socialization, University of Padova, Italy*

ABSTRACT

The current study aimed at exploring the impact of the modality in which numerical trainings proposed in kindergarten school. Participants were recruited from some Sardinian kindergarten schools and were then divided into three groups: a control group, which had to carry out the activities planned by the educational curriculum, and two experimental groups, which were proposed a psychoeducational mathematical enhancement training via either hard copies or multimedia software, respectively. Regardless of the format in which the training was proposed, results showed that the psychoeducational mathematical training lead to improved learning regardless of the format in which the training was proposed. Its positive effects in terms of performance improvement in both the experimental groups. Moreover, as evidenced by a follow-up assessment conducted six months after the end of the enhancement activities, the effect of the mathematical training was maintained over time. In conclusion, the implementation of specific psychoeducational programs aimed at improving numerical mathematical knowledge seems to be a crucial resource to promote learning in pre-schoolers.

KEYWORDS

Early numeracy learning; Psychoeducational Training; Kindergarten schools; Cognitive Empowerment; Educational technology

1. INTRODUCTION

In kindergarten schools, the promotion of specific activities aimed at enhancing the development of mathematics is frequently neglected. In fact, priority is often given to empower preparatory skills favoring the development of reading and writing expertise, such as methafonological awareness (Melhuish et al. 2008). Thus, this is not taking into account the fact that in children's everyday life numbers are crucial everywhere and, that daily life experiences should drive learning of preschoolers (Lucangeli et al. 2012) .

Mathematics is a subject that students often dislike and dread enough to get to real difficulties in learning. Overall, succeeding in mathematics is influenced by emotional, motivational and metacognitive factors (Caponi et al. 2012). In particular, the impact of the emotional dimension on math-related tests is supported by numerous studies that confirm the relationship between anxiety and success in mathematics, that is, the more students are anxious when tested on numerical cognition, the more they are prone to perform poorly (Newstead 1998; Rubinsten & Tannock 2010). Therefore, it is necessary that the first structured interaction with the numbers' world occurs in kindergarten school by means of specific playful activities. These activities have the goal to promote different aspects of numeracy learning, such as what a number is, how to represent its quantitative characteristics, how to express judgements about size (e.g., five cars are more than three cars), how to process calculation, in short, how to learn to process numerical information without any fear (Lucangeli et al. 2012).

There are several theoretical models explaining how to develop the ability to process an information related with numbers. According to several researchers, the notion of number/quantity is innate (e.g., Butterworth 1999), whereas authors such as Piaget and Inhelder (1958) state that developmental factors play a crucial role in promoting the development of the cognitive operations underlying number processing.

Among these operations, we find the ability to compare, classify and understand one-to-one correspondence and seriation, which, in turn, are crucial to learn cardinality and ordinality, which, in turn are essential to understand number word sequences.

Further empirical evidence based on the habituation procedure demonstrates that even infants are capable of identifying sets of different quantities, discriminating between collections of one to three discrete objects (Loosbroek & Smitsman 1990). Similarly, using the violation of expectation paradigm, Starkey, Spelke and Gelman (Starkey et al. 2004) documented that that six -to eight-month old children detect numerical correspondences between either two- or three-object arrays presented in audial and visual modalities, suggesting that infants as young as 6 months possess sensitivity to numerosity.

Krajewski and Schneider (2009) refer to early numeracy as the ability to operate with number word sequences and enumerate combined with mathematical–logical thinking skills, which is the core of mathematics development in preschoolers. Moreover, further studies highlighted the importance of visuospatial abilities (e.g., visuospatial working memory) in promoting different academic achievements such as numeracy in preschoolers and older children (Agus et al. 2015; Dehaene et al. 1993; Rinaldi & Girelli 2012). For instance, Agus et al. (2015) documented the positive effect of combined visuo-spatial and numerical trainings to empower numeracy learning in primary school. However, for what concerns the importance of the development of numerical skills in preschoolers many studies point out that early numerical skills predict successive arithmetic achievements in primary school (Booth & Siegler 2008; Cerda et al. 2015; Navarro et al. 2012). Espy et al. (2004) stated that skills in basic calculation are the best predictor of success in mathematics achievement at school, that is, students with underdeveloped numerical acuity are more likely to fail in mathematics and to develop low self-efficacy and self-esteem. For this reason, it is important to screen early mathematics achievement at preschool age, in order to implement specific psychoeducational interventions promoting successful scholastic performance and psychological well-being at school. In this regard, Aunio, Heiskari, Van Luit & Vuorio (2014) claim that differences in mathematical skills can be detected in kindergarten-age children before formal primary education. Moreover, the authors pointed out that without a specific intervention, preschoolers lacking relational skills in a numerical context and counting abilities cannot be corrected later in primary school. Thus, the risk is that these preschoolers will remain low-performers in mathematics and despite their effort; they cannot reach the performance level of their peers. Further empirical evidence confirms that children with low numerical knowledge in primary school can learn how to process numerical information slowly (Desoete et al. 2012; Missall et al. 2012), that is, they need longer time to develop mathematics skills and to learn the procedures driving number processing (Morgan et al. 2009).

In this perspective, Aubrey, Godfrey and Dahl (2006) point out the importance to implement early psychoeducational interventions aimed at enhancing numeracy learning in preschoolers at risk or with evident mathematical learning problems. In this regard, there is also ample (compelling) evidence of the benefits of the implementation of psychoeducational interventions in kindergarten school for children with and without atypical developmental characteristics (Magnuson et al. 2004; Sammons et al. 2004; Melhuish et al. 2008).

Distinguishing learning difficulties and specific learning disorders not easy (Tucci & Tressoldi, 2009). In order to discriminate a general difficulty due to a delay in terms of educational knowledge or to a real learning specific disorder, it is necessary identifying and separating the characteristics that can be traced back to a deficit and / or compromised profile from those which involve a simple and temporary slowdown in learning (Cornoldi 2007). Following the definition given by DSM V (American Psychiatric Association 2013) the diagnosis of a specific learning disorder requires the presence of persistent difficulties in reading, writing, arithmetic, or mathematical reasoning skills during formal years of schooling. Among symptoms are present in an inaccurate or slow way: effortful reading, poor written expression that lacks clarity, difficulties remembering number facts, or inaccurate mathematical reasoning. However, the diagnosis of specific learning disabilities such as dyscalculia can be conducted only in primary school age, after the end of the second grade. Nonetheless, as highlighted earlier, early interventions in kindergarten school are possible through specific and ad-hoc enhancements with the aim to strength crucial bases critical to the successive mathematics achievements.

Stressing the fact that the numeracy learning is a complex construct defined by different abilities, such as classification, comparisons among sets of stimuli to express quantity judgments, there is evidence that children benefit of different psychoeducational trainings aimed at empowering writing of numbers, calculation, representation of quantity, recognition of numbers (Molin et al. 2007; Wilson & Räsänen 2008;

Riccomini & Smith 2011). Such trainings may have specific connotations and effectiveness in terms of educational achievements and their efficacy depends on different factors related to the characteristics of the students involved (e.g., age, presence of deficit in academic achievement, learning style), the nature of the materials used, the form in which they are presented (e.g., computer-assisted versus pencil-and-paper) and social policy initiatives. Overall, according to Dehaene (2011) in order to be effective, a psychoeducational intervention aimed at enhancing numeracy learning must include activities promoting the sense of the number, which refers to the ability to quickly understand, estimate and manipulate numeric formats.; This is an essential feature of mathematical cognition and it is the crucial essence of several pre-school interventions (Malofeeva 2005).

With this background in mind, the aim of our study is to investigate the effect of presentation mode of a psychoeducational training for the development of numerical skills in kindergarten, proposing to children five years of activities presented in the paper - pencil mode, respectively, or by the use of computers. Specifically, we wanted to evaluate the effect of the above presentation of the training psychoeducational of numerical skills in relation to lexical area, pre-syntactic, semantic and counting, as well as in relation to intelligence fluid student.

The aim of our study is to test whether the implementation of psychoeducational training for the development of numerical skills in kindergarten provides an advantage for the pre-school students, who will possess more efficient numerical skills (not limited to math) that will be useful for the next steps in their education.

2. METHOD

2.1 Participants

Fifty-eight Italian children (mean age=64.5 months, ds=3.7), attending the last year of kindergarten in some small towns in the province of Nuoro and Cagliari (Sardinia), took part in the study after their parents had provided written informed consent for participation. The sample (f = 46.4 %) comprised typically developing children, showing no signs of cognitive or perceptual deficits. The research have a non-probability sampling and was conducted on the base of the ethical requests defined by the Italian Association for Psychology, thanks to the obtainment of the families' authorizations and consent forms. Children were divided into two experimental groups, who have made the same training to upgrade the numerical skills, one in paper - and - pencil mode (G1 n = 26), the other in the computerized version (G2 n = 19). Additional 13 participants in the research were included in the control group (G3). At the end of the project 50 participants out of 58 have completed all the surveys (pre training, post-training and follow-up).

2.2 Materials and Procedure

In order to have respectively a measure of fluid intelligence and of their numerical acuity, pre-schoolers were presented a standardized battery, constituted by the Raven's Colored Progressive Matrices (CPM, Raven 1958) and by the BIN (Numerical Intelligence Scale; Molin et al. 2007).

The CPM (Raven, 1958) can be used also for children in kindergarten (Italian adaptation, (Belacchi et al. 2008), tests, in their colored form, are easy to administer and easy to interpret in a clear way.

The BIN (Molin, Poli, & Lucangeli 2007) is composed of four subscales created in order to measure number and arithmetic knowledge. The four subscales are lexical, semantic, pre-syntactical and counting (Mascia et al. 2015), all these subscales have good psychometric characteristics with high test-retest reliability (Semantic subscale: r=.69; Lexical subscale r=.89; Pre-syntactic subscale: r=.79; Counting subscale: r=.74) (Sella et al. 2016).

The training program used was "L'intelligenza numerica I" (Lucangeli et al. 2003) and 'Sviluppare l'intelligenza numerica I" (Lucangeli et al. 2010) in pencil-and-paper format.

These programs are applied for typically developing children; the activities are presented like a game and range among many areas. They aim to improve the cognitive abilities related with numerical skills: counting, mental calculation, semantic processing, pre-syntactic processing, and lexical processing. The two programs present the same activities but in different format (pencil-and-paper and multimedial software). The programs contained many different modalities to support numerical achievement. For example, the promotion of counting from one to ten were supported with the use of a rhyme, moreover using the fingers and objects to help the achievements; similar activities are carried out by the software. Programs were created to allow to children to internalize calculation procedures in order to shift from physically to mentally actions in the numerical knowledge and its application. The trained educators administer both programs.

The children (n=26) were assigned to the first experimental group (G1) to perform activities in pencil-and-paper format; the other (n=19) composed the second experimental group who follow the same activities in the computerized format. Children in the control group (CG) carried out the regular curricular activities. Children were tested individually in two sessions (each sessions of twenty minutes) at pre-test (T1), post-test (T2) and follow up (T3). Each test was presented following the instructions contained in the original manuals (Belacchi et al., 2008; Molin, Poli, & Lucangeli, 2007). After the pre-test phase, children were randomly extracted from the original sample and matched for chronological age, after were presented the training activities in pencil-and-paper format (G1), in computerized format (G2) and in the control group (G3) that carried out the regular curricular activities proposed by their teachers. After 6 months from the post-test phase, a follow-up valuation was administered in the three groups (G1, G2 e G3).

3. RESULTS

In order to examine the development of skills in the course of the activities we were compared to the results achieved in the three time points (T1,T2 and T3) by calculating the linear correlation coefficient "r" of Pearson and later with the evaluation of differences between the averages with a Multivariate Mixed design Analysis of Covariance. Preliminary bivariate correlations (Table 1) were evaluated, these data confirm the presence of significant direct linear relationship between the size surveyed in the three time points, as shown in the literature (Molin et al. 2007; Mascia et al. 2015).

Table 1. Bivariate "r" Pearson Correlation

	Variable	1.	2.	3.	4.	5.	6.	7.	8.
1.	T1 LEXICAL AREA	1							
2.	T1 SEMANTIC	.506**	1						
3.	T1 COUNTING	.641**	.560**	1					
4.	T1 PRE-SYNCTATICAL	.511**	.632**	.577**	1				
5.	T1 CPM	.200*	.335**	.248**	.360**	1			
6.	T2 LEXICAL AREA	.656**	.461**	.465**	.449**	.185*	1		
7.	T2 SEMANTIC	.453**	.559**	.474**	.597**	.349**	.607**	1	
8.	T2 COUNTING	.487**	.436**	.618**	.394**	.281**	.510**	.486**	1
9.	T2 PRE-SYNCTATICAL	.517**	.570**	.503**	.718**	.367**	.579**	.734**	.506**
10.	T2 CPM	.356**	.372**	.332**	.417**	.495**	.335**	.424**	.338**
11.	T3 LEXICAL AREA	.498**	.382**	.450**	.391**	.221*	.565**	.450**	.373**
12.	T3 SEMANTIC	.419**	.412**	.438**	.433**	.291**	.484**	.569**	.474**
13.	T3 COUNTING	.549**	.349**	.609**	.412**	.230*	.616**	.507**	.706**
14.	T3 PRE-SYNCTATICAL	.401**	.359**	.521**	.520**	.159	.408**	.527**	.490**
15.	T3 CPM	.299**	.271**	.197*	.379**	.427**	.189*	.296**	.211*

	Variable	8.	9.	10.	11.	12.	13.	14.	
9.	T2 PRE-SYNCTATICAL	1							
10.	T2 CPM	.471**	1						
11.	T3 LEXICAL AREA	.525**	.342**	1					
12.	T3 SEMANTIC	.516**	.461**	.516**	1				
13.	T3 COUNTING	.554**	.386**	.605**	.591**	1			
14.	T3 PRE-SYNCTATICAL	.587**	.384**	.427**	.490**	.566**	1		
15.	T3 CPM	.372**	.387**	.323**	.399**	.346**	.398*	1	

** p<.01; * p<.05

It was subsequently applied an Analysis of Multivariate Covariance in order to verify that the groups did not differ in the pre -training survey (T1) in relation to the investigated dimensions. This analysis confirmed the absence of statistically significant differences between groups [Wilks' Lambda =. 799; $F_{(10;102)}$=1.210; p=.293].

In order to assess any changes in participants' skills during the implementation of the upgrading course, it was applied the Multivariate Analysis of Covariance with mixed design, in which as a factor among subjects is considered the group (G1, G2 , G3) and as within-subjects factor the time of the valuation (T1 , T2, T3). The covariate is the age of participants in the pre - test in months, as dependent variables repeated measures relating to the scales of the BIN and CPM. These analyzes showed a significant interaction effect between *group*valuation time* [Wilks' Lambda =. 374; $F_{(4;43)}$=17.986; p=.0001; $p\eta^2$ = .626]. Statistically significant differences in relation to the dimensions have been highlighted with the Post hoc comparisons (Fisher's Least Significant Difference); they are briefly indicated in Tab. 2.

Table 2. Principal results obtained with Analysis of Covariance with mixed design (Post Hoc Comparison LSD)

Group	Dimension	Relevation		Relevation	Mean differences (Standard error)
Training in pencil and paper format	LEXICAL AREA	T2	>	T1	12.796 (4.303)**
	COUNTING	T2	>	T1	20.174 (5.050)**
	COUNTING	T3	>	T1	20.653 (5.858)**
	PRE-SYNTACTICAL	T2	>	T1	22.817 (3.948)**
	PRE-SYNTACTICAL	T3	>	T1	18.618 (5.655)**
	CPM	T3	>	T1	17.895 (6.318)**
Training in computerized form	LEXICAL AREA	T2	>	T1	10.795 (5.025)*
	SEMANTIC	T3	>	T1	18.180 (6.905)**
	SEMANTIC	T2	>	T1	12.678 (5.275)*
	COUNTING	T3	>	T2	17.477 (5.817)**
	PRE-SYNTACTICAL	T2	>	T1	20.969 (4.611)**
	PRE-SYNTACTICAL	T3	>	T1	24.941 (6.604)**
	CPM	T3	>	T1	20.488 (7.378)**
Control group	SEMANTIC	T2	>	T1	16.018 (6.778)*
	PRE-SYNTACTICAL	T3	>	T1	20.878 (8.486)*
	PRE-SYNTACTICAL	T3	>	T2	17.504 (7.804)*

Table 2 highlights the significance of the differences between the average size of the investigated specifically in relation to the presented training both in print mode and in CD mode room, in relation to the three time points (T1, T2 and T3). Specifically, the area of the Pre syntax appears significantly greater at T3 in all experimental groups , but in specific the G1 appeared to have better performance specifically in the area of the Count , while the G2 specifically in semantics .

In any case, both modes of the training presentation appear to be effective in enhancing the numerical skills of pre-school age, which also maintain the follow-up survey.

4. DISCUSSION AND CONCLUSIONS

A wide literature stresses the importance of the effects and the effectiveness of psychoeducational trainings developed to improve working memory and early numeracy in kindergarteners (Kroesbergen et al. 2014). There is also evidence suggesting that trainings efficacy depends also upon the modality in which they are presented (Slavin 2013). However, a few studies are focused on the investigation of the long-term effects of the psychoeducational interventions promoting the development of the numeracy in preschoolers, as well as not so many training programs are addressed to children with typical and atypical development trajectories.
The current study was mainly aimed at exploring the impact of the presentation modality of a psychoeducational training promoting the empowerment of mathematics skills in children attending the kindergarten school. Furthermore, we were interested in investigating the possible long-term effect of the intervention.

Overall, compared with previous studies (Afshari et al. 2009; Jordan et al. 2007; Krajewski & Schneider 2009; Lefevre et al. 2010; Hasselhorn 2013), current findings seem to be very interesting.

As it was already documented in literature (Krajewski & Schneider 2009), the development of working memory capacity and the speed of access to long-term memory are precursors of a successful improvement of mathematics achievements in primary school too. In agreement with this trend of research and consistently with the study conducted by Mascia et al. (2015), current findings suggest that the positive impact of the proposed numeracy training is maintained even a few months after its conclusion, that is, when both control and experimental groups were only involved in the conduction of the curricular activities. Specifically, at follow-up step (i.e., T3) pre syntactical numeracy skills (i.e., appraising the ability to link numbers to their number representation and to order several quantities) were significantly greater in both the experimental groups (G1 e G2) than in the control one. This also suggests that in agreement with previous studies (Penna et al. 2002; Agus et al. 2015; Mascia et al. 2016). Overall, the variation of training presentation form (i.e., pencil-and-paper versus computer-assisted modality) did not impact the development of numeracy skills in preschoolers. Nonetheless, two exceptions deserve to be pointed out. First, at follow-up, compared to the other experimental and control groups, children who attended the pencil and paper training (G1) exhibited better counting performance (i.e., the ability to recite the number–words sequence forward and backward, as well as the knowledge of the order of Arabic digits from 1 to 5). Second, at follow-up, the experimental group exposed to the computer-assisted training showed better semantic knowledge about number (i.e., the ability to associate numerical sizes, dots and Arabic digits). This last finding suggests us to point out that if from the one hand technology tools allow to present a set of activities in an interactive way promoting the motivation in the pupils, that in turn learn, explore and then process new stimuli in a very active and joyful way (Vanderlinde et al. 2014); from the other hand the attainment benefits of technology-based interventions are currently limited and contradictory (Sandford et al. 2006).

Although National Council of Teachers of Mathematics of the USA some years ago stated that technology is essential in teaching and learning mathematics (Moeller et al. 2015), to our knowledge, so far a few studies have evaluated the use of technology-based numeracy trainings in supporting mathematics development in early childhood (Nutta 2013), but some literature shows that trainings based on technology supports have a great importance in the development of many different kinds of learning abilities (Meneses et al. 2012). As regards the empowerment of numerical and mathematical abilities using technology, a research showed that students who resolved the problems in the context of a computer story treatment had a considerable higher achievement than students who solved the problems in the context of a paper story and isolated word problems treatments (Gunbas 2015). Thus, the development of computer-based interventions seems to represent an excellent choice to promote the enrichment of specific cognitive skills underpinning scholastic achievements (e.g., counting, reading) in a playful fashion, where children learn while they interact with some avatars presented on the computer screen.

Most literature focuses the attention on the number line trainings, starting from the beneficial effect of paper–pencil tools on children's numerical development and their mathematics achievement (Klein et al. 2013; Moeller et al. 2015).

However, according to Pitchford (2015) technology can effectively promote the empowerment of mathematical skills in preschoolers if the software is carefully designed to actively engage the child in the learning processes and if the presented contents are developed consistently with the curriculum activities, which, in turn, must take in account the cognitive developmental stage reached by the user.

This fact sometimes can be due to limitations in its design and content (Yelland & Kilderry 2010) we can state, the in this case both modalities used as complementary to the curricular teacher activities are shown good results in numerical acuity enhancement in kindergarten.

REFERENCES

Afshari, M. et al., 2009. Factors Affecting Teachers' Use of Information and Communication Technology. *Online Submission*, 2(1), pp.77–104.

Agus, M. et al., 2015. The measurement of treatment effects in mathematical abilities: Comparing trainings in pencil-and-paper and computerised formats. In *XXI IMEKO World Congress*. IMEKO. Available at: http://www.scopus.com/inward/record.url?eid=2-s2.0-84951184841&partnerID=tZOtx3y1.

American Psychiatric Association, 2013. *DSM 5*, American Psychiatric Association.

Aubrey, C., Godfrey, R. & Dahl, S., 2006. Early mathematics development and later achievement: Further evidence. *Mathematics Education Research Journal*, 18(1), pp.27–46. Available at: http://link.springer.com/10.1007/BF03217428.

Aunio, P., Heiskari, P., Luit, J.E.H. van, & Vuorio, J., 2014. The development of early numeracy skills in kindergarten in low-, average- and high-performance groups. *Journal of Early Childhood Research*, 13(1), pp.3–16. Available at: http://ecr.sagepub.com/cgi/doi/10.1177/1476718X14538722.

Belacchi, C. et al., 2008. *Manuale CPM*, Firenze: Organizzazioni Speciali.

Booth, J.L. & Siegler, R.S., 2008. Numerical Magnitude Representations Influence Arithmetic Learning. *Child Development*, 79(4), pp.1016–1031. Available at: http://dx.doi.org/10.1111/j.1467-8624.2008.01173.x.

Butterworth, B., 1999. *The mathematical brain*, Macmillan.

Caponi, B. et al., 2012. Test MeMa. Valutare la metacognizione, gli atteggiamenti negativi e l'ansia in matematica.

Cerda, G. et al., 2015. Explanatory Model of Emotional-Cognitive Variables in School Mathematics Performance: A Longitudinal Study in Primary School. *Frontiers in Psychology*, 6. Available at: http://www.frontiersin.org/Journal/Abstract.aspx?s=346&name=educational_psychology&ART_DOI=10.3389/fpsyg.2015.01363.

Cornoldi, C., 2007. *Difficoltà e disturbi dell'apprendimento*. Il Mulino. Milano.

Dehaene, S., 2011. *The number sense: How the mind creates mathematics*, Oxford University Press.

Dehaene, S., Bossini, S. & Giraux, P., 1993. The mental representation of parity and number magnitude. *Journal of Experimental Psychology: General*, 122(3), pp.371–396.

Desoete, A. et al., 2012. Can we predict mathematical learning disabilities from symbolic and non-symbolic comparison tasks in kindergarten? Findings from a longitudinal study. *British Journal of Educational Psychology*, 82(1), pp.64–81. Available at: http://dx.doi.org/10.1348/2044-8279.002002.

Espy, K.A. et al., 2004. The contribution of executive functions to emergent mathematic skills in preschool children. *Developmental neuropsychology*, 26(1), pp.465–86. Available at: http://www.scopus.com/inward/record.url?eid=2-s2.0-3943075808&partnerID=tZOtx3y1.

Gunbas, N., 2015. Students' mathematics word problem-solving achievement in a computer-based story. *Journal of Computer Assisted Learning*, 31(1), pp.78–95. Available at: http://dx.doi.org/10.1111/jcal.12067.

Hasselhorn, 2013. Fostering early numerical skills at school start in children at risk for mathematical achievement problems: A small sample size training study. *International education studies*, 6(3), p.213.

Jordan, N.C. et al., 2007. Predicting First-Grade Math Achievement from Developmental Number Sense Trajectories. *Learning Disabilities Research & Practice*, 22(1), pp.36–46. Available at: http://doi.wiley.com/10.1111/j.1540-5826.2007.00229.x.

Klein, E. et al., 2013. Processing pathways in mental arithmetic--evidence from probabilistic fiber tracking. *PloS one*, 8(1), p.e55455.

Krajewski, K. & Schneider, W., 2009. Exploring the impact of phonological awareness, visual-spatial working memory, and preschool quantity-number competencies on mathematics achievement in elementary school: Findings from a 3-year longitudinal study. *Journal of Experimental Child Psychology*, 103(4), pp.516–531.

Kroesbergen, E.H., van 't Noordende, J.E. & Kolkman, M.E., 2014. Training working memory in kindergarten children: Effects on working memory and early numeracy. *Child Neuropsychology*, 20(1), pp.23–37. Available at: http://dx.doi.org/10.1080/09297049.2012.736483.

Lefevre, J.A. et al., 2010. Pathways to Mathematics: Longitudinal Predictors of Performance. *Child Development*, 81(6), pp.1753–1767. Available at: http://doi.wiley.com/10.1111/j.1467-8624.2010.01508.x.

Loosbroek, E. Van & Smitsman, A., 1990. Visual perception of numerosity in infancy. *Developmental Psychology*, 26(6), pp.916–922. Available at: http://doi.apa.org/getdoi.cfm?doi=10.1037/0012-1649.26.6.911.b.

Lucangeli, D., De Candia, C. & Poli, S., 2012. SVILUPPARE L'INTELLIGENZA NUMERICA 3.

Lucangeli, D., Poli, S. & Molin, A., 2003. *L'intelligenza numerica*, Trento: Erickson.

Lucangeli, D., Poli, S. & Molin, A., 2010. Sviluppare l'intelligenza numerica I.

Magnuson, K.A., Meyers, M.K. & Ruhm, C.J., 2004. Inequality in Preschool Education and School Readiness. *American Educational Research Journal*, 41(1), pp.115–157. Available at: http://aer.sagepub.com/cgi/doi/10.3102/00028312041001115.

Malofeeva, E. V, 2005. *Meta-analysis of mathematics instruction with young children*, ProQuest.

Mascia, M.L. et al., 2016. Enhancement in Mathematical Abilities: A System Approach. In G. Minati, M. R. Abram, & E. Pessa, eds. *Towards a Post-Bertalanffy Systemics SE - 25*. Contemporary Systems Thinking. Springer International Publishing, pp. 243–249. Available at: http://dx.doi.org/10.1007/978-3-319-24391-7_25.

Mascia, M.L. et al., 2015. The development and empowerment of mathematical abilities: The impact of pencil and paper and computerised interventions for preschool children. In *COGNITION AND EXPLORATORY LEARNING IN THE DIGITAL AGE (CELDA 2015)*. ERIC, pp. 59–68. Available at: http://files.eric.ed.gov/fulltext/ED562093.pdf#page=76.

Melhuish, E.C. et al., 2008. Effects of the home learning environment and preschool center experience upon literacy and numeracy development in early primary school. *Journal of Social Issues*, 64(1), pp.95–114. Available at:

http://doi.wiley.com/10.1111/j.1540-4560.2008.00550.x.

Meneses, J. et al., 2012. Internet in teachers' professional practice outside the classroom: Examining supportive and management uses in primary and secondary schools. *Computers & Education*, 59(3), pp.915–924. Available at: http://www.sciencedirect.com/science/article/pii/S0360131512000954.

Missall, K.N. et al., 2012. Concurrent and Longitudinal Patterns and Trends in Performance on Early Numeracy Curriculum-Based Measures in Kindergarten Through Third Grade. *Assessment for Effective Intervention*, 37(2), pp.95–106. Available at: http://aei.sagepub.com/cgi/doi/10.1177/1534508411430322.

Moeller, K. et al., 2015. Computers in mathematics education – Training the mental number line. *Computers in Human Behavior*, 48, pp.597–607.

Molin, A., Poli, S. & Lucangeli, D., 2007. *Batteria Intelligenza Numerica 4-6 [Battery for Numerical Intelligence]*, Trento: Erickson.

Morgan, P.L., Farkas, G. & Wu, Q., 2009. Five-Year Growth Trajectories of Kindergarten Children With Learning Difficulties in Mathematics. *Journal of Learning Disabilities* . Available at: http://ldx.sagepub.com/content/early/2009/03/19/0022219408331037.abstract.

Navarro, J.I. et al., 2012. Longitudinal study of low and high achievers in early mathematics. *British Journal of Educational Psychology*, 82(1), pp.28–41.

Newstead, K., 1998. Aspects of Children's Mathematics Anxiety. *Educational Studies in Mathematics*, 36(1), pp.53–71. Available at: http://link.springer.com/10.1023/A:1003177809664.

Nutta, J., 2013. Is computer-based grammar instruction as effective as teacher-directed grammar instruction for teaching L2 structures? *Calico Journal*, 16(1), pp.49–62.

Penna, M.P., Celani, E. & Bonfiglio, N.S., 2002. The Role of Knowledge Management as a Key Tool for Companies to deal with the Turbulent Environment: A Survey. In G. Minati & E. Pessa, eds. *Emergence in Complex, Cognitive, Social, and Biological Systems SE - 25*. Springer US, pp. 313–320. Available at: http://dx.doi.org/10.1007/978-1-4615-0753-6_25.

Piaget, J. & Inhelder, B., 1958. *The growth of logical thinking from childhood to adolescence: An essay on the construction of formal operational structures*, Routledge.

Pitchford, N.J., 2015. Development of early mathematical skills with a tablet intervention: a randomized control trial in Malawi. *Frontiers in psychology*, 6, p.485. Available at: http://www.ncbi.nlm.nih.gov/pubmed/25954236.

Raven, J.C., 1958. *Guide to using the Coloured Progressive Matrices*, Oxford, England: H. K. Lewis & Co.

Riccomini, P.J. & Smith, G.W., 2011. Introduction of response to intervention in mathematics. In R. G. & R. Newman-Gonchar, ed. *Understanding RTI in Mathematics. Proven methods and applications*. Baltimore: Paul H. Brookes Publishing Co, pp. 1–16.

Rinaldi, L. & Girelli, L., 2012. The role of number-space associations in preschoolers' numerical competence. *Giornale italiano di psicologia*, 39(4), pp.931–940.

Rubinsten, O. & Tannock, R., 2010. Mathematics anxiety in children with developmental dyscalculia. *Behavioral and brain functions : BBF*, 6(1), p.46. Available at: http://behavioralandbrainfunctions.biomedcentral.com/articles/10.1186/1744-9081-6-46.

Sammons, P. et al., 2004. The impact of pre-school on young children's cognitive attainments at entry to reception. *British Educational Research Journal*, 30(5), pp.691–712. Available at: http://doi.wiley.com/10.1080/0141192042000234656.

Sandford, R. et al., 2006. Teaching with Games: Using commercial off-the-shelf computer games in formal education. *Teaching with Games*, teachingwi, p.61. Available at: http://www.futurelab.org.uk/research/teachingwithgames/report_01.htm#1.

Sella, F. et al., 2016. Training numerical skills with the adaptive videogame "The Number Race": A randomized controlled trial on preschoolers. *Trends in Neuroscience and Education*, 5(1), pp.20–29. Available at: http://www.sciencedirect.com/science/article/pii/S2211949316300035.

Slavin, R.E., 2013. Effective programmes in reading and mathematics: lessons from the Best Evidence Encyclopaedia 1. *School Effectiveness and School Improvement*, 24(4), pp.383–391.

Starkey, P., Klein, A. & Wakeley, A., 2004. Enhancing young children's mathematical knowledge through a pre-kindergarten mathematics intervention. *Early Childhood Research Quarterly*, 19(1), pp.99–120. Available at: http://www.sciencedirect.com/science/article/pii/S0885200604000031.

Vanderlinde, R., Aesaert, K. & van Braak, J., 2014. Institutionalised ICT use in primary education: A multilevel analysis. *Computers & Education*, 72, pp.1–10. Available at: http://www.sciencedirect.com/science/article/pii/S0360131513002923.

Wilson, A.J. & Räsänen, P., 2008. Effective interventions for numercacy difficulties/disorders. *Encyclopedia of Language and Literacy Development*, pp.1–11.

Yelland, N. & Kilderry, A., 2010. Becoming numerate with information and communications technologies in the twenty-first century. *International Journal of Early Years Education*, 18(2), pp.91–106. Available at: http://dx.doi.org/10.1080/09669760.2010.494426 .

A VIDEO GAME FOR LEARNING BRAIN EVOLUTION: A RESOURCE OR A STRATEGY?

Luisa Fernanda Barbosa Gomez, Maria Cristina Bohorquez Sotelo, Naydu Shirley Roja Higuera and Brigitte Julieth Rodriguez Mendoza
Universidad Manuela Beltrán. Km 2 Centro Chia Cajicá, Colombia

ABSTRACT

Learning resources are part of the educational process of students. However, how video games act as learning resources in a population that has not selected the virtual formation as their main methodology? The aim of this study was to identify the influence of a video game in the learning process of brain evolution. For this purpose, the opinions of the video game players were categorized into two groups (learning and entertainment) through a qualitative analysis in ATLAS.ti software. Then, the correlation between the grade obtained in the exam and the advance of the game was assessed using a Spearman correlation test in SPSS. Finally, an analysis of variance was performed taking into account the opinions categories (learning and entertainment), the advance in the game and the score of the exam. We found a low correlation ($\rho = 0.336$) between the advance in the video game and the score in the exam. Next, we found no effect on how the players perceive the entertainment and the learning during the game in how well they perform neither in the exam nor in the advance of the video game ($p>0,05$). Therefore, it is clear for this specific case the need for different instructional strategies and integration to complement the role of a video game when learning brain evolution.

KEYWORDS

Video game, learning, virtual learning object

1. INTRODUCTION

We are living in the digital age. In this age, rethinking the way of teaching and learning is essential. As part of this transformation, new tools have emerged. Del Moral et al, (2010) states that opportunities for design, development and innovation offered by Web 2.0, along with support structures and collaborative tools to accompany the process of teaching and learning in the network, allow a reformulation of approach to e-learning, leading to an opening and constant change in the shared construction of knowledge that can establish a set of digital resources for educational purposes, which can be used in learning environments supported by technology, commonly known as virtual learning objects (VLO).

According to the above and within the educational purpose set out in the portal *Colombia Aprende* ("Colombia learns", 2016) a VLO must obey at least three components to ensure a structure of basic information: the definition of content to be treated, the structure of activities focused on learning and the contextualization of its elements. In addition, Cuervo (2011) noted that for a VLO to fulfill a significant educational structure and value it is necessary to accomplish the characteristics described in Figure 1.

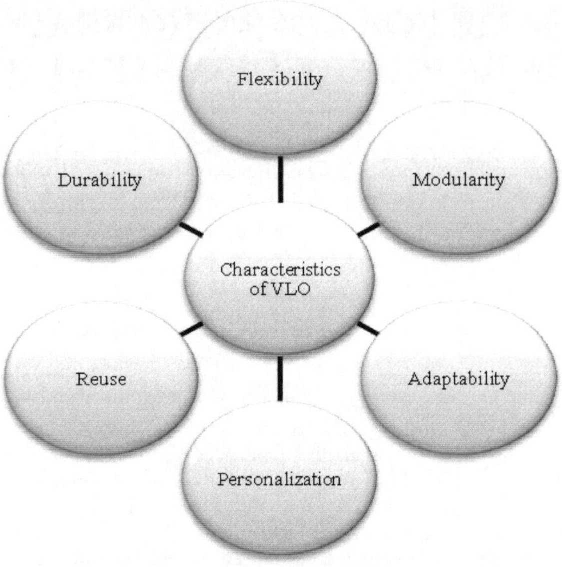

Figure 1. Characteristics of a good VLO as described by Cuervo (2011)

The features described in Figure 1 offer a structure that allows exploiting adequately the contents of a VLO (Del Blanco et al, 2011). This implies that as part of the modularity of a VLO, several tools can be used. For instance, video games or digital games. Video games appear in the school system as a way of including artifacts and own cultural symbols of this era. They are the icon of interactivity in virtual spaces, and offer the possibility of obtaining immediate response depending on the actions of users and the ability to handle large amounts of information along with their distant mass consumption. Because of this, video games are an alternative to the innovation and motivation characteristic of online educational environments.

Initial references of working with video games can be found by 1998, as described by Molinas (2005). In his work, part of the Grup F9 project developed in Spain, video games were used as a tool to achieve significant learning with students with learning difficulties. Nowadays, there are several cases of video games developed with specific curricular contents (Oblinger, 2006) that are used to teach. With them, it is proposed that students build knowledge and design strategies that involve higher order cognitive functions as attention, perception, memory, problem solving and understanding of some topics previously defined by the teaching and production teams.

Investigation related to video games in pedagogy focuses on primary and secondary education, as evidenced in numerous publications (Smith & Pellegrini, 2008). However, video game research focused on a college level is very poor. In general, there is a positive correlation between the "serious games" as mentioned by Rodriguez and Gomes (2013) and the impact of these on teaching and learning (Bai *et al.,* 2012; Ritterfeld *et al.*, 2009 and Kebritchi, *et al*., 2010). These studies found an influence of video games on the results in mathematics, and highlight the multimodality and interactivity of the game. On the other hand, there are also research studies that found little influence of video games on education (Friedman & Saponara, 2008; Ketamo & Suominen, 2008; Anetta *et al.*, 2009). One of these investigations specifically assessed comprehension of biology concepts and failed to find improvement after using video games.

In this document we describe the research conducted by our group of teachers in the framework of processes of virtual training, to question the role that digital content – specifically video games-, play in the learning process of students enrolled in a virtual course as part of their minor. These virtual courses are mandatory for all students. Given that virtual contents occupy a central place in the VLO, it is essential for the techno-pedagogical design of virtual courses to investigate the relationship between video games and the learning they promote. When asked for the learning and the quality of these courses one finds a gap between objectives and achievements, which contributes to unveil the relevance that video games have in online education, a field still under construction.

This research evaluates the influence a video game has on learning brain evolution and therefore contributes to the understanding of virtual education processes at a college level that use video games as an innovative and alternative strategy of teaching specific content.

2. BODY OF PAPER

2.1 Population

In this research we assessed the learning process of 431 students (17 - 26 years old) from the Manuela Beltran University (Bogotá, Colombia). As part of their minor, every student in the university has to take the virtual course in basic neuroscience, the one under study, which means the students belong to various disciplines.

2.2 Methods

We designed a game called "The brain evolution game" in order to teach brain evolution. We asked the students to play the game, and noted how far they reached on it. According to how many levels they were able to complete, we assigned a grade from 0 (the student did not complete any level) to 5 (the student finished the game). Then, we designed an exam that questioned concepts related to brain evolution. After the students played the game, we asked them to take the exam. Again, according to how many questions they answered correctly, we assigned a grade ranging from 0 (the student did not get any correct answer) to 5 (the student answered correctly all the questions). Next, we correlated these two grades and performed a Spearman's rank correlation coefficient in SPSS Statistics (SPSS Inc, version 17.0, Chicago).

Furthermore, we asked the students to rate their experience with the video game, writing their opinions in a forum. Then, we categorized those opinions. To do that, we created two main clusters, named "Entertainment" and "Learning". For the qualitative analysis we used the Atlas Ti software (version 7, USA) and classified each participant's opinion into one of three categories inside each cluster: "high", "medium" or "low". This means, for example, that one participant that expressed about the game as "[it was] an excellent experience, I had so much fun playing it and learned a lot about brain evolution" was categorized as "high" inside both the entertainment ("he had much fun") and the learning ("he learned a lot") clusters. Next, we analyzed the relationship between the categorization in each cluster and the grades in the game and the exam. For this, we performed a Krukal-Wallis test using the software Statistix (version 8, USA). In total, we analyzed 153 participations related to "entertainment" and 285 related to "learning".

2.3 The Brain Evolution Game

Definitions related to digital games vary. However, digital games do have in common that they all provide visual information to one or more players, accept input from the player(s), and use a set of programmed rules. All this inside a sensory interface and a story that adds emotional appeal (Oblinger, 2006). The games that are designed to teach something are also part of the category called "edutainment", which comes from the words "education" and "entertainment". Here, we studied a digital game called "The brain evolution game" that falls into the classification of edutainments as it tries to use entertainment with the development of purely curricular contents. Moreover, this game is a role game, where the player assumes the role of a creature (Oblinger, 2006). To further describe the game, we used the criteria presented by Gross-Salvat (2000) and summarized it in Table 1.

Table 1. Description of the brain-evolution-game according to the criteria used by Gross-Salvat (2000)

Product description		
Name	The brain evolution game	
Game description	The game consists of an avatar that should be controlled by the player using the arrow keys. The avatar starts as a round structure, representing a single-celled organism. The objective is to make the avatar "evolve". To evolve, the avatar must eat "nutritious food", and avoid "toxic food". Also, at the beginning of each level there is a 3 to 6-minutes video that gives information about evolution. During each level, a set of pop-up windows appear giving the player more information of the evolution and the nervous system of a particular group of animals. Moreover, during each level the player must answer several questions related to the given information. If the player manages to feed the avatar and answer the questions correctly, they complete the level. As the player completes a level, the avatar "evolves": it changes from a single cell to a lobster-like representation, to a fish, to an amphibian-like body, to a monkey, and finally reaches a cavern-man-like shape. The game has twelve levels with increasing complexity.	
Type	Simulation	
Language	Spanish	
¿How important is language for the player?	Very important.	
Pedagogical criteria		
Main type of contents in the game	Concepts	
Related area of knowledge	Natural sciences	
Conceptual content of the game	Evolution of living organisms, and the characteristics of their nervous system.	
Procedures	Psychomotor skills.	o Visual-motor coordination: High o Laterality: Low o Space organization: Medium
	Retention of information.	o Attention: High o Memory: High
	Creative skills.	NO
	Analytical skills.	NO
	Metacognitive skills.	NO

The brain evolution game was designed for teaching nervous system evolution, as part of a virtual course given to every student in the university. So, it can be further classified as a "*serious game*", an application designed and built by a group of professionals who have an intention and a pedagogical approach (Rodriguez & Gomes, 2013).

2.4 Playing and Learning

To assess how the Brain evolution game rendered specific knowledge to its players, we evaluated the grades players got in the exam and correlated them with how much they advanced in the game. The results are shown in Figure 2. If the game is a real edutainment, then one would expect to see a positive correlation between these two variables. However, we found a weak correlation (ρ=0,336; n=431, Spearman's rank correlation coefficient, SPSS Statistics) between them. The results indicate that either the game is not achieving the learning process it intends, or it is not appropriate to assess learning measuring the grade in an exam. Both possibilities have been discussed in several studies (Buckingham, 2008).

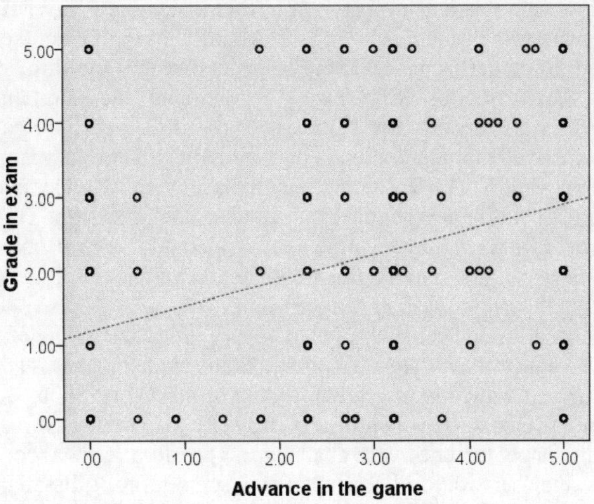

Figure 2. Relationship between the advance in the game the students had –measured as a grade according to how many levels they passed, and the grade they got in the exam. n=431

Several authors have shown that video games enhance the learning process of natural sciences. For instance, Kebritchi *et al.* (2010) showed an enhanced performance in tests that needed algebraic calculations in students that had previously played a video game. However, other authors (see Anetta *et al.,* 2009) have proven that when learning biology, the students that played a serious game did not show a better understanding of the concepts than a control group. Because we could not find a significant correlation between how far the students reached in the game and how well they performed in the exam, our results support the studies in the line of Anetta *et al.* (2009), in which the mere playing of a serious game does not improve the acquisition of concepts of the topic the video game is approaching.

One point that must be taken into consideration in the light of our results is game designing. Some studies that have found a positive correlation between video games and learning highlight as important characteristics the multimodality and the interactivity of the game. Although these two characteristics are also present in the brain evolution game, we did not find this correlation. Moreover, Kritzenberger (2010) discusses the characteristics that video games should have in order to improve the user experience. He concludes that one of the things that should be taken care of when designing serious games is that they should resemble as much as possible the commercial video games, given that serious games are often boring to users because they focus on the pedagogical dimension.

Next, we categorized the perception of the players in relation to the game, and assigned a level inside the clusters "entertainment" and "learning". We assessed the effect the categories had on how much the students advanced in the game and how well they performed in the exam. The results are represented in Figure 3 and Figure 4.

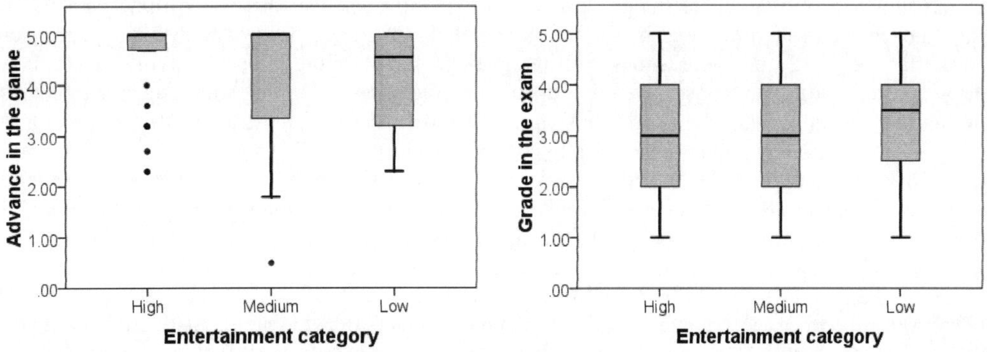

Figure 3. Advance in the game and grade in the exam according to the perception of entertainment players had during the game. n=153

One would expect to see a relationship between how entertaining a player finds a game and how far they reach on it. However, this was not the case for the Brain Evolution Game (see Figure 3) as no significant differences were found in the performance of the students that fell into three different entertainment levels (p=0,3078; n=153; Krukal-Wallis test; Statistix 8). Furthermore, the entertainment the player finds in the game does not affect how well they perform in the exam (p=0,4923; n=153; Krukal-Wallis test; Statistix 8).

It has been widely reported that motivation is one of the most important factors that drive learning. Some have said that "when motivation dies, learning dies and playing stops" (Gee, 2003). One of the definitions of motivation is the "learner's willingness to make an extended commitment to engage in a new area of learning (diSessa, 2000)". Good games should be highly motivated to many people. Although we found many students rating the game as "highly entertaining" this motivation they reported did not helped them improve neither in the advance on the game itself, nor in the exam.

This could be understood if one considers several possibilities. First, one of the most recurrent comments students made on the game was its slow response. Some authors propose that "entrainment, not to be confused with entertainment, which is the careful timing of moves, (...) the pace of the game, elicits a deep rooted connection with the character, which results in a sense of flow" (Squire, 2013). Without this sense of flow, the abilities are no longer matched with challenges. Therefore, a good video game must have these flow experiences; otherwise the user would likely experience some level of dissatisfaction with the game. In our case, we indeed found some dissatisfaction which could affect the engagement students had with the game and in that way with the contents on it. Secondly, game-based learning is not just creating games for students to play. It requires the design of learning activities that can incrementally introduce concepts, and guide users towards an end goal (Pho & Dinscore, 2015).

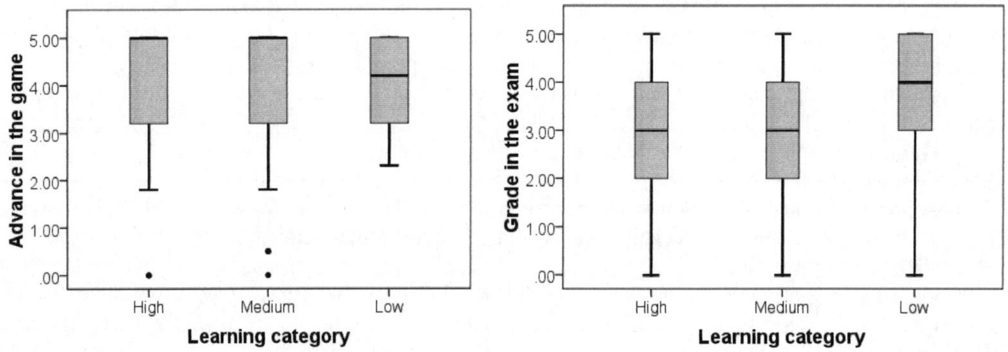

Figure 4. Advance in the game and grade in the exam according to the perception of learning players had during the game

In the Brain Evolution Game we did not find a relationship between the appreciation of learning a player had (i.e. how much they feel they learned) and the performance in the game (p=0,2316; Krukal-Wallis test; Statistix 8) or the exam (p=0,0709; Krukal-Wallis test; Statistix 8), as can be seen in Figure 4. If one considers that the behavior in an exam is a good measure of learning, then our results indicate that the game is not achieving the player's learning. At this point one must consider that the learning potential of games should be merged with how the game is used. As Van Eck (2006) describes: "simply using games may not be very effective; use is not synonymous with integration. What is more important is to consider how to add games to the educational tool set, blending them with other activities. Integration requires an understanding of the medium and its alignment with the subject, the instructional strategy, the student's learning style, and intended outcomes. Integration of games into curricula is much more likely to be successful than mere game use". Also, both meaning making and participation are key factors in the development and the application of a good video game. These genuine and deeply rooted learning opportunities can only be found in games that offer players the ability to construct goals, strategies, and theories about the game system (Squire, 2013).

One of the drawbacks to overcome in academic training processes including video games as the central element of learning is the difficulty of learning from games itself and the problem of establishing the relationships between video games and the curriculum content (Buckingham, 2008). With our study we find that, as Buckingham (2008) proposes, designing a video game should carefully think the way the curriculum contents are approached. We hypothesized that the Brain evolution game is not achieving the learning process it intends because it lacks an explicit relation between the learning objectives, the academic contents and the elements of the game.

The 2014 NMC Horizon Report lists games and gamification as a trend in higher education with an adoption timeframe of two to three years (Pho & Dinscore, 2015). We propose that, in this era of increasing gamification, where the idea is that video games can add an extra level of motivation and incentive to education activities, it is very important for teachers and game developers to consider the conditions that render actual game-based learning. Our results show that careful planning of games and related activities is crucial. Moreover, coming back to our initial question, we propose that video games can be a resource inside a learning strategy. As our results show, the mere act of playing a video game does not imply learning of specific curricular contents, so this resource should be used inside a planned learning strategy that goes beyond the act of playing.

3. CONCLUSION

In this study we did not find a positive influence of one video game in learning brain evolution. The correlations found are weak or non-existent between the advance in the game and the grade the students got in an exam designed to measure learning. Our results give information to take into account when designing VLOs and when intending to transform the relationships that take place in the virtual learning spaces: between the students and knowledge, content, learn and exams involved in the processes of massive formation in virtual education. Our results suggest that a video game is a learning resource that must be carefully planned inside a learning strategy in order to integrate the curricular content and in that way to successfully influence the learning process.

REFERENCES

Annetta L.A., Minogue J., Holmes S.Y. & Cheng M.T. (2009) Investigating the impact of video games on high school students' engagement and learning about genetics. *Computers & Education,* 53, 74–85.

Bai, H., Pan, W., Hirumi, A., & Kebritchi, M. (2012). Assessing the effectiveness of a 3-D instructional game on improving mathematics achievement and motivation of middle school students. *British Journal of Educational Technology*, 43(6), 993–1003.

Buckingham, D, 2008. *Más allá de la tecnología: Aprendizaje infantil en la era de la cultura digital*. Ediciones Manantial SRL, Buenos Aires, Argentina.

COLOMBIA APRENDE, sf. Objetivos Virtuales de aprendizaje e Informativos. Disponible en: http http://www.colombiaaprende.edu.co/html/directivos/1598/article-172369.html

Cuervo, M. et al, 2011. Objetos de aprendizaje, un estado del arte. *Proceedings Entramado*. Cali, Colombia, pp.176–189.

Del Blanco Á. et al, 2011. Análisis del uso del estándar SCORM para la integración de juegos educativos. Proceedings IEEE-RITA. USA. pp. 118.

Del Moral, E. et al, 2010. Objetos de aprendizaje 2.0: Una nueva generación de contenidos en contextos conectivistas. *Proceedings Revista de educación a distancia*, (25). Murcia, España.

diSessa, A. A. (2000). *Changing Minds: Computers, Learning, and Literacy*. Cambridge, Mass.: MIT Press.

Friedman, R. y Saponara, A. (2008). Novice and expert collaboration in educational software development: evaluating epplication effectiveness. *Journal of Interactive Learning Research*, 19 (2), 271-292. Chesapeake: AACE.

Gee, JP. (2003). What Video Games Have to Teach Us About Learning and Literacy. *ACM Computers in Entertainment*, 1 (1).

Gros-Salvat, B., 2000. *El ordenador invisible: hacia la apropiación del ordenador en la enseñanza.* Gedisa Editorial, Barcelona, Spain.

Kebritchi, M., Hirumi, A., & Bai, H. (2010). The effects of modern mathematics computer games on mathematics achievement and class motivation. *Computers & Education*, 55(2), 427–443.

Ketamo, H. & Suominen, M. (2008). Learning-by-Teaching in Educational Games. En J. Luca y E. Weippl (Eds.), *Proceedings of World Conference on Educational Multimedia, Hypermedia and Telecommunications 2008*, 2954-2969. Chesapeake: AACE.

Kritzenberger, H. (2010). User Experience in digital game-based learning and serious games: towards the role of media design. *Proceedings of World Conference on Educational Multimedia, Hypermedia and Telecommunications 2010*. Canadá, 29-30 de junio.

Molinas, I, 2005. *Memoria de elefante: interrogantes sobre la incorporación de los videojuegos en la enseñanza*. En: Litwin, E. Tecnologías educativas en tiempos de Internet. Amorrortu editores, Buenos Aires, Argentina.

Oblinger, D., 2006. Simulations, games and learning. *ELI White Paper*, Educase learning Initiative.

Pho, A. & Dinscore, A. (2015). Game-based learning. *Tips and trends: Instructional technologies committee*, spring 2015.

Richard Van Eck, 2006. Digital Game-Based Learning: It's Not Just the Digital Natives Who Are Restless. *EDUCAUSE Review*, 41 (2).

Ritterfeld, U, Shen, C., Wang, H., Nocera, L., Wong, WL. (2009). Multimodality and Interactivity: Connecting properties of serious games with educational outcomes. *Cyberpsychology and Behavior*, 16 (6), 691-697.

Rodríguez, C. & Gomes, M., 2013. Videojuego y educación: Una visión panorámica de las investigaciones desarrolladas a nivel internacional. *Revista de Curriculum y formación del profesorado*, Vol.17, No. 2, pp 479-494.

Smith, P. K. & Pellegrini, A. (2008). *Learning Through Play, Encyclopedia on Early Childhood Development*. Centre of Exellence for Early Childhood Development.

Squire, K. (2013). Video Games and Learning: Teaching and Participatory Culture in the Digital Age. *Alberta Journal of Educational Research*, 59 (1), 129-132

COMMUNICATION VULNERABILITY IN THE DIGITAL AGE: A MISSED CONCERN IN CONSTRUCTIVISM

Fusa Katada
Waseda University, Faculty of Science and Engineering
3-4-1 Okubo, Shinjuku-ku, Tokyo 169-8555 Japan

ABSTRACT

The current wave of globalization aided by ubiquitous computing necessarily involves interaction and integration among people and human institutions worldwide. This has led to a worldwide awareness that professionals in academia need to have effective communication skills. Such communication-driven academic discourse puts much demand on language education, particularly tied to English as a medium of global communication. There is, however, a critical but unidentified gap. The targeted students are technically and academically capable but often with general communication difficulties, and such a student population is growing. This poses a challenge to constructivist classroom that is marked by student-centered, interactive, and group-oriented learning. This paper reports on exploratory studies on the temperamental, autistic tendencies of university students carried out in Japan and their preference in academic subjects including the English language. Results indicate that the university students are in general more toward drawing into themselves; that is, they are neither sociable nor communicative. The survey also shows a clear preference for less communication-driven subjects within their major, as opposed to study of the more communication-driven English language. These findings indicate the necessity of calling for complementary constructivism that would accommodate a student population with communication vulnerabilities. As far as English classroom is concerned, the relevance of adopting ESP (English for Specific Purposes) is clarified, which focuses on the knowledge structure of the subjects that find the students' strength. ESP is expected to compensate for their communication vulnerabilities, and thus to offer a hint for a meaningful form of complimentary constructivism for educational settings.

KEYWORDS

Complementary Constructivism, Communication Vulnerability, Science and Technology, ESP

1. INTRODUCTION

Though the emergence of the educational concept of constructivism has its roots in the Socratic dialogue, its evolution is relatively new. The paradigm change, from behaviorism to constructivism, arose in the 1950s in accordance with an increasing awareness of each child's natural inclination toward an autonomous, active learner. Among most influential constructivists are Piaget, Dewey, Vygotsky, and Bruner, to name only a few. As Table 1, taken from Educational Broadcasting Corporation (2004), shows, constructivist classroom focuses on communication-driven learning that is student-centered, interactive, dialogue-based, group learning. Noteworthy constructivists in relation to the digital age are Seymour Papert, John D. Bransford, and Roger Shank. They are all leading experts on integrating computer technology in teaching within the environment of constructivism where children are considered active learners; they learn by doing from experience.

There is, however, a missed concern that has never been pointed out explicitly till today, namely the growing student population with communication vulnerabilities. The students are technically and academically competent but they are neither sociable nor communicative, and yet there is a demand on them for good communication skills. Under the constructivism environment how should communication-driven language classroom deal with such a student population? The digital age seems to be calling for complementary constructivism that can accommodate students with communication difficulties.

Table 1. The Paradigm Shift in Classroom

	Traditional classroom	Constructivist classroom
1	Curriculum begins with the parts of the whole. Emphasizes basic skills.	Curriculum emphasizes big concepts, beginning with the whole and expanding to include the parts.
2	Strict adherence to fixed curriculum is highly valued.	Pursuit of student questions and interests is valued.
3	Materials are primarily textbooks and workbooks.	Materials include primary sources of material and manipulative materials
4	Learning is based on repetition.	Learning is interactive, building on what the student already knows.
5	Teachers disseminate information to students; students are recipients of knowledge.	Teachers have a dialogue with students, helping students construct their own knowledge.
6	Teacher's role is directive, rooted in authority.	Teacher's role is interactive, rooted in negotiation.
7	Assessment is through testing, correct answers.	Assessment includes student works, observations, and points of view, as well as tests. Process is as important as product.
8	Knowledge is seen as inert.	Knowledge is seen as dynamic, ever changing with our experience.
9	Students work primarily alone.	Students work primarily in groups.

While the field of language education gathers diverse case studies for 'know-how' types of practical outcomes, this paper is qualitative in nature with dual purposes. One is to raise an awareness of the critical gap which communication-driven constructivism faces with respect to the learners with communication difficulties. The other is to claim the necessity of calling for a model that would complement such constructivist classroom. This is done by reporting a quantitative exploratory survey conducted by the author on the students' temperamental (dispositional) tendencies associated with sociability and communicability and their preference for academic subject (i.e. subjects within their major versus the English language). Results clarify the relevance of ESP (English for Specific Purposes) which, by definition, uses learning materials specific to the learners' fields. Given the students' general communicative vulnerabilities, the results suggest that the communicative demands in tertiary education in general (and ESP classed in specific) be minimized. The paper thus concludes that a 'complementary constructivism' should be called for that would suit the digital age, although a new model is yet to come.

2. FACTS CHALLENGING CONSTRUCTIVISM

2.1 Communication Vulnerability in Communication-Driven Discourse

There has been a worldwide awareness that scientists and engineers need to have effective communication skills. A survey carried out in the USA, for example, reports that engineers and professionals in the field of technology spend half of their workplace hours on communication-related activities (Vest, Long, and Anderson, 1996). In line with this report is the result of another survey carried out in Australia, which shows that employers in computer science seek effective communication skills in graduates (Gruba and Al-Mahmood, 2004). Magno (2014) likewise reports on employers' similar demands for college graduates in Southeast Asia such as in the Philippines. Furthermore, JABEE (Japan Accreditation Board for Engineering Education), which was established in 1999 and became the first Asian nation member of the Washington Accord in 2005, emphasizes the importance of internationally endurable communication skills for engineers.

As specific academic discourse gets more and more communication-driven, the learner-needs appear to include skills that are associated with sociability and communicability. For example, Rose, Katada, Sheppard, and Manalo (2014) identify three basic areas of learner-needs:

(a) work collaboratively,

(b) communicate with industry and academic professionals, and

(c) write technical reports and documents.

Among the three, (a) and (b) are concerned with internal attributes of the learners and well suit the constructivist pedagogical design which focuses on communication-driven, interactive learning. It is evident that these attributes must be taken into account.

A challenge then arises because it is often the case that the targeted group of learners exhibits the opposite, autistic, attributes. They are often unsociable and not very communicative. It is noteworthy that such a population marked by communication difficulties or autistic traits keeps on growing. Many external factors may drive this increase, such as the growing awareness of autism, changes in diagnostic criteria, and more advanced screening tools (Wing and Potter, 2002; Cornwall, 2015). Yet, there is evidence that the prevalence of such a student population is rising.

2.2 Negative Connotations and Positive Overtones of Autistic Traits

The number of students who are academically capable or even gifted but who simultaneously have general communication difficulties is ever growing. This can be seen in the teachers' familiar comments: "the students are extremely shy and silent," "it's difficult to get them to talk," "I cannot communicate with them," "their culture is different from mine." Often, the students are beyond simple shyness; they are said to have autistic traits. *Digital teens* and *troublesome online youth groups* are the terms used by Bishop (2014) in educational settings, which refer to young people at the extreme end of the spectrum of sociability. Another expression used in this context is *digital natives*, which can be interpreted as an indication for the emergence of a new generation with communication vulnerability in digital age.

Every culture may find expressions for unsociable, non-communicative behaviors. *Geek* is a familiar English word; *otaku* and *asupe* are the closest common Japanese equivalents, both newly invented. While these expressions have negative connotations, Japanese culture brings positive overtones to some traditional expressions of these traits. Most specifically, *shokunin-katagi* 'artisan spirit' is a highly-valued characterization of skilled craftsmen who are often socially reticent, but with high tenacity and drive. The nation's vitality in global competence is often attributed to these traits.

It has been observed that professionals in science and technology have the tendency toward *geekish* or *artisanal* temperaments (dispositions). Baron-Cohen et al. (1998), for example, report that there is an association between science/math skills and autistic conditions, which is confirmed by their subsequent report on the autism-spectrum quotient (AQ) (Baron-Cohen et al., 2001). Silberman (2001) also suggests a link between the 'geek syndrome' and 'math-and-tech genes'.

The problem arises then because, as aforementioned, scientists and engineers are typical professionals who are required to have effective communication skills. As we will see in the next section, a student population with communication difficulties is no longer atypical in present-day academic communities. In order to cultivate effective curriculum development, educators must be aware of this ironical gap between communication-driven academic discourse and the learners' non-communicative dispositional nature.

2.3 The Prevalence on Campus

Unsociable, non-communicative temperaments and behaviors mark people with *developmental disorders,* which have come to be acknowledged only recently. Symptoms of developmental disorders are diverse, including ADHD (attention deficit hyperactivity disorder), HFA (high functioning autism), and AS (Asperger syndrome). With the new diagnostic standards of the *APA (*American Psychiatric Association) (1994) (see also WHO, 1990; 2007), developmental disorders have been subsumed under the label *ASD* (autism spectrum disorders), which is a continuum notion that ranges from the least to the highest degree of affectedness. Under the continuum interpretation, ASD is no longer perceived as a rare disorder.

Statistically, the prevalence of ASD keeps on increasing. In the USA 10% of the adult population may count as having ADHD alone (Hoshino, 2011). In California, the population affected by geek syndrome increased threefold during the 1990s and 85% of them are children (Silberman, 2001). As aforementioned, many factors are involved in this increase and an interpretation of the increase calls for careful attention (Honda et al., 2005). Nonetheless, a generally agreed view is that the affected population continues to grow.

For educational settings, the Ministry of Health, Labor and Welfare of Japan (2005-2006) reported that, out of 189 adults with ASD, two of them had graduate school degrees, 50 were four-year college graduates, and 16 were two-year junior college graduates. This totals nearly 40% of the affected individuals who had received a college education. Moreover, 117 of them (that is, over 60%) spent their entire school-lives in regular classes, not in classes with special needs. This indicates that the student population with ASD is large enough on regular campuses. I anticipate that such a situation is a worldwide reality.

Three areas of affected behavior typical of ASD are: (a) sociability, (b) communication, and (c) imagination (flexible thinking), which in this paper are subsumed under a single term 'communication vulnerability'. In constructivist classrooms, the students' communication vulnerability should be acknowledged as a voice for a new type of learner-needs.

3. EXPLORATORY SURVEY ON TEMPERATMENTAL TENDENCIES OF UNIVERSITY STUDENTS

Based on the established necessity of understanding learners' internal attributes in educational settings, I conducted an exploratory survey on temperamental tendencies and academic attitudes and behaviors, with special attention paid to one group of the target learners, namely students in science and technology. This section reports on part of the survey relevant to the issues raised in this paper.

3.1 Structure and Form of the Survey

The survey was conducted in the form of questionnaire consisting of Part I and Part II with three main purposes (1) – (3) stated below.[1] Part I, consisting of two categories (a) and (b), is directly linked to purpose (1); it is then expected to lead to achieving purpose (2). Part II, consisting of five categories (c) – (g), is linked to purpose (3); it is designed to see if the students' temperamental tendencies appear to pattern with their other academic behaviors. Subjects were two groups of undergraduate students: Group (1) consisting of science and technology majors (S&T) and Group (2) consisting of various other majors (Mixed).

<Part I>

category (a) 50 questions to measure the autism-spectrum quotient (AQ) (Baron-Cohen, at al., 2001)
category (b) 10 questions about the students' preference for academic subjects

<Part II>

category (c) 5 questions about critical thinking, taken from MSLQ (motivated strategies for learning questionnaire) (Pintrich and De Groot, 1990)
category (d) 9 questions from the self-efficacy section of MSLQ (Pintrich and De Groot, 1990)
category (e) 18 questions to measure Asian students' cognitive attitudes (Stapleton, 2002)
category (f) 8 questions out of 33 to major effects of critical thinking attitudes to decision making processes (Hirayama and Kusumi, 2004)
category (g) 24 questions on two types of self-control (Kruglanski, et al., 2000)

<Purposes>

(1) Capture temperamental tendencies of the undergraduate students and their preference in academic subjects including the subjects of their major and the English language.
(2) Construct an effective curriculum that fills in the gap between communication skills development and the students' characteristics associated with communication vulnerabilities.
(3) Examine whether the students' temperamental tendency is correlated with their other academic attitudes such as critical thinking, self-efficacy, etc.

<Subjects>

Group (1): 250 undergraduate students of science and technology (S&T Group)
Group (2): 200 undergraduate students of various majors (Mixed Group)

This paper limits itself to Part I only, given that the theme underlying Part II is beyond the scope of this paper.

---

[1] The survey has been expanded and conducted in developing countries such as in the Philippines (2015-2016), where linguistic backgrounds are far more complicated in both their mother-tongues and languages of education. Results have many implications for thought and language, nations' vitality, and most especially where English is situated. In my estimation, these issues are quite important when deploying language policy in education for the coming century. However, they are beyond the scope of the main concerns of this paper, and I leave relevant discussion to another opportunity of presentation.

3.2 Background for Part I

Baron-Cohen et al. (2001) constructed 50 questions in English as a self-administered instrument to assess the degree to which an adult with normal intelligence has traits associated with the autistic spectrum. This English version was transformed into a Japanese version by Wakabayashi et al. (2004). Both versions have been standardized with AQ (the autism-spectrum quotient) ranging from 1 to 50.

The AQ score of higher than 32 ($\geq$ 33) is a useful cut-off point for distinguishing individuals with clinically significant levels of autistic traits. This is based on the research results that, while 80% of adults with AS (Asperger syndrome) and HFA (high functioning autism) scored above 32 on the AQ scale, only 2% of the controls did so. In the same manner of standardizing, 26 is the score that can be interpreted as a cut-off point for no autistic traits. That the subject population with AS/HFA scored significantly higher than the controls in their surveys is shown in two distinct, maximally separated curves in Figure 1 in the following section3.3.1. The rightmost curve is for the population with AS/HFA and the leftmost is for the controls.

In the present report, category (a) of Part I consists of 50 questions adopted from the Japanese version to assess university students' autistic traits. It was expected that Group (1) students of science and technology (S&T) will show a higher degree of autistic traits than Group 2 students of various majors (Mixed).

Category (b) consists of 10 questions asking for the students' preferences for academic subjects including English. This is to probe where in academic domains the students' strength lie not only technically but also emotionally. It was expected that results will suggest pedagogical directions for curriculum design, especially in reference to communication-driven language subjects such as English and less-communication driven, knowledge-centered subjects such as mathematics, physics and chemistry.

3.3 Results and Analyses

3.3.1 Part I: Category (a)

The result in category (a) of the exploratory survey is shown in Table 2, which is overwritten in Figure 1 so that it can be easily seen in reference to the standardized interpretation of autistic traits explained above in section 3.2.

Table 2. AQ score ranges

Group	< 26	26 ≤	30 ≤	33 ≤	Total
(1) S&T	174 (69.6%)	76 (30.4%)	32 (12.8%)	18 (7.2%)	250 (100%)
(2) Mixed	109 (54.5%)	91 (45.5%)	41 (20.5%)	13 (6.5%)	200 (100%)

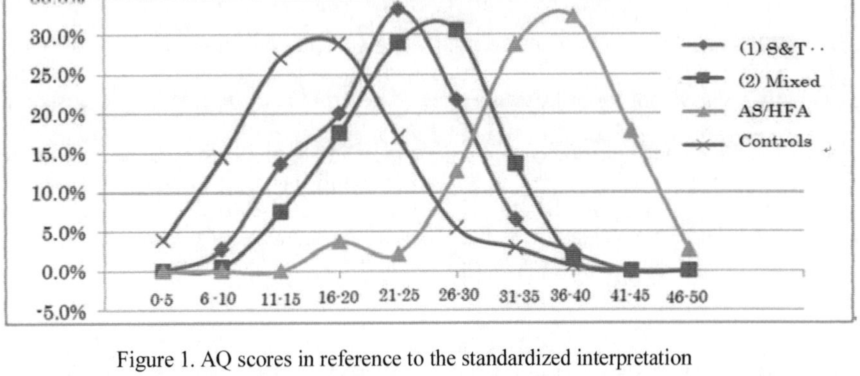

Figure 1. AQ scores in reference to the standardized interpretation

As Table 2 shows, those who scored higher than 32 (≥ 33) on the AQ scale appeared as: [S&T : Mixed] = [7.2% : 6.5%]. This indicates that there is no significant difference in clinically significant levels of autistic traits between the two groups. These percentages, however, are significantly higher than 2%, the corresponding standardized figure for the controls. Also noted in Figure 1 is that, in all score ranges up to 36-40, Group (2) (Mixed majors) scored slightly higher than Group (1) (Science & Technology majors). This is contrary to our expectation.

Figure 1 also shows that both of the two student groups fall between the controlled adults and the AS/HFA-diagnosed adults. This indicates that the students tend to draw into themselves more than the controlled adults do. This might be due to the youth-specific autistic tendency, which is consistent with the observation reported by previous studies (Baron-Cohen et al., 2001 and Wakabayashi et al., 2004). For the purpose of this paper, it is appropriate to interpret that the university students in general, regardless of their majors, are not particularly communicative. Such temperamental tendency is not in harmony with communication-driven constructivist classroom and must be taken into account when pedagogical designing takes place.

3.3.2 Part I: Category (b)

Unlike the results in category (a), the two groups appeared to exhibit a clear contrast in category (b) their preference for academic subjects. To the extent that is relevant in this paper, the results restricted to English, physics/chemistry, and mathematics are shown in Table 3.

Table 3. Preference for Academic Subjects

Group		English	Physics/Chemistry	Mathematics
(1) S&T	favored (+like)	87 (34.8%)	176 (70.4%)	171 (68.4%)
	unfavored (−like)	163 (65.2%)	74 (29.6%)	79 (31.6%)
	HT	0	60.96	50.06
(2) Mixed	favored (+like)	81 (40.5%)	73 (36.5%)	99 (49.5%)
	unfavored (−like)	119 (59.5%)	127 (63.5%)	101 (50.5%)
	HT	0	0.52	2.92

In Group (1) (science & technology majors), less than 35% of the students named English as their favorite subject, whereas over 65% responded that English is not a subject they favor or like. The majority of the students in science and technology appeared to feel that English is a hard subject to deal with. Noteworthy is a turnabout effect between English and hard science subjects. That is, the ratio of [35% (+like) vs. 65% (−like)] for English gets reversed into [70% (+like) vs. 30% (−like)] for physics/chemistry and mathematics. Under the null hypothesis that there is 'no difference with respect to English', this turnabout is salient enough going beyond the usual hypothetical range, as shown by extremely high HT (hypothesis testing) values: about 61 for physics/chemistry and 50 for mathematics.

One may say that this is not a surprise since the students are of science and technology major whose strength should lie in hard science subjects. Such rather unsurprising result, however, is a significant message for constructivist classroom for at least this targeted group of students.[2] This is discussed in the next section 3.4.

By contrast, the reversal phenomenon did not appear in Group (2) (mixed majors). In Table 3, the ratio of [(+like) vs. (−like)] goes from [40.5% vs. 59.5%] for English to [36.5% vs. 63.5%] for physics/chemistry to [49.5% vs. 50.5%] for mathematics. As HT values lower than 3.0 (critical value) for these hard science subjects show, the null hypothesis holds here; that is, for students of mixed majors there is no significant difference in the their preference between English and the hard science subjects.[3]

[2] It may not be so unsurprising as we think when cross-cultural data come into play. In fact, the survey carried out in the Philippines did not show such a drastic contrast between English and the hard science subjects in the group of students with similar science majors. Many complicated factors interplay to yield contrastive results between the two distinct cultures, and these themes are under careful inspections, and I leave extended discussion on comparative studies to another opportunity of presentation.

[3] Given the main issue of this paper being hard science majors, I leave detailed discussion on mixed majors to another opportunity of presentation.

3.4 Implications for Complementary Constructivism and ESP

The autistic traits measured by AQ did not appear to be tangibly attributable to science and technology majors. However, compared to the standardized controls, a significant number of the students, regardless of their majors, attained high scores on the AQ scale. In other words, it is general tendency that the university students draw into themselves; that is, they are neither sociable nor communicative. The survey appeared to show that such temperamental (dispositional) tendency associated with communication vulnerabilities is an issue relevant to tertiary education in general and must be taken into account for pedagogical designing.

In ordinary English language classroom, students of science and technology come to face double challenges; they are by nature neither communicative nor fond of English, even though English is the medium of global communication in the digital age and they need it. Supplementing these disadvantages, however, they have an advantage; that is, they are strong in hard science subjects.

Implications for constructivist language classroom seem to be clear. First of all, English language education (ELE) in tertiary education should be ESP (English for Specific Purposes), which by definition focuses on materials in the academic domains where targeted students' strength lies. ESP classroom for science and technology majors naturally uses materials from basic mathematics and physics/chemistry since these are the subjects that find the students' strength. The conceptual knowledge of these subjects functions as a cushion to reduce uncomfortable feelings or fears that the majority of the science students have towards communication-driven English classroom. The knowledge of hard science materials can be expected to compensate for the weakness they feel towards communication.

Second, autistic traits are most of the time beyond the individual's control. Thus, even though ESP is ultimately communication-oriented, it should not be unreasonable pedagogically if the demand on the students for sociability and communicability is minimized. ESP should rather concentrate on the universal knowledge of academic subjects in their major because understanding and explaining structured knowledge of the specialized fields do not require extensive human interaction, which is the learners' weak area. Less demanding human communication activities would hopefully function as an incentive to improve the learners' general communicative competence, which certainly is an essential ability for survival.

Finally, as pointed out by a reviewer, another medium of communication mediated by computers is on the rise. It is reported by McDowell (2015) that, through computer-mediated communications, learners diagnosed as having Asperger syndrome have opportunities for meaningful participation in group-work. Ironically, such a communication form and a generation with communication vulnerability are both the 'products' of digital age that are in harmony with each other. ESP and computer-mediated communication together may offer a hint to develop a meaningful form of complementary constructivism in education.

4. CONCLUSION

The emphasis of the field of language education has been on practical outcomes. This paper, by contrast, is qualitative in nature backed up by quantitative exploratory survey results. It demonstrated that there is a new type of concern, communication vulnerability in university students, which poses a challenge to communication-oriented constructivist classroom. Complementary constructivism must therefore be called for. Focusing on students of hard science majors and their communicative needs, the paper has shown that ESP (English for Specific Purposes) can be a solution. Although practical models are yet to come, ESP, together with some form of computer-mediated communication, is worth exploring for the development of potential models of complementally constructivist classroom in the digital age.

ACKNOWLEDGEMENT

This study is supported by Japan Society for Promotion of Science (JSPS), Grant-in-Aid for Exploratory Research No. 25590289 (2013-2016): Principal Investigator: Fusa Katada. My appreciation goes to participants of the survey for their understanding and cooperation. I would also like to thank two anonymous reviewers for their valuable comments on an earlier version of this paper. All shortcomings are mine.

REFERENCES

American Psychiatric Association: APA, 1994. *Diagnostic and Statistical Manual of Mental Disorders-IV: DSM-IV.*

Baron-Cohen, S., Bolton, P., Wheelwright, S., Short, L., Mead, G., Smith, A., and Scahill, V., 1998. Autism Occurs More Often in Families of Physics, Engineers, and Mathematics. In *Autism*, Vol. 2, pp 296-301.

Baron-Cohen, S., Wheelwright, S., Skinner, R., Martin, J., and Clubley, E., 2001. The Autism-Spectrum Quotient (AQ): Evidence from Asperger Syndrome/High-Functioning Autism, Males and Females, Scientists and Mathematicians. In *Journal of Autism and Developmental Disorders*, Vol. 31, pp 5-17.

Bishop, J., 2014. Digital Teens and the 'Antisocial Network': Prevalence of Troublesome Online Youth Groups and Internet Trolling in Great Britain. In *International Journal of E-Politics*, Vol. 5, No. 3, pp 1-15.

Cornwall, W., 2015. Autism Rates Are Up, but Is It Really on the rise? In *Health*. DOI: 10.1126/science.aaac8889.

Educational Broadcasting Corporation, 2004. Concept to Classroom: How does This Theory Differ from Traditional Ideas about Teaching and Learning? Retrieved from http://www.thirteen.org/edonline/concept2class/constructivism/index_sub1.html on 19 June, 2016.

Gruba, P. and Al-Mahmood, R., 2004. Strategies for Communication Skills Development. In *Proceedings of the Sixth Australasian Conference on Computing Education*, Vol. 30, pp 101-107.

Honda, H., Shimizu, Y., Imai, M., and Nitto, Y., 2005. Cumulative Incidence of Childhood Autism: A Total Population Study of Better Accuracy and Precision. In *Developmental Medicine and Child Neurology*, Vol. 47, No. 1, pp 10-18.

Hirayama, R. and Kusumi, T., 2004. Effects of Critical Thinking Attitudes to Decision Making Processes. In *Studies on Educational Psychology*, Vol. 52, pp 186-198. (written in Japanese)

Hoshino, Y., 2011. *Adults Who do not Recognize Developmental Disorders: Volume for Workplace*, Tokyo: Shodensha Shinsho. (written in Japanese)

Kruglanski, A.E., Thompson, E.P., Higgins, E.T., Atash, M.N., Pierro, A., and Shah, J.Y., 2000. To "Do the Right Thing" or To "Just Do It": Locomotion and Assessment as Distinct Self-Regulatory Imperatives. In *Journal of Personality and Social Psychology*, Vol. 79, No. 5, pp 793-815.

Magno, J., 2014. Needed Skills in the Workplace: A Survey of Employers' Perceptions of the Linguistics and Literature Majors. Paper presented at International Conference on Applied Linguistics and Language Education 2014. De La Salle University, Manila, Philippines. October 16-18, 2014.

McDowell, J., 2015. "A Black Swan in a Sea of White Noise: Using Technology-Enhanced Learning to Afford Educational Inclusivity for Learners with Asperger's Syndrome. In *Social Inclusion*, Vol. 3 No. 6, pp 7-15. DOI: 10.17645/si.v3i6.428.

Pintrich, R.R. and DeGroot, E.V., 1990. Motivational and Self-regulated Learning Components of Classroom Academic Performance, In *Journal of Educational Psychology*, Vol. 82, pp 33-40.

Rose, R., Katada, F., Sheppard, C., and Manalo, E., 2014. Addressing Challenges in a Large-scale ELT Program: Learner Needs, Teaching Approaches, and Learner Assessment. In *AILA World Congress 2014 Abstract Book,* p 50.

Silberman, S., 2001. The Geek Syndrome: Autism - and Its Milder Cousin Asperger's Syndrome - is Surging among the Children of Silicon Valley. Are Math-and-Tech Genes to Blame?, *Wired* 9.12, December 2001.

Stapleton, P., 2002. Critical Thinking in Japanese L2 Writing: Rethinking Tired Constructs, *ELT Journal* Vol. 56, No. 3, pp 250-257.

Vest, D., Long, M., and Anderson, T., 1966. Electrical Engineers' Perceptions of Communication Training and Their Recommendations for Curricular Change: Results of a National Survey. In *IEEE Transactional Communication*, Vol. 39, No. 1, pp 38-42.

Wakabayashi, A., Tojo, Y., Baron-Cohen, S., and Wheelwright, S., 2004. The Autism-Spectrum Quotient (AQ) Japanese Version: Evidence from High-Functioning Clinical Group and Normal Adults. In *The Japanese Journal of Psychology*, Vol. 75, No. 1, pp 78-84. (written in Japanese)

Wing, L. and Potter, D., 2002. The Apidemiology of Autistic Spectrum Disorders: Is the Prevalence Rising? In *Ment. Retard. Dev. Disabil. Res. Rev.,* Vol. 8, pp 151-161. DOI: 10.1002/mrdd.10029.

World Health Organization: WHO, 1990/2007. *Statistical Classification of Diseases and Related Health Problems-10: ICD-10*, International Statistical Institute: ISI.

ONLINE LEARNERS' NAVIGATIONAL PATTERNS BASED ON DATA MINING IN TERMS OF LEARNING ACHIEVEMENT

Sinan Keskin[1], Muhittin Sahin[2], Adem Ozgur[3] and Halil Yurdugul[2]
[1]*Yuzuncu Yil University*
Education Faculty, Department of Computer Education and Instructional Technology, Van, Turkey
[2]*Hacettepe University*
Education Faculty, Department of Computer Education and Instructional Technology, Ankara, Turkey
[3]*Usak University*
Education Faculty, Department of Computer Education and Instructional Technology, Usak, Turkey

ABSTRACT

The aim of this study is to determine navigational patterns of university students in a learning management system (LMS). It also investigates whether online learners' navigational behaviors differ in terms of their academic achievement (pass, fail). The data for the study comes from 65 third grade students enrolled in online Computer Network and Communication lesson in a state university. As the online learning environment, Moodle, an open source software, is used in this study. Navigational log records derived from database were converted into sequential database format. According to students' achievement (pass, failure) at the end of the academic term, these data were divided in two tables. Page connections of the users were transformed into interaction themes namely, homepage, content, discussion, messaging, profile, assessment, feedback and ask the instructor. Data transformed to sequential patterns by the researchers were organized in navigational pattern graphics by taking frequency and ratio into consideration. To test the difference between obtained patterns ratio test was conducted by means of z statistics. The findings of the research revealed that first and second order navigational patterns of passed and failed students in the online learning environment had similar features, but passed students allocated more time to interaction process.

KEYWORDS

Navigational pattern, data mining, online learner

1. INTRODUCTION

With the spread of ICT, its usage in the educational contexts has become prevalent. Especially by the virtue of Web 2.0 technologies, there has been significant progress in the user-system interaction. The principal aim of these technologies is to support learners' learning process and increase their learning performance (Richey, Silber, & Ely, 2008). Web technologies draw attention especially in terms of providing opportunities for time and place independent learning, supporting learners anywhere and anytime, updating teaching materials instantly, having an adaptive nature in accordance with learners' needs (Ally, 2008). Although they offer various advantages, it has been well accounted that self-directed students make better use of these technologies (Grow, 1991; Demir, Yasar, Sert, & Yurdugul, 2014). This fact can be interpreted in such a way that online learning environments may be disadvantageous for those individuals differing from each other in terms of features such as readiness toward online learning, self-directed learning and motivation. With the help of intelligent, adaptive and personalized learning environments, these disadvantages can be minimized through providing feedback and interventions appropriate for individual needs.

The commonly accepted definition of the term interaction is mutual events that's requires two or more interrelated objects and actions (Wagner, 1994). Interaction occurs when these objects and actions influence of each other. Therefore, interaction occurs not only among individuals but also among objects. Accordingly, Moore (1989) states that learning activities present three different interaction types, which are between I) learning and content, II) learner and teacher III) learner and learner. Today, the learning environments are not only in the form of face-to-face classroom settings but also in the form of online platforms. During their experiences in the online learning environment, the users leave traces in relation to their interactions. Recently, researchers from different disciplines have developed methods to analyze and interpret these traces (Martin & Sherin, 2013). Learning analytics refers to the analysis of interactions of learners in the online learning environment and the interpretations of these analyses to have a better understanding of the learning environment and to improve it, which includes the measurement of the data, gathering and analysis it, and reporting the findings (Siemens & Long, 2011; Ferguson 2012). The aim of learning analytics is organizing existing information and explore meaningful knowledge in learning communities' and instruction processes.

Students' having interaction with the learning environment and activities has a positive effect on completing learning tasks (Ma, Han, Yang, & Cheng, 2015). One of the methods to empower and increase that interaction is to recreate learning environments in accordance with the individual characteristics and needs. Teaching content, methods and media should be in consonant with learners' characteristics to get the best benefit from learning environment (Rezaei, & Katz, 2004). To put it another way, providing learners with instructional technology applications is not sufficient to ensure an efficient learning climate. These environments presented to learners must be also suited to individual characteristics. Numerous online learning and evaluation environments are constructed to serve various purposes. Learners navigation behaviors in this environment also varies according to various individual characteristics. Cognitive styles (Chen, & Ford, 1998; Chen, 2010; Ford, & Chen, 2000), gender (Roy, & Chi, 2003), ethnic groups (Lu, Yu, & Liu, 2003); experience (Roy, & Chi, 2003), prior knowledge (Rezende, & Souza Barros, 2008) can be given as examples for these individual characteristics. These differences observed in the navigational patterns not only effect learners' learning performance but also give important recommendations about what kind of personalization and adaptation should be for more efficient and effective learning environment.

In literature there are many studies related to learners' interaction behaviors and navigation patterns. In Chen's (2010) study, a web-based learning system is offered to 105 undergraduate students. Navigational behaviors of the students are detected through log records in system. The results of the study show that students who have different cognitive styles exhibit similar behaviors in linear learning approach, but students make use of different navigation tools in accordance with their cognitive styles. Rezende and Souza Barros, (2008) investigate navigational patterns in terms of learners' prior knowledge. Their study reveals that there is a different navigational patterns for learners according to different prior knowledge. Those who have more prior knowledge have more systematic and organized behaviors and those who have less prior knowledge display less organized behaviors; in other words, their navigation behaviors indicate that they lost their way in the system. In the study conducted by Puntambekar and Stylianou (2005), learners' navigation behaviors in a multimedia setting is examined to provide them different learning support. Students have four different types of navigation in learning system. It has been proved that giving support according to their navigational behaviors, has a positive impact on learners' achievement.

Interactions of learners in an online learning environment are derived from log records and they are expressed as navigation. The aim of the current study is to investigate navigational patterns of university students in a learning management system. Having a close review of the literature, it has been found that there is a research gap in the relation between online learners' navigational patterns and their learning performance. To fill the void, the study aims to examine whether there is a potential difference in navigational patterns of the learners in terms of their academic achievement (pass, fail).

template is a set of styles and page layout settings that determine the appearance of a document. This template matches the printer settings that will be used in the proceeding and the CD-Rom. Use of the template is mandatory.

2. METHOD

2.1 Participants

This study, aiming at investigating navigational patterns of learners in a LMS, draws on the data collected from 65 university students, who registered to Computer Networks and Communication class in a state university.

2.2 Online Learning Environment

As the online learning environment, Moodle, an open source software, is used in this study. Moodle which has a serial database keeps the record of users' all interaction with the system. Moodle was arranged in accordance with the objectives of the class and weekly course content and assessment activities were reconstructed by the lecturer. Within the context of the course, the functions of Moodle such as providing learning content, discussion, messaging, assessment, feedback, profile and schedule were utilized. Learners used LMS for a class period and log records in regard to this usage were kept in the database. Navigational patterns of the learners while using these tools were categorized under 8 themes by the researchers namely, homepage, content, discussion, messaging, profile, assessment, feedback and ask the instructor.

2.3 Data Evaluation

Moodle records the data based on LMS user interaction sequentially in the database. Navigational log records derived from database were converted into sequential database format. In the following table, information related to users' login id, user name, date, time, link of the visited page and duration spent on the page are presented. According to students' achievement (pass, failure) at the end of the academic term, these data were divided in two tables. Afterwards, the tables were reorganized to show how long each user spent time on which internet pages sequentially in a single login. With the available data, 437 alternate logins in relation to passed and 227 alternate logins with regard to failed students were found. Page connections of the users were transformed into interaction themes namely, homepage, content, discussion, messaging, profile, assessment, feedback and ask the instructor. After the processes mentioned above were carried out, the data, as presented in Figure 1, were made prepared to be analyzed. Users differed from each other in terms of the number of navigational steps and time they spent on the system in every unique login. The present study investigates the patterns users follow in the first four steps with regard to system interaction. Additionally, sequential navigations in the same theme were merged.

Sira	ID	session	date	theme1	time1	theme2	time2	theme3	time3	theme4	time4	theme5	time5
32	23392	1RMDZ1j6c	4.03.14	HOMEPAGE	41	CONTENT	7	HOMEPAGI	14	CONTENT	4829	ASSESMEN	1890
3	517	0939N8Par	15.03.14	HOMEPAGE	185	ASSESMEN	6	HOMEPAGI	5	CONTENT	326	ASSESMEN	948
667	34134	wtDQ8S75J	10.03.14	HOMEPAGE	8	FORUM	8	CONTENT	5	HOMEPAGI	6	CONTENT	934
318	21181	hMa3NMC	2.03.14	HOMEPAGE	13	DONUT	12	HOMEPAGI	13	PROFIL	21	CONTENT	847
181	31611	bIFvnQ3k6	9.03.14	HOMEPAGE	7	CONTENT	1103	ASSESMEN	652	CONTENT	10	ASSESMEN	792
247	29665	DxylaUe2JE	8.03.14	HOMEPAGE	65	CONTENT	127	PROFIL	26	HOMEPAGI	13	CONTENT	781
392	19206	KJaqVmHM	28.02.14	HOMEPAGE	18	CONTENT	2105	ASSESMEN	454	CONTENT	29	ASSESMEN	756
257	38290	Ekv3bfG9JC	12.03.14	HOMEPAGE	29	CONTENT	51	HOMEPAGI	56	CONTENT	352	ASSESMEN	706
310	39685	h0EYciovYu	13.03.14	HOMEPAGE	5	CONTENT	10	HOMEPAGI	7	FORUM	29	CONTENT	611
241	1520	dQKqCSum	16.03.14	HOMEPAGE	55	ASSESMEN	75	HOMEPAGI	16	CONTENT	194	ASSESMEN	581
496	20935	PVYDHgX6	2.03.14	HOMEPAGE	12	CONTENT	7	FORUM	213	CONTENT	848	ASSESMEN	517
209	34497	chJfvxnHVv	10.03.14	HOMEPAGE	64	CONTENT	2643	ASSESMEN	1596	HOMEPAGI	57	FORUM	474
250	15847	e71eZwjFai	26.02.14	HOMEPAGE	10	CONTENT	32	FORUM	212	HOMEPAGI	179	CONTENT	464
210	17311	CHqmd8Bn	27.02.14	HOMEPAGE	22	ASSESMEN	7	HOMEPAGI	6	CONTENT	267	ASSESMEN	427
365	22905	JICBW00UH	3.03.14	HOMEPAGE	14	ASSESMEN	8	HOMEPAGI	16	CONTENT	320	ASSESMEN	365
703	20771	xvl9EYfC72	2.03.14	HOMEPAGE	44	CONTENT	165	HOMEPAGI	13	CONTENT	223	FORUM	271
601	3111	ttGLkWJ9z	17.03.14	HOMEPAGE	23	CONTENT	146	HOMEPAGI	21	ASSESMEN	7	CONTENT	231
457	25880	nXo80Lc2vI	5.03.14	HOMEPAGE	24	CONTENT	258	HOMEPAGI	5	CONTENT	911	FORUM	209
527	15023	R7RXBcQzD	26.02.14	HOMEPAGE	40	EGITMENE_	8	FORUM	8	PROFIL	7	FORUM	150
661	30225	WLtzXuoTY	8.03.14	HOMEPAGE	18	CONTENT	1090	HOMEPAGI	5	ASSESMEN	601	CONTENT	127
740	17192	z4HtscePyL	27.02.14	HOMEPAGE	33	CONTENT	285	ASSESMEN	272	CONTENT	56	ASSESMEN	97
416	23911	IMK4wynBt	4.03.14	HOMEPAGE	39	CONTENT	698	ASSESMEN	286	CONTENT	24	ASSESMEN	88

Figure 1. Sample data table

Data transformed to sequential patterns by the researchers were organized in navigational pattern graphics by taking frequency and ratio into consideration. To test the difference between obtained patterns ratio test was conducted by means of z statistics. The steps of the process follow as such: a) In the first order analysis, frequencies related to which themes login students tend towards afterwards were detected and index values were obtained by dividing the frequencies into total number of logins in each system (passed -failed students). b) Later on, students' tendency towards the second order navigations after each theme in the first order was computed using index values based on frequencies again.

3. FINDINGS

Within the scope of the research, navigational patterns of students who passed and failed the course were revealed. Patterns were examined in first order and second order navigations. These patterns are presented with the ratios in Figure 2.

First and second order navigational patterns of online students and index values based on login frequencies are displayed in Figure 2. It has been shown that in both achievement groups the primary preference of online learners is to form an interaction with the content and later have an interaction with other students in discussion. Therefore, within the scope of the current study, second order navigations are limited to merely navigations after content and discussion. Passed students after having content interaction (excluding those for homepage and log out) tended towards discussion or assessment in the second order navigations. Passed students preferring discussion in the first order navigations opted for content interaction in the second order navigations. While ranking determined a cutpoint by the researchers. This cutpoint is %10.

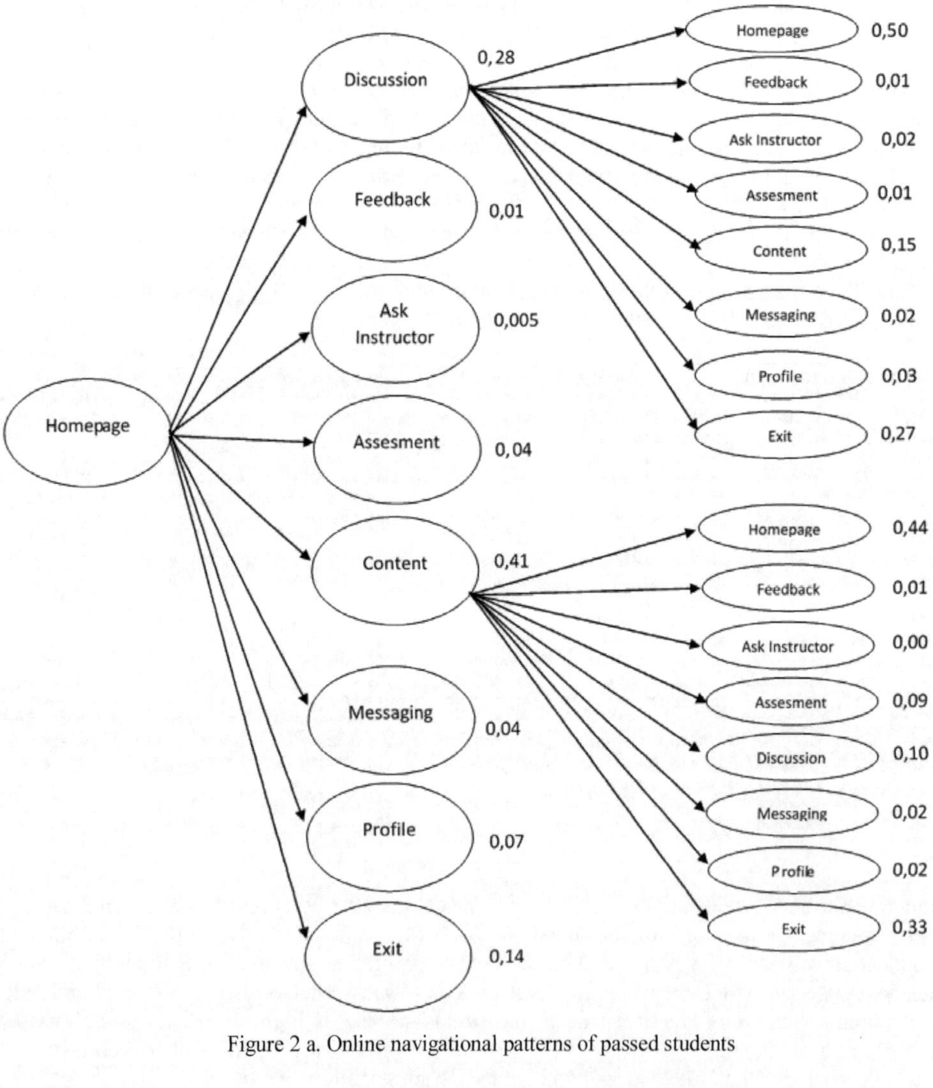

Figure 2 a. Online navigational patterns of passed students

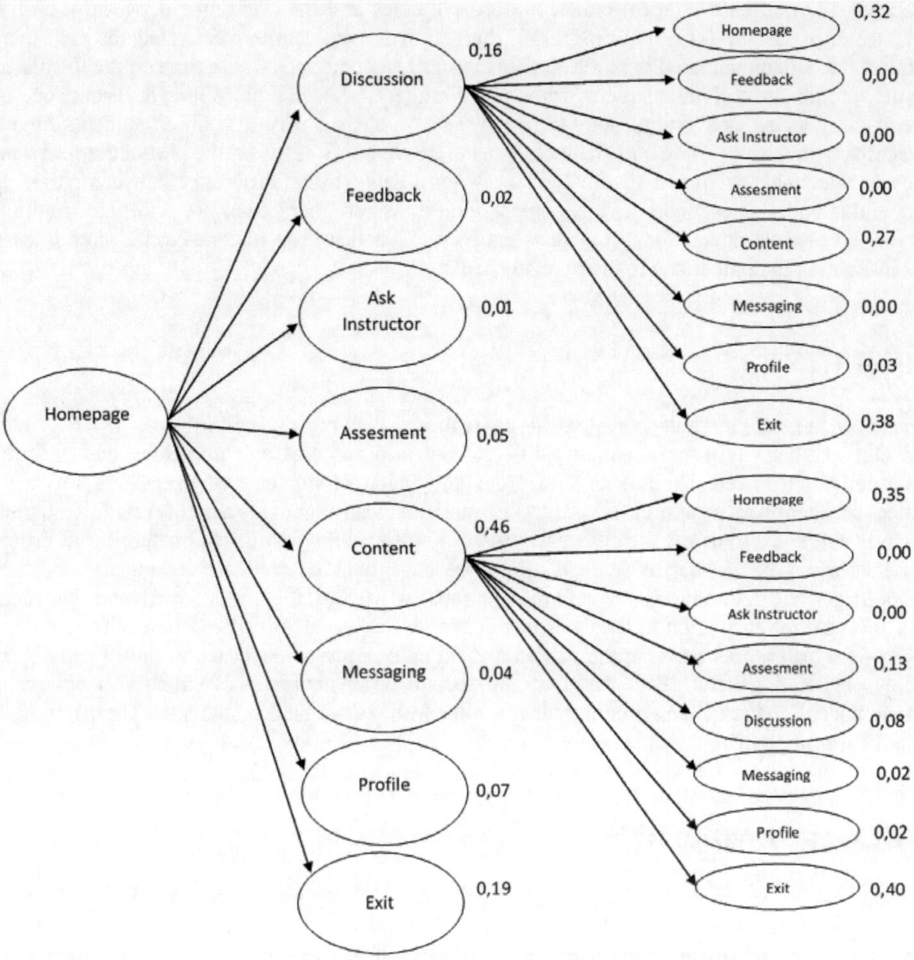

Figure 2 b. Online navigational patterns of failed students

As you can see figure 2.a and 2.b figures numbers represent percentages. For example 28 percent of the passed students link from homepage to discussion page. For the failed students this percentage is 16.

In addition to this, it has been revealed that passed students logged in more and had more content interaction in comparison to failed students. In accordance with students' academic achievement, themes and length of time spent were also investigated. Average times (seconds) of students spent on the pages in the second order and differences are presented in Table 1.

Table 1. Times (Seconds) of learners spent on the page in the second order

	Content	Discussion	Messaging	Profile	Assessment	Feedback	Ask Instructor
Passed	588,24	102,16	30,89	39,84	303,47	16,67	31
Failed	495,25	109,35	9,25	30,40	614	22,60	6,67
Differences	92,99	-7,19	21,64	9,44	242,47	-5,93	24,33

The average time learners spent on second order themes and the difference between passed and failed students are displayed in Table 1. Considering the length of time learners allocated for each theme, it has been shown that when compared to failed students, passed students spent more time on the themes of content, messaging, profile and ask the instructor while failed students allocated more time to discussion, assessment and feedback themes. This finding may be interpreted in such a way that failed students might find the assessment activities demanding and challenging as more time was spent on the part of them. As can be seen from the navigational patterns in Figure 2, there is not a navigational difference between passed and failed students and in both achievement groups, content and discussion interactions are prioritized in the first order navigation. Of the two interactions, content is more crucial and passed students spend more intense time on content interaction in comparison to their counterparts.

4. RESULTS

The results of the current study revealed the navigational patterns of learners in LMS. The research also showed that whether navigational patterns differ or not in terms of academic achievement of the learners. Navigational patterns were handled as first order and second order and whether there was a significant difference between these patterns according to students learning achievement was investigated. Z-test statistic was employed to detect the difference. According to results of the test, no significant difference was found between passed and failed students. Both passed and failed students are mostly visit content and discussion pages in the first order navigation. Additionally, whether there was a difference between the time learners allocated for each login in terms of their academic achievement was examined. The findings showed that there were differences between the passed and failed students with regard to time spent on each login. The study yielded a general result that first and second order navigational patterns of passed and failed students in the online learning environment had similar features but passed students allocated more time each pages in the learning environments.

5. RECOMMENDATION

The current study investigates the navigational patterns of online learners in terms of their achievement. The findings of the research may have a potential for the design of intelligent tutorial systems. According to characteristics and navigations of the learners, intelligent tutorial systems involve intervention and adaptive mechanisms. In the light of the results of the study, although learners differ in terms of their achievement, they draw upon similar ways in the online learning environments but they differentiate in the sense of time they allocate for interaction. Accordingly, especially for those who perform poor in the school the interactions of the learners with the system can be enriched with online learning agents and the interventional feedback suitable for interaction period. So learners can be directed to deep learning.

REFERENCES

Ally, M. (2004). Foundations of educational theory for online learning. *Theory and practice of online learning*, *2*, 15-44.

Chen, S. Y., & Ford, N. J. (1998). Modelling user navigation behaviours in a hyper-media-based learning system: An individual differences approach. *Knowledge organization*, *25*(3), 67-78.

Chen, L.H. (2010). Web-based learning programs: Use by learners with various cognitive styles. *Computers & Education, 54*. 1028-1035p.

Demir, Ö., Yasar, S., Sert, G., & Yurdugül, H. (2014). Examination of the Relationship between Students' Attitudes towards Computer and Self-Directed Learning with Technology. *Egitim ve Bilim*, *39*(176).

Ferguson, R. (2012). Learning analytics: drivers, developments and challenges.*International Journal of Technology Enhanced Learning*, *4*(5-6), 304-317.

Ford, N., & Chen, S. Y. (2000). Individual differences, hypermedia navigation, and learning: an empirical study. *Journal of educational multimedia and hypermedia*, *9*(4), 281-312.

Lu, J., Yu, C. S., & Liu, C. (2003). Learning style, learning patterns, and learning performance in a WebCT-based MIS course. *Information & Management*, *40*(6), 497-507.

Grow, G. O. (1991). Teaching to learners to be self-directed. *Adult education quarterly, 41*(3), 125- 149. http://aeq.sagepub.com/

Ma, J., Han, X., Yang, J. ve Cheng, J. (2015). Examining the necessary condition for engagement in an online learning environment based on learning analytics approach: The role of the instructor. *Internet and Higher Education, 24*. 26–34p.

Martin, T., & Sherin, B. (2013). Learning Analytics and Computational Techniques for Detecting and Evaluating Patterns in Learning: An Introduction to the Special Issue. *Journal of the Learning Sciences, 22*(4), 511-520. doi: 10.1080/10508406.2013.840466

Moore, M.G. (1989). Editorial: Three types of interaction. American Journal of Distance Education, 3 (2). 1-7p.

Puntambekar, S., & Stylianou, A. (2005). Designing navigation support in hypertext systems based on navigation patterns. *Instructional Science*, *33*(5-6), 451-481.

Rezaei, A.R. ve Katz, L. (2004). Evaluation of the reliability and validity of the cognitive styles analysis. *Personality and Individual Differences 36.* 1317-1327p.

Rezende, F., & de Souza Barros, S. (2008). Students' navigation patterns in the interaction with a mechanics hypermedia program. *Computers & Education*,*50*(4), 1370-1382.

Richey, R. C., Silber, K. H., & Ely, D. P. (2008). Reflections on the 2008 AECT Definitions of the Field. *TechTrends, 52*(1), 24-25.

Roy, M., & Chi, M. T. (2003). Gender differences in patterns of searching the web. *Journal of educational computing research*, *29*(3), 335-348.

Siemens, G., & Long, P. (2011). Penetrating the Fog: Analytics in Learning and Education. *EDUCAUSE review*, *46*(5), 30.

Wagner, E.D. (1994). In support of a functional definition of interaction. *American Journal of Distance Education, 8*(2), 6–26.

AMAZED BY MAKING: HOW DO TEACHERS DESCRIBE THEIR PBL EXPERIENCE

Dalit Levy[1] and Olga Dor[2]
[1]*Zefat Academic College, Zefat, Israel*
[2]*Kibbutzim College of Education, Tel Aviv, Israel*

ABSTRACT

This paper is based on data gathered in a study conducted during the 2015 school year, in a reputable Israeli high school experimenting project-based learning (PBL) as part of an innovative pedagogy for the information age. The overall research goal was to investigate the teachers' views of PBL and the ways by which these views have changed following the experience of designing, teaching, and evaluating PBL activities. Among the results, one noticeable theme has crystallized throughout the qualitative analysis: our participants felt excited about their in-school experiences with PBL, and expressed their enthusiasm and satisfaction repeatedly. The focus in this paper is therefore on the emergent theme of *excitement* and on its links to the realm of *making*.

KEYWORDS

High School; Making; Multi-cultural; Pedagogical Innovation

1. INTRODUCTION

"I think it's an amazing experience for kids *to make* this, I really got excited. And something here is very authentic", summarized one teacher the previous several weeks she had spent with her ninth graders, dealing with history by way of PBL – Project-Based Learning. "He *made* an amazing thing in the products evening. I'm out of words… I am shaking as I speak", added a social studies teacher in a staff meeting. Both citations were documented in a participant-observation conducted at the end of the 2015 schoolyear. What brings these teachers to feel so excited and to express their feelings to such extent? Based on a recent ethnographic study conducted in an Israeli high school branded as a school of excellence in science and technology, we suggest that at least part of the answer lies in experiencing the culture of *making*. What is known as 'the maker movement' has been dramatically expanding over the past decade, and a growing community of educational researchers and leaders see in making great potential for students, teachers, and schools (Blikstein, 2013; Kafai & Peppler, 2010).

The study here presented focused on the implementation of PBL in the school (Gerogiannis & Fitsilis, 2006) as part of an innovative pedagogy this school is experimenting in the last three years, titled 'multi-layered learning in a changing reality' (Eyal, Sivan, Almi-Melman & Cohen, 2015). PBL is often presented as a powerful educational approach for the knowledge age (McDonald, 2008; Gerogiannis & Fitsilis, 2006; Rosenfeld, 1999). It is thought of as especially appropriate for providing opportunities for collaborative experiential learning (Levy, in press; Weinberger, Stegnmann, & Fischer, 2007) as well as for students to be actively engaged in knowledge construction processes (King & Puntambekar, 2003) and to experience the maker movement (Vossoughi & Bevan, 2014). However, teachers who have been conventionally educated and trained, might find such an approach challenging (Levy & Baratz, 2013). The current research goal was therefore to investigate the teachers' views of PBL and the ways by which these views have changed following the experience of designing, teaching, and evaluating PBL activities (Dor, 2016).

Indeed, interesting results emerged from the inductive analysis of the data gathered through semi-structures interviews as well as participant observations in teachers' reflective meetings. The emergent core categories consisted of PBL-centered views, students-centered views, and teachers-centered views. The latter core category included expressions of enthusiasm, excitement, and satisfaction by the participants, like those arising from the two citations above. This paper will focus mainly on the excitement sub-category and its connection to the theme of *making*.

2. 'MULTY-LAYERED LEARNING' AS AN INNOVATIVE PEDAGOGY

The high school is a unique educational institute located in the heart of Tel Aviv, comprising middle school (grades 7-9), high school (grades 10-12), and a technological college (two years undergraduate programs in practical engineering). The school promotes excellence in math, science and technology and fosters arts through its reputable art center. As an educational institute placed within one of the busiest high-tech quarters contributing to describing Israel as a start-up nation (Senor & Singer, 2009), one of the school's flags is "educating the next generation of Israeli high-tech entrepreneurs" (as is cited in the school's website). Most of the eight hundred students come from families of immigrants from Russia and the former Russian territories. Therefore, the school emphasizes multi-culturalism and diversity hand in hand with fostering the Jewish Israeli identity. Only fifth of the students live in Tel Aviv, and the others come from cities and towns in the close periphery.

The school seeks to maintain an open system of inter-relationship with the surrounding communities. As part of such goal, an innovative approach has been formulated by the school and suggested for piloting. The approach title, 'multi-layered learning in a changing reality', denotes the school's aim to develop and implement a model of learning constructed of multiple layers of pedagogical, organizational, and technological parts (Eyal, Sivan, Almi-Melman & Cohen, 2015). The overall model was approved by the ministry of education for experimentation in 2014.

The innovative pedagogical model is based on a three-phase cyclic process including (a) Integration into the multi-cultural and dynamic reality; (b) Interpretation and choice of leading values; and (c) Making, creating, and contributing to the communities surrounding the school (see Figure 1).

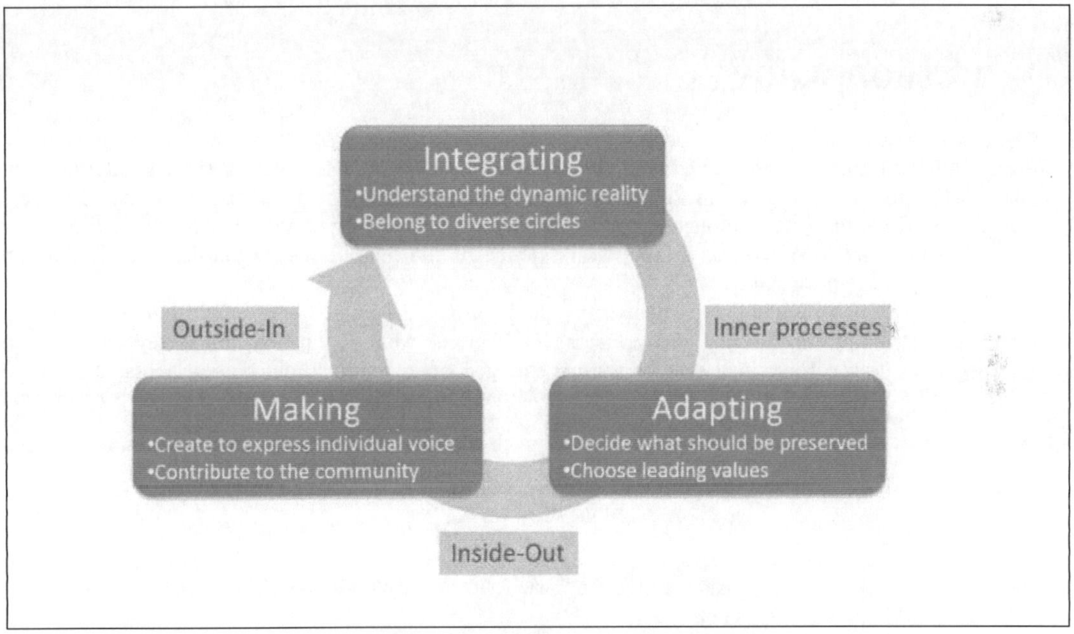

Figure 1. Principles of the 'Multi-Layered Learning' Pedagogy

By 'multi-layered learning in a changing reality', this innovative pedagogy (Levy & Baratz, 2013) reflects a process of teaching, learning, and assessment that is sensitive to the changing reality of the knowledge age in which the process takes place (McLoughlin & Lee, 2008). The technology-enhanced model (Pilkington, 2015) implemented in the school in the last three years is characterized by complexity, flexibility, relevancy, and producing. These characteristics have been evident in the curriculum as well as in the learning environment, the school culture, the organizational structure, and the teachers' role definition.

Project-Based Learning (PBL) is an important layer of the model, alongside other layers such as using tablets regularly by students and teachers; integrating R&D into school hours; cooperation with high tech companies; continuous professional development; and more. PBL is often defined as a pedagogical method in which a real-life or authentic problem or situation is presented to students for investigation, analysis, solution, synthesis and evaluation (McDonald, 2008). It is therefore common to use PBL to denote Problem-Based Learning rather than Project-Based Learning. In both approaches, the students work individually or in groups, while the teacher acts as facilitator, coach, and sometimes even as a fellow learning partner rather than traditional instructor or tutor. In addition, the notion of group work is central to both Problem-Based Learning (Lambros, 2004) and Project-Based Learning (Livingstone & Lynch, 2002), as collaborative processes cultivate an active and interactive rather than passive approach to learning in ways that promote creativity, critical thinking and experiential learning (Barfield, 2003). The main difference between Problem- and Project-Based Learning exists in the notion of *making* which is far more prominent to the latter. In the innovative model experimented in the school, and in the research here described, PBL indeed denotes Project-Based Learning.

Introducing PBL into this school is further justified by its inherent diversity as well as the learning requirement from students to develop a broader and deeper understanding of how high tech organizations and entrepreneurs work, and how they utilize technology to improve their products in particular and the society in general. As a preparation for implementing PBL in the school, leading teachers have participated in workshops in High-Tech High in San Diego, and an in-school professional development program has been designed to deal with the changing role of the teacher as a mentor of project-based learning processes. The second author participated in these pedagogical ventures as one of the school's leading teachers during 2014, and later on developed an ethnographic research plan in her school as part of her Master of Education studies, supervised by the first author (Dor, 2016). The overall research aimed at documenting the implementation of PBL in the school through the eyes of the participating teachers. The research methodology is briefly presented next.

3. METHODOLOGY

The research combined participant observations and semi-structured interviews. The observations aimed at documenting educators meetings and their discussions of their experiences with PBL. The interviews were conducted with ten teachers using PBL in a variety of subjects during the 2015 school year. During that school year, two interviewees implemented PBL for the first time, four had two years of experience, and four had a longer experience of three or four years. Three of the interviewees were also part of the school pedagogical management staff.

The researchers used an inductive analysis method (Guba & Lincoln, 1989), in which they carefully read the data, reflected on the meaningful expressions, and colored what they interpreted as keywords (Leech & Onwuegbuzie, 2007). The primary categories that emerged were then highlighted and elaborated on. Finally, a list of fifty categories was formulated and restructured as a categorical system consisting of three core categories:

- I. PBL-centered views
- II. Students-centered views
- III. Teachers-centered views

Each of the three core categories further contained first level sub-categories. For example, the first level sub-categories of the third core category termed 'Teacher-centered views' were formulated as follows.

- III-P. Personal
- III-R. Requirements
- III-S. Support
- III-T. Teamwork

As a last analytic step, each first level sub-category was reorganized to contain 2nd level sub-categories (Leech & Onwuegbuzie, 2007). Figure 2 below visualizes the core structure created in the study (Dor, 2016), along with the first level sub-categories.

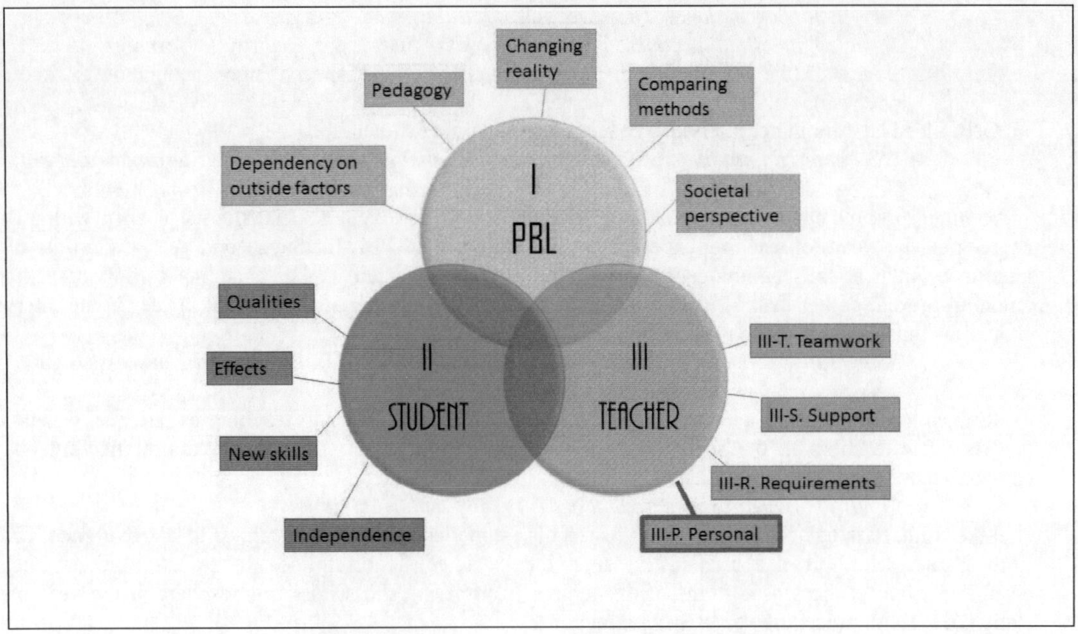

Figure 2. Core Categories and First Level Sub-Categories

The complete emergent system of categories is not presented here in details due to space limitations, but let's look for example at the 2nd level sub-categories that were classified as III-P or 'Personal' (highlighted in Figure 2 above). This sub-category contains expressions hinting at different types of personal considerations, characteristics, and feelings by the participating teachers. Three such types were found:

III-P.1	Teacher's individual character as related to success
III-P.2	Teachers expressing excitement
III-P.3	Teachers manage to change the educational reality

One noticeable type of the 'personal' teachers-centered views (coded III-P.2) comprises expressions of enthusiasm, excitement, and satisfaction by the participant teachers, like those arising from the two citations presented in the Introduction. In both cases, the excitement seems to be related with *producing* and *making*, which, as has been stated above, is regarded as a noticeable characteristic of Project-Based Learning (King & Puntambekar, 2003; Gerogiannis & Fitsilis, 2006). The following Results section will bring additional evidence linking excitement and *making*.

4. RESULTS: TEACHERS EXPRESSING EXCITEMENT

The theme of excitement was evident in all the observations and interviews conducted throughout the year of the study. Moreover, the participants described their experience with PBL in their classes using strong adjectives such as 'amazing', 'joyful', 'authentic', and 'powerful'. The teachers used such adjectives to describe both the learning processes and the products of these learning-by making processes.

One example can be found in Orly's interview (all names are pseudonyms). Orly is teaching history and social studies for ten years. She is in her forties and holds a B.A. degree. At the time of the interview she implemented PBL for the first time as part of history lessons devoted to the years of WWII and the holocaust. The projects of her students were creations related to what is known in Israel as "righteous among the nations" – an honorific used to describe non-Jews who risked their lives to save Jews. Here is one citation from the beginning of her interview:

"*It was just exceptional. They loved it. What they made... is just astonishing. Yesterday I received the final product from one student. She wrote a diary – seven pages, A4 pages!!!*" (the exclamation marks denotes Orly's tone of speech, emphasizing how excited she was).

Orly added later on in her interview, reflecting on what that student did:

"*She entered into that period; she investigated that period, as if she was writing a diary of her own life between 1925 and 1945. It is so special. It is a book. A readymade book!!!*".

Another example can be found in Abby's interview. Abby is a young social studies teacher, with a B.Ed. degree and five years of teaching experience. She implemented PBL for the second year at the time of the interview. Right at the beginning of the interview, Abby reflected on her changing role as a mentor, a guide-on-the-side rather than a sage-on-the-stage (King, 1993). Abby also commented later in the interview about how much she loved the making process:

"*Something about YOU decide what to focus on, about YOU construct the process, is very very powerful... I just love it*".

Ruth, a Biology teacher with an M.A. degree and twenty-one years of teaching experience, was among the very few teachers in the school that implemented PBL for three or four years. Reflecting on her comprehensive experience, she said:

"*I felt I'm realizing my personal desire, really and truthfully*".

Like Ruth, Sara has twenty-one years of teaching experience and three years of PBL experience. Unlike Ruth, Sara teaches bible, a humanistic rather than a scientific discipline. Regardless of their teaching discipline, both teachers used terms of excitement. Comparing the school's atmosphere at the year of the study (2015) with preceding years, Sara claimed:

"*The making this year is massive, because of the expansion* (of PBL) *and because of the huge making of teachers that engage and get excited and make*".

As a last example, we quote Sharon, a language arts teacher in her forties, with an M.A. degree and fourteen years of teaching experience. She implemented PBL for the second year at the time of the interview, and summarized her experience with satisfaction:

"*When you see that you truly did something meaningful with the students you feel satisfaction*".

When then asked if she enjoyed implementing PBL, Sharon answered:

"*Yes. I don't speak about fears, on the contrary, I speak about what's next now, what's next... we are preparing now the photography exhibition*".

At the end of the interview, Sharon mentioned again the theme of satisfaction hand in hand with the theme of excitement:

"*We must get the students excited. If we don't manage to get ourselves excited we won't be able to get the students excited and our teaching will be just boring, and I also won't be satisfied of myself*".

In addition to the examples brought above, all taken from interviews data, many more expressions hinting at excitement, satisfaction, enthusiasm etc. were documented in formal and informal staff meetings. Here is a brief list of quotes:

- "*The students succeeded to have uniforms of the Red Army with medals, partisans. They organized a real show and each student had a role. Amazing*" (History teacher)
- "*I'm truly amazed by the depth and the richness of the project, you see a very thoughtful making, that interdisciplinary, and it is very spectacular... I have a lot of satisfaction, in particular after twenty years of teaching*" (Art teacher)
- "*You surprised me; it was touching to see the integration of languages art and sports. It is not obvious to combine these two disciplines. I loved it so much*" (unspecified teacher)

Together with the pair of quotes that appear in this paper's Introduction section, the above quotes contain a collection of excitement-related terms. Furthermore, these *excitement*-related quotes also mention *making* in various forms. We interpret this duality as a possible explanation of the phenomena here presented, and suggest that one reason for the *excitement* our participants felt while experiencing PBL was their immersion into a culture of *making* (Vossoughi & Bevan, 2014).

5. CONCLUSION

Based on observations, interviews, and analyses of these qualitative data, one of this study's emergent findings highlights the links between teachers' excitement with regard to implementing PBL and practices of making across diverse disciplines within school setting. Excitement on teachers' side seems to be a noticeable advantage of the innovative pedagogy titled 'multi-layered learning in a changing reality' (Eyal, Sivan, Almi-Melman & Cohen, 2015), as well as other advantages found in our overall study but were not dealt with here. To better understand the reasons for this excitement, and to establish the connection between excitement and making, more research is needed.

Like in other cases of introducing innovative pedagogies into educational institutions (for example, Levy & Schrire, 2015), in parallel to the advantages mentioned with regard to PBL and the culture of making, the participants of this study also reported numerous challenges. These include difficulties in organizing for collaborative learning, tensions related to alternative assessment needed for evaluation of teamwork and products as opposed to traditional high stake evaluation (Nevo, Shaw, Greene, Mark, 2006), the unwillingness of some to embrace change, and more. Interestingly, other studies also report on another challenge relevant to the theme of excitement we focused at, namely over-enthusiasm of the experienced personal and its effect on novices (McDonald, 2008). No traces of such a challenge were found in our data, and the reason might be that even the most experienced participated in this study were with only three or four years of experience.

Excitement experienced by teachers in their daily practice seems to serve as a strong motivating force for both the teachers and their students. Therefore, we believe the finding focused at in this paper is of relevance far beyond the limited scope of this case study.

REFERENCES

Barfield, R. L. 2003. Students' Perceptions of and Satisfaction with Group Grades and the Group Experience in the College Classroom. *Assessment and Evaluation in Higher Education*, 28 (4), 354-369.

Blikstein, P. 2013. Digital fabrication and 'making' in education: The democratization of invention. In J. Walter-Herrmann & C. Büching (Eds.), *FabLabs: Of Machines, Makers and Inventors.* Bielefeld, Germany: Transcript Publishers, pp. 1-21.

Dor, O. 2016. *What is significant in "Significant Learning"?* Unpublished M.Ed. Research Project (in Hebrew). Kibbutzim College of Education, Tel Aviv, Israel.

Eyal, L., Sivan, M., Almi-Melman, S., and Cohen, I. 2015. *Not only Technology: The 'Multi-Layered Learning' Pedagogy – an Evaluation of the Experimental Program.* Research Report (in Hebrew). Shevach-Moffet High School. Retrieved July 11, 2016 from http://shevach-moffet.com/index.php/36-2012-10-11-13-11-06/2012-10-11-13-17-34/330-2015-12-30-04-26-55

Gerogiannis, V. and Fitsilis, P. 2006. A Project-Based Learning Approach for Teaching ERP Concepts. *Int. J. of Learning*, 5, 12, 261-268. Retrieved July 10, 2016 from http://dde.teilar.gr/publications/106/106fulltext.pdf

Guba, E.G. and Lincoln, Y.S. 1989. *Fourth Generation Evaluation.* Sage Publications, London, UK.

Kafai, Y. B., & Peppler, K. A. 2010. Youth, technology, and DIY developing participatory competencies in creative media production. *Review of Research in Education,* 35 (1), 89-119.

King, A. 1993. From Sage on the Stage to Guide on the Side. *College Teaching*, 41 (1), 30-35.

King, F. & Puntambekar, S. 2003. Asynchronously Conducted Project-Based Learning: Partners with Technology. *International Journal on E-Learning* 2 (2), 46-54. Norfolk, VA: AACE.

Lambros, A. 2004. *Problem-Based Learning in Middle and High School Classrooms.* Thousand Oaks, CA: Corwin Press Inc.

Leech, N. L., & Onwuegbuzie, A. J. 2007. An Array of Qualitative Data Analysis Tools: A Call for Data Analysis Triangulation. *School Psychology Quarterly*, 22 (4), 557-584.

Levy, D. In Press. Collaborative Conceptual Change in the Computer Science Classroom. In M. Schoenfeld & D. Griest (Eds.), *Collaborative Learning in a Global World.* Charlotte, NC: IAP (Information Age Publishing Inc.)

Levy, D. and Baratz, L. 2013. How do Teacher Educators Relate the Term "Pedagogical Innovation" to their Use of Educational Technology. Paper presented at *the 5th International Conference on Education and New Learning Technologies - EDULEARN13*, Barcelona, Spain.

Levy, D, & Schrire, S. 2015. Developing a Massive Open Online Course (MOOC) at a College of Education: Narrative of Disruptive Innovation?, *Current Issues in Emerging eLearning* 2 (1), Article 8. Retrieved October 10, 2016 from http://scholarworks.umb.edu/ciee/vol2/iss1/8

Livingstone, D., & Lynch, K. 2002. Group Project Work and Student-Centred Active Learning: two different experiences. *Journal of Geography in Higher Education*, 26 (2), 217-237.

McDonald, B. 2008. *Reflections on Graduate Student PBL Experiences.* Trinidad, West Indies: University of Trinidad and Tobago, O'Meara Campus. Retrieved July 10, 2016 from_http://files.eric.ed.gov/fulltext/ED503435.pdf

McLoughlin, C. & Lee, M. J. W. 2008. The Three P's of Pedagogy for the Networked Society: Personalization, Participation and Productivity, *International Journal for Teaching and Learning in Higher Education*, 20 (1), 10-27.

Nevo, D., Shaw, I., Greene J.C., Mark M.M. 2006. (Eds.). *Evaluation in Education. The SAGE Handbook of Evaluation*. SAGE: Los Angeles, London, New Delhi, Singapore &Washington DC.

Pilkington, R. 2015. *Discourse, Dialogue and Technology Enhanced Learning*. NY: Routledge.

Rosenfeld, M. 1999. Understanding the Surprise in PBL: An Exploration into the Learning Styles of Teachers and Their Students. Paper presented at the *8th EARLI Conference.* Gothenburg, Sweden.

Senor, D. and Singer, P. 2009. *Start-up Nation: The Story of Israel's Economic Miracle*. Twelve, New York, NY.

Vossoughi, S. & Bevan, B. 2014. *Making and Tinkering: A Review of the Literature*. National Research Council Committee on Out of School Time STEM: 1-55. Accessed October, 10 2016 from http://sites.nationalacademies.org/cs/ groups/dbassesite/documents/webpage/ dbasse_089888.pdf

Weinberger, A., Stegnmann, K., and Fischer, F. (2007). Knowledge Convergence in Collaborative Learning: Concepts and Assessment, *Learning and Instruction*, 17, 416-426.

GROUP WORK AND THE IMPACT, IF ANY, OF THE USE OF GOOGLE APPLICATIONS FOR EDUCATION

Jannat Maqbool
Waikato Institute of Technology, Hamilton, New Zealand

ABSTRACT

The use of group work in teaching practices has been well supported in educational theories however the researcher has experienced a number of issues or areas of concern in having students work in groups to complete a major assessment for a second year Project Management course at a leading polytechnic in New Zealand. Factors potentially influenced by the majority of students having English as their second language, the inexperience of the Lecturer in facilitating group work and the lack of tools available to or recommended for students to use in facilitating collaboration and managing the administrative aspects of group work. For the purposes of the present research there are two primary areas of interest. Firstly, the problematic experience of students in coordinating or managing the administration element of group work involving scheduling meetings, corresponding, communicating and managing documentation, and further incorporating the challenges of collaborating as a group to produce a coherent and cohesive group work output or outcome. Students were required to use a web-based portal or wiki developed using Google Applications to assist in coordinating group effort, managing documents and communication, and collaborating to develop the required output in completing the group assignment. The research is aimed at identifying and clarifying what, if any impact, using Google Sites has on group work within a cohort of students undertaking the project management course.

KEYWORDS

Group work, Google, Google Sites, Collaborative Learning

1. INTRODUCTION

The use of group work in teaching practices has been well supported in educational theories pertaining to the "importance of interaction between social, affective and cognitive states in development and learning" (Blatchford, 2003). Group work aims to develop intellectual understanding, abilities and skills; communication, cooperative and teamwork skills; personal and professional growth; and reflective practices as well as encourage those involved in group work to be more independent and take ownership of their own learning (University of Sydney. 2015).

A major component of a second year Project Management course, offered as part of a Bachelor of Applied Management or Graduate Diploma programme at a leading polytechnic in New Zealand, is a Group Assignment which forms 30% of the students' final grade. The Group Assignment requires students to work together, in groups of four or five, for the majority of the semester and deliver a project plan for a project idea as the group output.

The paper also requires students to complete a summative assessment half way through the semester and another at the end of the semester, in the form of a Test and Exam. Both assessments are individual assessments and weighted at 25% and 30% respectively. During the semester students also participate in two online forum discussions as a group and this is assessed at 15% of their module mark. By the end of the semester students should understand the basic principles and terminology of the profession of project management and how to apply these to create project plans.

In previous semesters a number of issues and areas of concerns were identified related to the group work component of this course. Some of these issues were: group members not pulling their weight, break downs in communication, lack of cohesion in the final output, alienation and/or exclusion of group members, general confusion regarding objectives and progress, versioning issues and files being lost, and dominance and power struggles between students. From the assessor's perspective, there were also issues related to the inability to effectively gauge individual contribution. Research suggests that these are rather common concerns amongst educators.

Factors that contribute to these issues and concerns include the fact that the majority of students are second language speakers of English, the convenor's inexperience at facilitating group work and the lack of tools available to or recommended for students to use in facilitating collaboration and managing the administrative aspects of group work. Postholm (2004) also identified difference in living conditions, education, life and work experience as having an influence.

This research is primarily interested in the problematic experience of students in coordinating or managing the administration element of group work, including scheduling meetings, corresponding, communicating and managing documentation, and further incorporating the challenges of collaborating as a group to produce a coherent and cohesive output.

2. THE STUDY

Students were required to use a web-based portal, or wiki, to assist in coordinating group effort, managing documents and communication, and collaborating to develop the required output in completing the group assignment.

The term Computer Supported Collaborative Learning (CSCL) may be used in this context. The purpose of which, is to provide a setting that supports collaboration amongst students to "enhance their learning processes, facilitate collective learning or group cognition" (Resta and Laferriere, 2007).

The tool they used was applications provided by Google which includes applications for email, calendar, real-time word processing, file and document storage, instant messaging and Voice of Internet Protocol (VOIP), and Google Sites which can be used to develop a structured wiki. All of these can be accessed online, from any device with an Internet connection and can provide "a whole new way to work together online" (Google, 2016).

Development of a wiki was the first deliverable of the group assignment and represented 20% of the overall group assignment mark. This component of the assignment was designed as a scaffolding exercise to enable students to experience working together as a group to deliver an output as a minor project within the overall group assignment. In their groups and supported by the researcher in the role of facilitator students would be involved in constructing knowledge and working through a problem-based activity in developing the platform for use in their group assignment. The students ability to work as a group as evidenced through group work and participation represented 30% of the overall group assignment mark.

To assist with the group work component of the assignment students were introduced to Bruce Tuckman's (1965) "forming-storming-norming-performing" model of group development soon after they were divided into groups. The model was explained from a theoretical perspective and then illustrated in terms of its application to the module where students were required to work together in groups to complete a major assessment. At the following weeks session students were asked to work in their assigned groups and construct a bridge from wooden sticks and other material. This exercise was designed to start the group thinking about how the group development model applied to their situation as an illustration of at least the initial stages of the model.

The research is aimed at identifying and clarifying what impact using Google applications has on group work when it's used to manage documents, communication and collaboration, amongst other elements of project administration.

It is envisaged that the use of a tool will also facilitate more effective assessment of individual contribution and overall participation in group work. The use of technology to screen individual contribution and/or group contribution may assist in reducing the incidence of social loafing; exerting less effort when working in a group than they would working alone (Deal, 2009).

The pilot study aimed to assist with the development of a further research protocol, the evaluation of research instruments, and the feasibility of the proposed research, given the researcher's inexperience at conducting research and dealing with the "unknown" with respect to the cohort's ability to learn to use, and willingly adopt the proposed tool.

The researcher made observations during the course of the semester and held a focus group session at the end with a random selection of the cohort as a representative sample.

3. DATA COLLECTION

The study involved thirty three students, divided into seven groups of between 4-5 students in Week 3, of a 14 week semester. Members of the student cohort were undertaking a Graduate Diploma in Operations and Production, Sales and Marketing or Event Management. Three of the students were domestic students and the remainder of the cohort was made up of international students from India (24) and China (6).

There was a considerable amount of diversity in the students' ethnic and cultural background, work experience, subject major of previous qualification, subject major in their current course of study and their spoken English proficiency. This information was obtained as part of an icebreaker exercise in Week 1 when students were asked to introduce themselves to the class. Furthermore, one of the course requirements was that students learn to use MS Project, and through observing the first three weeks of computer lab sessions the researcher identified that there was also considerable variation in the ability of members of the cohort to use computer software. The researcher then considered this variance and the diversity amongst students when dividing students into groups in an effort to ensure that the makeup of each group was similar and that no group had a seemingly unfair advantage or disadvantage when compared to another.

The cohort attended a three hour session each week. The first two hours were undertaken in a seminar style environment that has seating for up to 40 students. The first hour of this session was a lecture where the researcher covered theoretical subject matter. The room then enabled students to rearrange furniture into a setting more suited to group work, and to comfortably interact and work within their groups on the group assignment for the last hour. Students were then moved to a computer lab for the final hour of the weekly session where they learnt to use MS Project for the first half of the semester and were able to then use this time to work on their group assignment online during the second half of the semester.

From a qualitative primarily exploratory perspective, the researcher in their role as facilitator was able to talk to and observe students during these weekly face-to-face in class group work sessions. Although the majority of the group work was conducted by students outside of the classroom the weekly sessions did enable the researcher to observe interactions amongst members of the group and identify strengths and weakness amongst the group, which students participated in and contributed more to the discussion, which students tended to dominate, how the group went about assigning tasks to members, and how they planned to use, if at all, the tools available to them to facilitate collaboration, communication and document management. Students were able to ask the researcher questions in clarifying their understanding of the assessment requirements, whether their application of the theoretical principles of project management in developing the project plan were sound, any questions or concerns regarding the suite of Google applications and how to access and/or use the platform for the purposes of completing the required group assignment output. This latter element was more common during the second half of the semester when the computer lab sessions were able to be used to work on the group assignment in the Google applications environment.

It was important for the researcher that during the one-hour (and then two hour) group work component of the weekly sessions they remain in the role of a facilitator only and use the time to observe groups as they worked through the stages of group development, used the Google platform and developed the assessment requirements.

The researcher was also able to view a log of recent activity on each Google Site. This provided the name of the user logged in, the date and time of the activity, and a summary of the activity undertaken. There was however no indication of how long the user had been logged in and there appeared to be, perhaps due to the researchers own inexperience with the software platform, no way to extract this data for analysis and reporting purposes.

After the group assignment was submitted students were asked to attend a focus group session. Attendance was voluntary and the researcher did not themselves select students to participate. The representative sample was made up of 20 students who were available at the time of the focus group session and willing to participate in the research. Students were provided with a Participant Information Sheet and asked to sign a Participant Consent Form.

The focus group was designed to gain a deeper understanding of student perceptions, and any underlying reasons, motives or influencing factors, related to the impact on group work, if any, of the sample using Google applications for project administration and facilitating collaboration and communication in completing the group assignment assessment. The sessions provided an opportunity to ask specific questions to build on evidence obtained from the researchers own observations.

4. RESULTS

The pilot study, as the research can now be referred, found that the adoption of the collaborative nature of the tool was ad hoc amongst groups. There was only evidence of one group that worked online simultaneously, from separate locations, at various times, during the semester to collaborate on and develop the assignment output. This group developed the site and assignment output primarily through online collaboration. There was evidence, as observed using the Recent Activity information in the Google Site, of every group member participating and making a contribution. This group work was not evident as predominately during class room group work sessions given two of the five group members were not able to attend most weeks of the semester due to the hours they were working in paid employment. Interestingly one group member, who was present in the focus group, made significantly more online contributions than they did during in-class group work sessions. For this student, English was a second language and the somewhat confrontational nature of face-to-face group discussion was something that they were not accustomed to. Hence, they found the online environment 'safer' and were more willing to actively participate and contribute. This group member was a female and the other group members were male.

Two members of the group also commented that it was useful to be able to tag the researcher using the comments feature on pages in the Google Site if they required some assistance, feedback or clarification with respect to a piece of work.

This group was also the only group that used Google Hangouts in conjunction with Google Sites and a member of the group identified that they found it useful being able to have their Google Hangouts conversation running at the same time as working on a Google Doc within the Google Site. This was important as not all the group members were able to meet on a regular basis in person and so having an online environment that enabled the members to discuss content and develop it at the same time was essential to allowing the group to complete the assessment requirements.

With respect to Google Hangouts however the group members felt that they were not able to freely communicate using the platform, with the knowledge that the lecturer had access to their conversations. Thus, they were very careful in regards to what they said. There was also initially a disparity in the amount of effort members were investing in completing the assignment. One member then commented that being able to view the Recent Activity statistics was useful in identifying who was not contributing enough so that they could raise their concern with members in question. This helped ensure everyone was actively and effectively participating in the group assignment at least toward the end of the semester. Overall the group was awarded a B grade for the assessment as although the mark awarded for group work/participation was considerable compared to many of the other groups the standard of the final project plan was much lower than that required for an A grade.

Another group discussed each component of the assignment output at a face-to-face session each week, agreed on what would be written for that component in the assignment and then assigned the task of developing the Google Doc to a different group member each week. In this way, as explained by the Group Leader present at the focus group, they worked to ensure that everyone contributed to the assignment and worked as a team in producing the required output. During assessment, each member's contribution was clear because the researcher could see who had participated in the online environment. The researcher was also able to observe similar cohesion during in-class group work sessions. As a result, their group output was cohesive; similar font and formatting, as well as language style, was used throughout.

This group was also the only one that had some fun with the online environment; they customised the template with group images, a team name, a calendar illustrating when meetings were to be held, and a well-structured sitemap that was aligned with their assignment. They also used a task management feature in the wiki template to list, assign and check off tasks as they were completed in developing the Google Site and their group assignment output. The students were able to identify that the group members' positive outlook and willingness to cooperate as well as meeting face-to-face and discussing the requirements are the reasons they were able to work together so effectively. Other factors that may have influenced this group is that a domestic student and an exchange student from South America were members of the group. The domestic student may have had previous learning experience that utilized collaborative instruments. The exchange student was eager and motivated to understand the Kiwi way of learning. She was also very interested in getting to know people from different cultures and backgrounds. One member of the group felt that face-to-face sessions were essential since for most of the members of the group English was a second language and so these sessions facilitated each member's comprehension of the requirements of the assessment, the theory covered by the researcher in lectures and how it applied to the project. The group also initially experienced difficulty in configuring the site and a member of the group admitted they initially questioned why use of the site in completing the group assignment was required at all. The group then moved through this by watching instructional videos together and then working together to configure and customize the environment. Members of the group present at the focus group acknowledged that they then soon came to appreciate the ability to upload documents and have other members of the group review them and make comments or suggestions. Although there was only little evidence of the group members working simultaneously the group did use the Google Site regularly for document management and some collaboration during the semester and although they did not use Google Hangouts the group did include screenshots from instant messaging conversations from an online communication application they were using to communicate outside of face-to-face sessions. The application used was Facebook including Facebook Messenger since all members of the group had access to and were familiar with it. Interestingly there were far fewer instances of online messaging then face-to-face meetings, the minutes of which were also stored in the Google Site, since all members of the group were able to commit to weekly meetings and attend in-class group work sessions perhaps due to the fact that only one member of the group was a part-time student and in paid employment. This group was awarded an A plus grade as their overall group assignment mark.

A third group recognized the role that developing the Google Site played as a minor project to enable the group members to experience working as a group in delivering an output in order to identify individual strengths and develop an agreed and effective approach to working as a group. One member commented that the group had at times discussed the group development model at weekly group meetings in order to identify at what stage the group was at in terms of the various stages of the model. The researcher had also observed this group during the storming stage as they worked on building the bridge during a class group work session. At that time two members of the group dominated as leaders however when reviewing the groups' profile page in the Google Site part way through the second half of the semester it was interesting to find that another member of the group had been assigned the role of Group Leader. When prompted to talk to this during the focus group the appointed Group Leader was present and advised that the group had agreed that given the timeframe available to meet the assessment requirements and the conflict that had arisen and was most likely going to continue with respect to the two members of the group dominating the in-class group work session that week the group had decided the best way forward in order to move through the norming and to the performing stage of the group development model someone other than the two dominating students needed to lead the group. They went on to explain that the group leader was chosen based on that members ability to get the group to work together to produce the Google Site, using this component of the group assignment as a further test of individual member strengths and weaknesses. This group did then attempt to work collaboratively in the online platform to develop the assessment requirements however their use of the Google Site environment was disparate. The group used WhatsApp Messenger to communicate outside of face-to-face sessions, since the majority of the group was familiar with this application. Evidence of this, as witnessed from screen-prints taken from the application and uploaded on the groups Google Site, illustrated that such communication was irregular and mostly involved arranging meetings, chasing up group members who had not turned up for a meeting or who failed to complete an assigned task, and confirming assignment requirements. This group was awarded a C plus grade for the group assignment.

There was only one other group that mentioned the group development model. Members of this group that were present at the focus group acknowledged that they were not be able to move past the storming stage and were in fact very rarely using the online environment they were requested to configure for communication, collaboration and document management. The researcher was able to see this reflected in the Recent Activity statistics from the Google Site where it appeared that only one or two members of the group were in fact logging in to the environment. The Google Site itself was not created and configured till well into the Semester and the researcher saw no evidence of the group working collaboratively, on the site itself or on a document accessible through the site, in this environment. This group was however still able to produce a project plan for assessment, as the final project plan is required in in printed form, but it lacked cohesiveness not only in terms of format and style but also in terms of many aspects of the content itself and in the application of project management principles to the project idea. The researcher observed that during class room group work session's one member of the group dominated and much of the time was spent assigning tasks with little or no time allocated to understanding relevant theory and discussing its application to the project idea. The group also did not upload screen prints of online messaging or communication to their Google Site as evidence of group communication. This together with the general lack of evidence of group work and participation of every member of the group and the quality of submitted project plan resulted in the group being awarded a C minus grade overall for the group assignment.

The remaining three groups mostly only used the Google Site to upload documents developed offline or to develop parts of the required project plan as separate documents that were then combined as a printed version for submission. Their sites were also simple in structure however activity, albeit still minimal at times, was more frequent and involved all members of the group. The researcher also observed, during in class group work sessions, that there was evidence of the group having moved to the norming if not performing stage, in one case, of the group development model. As such there was discussion, acknowledgement and acceptance of individual contribution, and on occasions when the researcher was asked to take part in or contribute during group work sessions there was evidence of group cohesion. As a result, these three groups were awarded a higher mark for the group work/participation component of the assessment and this together with their mark for the group assignment output, although not as comprehensive or cohesive as the first two groups, resulted in two of the groups being awarded a B minus and one a C overall for the group assignment. One of these groups commented that having all the relevant files and documents stored centrally was useful given members of the group were rarely in contact face-to-face outside of class. They were able to use a section titled "research" to file documents and links that they had found useful in further understanding course material or that would be useful in developing the group assignment output. Other members of the group were able to access the same resources and work with the material. One of the groups also used a calendar feature within a Google Sites template to highlight when members of the group were available to work on the assignment and when they were involved in other activities such studying for or working on assessments for other subjects or working. This group also started to use a task management feature of the same template to list and assign tasks to be completed in developing the project plan. These groups all used Whats App Messenger to communicate outside of comments in the Google Site, primarily used for communicating with the researcher, and face-to-face sessions. When a member of the group present at the focus group was asked why the group had not used Google Hangouts the response generated further conversation with other members of the focus group around student preferences for using an application they were familiar with and that was easily accessible on a smartphone.

Interestingly, a small percentage of students found gaining access to the Google platform a little difficult, given they did not have an existing Gmail account with which they could login to the Google platform. The lecturer had mistakenly assumed that all the students would have a Gmail account. Google Sites is also apparently not well suited to use on a smartphone.

During the focus group, students also pointed out that it was a hassle to draft their content in MS Word and then upload and edit in Google Docs so as to present it as part of the group assignment output in a single document. These students were not using the Google Docs space to its full potential. Instead, they were worked individually and then pulled their contributions together for the purpose of assessment. As a result, the majority of the finished document lacked cohesion. Students were unaccustomed to using Google Docs and preferred to work with the familiar MS Word on computers at the Polytechnic or at home. The MS Word document at times reformatted automatically when imported to Google Docs which added to the confusion and unwillingness to adopt Google Docs as a tool.

The students also suggested that should the Google platform be used as part of the learning environment, that the content available to students should be customised. They felt overwhelmed by the application options and likened it to "opening a can of worms". Students felt that generic videos from YouTube or other material off the Internet were not helpful to their understanding of setting up, configuring or using a Google Site to facilitate the group work component of the group assignment. Students suggested that in the future it would be beneficial for the lecturer to provide video tutorials for students to refer to, which are tailored to the use of the Google platform and suite of applications for this module.

5. DISCUSSION

This study has confirmed for the researcher that there are a number of elements at play that influence how successful a group is in working together and delivering a group output.

The research has identified that those students who used Google Sites and related applications to coordinate schedules, manage documents, communicate and collaborate, according to the students, had a positive impact on their group work and on improving the cohesiveness of the assignment output. It is apparent however that using the suite of applications alone is not on its own the only aspect of such an assessment that students need to be aware of and that they should focus on if they are seeking an A grade.

The research further identified that many students were comfortable using Google Sites as a tool to assist with project administration, once they had spent some time learning how to use it and were provided with, or directed to, sufficient guidance and support.

One group did not complete the setup of their groups Google Site until well into the semester while some who had done so earlier on, used it in a way that was unintegrated into their group work. This may be due to their limited aptitude and as the researcher identify due to the lack of tailored instruction and supporting material from the lecturer.

Some students were confused and questioned the purpose of using such a tool to assist with group work and how they would be assessed for the time and effort spent on learning and developing the tool and for using it. Many students preferred therefore to use an application they were already familiar with to manage communication outside of face-to-face group work sessions and meetings.

There was also evidence of the benefit of providing the cohort with a brief outline of one example of a theory related group development with some students acknowledging the importance of focusing on getting the group work component working well in completing the assessment requirements to an acceptable standard.

6. LIMITATIONS

Ethics approval was not granted by the institution until the final week of the semester, hence a comparison of attitudes and experience of group work before and after the use of the online platform could not be effectively gathered.

The lecturer, as researcher, should have taken a more systematic approach to observing students by keeping a weekly reflective research journal, to capture perspectives on group work. If ethics approval was obtained closer to the semester start date students could also have been asked to maintain a weekly reflective journal of their experience in working as a group as the groups moved through the group development model and as the groups took up using the Google applications suite. Students would also have then not been pressured to feedback an entire semesters experience in one focus group and the possibility of a significant and/or useful element of their experience being forgotten would have been minimized.

While this study was conducted based purely on qualitative data, a mixed method could be used to analyse each student's usage data from the recent activity log and document version history in each Google Site. Data could then be used to support the researcher's observations as well as student feedback captured in a reflective journal during the semester and at a focus group discussion. A questionnaire could also be used to assist with sample selection for the focus group and for collecting quantitative data to support evidence obtained through qualitative methods. Multiple methods would have contributed towards a clearer understanding of the students' group work experiences and the impact, if any, of using Google applications.

7. CONCLUSION

Following the pilot study a more in-depth literature review was conducted of existing research and findings in the field of education research concerned with collaborative learning and group work, as well as related pedagogy, and the use of teaching and learning technologies and in particular Computer Supported Collaborative Learning (CSCL), including consideration of appropriate research methods and instruments, in tertiary education.

The experience and initial findings of the pilot study together with the results of this literature review will be used to develop a research design for further research. It is envisaged that by using a mixed method approach in the future greater insight and stronger more robust evidence will be obtained in addressing the research question.

An important final note is that ideally in the future the bulk of any quantitative data collected should be conducted once the Group Assignment has been assessed and the final overall mark for the course has been moderated and finalized. This would avoid any possible distortion of student responses and feedback pertaining to the students assumption that their partaking in the research and the response or feedback they provide therein having any weighting on their final assessment result.

REFERENCES

Blatchford, P. (2003). Toward a social pedagogy of classroom group work. *International Journal of Educational Research*, 39 (1-2), 153-172.

Deal, A. (2009). *A Teaching with Technology White Paper – Collaboration Tools*. Retrieved from https://www.cmu.edu/teaching/technology/whitepapers/CollaborationTools_Jan09.pdf

Google. (2016). New to Google Apps? Learn the Basics. Retrieved from https://support.google.com/a/answer/3035792?hl=en

Hall, D. & Buzwell, S. (2013). The problem of free-riding in group projects: Looking beyond social loafing as reason for non-contribution. *Active Learning in Higher Education*, 14(1), 37-49.

National Institute for Science Education. (1997). *What is Collaborative Learning?* Retrieved from http://archive.wceruw.org/cl1/CL/moreinfo/MI2A.htm

Postholm, M. B. (2008). Group work as a learning situation: a qualitative study in a university classroom. *Teachers and Teaching*, 14(2), 143-155

Resta, P. & Laferrière, T. (2007). Technology in support of collaborative learning. *Educational Psychology Review*, 19, 65-83.

Tuckman, B. (1965). Developmental Sequence in Small Groups'. Psychological Bulletin, 63 (6), 384-99.

University of Sydney. (2015). *Learning and Teaching group work guide for staff.* Retrieved from http://sydney.edu.au/education_social_work/groupwork/

FRACTANGI: A TANGIBLE LEARNING ENVIRONMENT FOR LEARNING ABOUT FRACTIONS WITH AN INTERACTIVE NUMBER LINE

Magda Mpiladeri, George Palaigeorgiou and Charalampos Lemonidis
Department of Primary Education, University of Western Macedonia, Greece

ABSTRACT

Tangible user interfaces (TUIs) are frequently used to teach children abstract concepts, in science and mathematics. TUIs offer a natural and immediate form of interaction that promotes active and hands-on engagement and allows for exploration and reflection. Tangible objects are representational artifacts in their essence, and they increase the representational power, which is a much needed quality in fraction teaching. By exploiting research into the external representations for learning, tangibles and embodied learning, we have designed an interactive tangible number line, named Fractangi, as a conceptual metaphor for helping students to understand and exploit fractions by acting with their hands. A pilot study was conducted in a Department of Primary Education with 65 undergraduate students in order to extract preservice teachers' views on the usability and learning effectiveness of the proposed tangible interface. Preservice teachers' views were extremely positive, in regards both to the context of usage (tangibility, gamification), and to the content of the interaction (learning interactions were considered better than traditional forms of teaching). Fractangi seems able to transform an unpopular learning topic to an enjoyable learning experience.

KEYWORDS

Tangible User Interface, Fractions, Number Line, Embodied Learning, Ubiquitous Computing

1. INTRODUCTION

Many researchers have suggested that tangible user interfaces (TUIs) have a great potential for supporting children's informal and formal learning because they leverage both familiar physical artifacts and digital computation. Tangibles are frequently used to teach children abstract concepts, in science and mathematics (Manches et al. 2010, McNeil et al. 2009). For example, Button Matrix (Cramer & Antle, 2015) uses coupled tactile, vibration and visual feedback to highlight features of a physical experience with arithmetic concepts and cue reflection on the links between the physical experience and mathematical symbols. Tangibles are able to offer a natural and immediate form of interaction that is accessible to learners, promotes active and hands-on engagement, encourages exploration and reflection, provides learners with tools to think with, enables learning abstract concepts through concrete representations while also offering collaborative opportunities for learners (Antle & Wise, 2013). Research has highlighted that technological tools for children need to be exciting, support exploration, inspire creativity, grow curiosity, stimulate interaction, and collaboration with peers, while being intuitive to use (Sylla et al. 2015). These are exactly the opportunities offered by TUIs for education through their natural support for collaborative activities, physical interactions, and external representations (Schneider et al. 2011).

While similar efforts have been made in many fields of mathematics, just few educational applications aim at learning about fractions. Fractions knowledge is a difficult to grasp domain, given the complex conceptual content and the frequent students' misconceptions. In this study, we have created a tangible learning environment called Fractangi, which aims to help students understand fractions with the help of a tangible interactive gamified number line. After a brief literature review, we will describe the design and operation of the tangible explorative interface, and then the results of a pilot study.

2. LITERATURE REVIEW

2.1 Learning about Fractions

Fractions instruction is usually a challenge for the teachers, since it is an object with complex conceptual content. Main fraction knowledge include the facts that fractions represent a part of an object or parts of a set of objects, they can be represented by fractional symbols, and that they are numbers that reflect numerical magnitudes (Jordan et al, 2013).

However, students often meet difficulties, as they cannot overcome the belief that the whole number properties are not applicable for all numbers in all cases and, even in high-school, many students are unable to understand that there are infinite numbers between any two fractions (Vamvakoussi and Vosniadou, 2010). In addition, many students encounter fractions as "meaningless symbols" or view numerator and denominator as separate numbers and not as a unified whole (Fazio and Siegler, 2011). Apart from these, some weaknesses in conceptual understanding can also be identified by the variability of strategies used by students, even in the case of the same problems and procedures (Lemonidis, 2015; Siegler et al, 2013). Due to such misconceptions, many teachers tend to work with fractions entirely as part-whole concepts (Lee, 2012). However, it is difficult for students to reconcile the part-whole model with the fact that fractions are continuous and infinitely divisible (Riconscente, 2013) and, consequently, more learning obstacles appear.

Among various teaching approaches suggested in contemporary bibliography, the most effective method to understand that fractions are numbers seems to be their representation on a number line. As Siegler et al, (2011) state "numerical development involves coming to understand that all real numbers have magnitudes that can be ordered and assigned specific locations on number lines". As a result, the number line model is suitable for fractions comprehension, as it offers significant benefits compared to other representational models. For instance, it offer advantages over the area models (such as pizza and rectangles) since it is much easier to divide the whole into equal parts; only length is involved, and hence addition and subtraction of fractions are more easily modeled on the number line (Wu, 2011).

Consequently, the number line is an advantageous tool for the understanding fractions as number magnitudes and that's why we selected this representational approach to become the basis of our tangible environment.

2.2 Tangibles and Embodiment in Mathematics

Mathematical cognition is embodied in two senses: it is based on conception and action, and is founded on the natural environment (Alibali & Nathan, 2012). Original human experiences are with objects met in nature and not with symbols. So, from the perspective of embodied learning, people interactions with physical objects create the foundation for subsequent "construction" of non-physical entities, contained in formal mathematical definitions (Moore-Russo et al, 2014). For example, when students talk about the concepts they learn, they often express new knowledge with gestures and bodily expressions proving that gestures are an integral part of communication about mathematical concepts (Abrahamson et al, 2012). So, when a student "becomes a thing itself," researchers assume that has a completely different kind of experience from a student who just watches, because the embodied learning promotes links between physical activities and mathematics, in a way that observation cannot do. As Birchfield claimed (2015), embodied learning is kinesthetic, multimodal and collaborative. In the definition above, the term "kinesthetic" means that each student interacts with the physical space using movements of his entire body, while the term "multimodal" refers to the fact that students see, hear and touch their "experiences". According to Moore-Russo, Ferrara & Edwards (2014), the motor system is involved in learning in diverse ways such as whole body movements, gestures, gaze, head movements, body postures, object manipulation, rhythm, etc. Similarly, the means of interaction can be tangible, such as voice, hands and body, or external, such as a computer screen, pencil, electronic devices, manipulative material for mathematics etc.

Physical objects have been traditionally used in kindergartens and elementary schools to introduce young learners to abstract concepts such as quantity, numbers, base ten, etc. Interestingly, there is another stream of research which supports that physicality is not important and offer evidence where children do not transfer performance from physical to symbolic representations of problems (McNeil et al 2009). However, a recent meta-analysis found that the use of physical manipulatives in math education tends to improve retention, problem solving, and transfer (Carbonneau, Marley, & Selig, 2013). Additionally, the context of use seems also to have detrimental effects. For example, unconstrained physical manipulation is probably suboptimal for learning (Stull et al. 2013) or high interactivity may be overwhelming and also lower learning performance (Stull et al. 2012).

Summing up, tangibles seem to offer great opportunities for learning since they constrain input alternatives and thus reduce modality on the interface, they promote sensory engagement which is the natural way students learn, they facilitate spatial tasks through the inherent spatiality of their existence, they offer opportunities for coupling the control of the physical object and the manipulation of its digital representation and they promote group learning by providing a multi-hand interface that does not give control to one person.

3. FRACTANGI: INTERACTIVE NUMBER LINES

Tangible objects are representational artifacts in their core essence, and combine some form of external representation with physical objects. Hence, they increase the representational power which is a much needed quality in fraction teaching. By exploiting research into the external representations for learning, tangibles and embodied learning, we have designed an interactive tangible number line as a conceptual metaphor for helping students to understand and exploit fractions by acting with their hands.

The tangible interface consists of a rectangular wooden structure with a length of 130 cm and width of 30 cm. On the bottom side, there is a lane with metal points along its length and a little wooden car, which can be moved along the lane and is fastened with a strap that resists moving and always returns it to its initial position. All along the main lane there are 14 points, which act like "buttons" and can be clicked by players to indicate the respective answer during the game. Above the first lane, there are 3 colorful ones which correspond to number lines divided into 3, 4 or 5 parts. In this area there is also a vertical "marker" that can be moved right or left to enable the players to study the equivalences between the different number lines. The basic number line is located just above the first lane and ranges from 0 to 2. Similarly, under the main lane, the distance is also presented in meters, so as to offer various symbolic representations.

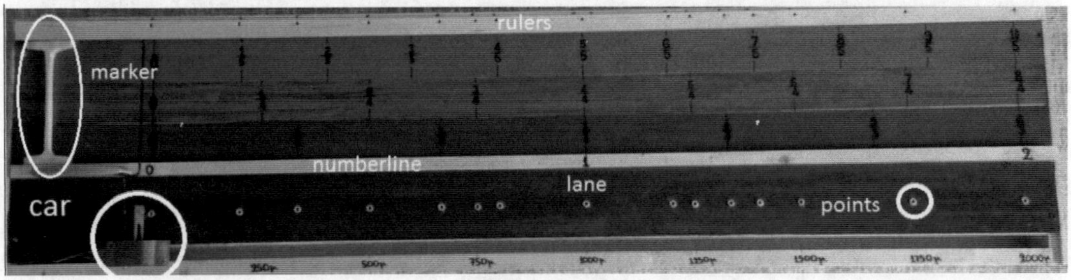

Figure 1. Fractangi

The game script describes that 20 runners from various countries had begun a race of 2 kilometers, which stopped due to heavy rainfall. At that time, each athlete had reached a specific position which was written down in cards. Students have to become the drivers of the wooden car and carry each athlete from the start to the point where they had stopped. Their runners' last position is given as a fraction of the main lane or in some cases as a fraction in relation to the position of other runners.

Athletes are depicted on the cards together with a name, the flag of their home country, and their last position as a fraction, a decimal number, and/or another virtual representation. The runners' names rhyme humorously with the names of the countries, so as to offer a more appealing experience to the students. Students have to put the card on the back of the car, transfer the athletes to their last position and press the metal protrusion located in the side of the car in order to check their answers. The device either congratulates the student or gives her feedback for finding the right answer. When the students find the correct answer, they place the card in holes at the upper edge of the construction, so as to be able to compare it later with the other runners.

The construction exploits cheap prototyping hardware (Makey Makey) and is controlled by a Scratch 2.0 program so as to be easily replicated by school instructors.

Figure 2. Fractangi Playing

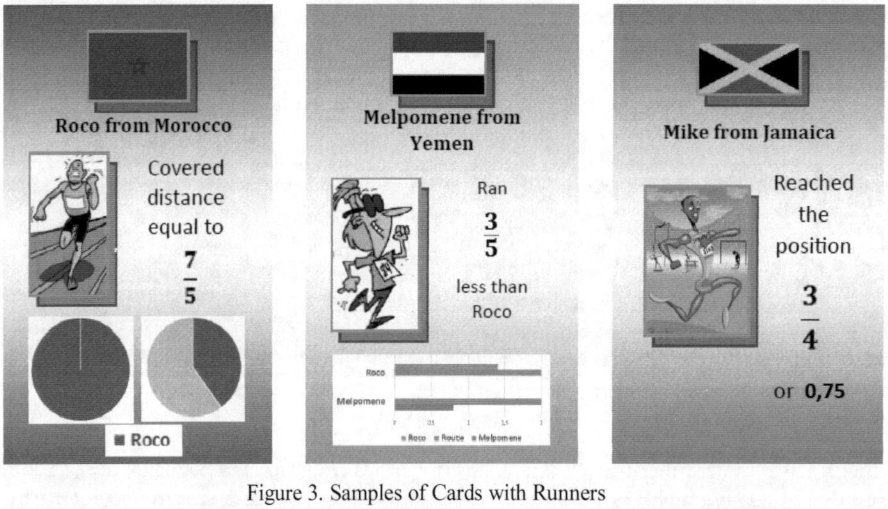

Figure 3. Samples of Cards with Runners

The game's objective is to engage the students in a variety of actions and cognitive processes, such as placing simple and improper fractions on number lines, interacting with various representations of fraction magnitudes (areas, decimal numbers and bar charts), comparing fractions, converting fractions into other equivalent representations and, finally, making operations with fractions (mainly addition and subtraction).

4. METHOD

A study was conducted in order to extract preservice teachers' views on the usability and learning effectiveness of the proposed tangible interface. The study was conducted in the context of a tangible and mixed reality educational spaces exhibition. Sixty five students of a Department of Primary Education participated in the study, 14 men and 51 women. The sampling was random and voluntary from the perspective of participants.

Every time a group of students approached the researchers, they explained the game rules and, then, asked them to get involved in the game. Participants usually played the game in groups of 3 to 4 people, but in few cases individually too. The mean usage of the environment was 20 to 30 minutes.

We employed both quantitative and qualitative measures. A questionnaire with 10 Likert type questions was used for evaluating the interface in 5 axes: usability, innovation, enjoyment, addressing learning objectives and future use. Ten of the participants voluntarily participated to a semi-structured interview process. The interview questions focused on the differences between the learning processes promoted by Fractangi, compared to traditional forms of teaching fractions.

5. RESULTS

5.1 Quantitative Data Analysis

The following table (Table 1) presents 65 students' responses in the closed-type questionnaire. The quantitative evaluation of the tangible environment was very positive. It can be concluded that the overwhelming majority of the students considered the tangible interface as useful, easy and enjoyable, both for themselves and their prospective students. And this becomes even more important, if we consider that fractions are a difficult and unpopular subject. Preservice teachers claimed that Fractangi is able to achieve its learning objectives, can help student exercise with fractions and fits well to the school's curriculum. The vast majority of the students also claimed that the interface offers interactions that were not possible in the past, provides understanding that is not easily achieved with traditional teaching means and, also, the feedback provided for the students' actions is satisfactory. It is particularly encouraging that students not only stated that they would like to test Fractangi in the classroom, but also that they would like to be in a position to create their own respective interfaces.

Consequently, preservice teachers' views for Fractangi were very positive, in regards both to the context of usage (tangibility, gamification), and to the content of the interaction (better learning interactions than traditional forms of teaching).

Table 1. Students' Responses to the Statements of the Questionnaire

Fractangi:	Totally Disagree	Disagree	Neither Agree Nor Disagree	Agree	Totally Agree
The use of the device was difficult.	2 (32,3%)	32 (49,2%)	7 (10,8%)	4 (6,2%)	1 (1,5%)
Students will find the interface enjoyable and they will be actively engaged with it.	0 (0%)	0 (0%)	0 (0%)	25 (38,5%)	40 (61,5%)
The learning objectives regarding fractions can be achieved through Fractangi.	0 (0%)	0 (0%)	1 (1,5%)	29 (44,6%)	35 (53,8%)
The device addresses the school's curriculum aims.	1 (1,5%)	0 (0%)	7 (10,8%)	34 (52,3%)	23 (35,4%)
The device allows students to make mistakes and gives them appropriate feedback.	0 (0%)	3 (4,6%)	4 (6,2%)	36 (55,4%)	22 (33,8%)
Students will probably prefer traditional teaching methods, as they will learn more that way.	35 (53,8%)	25 (38,5%)	1 (1,5%)	3 (4,6%)	1 (1,5%)
The device provides knowledge in such a way that could be hardly achieved in the classroom by traditional means.	0 (0%)	5 (7,7%)	11 (16,9%)	29 (44,6%)	20 (30,8%)

The interface is innovative and provides interactions that were unachievable in the past.	0 (0%)	0 (0%)	1 (1,5%)	31 (47,7%)	33 (50,8%)
I would like to experiment the device with students.	0 (0%)	0 (0%)	1 (1,5%)	27 (41,5%)	37 (56,9%)
I would like to be able to create such devices.	0 (0%)	0 (0%)	0 (0%)	20 (30,8%)	45 (69,2%)

5.2 Qualitative Data Analysis

The questions posed to the ten interviewees aimed at gathering qualitative data for the five axes of the questionnaire.

Regarding the innovation of the interface and its differences to traditional teaching methods, all students claimed that they find Fractangi very innovative. Also, they supported that Fractangi will be even more enjoyable for students thanks to its playful nature, which will undoubtedly stimulate children's interest, and will motivate them.

"It's very innovative and different in comparison to just listening to the teacher"

"It is innovative and quite helpful... it is a game, in which children will strive to participate, it will capture their interest and will become a creative activity"

"It is pleasant, interesting and has a lot of fun"

When participants were asked about whether a student could learn about fractions with Fractangi, everyone responded positively. Two undergraduates claimed that the tangible device probably is more intended for practicing in fractions, so they would use it complementary to conventional teaching in classroom.

"Students can obtain an enhanced sensitization of numbers, since they see the fractions in front of them"

"They see in front of them what the fractional unit is as well as its relationship with other fractions, so they will develop a better understanding"

"The game involves distances, which are familiar to students, and that will help them a lot to learn"

"It helps kids to learn, because although it is an embodied game, it is not abstract but focuses on specific learning objectives. I would definitely prefer Fractangi as a supplement to traditional teaching in the classroom"

It is important that although participants found the tangible device easy to use, interesting and playful at the same time, they said that the activities demanded a lot of cognitive effort.

"You stress your mind, but that's the point"

"There is an inherent difficulty in fractions, but that's the case. You aren't just placing the athletes; you have to work your mind in order to do it"

"...it cleverly asks students to simplify fractions and do fraction operations, since it asks them to calculate distances, by saying 'he is in front of somebody by a fraction'"

Some undergraduates confronted difficulties in putting the athletes in the right position, while during practicing, they also clarified issues around fractions that they had not comprehended in the past. The representations of the fractions were considered adequate and useful, both the ones that existed on the device and the ones presented on the cards.

"It offers good representations, you can see the equivalences and you can easily make conversions and simplifications."

"The cards are necessary and help a lot, because you can see the comparisons between runners and you can understand the relationship between fractions"

When asked to consider changes that should be made in order to improve the tangible device, all ten participants answered that they wouldn't change anything, while some argued that Fractangi should be even sold as a commercial game.

"It is very impressive, it has nice colors and it immediately caught my attention."

"It is robust because it is made of wood and you are not afraid to play. It could be sold as a toy. It is very well made"

A small concern stated was that the large size of the device may impede its usage for shorter kids. However, this can easily be overcome since two or more students can work together in choosing the position by just touching each other. As expected, a participant underlined that one device alone cannot address the needs of a classroom as its usage is intended for 4-6 individuals. He argued that if there are no other devices, that could be a deterring factor for using it in a classroom.

An important observation of the authors was that some participants, who faced considerable difficulties in carrying out the required operations with fractions, could continue its usage only with the explicit help of the researchers. Hence, if there was no presence of a researcher, some players would probably "stuck" at a point and would not manage to complete the game successfully. This means that despite the positive assertions for the feedback system, there is room for improvement. The device aims at letting the students to become autonomous in their play; the interaction should occur between them and the device, without requiring the researcher's or teacher's presence during the game play.

6. DISCUSSION

Low cost rapid prototyping hardware together with the uprising trend of arts and crafts fairs, tinkering and inventing have created a new trend of creating tangible technologies for learning. Researchers but also teachers and students can create or replicate tangible devices as Fractangi easily and, hence, the focus now is on the effective exploitation of physical interfaces or on identifying adequate embodied metaphors and realizing them into interaction models. Our pilot study indicated that Fractangi is a tangible environment that manages to transform exercising with fractions to an enjoyable and effective learning experience. Preservice teachers were enthusiastic with its instructional possibilities and also wanted to be able to create such devices by themselves.

Our study has several limitations. The most important one is that we present the perceived evaluations of preservice teachers. Although their views are a good indicator for the acceptability of the proposed interface from teachers, they cannot offer definite answers for the learning effectiveness of the device for students. Additionally, we do not analyze the underlying embodied mechanism for learning. Our hypothesis is that the Fractangi provokes students to develop a significant number of gestures that help them codify and understand better fractions and their equivalences and operations. This is the basic aim of our future research with Fractangi.

REFERENCES

Abrahamson, D. et al, 2012. You're it! Body, action, and object in STEM learning. *Proceedings of the International Conference of the Learning Sciences: Future of Learning (ICLS 2012)*. Vol. 1, pp. 283-290.

Alibali, M. W. and Nathan, M. J., 2012. Embodiment in Mathematics Teaching and Learning: Evidence From Learners' and Teachers' Gestures. *Journal of the Learning Sciences*, Vol. 21, No. 2, pp 247–286.

Antle, A. N. and Wise, A. F., 2013. Getting down to details: Using theories of cognition and learning to inform tangible user interface design. *Interacting with Computers*, Vol. 25, No. 1, pp 1-20.

Antle, A. N. et al, 2011. Embodied Interaction: Theory and Practice in HCI. In *Proc. CHI*, Vol. 11.

Ayala, N. A. R. et al, 2013. Kinesthetic Learning Applied to Mathematics Using Kinect. *Procedia Computer Science,* Vol 25, pp 131–135.

Birchfield, D., 2015. *Smallab learning*. Retrieved August 12, 2015, from http://smallablearning.com/embodied-learning/

Carbonneau, K. J. et al, 2013. A meta-analysis of the efficacy of teaching mathematics with concrete manipulatives. *Journal of Educational Psychology*, Vol. 105, No. 2, pp 380.

Cramer, E. S. and Antle, A. N., 2015. Button Matrix: How Tangible Interfaces can Structure Physical Experiences for Learning. *Proceedings of the Ninth International Conference on Tangible, Embedded, and Embodied Interaction*. ACM, pp. 301-304.

Fazio, L. and Siegler, R. S., 2011. *Teaching fractions*. International Academy of Education.

Jordan, N. C. et al, 2013. Developmental predictors of fraction concepts and procedures. *Journal of Experimental Child Psychology*, Vol. 116, No. 1, pp 45-58.

Lee, Y.L., 2012. *Using computer games to learn fractions* (Doctoral dissertation, University of Otago).

Lemonidis, C., 2015. *Mental Computation and Estimation: Implications for Mathematics Education Research, Teaching and Learning*. Routledge.

Manches, A. et al, 2010. The role of physical representations in solving number problems: A comparison of young children's use of physical and virtual materials. *Computers & Education*, Vol. 54. No. 3, pp 622-640.

McNeil, N. M. et al, 2009. Should you show me the money? Concrete objects both hurt and help performance on mathematics problems. *Learning and Instruction*, Vol. 19, No. 2, pp 171-184.

Moeller, K. et al, 2015. Computers in mathematics education–Training the mental number line. *Computers in Human Behavior*, Vol. 48, pp 597-607.

Moore-Russo, D. et al, 2014. *Emerging Perspectives on Gesture and Embodiment in Mathematics*. Information Age Publishing, Charlotte, NC.

Riconscente, M., 2013. *Mobile Learning Game Improves 5th Graders' Fraction Knowledge and Attitudes.* GameDesk Institute, Los Angeles.

Schneider, B. et al, 2011. Benefits of a tangible interface for collaborative learning and interaction. *In IEEE Transactions on Learning Technologies*, Vol. 4, No. 3, pp 222-232.

Siegler, R. S. et al, 2013. Fractions: the new frontier for theories of numerical development. *Trends in cognitive sciences*, Vol. 17, No. 1, pp 13-19.

Siegler, R. S. et al, 2011. An integrated theory of whole number and fractions development. *Cognitive psychology*, Vol. 62, No. 4, pp 273-296.

Stull, A. T. et al, 2013. Usability of concrete and virtual models in chemistry instruction. *Computers in Human Behavior*, Vol. 29, No. 6, pp 2546–2556.

Stull, A. T. et al, 2012. Representational translation with concrete models in organic chemistry. *Cognition & Instruction*, Vol. 30, No. 4, pp 404–434.

Sylla, C. et al, 2015. Play platforms for children's creativity. *In Creativity in the Digital Age*, pp. 223-243.

Vamvakoussi, X., and Vosniadou, S., 2010. How many decimals are there between two fractions? Aspects of secondary school students' understanding of rational numbers and their notation. *Cognition and instruction*, Vol. 28, No. 2, pp 181-209.

Wu, H., 2011. *Teaching fractions according to the Common Core Standards*. Retrieved February, 24, 2014.

EVALUATION OF LEANING UNIT DESIGN WITH USE OF PAGE FLIP INFORMATION ANALYSIS

Izumi Horikoshi[a], Masato Noguchi[b] and Yasuhisa Tamura[b]
[a]*Graduate School of Information Science, Sophia University, Japan*
[b]*Dept. Information & Communication Sciences, Sophia University, Japan*

ABSTRACT

In this paper, the authors attempted to evaluate design of leaning units with use of Learning Analytics technique on page flip information. Traditional formative assessment has been carried out by giving assignments and evaluating their results. However, the information that teacher can get from the evaluation is limited and coarse-grained. The authors set a research question that whether one can evaluate relation between learning objectives of learning units and the learners' actual activities in the units from page flip histories. The experimental result showed that the intensity of relation between the assignments and learning materials were different for each unit. Quantitatively, the correlation coefficients between "p-value of chi-square tests between range of page flip count and grade of assignment" and "proportion of number of questions in an assessment with reference page" was -0.889. With use of this relation, the authors attempted to evaluate design of units, and found out that the thing that may be critical to get high grade in an assignment of a certain unit was how many times they refer to their text book, though this assignment was designed for assessment of learners' skills to use or apply the learned knowledge. If teacher can get such suggestion as feedback, it is possible to utilize for formative assessment.

KEYWORDS

Learning Analytics, Formative Assessment, Learning Objective, Learning Log, Page Flip

1. INTRODUCTION

1.1 Digitization in Education and Learning Analytics

In the age of paper-based learning environment, learning records were limited in respects of both quantity and variety. It consisted of only results of exams, grades of assignments or course histories; even they were usually written with pencil or ink on paper. In 1990s, with the introduction of computers into schools, learning record data had been moved into machine-readable form. In 2000s, Learning Management System (LMS) had been spread, and many types of learning activity logs were collected. Finally, in 2010s, usage of laptop or tablet PCs has become common in even K-12 education. It enables to record or collect various fine-grained learning activity logs. It is notable that these modern logs contain client-side activities, e.g. page flip, process of answering, eye-track, voice and environmental sound, and GPS information. In the future, even physiological data like blood pressure, sweating or heartbeat will be treated as "learning activity logs".

Along with the trend on digitization in education, Learning Analytics (LA) has become a major area in learning science and learning technology research. Ferguson (2012) described a definition of Learning Analytics as follows: "Learning analytics is the measurement, collection, analysis and reporting of data about learners and their contexts, for purposes of understanding and optimizing learning and the environments in which it occurs." Ferguson does not refer to "report to whom" in her definition of LA. However, some target to report can be assumed, for example learners, teachers, or schools, and the authors think their needs in LA depend on each target. For example, learners want to know their own grade or position in their class, while teachers want to know whether their lectures worked as they had intended.

1.2 Learning Analytics and Formative Assessment

In this paper, the authors focus on utilizing LA for formative assessment, in other words, LA for teachers. Bloom (1971) described a definition of the formative assessment as follows: "the use of systematic evaluation in the process of curriculum construction, teaching and learning for the purpose of improving any of these three processes." This Bloom's definition of formative assessment is very similar to Ferguson's definition of LA, especially on its purpose.

Traditional formative assessment has been carried out by giving assignment or quiz and evaluating their results. However, assignment or quiz is not more than once a unit and therefore information for the teachers is limited and coarse-grained. Therefore, teachers observe their learners carefully to get further information. However, it is difficult to get what they did or said, much less what they thought or what they learned. In cognitive science area, there are many methods to estimate such cognitive information. These methods are able to give fine-grained information. However, it needs qualitative assessment and it is also heavy workload to carry out these assessment or observation in practice.

However, as mentioned in Section 1.1, fine granularity learning data has been recorded in machine-readable form. In LMS based environment, some kinds of LA are already at practical stage, and some LMSs have functions such as summary of login history/ course history/ grade, visualization of their week units, or recommendation of related courses. Educational applications also have had functions to visualize information of same kind. Some leading-edge LMSs or applications have functions such as evaluation of design of courses, units or learning materials by analyzing learning logs. That is, for example, to verify whether learners who take a certain course were target learners as expected, or to analyze the reason why many learners chose or wrote wrong answer in a certain problem.

One factor of the learning design that the authors have focused on is learning objective. As often said, learning objective of some units are acquisition of knowledge or theory while that of other units are application of them. In Japan, Ministry of Education, Culture, Sports, Science and Technology (MEXT) has been conducting the National Assessment of Academic Ability (NAAA) in mathematics and language for Grades 6 and 9 every year. According to OECD (2015), NAAA consists of two types of assessments: assessment on learner learning (subject knowledge; problem Type-A) and learner achievement (practical use of knowledge and skills; problem Type-B). Shirouzu (2015) mentioned that "problem Type-B" is roughly corresponding to TIMSS or PISA literacy problems respectively."

There are some researches or practice of utilizing learning data to assessment, and Ripley (2007) reported update on research, policy and practice, and the author of that paper called such assessment as "e-assessment".

1.3 Page Flip History

Among various data in Learning Analytics, the authors have focused on "page flip" log of learning materials. Page flip log or page transition log is the information when and in what order the learners flipped pages, and the authors called the sequence of page flip log "page flip history". This page flip history could not available from paper-based textbooks or other materials. In other words, teachers using paper-based textbooks conduct lessons on the assumption that their learners follow the teacher. However, if teachers use digital textbooks on client PCs, page flip history of each learner can be visualized by equipping function to collect page flip information.

There are many researches that focused on a kind of page flip history. Nicholas (2010) reported analysis of transactional logs obtained from the MyiLibrary platform regarding 127 UK universities. Also, in Japan, Kyushu University has carried out whole-university project to collect and analyze learning data from LMS (Moodle) and the e-book system (BookLooper) (Kyushu University Learning Analytics Center 2016). Objectives of their studies are as follows: (1) improving of learning materials, (2) analyzing learning patterns, (3) detecting students' comprehensive level, (4) predicting final grades, and (5) recommending e-books in accordance with personalization (Mouri 2016).

1.4 Research Question

The purpose of this research is to verify research question that we can evaluate design of learning units from page flip history of the units. Especially, the authors focused on the point whether we can evaluate relation between learning objectives of the learning units and the learners' actual activities in the units. If this relation can be visualized and evaluated, it leads to enable the quantitative formative assessment from fine granularity data with light workload.

2. METHODS

2.1 Target Courses, Units and Subjects

The authors set two target courses. Both courses were held in Sophia University, Japan, and one of the authors was in charge. Target courses, units, and the number of subjects are shown in Table 1.

Table 1. Information of Target Unit

Course	Unit ID	Unit	Date	Number of Subjects
Information Literacy	IL518	Journal search	May 18, 2015	71
	IL601	Numerical data	June 1, 2015	64
Learning Technology	LT519	Instructional Design	May 19, 2015	37
	LT526	Test and Feedback	May 26, 2015	34

The Information Literacy course was entry level for 1st year students, so contents were rather easy. In contrast, Learning Technology course was for 3rd year students, so contents were relatively difficult.

2.2 Data Acquisition Scheme

As previously reported (Horikoshi 2015), the authors focused on page transition of PowerPoint slide, because an author (Tamura) mainly uses PowerPoint in his lectures. And the other author of that paper (Yamazaki) developed the scheme and function to detect and transfer page flip logs automatically. This function is implemented in JavaScript, therefore the authors converted the original materials (Power Point files) into HTML and JPEG files, and added the JavaScript above. Page flip logs and other information are sent to Learning Record Store (LRS), when each subject changed pages. The items stored in LRS are as below:

- Actor: student's ID
- Verb: lunched/ experienced
- Page: page number
- Date: date and times

2.3 Procedure

In the target classes, the author (Tamura) held lectures as usual with use of these materials. Subjects access the proposing materials, and page flip logs were transferred into LRS, when each subject changed pages in the classes. Then, learners were given assignments.

3. RESULT

3.1 Page Flip History and Page Flip Count

An example of page flip history is shown in Figure 1. In this figure, vertical axis shows slide page number and horizontal axis shows time (maximum of 90 minutes), and the thick line shows a history of a teacher while other thin lines show subjects'.

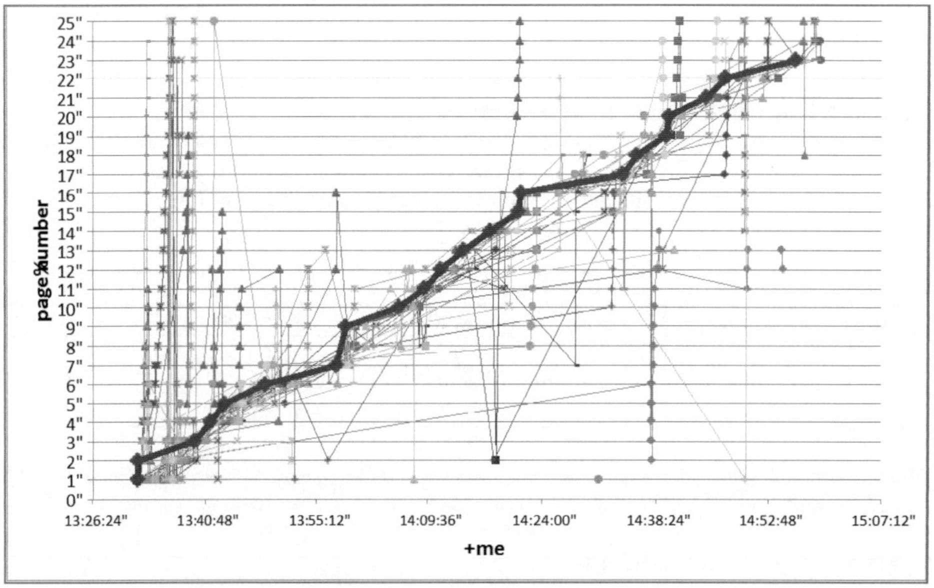

Figure 1. Example of Page flip history (LT526)

"Page flip count" is the number of page transition times. In this paper, the authors define the "page flip count" specially as follows: transition only from a certain page to other page. Some examples of fit/unfit case are as below:

· fit case: from page3 to page4

· unfit case: from page3 to page3 (click a link of current page)

3.2 Correlation between Page Flip Count and Grade

At the beginning of analysis, the authors determined the strength of a correlation between the page flip count and grade of assignment of each unit, for there might be general hypothesis that learners who refer to their text book many times are diligent, and they are able to get high grade at assignment of that unit. Scatter plot of the page flip count versus grade of assignment and correlation coefficients between them are shown in Table 2 and Figure 2.

Table 2. Correlation coefficients between page flip count and grade of assignment

Unit ID	Correlation coefficient	p-value
IL518	0.122	0.360
IL601	0.195	0.142
LT519	-0.142	0.409
LT526	-0.207	0.263

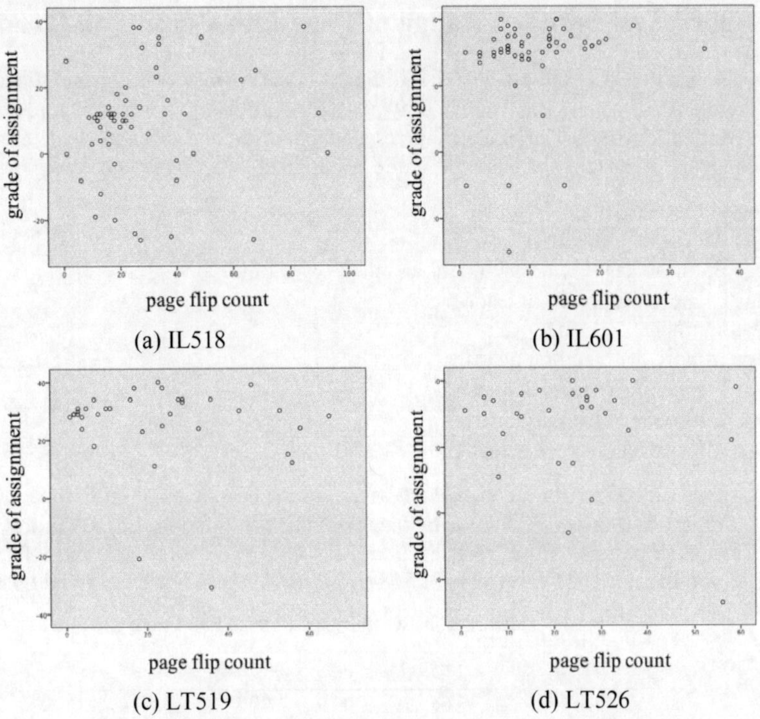

Figure 2. Scatter plot of page flip count vs. grade of assignment

As observed from Figure 2 and Table 2, there was no significant correlation between page flip count and grade of assignment. This result means even if learners referred to their text book many times, they cannot always get high grade at assignment. This is visually shown in Figure 3. Figure 3 shows page flip history of each learner in a unit (LT526), and the histories are ordered from upper left to lower right by their grades (history of the top left is the teacher's). Blank cells show learners who were absent from the class. For example, the learner in the 3rd cell from the right on the top raw is the second in grade of assessment while he or she was absent from the class.

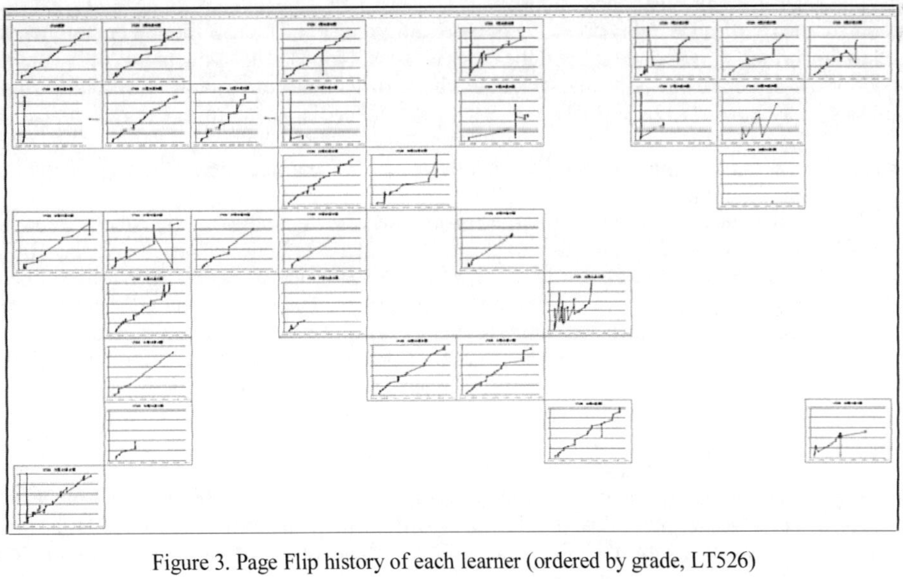

Figure 3. Page Flip history of each learner (ordered by grade, LT526)

3.3 Chi-Square Test between Range of Page Flip Count and Grade

As mentioned in Section 3.2, there was no significant correlation between page flip count and grade of assignment, therefore the authors verified whether there is a significant variation in grade by range of page flip count. The verification is performed using cross-tabulation and independent chi-squared test. For cross-tabulation, page flip count and learners' grade are divided into ranges as below:

Page flip count

- Range A: less than teacher's flip
- Range B: more than teacher's flip and less than twice of teacher's
- Range C: more than twice of teacher's

Grade of assignment

- Range 1: more than the first quartile
- Range 2: more than the median
- Range 3: more than the third quartile
- Range 4: less than the third quartile

The result of chi-square test of independence based on the cross-tabulation is shown in Table 3. Table 3 shows there is a significant variation in grade by range of page flip count in IL518 and IL601, but not in LT519 and LT526. This result possibly arose from difference between two courses (IL and LT). However, there are still difference even in same course, between IL518 and IL601 or between LT519 and LT526.

Table 3. Chi-Square Test between Range of Page Flip Count and Grade

Unit ID	χ^2	p-value
IL518	28.19	0.000
IL601	14.26	0.027
LT519	8.34	0.214
LT526	4.58	0.599

3.4 Relation between Assignment and Learning Materials

Based on the result in Section 3.3, the authors hypothesized that the intensity of relation between the assignments and learning materials are different for each unit, and the p-value of chi-square test in Section 3.3 reflects this intensity. As mentioned in Section 1.2, learning objective of some units are acquisition of knowledge or theory while learning objective of other units are application of them. For simplicity, the authors referred to the former units as Type-A, and the latter units as Type-B. The assignments of the units Type-A are designed for assessment whether learners acquired the knowledge lectured in the class, and assignments with such purpose may have reference pages in the learning materials. In contrast, the assignments of the units Type-B are designed for assessment of learners' skills to use or apply the learned knowledge, and assignments with such purpose may not have direct reference pages in the learning materials, or perhaps it may not be critical how many times they refer to their textbook to get high grade in assignment.

This hypothesis consists of following two elements; (a)Whether some questions have reference page and the others do not, and proportion of number of questions in an assessment with reference page differ from each unit, and (b) Whether there is correlation between p-value of chi-square tests between range of page flip count and grade of assignment and proportion of number of questions in an assessment with reference page.

First, the authors examined each assignment to verify (a), and evaluated proportion of number of questions in an assessment with reference page. The result of this evaluation is as follows: IL518 (20%), IL601 (10%), LT529 (5%), LT526 (0%). Proportion of number of questions in an assessment with reference page is given in parenthesis. This result demonstrated that the proportion of number of questions in an assessment with reference page differ from each unit, and this indicates that (a) is verified. Therefore, in second, the authors determined the correlation coefficients between the "p-value of chi-square tests between range of page flip count and grade of assignment" and the "proportion of number of questions in an assessment with reference page" to verify (b). Scatter plot of the p-value of chi-square tests versus the proportion is shown in Figure 4, and correlation coefficients between them was -0.889. It shows there is strong negative correlation between them, and this indicates that (b) is verified.

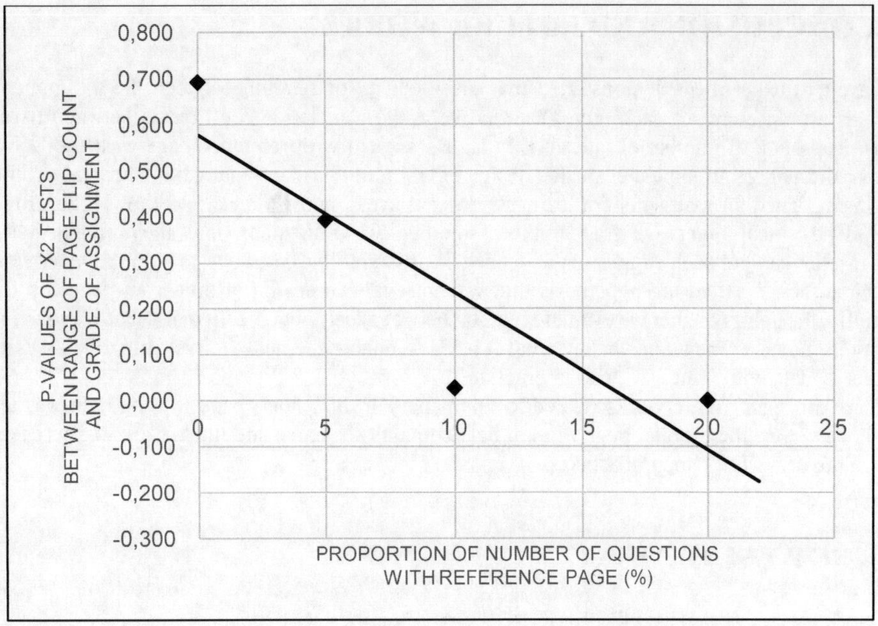

Figure 4. Scatter plot of "p-value of chi-square tests between range of page flip count and grade of assignment" and "proportion of number of questions in an assessment with reference page"

4. DISCUSSION

The result in Section 3.4 demonstrates that the intensity of relation between the assignments and learning materials are different for each unit. Also, Figure 6 and correlation coefficients in Section 3.4 show that larger proportion of number of questions with reference page the units have, more significant the p-values of chi-square tests are. That is, as mentioned in Section 3.4, intensity of relation between range of page flip count and grade of assignments reflects the intensity of relation between the assignment and learning material. Based on these results, it is suspected that it is possible to provide formative assessment from page flip history. In other words, it is possible to evaluate whether the lectures or assignments worked as teacher or designer intended from these two intensity of relation.

The intensity of relation between the assignment and learning material is quantitatively evaluated as the "proportion of number of questions in an assessment with reference page", and it may represent intention of learning design. By contrast, the intensity of relation between range of page flip count and grade of assignments is quantitatively evaluated as the "p-value of chi-square test between range of page flip count and grade of assignment", and it may represent how the lectures or assignments worked actually. If these two intensity of relation are comparable with each other, this may appear as negative correlation coefficients.

Therefore, in order to evaluate a certain unit from these correlation coefficients in terms of formative assessment, you should focus on whether a point of scatter plot shown in Figure 4 is on the regression line. For example, as observed from Figure 4, the point of IL601 is outliner. This shows that the "proportion of number of questions in an assessment with reference page" is small in this unit, though intensity of relation between range of page flip count and grade of assignments is strong. In this case, it is suggested that the thing that may be critical to get high grade in this assignment was how many times they refer to their text book, though an assignment of this unit was designed for assessment of learners' skills to use or apply the learned knowledge. If teacher can get this suggestion as feedback, it is possible to utilize for formative assessment; for example, a teacher improves his assignment as designed for assessment of learners' skills to use or apply the learned knowledge.

5. CONCLUSION AND FUTURE WORKS

The result of experiment demonstrated that the intensity of relation between the assignment and learning materials are different for each unit. Quantitatively, the correlation coefficients between p-value of $\chi 2$ tests versus proportion of number of questions in an assessment with reference page was -0.889. With use of this relation, the authors attempted evaluated design of learning units, and found out that an assignment of a certain unit was designed for assessment of learners' skills to use or apply the learned knowledge. However, the thing that may be critical to get high grade in this assignment was how many times they refer to their text book.

If teacher can get such suggestion as feedback, it is possible to utilize for formative assessment. It shows that the authors verified the hypothesis that we can evaluate design of unit from page flip history the unit, especially, the point whether we evaluate relation between learning objective of the unit and the learner's actual activity in the unit. The author believe that it leads to enable the quantitative formative assessment from fine granularity data with light workload in practice.

There are some future works related to this paper. In this paper, page flip log data was use as page flip counts. However, the original page flip log data contains sequence and time span. So, there is a possibility to analyze the data from temporal aspects.

ACKNOWLEDGEMENT

This work was supported by JSPS KAKENHI Grant Number 26282059.
The authors also thank to Mr. Kimiaki Yamazaki, TEK Software to develop page flip acquisition scheme.

REFERENCES

Bloom, B. et al., 1971. *Handbook on Formative and Summative Evaluation of Student Learning.* McGraw-Hill, New York, USA.

Ferguson, R., 2012. Learning analytics: drivers, developments and challenges. *International Journal of Technology Enhanced Learning*, Vol. 4, No. 5-6, pp.304-317.

Horikoshi, I., et al., 2015. Learning Style Verification with use of Questionnaire and Page Flip History. *Proceedings of the 23rd International Conference on Computers in Education.* Hongzhou, China, pp.627-636

Kyushu University Learning Analytics Center, 2016. Retrieved from http://lac.kyushu-u.ac.jp/e/

Mouri, K., et al,. 2016. Profiling High-achieving Students for E-book-based Learning Analytics. *Proceedings of Cross-LAK 2016.* Edinburgh, UK, pp.1-5.

Nicholas, D., et al., 2010. E-textbook use, information seeking behaviour and its impact: Case study business and management. *Journal of information Science,* Vol. 36, No.2, pp.263-280.

OECD, 2015. *Education Policy Outlook: Japan.* OECD Publishing, Paris, France. Retrieved from http://www.oecd.org/edu/Japan-country-profile.pdf

Ripley, M., 2007, E-assessment: An update on research, policy and practice. Bristol: Futurelab, Bristol, United Kingdom. Retrieved from https://www.nfer.ac.uk/publications/FUTL64/FUTL64.pdf

Shirouzu, H., et al., 2015. Proposing an Alternative Framework for the Assessment of Collaborative Problem Solving. *Proceedings of CSCL 2015.* Gothenburg, Sweden, pp.839-840.

EINSTEIN'S RIDDLE AS A TOOL FOR PROFILING STUDENTS

Vildan Özeke[1] and Gökhan Akçapınar[2]

[1]*Gaziosmanpaşa University, Turkey, Faculty of Education, Department of Computer Education and Instructional Technology*

[2]*Hacettepe University, Turkey, Faculty of Education, Department of Computer Education and Instructional Technology*

ABSTRACT

There are many computer games, learning environments, online tutoring systems or computerized tools which keeps the track of the user while learning or engaging in the activities. This paper presents results from an exploratory study and aims to group students regarding their behavior data while solving the Einstein's riddle. 45 undergraduate students were given this logic puzzle as a complex cognitive task without any time limitation. After completing the task, they were asked to report their mental effort. While grouping the similar students, cluster analysis with X-Means algorithm was used. Features such as task performance, puzzle's difficulty levels, item movements inside and between the puzzle's sections, duration and a total number of incorrect moves were used while grouping students. At the end of the lab session, six out of forty-five participants solved the puzzle and find the correct answer, on the other hand, other students reached different completion levels. Based on cluster analysis students grouped into three different clusters, Cluster_0, Cluster_1 and Cluster_2. Cluster_2 was the successful group with the highest score, lowest moves and errors, medium level of mental effort in the shortest time period. Cluster_0 had the medium level of success with highest moves and errors, the highest level of mental effort in the highest time period. Cluster_1 was the least successful group with the lowest score, medium level of moves and errors and lowest level of mental effort.

KEYWORDS

Student profiling, clustering, educational data mining, complex cognitive task, mental effort, logic puzzle

1. INTRODUCTION

Computerized tools allow researchers to collect all kind of data about interaction between the user and the system in an unobtrusive way without disturbing the user (Khenissi et al., 2015). By analyzing data - obtained from these tools - with the help of data mining techniques can be used in different areas. One of this application area is grouping users based on their similarities (personal preferences, characteristics, etc.). Grouping similar users (user profiling) can be used for many purposes in many domains such as business for marketing strategies and personalized advertising, or gaming industry for categorizing the players (e.g. casual players, weekenders, social players, big spenders, decorators etc.) (Bienkowski et al., 2012). In educational setting, user profiling has been used to increase the learning performances and effectiveness when organizing adaptive/individualized learning environments (Bienkowski et al., 2012), in intelligent tutoring systems to present adaptive interaction support, to create online study groups according to clustering results (Kardan and Conati, 2011).

Learner profiling is usually conducted by analyzing the learner logs retrieved from e-learning environments (Wang and Liao, 2011, Akçapınar et al., 2016) or educational games (Hawlitschek and Köppen, 2014) with data mining and machine learning algorithms (Bienkowski et al., 2012). Apart from these studies, in the present study we used a logic puzzle (Einstein's Riddle) as a data collection tool with the aim of grouping similar students. Correlation between students' self-reported mental effort scores and log based features was also investigated for each cluster.

1.1 Einstein's Riddle as a Complex Cognitive Task

Solving a logic puzzle is required to use high-level cognitive skills (e.g. reasoning, problem-solving, analytical/critical thinking, etc.) and cognitive processes (e.g. attention, coding, storing, mental shifting, mental effort etc.) together. Cognitive competence of a person was formed by cognitive skills which allow individuals to distinguish objects, events or stimuli, to identify and categorize the concepts, to build issues, rules and make them "problem solvers" with high-level mental processing (Otero et al., 2012).

Therefore, these puzzles can be used to assess cognitive skills of students and to profile their cognitive traits and situations. Moreover, we can also categorize them as "*complex cognitive task*" according to Wood's (1986) task complexity definition. As stated by Wood, there are three types of task complexity: a) component, b) coordinative, and c) dynamic complexity. The component complexity is a function of the number of information cues to be processed and the number of acts which need to be executed during the task performance (e.g. chess game). As the numbers increase the task complexity increases. The coordinative complexity related to the power of relationships (strong/weak) between task inputs (information cue & required acts) and task products. While the learner performed acts in one part of the task, several other acts need to be performed concurrently (e.g. radio assembly). The dynamic complexity refers to the change in time of both task inputs/outputs, and the relationships between them (e.g. decision making). For example, air-traffic controlling used to be known as complex cognitive tasks which include these three types of task complexity. According to Wood (1986), total complexity of a task derives from these three types of complexity.

There are rules, hints and puzzle items as information cues in Einstein's riddle (see Figure 1), and learners have to act between areas by dragging and dropping, clicking and checking the boxes simultaneously. All these actions can be considered as component and coordinative complexity. Some hints may need to be returned and to read again for solving the puzzle and the participant need to uncheck/recheck it for the upper-level boxes and this situation can be considered as dynamic complexity.

Finally, it is important to track and record the cognitive processing of a learner while s/he was engaging with a cognitive task. The aim of this study is to determine user behavior and to name their profiles by using a computerized complex cognitive task.

2. METHOD

2.1 Study Design

This is an exploratory design study conducted with 45 undergraduate students (24 females and 21 males) in the Computer Education and Instructional Technology (CEIT) Department in a state-funded university in Turkey. Participants' ages ranged between 20 and 27 with the mean of 21.92 (SD = 1.47). Each student has completed the computer-based task on their own without any time limitation. The minimum and maximum duration for all participants were between 5 and 39 minutes (M = 19.88, SD = 8.02). All participants were a volunteer and dealt with the task in a computer laboratory. The instructions were given by the authors and there was no time limitation for completing the task. The participants were informed about they have a right to quit the task anytime they want. After completing the task, they have asked to self-reported their amount of mental effort.

2.2 Material

The complex cognitive task used in a study is known as Einstein's five-house riddle (see Appendix). There is no evidence about who invented the puzzle but it is very popular among logic puzzles. In general, different kind of animals and cigarette brands are used as a puzzle items. Because of educational concern of the study, we have changed cigarette brands with car brands. The authors developed a computerized version of this puzzle. The tool was developed using C# programming language on Windows Presentation Foundation (WPF) platform. Event based logging system was also implemented. Therefore, the tool is able to log all events (check, uncheck, move, etc.) during the session with a timestamp. Following information was given to the students as part of the puzzle: rules to be considered, fifteen hints, and a question. They can click the checkbox in front of the hint when they think they have used that information to solve the puzzle and it turns red as seen in the "hints" area in Figure 1. They can drag and drop each of the "puzzle items" over the "solution matrix" (from Section A to Section B), they can also move items inside the section A and section B as they prefer. In the "hints" section there are two more buttons: "Restart" (works as a reset) and "Finish" (to use after completing the task or when they would like to quit).

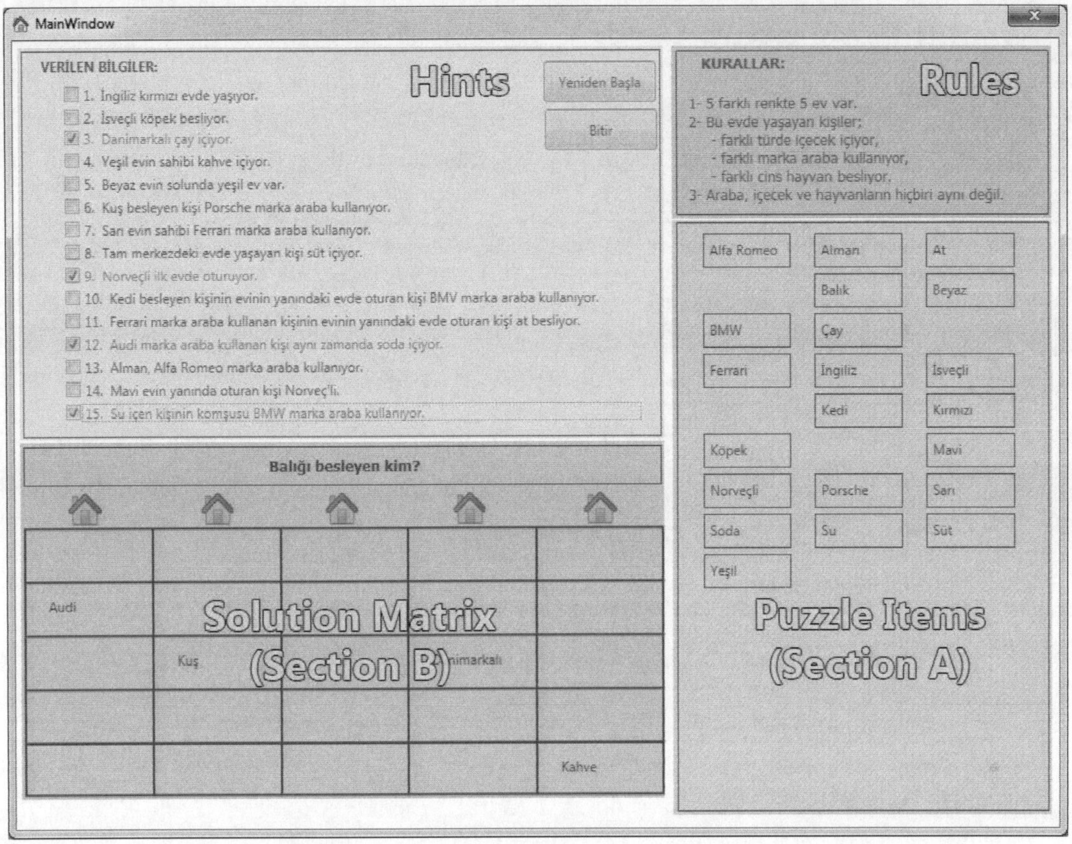

Figure 1. A screenshot from the computerized version of Einstein's five-house riddle

Merrill (2006a, 2006b) suggests researchers to create rubrics for the evaluation of task performance, and to calculate different performance levels at the end of the process. According to Merrill (2006a, 2006b) the number of transactions/steps where the complexity ascends should be stated in order to be able to assess the performance levels for complex tasks. A rubric scale was developed to calculate the performance score of participants (over 100 points). There are four levels to get the final answer. Level 1 has the basic boxes to fill. While the level increases the puzzle requires more attention and the scores of the boxes increase. There are 25 boxes to fill while solving the puzzle and all truly filled box adds some points to the participant's overall score. While calculating the total score of the participants the scale given in Table 1 was used.

Table 1. Calculating the performance score over 100 points

Difficulty level	Count of boxes	Points for each	Total Point
Level 1	3 boxes	1 point	3
Level 2	8 boxes	3 points	24
Level 3	6 boxes	5 points	30
Level 4	7 boxes	6 points	42
The answer	1 box	1 point	1

2.3 Rating Scale Mental Effort (RSME)

Zijlstra (1993) gave some visual search tasks to his driver participants and then measured their mental effort in his dissertation. The vertical scale has a range between 0-150 points from "hardly any effort" to "extreme effort". According to Zijlstra (1993; pp.34-35) the amount of the effort depends on the following three variables as a) the demands of the task, b) subject's available performance potential and c) the duration of the activity (time-on-task). The reliability of the scale was $r = .81$ in a laboratory setting and $r = .71$ in a real work setting. The participants self-reported their mental effort after finishing the task.

2.4 Features

Computerized version of the puzzle is able to log every action done by the students. Each session was logged in separate log files. Student's ID was used as a unique identifier to join different data sources. Analysis data generated automatically by the developed preprocess tool. The dataset used in the cluster analysis consisted of 45 students' usage data with 11 features. Four of them related to student's moves inside the game. Four of them related to student's achievements across the different levels. One is a number of error (incorrect placements) done by the student. One is game duration. And the last one is showed the highest score achieved by the student during the game. List of the features and their explanations can be seen in Table 2.

Table 2. Description of features

Feature	Description
AA[a]	Total number of moves inside section A (item area)
AB[a]	Total number of moves from section A to B
BA[a]	Total number of moves from section B to A
BB[a]	Total number of moves inside section B (solution area)
L1	Total number of correct placements in Level 1 difficulty
L2	Total number of correct placements in Level 2 difficulty
L3	Total number of correct placements in Level 3 difficulty
L4	Total number of correct placements in Level 4 difficulty
Duration	Total time (minutes) spent in puzzle
Error	Total number of incorrect moves
Score	Highest score achieved during the session

[a] Section A and Section B can be seen in Figure 1.

2.5 Data Analysis

Data analysis was performed by using cluster analysis. Cluster analysis is widely used in educational data mining studies to identify similar groups of students. X-Means was used as a clustering algorithm; it is a modified version of the K-Means. Unlike K-Means algorithm, X-Means does not need to perform any clustering a-priori. It directly finds the optimum number of clusters from the data by using Bayesian Information Criteria (BIC) (Pelleg and Moore, 2000). X-Means algorithm was selected since we have no a priori knowledge about the number of hidden groups in the data. Cluster analysis was performed RapidMiner data mining software with process given in Figure 2. Cosine similarity measure was used as a distance metric and all features were converted to z-scores before the analysis.

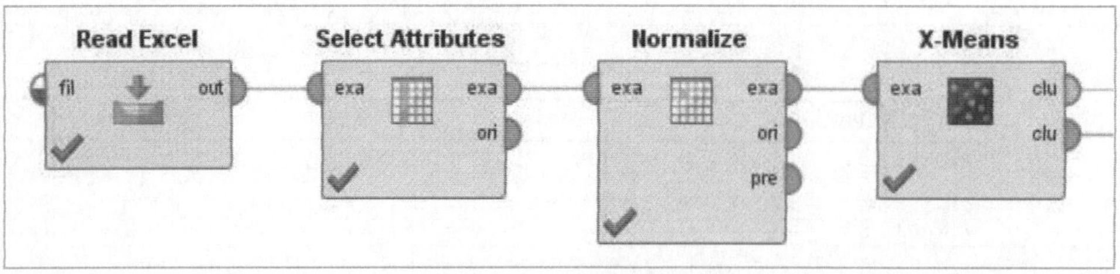

Figure 2. Cluster analysis process

3. RESULTS

As a result of the cluster analysis three different groups of students were obtained, Cluster_0, Cluster_1 and Cluster_2. According to cluster means given in Table 3 and Figure 3, Cluster_0 spent more time during the task than Cluster_1 and Cluster_2. Cluster_0 also had the most moves inside and between the sections (item and solution area), had the most errors but got average level of success. We can infer that Cluster_0 really did their best to accomplish the task. On the other hand, Cluster_2 was the one who spent the minimum time and had the minimum moves with minimum errors. Cluster_2 got the highest success in contrast with Cluster_1. However, Cluster_1 was the least successful group with medium errors. They had very close values to Cluster_2 in terms of moves between sections with only a distinct difference that Cluster_1 had more moves inside section A than Cluster_2. Their performance duration was similar.

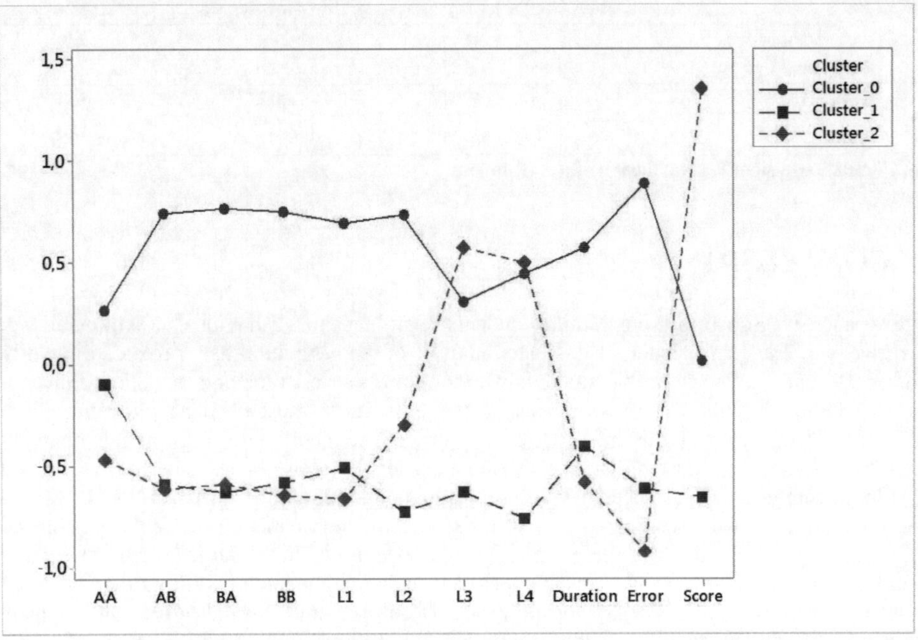

Figure 3. Normalized cluster centroids

Six of the participants placed all of the 25 items correctly and find the answer. Four of them are in the Cluster_2, two of them in Cluster_0. Other participants, however, reached the different level of completion. Their scores range from 8 to 93 (M = 43.0, SD = 21.0).

Table 3. Cluster means and standard deviations for all features

Feature	Cluster_0 (n = 18)	Cluster_1 (n = 18)	Cluster_2 (n = 9)
AA	29.4 (38.5)	15.4 (24.1)	4.8 (6.9)
AB	59.9 (18.8)	34.1 (9.0)	34.3 (10.5)
BA	25 (13.1)	5.8 (6.3)	5.4 (6.2)
BB	61.5 (32.3)	21.9 (12.2)	21.3 (15.8)
L1	7.6 (2.6)	4.4 (1.8)	4.2 (2.2)
L2	14.6 (6.7)	5.3 (2.5)	8.3 (2.3)
L3	6.2 (4.6)	2.2 (2.0)	6.7 (1.2)
L4	6.6 (3.7)	2.1 (1.5)	6.6 (1.4)
Duration	25.3 (5.9)	16.7 (7.7)	15.4 (6.4)
Error	111.4 (30.2)	47.8 (22.5)	35.3 (21.3)
Score	50.7 (22.9)	31.7 (15.5)	88.1 (14.1)

In terms of mental effort, students in Cluster_0 self-reported more average mental effort (M = 77.22, SD = 30.64) than those in Cluster_2 (M = 70.55, SD = 22.70) and Cluster_1 (M = 56.94, SD= 21.77). Cluster_1 reported the minimum mental effort. A Pearson product-moment correlation coefficient was computed for each cluster to assess the relationship between the log based features and students' self-reported RSME scores. When results in Table 4. were examined, statistically significant correlations can be observed only in Cluster_0. In this group, there was a moderate positive correlation between RSME and Total Moves variables. For this group increases in moves were correlated with perceived mental effort. There was also a moderate positive correlation between RSME and Score variables.

Table 4. Correlations between RSME scores and log variables for each cluster

	Rating Scale Mental Effort (RSME) Scores		
Feature	Cluster_0 (n = 18)	Cluster_1 (n = 18)	Cluster_2 (n = 9)
Total Moves	.480*	-.195	.376
Total Errors	-.077	.051	.258
Score	.499*	-.078	.364
Duration	.443	.123	.188

*Correlation is significant at the 0.05 level (2-tailed).

4. CONCLUSION

In this paper, we aimed to group similar students regarding their behavior data while solving the complex cognitive task (Einstein's riddle). The cluster analysis of the behavioral data revealed three different groups, Cluster 0, 1 and 2. We found that students who took the shortest time and made less moves in solving the puzzle obtained the highest scores (Cluster_2) while students who took the longest time and more moves obtained moderate scores (Cluster_0). Obviously one of the most interesting findings obtained here is that, although Cluster_1 and Cluster_2 are most distinct clusters in terms of performance, students in these clusters has a lot in common. For instance, they both have the minimum number of interactions; both spend a shorter time on the puzzle when compared to Cluster_0. If we didn't include students' performance in cluster analysis, most of the students in these clusters could be assigned to the same cluster. This finding shows the importance of the performance metrics in educational data mining studies while extracting student profiles.

Paas and Merriënboer (1993) formulized performance and mental effort and named as "mental efficiency". If an individual gets higher performance with the lowest mental effort they said "higher mental efficiency", despite that lowest performance with the highest mental effort was called as "lowest mental efficiency" (Paas et al., 2003). Sometimes they used speed (task duration while completing the task) as a secondary metric in addition to the mental effort. The complexity and mental effort are generally correlated with each other, mental effort usually be treated as indices of cognitive load (Clark and Elen, 2006). In terms of mental effort scale scores, students in Cluster_0 reported highest mental effort when compared to students in other clusters. One possible explanation of this could be as students in this cluster take the task seriously and tried to do their best. It is a limitation of this study not to use other tests to measure attention/sustained attention. In further studies such cognitive preferences should be carried out to the research design.

For an optimal solution 25 moves from Section A (item area) to B (solution matrix) could be enough to solve the puzzle however average moves of the students in Cluster_0 seven times higher than that and most of these moves occurred in the solution area while changing the item one place to another. Students who have higher performances have less mouse clicks and moves than others. Unintentional mouse movements may be used for measuring the degree of concentration or frustration of learner (Khenissi et al., 2015).

According to Alloway et al. (2009), learners with low-level working memory give up the complex tasks without struggling with it. In our study, the lowest performance of Cluster_1 may be a result of participants' low level working memory, since, Cluster_1 has similar moves and duration like Cluster_2, yet, in terms of performance there is a huge difference between them. In further studies obtained clusters can be analyzed in terms of working memory capacity.

This study showed to possible usage of the logical reasoning puzzle as a student profiling tool. It may be the first time to use logical reasoning puzzles to measure the cognitive skills of learners. In the literature there were examples which used games and learning environments/materials for measuring. The path to solving the puzzle and the decisions the students make may be related to learners' cognitive skills (Taiyu and Kinshuk, 2009). However, further studies are needed to understand the characteristic of these students in more details in terms of more cognitive preferences. These puzzles also can be used while determining the at-risk students (as Cluster_1 in our study). Teachers provide individualized advice to the learners according to their clusters (Alfredo et al., 2010). We can use these puzzles to create learner profiles in adaptive systems. Furthermore, as mentioned by Rodrigo et al. (2008) obtained results can in the future be used to design a prediction model that is capable of detecting different learner profiles. While predicting the learner behavior and describing their peculiarities we can create models by using the captured log files and recorded data structures as the trails of learner actions (Jovanovic et al., 2012).

REFERENCES

Akçapinar, G., Altun, A. & Aşkar, P. 2016. Çevrimiçi Öğrenme Ortamındaki Farklı Öğrenci Profillerinin Kümeleme Yöntemi ile Belirlenmesi. *Eğitim Teknolojisi Kuram ve Uygulama,* 6, 46-64.

Alfredo, V., Félix, C. & Àngela, N. 2010. Clustering Educational Data. *Handbook of Educational Data Mining.* CRC Press.

Alloway, T. P., Gathercole, S. E., Kirkwood, H. & Elliott, J. 2009. The cognitive and behavioral characteristics of children with low working memory. *Child Dev,* 80, 606-21.

Bienkowski, M., Feng, M. & Means, B. 2012. Enhancing Teaching and Learning Through Educational Data Mining and Learning Analytics: An Issue Brief. Washington, D.C.

Clark, R. E. & Elen, J. 2006. When less is more: Research and theory insights about instruction for complex learning. *In:* Elen, J. & Clark, R. E. (eds.) *Handling Complexity in Learning Environments: Theory and Research.* Oxford, UK: Elsevier.

Hawlitschek, A. & Köppen, V. Analyzing Player Behavior in Digital Game-Based Learning: Advantages and Challenges. 8th European Conference on Games Based Learning: ECGBL2014, 2014 Berlin, Germany. Academic Conferences and Publishing International, 199-206.

Jovanovic, M., Vukicevic, M., Milovanovic, M. & Minovic, M. 2012. Using data mining on student behavior and cognitive style data for improving e-learning systems: a case study. *International Journal of Computational Intelligence Systems,* 5, 597-610.

Kardan, S. & Conati, C. A Framework for Capturing Distinguishing User Interaction Behaviours in Novel Interfaces. The 4th International Conference on Educational Data Mining (EDM 2011), 2011 2011. Eindhoven, the Netherlands.

Khenissi, M. A., Essalmi, F., Jemni, M. & Kinshuk 2015. Learner Modeling Using Educational Games: A Review of the Literature. *Smart Learning Environments,* 2, 1-16.

Merrill, M. D. 2006a. Hypothesized performance on complex tasks as a function of scaled instructional strategies. *In:* Elen, J. & Clark, R. E. (eds.) *Handling Complexity in Learning Environments: Theory and Research.* Oxford, UK: Elsevier.

Merrill, M. D. 2006b. Levels of instructional strategy. *Educational Technology,* 46, 5-10.

Otero, W. I., Petch, J. & Catapan, A. H. 2012. Developing high-level cognitive skills in distance education. *InterSciencePlace: Revista Cientifica Internacional,* 20, 41-57.

Paas, F., Tuovinen, J. E., Tabbers, H. & Van Gerven, P. W. M. 2003. Cognitive Load Measurement as a Means to Advance Cognitive Load Theory. *Educational Psychologist,* 38, 63-71.

Paas, F. G. W. C. & Merriënboer, J. J. G. V. 1993. The efficiency of instructional conditions: An approach to combine mental effort and performance measures. *Human Factors: The Journal of the Human Factors and Ergonomics Society,* 35, 737-743.

Pelleg, D. & Moore, A. W. 2000. X-means: Extending K-means with Efficient Estimation of the Number of Clusters. *Proceedings of the Seventeenth International Conference on Machine Learning.* Morgan Kaufmann Publishers Inc.

Rodrigo, M., Anglo, E., Sugay, J. & Baker, R. Use of unsupervised clustering to characterize learner behaviors and affective states while using an intelligent tutoring system. International Conference on Computers in Education, 2008. 57-64.

Taiyu, L. & Kinshuk 2009. Cognitive Profiling in Life-Long Learning. *In:* Patricia, L. R., Gary, A. B., Judith, V. B., Caroline, H., Lorraine, J. & Karen, D. S. (eds.) *Encyclopedia of Distance Learning, Second Edition.* Hershey, PA, USA: IGI Global.

Wang, Y.-H. & Liao, H.-C. 2011. Data mining for adaptive learning in a TESL-based e-learning system. *Expert Systems with Applications,* 38, 6480-6485.

Wood, R. E. 1986. Task complexity: Definition of the construct. *Organizational behavior and human decision processes,* 37, 60-82.

Zijlstra. 1993. *Efficiency in work behaviour: A design approach for modern tools (Unpublished doctorate dissertation).* TU Delft, Delft University of Technology.

APPENDIX

Einstein's riddle

The situation

1. There are 5 houses in five different colors.
2. In each house lives a person with a different nationality.
3. These five owners drink a certain type of beverage, drive a certain brand of car and keep a certain pet.
4. No owners have the same pet, drive the same brand of car or drink the same beverage.

The question is: *Who owns the fish?*

Hints

1. The Brit lives in the red house
2. The Swede keeps dogs as pets
3. The Dane drinks tea
4. The green house's owner drinks coffee
5. The green house is on the left of the white house
6. The person who drives Porsche rears birds
7. The owner of the yellow house drives Ferrari
8. The man living in the center house drinks milk
9. The Norwegian lives in the first house
10. The man who drives BMW lives next to the one who keeps cats
11. The man who keeps horses lives next to the man who drives Ferrari
12. The owner who drives Audi drinks mineral-water
13. The German drives Alfa-Romeo
14. The Norwegian lives next to the blue house
15. The man who drives BMW has a neighbor who drinks water

Short Papers

Gap in pagination due to formatting issues.

Pages 181-278

CONNECTIVIST COMMUNICATION NETWORKS

Ingolf Waßmann, Robin Nicolay and Alke Martens
University of Rostock, Institute of Computer Science
Albert-Einstein-Str. 22, 18059 Rostock, Germany

ABSTRACT

Facing the challenges of the digital age concerning lifelong learning, this contribution presents an approach to dynamically establish Connectivist communication networks. According the statement "the pipe is more important than the content within the pipe" by Georg Siemens, learning in digital age includes the connection of people to share required information. For this purpose, the Wiki-Learnia learning platform, which collects context information about users, is combined with the InterLect software, which identifies topics and semantic relations of contents. Based on mapping of both data sources, a wide range of matched users can be found for a specific content-related communication channel. By analyzing the course of conversation at runtime, participants can adaptively be added and removed from communication. Consequently, the presented solution serves as a just-in-time learning approach for finding direct help by experts.

KEYWORDS

Context-aware Communication, Connectivism, Topic Modeling

1. INTRODUCTION

Caused by the penetration of digital information and communication technologies in all areas of life, people of the *digital age* (Castells 1999) are faced with ever-changing demands and decreasing *half-life of knowledge* (Siemens 2005) (Gonzales 2004), that lead to the need of a continuous learning process in terms of *lifelong learning*. Castells talks about the *Network Society* "[...] where the key social structures and activities are organized around electronically processed information networks. [...] It's about social networks which process and manage information [...]" (Castells 2001). This view is shared by Georg Siemens and Stephen Downes, who examined the limits of current learning theories in view of rapidly progressing technology and its implications for learning processes in digital age (Siemens 2005) (Downes 2012). In their approach called *Connectivism*, they depict learning as "[...] the ability to construct and traverse those networks [...]" (Downes 2007). It's about connecting with people in a network to share specialized knowledge and experiences ("collecting knowledge through collecting people" (Stephenson 1998)).

In order to support these processes, we have the goal to combine two powerful tools. On the one hand, the learning platform Wiki-Learnia (chapter 2) uses Web 3.0 technologies in order to create and find user-centered learning contents and people (Waßmann et al. 2014). On the other hand, the InterLect tool (chapter 3) semantically analyzes textual contents in order to detect main topics and semantic relations between materials (Nicolay et al. 2015). A combination of both tools (chapter 4) will deliver *Connectivist communication networks* consisting of experts for direct help. The high potential of such an approach was revealed by the evaluation of a similar solution from the Open Universiteit Nederland, which figured out positive effects on the level of relationship characteristics and mutual support (Fetter et al. 2012).

2. WIKI-LEARNIA

Designed as a social network, Wiki-Learnia automatically tracks *primary* context information (Dey and Abowd 1999) like user ID (Who is?), visited pages (Where is?), activities (What is?) and time (When is?). Based on this data, Wiki-Learnia can take into account several *secondary* contexts' information that are manually given by the user or automatically reasoned by the system. These include *background* information like age, languages and social connections; *preferences* such as media type, maximum expenditure of time and learning/didactic concept; *knowledge* in terms of completed Wiki-Learnia modules, experiences, skills etc.; and *learning targets* that are divided into general interests as well as coarse- and fine-grained targets according to (Mayer et al. 2009).

Besides the user model, Wiki-Learnia offers a collaborative editor to create semantically processed learning data. At the beginning of the underlying content structure, there's a *learning object (LO)* that includes learning material like an image, a PDF or a video, that will be enriched with metadata such as name, description and keywords. Furthermore, an ordered list of LOs (a *learning path*) with additional meta-information forms a *learning unit (LU)*. Among other things, it's defined by required knowledge (pre-condition) and fine-grained learning targets (post-condition) which is the basis to semantically connect LUs (post-condition of a LU could be pre-condition of another one etc.). The same principle is used on higher levels: several, ordered LUs form a *learning module (LM)* which in turn depicts coarse-grained learning targets as well as pre- and post-conditions. Any longer, completing numerous LMs can satisfy long-term targets defined by general interests.

Taking into account the ideas of Connectivism, authors can add users in terms of profile pages with attached bulletin boards, and communication channels like text and video chat, or forums as so-called *learning connections* to LUs and LMs. In this way, people are connected with other users with same learning targets and background knowledge for cooperative learning. Besides to this static approach, there's also a mechanism to dynamically connect people regarding specific context information as explained in (Waßmann et al. 2016). The presented approach takes into account inter alia the content that users are visiting at runtime. While the current algorithm just adds users with exact matches of LOs, LUs or LMs, the tool described below can find more participants dealing with similar topics.

3. INTERLECT

InterLect analyzes sequences of lecture content (such as sets of lecture slides) and extract semantic topics as well as relations to approximate the underlying expert model of a docent (Nicolay et al. 2016). To examine semantic topics we use "Latent Dirichlet Allocation" introduced by (Blei et al. 2003). To reconstruct semantic structures, we examine relations between topics on lecture material, such as temporal proximity and topics sharing the same resources. The expert model then can be approximated as simplified "Topic-Map" (Marius et al. 2008) (Fig. 1).

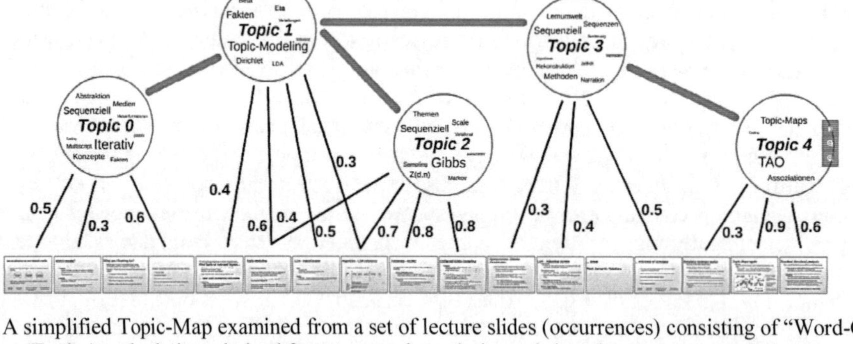

Figure 1. A simplified Topic-Map examined from a set of lecture slides (occurrences) consisting of "Word-Clouds" (Topics) and relations derived from temporal proximity and shared resources (associations)

Latend-Dirichlet-Allocation (LDA) is the most widespread algorithm used for Topic-Modelling of unsorted sets of documents. In our case documents are ordered sequences of lecture slides containing lecture information. LDA is performed by Gibbs Sampling (Darling 2011). LDA infers a set of topics T from a set of Slides S with a overall vocabulary V. Therefore LDA calculates Topics t as a discrete distribution on the probability of appearance for all words v of V. On top, LDA provides a distribution of topics and their probabilistic intensity for all slides s of S. Condensed, every slide has a distribution over the intensity of participating topics while topics are defined by most relevant terms on that topic.

To refine our inferred topics, on the first hand, we increase the proportion of relevant phrases using a set of filters to reduce the vocabulary, such as unification of upper- and lowercase, removal of stop words, stemming of grammatically deformations, and the removal of numbers, to short terms, and high frequent words. On the second hand, we currently looking into an inclusion of meta-information provided by the lecturer using Labeled LDA (Ramage et al. 2009) and meta-information derived from the slide's layout, such as increasing a relevance weights for visually highlighted terms.

In difference to the common use case of "LDA" (analyzing unsorted documents), information in a lecture contain an intended teaching path derived from docent's expert knowledge. This path allows us to assume relational implications, such as semantic relationships between topics appearing on common slides or close temporal proximity; bottom-up dependencies indicating a pre/post condition between topics that follow each other; and scopes by co-occurring topics commonly on many slides.

4. CONNECTIVIST COMMUNICATION NETWORKS

Consequently, InterLect analyzes lecture material regarding relevant words and relations that are derived from observed teaching paths to deliver an associated meta-network. As a next step, we include the algorithm into Wiki-Leania to identify topics and relations of existing LOs, LUs and LMs. We evaluate, how LOs can be summarized into LUs and include information from observed teaching paths to connect LUs via generated pre- and post-conditions into lecture-supporting LMs. Considering this initiation phase, InterLect then is able to autonomously identify semantic relations between new material and the training set.

These circumstances enable Wiki-Learnia to enhance the described static approach (chapter 2) of connecting people in Connectivist communication networks. Learners get in touch with like-minded users and experts by manually searching for content-associated LUs and LMs. The actual algorithm simply compares the search term with given, author-generated keywords that are statically attached to the material. InterLect can be used to automatically find and update those tags in order to guarantee an optimized finding of fitting contents with associated learning networks.

Furthermore, there's a dynamic approach do automatically establish Connectivist communication channels which is described in (Waßmann et al. 2016). Implemented as a live chat that will be initialized by a person seeking for help, the current prototype automatically adds users founded on given keywords of same content history, knowledge and learning targets. InterLect can also figure out persons dealing with topic-related material that's not included in this set: *not yet semantically processed content* (e. g. new created articles or uploaded files), and *public statements* within the social network of Wiki-Learnia like bulletin board messages, forum replies or comments. As a consequence, a wider range of matching users can be added into the Connectivist learning networks.

In (Van Rosmalen et al. 2008) the authors present a similar solution that automatically adds fitting users to a dedicated wiki page in order to collaboratively work out the solution for an asked question. In contrast, our approach presents synchronous communication channels that enable content-related live discussions regarding underlying LOs, LUs or LMs. By analyzing topics of the chat conversation at runtime (using InterLect), participants will automatically be added and removed from the dynamic channel. Also individual preferences of the initiator like spoken languages, role within the system (e. g. learner, author, tutor) and social connections are considered by the algorithm. Besides problem-based learning groups, our solution includes further use cases like author meetings, tutoring and assessment.

5. CONCLUSION

The idea of combining the two applications Wiki-Learnia and InterLect has revealed the high potential regarding an improved mechanism to establish Connectivist communication networks. While the former one collects different context information of users, the latter one identifies semantic meta-information of contents. By mapping both data, people with similar interests or problems can dynamically get in contact in context-aware communication channels for discussions, learning and other things. In terms of Connectivism, the presented solution supports the automatic creation of expert networks to enhance the exchange of information. This delivers a just-in-time learning approach to overwhelm the challenges of digital age. In future, the solution might gain in importance due to the upcoming *forth industrial revolution* (Schwab 2016), which intensifies the application of IT in work and life processes.

In further work, synonym databases (e.g. OpenThesaurus) can be used to enhance the search algorithms. Combined with technologies like Tin Can API also external sources and platforms can be analyzed in order to overcome network boundaries. Besides to the presented cooperation between both applications, there're some more scenarios that will be pursued in future. Among other things, this includes automatic semantic tagging and automatic pre- and post-condition acquisition of LMs, LUs and LOs that can lead to a automatic creation of learning paths with adaptively exchangeable learning contents.

REFERENCES

Blei, D. et al, 2003. Latent Dirichlet Allocation. *The Journal of Machine Learning Research*, 3. pp. 993-1022.

Castells, M., 1999. *The Information Age, Volumes 1-3: Economy, Society and Culture*. Cambridge (Mass.); Oxford: Wiley-Blackwell.

Castells, M., 2001. Identity and change in the network society. Conversation with Manuel Castells. *Institute of International Studies, UC Berkeley*, http://globetrotter.berkeley.edu/people/Castells/castells-con4.html, Retrieved 05/06/2016.

Darling, W., 2011. A Theoretical and Practical Implementation Tutorial on Topic Modeling and Gibbs Sampling. *Proceedings of the 49th Annual Meeting of the Association for Computational Linguistics. Human Language Technologies.*

Dey, A. K. and Abowd, G. D., 1999. Towards a Better Understanding of context and context-awareness. *Technical Report GIT-GVU-99-22*, Georgia Institute of Technology, College of Computing.

Downes, S., 2007. What Connectivism Is. *Half an Hour Blog,* http://halfanhour.blogspot.de/2007/02/what-connectivism-is.html, Retrieved 07/06/2016.

Downes, S., 2012. Connectivism and Connective Knowledge: essays on meaning and learning networks. *Stephen Downes Web*, http://www.downes.ca/files/books/Connective_Knowledge-19May2012.pdf, Retrieved 05/06/2016.

Fetter, S. et al, 2012. Using peer-support to connect learning network participants to each other: an interdisciplinary approach. *In International Journal of Learning Technology*, 7(4), 378-399.

Gonzalez, C., 2004. The Role of Blended Learning in the World of Technology. http://www.unt.edu/benchmarks/archives/2004/september04/eis.htm, Retrieved 11/12/2015.

Marius, L. et al, 2008. ISO 13250-2: Topic Maps – Data Model. Available at: http://perma.cc/MPT4-MVLM.

Mayer, H. O. et al, 2009. *Lernzielüberprüfung im eLearning*. Walter de Gruyter GmbH & Co KG.

Nicolay, R. et al, 2015. InterLect – Lecture content Interface. *7th International Conference on Computer Supported Education*. Lisbon, Portugal, pp. 269-276

Nicolay, R. et al, 2016. Visualisierung konzeptuellen Lernens durch semantische Vernetzung sequenzieller Lehrinhalte. *To appear: GI-Edition - Lecture Notes in Informatics (LNI) 2016. Digitalisierung in Lehre und Lernen: Des Kaisers neue Kleider?!.*

Ramage, D. et al, 2009. Labeled LDA: A Supervised Topic Model for Credit Attribution in Multilabeled Corpora. *Proceedings of the 2009 Conference on Empirical Methods in Natural Language Processing*. Stroudsburg, USA, pp. 248-256.

Schwab, K., 2016. *The Fourth Industrial Revolution*. World Economic Forum.

Siemens, G., 2005. Connectivism: A learning theory for the digital age. *In International journal of instructional technology and distance learning*, 2(1), pp. 3-10.

Stephenson, K., 1998. What knowledge tears apart, networks make whole. *In Internal Communication Focus*, 36, pp. 1-6.

Van Rosmalen, P. et al, 2008. A learner support model based on peer tutor selection. *In Journal of Computer Assisted Learning*, 24(1), 74-86.

Waßmann, I. et al, 2014. Learning through life. *In eleed Journal*, Iss. 10.

Waßmann, I. et al, 2016. Context-aware communication channels in e-learning. 10th *International Technology, Education and Development (INTED) Conference Proceedings.* Valencia, Spain, pp. 4099-4109.

LEARNING AND SKILLS DEVELOPMENT IN A VIRTUAL CLASS OF EDUCOMMUNICATION BASED ON EDUCATIONAL PROPOSALS AND INTERACTIONS

Maria Cristina Bohorquez Sotelo, Brigitte Julieth Rodriguez Mendoza, Sandra Milena Vega, Naydu Shirley Roja Higuera and Luisa Fernanda Barbosa Gomez
Universidad Manuela Beltrán. Km 2 Centro Chia Cajicá, Colombia

ABSTRACT

In the present paper we describe the analysis of qualitative and quantitative data from asynchronous learning networks, the virtual forums that take place in VirtualNet 2.0, the platform of the University Manuela Beltran (UMB), inside the course of Educommunication, from the master of Digital technologies applied to education. Here, we performed a multimodal investigation to assess, identify and describe according to the interactions and participations, the characteristics of the asynchronous learning networks (ALN), in order to consider it as a collaborative strategy in the virtual formation.

KEYWORDS

ALN, Virtual Forum, Dialogic-Collaborative Learning

1. INTRODUCTION

It is frequent inside the virtual courses of the UMB the use of forums as resources that favor learning and skills development, as evidenced in the course object of this study. All activities are made using the forums, in which the teacher proposes a discussion based on some readings related to the topics of the course. For this reason, in this research we question about the learning and the skills strengthened in these virtual spaces. Specifically, we question if the dialogs, discussions and reflections made through the forum contribute in the theoretical constructions related to educommunication. Do they reach their learning objectives? Is it possible to consolidate a learning community through the forums and the dialogic exchange? Those approaches are reflections and problems that teachers and students face in the virtual spaces, so they are considered to orient the investigation and contribute to the design of virtual classes of theoretical courses.

2. BODY OF PAPER

2.1 Theoretical Fundaments

Learning theories, from the conductism (Skinner, 1974) to the social learning (Bandura, 1977), have gone though the constructivist and cognitivist trends, adopting a basic psychological perspective. In spite of some of them already taking into account the interactions, they highlight the interpersonal relations that intervene in the imitation and modeling centered in the study of cognitive processes, in which observation is a source of learning.

Wenger (2004) proposes a social learning theory, tightly related to the community of practice, whose conceptualization is developed to make explicit how learning is presented and how knowledge is generated inside these communities. The interest of this research focuses on the learning that takes place in the Educommunication course that brings together (virtually) the students and the teacher through a participation in which their members share their experiences and skills regarding the topic that brings them together.

Garibay and Concari (2013) made an analysis of the interactions that take place in the forums of a civil engineer course. They used the categories of analysis proposed by Garrison, et al (1999) in order to measure the learning that takes place in the community of inquiry, the same that are used in the interactions that take place in the forums analyzed in this study. Finally, to support this analysis we take into account the investigation made by Coll et al, (2011), where the authors set out and define specific profiles of participation and attendance of the teacher in the asynchronous collaborative learning spaces, that can consolidate as learning communities. Their goal is to go beyond with a multimodal proposal based on social participation and in four components: meaning, practice, engaged communities and identity.

2.2 Methodological Design

2.2.1 Population

This project is performed with 17 students of a virtual Educommunication class as part of the master in Digital technologies applied to education that takes place in the VirtualNet 2.0 platform of the UMB. This course took place in the academic term of May-July.

2.2.2 Materials

Inside the virtual course, the teacher gives the students six academic papers divided into three forums. The Table 1 shows the articles and how they were organized:

Table 1. Papers used in the Educommunication Class

Forum 1	Forum 2	Forum 3
1. Fernández, A. (2012). 2. Coslado, Á. (2012) 3. Matilla, A. (2006).1	1. Barbero, J. (2003). 2. Huergo, J. (2007)	1. Valderrama, C. y Espitia, U. (2009).

2.2.3 Techniques

The current analysis uses the scientific method of investigation directed to the study of descriptive cases, to achieve a methodological approach that allows analyzing and understanding the activities that intervene in the interaction and the communication strategies inside the virtual class. The techniques used for this study are:

1. The dialogic learning: For this, it is necessary to define the working methodology and the objectives on each forum to focus the discussion and define the goals and expectations that each participant should achieve. This allows having a guide to conduct the process of participation and dialogue.
2. The deepening into the dialogue using threads of reasoning. This explores the conceptualizations proposed, to evaluate what has been discussed with the objective of driving the students to re-evaluate and strengthen its argumentation.

2.2.4 Procedures

In the current investigation we will implement a mix multimodal approach. We revised the contributions, participations and dialogic development en each forum, according to the following criteria:

1. Check for the number of participations of each of the students that interacted
2. Establish the categories to assess in the cognitive, social and content-related support
3. Evaluate the cognitive, social and content-related support of each contribution from students
4. Tabulate the structural information taking into account the cognitive and social categories.
5. Graph the structural analysis using the Atlas Ti software (version 7, USA)

2.3 Results and Analysis

This study involves a quantitative analysis that allows obtaining the structure of the interaction network that is established in the community. This network is performed using some basic elements of the Analysis of social networks (ARS), the density index and the cohesion index. In the Figure 1, 2 and 3 it can be observed the interactions that took place in the three forums proposed during the course development.

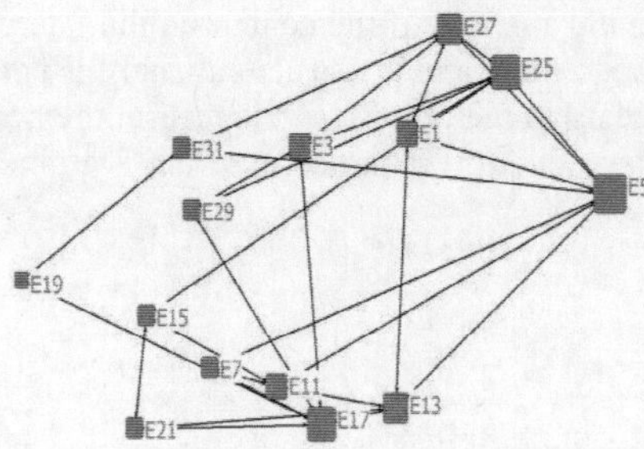

Figure 1. Structural analysis of forum 1

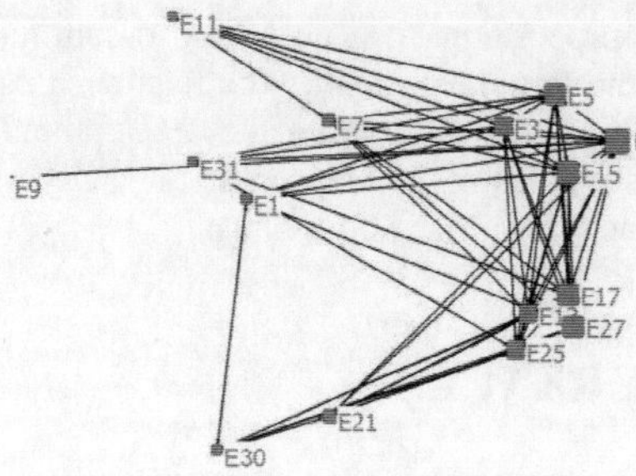

Figure 2. Structural analysis of forum 2

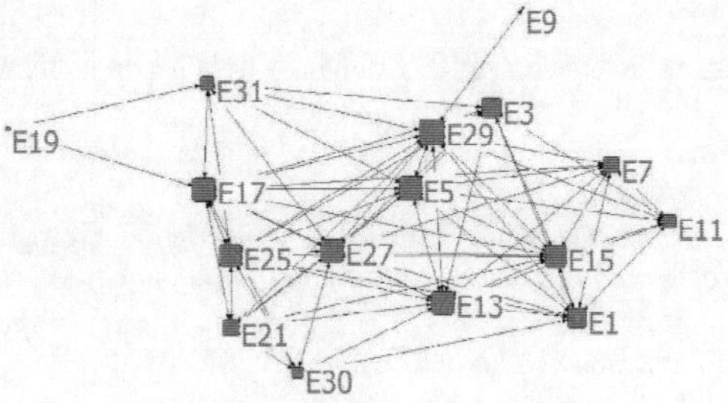

Figure 3. Total structural analysis

In the Figures 1 to 3 each student is represented by a node and its interactions by the arcs (lines) in the graph. When one compares the centrality and the role that each student assumes inside the community in forum 1 (see Figure 1) there are three main nodes (E5, E25 and E17) that correspond to the persons that interact permanently in the discussion and that in this forum take on the role of the teacher support as described by Coll(2011). According to this role, the students orient the discussions and encourage self debate inside the communities where dialogic learning takes place.

There is a group of students located in intermediate locations (nodes E13 and E27) that are not in the periphery and therefore participate with some frequency in the discussions. Additionally, we find that a great number of people in forum 1 have a scarce participation. This situation changes in forum 2, as seen in Figure 2. This transit from the situation in forum 1 to the situation in forum 2 allows a consolidation of a learning community.

When we consider all possible interactions that take place inside the class (see Figure 3) we observe a more distributed centralization, what means that in terms of meaning negotiations the biggest part of the students reach the same learning levels.

3. CONCLUSION

Through the proposed discussions in the forums and from previous discussions the learning communities are consolidated. The resource of group and asynchronous discussions make sense in the processes of virtual formation after a first moment of appropriation and identity consolidation in the community. In a first moment, the people that assume a central in the community are scarce and therefore there is a need to accompany the collaborative strategies with other activities that, on the one hand, contribute to the recognition of the people that take part in the communities, and on the other hand potentiate the scope of the learning objectives proposed in virtual education.

We propose that it is necessary to continue the study and the analysis of the content in the interventions inside the forums to identify the relationships that exist between them and the structural analysis performed here. This could account for the development of skills according to the objectives planned in the pedagogic designs in e-learning and propose the study of ARS as an alternative of evaluation in virtual learning spaces and in activities based on forums.

REFERENCES

Barbero, J., 2003. Saberes hoy: diseminaciones, competencias y transversalidades. *Revista iberoamericana de Educación* 32, España, pp. 17-34.

Coll, C. et al, 2011. Perfiles de participación y presencia docente distribuida en redes asíncronas de aprendizaje: la articulación del análisis estructural y de contenido. Proceedings Revista de Educación, Barcelona, España, pp. 657-688

Coslado, Á.B., 2012. Educomunicación: desarrollo, enfoques y desafíos en un mundo interconectado. *Foro de Educación 10*, pp. 157–175.

Fernández, A.A., 2012. Educomunicación, ciudadanía y medios escolares: entrevista con cinco investigadores latinoamericanos. *[Con] textos 1*, pp. 11–18.

Garibay, M. et al, 2013. Análisis de foros virtuales con empleo del programa" Atlas. ti."Proceedings. *Revista Iberoamericana de Tecnología En Educación Y Educación En Tecnología v11*. La plata, Argentina, pp. 54–65.

Garrison, D. R., Anderson, T., & Archer, W. (1999). Critical inquiry in a text-based environment: Computer conferencing in higher education. *The internet and higher education,* 2(2), 87-105.

Huergo, J., 2007. Los medios y tecnologías en educación. La Plata, Argentina, pp. 1-21.

Matilla, A.G., 2002. Educomunicación en el siglo XXI. *Comunicación Educativa y Cultura Popular (UNED), Salamanca, España,* pp 1-15.

Vásquez, U.E., 2009. Hacia una apertura política del campo comunicación-educación. *Nómadas,* Bogotá, Colombia, pp.164–179.

Wenger, E. (2004). Knowledge Management as a doughnut: Shaping your Knowledge strategy trough communities of practice. *Ivey Business Journal Online*, Canada, pp.1.

THE RELATIONSHIP AMONG ICT SKILLS, TRADITIONAL READING SKILLS AND ONLINE READING ABILITY

I-Fang Liu and Hwa-Wei Ko
National Central University, Taiwan

ABSTRACT

Perspectives from reading and information fields have identified similar skills belong to two different kind of literacy being online reading abilities and ICT skills. It causes a conflict between two research fields and increase difficult of integrating study results. The purpose of this study was to determine which views are suitable for describing the essence of online reading. A path' analysis model was proposed to verify different views. 376 children (4th grade to 6th grade) from three primary schools were recruited as participants. The results show that approximately half of the variance related to online reading ability could be explained by ICT and paper-based reading skills. However, online reading depends less on ICT skills. Paper-based reading skills remain the main basis for online reading.

KEYWORDS

Online reading ability, Item response theory, ICT skills

1. INTRODUCTION

Online information has gradually become a popular reading source over the two decade. Given this trend, issues concerning skills required for online reading and on whether those skills differ from those used for paper reading have been frequently researched. Though most scholars agree that online reading abilities are more complex than paper reading abilities, different definitions have been proposed. Some scholars, who focus on digital environment, define online information processing skills as information and communications technology (ICT) skills/digital literacy/Information literacy (Eisenberg, 2010; Karchmer, 2001). For example, the United Nations Educational, Scientific and Cultural Organization (UNESCO) notes that information in the digital environment is not merely passively accepted. People have to develop the capability to find information in plenty of hypertexts, assess its credibility, and decide whether to accept the information, or continue searching for more relevant information (Catts, Lau, Statistics, & Programme, 2008). The ISTE's (International Society for Technology in Education) (2007) digital literacy indicators for elementary school students, include: (1) the capacity to locate, organize, analyze, and integrate vast amounts of information based on ethics; (2) the capacity to appropriately evaluate and select information sources and digital tools depending on the task at hand; and (3) the capacity to process data and report results.

Others believe that online reading required both ICT skills and traditional reading skills (Leu, Kinzer, Coiro, & Cammack, 2004; OECD, 2010; Schmar-Dobler, 2003). In the 2009 PISA online reading comprehension test, the capabilities required for paper reading were still viewed as the definitions of reading ability. Besides those paper reading abilities, formulating keywords, assessing relationships between hyperlinks, selecting high-quality texts from online texts, integrating hypertexts within open textual boundaries, and retrieving specific facts from websites were identified as new skills for online reading. Furthermore, ICT skills, including using site maps and mouse operation such as scrolling on a page, and clicking on a hyperlink, have been defined as online reading skills (OECD, 2011). The redefinition of online reading ability by PIRLS was similar to that by PISA. Original paper-based reading ability definitions created by the PIRLS and e-PIRLS, were retained, though the e-PIRLS highlights differences between paper-based and online texts, with definitions focusing on web page information localization; the inferences of relationships between content and reading purposes; comparisons and connections between content displayed on multiple web pages to form a general understanding; and the evaluation of credibility, viewpoints, and potential impacts on reader webpage comprehension (Mullis, Martin, & Sainsbury, 2013).

Leu et al. (2015) referred to reading literacy changes brought about by ICTs as "new literacies of online research and comprehension." In this view, online reading within the limits of hypertext, such as email or web pages, is actually very similar to paper reading. The differences between the two lie in the mechanisms required when reading for problem solving and for searching information in the case of online reading. In other words, online reading requires not only traditional reading skills but also skills in searching, evaluating, and integrating information to form a new comprehension that extends beyond the original information. Therefore, they believed that online reading skills include traditional reading skills and ICT skills but differ from both sets of skills. The ORCA online reading comprehension test, which conducted by this view, included locating, evaluating, synthesizing, and writing for communication purposes abilities (Coiro, & Kennedy, 2011). Although the definition of these abilities was not base on traditional reading ability like PISA or e-PIRLS, it was quite similar with ICT skills.

Association with Information-seeking changes traditional definitions of reading ability. Seeking and browsing become two major components of online information processing. Therefore, localizing and navigating the search process, assessing relevant and trustworthy information, and integrating fragmented information obtained through the browsing process are more emphasized in the online reading environment (Henry, 2006; Rouet, Ros, Goumi, Macedo-Rouet, & Dinet, 2011). However, these abilities can also be defined as ICT skills frequently. Ultimately, the overlap between online reading abilities and ICT literacy leads to speculation that two sets of skills are similar. Furthermore, comparable skills that belong to two different forms of literacy also create a conflict between the two different research fields.

Perspectives from different fields have diversified the essence of online reading ability, and different scholars present different perspectives, which make it difficult to integrate and compare the study results. Therefore, it is necessary to determine which view most appropriately defines online reading abilities. If the view that ICT skills are similar to those of online reading holds true, it is no longer necessary to address such issues using different terminology. However, if the view that online reading skills are not equivalent to ICT skills holds true, exploring how much traditional reading abilities and ICT skills are implicated in online reading abilities will help us better understand the essence of online reading skills. In relation to undergraduates, elementary school students need more instruction on online reading skills, which has rarely been investigated. Age can also significantly predict paper-based reading comprehension (Cain, Oakhill & Bryant, 2004; Verhoeven, & van Leeuwe, 2008). In this way, elementary school students were used as subjects.

2. METHODS

2.1 Participants

A total of 384 children from three primary schools in northern Taiwan were recruited as participants. Overall, 121 children were in fourth grade, 115 were in fifth grade, and 148 were in sixth grade. Children diagnosed with specific learning disorders or disabilities were excluded from the study. In the Taiwanese schooling system, children start to learn how to use computers in third grade. Thus, all of the children had at least one year of computer experience.

2.2 Assessment

2.2.1 Chinese Reading Comprehension Test (CRCT)

The student participants were subjected to the Chinese reading comprehension test compiled by Lin and Chi (2002) to measure their paper reading abilities. The test is the normal reference paper test with pencil and is conducted in a group, with split-half reliability of 0.95. The test consists of 12 articles and 100 multiple-choice questions (49 questions for narrative articles and 51 questions for descriptive articles). It tests proficiencies including phonological processing, semantics, syntax, the understanding of basic facts, comparative analysis, integration and interpretation, and inference, with one point for one correct answer on one question and a perfect score of 100 points.

2.2.2 Chinese Online Reading Comprehension Test (CORT)

This online reading ability test that was constructed according to the item response theory (IRT), was developed by the authors to measure the online reading ability (Liu & Ko, 2015). The test contains 25 questions (3 coordination questions and 22 multiple-choice questions) divided into the 3 cognitive aspects of searching, evaluating, and integrating. The test contains texts, figures, and tables. In addition to proper nouns, the word frequency was based on the 3500 words that are commonly used by elementary school students in Taiwan; the proportion of words that fall outside of these 3500 words was lower than 10%. The text types included web pages, search result lists, E-mails, and discussion boards, and the ICT skills needed by the four text types were all included in the curriculum specifications of the elementary school students in Taiwan. The text was rendered with either static or dynamic questions; the static questions rendered the web page in the form of an image, whereas the dynamic questions rendered an actual web page. The item response theory (IRT) reliability value of the test was 0.78, and the test was administered via a computer network. The test score was estimated based on the probability of the students' correctly answering each question using IRT, then converted into a domain score, with the highest score being 100 points.

2.2.3 ICT Skills Questionnaire

The online information search strategy inventory (OISSI) compiled by Tsai (2009) was adopted for the self-evaluation of the online information search capabilities of the students. A 6-point Likert scale was used in the questionnaire, which has a reliability coefficient of 0.85. Aspects of the OISSI focus on behavior, procedure, and metacognition with 25 questions. Two sub-aspects of control and disorientation were contained in the behavioral aspect, the procedural aspect included trial and error and problem-solving skills, and the 3 sub-aspects of purposeful thinking, target selection, and evaluation were contained in the metacognitive aspect.

2.3 Procedure

The test procedure in this study included an online group test and a paper group test. The online group test included an online reading test and the OISSI questionnaire, completed in 2 class periods in the school's computer classroom. In the first class period, the online reading comprehension test was conducted; at the beginning of the test, students were provided with account numbers to log in. Upon completion of login, the students were instructed on the purpose of the test and how to take the test. After ensuring that the students had no questions, the test began. The time for the test was 30 minutes, excluding the time for login and instruction. In the second class period, the online information search strategy questionnaire was administered, with the same login procedure and instruction as described above. A total testing time of questionnaire was 15 minutes. The paper and pencil group test was performed in the students' original classroom and administered sequentially according to the procedure developed for the Chinese reading comprehension test program. The investigator first explained to the students the purpose and method of the test according to the guidance on the test manual; then, the test paper and answer sheet were issued for students to begin. The total testing time was 60 minutes.

3. RESULTS

A path model was proposed to clarify the relationships between online reading abilities, paper reading abilities, and ICT skills. In the hypothesis model, paper-based reading skills have a direct impact on ICT and online reading abilities, and ICT skills also have a direct impact on online reading abilities. Grade had a direct impact on paper reading ability and ICT skills and an indirect impact on online reading ability. The predicted power level reflects similarities between sets of skills. If the view that ICT skills are very similar to online reading ability is supported, then ICT skills will have rather high explanatory power for online reading ability. If ICT skills only provide a low level of explanatory power that is lower than that of the traditional reading ability and the 2 sets of skills are not able to provide a high joint explanatory power on online reading ability, then online reading ability is more consistent with the new literacy concept proposed by Leu et al., i.e., online reading ability includes the components of traditional reading skills and ICT skills but is different from the 2.

A structural equation model path analysis was conducted to test for fitness between the data and path model. The model and the standardized parameters describes in Figure 1. The results show that X^2 (df =1, N = 376) = 0.255, p = .613 (AGIF=.997, CFI = 1.00, RMSEA= .000), indicating that the model fit the data well. The model shows that paper-based reading comprehension is the strongest predictor of online reading comprehension, whereas ICT skills play a significant but minor role. Paper reading comprehension also significantly predicts children's ICT skills. Grade variables show a positive and direct association with paper reading scores and are indirectly related to online reading through paper-based reading comprehension. Nevertheless, grade variables are non-significant in terms of ICT skills. The models accounted for 45% of the variance. The results from the path analysis suggested that both paper reading and ICT skills accounted for variation of online reading. Furthermore, the effect of paper reading comprehension was more than ICT skills. Model, confirming the perspective that online reading comprehension include paper reading comprehension and ICT skills but different from both of them, was met. However, the grade variable failed to explain ICT skill levels.

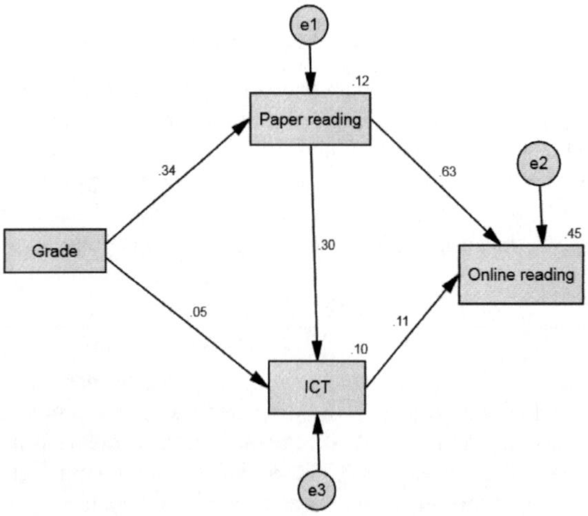

Figure 1. The path model showing relationships between paper reading comprehension, grades, ICT skills, and online reading comprehension

4. CONCLUSIONS AND IMPLICATIONS

The purpose of this study was to clarify the relationships among traditional reading abilities, online reading ability and ICT skills. The results showed that online reading ability contains components of ICT skills and traditional reading skills, which explain almost half of the variance in online reading ability. The explanatory power of traditional reading abilities is significantly higher than that of ICT skills. Furthermore, ICT skills contain components of traditional reading skills. Consequently, the results supported the online reading mode as it has been redefined by international organizations such as PISA and ePIRLS, i.e., retaining part of the traditional definition and including ICT skills. Online reading skills have little similarity to ICT skills and are more like traditional reading skills. The new literacy concept proposed by Leu et al. is generally acceptable either, but the importance of ICT skills is not as high as they suggested. Traditional reading skills remain the main basis for online reading. In addition, ICT skills do include components of reading ability although in most of definitions of ICT literacy, reading is not mentioned.

Ultimately, the trend of online reading ability and ICT skills advancing with a student's grade level is less pronounced than that associated with traditional reading abilities. Though access and usage of Internet at home or school is rapid growth, this result shows that convenient access is not sufficient to empower students to be capable of online reading ability. It is important for teaching online reading and ICT skills in school so that students have the opportunity to become familiar with those skills.

In this study, we clarify the relationships among traditional reading ability, online reading ability and ICT skills, and the results show that, with the increasing proportion of online reading, traditional reading ability is still an important "literacy" in the digital age. The authors suggest that it is necessary to increase the class time spent on online reading after reader have a fair level of traditional reading ability. However, online reading ability still has approximately one-half of the variance that could not be explained by ICT skills and traditional reading skills. How to more precisely define the capability components that were not explained should be the topic of future investigations.

REFERENCES

Cain, K., Oakhill, J., & Bryant, P. (2004). Children's Reading Comprehension Ability: Concurrent Prediction by Working Memory, Verbal Ability, and Component Skills. Journal of Educational Psychology, 96(1), 31–42.

Catts, R., & Lau, J. (2008). Towards information literacy indicators. UNESCO: Paris

Eisenberg, M. B. (2010). Information literacy: essential skills for the information age. *Journal of Library & Information Technology, 28*(2), 39-47.

Henry, L. A. (2006). SEARCHing for an answer: The critical role of new literacies while reading on the Internet. The Reading Teacher, 59(7), 614–627.

Karchmer, R. A. (2001). The journey ahead: Thirteen teachers report how the Internet influences literacy and literacy instruction in their K-12 classrooms. Reading Research Quarterly, 36, 442-467.

Liu, I. F., Ko, H. W. (2015). Development online reading skill test to assess elementary students' online reading performance. *Psychology testing, 61*(4), 509-532. (In Chinese)

Leu, D. J., Forzani, E., Rhoads, C., Maykel, C., Kennedy, C., & Timbrell, N. (2015). The New Literacies of Online Research and Comprehension: Rethinking the Reading Achievement Gap. Reading Research Quarterly, 50(1), 37–59. http://doi.org/10.1002/rrq.85

Leu, D. J., Kinzer, C. K., Coiro, J. L., & Cammack, D. W. (2004). Toward a theory of new literacies emerging from the Internet and other information and communication technologies. Theoretical Models and Processes of Reading, 5, 1570–1613.

Lin, B. G., & Chi, P. H. (2002). Test of reading comprehension. Taipei: Ministry of Education. (In Chinese)

Mullis, I.V.S., Martin, M.O., & Sainsbury, M. (2013). PIRLS 2016 Assessment Framework. Chestnut Hill, MA: TIMSS & PIRLS International Study Center, Boston College.

OECD (2010). PISA 2009 Results: What Students Know and Can Do - Student Performance in Reading, Mathematics and Science (Volume I). OECD, Paris.

OECD (2011). PISA 2009 Results: Students on Line: Digital Technologies and Performance (Volume VI). Retrieved December 29, 2013, from http://dx.doi.org/10.1787/9789264112995-en

Rouet, J-F., Ros, C., Goumi, A., Macedo-Rouet, M., & Dinet, J. (2011). The influence of surface and deep cues on primary and secondary school students' assessment of relevance in Web menus. Learning and Instruction, 21(2), 205–219. http://doi.org/10.1016/j.learninstruc.2010.02.007

Schmar-Dobler, E. (2003). Reading on the Internet: The link between literacy and technology. Journal of Adolescent & Adult Literacy, 47(1), 80–85.

Tsai, M.-J. (2009). Online Information Searching Strategy Inventory (OISSI): A quick version and a complete version. Computers & Education, 53(2), 473–483. http://doi.org/10.1016/j.compedu.2009.03.006

Verhoeven, L., & van Leeuwe, J. (2008). Prediction of the development of reading comprehension: a longitudinal study. Applied Cognitive Psychology, 22(3), 407–423.

TOWARDS CONCEPT UNDERSTANDING RELYING ON CONCEPTUALISATION IN CONSTRUCTIVIST LEARNING

Farshad Badie
Center for Linguistics, Aalborg University, Rendsburggade 14, 9000 Aalborg, Denmark

ABSTRACT

This research works within the framework of constructivist learning (based on constructivist epistemology) and examines learning as an activity of construction, and it posits that knowledge acquisition (and learning) are transformative through self-involvement in some subject matter. Thus it leads, through this constructivism to a pedagogical theory of learning. I will mainly focus on conceptual and epistemological analysis of humans' conceptualisations based on their own mental objects (schemata). Subsequently, I will propose an analytical specification of humans' conceptualisations and understandings over their mental structures in the framework of constructivism, and I will clarify my logical [and semantic] conceptions of humans' concept understandings. This research focuses on philosophy of education and on logics of human learning. It connects with the topics 'Cognition in Education' and 'Mental Models'.

KEYWORDS

Constructivism, Concepts, Concept Understanding, Conceptualisation, Interpretation, Conceptual Learning

1. INTRODUCTION

Perceived by a very general definition, the act of learning is identified as related to acquiring or modifying knowledge. Learning can be seen as the involvement of the self in increasing knowledge about a thing/phenomenon. We can interpret learning as a process that causes changes in a human's mind. The learner is someone who attempts to learn something and to acquire knowledge on that thing, and the mentor is someone who opens the world to the learner and opens the learner to the world. All the characteristics mentioned are conducive to interpreting learning as the 'activity of construction'. In this article I will focus on the constructional dimension of learning. At this point I feel the need to focus on describing and specifying 'knowledge'. Regarding [Furst (1956), Krathwohl (2002)], knowledge has a strong relationship with recognition [and understanding] of materials, ideas, methods, processes, structures and settings. Accordingly, a body of knowledge may cover (satisfy) multiple branches like, e.g., terminologies, ways and means, trends and sequences, classifications, methodologies, universals and abstractions, quantifications and qualifications, conditionings, principles and generalisations, and theories and structures. I may conclude that knowledge acquisition [and, respectively, learning] processes consist of a sort of 'transformation functions' from reality into the sets and categories of various disciplines and systematic enterprises. I have focused on this subject in [Badie (2016a), Badie (2016b)]. According to these papers, a human being has the ability to deal with different disciplines and systematic enterprises, and can transform them in her/his mind. I shall interpret these transformations as the outcomes of the self-involvement in increasing knowledge about a subject matter. In human systems, a learner is an intentional participant (agent) and attempts to know more about something in order to construct her/his knowledge about that thing. Any human has a background knowledge and tackles to carry on constructing knowledge over her/his existing knowledge. S(he) attempts to develop her/his knowledge constructions and to get the opportunity to attain deeper comprehensions and understandings. *Constructivism* is a philosophy that forms the backbone of this research. It is a learning philosophy and a pedagogical theory of learning that can also be realised as a model and a theory of knowing with separate roots in philosophy, psychology and cybernetics. According to the existential element of constructivism, the construction of knowledge is an active process, but the activity itself can be described in terms of individual cognition [and personal understanding] in different processes, see [Phillips (1995)]. As for Piaget's developmental theory of learning[1], constructivist learning is concerned with how the individual learner goes about the construction of knowledge in her/his own cognitive apparatus. This article will – conceptually and epistemologically – analyse human understanding and conceptualisation based on the proper foundation that has been provided by the constructivist model of knowing (and constructivist epistemology). I will focus mainly on the analysis of humans' schemata-based concept representations, where schemata form humans' mental structures. In my opinion, the central focus of constructivist knowledge acquisition and learning is on schemata-based conceptual representations and conceptualisations. Accordingly, this article will propose an analytical description of humans' schema-based understandings [of concepts] in the ground of their conceptualisations and in the framework of constructivism. Before offering specifications, I shall describe what I mean by the act and the process of constructivist knowledge acquisition and learning with regard to concepts. The following definition draws out the key elements of constructivist knowledge acquisition and learning, which have individual and social implications for humans, see [Watkins (2002)]. "Knowledge acquisition is the reflective activity which enables the humans to draw upon their previous experiences [and background knowledge] to conceptualise [and, respectively, to realise and to understand in order to] evaluate the present, so as to build up and shape future actions and to construct [and, subsequently, to develop the construction of] new knowledge". At this point I shall emphasise that there is, obviously, no reason to claim that concept construction, as such, must be based on the processes described by constructivism. The aim of this study is that I will use constructivism to describe human concept construction as a kind of 'conditional reasoning' in a learning context, and, accordingly, I am trying to analyse concept construction in that context relying on constructivist epistemology. Therefore, in my opinion, constructivism could provide a proper base of description of the concept construction process, if it is seen as an individual's conditional reasoning in a learning context.

2. CONCEPTUALISATION AND CONCEPT UNDERSTANDING

According to constructivist knowing [and learning], human beings' mental structures manifest themselves in the form of mental objects (schemata[2]), see [Bartlett (1932), Parker (2008)]. Schemata conceptually represent the constituents of human's thoughts for knowledge acquisition with regard to her/his perception of [parts of] the world. Regarding [Piaget (1952)], a schema is a "cohesive, repeatable action sequence possessing component actions that are tightly interconnected and governed by a core meaning". In constructivist learning and constructivist knowledge acquisition, schemata—in a broad sense—support humans in constructing concepts, developing (forming[3] and reforming) their constructed concepts, in providing their semantic interpretations and in processing their meaning construction. I shall, therefore, conclude that a human's elucidation, explication and explaining abilities all get supported by her/his schemata. Subsequently, relying on semantic interpretations, humans get concerned with meanings of their mental entities associated with different objects/phenomena. In my opinion, schemata determine the locus of meanings and thus support world descriptions and reinforce the structural and descriptive analysis of mental entities. Moreover, the semantics as the scrutiny and the analysis of meanings could focus on various conditions for definitions of truth. Then, it connects with humans' inferences and reasonings which attempt to give satisfying conditions for definitions of truth. Accordingly it seems possible to conclude that humans' inferences are given shapes over their designed schemata. In my conceptual approach, a concept is a linkage between the mental representations of linguistic expressions and the other mental images (e.g., representations of the world, representations of inner experiences) that a human has in her/his mind, see [Götzsche (2013)]. Considering this idea of concepts, humans may be said to transform the collection of (*i*) linguistic expressions, (*ii*) images of the world, and (*iii*) their interrelationships in the form of [psychological] entities and utilising generic and specific labels. I could say that concepts might be understood to be representations of actualities and objectivities in humans' minds, and those representations can affect humans' reasoning processes.

[1] Jean Piaget (1896 - 1980) was the originator of constructivism. He was the first psychologist to make a systematic study of cognitive development and developmental theory of learning, see www.piaget.org/aboutPiaget.html.

[2] Piaget argued that all learning was mediated by the construction of mental objects that he called schemata. Schemata gradually develop into more conceptual mental entities.

[3] See http://teachinghistory.org/teaching-materials/teaching-guides/25184

2.1 Understanding, Explanation and Conceptualisation in the Framework of Constructivism

From the constructivist learning perspective, human beings focus on knowledge construction and on developing the constructed knowledge over their background knowledge. The most significant objective of constructivism is producing one's own understanding of the world, see [Husén (1989), McGawand Peterson (2007), Keith Sawyer (2014)]. Let me take into consideration the SOLO[4] taxonomy in order to focus on understanding in the framework of constructivism. According to SOLO, the sequence 'pre-structured knowledge → uni-structured knowledge → multi-structured knowledge → related knowledge → extended abstracts' represents a flow from shallow understanding to deep understanding, see [Burville Biggs (1982)]. A shallow understanding of an object may support humans in identifying some isolated facts and matters related to that object. On the other hand, a deep understanding of an object supports humans in linking lots of related facts as conceptions [about a certain object] and in linking those conceptions to other complicated conceptions. Additionally, deep understanding of an object supports analysing, justifying, criticising, hypothesising and theorising about that object. Before getting into details I shall emphasise that 'understanding' is a very complicated term in philosophy, psychology and cognitive science. In my opinion, there cannot be any absolute and comprehensive description for understanding, but there can be acceptable descriptions of 'realisations of understanding'. Actually, there could be a very strong relationship between 'understanding' and 'explanation'. Explanation (i.e. the actual process of explaining something) can shed light on the produced personal understandings of that thing. I have assumed that humans' linguistic expressions and the produced meanings [based on humans' conceptions], strongly support knowledge construction processes and understanding in the framework of constructivist learning. Thus, an explanation could also be assumed to be the actual explanation of expressions and meanings. Therefore, humans rely on their own explanations in order to shed light on their produced personal comprehensions and understandings.

At this point I focus on the term 'conceptualisation' in order to provide a supportive specification of understanding. In [Badie (2016b)] I have described conceptualisation as "a uniform specification of separate understandings [of concepts]". I concluded that a specific conceptualisation provides a global (a universal) manifestation of local concept understandings. Furthermore, a human's grasp of concepts provides a proper foundation for generating her/his own conceptualisations. So the personal conceptualisation could be elaborated by the outputs of the processes of concept formation [and reformation] with regard to the basis that is provided by the individual realisation. When a human forms her/his conception (as an outcome of her/his constructed concept) from its attributes, qualities, properties and its relationships with other conceptions, s(he) gets to know [and gets to understand] more than just some isolated facts about that conception [and of that concept]. This qualifies deep knowledge acquisition rather than superficial knowledge acquisition over concepts. Note that [Parker (2008)] has also (from another point of view) focused on this subject in analysing inductive teaching strategies.

A person who understands something, directly or indirectly, gets concerned with the taxonomy of various concepts. I have focused on the last statement from the structuralist point of view. The structuralist description and analysis of understanding supports me in explaining a variety of facts about 'understanding' and 'understanding something'. The individual who understands something, needs to move through a chain of various related concepts. Then, we could see 'Concept' and 'Generality' as two significant aspects that support the structuralist account of understanding. According to [Kuczok (2014)], the notion of conceptualisation pertains to central terms in cognitive linguistics. According to [Langacker (1991)], it can be defined as the locus of meaning or even equated with meaning in lexical semantics, which should describe abstract entities like thoughts and concepts through structural analysis. So, considering the analysis of schemata and the humans' mental structures, I conclude that conceptualisations are highly dependent on schemata.

3. SEMANTICS OF CONCEPT UNDERSTANDING

In this section I clarify my logical conceptions of understanding and focus on logical description of understanding concepts through the lenses of semantics. The conclusions will be used for designing a

[4] Structure of Observed Learning Outcomes (SOLO) taxonomy is a proper model that can provide a structured framework for who acquires knowledge in order to promote the efficiency of her/his knowledge acquisition.

semantic representation of humans' concept understanding. Suppose that a person undertakes to acquire knowledge about a concept and to understand it. Then understanding is a type of relation between person and concept. Therefore, this relation transforms the characteristics, attributes and qualities of that concept into the person's mind. It also transforms the properties of that concept and its relationships with other concepts into mind. I interpret an understanding[5] as the limit (or as the type) of a conceptualisation. Considering understanding as a limited conceptualisation, it could be explained as a kind of process of forming [and reforming] concepts. So, an understanding focuses on concepts on the basis that is provided by a conceptualisation. Then, one who undertakes to understand something, needs to have that thing conceptualised. As mentioned, a conceptualisation provides a global manifestation of local understandings. Therefore, all understandings (of concept *C*) are conceptualisations (of concept *C*). Therefore, understanding *C* has been interpreted as the subset of conceptualising *C*. But not all conceptualisations are understandings. In fact, all conceptualised concepts may not be understood, but all understood concepts have been conceptualised. Considering the person *P* and the concept *C*, "*P* understands *C*" then: "*P* conceptualises *C*".

Now I shall draw your attention to the concept formation process. Relying on concept formation processes, a person gets concerned with manipulating, formatting, classifying and structuring concepts. Accordingly, these processes all provide supportive foundations for her/his concept understanding process. Concept formation and concept reformation are the salient products of conceptualisation in constructivist learning. From the methodological point of view, the person needs to focus on the attributes, characteristics, qualities and properties of something in order to consider it as an instance of the concept *C*. One person may have focused on formation of *C* before acquiring knowledge about it, and thus, s(he) reconsiders her/his initial formations after reconstructing her/his knowledge in order to reform *C* in her/his mind. On the other hand, another person may not have focused on *C* before the knowledge construction is processed, and then s(he) can form *C* with insights based on acquired knowledge. I have identified the sequence '*Concept Formation → Concept Transformation → Concept Reformation*' as the main foundation of the concept construction within meaning constructions, see [Badie (2015a), Badie (2015b)]. Note that the formed concepts could be affected by acquired knowledge within constructivist discussions, dialogues and interactions in order to be transformed and to support concept reformations. Therefore, understanding constructed (or reconstructed) concepts could be realised to be the limit of conceptualisation. Then, the person gets concerned with the attributes, characteristics, qualities and properties of concepts in order to distinguish them when they belong to different categories. In fact, s(he) identifies, specifies and relates the generalised concepts. Subsequently, as a salient product of understanding, s(he) could be able to make her/his personal labels and identifiers for identifying the [understood] concepts. These labels could be employed in categorising different things.

Moreover, by engaging the personal interpretation the person explicates what s(he) means by the concept *C*. The interpretations make bridges between a person's 'expressions and explanations' and 'semantics and meanings'. Taking semantics into my analysis, it's possible to infer that someone who has focused on the concept *C*, needs to provide a manner of determining the truth values of her/his statements, expressions, theories and explanations concerning *C*. Consequently, I identify all understandings [of concept *C*] as the interpretations [of concept *C*]. Therefore, understanding *C* has been interpreted (and is expressed) as the subset of interpreting *C*. But, all interpretations are not understandings. In fact, all interpreted concepts could not be understood, but all understood concepts certainly have been interpreted. Considering the person *P* and the concept *C*, " *P* understands *C* " then: " *P* interprets *C* ".

More specifically, the collection of the rules and the processes that manage different terms and descriptions in linguistic expressions, do not (and cannot) have any meaning until the non-logical parts[6] and constructors of the language are given interpretations and are interpreted. The interpretations prepare the person for producing her/his personal meaningful [and understandable] concept descriptions. By learning and acquiring knowledge in the framework of constructivism, a human being attempts to provide a way to determine the truth values of the non-logical parts through her/his conceptions. Consequently, **(I)** the understanding (as a conceptualisation) focuses on the domain of conceptualisation. Actually, it conceptualises the objective of conceptualisation, and, respectively, focuses on the objective of understanding. Therefore, the understanding focuses on the domain of understanding. **(II)** The understanding (as an interpretation) focuses on the domain of interpretation. In fact it focuses on the objective of interpretation, and, respectively, on the objective of understanding. Therefore, the understanding focuses on

---

[5] See www.cocon.com/observetory/carlbereiter

[6] The words like, e.g., *and, or, not, since, then, so, all, every, any*, have logical consequences and are identified as the logical parts (words) in a natural language with regard to classical symbolic logic and predicate logic.

the domain of understanding. **(III)** The understanding (as a conceptualisation) conceptualises the concepts belonging to the domain of conceptualisation. Therefore, the understanding understands the concepts (works on the concepts). **(IV)** The understanding as an interpretation interprets the concepts belonging to the domain of interpretation. Therefore, the understanding understands the concepts (works on the concepts).

4. CONCLUSIONS AND FUTURE WORK

Constructivist learning is concerned with how the individual learner goes about the construction of knowledge in her/his own cognitive apparatus. Conceptually and epistemologically I have focused on analysis of human understanding and conceptualisation. I have been concerned with human concept representations over her/his schemata. Schemata support humans in constructing concepts, and developing their constructed concepts, in providing their semantic interpretations and in processing their meaning construction. According to this research, conceptualisation provides a global (a universal) manifestation of local concept understandings. Consequently, I have focused on a more specific logical description of conceptualisations and concept understandings based upon individual constructed concepts. The conclusions have been applied in a logical and semantic description and representation of 'concept understanding'. This research has formed a building block of my PhD research, which is dealing with Semantic Analysis of Constructivist Concept Leaning. In future research, I will, logically and semantically (mainly based on Description Logics), focus on formalising and analysing humans' concept understanding and on proposing a semantic model for concept understanding in the framework of constructivism.

REFERENCES

Badie, Farshad, 2015a. *A Semantic Basis for Meaning Construction in Constructivist Interactions*. Proceedings of the International Conference on Cognition and Exploratory Learning in Digital Age (CELDA). Dublin, Ireland.

Badie, Farshad, 2015b. *Towards A Semantics-Based Framework For Meaning Construction in Constructivist Interactions*. Proceedings of the 8th Annual International Conference of Education, Research and Innovation (ICERI). Seville, Spain.

Badie, Farshad, 2016a. *A Conceptual Mirror: Towards A Reflectional Symmetrical Relation Between Mentor And Learner*. Proceedings of the 3rd International Conference on Education and Psychological Science (ICEPS): International Journal of Information and Education Technology. Florence, Italy.

Badie, Farshad, 2016b. *Concept Representation Analysis in the Context of Human-Machine Interactions*. Proceedings of the 14th International Conference on e-Society (ES). Algarve, Portugal.

Bartlett F. C., 1932. *A Study in Experimental and Social Psychology*. Cambridge University Press.

Burville Biggs, John, 1982. *Evaluating the quality of learning: the SOLO taxonomy (Structure of the Observed Learning Outcome)*. Educational Psychology.

Furst M. D., Hill E. J., Krathwohl W. H., Bloom D. R. And Engelhart B. S., 1956. *Taxonomy of Educational Objectives: The Classification of Educational Goals*. Handbook I: Cognitive Domain. New York: David McKay Company.

Götzsche Hans, 2013. *Deviational Syntactic Structures*. Bloomsbury Academic: London / New Delhi / New York / Sydney.

Husén T. and Postlethwaite T.N., 1989. *Constructivism in Education*. The International Encyclopaedia of Education. Oxford/New York: Pergamon Press.

Keith Sawyer R., 2014. *The Cambridge Handbook of The Learning Sciences*. Cambridge Handbooks in Psychology.

Krathwohl David R., 2002. *A Revision of Bloom's Taxonomy: An Overview*. Theory Into Practice. Routledge Publishers.

Kuczok, Marcin, 2014. *The Conceptualisation of the Christian Life in John Henry Newman's Parochial and Plain Sermons*. Cambridge Scholars Publishing.

Langacker, R, 1991. *Foundations of Cognitive Grammar*. Stanford University Press, Stanford, CA. .

McGawand Peterson, P., 2007. *Constructivism And Learning*. International Encyclopaedia of Education, Oxford: Elsevier.

Parker W. C., 2008. *Pluto's Demotion and Deep Conceptual Learning in Social Studies*. Social Studies Review.

Phillips, D. C., 1995. *The Good, the Bad, and the Ugly: The Many Faces of Constructivism*. Educational Researcher.

Piaget, J., & Cook, M. T., 1952. *The Origins of Intelligence in Children*. New York, NY: International University Press.

Watkins Chris, Carnell Eileen, Lodge Caroline, Wagner Patsy And Whalley Caroline, 2002. *Effective Learning*. National School Improvement Network.

E-LEARNING IN CHEMISTRY EDUCATION: SELF-REGULATED LEARNING IN A VIRTUAL CLASSROOM

Rachel Rosanne Eidelman and Yael Shwartz
Weizmann Institute of Science, Israel

ABSTRACT

The virtual Chemistry classroom is a learning environment for students that are willing to study Chemistry, but have no opportunity to do so at school. The program launched in 2015, and currently, there are 22 students in the 11th grade and 80 students in the 10th grade.

This study investigates and characterizes the virtual learning environment, students' learning profiles and self-regulated learning processes, and tries to establish a connection between these variables.

Self-regulated learning skills (SRL) help cope with learning and learning progression. Comparing students' SRL skills and strategies whilst studying Chemistry in two different learning environments (face to face and virtual classrooms), may result in answering the questions: what are the needed skills and strategies in order to be successful in the virtual Chemistry environment, and can one predict which student will do well studying in a virtual learning environment, based on their SRL profile? Can these skills be developed in a virtual environment using aids, and what aids can contribute to acquisition of SRL skills?

Initial results indicate that there are small differences in some SRL categories between control and intervention groups. Significant differences were found in intervention students chat activity over time, and in their ability to answer different level questions (categorized by Bloom's Taxonomy). These findings were used to build a student profile and advance understanding of the correlation between course characteristics and the SRL of students in the program. The students will be followed over a period of 3 years, and the link between SRL and their ability to answer higher level questions in Chemistry will be further investigated.

KEYWORDS

Chemistry education; E-learning; Virtual learning environments; Self-regulated Learning; High-Order thinking skills

1. INTRODUCTION

E-learning is becoming a major tool in the educational world, and therefore holds great importance. This study deals with the construction and implementation of a virtual Chemistry class for high school students. The virtual Chemistry classroom is a solution for those students that are willing to expand their knowledge of Chemistry, but have no opportunity to do so in their school.

Tallent-Runnels, et al. (2006), summarize 76 research papers regarding students encountering E-learning and conclude that students preferred flexibility, convenience and autonomy of individual pacing, although it required self-management. It was found that E-learners had the same level of both comprehension and higher thinking skills as their peers who studied in a face-to-face classroom environment.

Self-regulated learners (SRL) are defined as those who proactively seek out information, and take the necessary steps to master it (Zimmerman, 1990). Self-regulated learners are conceptualized as metacognitive, since they plan, set goals, organize, self-monitor, self-evaluate during the learning process. They are motivated and hold high self-efficacy, engage in self-attributions and have intrinsic task interest, and are behaviorally active participants in their learning processes (Zimmerman, 1989; 1990; 2008; Pintrich & De Groot, 1990). Self-regulated learning skills are important in all learning environments, especially in a virtual learning environment, since it lacks the immediate ability to seek help from teachers (Cho, 2004; O'Neill, Singh & O'Donoghue, 2004; Tsai, 2011). It is equally important to challenge high achievers, to help them gain deep understanding of the material, and to support low achievers in monitoring and regulating their learning (Kramarski & Michalsky, 2013). In order to self-assess SRL skills, a Likert type questionnaire, containing 80 items attributed to ten different categories was developed by Weinstein, Palmer & Shulte, (2002): Learning and Study Strategies Inventory (LASSI). In this research, a modified and translated form of the LASSI questionnaire was used, with 48 items related to six categories out of the original ten categories: attitude and interest; concentration and attention to academic tasks; motivation, diligence, self-discipline, and willingness to work hard; use of support; time management principles for academic tasks; test strategies and preparing for tests.

The main purposes of this research are to follow the development of student's SRL skills studying Chemistry in a virtual environment, to portray the characteristics of a student suitable for studying in such an environment and to determine the efficiency and necessity of virtual learning of Chemistry.

2. COURSE DESCRIPTION

A three year virtual Chemistry course was designed, in which each student attending, had weekly synchronic and a-synchronic lessons, tutoring online lessons, home-labs and science camps (containing inquiry labs and lectures). All assignments for the virtual Chemistry course were designed with consideration for the development and progress of SRL and thinking skills according to Bloom's Taxonomy (Collins et al 1992; Churches, 2008).

3. THE RESEARCH

3.1 Research Questions

1. What are the characterizations of the virtual Chemistry course (teaching, student profile and development and course changes)?
2. What are the characterizations and differences between SRL of the research participants (9th grade science students, 10th grade face-to-face Chemistry classroom students and 10th grade virtual classroom Chemistry students).
3. Is there a correlation between the intervention students' (the 10th grade students' in the virtual Chemistry class who chose to major in Chemistry) SRL and the level of success in the virtual Chemistry course?

3.2 Method

3.2.1 Participants

Table 1. Research groups

Phase	1		2
Group	**Pre**	**Control**	**Intervention**
N	109	17	24
Grade	9	10+11	10+11
Purpose	baseline scores	comparison	Research
LASSI questionnaire	end of 9th grade	-End of 9th grade ; -After experiencing a computerized unit; -After the first semester of the 11th grade	-Beginning of the 10th grade; -End of the 10th grade; -After the first semester of 11th grade

3.2.2 Instruments and Analysis

Tests, graded assignments and questionnaires, paired comparison tests for each student, t-test comparisons between the research groups, and a-parametric tests within the intervention group were used as the quantitative means of analysis. Analyzing chat conversations and in-depth interviews are the qualitative means of analysis (Beyth-Marom, & Ellis, 1986; Chi, 1997; Shkedi, 2011).

4. RESULTS AND DISSCUSION

No significant differences were found between the t-test analyses and a-parametric tests performed for the two groups in order to track individual differences per student, and between the intervention and control group after answering the first unit a-synchronic assignments. This result indicates that the starting point for all students is the same at the beginning of the research.

Overtime, significant differences in the ability of the intervention students' to answer different types of questions, of different thinking skill levels according to Bloom's Taxonomy were found as shown in Table 2.

Table 2. Means and significance of development of thinking skills (full 10th grade; one semester 11th grade)

	Means and significance of question category					
grade	Knowledge	Comprehension	Application	Analysis	Synthesis	Evaluation
10	83.427***	72.549***	77.001**	70.027***	42.906*	44.679**
11	78.003	79.222**	71.677***	n.r.[1]	86.271*	90.973***

*p<.05. **p<.0005. ***p=.0001. p (significance)

[1] Since there was only one question in this category no repeated measure calculations were possible.

4.1 Student Profile

Students were divided in three groups (high, medium and low achievers) according to their 10th grade annual scores. A weak but significant positive correlation between effort mark (calculated with consideration to all non-mandatory tasks, in order to establish effort hierarchy amongst students) and final grade of 10th grade was found (Pearson Correlation Coefficients 0.40232, p < 0.0305). There was no correlation between LASSI category grades and effort mark, or between LASSI category grades and final 10th grade score.

4.2 Chat and Forum Messages

Student's messages from the chat area during the synchronic lesson were counted and analyzed. Results shown in figure 1a are significant (Pearson coefficient = 0.65, p < 0.0118). Students who were more active in the chat achieved a higher final grade at the end of the first year (10th grade). Figure 1b shows significant correlation between the number of votes cast by students in the synchronic lesson and the number of messages posted in the chat area during these lessons (votes in the synchronic lesson are students' answers to a multiple choice question (arranged as a poll question). Students cast their vote; the teacher reveals the results and explains the answer) (Pearson coefficient = 0.70, p < 0.00000172). These results indicate that the more students' are involved during the synchronic lesson (by messaging and voting) their grades improve.

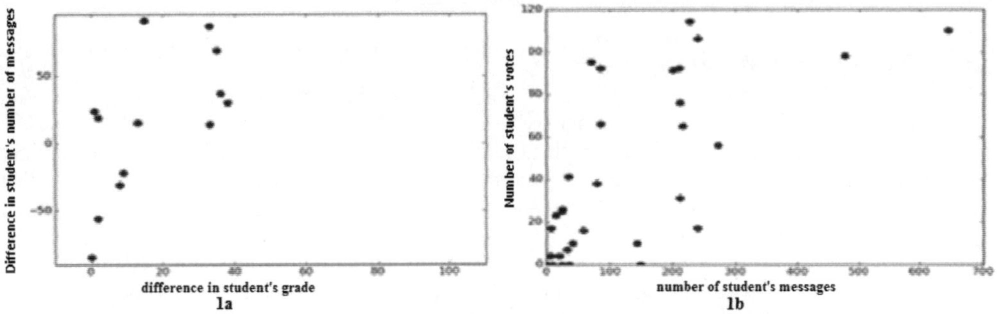

Figure 1. a. Correlation in students' number of messages vs. difference in students' final grades; b. Number of students' votes vs. number of students' messages in synchronic lessons

All students' chat messages during the first year (10th grade) were counted and sorted into five categories according to their content (1. Chemical content messages 2. Technical content messages 3. Social content messages 4. Administrative content messages 5. Other; see figure 2a).

Differences were found between students' messages throughout the year, indicating that changes in their messaging habits and terminology took place. There has been a continuous rise in Chemistry content related messages in the chat area during the synchronic lessons in the first year (10th grade) as seen in figure 2b, as well as a general reduction in technical content-related messages during the first term of the first year (10th grade) (see figure 2c). A continuous rise in social content-related messages during the first year (10th grade) occurred (see figure 2d). This finding indicated formation of a social network between the students.

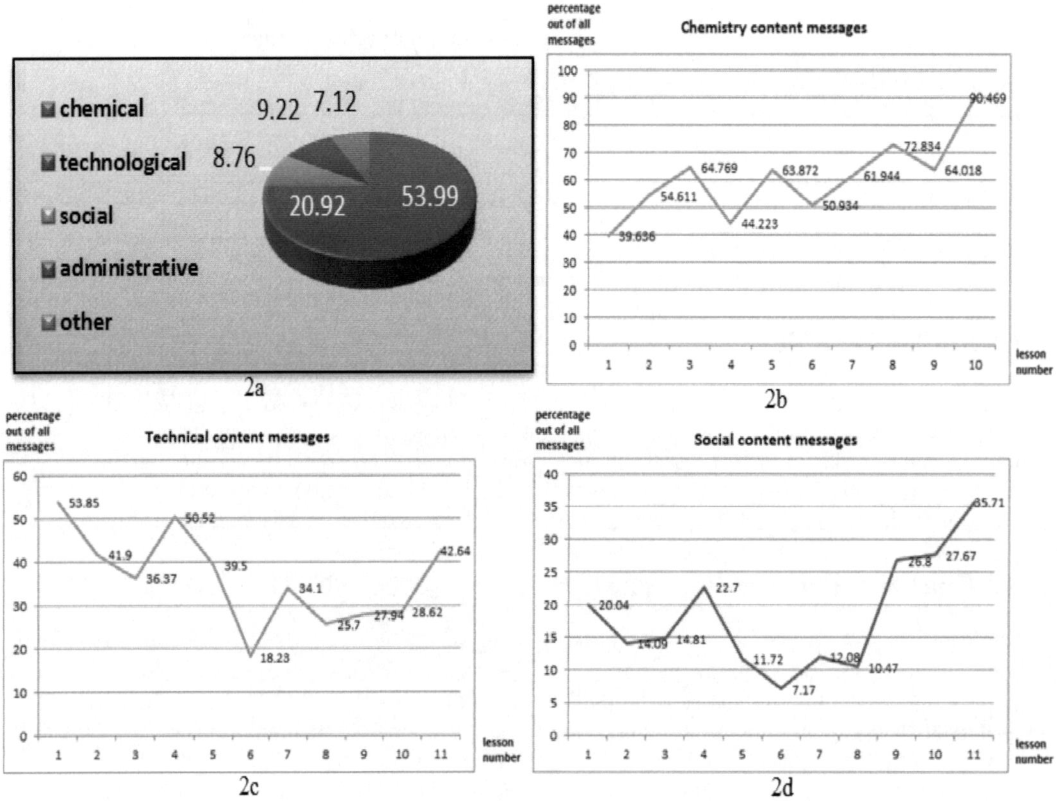

Figures 2a-2d. a. Relative percentages of chat messages per category (10th grade) in synchronic lessons; b. Percentage of Chemistry content messages; c. Percentage of Technical content messages; d. Percentage of Social content messages

4.3 LASSI Questionnaires

The average score of the pre-group students (N=109) of the modified LASSI questionnaire in each of its categories was used to set a baseline and track SRL differences (per group) and SRL skill development (per student). Distribution of the LASSI questionnaires took place as indicated in table 1. A Wilcoxon a-parametric test was performed for each student in the intervention and control groups in order to track changes that have occurred in the period of 1.5 years. No significant differences between students in the three research groups at the beginning of 10th grade (PRE-LASSI questionnaire) were found. All students, in all groups, seem to possess the same level of SRL according to the six categories of the modified questionnaire. In table 3, the significant mean score differences for the LASSI questionnaires for each research group are presented (Wilcoxon a-parametric test).

Table 3. Differences between means of LASSI questionnaires: control and intervention-group

	(PPOST)-PRE mean difference	(PPOST)-POST mean difference
Control group	N = 15	N = 14
concentration and attention to academic tasks	0.450**	
motivation, diligence, self-discipline, and willingness to work hard	-0.350*	
Intervention group	N = 7	N = 8
motivation, diligence, self-discipline, and willingness to work hard	-0.339*	
use of support techniques and materials		0.250*

*S<.05. **S<.003 Wilcoxon signed rank S (significance)

In the control group, significant differences were found between the end of first semester of 11th grade, PPOST-LASSI questionnaire, and the beginning of the 10th grade (PRE-LASSI questionnaire): A positive significant change in concentration and attention to academic tasks: $p < 0.003$; a negative significant change in motivation: $p < 0.0310$. In the intervention group, there are significant differences over the same period, in one category: A negative significant change in motivation: $p < 0.05$. In addition, a positive significant change in use of support techniques and materials was observed between the PPOST LASSI questionnaire and the POST-LASSI questionnaire: $p < 0.05$.

5. CONCLUSION

The virtual Chemistry class enables students to study Chemistry while developing SRL during their studies and although the students were from all over the country, social networking took place. According to Piller, (2014), one of the biggest challenges in on-line environments is not only to initially engage students but also to sustain the motivation throughout the course. In both groups (control and intervention), motivation declined (more so for the control group). Several factors may explain this: students may have chosen poorly, resulting in disappointment; novelty decreased over time; difficulties in coping with subject matter (increasing level of difficulty and time issues). For the intervention group, one may add: bad synchronization with school schedule, need for more interaction in the learning process (teacher and peers), and technological problems. In the control-group alone, the positively significant change in concentration and attention to academic tasks can be a result of the fact that the groups' preparation for their matriculation exams at the end of this year (as opposed to the intervention group that are to be tested at the end of the 12th grade). In the intervention group alone, the positively significant change in use of support techniques and materials can possibly be explained by understanding the nature of learning processes in the program: students are more resourceful and use external resources (such as, internet links and searches) in order to find relevant material to support their studies in any topic, and use the internal course resources more than other students. Students possessing higher SRL skills seem to do better than students with lower SRL skills. These students who are more involved use the provided course materials and summarize the lessons, all of which have a positive effect on the students' scores.

Future research will supply more sufficient results and it is hoped to support evidence collected until now regarding the connection between the students' SRL and the level of success in the virtual Chemistry course.

ACKNOWLEDGEMENT

This research was funded with the aid of the Davidson institute in the Weizmann institute of science and the Meital research fund.

REFERENCES

Beyth-Marom, R. and Ellis, S. (1986). *Quantitative vs. qualitative methods: An ambiguous, inexclusive and dysfunctional distinction*. The Open University of Israel, 13 pp.

Chi, M. (1997). Quantifying Qualitative Analyses of Verbal Data: A Practical Guide. *The Journal Of Learning Sciences, 6*(3), 271-315.

Cho, M.-H. (2004). The Effects of Design Strategies for Promoting Students' Self-Regulated Learning Skills on Students' Self-Regulation and Achievements in Online Learning Environments. *Association for Educational Communications and Technology*.

Churches, Andrew. "Bloom's taxonomy blooms digitally." Tech & Learning 1 (2008) http://teachnology.pbworks.com/f/Bloom%5C's+Taxonomy+Blooms+Digitally.pdf.

Collins, A., Greeno, J., Resnick, L., Berliner, B., & Calfee, R. (1992). Cognition and learning. *B. Berliner & R. Calfee, Handbook of Educational Psychology, New York: Simon & Shuster MacMillan*.

Kramarski, B., & Michalsky, T. (2013). Student and teacher perspectives on IMPROVE self-regulation prompts in web-based learning. In *International handbook of metacognition and learning technologies* (pp. 35-51). Springer New York.

O'Neill, K., Singh, G., & O'Donoghue, J. (2004). Implementing eLearning Programmes for Higher Education: A Review of the Literature. *Journa of Information Technology Education, 3*.

Piller, Y. (2014). Self-Regulated Learning Online: Motivation The Review of the Literature.

Pintrich, P. R., & De Groot, E. V. (1990). Motivational and self-regulated learning components of classroom academic performance. *Journal of Educational Psychology, 82*(1), 33.

Shkedi, A. (2011). The meaning behind the words. Methodologies of qualitative research: Theory and practice. Ramot, Tel Aviv University. [Hebrew]

Siegel, S., & Castellan, N. (1981). (1988) Nonparametric statistics for the behavioral sciences. *NewYork: McGraw-Hill.*

Tallent-Runnels, M. K., Thomas, J. A., Lan, W. Y., & Cooper, S. (2006). Teaching Courses Online: A Review of the Research. *Review of Educational Research, 76*(1), 93–135.

Tsai, C.-W. (2011). Achieving effective learning effects in the blended course: A combined approach of online self-regulated learning and collaborative learning with initiation. *Cyberpsychology, Behavior, and Social Networking, 14*(9), 505-510.

Weinstein, C. E., Palmer, D. R., & Shulte, A. C. (2002). *LASSI: Learning and Study Strategies Inventory* (2nd ed.). Clearwater, FL USA: H&H Publishing Company, Inc.

Zimmerman, B. J. (1989). A Social Cognitive View of Self-Regulated Academic Learning. *Journal of Educational Psychology81*(3), 329-339.

Zimmerman, B. J. (1990). self regulating learning and academic achievment: an overview. *educational psychologist, 25*(1), 3-17.

Zimmerman, B. J. (2008). Investigating Self-Regulation and Motivation: Historical Background, Methodological Developments, and Future Prospects. *American Educational Research Journal, 45*(1), 166 –183. doi: 10.3102/0002831207312909.

RELATIONSHIP OF MOBILE LEARNING READINESS TO TEACHER PROFICIENCY IN CLASSROOM TECHNOLOGY INTEGRATION

Rhonda Christensen and Gerald Knezek
Learning Technologies, University of North Texas, USA, 3940 Elm St. #G-150, Denton TX USA 76207

ABSTRACT

Mobile learning readiness as a new aspect of technology integration for classroom teachers is confirmed through the findings of this study to be significantly aligned with well-established measures based on older information technologies. The Mobile Learning Readiness Survey (MLRS) generally exhibits the desirable properties of step-wise increases in readiness as teacher competence grows. The MLRS and other measures are presented as a basis for beginning the development of a classification framework to assist in targeting types of professional development to ensure effective integration of mobile learning into classroom environments.

KEYWORDS

Mobile learning readiness, professional development, technology integration

1. INTRODUCTION

Mobile learning in the classroom has become increasingly common throughout the world. The ways in which mobile learning devices are implemented vary greatly, from school provided devices for each student to "bring your own device" programs. Determining the best strategies for successfully implementing mobile devices in order to improve learning is an important topic needing systematic research. How best to empower teachers to guide student learning with mobile devices is an urgent problem to be addressed.

A paradigm shift is required for teachers to effectively integrate mobile devices in classroom learning. Simply owning mobile technologies does not guarantee effective use in education by students and teachers. Teachers must have supportive training on the pedagogy of integrating these devices as well as useful strategies for classroom management that will enable the teachers to feel confident in their classroom instructional environment. "Current pedagogical approaches are not appropriate for mobile learning and for the new generation of learners. There must be an instructional paradigm shift that promises to fundamentally change the way students learn" (UNESCO, 2012). Successful teacher implementation of emerging technologies in education requires well-planned, on-going professional development and support (Muir, Knezek, and Christensen, 2004) guided by data-driven decisions.

Researchers have demonstrated that teacher quality is dependent on effective and ongoing professional development (PD) opportunities (Desimone, 2009). The learning environment, especially regarding technology, has changed in the last decade and teachers who have been in the classroom for many years may not have the PD support needed to transform their practices to meet the needs of the newer learning environments (Johnson, 2013). While online PD programs have an important role in the professional development of teachers (Dede, et al 2009; Surrette and Johnson, 2015), determining which teachers may or may not be successful in that type of learning environment is important for effective PD leading to successful implementation of a classroom-based mobile learning environment.

This paper examines emerging mobile learning constructs and their relationships to teachers' abilities to integrate technology into the classroom. The relationship of four dimensions of mobile learning readiness and preference for face-to-face, blended, or online professional development are also explored, along with associations with years of classroom teaching. Aggregate findings are suggested as useful toward the development of a framework that will aide the identification and measurement of attributes important for guiding educators in extending traditional technology integration skills into the realm of mobile learning.

2. THE STUDY

2.1 Methods

2.1.1 Participants

Educators from grades K-12 in a large school district in the southwestern US were invited to submit data related to mobile learning readiness in the fall of 2015. Of the 1,430 respondents, slightly fewer than half (n = 640, 44.8%) reported teaching at the elementary level with the remainder representing middle school (n = 370, 25.9%), high school (n = 404, 28.3%), or undesignated (n = 16, 1.1%). Almost two-thirds of the respondents (61.5%) had been teaching seven or more years.

2.1.2 Instrumentation

Participants were administered a battery of instruments including the Mobile Learning Readiness Survey (Christensen and Knezek, under review) designed to measure whether teachers feel prepared to introduce and teach with mobile devices in their classrooms. Twenty-eight (28) Likert-type items representing four factors were responded to by participants on a scale of 1 = Strongly Disagree to 5 = Strongly Agree. The reliabilities for four scales produced from this instrument, for this set of data are listed in Table 1.

Table 1. Internal Consistency Reliabilities for Four Scales of the MLRS

	Cronbach's Alpha	No. of Items
Factor 1 (Possibilities)	.92	8
Factor 2 (Benefits)	.91	10
Factor 3 (Preferences)	.79	5
Factor 4 (External Influences)	.61	4

Stages of Adoption of Technology (Christensen, 1997) is an instrument also administered to the teachers. Stages is a self-assessment of a teacher's level of adoption of technology, There are six possible stages in which educators rate themselves: Stage 1 - Awareness, Stage 2 - Learning the process, Stage 3 - Understanding and application of the process, Stage 4 - Familiarity and confidence, Stage 5 - Adaptation to other contexts, and Stage 6 - Creative application to new contexts.

2.2 Results

2.2.1 Teachers' Levels of Technology Integration

As shown in Table 2, the greatest number of educators (n = 454, 31.7%) reported being in Stage 4 followed by a large number in Stage 5 (n = 397, 22.4%). The mean Stage for this group of respondents was 4.51 (SD = 1.10) out of maximum of 6. There were very few in Stage 1. The group mean values for Stages by elementary, middle school and high school levels were: elementary teachers = 4.45 (SD = 1.06), middle school teachers = 4.41 (SD = 1.12), and high school teachers = 4.68 (SD = 1.13). These group mean values were significantly different (p = .001) with high school teachers being significantly higher than elementary and middle school teachers in post hoc analyses ($p < .05$).

Table 2. Frequencies of Stage of Adoption for 1,430 Participants

Stage	Frequency	Percent
Stage 1 - Awareness	6	.4
Stage 2 - Learning the process	40	2.8
Stage 3 - Understanding and application of the process	213	14.9
Stage 4 - Familiarity and confidence	454	31.7
Stage 5 - Adaptation to other contexts	397	27.8
Stage 6 - Creative application to new contexts	320	22.4
Total	1430	100.0

2.2.2 Association of Mobile Learning Readiness and Levels of Technology Integration

An analysis of variance contrasting Mobile Learning Readiness by Stages of Adoption of Technology determined that all four factors were significantly different ($p < .0005$) based on the Stage of Adoption of Technology reported by the teacher. The Pearson Product Moment Correlations of Stages with each of the mobile learning readiness factors were F1: *Possibilities* = .28 ($p < .01$), F2: *Benefits* = .16 ($p < .01$), F3: *Preferences* = .21 ($p < .01$), and F4: *External Influences* = .13 ($p < .01$). The development of higher MLRS attributes was found to have a linear relationship with Stages of Adoption for all four factors, as shown in Figure 1. Factors 1-3 had relationships in the range of small to moderate according to guidelines by Cohen (1988) while Factor 4's relationship is significant although the strength of the relationship was small (Cohen, 1988).

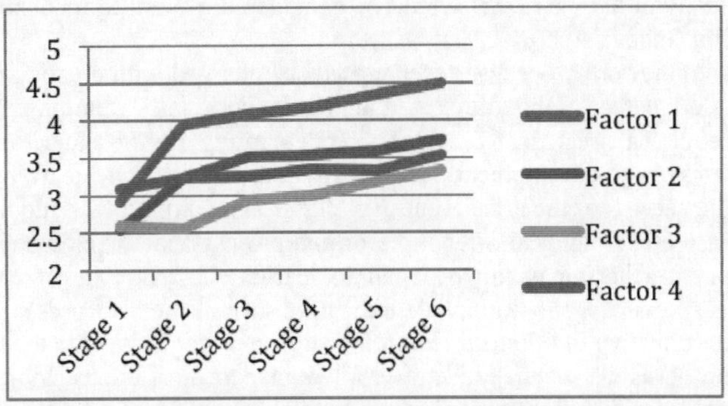

Figure 1. Teachers' Mobile Learning Readiness by Stages of Adoption of Technology

2.2.3 Association of Mobile Learning Readiness and Preference for Style of Professional Development

Participants were asked to select their preference for professional development related to technology integration. Their selection options were face-to-face, blended and online learning. The majority of respondents (53%, n = 755) preferred a blended style of professional development with the next largest percentage being face-to-face (28%, n = 395) and only 20% (n = 279) preferring online.

Analysis of variance was computed for the four factors of the MLRS by preferred professional development format. There were significant ($p < .01$) differences based on style of preferred learning for each of the four factors. A series of three regression analyses using dummy-coded variables for face-to-face, blended, and online professional development preference confirmed not all constructs contributed equally to preference for a specific form of professional development (PD). For face-to-face preference, Factor 1, *Possibilities,* (p = .021, Beta = -.082) and Factor 3, *Preference,* ($p < .0005$, Beta = -.186) contributed significantly while for Blended PD preference, only Factor 3, *Preference,* contributed significantly ($p < .05$, Beta = .080). For Online, Factor 3, *Preference,* ($p = .002$, beta = .111) contributed significantly. Note that for the group who preferred face-to-face PD, their areas of significant association with mobile learning readiness were negative. The trend across these findings is that F3: *Preference* is an important discriminator (positive or negative) for each of the types.

2.2.4 Association of Mobile Learning Readiness and Years of Teaching

A regression analysis was used to determine the strength of association of the MLRS factors with years of teaching. The overall association was significant ($p = .030$) and F2, *Benefits,* was an individually significant contributor ($p = .007$) with an inverse relationship (Beta = -.115). Apparently the greater the number of years in teaching, the lower the perceived benefits of mobile learning in the classroom. This point was reconfirmed with the calculation a Pearson r for the two of r = -.079 ($p = .003$), and could possibly be an indicator of age due to the relationship between age and years of teaching (Christensen, Knezek and Tyler-Wood, 2016).

3. CONCLUSION

Mobile learning readiness as a new aspect of technology integration is confirmed through the findings of this study to be significantly aligned with well-established measures based on older information technologies and generally exhibits the desirable properties of step-wise increases in readiness as teacher competence grows. Different demographics and professional development preferences align more closely with subsets of the four constructs measured by the MLRS; in particular, F3: *Preference* is an important discriminator (positive or negative) for teachers who prefer face-to-face, blended, or online professional development, and F1: *Possibilities* has the highest Pearson Product Moment Correlation ($r = .28$ ($p < .01$), with Stages of Adoption of Technology, the general measure of level of technology integration used in this study. These and other relationships would occur so rarely by chance that we conclude they are real although the magnitude of the associations are typically in the range that would be considered a small to moderate effects according to the guidelines provided by Cohen (1988).

These findings are noteworthy because teachers will be charged with creating a learning environment to accommodate multiple types of mobile devices that will be constantly changing. These changes in the way instruction occurs require a great deal of professional learning by the educators. Preference in the way teachers acquire professional development for the integration of mobile learning in the classroom is an important factor in the success of the effectiveness of classroom learning with mobile devices. Because many school administrators are beginning to offer more online professional development for their educators, it is useful to know which teachers may not be open to learning in that type of online environment. When planning PD, a needs assessment should include indicators such as the ones presented in this paper as a guide to delivering the most effective PD. Future research in this area might include the comparison of gender and preferences for online PD as well as the grade level in which educators are teaching.

This study is considered just the first step toward the construction of an explanatory framework that will eventually incorporate the rapidly expanding field of mobile learning into traditional technology integration schema. One step is to be able to measure different aspects of the domain and show that those aspects relate in expected ways to established measures. This paper reports on positive initial indications toward that broader goal.

REFERENCES

Christensen, R., 1997. *Effect of technology integration education on the attitudes of teachers and their students*. Doctoral dissertation, University of North Texas.

Christensen, R. and Knezek, G, under review. Validating the Mobile Learning Readiness Survey.

Christensen, R., Knezek, G., and Tyler-Wood, T., 2016. Age differences in teacher confidence in integrating technology in STEM classrooms. In *Proceedings of the Hawaii International Conference on Education*, Honolulu, HI.

Cohen, J., 1988. *Statistical power analysis for the behavioral sciences*. Hillsdale, NJ: Erlbaum.

Dede, C. et al, 2009. A recent agenda for online teacher professional development. *Journal of Teacher Education*, Vol. 60, pp 8-10.

Desimone, L., 2009. Improving impact studies of teachers' professional development: Toward better conceptualizations and measures. *Educational Researcher*, Vol. 38, No. 3, pp 181-199.

Johnson, C.C., 2013. Educational turbulence: The influence of macro and micro policy on science education reform. *Journal of Science Teacher Education*, Vol. 24, No. 4, pp 693-715.

Muir, M., Knezek, G., and Christensen, R., 2004. The power of one to one: Early findings from the Maine Learning Technology Initiative. *Learning and Leading with Technology,* Vol. 32, No. 3, pp.6-11.

Surrett, T.N., and Johnson, C.C., 2015. Assessing the ability of an online environment to facilitate the critical features of teacher professional development. School Science and Mathematics, 115(6), 260-270.

UNESCO, 2012. *Working paper series on mobile learning: Turning on mobile learning in North America*. UNESCO, Paris: 2012.

HUMAN COMPUTER INTERACTION (HCI) AND INTERNET RESIDENCY: IMPLICATIONS FOR BOTH PERSONAL LIFE AND TEACHING/LEARNING

Linda Crearie
School of Engineering & Computing, University of the West of Scotland
High Street, PAISLEY, PA1 2BE, United Kingdom

ABSTRACT

Technological advances over the last decade have had a significant impact on the teaching and learning experiences students encounter today. We now take technologies such as Web 2.0, mobile devices, cloud computing, podcasts, social networking, super-fast broadband, and connectedness for granted. So what about the student use of these types of technologies? Is there a blurring of the distinction between using them for academic purposes versus social use in their everyday lives? If so, what lessons can Higher Education learn from the fields of HCI and User Experience Design (UXD) about improving engagement through using familiar, intuitive and exciting interactions with technology?

One of the factors driving the development of new pedagogies associated with the use of technologies for learning is a concern that there may be differences between the way that students use technologies today for socialising, working and learning. This paper describes the experiences of undergraduate students within the School of Engineering and Computing at the University of the West of Scotland. Initially under the auspices of a UK Higher Education Academy (HEA) Digital Literacies project, groups of students have completed activity maps to show how they used modern technologies for educational and personal purposes, and whether Visitor or Resident behaviour is exhibited. An analysis of these maps may prove interesting showing which tools are most popular and which are niche-focussed in order to assess the implications for student engagement and enjoyment of learning.

KEYWORDS

HCI, Pedagogies, Internet Residency, Digital Literacies, Visitor, Resident

1. INTRODUCTION

The world we live in is becoming increasingly digital. Students are increasingly immersed in this digital world, in both academic and personal contexts, where they often have a wealth of data and information instantly available to them wherever they happen to be. Visitors use the internet as a tool, accessing information as required and logging off without leaving a trace, whereas Residents live a proportion of their lives online, using the internet socially and leaving a digital trace. But how do they use this in their learning, and how can this be improved? Students today are very much at ease with digital technologies such as laptops, smartphones and tablet and other mobile devices. Innovations and advances in technologies are changing the way that students learn and the way that they are taught as well as impacting on their everyday lives. The rapidly increasing technological advances that have taken place since the millennium have changed what we think of as literacy in terms of 'Digital Literacies'.

Many educational experts such as Prensky (Prensky, 2001) refer to the E-Generation or D-Generation who have mastered the digital competencies that are essential for students today. The pace of technological change is continuing to increase dramatically and the impact may be difficult to manage successfully. In a technological sense we are living in exciting time and Higher Education (HE) now has the opportunity to harness the potential to provide a better learning environment for students.

Rapid advances in digital technologies and the Internet, and the subsequent continual increase in use by students has been having a very significant impact on how students use these technologies, when they use them, and what they use them for. As digital technologies and literacies converge many different disciples such as Human Computer Interaction (HCI) and User Experience Design (UXD) have become particularly relevant since how we interact with technology is becoming increasingly important if we want to ensure that student engagement and satisfaction is prioritised. In respect to higher education, JISC provides a definition of Digital Literacies as "those capabilities which fit an individual for living, learning and working in a digital society" and goes further than simply considering IT-related skills by including digital behaviours, practices and identities (JISC, 2014). In the early days of interacting with the Internet, Web 1.0 consisted mainly of information that was relatively static (read only) with limited user interaction. Users typically were looking up information or buying online (Visitor behaviour). Web 2.0 introduced more interactivity and the Social Web evolved to allow users to have 'presence' online (Resident behaviour – leaving a social trace) to connect with other people enhancing collaboration and connectedness through creating and sharing. Interactions evolved to become more personalised. Social media are primarily web-based communication tools enabling people to interact with each other by sharing and consuming information. (Moreau, 2016). Facebook and Twitter dominate at present, but mobile apps such as Snapchat are proving popular. Others include Linkedin, YouTube, Instagram, Pinterest, Tumblr, Vine, Reddit and Flickr. The Pew Internet Project's research on social networking in US (Pew, 2014) estimates that 46% internet users are "creators" posting original materials, 41% are "curators" reposting materials found on the web, 28% online adults use LinkedIn and 23% use Twitter. The type of tool used often impacts on behaviour, e.g. young people often use Tumblr people to re-blog from people they follow but are less likely to generate original content. As the rate of technological change increases the amount of time it takes for tools such as these to become mass market is reducing dramatically: television took 30 years to reach mass audiences, broadband took 3 years, in 2006 18-29 year old's social networking use jumped from 9% to 49%, and 28% of smartphone users use a social networking site daily, (Pew, 2014). The social web offers a world of endless information. A consequences may be information/cognitive overload leading to users becoming overwhelmed, constantly being immersed in an online world of constant interaction. Web 3.0 is the next stage of the evolution and is still evolving, encompasses elements such as Internet of Things, Semantic Web, Big Data, Smart/Intelligent Devices, AI, Virtual Worlds, mobile entertainment etc. - 'Connected Mobile Intelligence'. The shift toward mobile, semantic processing of data offers more personalised results. Some experts predict virtual and physical worlds will convergence with the web becoming an integral part of daily lives.

2. WHITE & LE CORNU'S VISITORS & RESIDENTS

"Using visitors and residents as a lens can help reveal underlying approaches and attitudes, which in turn, can help us support and engage the people we work with.", Dave White (White et al, 2011). In 2001, Prensky (Prensky, 2001) described the arrival and rapid dissemination of digital technology towards the end of the 20th century as a "singularity" - an event which changes things so fundamentally that there is no going back. He uses the term 'Digital Natives' to describe this new generation of student who are the first generations to grow up with this new technology, immersed in the computing environment to such an extent that that there are substantial implications for education. By contrast 'Digital Immigrants' as those not born into the digital world but who have adopted many or most aspects of the new technology - as they learn to adapt they retain 'a foot in the past'. In other words "older folk were socialised differently from their kids and are now in the process of learning a new language which uses a different part of the brain". David White and Alison Le Cornu who headed the HEA project **'Working with new forms of online practice in the disciplines: The challenges of web residency,** discussed in this paper, propose a continuum of 'Visitors' and 'Residents' as a replacement for Prensky's Digital Natives and Immigrants. **Visitors** are unlikely to have persistent profiles online projecting their identity, are concerned about privacy and identity theft, may view social networking as trivial and narcissistic, feel that if you have a 'real' social you wouldn't need online (visibility is the differentiator with residents - e.g. may use e–mail/Skype but wary of Facebook profiles), anonymous; activity invisible apart from databases running Web sites they use, think off–line: users (not members) of Web and don't value 'belonging online'. **Residents** live a proportion of their lives online, have blurred distinction between online and off–line, are happy to go online to spend time with others, consider they 'belong' to a community online, have a social networking profile, are comfortable expressing their persona online, view the Web as a place to express opinions where relationships are formed, use 'tools' but also maintain and develop a digital identity, have aspects of persona remain when logged off e.g. status updates, sharing, posts etc., value online activity in terms of relationships as well as knowledge and blog posting is an expression of identity and a discussion of ideas.

The aim of the project was to encourage teaching staff to reflect on practices and consider strategies for integrating technology into their learning and teaching. The specific disciples under consideration include Arts and Humanities, Social Sciences, Health and Social Care, Science, Technology, Engineering and Mathematics (STEM). The original Visitors and Residents project was JISC funded (White et al.) and suggested that people behave in different ways when using technology, depending on their motivation and context rather than age or background hence producing a much wider model of online behaviour. In order to better understand online activities of students, they were asked to produce activity maps to describe their online activity on a graph with axis representing 'Visitor' to 'Resident' activity and 'Personal Use' to 'Study/Work' purpose. A typical map is shown in figure 1.

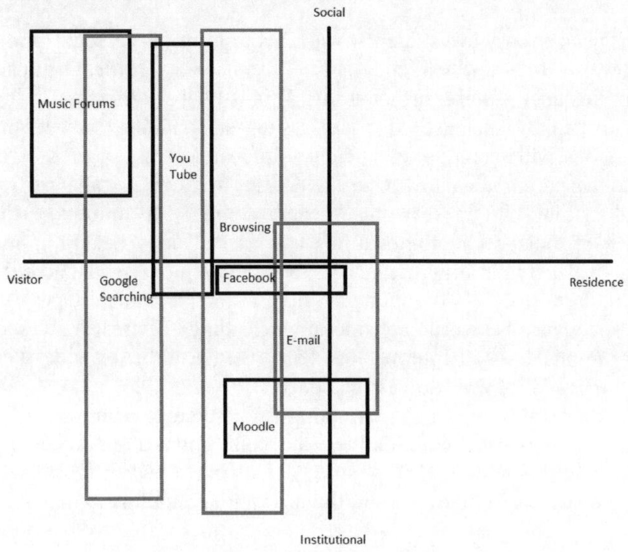

Figure 1. Student Activity Map

A number of strategies used in web residency were identified including: social media used to develop high collaboration, using 'open' practices to gain visibility and build reputation, building professional profiles and resources, and being 'Out on the Web'. Activity tended to remain mainly in 'Visitor' mode. This mode of activity was most common within this group. Some maps exhibit a flipped 'L' shape. This was slightly less common but nevertheless significant within the group and worth noting. The spread of activity for School of Engineering & Computing students is shown in Figure 2.

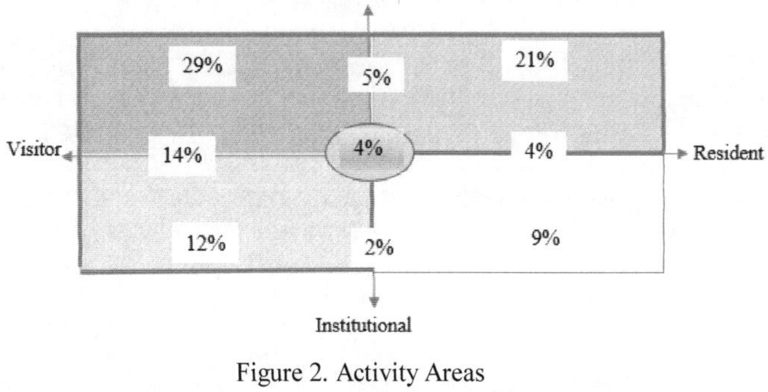

Figure 2. Activity Areas

Activity is primarily in the visitor mode (60.5%) with resident use at 39.5%. This would suggest that students are not particularly resident. Following discussions with the students, it transpired that many had privacy/security concerns which influenced this. Being knowledgeable is likely to have played a part in the decision-making process for them. An analysis of the tools which featured most in the activity maps of computing students suggests a fairly even mix of tools focussed around work and social activities. The use of Moodle is highest which is not surprising since students are required to use this to access online teaching materials and email is also mandatory. YouTube and Facebook are top of the tools used mainly for personal use, although there is some overlap with university work.

3. CONCLUSION

There are many influences on how students work, both from a personal and institutional perspective. Academically, the level of Internet Residency is likely to have a significant impact on learning, motivation and engagement, but this does require further study. This is likely to increase in importance as technological advances continue to rapidly increase in pace. Issues surrounding security/privacy and trust features frequently in discussions with computing students. Student awareness of the risks involved in 'resident mode' do appear to be paramount and ensuring privacy may encourage participation. Students already frequently create their own group learning spaces, some with minimal academics input. Providing individualised choice of tools, technologies and environments may benefit individual students and avoid overwhelming them – balancing information access, but avoiding overload, and encouraging appropriate time spent on tasks without overload. Computing/IT may attract particular types of students with particular learning strategies so it may be worth considering extending this research to other discipline. A better understanding of the implications of Internet Residency is vital to better understand the student psyche and online behaviour – the psychology of life in cyberspace.

Online presence is becoming increasingly important for students with a shift to the individual as distinct from the institution. The networks, communities and connections the student has are both academic and personal with a blurring of boundaries. The ubiquitous nature of the web allows opportunities for students to take learning and professional attributes beyond the institution to the world outside. By engaging the web in a more Resident mode, students may be in a better position to be able to use digital technologies to work, research, learn, influence and live in the ever-advancing digital world.

It may be useful when we consider the motivation of students as learners engaging with the web to pay particularly attention to learner-owned strategies and literacies – approaches to finding and sharing information, collaboration online and other techniques which students have developed in the digital world outside of their institutional environment – using tools and techniques that are familiar and that work for them individually are likely to be most successful in an educational context.

REFERENCES

JISC. (2012) Developing Digital Literacies. 1-2, retrieved from http://www.jisc.ac.uk/full-guide/18655.

Moreau E. (2016). About Tech, The Top 25 Social Networking Sites People Are Using. Retrieved from: http://webtrends.about.com/od/socialnetworkingreviews/tp/Social-Networking-Sites.htm.

Prensky M. (2001) Digital Natives, Digital Immigrants, From *On the Horizon* (MCB University Press, Vol. 9 No. 5, October 2001. 1-2)

Pew Research Center. (2014). Social Networking Fact Sheet, Highlights of the Pew Internet Project's research related to social networking, 2014. Retrieved from http://www.pinternet.org/fact-sheets/social-networking-fact-sheet

White, D., Le Cornu, A. (2011). Visitors and residents: A new typology for online engagement. *First Monday*, 16(5), 2-4. Retrieved from http://firstmonday.org/article/view/3171/3049

White, D., Connaway, L., S., Lanclos, D., Le Cornu, A., & Hood, E. (2012). Digital Visitors and Residents: Progress report. JISC, University of Oxford, OCLC, and University of North Carolina. Retrieved from http://www.jisc.ac.uk/media/documents/projects/visitorsandresidentsinterim%20report.pdf

A PORTFOLIO FOR OPTIMAL COLLABORATION OF HUMAN AND CYBER PHYSICAL PRODUCTION SYSTEMS IN PROBLEM-SOLVING

Fazel Ansari * and Ulrich Seidenberg **
*Post-Doc Researcher *, Professor ***
Institute of Production and Logistics Management,
Department of Business Administration, School of Economic Disciplines, University of Siegen, Germany

ABSTRACT

This paper discusses the complementarity of human and cyber physical production systems (CPPS). The discourse of complementarity is elaborated by defining five criteria for comparing the characteristics of human and CPPS. Finally, a management portfolio matrix is proposed for examining the feasibility of optimal collaboration between them. The optimal collaboration refers to the exchange of knowledge, reciprocal learning, and interaction of human and CPPS in smart factories. The proposed portfolio matrix provides feasibility check rules to trigger the transition towards ideal state of human and CPPS collaboration in Industry 4.0.

KEYWORDS

Human, CPPS, Complementarity, Problem-solving, Portfolio Matrix, Industry 4.0

1. INTRODUCTION

Industry 4.0 revolution and evolution of industrial internet is going to become a mega-trend, connecting various disciplines. Technological enhancement involves changes in human-technology interactions, whether technology guides human or human guide technology (Jäger et al., 2014). In addition, the emergence of cyber physical production systems (CPPS) raises several challenges for industries with regard to potential changes in processes, systems, human-based skills and organizational competencies (Acatech, 2013). CPPS are new types of production systems which are characterized as Feedback Systems that are ideally intelligent, real time, adaptive and predictive, networked and/or distributed, possibly with wireless sensing and actuation, and also possibly in loop with human (Lee & Seshia, 2015). Anticipating the trends of the 4th industrial revolution and evolution of CPPS, there will likely be a shift from a need for "data workers" to a need for "decision-makers". For instance, an operator in the future will not only run and monitor the performance of an industrial machine; rather he/she will customize machine performance under various requirements such as energy consumption. The transition is, therefore, assumed from low level operation to (high level) decision endeavors. The operator should check the output of the machine, interact with the system and make evidence based decisions considering quality, time and cost factors. This raises some questions: Which skills and competences should workers hold for problem-solving? How can we employ artificial intelligence (AI) solutions to facilitate human-machine interactions? What will be the Industry 4.0's conditions and requirements of human learning and didactical conceptions?

This paper exploits the previous studies of the authors on investigating two perspectives of human approaches of problem-solving, first synoptic and incremental, and second heuristics and meta-heuristics (Ansari et al., 2016a) and (Ansari et al., 2016b). In particular, we firstly examine and compare the characteristics of human and intelligent machines and/or production systems (i.e. CPPS) from the perspective of complementarity (Cf. Section 2). Secondly, we go beyond of the state-of-the-art by providing a portfolio matrix for characterizing the optimal collaboration between human and CPPS depending on the qualification level and degree of autonomy, respectively (Cf. Section 3). Finally, we emphasize on complementarity of human and CPPS whereby not only CPPS learn from human behavior and decision-making instances via advanced machine learning approaches, but also human can learn from CPPS behavior through communication.

2. COMPLEMENTARITY OF HUMAN AND CPPS

The human-machine interaction is an integral part of today's industrial operations. The tendency to proliferate CPPS in research laboratories and smart factories (Acatech, 2013), depending on the technology readiness level (TRL) (EC, 2016), raises uncertainty about the role of human in a CPPS environment (Jäger et al., 2014). Despite societal challenges and philosophical accounts on human substitutability, we approach the discourse of complementarity of strengths and weaknesses of human and CPPS from the perspective of knowledge exchange, reciprocal learning, and synergistic problem-solving. Hence, we have identified five criteria which may influence on complementarity of human and CPPS in smart factories, namely C1. Cost, C2. Flexibility with regard to fulfillment of various tasks and temporal availability, C3. Capacity with regard to mechanical (physical) job, information processing and problem-solving, C4. Performance variation, and C5. Quality variation with regard to mechanical job and decision-making. Table 1 compares the characteristics of human and CPPS with respect to the aforementioned criteria. It has been inspired and partially adopted from (Blohm et al., 2016) in which the characteristics of human and conventional production systems were compared with regard to mutual substitutability.

Table 1. Comparison of Human and CPPS in the context of Industry 4.0

Comparison Criterion (C)	**Human**	**CPPS**
1. Cost	**High cash expenses and mostly fixed cost,** depending on the number and the qualification of employees (within certain limits variable cost is applied due to compensation of wages for the involvement of manpower in a different operation area).	**High fixed cost** which tends upward especially due to increasing investments and service costs within the life time because of complexity of the computational and embedded controlling components.
2. Flexibility with regard to		
2.1 Fulfillment of various tasks	**High flexibility** which can be advanced through further (vocational) education and training.	**Medium to high** flexibility which depends on the advancement of the algorithms, adaptiveness e.g. to changes of processes, information and work orders, and degree of learnability.
2.2. Temporal availability	**Relatively low** (can be increased in case of readiness to flexible working hours and shifts).	**High** (24-hour operation is feasible).
3. Capacity with regard to		
3.1. Mechanical job	**High inter-individual differences and diversities,** efficiency limited through physiological conditions and mental ability, while both can be influenced by training.	**No technological limit.**
3.2. Information Processing	**Time-intensive** in access (mental and physical) databases. **Unreliability** in information storage and retrieval. **Ability** in error detection and correction routines.	**Moderate to high time-effectiveness** in processing algorithms, storage and retrieval. **Reliable in large scale** information storage. **Moderate to high ability** in error detection and (auto-)correction.
3.3. Problem-solving	**Advantages** … in solving ill-structured problems. … in managing exceptions. … in problem-modeling and -solving on the first occurrence (depending on the complexity of the problem and individual mental ability). … in collaborative and heuristic problem-solving.	**(Medium to High degree of) Advantages** … in learning and formalization of trouble-shooting process (depending on the advancement of the machine learning algorithms). … detection and correction of repeated problems (depending on the repeating rate). … prediction of standard problems based on continuous monitoring of functional and environmental parameters.
4. Performance	**Relatively high** (depending on individual capacity,	**Very low** (depending on lifetime, associated

Comparison Criterion (C)	Human	CPPS
variation	motivation and commitment). **High possibility** of work fatigue and job dissatisfaction.	degradation rate and service quality).
5. Quality variation with regard to		
5.1. Mechanical job	**High inter-individual differences and diversities** which can be improved by training and job satisfaction.	**Very low.**
5.2. Decision-making	**High inter-individual differences and diversities** depending on problem-solving abilities, competences, experiences and qualification level. The complexity and sensitivity (risk) of the decision may affect it.	**Low to moderate** depending on the quality of data (affected by disturbances and noises), preciseness of algorithms, degree of preparation by human, and complexity of the problem field. The quality can be improved after training the system with (relatively large) data-sets.

3. PORTFOLIO MATRIX FOR OPTIMAL COLLABORATION BETWEEN HUMAN AND CPPS

Taking into account the discourse of complementarity of human and CPPS (Cf. Table I), it is vital to identify the areas in which human and CPPS may collaborate to exchange knowledge, interact and learn. For this purpose, we have established a management portfolio matrix (Cf. Figure 1). The portfolio matrix identifies four zones and the transition rules between them, depending on the human qualification levels (Low or High) and autonomy degree of CPPS (Low or High).

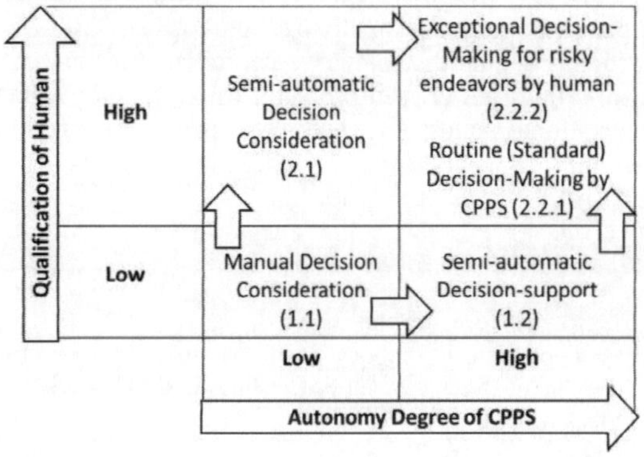

Figure 1. Portfolio matrix for optimal collaboration of Human and CPPS

The collaboration of human and CPPS is, therefore, identified according to the combination of qualification level and autonomy degree as follows:

- Low-Low (Zone 1.1) which addresses manual decision consideration through analysis of a problem space and identification of decision alternatives.
- Low-High (Zone 1.2) which refers to semi-automatic decision support by deployment of advanced assistance and recommendation systems.
- High-Low (Zone 2.1) which concentrates on semi-automatic decision consideration by highly qualified personnel through analysis of information and notifications provided by information systems.
- High-High (Zone 2.2) which is divided into two sub-areas as:
  - Routine (standard) decision-making by CPPS, i.e. autonomous decision-making with regard to low risk and non-sensitive endeavors such as shifting maintenance milestones (Zone 2.2.1)

- Exceptional decision-making by human, i.e. supervised decision-making with regard to risky endeavors such as purchasing a new machine (Zone 2.2.2).

The feasibility of incremental transition is examined by applying certain rules which are summarized below:

- Rule I - If the advancement of the TRL and utilization of AI is achieved, then transition from 1.1 to 1.2 is feasible.
- Rule II - If the Industry 4.0's requirements for goal-oriented and effective personnel training, assessment and selection are fulfilled, then transition from 1.1 to 2.1 is feasible.
- Rule III - If the Industry 4.0's requirements for effective personnel training, organizational change and reduction of risks for employing intelligent systems are fulfilled, then transition from 1.2 to 2.2 is feasible.
- Rule IV- If the technology maturity and reliability is highly improved through technology enhancement via in-house development or outsourcing, then transition from 2.1 to 2.2 is feasible.

4. CONCLUSION AND OUTLOOK

This paper discusses the complementarity of human and CPPS and provided a portfolio matrix for characterizing the optimal collaboration between them. While we emphasize on the fact that the transition to Industry 4.0 will result in substantial changes in the human work place, we stress that the interaction of human and CPPS during problem-solving processes promotes knowledge exchange and reciprocal learning. In the context of Industry 4.0, the tendency is to substitute human with CPPS in standard and routine decision situations. CPPS, also, generate information that has to be understood, interpreted, evaluated, verified and used by employees. Thus, the proposed portfolio matrix lays the ground for identifying the strategies for supporting the transition to the ideal state of smart factory model which is distinguished by collaboration of highly qualified personnel and highly autonomous CPPS.

Moreover, the portfolio matrix not only identifies the need to create artificial algorithms and software solutions for digitalization of human kind of problem-solving, but also indicates the demand to establish an Industry 4.0's work-based learning mechanism for training human resources towards holding new job roles which may involve multiple levels of problem-solving.

With the intent of promoting interdisciplinary research in Industry 4.0, the future work is aimed at identification of the semantic linkage between problem, solution and problem-solver characteristics through consideration of the organizational factors (e.g. enterprise size, human resource capacity, branch specificity, organizational culture), learning concepts, and machine learning approaches.

REFERENCES

Jäger, A., Sihn, W., Ranz, F. and Hummel, V.: Implications for Learning Factories from Industry 4.0 - Challenges for the Human Factor in Future Production Scenarios, In Proceedings of 4th Conference on Learning Factories, KTH Royal Institute of Technology, Stockholm, Sweden, 2014.

Acatech, Final Report of the Industry 4.0 Working Group: Recommendations for Implementing the Strategic Initiative Industry 4.0, acatech – National Academy of Science and Engineering, Germany, 2013.

Lee, E. A. and Seshia, S. A.: Introduction to Embedded Systems, A Cyber-Physical Systems Approach, 2nd Edition, 2015.

Ansari, F., Fathi, M. and Seidenberg, U.: Problem-Solving Approaches in Maintenance Cost Management - A Literature Review, Journal of Quality in Maintenance Engineering, Vol.: 22, Issue: 4, Emerald, 2016.

Ansari, F., Schenkelberg, K., Seidenberg, U. and Fathi, M.: Problem-Solving Approaches in the Digital World: Synoptic Formalism, Incrementalism and Heuristics, Encyclopedia of Computer Science and Technology, 2016 (In review process).

European Commission, Horizon 2020 Work Programme 2016-2017 – General Annexes, Brussels: European Commission, 2016, Retrieved from:

http://ec.europa.eu/research/participants/data/ref/h2020/other/wp/2016_2017/annexes/h2020-wp1617-annex-g-trl_en.pdf (Accessed on 05.09.2016)

Blohm, H., Beer, T., Seidenberg, U. and Silber, H.: Produktionswirtschaft (Production Management), 5th Ed., Verlag Neue Wirtschafts-Briefe, Herne 2016.

INNOVATIVE COLLABORATIVE LEARNING STRATEGIES FOR INTEGRATED INTERACTIVE E-LEARNING IN THE 21ST CENTURY

Barbara Son
California State University at Los Angeles
5151 State University Drive, Los Angeles, CA 90032, USA

ABSTRACT

There is a constant challenge for online programs, instructional designers and instructors to tailor eLearning materials for different learning styles. We examined this issue by closely looking at the innovative interactive learning models at the previous AACE Conferences (Son & Goldstone, 2011, Son & Goldstone, 2012, Son & Simonian, 2013, Son & Simonian, 2014). At the current Conference, we will discuss how learner-centered collaborative learning should be designed to improve these models using the example of a global online MBA course at Anaheim University. Using international economics as the subject matter, we will closely examine innovative collaborative learning strategies which are vital in cultivating highly active, engaging and applied learning in global economic classrooms in the 21st century.

KEYWORDS

Collaborative Learning, Integrated Interactive E-Learning, E-learning Paradigm, Pedagogy in International Economic Affairs

1. INTRODUCTION

How can we teach rising complex international economic affairs effectively in the 21st century global online classrooms? We need to pursue a new e-learning paradigm to foster learners with innovative and critical global thinking. Fast growing global digital world and rapid progress in multimedia instructional technology are facilitating a significant paradigm shift from traditional learning to learner centered active learning. Active learning paradigm in international economic affairs supports collaborative and engaged learning.

Online international economic curricula should be designed to constantly draw forth active learning feedback to facilitate learner-centered global economic classrooms. As students demand more flexible and responsive digital tools to access their learning materials, global online classrooms have to deliver more learner-friendly complex content effectively. In addition, global economic online programs, instructional designers and instructors ought to tailor eLearning materials for different learning styles. We examined these challenges by closely looking at the innovative interactive learning models at the previous AACE Conferences (Son & Goldstone, 2011, Son & Goldstone, 2012, Son & Simonian, 2013, Son & Simonian, 2014).

At the current Conference, we will discuss how learner-centered collaborative learning should be designed to improve these models. Using international economics as the subject matter, we will closely examine innovative collaborative learning strategies which are vital in cultivating highly active, engaging and applied learning in global economic classrooms in the 21st century.

2. NEW PARADIGM IN THE 21ST CENTURY GLOBAL E-LEARNING

In the evolving complex global environment, international economic affairs are entangled with multi-disciplinary problems. Accordingly, the scope of international economic affairs in the globalization era has to be broadened, and integrated flexible learning needs to be incorporated into student-centered nurturing pedagogy (Giles, 2009). Under this approach, online learners are able to:

- Collaboratively work together to understand the complex international economic affairs using flexible learning tools;
- Understand multi-disciplinary concepts through team online discussions and interactive online exercises;
- Develop collaborative learning through diverse applied e-learning activities; and
- Contribute to the innovative team solutions to multi-faceted global economic problems.

To successfully obtain these learning outcomes, academic institutions have to implement a new paradigm in the 21st century global e-learning as depicted below. They have to direct global economic online programs, instructional designers and instructors to develop innovative pedagogical techniques under the new paradigm. Active learning paradigm in international economic affairs supports collaborative and engaged learning through case studies, simulations, games, role-playing, policy debates, service learning, study abroad, film, interactive technology, and team discussions (Shaw, 2010). Online instructors need to constantly draw forth learning feedback to facilitate student-centered collaborative learning activities that can really engage and motivate even the most passive learners. This creates the continuous active learning cycle.

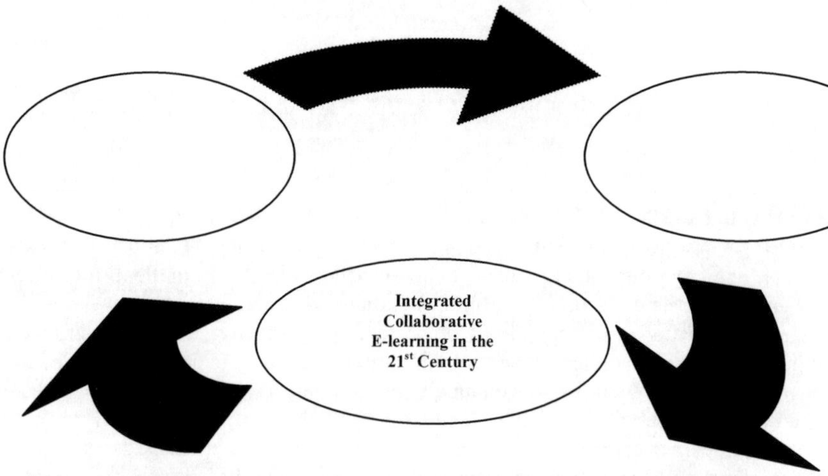

Figure 1. New Paradigm in the 21st Century Global E-Learning

2.1 Innovative Flexible Learning Tools in Global Online Classrooms

In the 21st century global classrooms, instructional technology is one of major pedagogical techniques for the active learning. Through flexible interactive tools, active learning encourages engaged learning and critical thinking skills (Giles, 2009). To assist innovative and collaborative lessons, we adopt flexible multimedia learning tools in our international economics class. Our online MBA students who are mostly global business professionals engage in highly interactive lectures, collaborative problem solving, and group project forums through a state-of-the-art customized web-based portal, iPod, streaming video webcast, and video podcasts (Anaheim University, 2015). We help them practice different learning tools flexibly in order to comprehend complex international economic affairs. In real-time online webcam classes, we facilitate innovative and collaborative learning through the latest high definition video webcam technology.

2.2 New Innovative Pedagogical Techniques

Learner-centered nurturing pedagogy in international economic affairs must address the complex and dynamic transformations of global environment. Active learners in international economic affairs need to identify and analyze the impact of various global variables and explore innovative policy ideas. To facilitate these learning outcomes, innovative pedagogical techniques must be incorporated into online economic curricula. In our online economics class, we apply flipped learning pedagogical techniques through asynchronous video lectures and active problem solving activities. Flipped learning combines constructivist learning theory which promotes authentic problem solving and behaviorist learning theory that emphasizes frequent practices (Roach, 2014). Instructors play as active learning facilitators to help students develop cognitive learning and practice experiential applied learning (Ash & Clayton, 2009). Online instructors and active learners have to be active learning partners to keep 'Integrated Collaborative Learning Cycle' (Figure 2) moving forward. We integrate innovative case exercises into interactive and collaborative lessons to deliver integrated learning environment. Our students realize actual roles they collectively play in the international economic affairs. We emphasize collaborative and experiential learning from which active learners gain perspectives toward tightly interwoven global issues, have empathy for others, and develop insights into challenges of others (Gibson & Shaw, 2010).

2.3 Integrated Collaborative E-learning in 21st Century

To build high order thinking and analytical skills, active learners in international economic affairs need to synthesize multidisciplinary components, to prescribe policy ideas, to predict future policy changes, and to evaluate potential policy outcomes. To fulfill these learning objectives, international economic curricula should adapt the pillars of four vital performing areas - innovative collaborative lessons, flexible multimedia learning tools, customized active learning activities, and integrated learning environment. We present these interwoven vital areas in the integrated collaborative e-learning model as shown in Figure 2.

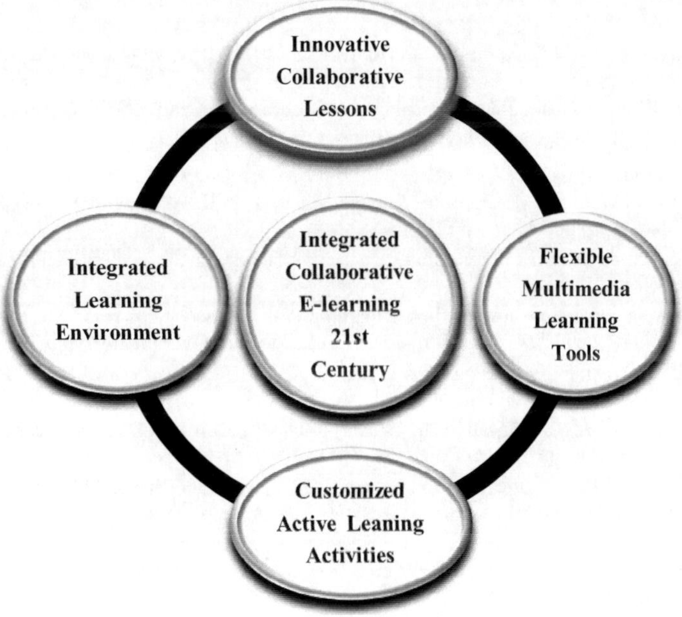

Figure 2. Integrated Collaborative E-learning Model

Integrated collaborative learning in our international economic class require instructors and students to take higher responsibilities towards leaning environment. They commit high levels of learning activity preparation and participation. They collaborate together to ultimately create an integrated learning environment which nurtures engaged, authentic and applied learning process. As we have earlier examined, collaboration, innovation and creativity are vital components in the 21st century learning paradigm. To enhance these components, we integrate various pedagogical techniques into our customized active learning activities. Flexible multimedia learning tools that are integrated into our innovative collaborative lessons help us foster these activities in the integrated learning environment.

3. CONCLUSION

Our students who are global business professionals have tremendously contributed to the building of the integrated learning environment. This is one of the four vital components in the integrated collaborative e-learning model. The integrated collaborative e-learning is nurtured by evolving innovative collaborative lessons, flexible multimedia learning tools, and customized active learning activities. International economic curricula should adapt these four interwoven components to constantly keep 'Integrated Collaborative Learning Cycle' (Figure 2) moving forward. This facilitates learner-centered global economic classroom (Son & Goldstone, 2010).

In the fast moving 21st century global environment, international economics courses require innovative pedagogies and multidisciplinary learning as we examined. Online economic classrooms must apply innovative pedagogical techniques to facilitate student-centered active learning. Active teaching and learning process is facilitated by continuous assessment of learning outcomes in the continuous collaborative learning cycle. We presented innovative collaborative learning strategies to improve our previous integrated e-learning models (Son & Goldstone, 2011, Son & Goldstone, 2012, Son & Simonian, 2013, Son & Simonian, 2014). Significant progress will only occur when all four components in the integrated collaborative e-learning model are leveraged to work together in an integrated manner.

REFERENCES

Anaheim University, 2015. *Student Resources*. Retrieved from https://www.anaheim.edu/student-resources/online-discussion-forum

Ash, S. and Clayton, P., 2009. Generating, Deepening, and Documenting Learning: the Power of

Critical Reflection in Applied Learning. *Journal of Applied Learning in Higher*

Education, Vol.1, Fall, pp. 25-48.

Gibson, K. and Shaw, C.M., 2010. *Assessment of Active Learning*. In R. A. Denemark (Ed.), The International Studies Encyclopedia. Blackwell Publishing.

Giles, M., 2009. Teacher as 'learner': A case study of teaching international economics and finance. *eCULTURE* Vol. 2, The Berkeley Electronic Press.

Roach, T., 2014. Student perceptions toward flipped learning: New methods to increase interaction and active learning in economics. *The International Review of Economics Education*, Vol.17, September, pp. 74-84.

Shaw, C.M., 2010. *Designing and Using Simulations and Role-Play Exercises*. In R. A. Denemark (Ed.), The International Studies Encyclopedia. Blackwell Publishing.

Son, B. and Goldstone, B., 2010. Innovative Approaches to Quality Delivery: Best Practices at the Top-Ranked Global MBA Online Program in Japan. *Global Learn Asia Pacific 2010 Conference*. Malaysia.

Son, B. and Goldstone, B., 2011. Innovative Approaches to Integrated Interactive e-Learning for Working Professionals: Pepperdine Online and DeVry Online. *Global Learn Asia Pacific 2011 Conference*. Melbourne, Australia.

Son, B. and Goldstone, B., 2012. Innovative Live Lecture Strategies for Integrated Interactive e-Learning at DeVry Online. *AACE Proceedings of Global TIME 2012 — Online Conference on Technology, Innovation, Media & Education*. Chesapeake, VA, pp. 184-190.

Son, B. and Simonian, M., 2013. Using Integrated Multimedia Learning in Cyber-Classrooms: Transforming "Dull Economics" into "Fun" Economics." E-LEARN 2013 - World Conference on E-Learning. Las Vegas, Nevada, pp.21-24.

Son, B. and Simonian, M., 2014. Using Mobile Learning to Enhance Innovative Interactive Learning at DeVry Online. *EdMedia-- World Conference on Educational Multimedia, Hypermedia and Telecommunications*. Chesapeake, VA, pp. 546–552.

EDUCATIONAL CRITERIA FOR EVALUATING SIMPLE CLASS DIAGRAMS MADE BY NOVICES FOR CONCEPTUAL MODELING

Mizue Kayama, Shinpei Ogata, David K. Asano and Masami Hashimoto
Faculty of Engineering, Shinshu University, Japan

ABSTRACT

Conceptual modeling is one of the most important learning topics for higher education and secondary education. The goal of conceptual modeling in this research is to draw a class diagram using given notation to satisfy the given requirements. In this case, the subjects are asked to choose concepts to satisfy the given requirements and to correctly extract the relations between objects and services. In this paper, we aim to propose criteria for evaluating conceptual modeling errors made by university freshmen. To achieve this research goal, we quantitatively analyzed class diagrams made by novice learners. Based on the results of three types of experiments, we propose 12 criteria, which are divided into 4 types, for evaluating class diagrams made by novices.

KEYWORDS

Conceptual modeling, class diagram, criteria, quantitative analysis, novice education

1. INTRODUCTION

Not only in undergraduate or graduate schools but also in pre-university education, conceptual modeling is one of the most important learning topics. These days, educational methods or learning courses related to conceptual modeling have been explored in many educational institutes, academic conferences and academic journals [Bezivin 2009, Börstler 2004, Fuller 2010, Kramer 2007, Moisan 2010, Sendall 2003]. The goal of conceptual modeling in this research is to draw a class diagram using given notation to satisfy the given requirements. In this case, the subjects are asked to appropriately capture the given requirements. This means the students need to choose concepts to satisfy the given requirements and to correctly extract the relations between objects and services.

In this paper, we aim to propose criteria for evaluating conceptual modeling errors made by university freshmen. To achieve this research goal, we quantitatively analyzed class diagrams made by students. During this analysis, we asked ourselves "What kind of criteria are suitable for novice learners when they create conceptual models? " and "Are there any differences between the scores of novice learners with and without programming knowledge? " There are two differences between previous research and our research. The first difference is our subjects. We focus on university freshmen and pre-university students, who have not taken any kind of CS specific courses. The other difference is the empirical and continual research method. We have been engaged in this research since 2007 [Hara 2007, Masumoto 2012].

2. RESEARCH METHODS

We define conceptual modeling as a way of thinking to solve problems using engineering methodology. In the first semester for university freshmen, students have to take a conceptual modeling course to express services and objects in the real world using a class diagram. The modeling targets in this course are not limited to artificial systems or services which can be executed on computers. The reason for this rule is to have our novice learners concentrate on modeling without programming.

Figure 1 shows an example class diagram used in this research. A hotel is modeled based on the simplified class diagram notation. We use a class diagram which is a simplified standard class diagram defined using UML2.x. Our simple class diagram has the minimum essential elements for conceptual modeling. The minimum essential elements are classes and bi-directional associations. For each class, a name and some attributes are listed, while no attribute types, method names, arguments, return types or visibilities are used. For each association, two names and two multiplicities with four types (0..1, 1, 1..*, *) are used, while no role, inheritance, aggregation, composition or dependency are used. The only association used in this diagram is a simple association between two peer classes. This association represents a pure structural relationship between two peers.

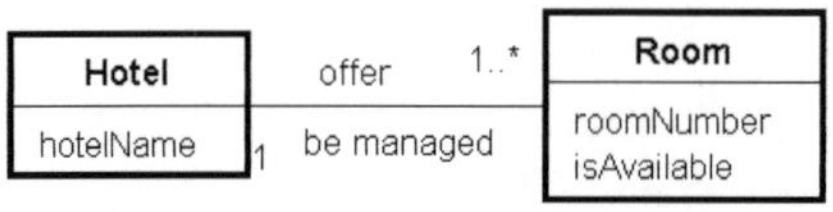

Figure 1. A class diagram with simplified notation

Our subjects were 174 university students who were novices at conceptual modeling. These subjects were divided into two groups based on their computer science knowledge. Table 1 shows their profiles. All subjects were required to answer the questions individually. They were not allowed to discuss the questions with each other or to solve the problems in groups.

Table 1. Subject Group Profiles

Group Name	11T	12T
Number of subjects	86	88
Year	Sophomore	Freshmen
Pre-acquired knowledge about computer science (number of semesters)	Algorithmic thinking (0.5) Conceptual Modeling (0.5) Algorithm & data structure (1) C language programming (2)	None
Experiment period	Second semestar in Second year	First semestat in first year
Course type	Elective	Required

Our experiment expands on this learning method by using three tests: a model reading test, a model creation test and a model modification test. In the model reading test, students are given requirements and a diagram. The students answer questions related to the diagram to check their understanding of conceptual modeling. By doing this test, we can confirm the students' fundamental knowledge about conceptual modeling. In the model creation test, students are asked to draw a complete simple class diagram that satisfies given requirements to check their understanding of and appropriate abstraction. In the model modification test, students have to indicate some inadequate elements in the given samples. They are also required to draw a revised model to check their understanding of conceptual modeling, requirement analysis and appropriate abstraction.

Before these tests, the instructor asked his students the names of the essential elements in a simple class diagram to confirm their level of understanding. Two instructors were engaged in the course management. They planned the learning contents of this course and gave our subjects lectures. Then, we analyzed the subjects' answers and discussed the results.

3. EXPERIMENTAL RESULTS

3.1 Model Reading Test

The goal of this test is to check the conceptual modeling capability of students. In this test, students point out the differences between a given diagram and the problem statements. Four problems (P) were given to students.

The trend of the percentage of problems answered correctly is the same for both groups. The students' level of understanding decreases as follows: class > association > multiplicity > attribute. The average total scores and in particular the attribute related problem scores of these two groups show a significant difference. So, the level of understanding about "attribute" is much lower than for other elements (class, association, multiplicity) for both groups.

3.2 Model Creation Test

The goal of this test is to check the requirement analysis capability and the appropriate abstraction capability.

Figure 3 shows the percentage of students who drew the class diagram correctly and incorrectly in this test for the two groups. The 12T group has a higher score than the 11T group. The average total scores and variances of these two groups show a significant difference.

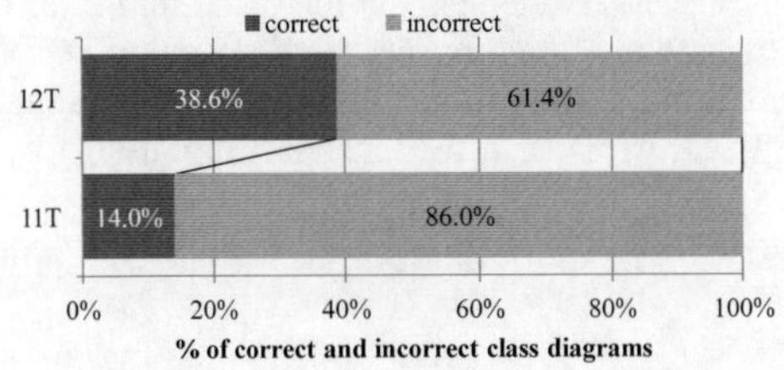

Figure 2. Percentage of students who drew the class diagram correctly and incorrectly in the model creation test for the two groups

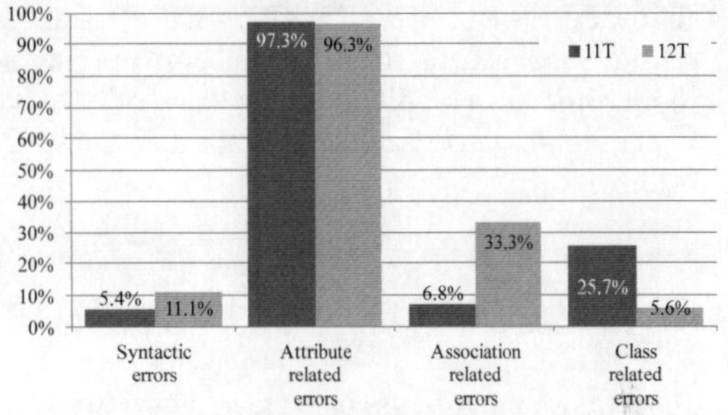

Figure 3. Percentage of the four error types that occurred in the model creation test

At first, we categorized the answers which had some errors based on the three error types from previous research. In total, we extracted four types of errors: syntactic errors, attribute related errors, association related errors and class related errors. Figure 3 shows the percentage of the four error types that occurred in the model creation test. For the 11T students, the number of incorrect answers was 74. For the 12T students, the number of incorrect answers was 54.

In this experiment, we found that attribute related errors are the most common type of error made by novice learners. In both groups, over 95% of the incorrect answers had this type of error. For the 11T group, which has programming knowledge, the percentage of class related errors is relatively higher. On the other hand, 12T group, which has no programming knowledge, shows a higher percentage of association related errors.

We analyzed these 4 types of errors in more detail. The class related error has two detailed subcategories:

1. There are some classes which have different abstraction levels in one diagram.
2. There are more than two classes whose names or attributes have the same meaning in one diagram.

The attribute related errors had six detailed error categories:

1. A class does not have any attributes (No attribute). This error also is included the syntactic error.
2. Two or more classes have the same set of attributes (Same attribute). "Same" means that each attribute has the same range of values.
3. An attribute is defined as not "name" but "value" (Value attribute).
4. Attributes which are actions or methods are listed (Behavioral attribute).
5. The meaning of both an attribute and the multiplicity of an association is overlapped (Overlapped property).
6. Duplicated attributes are used (Duplicated attribute).

The association related error type includes some class diagrams which have no association name or multiplicity and have inadequate association name or multiplicity. This type has four detailed error categories.

1. There are no association names. This error also is included the syntactic error.
2. Inadequate association name is given.
3. There are not two multiplicities for one association. This error also is included the syntactic error.
4. Inadequate multiplicity is given.

3.3 Model Modification Test

The goal of this test is to check the ability of conceptual modeling, requirement analysis and appropriate abstraction. In all five problems, students need to point out the mistakes in each class diagram and describe why they are incorrect. Then, they are asked to modify the class diagram to correct the mistakes. P1 has association related errors, which are inadequate multiplicity and duplicate association names. P2 has an attribute related error, where the attribute name is defined as a value instead of a property. P3 has an association related error, which is inadequate multiplicity. P4 has an association related error, which is the lack of association names. P5 has a syntactic error, which is redundant multiplicity.

The trend of the percentage of questions answered correctly is the same for both groups. The highest percentage of correctly corrected errors was for the syntactic error (P1) and the association related error (P4). The lowest percentage was for the association related error (P3). Their level of understanding decreases as follows: P1 > P4 > P2 > P5 > P3. Both P1 and P4 are lacking necessary elements in the diagram. P2, P5 and P3 have inadequate elements in the given diagrams. This means that the "inadequate description" error is more difficult to modify than the "lack of necessary element" error. The average total scores and variances of these two groups are statistically the same. Only the P3 scores of these two groups show a significant difference.

4. DISCUSSION

Here we want to discuss our research questions.

4.1 Question 1

What kinds of criteria are suitable for novice learners when they create conceptual models with simple class diagrams?

We propose 12 criteria, which are divided into 4 types, for evaluating simple class diagrams made by novices for conceptual modeling based on the results we mentioned above. Table 2 shows the proposed criteria. The frequency of occurrence is different for each item. However, by using these items we can check the level of understanding for conceptual modeling of novice learners. Therefore, conceptual modeling instructors can develop their course for novices with these criteria. An example of each criterion is shown in Figure A1 in the Appendix. These examples were made based on our students' answers. To explain each criterion exactly in these Figures, the authors simplified the students' answers.

Table 2. Criteria for Evaluating Simple Class Diagram made by Novice for Conceptual Modeling

Error types	Criteria
Syntactic error	Inadequate notation.
	Lack of necessary element [association and multiplicity].
	Lack of name of necessary element [class, attribute and association].
Class related error	There are some classes which have different abstraction levels in one diagram.
	There are two or more classes whose names or attributes have the same meaning in one diagram.
Attribute related error	The same attributes are used in more than two classes.
	The attribute name is defined as a value instead of a property.
	An attribute that describes an action is used.
	An attribute that has the meaning of multiplicity is used.
	Duplicated attributes are used.
Association related error	Inadequate association name.
	Inadequate multiplicity.

4.2 Question 2

Are there any differences between the programming-known group and the not-known group in terms of their level of understanding of conceptual modeling?

In the model reading test, there are no significant differences between the 11T group and the 12T group in terms of the percentage of questions answered correctly. Especially, the trend of the percentage of problems answered correctly is statistically the same for both groups. The average of the percentage of questions answered correctly by the 12T group is higher than the average of the 11T group. However, there are no statistically significant differences between any scores.

In the model creation test, there is a statistically significant difference between scores of the 11T group and the 12T group. Firstly, The percentage of problems answered correctly by the 12T group which has no programming knowledge is higher than the 11T group which has programming knowledge. Though these two groups were given the same contents and the same length of lectures about conceptual modeling, the 12T group which has no programming knowledge showed a higher score in creating models based on the given requirements. Secondly, about the percentage of the four error types that occurred in this test, for the 11T group the percentage of class related errors is high. On the other hand, the 12T group shows a high percentage of association related errors. Whereas the association related errors are relatively superficial mistakes, the class related errors are quite essential mistakes in conceptual modeling using class diagrams. These types of errors are concerned with abstraction level control. This fact means that programming knowledge has no effect on the ability to control abstraction levels. And finally, about the percentage of attribute related error types in this test, for the 11T group, the percentage of no attribute errors and behavioral attribute errors is about 20%. Duplicated attribute errors occurred only in the 12T group. The behavioral attribute errors occurred only in the 11T group. We think this fact is caused by structured programming knowledge which includes functions. If they draw a class diagram with methods, students in the 11T group would get a higher score on this test. Therefore, it is better to teach conceptual modeling with this notation before programming. However, the total trend of our 12 criteria seems to be the same for both groups.

5. CONCLUSION

Our research questions are "What kind of criteria are suitable for novice learners when they create conceptual models?" and "Are there any differences between the scores of novice learners with and without programming knowledge?"

In this paper, we propose criteria for evaluating conceptual modeling errors made by novices based on the results of three experiments. Overall, based on our experiments, programming knowledge seems to not directly affect conceptual modeling ability. If so, conceptual modeling education in this notation for university freshmen is reasonable. In this case, the instructors should consider our 12 criteria listed above. The effects of these matters for the proposed conclusions need to be considered in future work. Also, we need to discuss the relation between diagram notation and education timing more carefully.

REFERENCES

Bezivin, J. et al, 2009. "Teaching Modeling: Why, When, What?", *Proc. of the MODELS 2009*, pp.55-62.

Börstler, J., Michiels, I. and Fjuk, A., 2004. "ECOOP 2004 Workshop Report: Eighth Workshop on Pedagogies and Tools for the Teaching and Learning Object-Oriented Concepts", *ECOOP 2004 Workshop Reader*, pp.36-48.

Fuller, R.M., Murthy, U. and Schafer, B.A., 2010. "The effects of data model representation method on task performance", *Information & Management*, Vol.47, No.4, pp.208-218.

Hara, Y. et al, 2007. "A Basic Study of an Educational Environment for Modeling and Abstraction", *Proc. of the ESS 2011*, pp.16-1-16-5, 2011.

Kramer, J., 2007. "Is Abstraction The Key To Computing?", *In CACM*, Vol.50, No.4, pp.37-4.

Masumoto, K. et al, 2012. "A Basic Study of Teaching Methods for Model-Based Design with Error Analyses of Beginners - in the case of the class diagrams–", *Proc. of the ESS 2012*, pp.101-109.

Moisan, S. and Rigault, J.P., 2010. "Teaching Object-Oriented Modeling and UML to Various Audiences", *Proc. of the Educators' Symposium at MODELS 2009*, pp.40-54.

Sendall, S., 2003. "Model Transformation: The Heart and Soul of Model Driven Software Development", *In IEEE SOFTWARE*, Vol.20, No.5, pp.42-45.

DIGITAL NATIVES AND DIGITAL DIVIDE: ANALYSING PERSPECTIVE FOR EMERGING PEDAGOGY

Uriel U. Onye[1] and Yunfei Du[2], Ph.D.
[1]*Ph.D. Candidate*
[2]*Associate Professor*
Department of Library and Information Science, College of Information University of North Texas (UNT), USA

ABSTRACT

This paper addresses the concepts of digital natives and digital divide from the perspective of the digital outsiders (part of digital natives). It takes a critical look at the implications of available ICT in both developed and underdeveloped countries in the fight against digital divide. The major contribution to literature is by drawing attention to the inevitability of technology mediated learning and the need to embrace ICT adapted to countries strengths and weaknesses in the fight against digital divide. However, data used for this study significantly reveal how digital natives in the developed countries and digital outsiders in underdeveloped countries could achieve digital diffusion, especially those from underdeveloped countries with highly limited opportunities. As a result, there is no contesting the future of educational pedagogy depends on technology. Hence, people must take advantage of available technology in designing pedagogy. In the end, digital divide is relative and should apply differently in both developed and underdeveloped regions to enable rapid and sustainable digital diffusion despite the odds confronting digital natives globally.

KEYWORDS

Digital natives, digital divide, digital outsiders, educational pedagogy, bridging the gap

1. INTRODUCTION

When Prensky claimed to have recognized a pattern change in the learning behavior of people belonging to a certain age group, little did he know that learning pedagogy was about to witness a paradigm shift unparalleled in recent history. He regarded children born from the 1980's downwards as 'digital natives' while people from earlier generations became the 'digital immigrants'. The evolutionary effects of information technology (ICT) created a contrast between the two groups leaving the impression that the education system in place did not capture the learning needs and abilities of the digital natives (Prensky, 2001). Chains of debate concerning the claim erupted in both academic and professional quarters engulfing research questions and answers. Numerous debate among educators, academics and professionals took different perspectives in what later became the problems and solutions surrounding digital natives. The major problem confronting us today is that of 'digital divide' which symbolizes the inequalities in social, political, cultural and economic classification of people, families, communities and races into 'haves' and 'have nots'. In other words, Van Dijk (2006) puts it as the unequal distribution of access to information communications technology (ICT) between society's 'haves' and 'have-nots'.

Hence, prevailing factors against 'digital diffusion' increased the concept of digital divide, thereby forcing 'digital inclusion' into a major channel of bridging 'digital gap'. Today, digital inclusion has emerged into a model for neutralizing the divisions of digital divide between the digital haves and have nots. As a result of digital inclusion initiative, 100% of public schools in the U.S now provide internet access for students (Attewell, 2001). This solution is major boost to digital diffusion campaign. Unfortunately, digital divide goes beyond access to computer and internet, to include what has escaped the minds of people, "that some greater portion of these digital natives are not included in the digital divide paradigm because their demographics are outsides the boundaries constituting Prensky's digital natives." This paper refers to them as "digital outsiders" because they are the excluded component of an all-inclusive digital native paradigm.

2. INCLUDE AND DIFFUSE: THE OUTSIDERS CROSS

Researchers agree that access to ICT suffer from different types of inequalities throughout the developed countries of Europe and America (Selwyn, 2006). Judging from an international perspective, Mariscal (2005) describes the contrast in ICT access as huge when underdeveloped countries are compared with developed countries. As a result, digital inclusion is no longer a fight to bridge the gap between the rich and the poor (Howland, 1998), but to enable diffusion between the 'information rich' and the 'information poor' for everyone (Black, 1986; Doctor, 1991). Unfortunately still, the evolving nature of ICT combined with classism keeps the gap between the 'haves' and 'have nots' in constant expansion. Selwyn (2006) agrees with the factors that contribute to the continued expansion (digital divide) to include the inability and unlikelihood of members of certain social groups to meaningfully engage with new technologies. In other words, demographics with non-availability of computers and broadband internet connection at home and schools plus the required skill and knowledge to meaningfully use ICT (Hesseldhl, 2008).

This brings in the open conditions of the "digital outsiders" who are members of digital natives by definition, but are far removed from the operational standards of 'digital divide'. These groups have not by any means being digitally diffused through any digital inclusion programs. Lack of external digital inclusion programs has lowered the rate at which they are digitally diffused with the rest of the natives. In many case, all attempts to use ICT comes from the outsiders efforts to close the digital divide. It goes that 'jumping the bridge' sequels 'bridging the gap' as a means to enable members achieve digital diffusion in the absence of guided digital inclusion program as seen in the developed countries. Thus, jumping the bridge, becomes an effective way of curbing digital divide and ensuring digital diffusion is possible from the outsiders perspective and ICT needs. The aim is to bridge the digital divide and enable digital diffusion with the rest of the natives. Ironically, although the outsiders are not included in digital inclusion programs, they find it imperative to devise a method best adapted to their ICT problems and needs. Thus, 'jumping the bridge' describes the outsiders version of 'digital inclusion' which serve as channel for members to stay connected in the digital age. As seen in Africa, diffusion of cellphones suggest a reliable means of curbing digital divide and boosting mass mobilization for ICT (Buys, Dasgupta, Thomas and Wheeler, 2009).

3. DATA OUTCOME

The first set of tables show the use of both internet and mobile connections of different school age of digital natives in the U.S. While the second table compares internet landlines and mobile network acceptance in Africa. Campaigns against digital divide in the U.S emanated such programs as digital inclusion and digital diffusion. The programs includes free access to every school child to computers, internet and Wi-Fi connections in all public schools. However, it is an achievement only possible in areas where internet connection is not limited to mobile network. In Africa the case is different. Poor landlines begat dysfunctional ICT access in most public schools. On the contrary, the penetration of mobile networks in areas previously inaccessible to ICT has created a surge in cellphones ownership by members.

Tables 1 & 2. Shows the educational use of internet and mobile network by different levels of students in the U.S (Source: Pew Research Center, 2015)

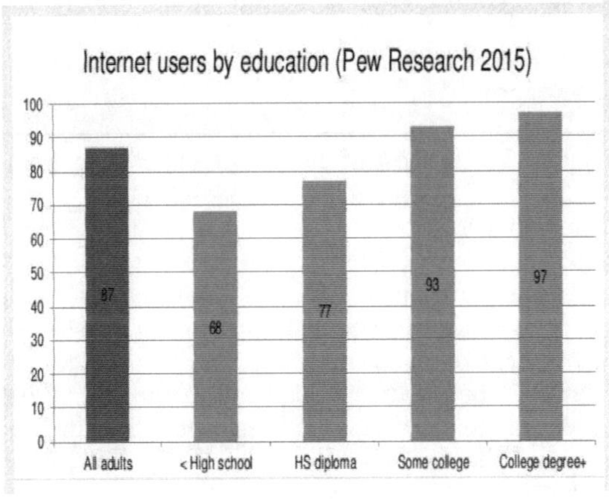

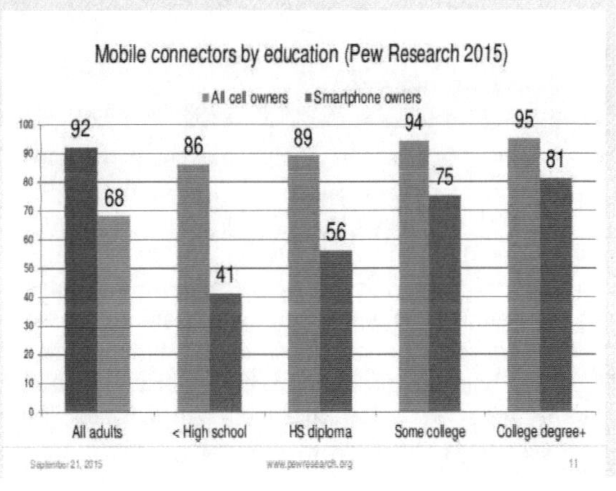

Tables 3 & 4. Shows a comparative use of mobile network and landlines in Africa (Source: Pew Research Center, 2015)

Cell Phone Ownership Surges in Africa

Adults who own a cell phone

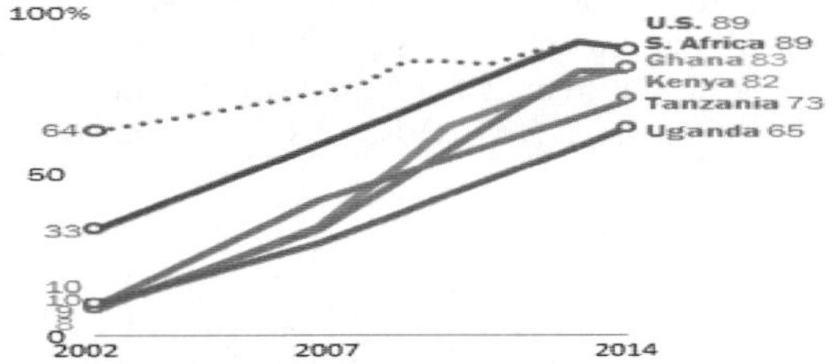

Note: U.S. data from Pew Research Center surveys.

Source: Spring 2014 Global Attitudes survey. Q68.

PEW RESEARCH CENTER

Very Few Africans Have Landlines

Do you have a working landline in your household?

	No	Yes
Senegal	94%	6%
South Africa	94	6
Kenya	97	3
Tanzania	98	2
Ghana	96	1
Nigeria	97	1
Uganda	98	1
MEDIAN	97	2
U.S.	40	60

Note: Percentages based on total sample. Median percentage excludes the U.S.

Source: Spring 2014 Global Attitudes survey. Q160 & LL.

PEW RESEARCH CENTER

Internet and cellphone uses in select African countries indicate an effort by digital outsiders to re-integrate themselves with technology. "By personal efforts of the outsiders" reference is made to the group individual acquisition of mobile devices and use of mobile network without any planned inclusion initiative from any sources. That's why when comparing the trends in landlines and mobile network in Africa, evidence show how mobile network is championing the future of ICT in the region. Landline use in the U.S is over 80% while in Africa the highest country with landline network is Senegal with 6% and the lowest are Ghana, Nigeria and Uganda with 1% respectively. On the other hand, mobile network by cellphone ownership indicate the following: U.S. has 89%, South Africa 89%, Ghana 83%, Kenya 82%, Uganda 65% and Tanzania 73%. The trend shows that most underdeveloped countries that have introduced mobile telecommunications market have been able to achieve ICT penetration (Mariscal, 2015).

Tables 5 & 6. Shows different capabilities of mobile network uses in Africa in perspective

Young More Likely to Use Cell Phones for Texting, Taking Pictures or Video

Adult cell phone owners who used a cell phone in the past 12 months to ...

	Send text messages			Take pictures or video		
	18-34	35+	Diff	18-34	35+	Diff
	%	%		%	%	
Ghana	65	34	+31	62	33	+29
Senegal	84	56	+28	61	39	+22
Nigeria	89	67	+22	68	42	+26
Uganda	66	52	+14	51	20	+31
Tanzania	97	84	+13	62	41	+21
Kenya	93	83	+10	62	44	+18
South Africa	98	92	+6	69	51	+18

Note: All age differences are statistically significant.

Source: Spring 2014 Global Attitudes survey. Q74a-b.

PEW RESEARCH CENTER

Texting, Taking Pictures and Videos Most Common Use of Cell Phones in Africa

Adult cell phone owners who used a cell phone in the past 12 months to ...

	Send text messages	Take pictures or video	Make or receive payments	Get political news	Access social network	Get health info	Look/ apply for a job	Get consumer info
South Africa	95%	60	15	18	31	15	19	14
Tanzania	92%	53	39	21	19	11	14	12
Kenya	88%	54	61	28	28	19	26	14
Nigeria	80%	57	15	28	35	23	15	14
Senegal	70%	50	30	19	19	17	12	14
Uganda	60%	37	42	23	14	20	14	16
Ghana	51%	48	15	18	15	11	9	8
MEDIAN	80%	53	30	21	19	17	14	14

Source: Spring 2014 Global Attitudes survey. Q74a-h.

PEW RESEARCH CENTER

The figure shows great achievement for those regions despite most of the integration coming from the outsiders strive to survive digital divide in regions bereft of ICT options. Taking advantage of mobile network to bridge gaps in technology is a commendable step that makes the region stand peculiar in the fight against digital divide (Poushter and Oates, 2015). Table 2 & 3 shows the most common uses of cellphones in African schools indicating a meaningful application of mobile technology for information sharing and a mechanism to fight digital divide. Mobile network as the dominant ICT provider in most regions of Africa unveils the dominant digital divide and possible diffusion methods that could be supported by the technology already in use by people. Such implication can transform ICT policy and propel the trajectory of educational pedagogy if well understood and utilized. Moreover, it reemphasizes the suggestion that integrating technology already in use will bridge gaps in digital divide in those region (Savery and Duffy, 2001).

4. IMPLICATION FOR ONLINE PEDAGOGY

Several intervening measures have arisen over the years as pedagogy confronts technology. Pew Research Center describes the future of education as becoming one with technology. What this indicates is that the direction of technology knows no bounds, and if well harnessed technology can direct the trajectory of learning pedagogies to accommodate all peoples regardless their ICT skills for meaningful purpose and personal empowerment (Kim and Kim, 2001). Since information communications technology is changing radically, it is also transforming traditional learning methods and instructional patterns (Lage, Platt and Treglia, 2000). Technology is putting different pedagogical philosophy to test, and has become a crucible polishing both content and context of educational delivery channels irrespective of demographic differences. It then holds that integrating technology with educational pedagogy cannot be obstructed without detrimental consequence to emerging educational channels such as digital learning, online learning, cloud-based learning, e-learning and even traditional learning settings. Regardless of the angle of ones perception, technology has become both the question and answer to the future of ICT directed educational pedagogy.

The percentages of students from African countries that utilize mobile network for information sourcing and sharing other than texting and calls leaves impressive feelings that countries in Africa could utilize method of the people in closing the level of digital divide facing the area. Mostly, in African countries the digital outsiders method of diffusion base on a communication needs and does not reflect actual inclusion. The cost of equipping schools with computers and Internet access cannot be realized by the locals themselves, but requires government intervention to achieve. Unfortunately, most digital inclusion programs that receive government funding take place in regions advanced in technology such as Britain, Canada and the United States. Chon (2001) laments the situation whereby developed countries are the ones benefiting from internet far more than the underdeveloped countries due to a lack of both human and material mechanisms. This contributes to the levels of technology delinquency in most countries of Africa. A condition so bad that hardly does any university in that region boast of supportive tools capable of successful hosting of functional online programs. How then are schools expected to adopt innovative pedagogy and implement online learning education without computers and Internet access? What could have been the fate of African countries if ICT excluded mobile network technology? Maybe the people will have one choice to migrate abroad or stagnate at home. Instead, underdeveloped countries are locally curbing digital divide with limited ICT options available. This pattern of bridging the gap by digital outsiders in Africa is a milestone achievement reflecting how India and China narrowed down digital divide by effectively taking advantage of available ICT the region (Chon, 2001).

5. CONCLUSION

This paper addresses digital divide as it pertains the evolution of Prensky's assertion of digital natives. The study agrees with Hohlfeld, Ritzhaupt, Barron and Kember (2008) that digital divide (DD) is a multilayered phenomenon. However, we have seen a different class of digital natives which is herein referred to as the 'digital outsiders' emerge in most underdeveloped countries. These digital natives shouldn't be neglected because Schlomab (2004) digital divide is not just for individuals and groups in the developed countries alone. It is therefore important to employ caution as a yardstick when determining what presently constitutes and defines digital divide in general. Basically, all efforts should be channeled towards bridging all digital gaps in technology access globally. Researchers and educationists can learn from the digital natives use of 'Mobile Network/ Social Medias' in the struggle to improve emerging educational pedagogy, especially online education. The collective efforts towards bridging digital gap between the 'haves' and 'have nots' has significantly contributed to changes in technology-use-behavior of these actors and campaigners for technology driven educational pedagogy. The outcomes include integrating technology with instructional materials and the evolving pattern of research in different online learning, cloud learning and SMART learning programs.

Based on the inconclusive description of digital divide which Hohlfed et al., (2008) said to have grown from access to computer hardware and software, internet and technology support within schools, to broadband computer internet connection at home and skills and knowledge to use ICT (Attewell, 2001; Hesseldah, 2008). The variances in what constitutes digital divide makes any single definition incapable of serving as a global indicator for the assessment of digital divide and ICT inequalities. All the same, different regions are devising ways to bridge the divide and diffuse pedagogy with available technologies. Digital access based on internet via computer and mobile network connections has different implications and practical outcomes for developed countries and their underdeveloped counterpart. The possibility for all public schools in the United States to provide 100% computers and internet access for students is unrealistic when used as yardstick in assessing the conditions of educational pedagogy in underdeveloped countries facing numerous challenges caused by sporadic innovations in the areas of ICT. However, notwithstanding numerous technology challenges confronting African countries, the digital outsiders irrespective of dearth landlines connectivity are making maximum use of limited but growing mobile network technology in bridging digital divide, albeit, to a recognizable extent of neutralizing the inequalities between developed and underdeveloped countries (James, 2013).

Finally, this study used existing data on the distribution of ICT in developed and underdeveloped countries for comparative analysis bothering on achievable educational pedagogy innovations factored on the position of ICT in the regions involved. However, more efforts should focus on ways educational pedagogy could be transformed with mobile network and devices that can match the innovations achieved in the developed countries with computers and internet access in schools. Using the figures data, ICT distribution in the various regions can be used to achieve customized innovation in educational pedagogy for locations deprived of ICT diffusion (Poushter, and Oates, 2015). Consequently, the influence of individualism on digital divide (Vandenbroek, Verschelden, Boonaert and Haute, 2007), reflects on the figures evidence that the digital outsider's method of digital inclusion (mobile technologies) could someday transform pedagogy in those regions.

REFERENCES

Attewell, P. (2001). Comment: The first and second digital divides. *Sociology of education*, *74*(3), 252- 259.

Black, K. (1986). The information poor. *RQ*, *25*(4), 517-518.

Buys, P., Dasgupta, S., Thomas, T. S., & Wheeler, D. (2009). Determinants of a digital divide in Sub Saharan Africa: A spatial econometric analysis of cell phone coverage. *World Development*, *37*(9), 1494-1505

Chon, K. (2001). The future of the Internet digital divide. *Communications of the ACM*, *44*(3), 116-116.

Doctor, R. D. (1991). Information technologies and social equity: Confronting the revolution. *Journal of the American Society for Information Science*, *42*(3), 216.

Hohlfeld, T. N., Ritzhaupt, A. D., Barron, A. E., & Kemker, K. (2008). Examining the digital divide in K-12 public schools: Four-year trends for supporting ICT literacy in Florida. *Computers & Education*, *51*(4), 1648-1663.

James, J. (2016). Mobile Phone Use in Africa: Implications for Inequality and the Digital Divide. In *The Impact of Mobile Phones on Poverty and Inequality in Developing Countries* (pp. 89-93). Springer International Publishing.

Kim, M. C., & Kim, J. K. (2001). Digital divide: Conceptual discussions and prospect. In *The Human Society and the Internet Internet-Related Socio-Economic Issues* (pp. 78-91). Springer Berlin Heidelberg.

Lage, M. J., Platt, G. J., & Treglia, M. (2000). Inverting the classroom: A gateway to creating an inclusive learning environment. *The Journal of Economic Education*, *31*(1), 30-43.

Mariscal, J. (2005). Digital divide in a developing country. *Telecommunications policy*, *29*(5), 409-428.

Poushter, J., & Oates, R. (2015). Cell phones in Africa: communication lifeline. *Washingston DC: Pew Research Centre.*

Prensky, M. (2001). Digital natives, digital immigrants part 1. *On the horizon*, *9*(5), 1-6.

Savery, J. R., & Duffy, T. M. (1995). Problem based learning: An instructional model and its constructivist framework. *Educational technology*, *35*(5), 31-38.

Schloman, B. F. "The digital divide: how wide and how deep?" *Online journal of issues in nursing* 9, no. 2 (2004): 7.

Selwyn, N. (2006). Digital division or digital decision? A study of non-users and low-users of computers. *Poetics*, *34*(4), 273-292.

Sidney Howland, J. (1998). The 'digital divide': Are we becoming a world of technological 'haves' and' have-nots?' *The Electronic Library*, *16*(5), 287-289.

Van Dijk, J. A. (2006). Digital divide research, achievements and shortcomings. *Poetics*, *34*(4), 221-235.

Vandenbroeck, M., Verschelden, G., Boonaert, T., & Haute, L. V. (2007). Changes in the digital divide: a case from Belgium. *British Journal of Educational Technology*, *38*(4), 742-743.

E-LEARNING SYSTEM USING SEGMENTATION-BASED MR TECHNIQUE FOR LEARNING CIRCUIT CONSTRUCTION

Atsushi Takemura
Tokyo University of Agriculture and Technology 2-24-16, Naka-cho, Koganei-shi, Tokyo 184-8588, Japan

ABSTRACT

This paper proposes a novel e-Learning system using the mixed reality (MR) technique for technical experiments involving the construction of electronic circuits. The proposed system comprises experimenters' mobile computers and a remote analysis system. When constructing circuits, each learner uses a mobile computer to transmit image data from the circuit to the analysis system during experiment. The remote analysis system performs automated segmentation and recognition of the circuit image and automatically supplies the user with virtual measurement and the circuit behavior simulation using a segmentation-based MR technique. This proposed system is beneficial for practical use in that an experimenter who lacks sufficient circuit components, measurement instruments, or experimental facilities can learn to construct practical circuits and evaluate their behavior. The usefulness and effectiveness of the proposed system was evaluated by analyzing circuits made by 42 university students in a class. Results showing positive responses, which indicate the usefulness of the proposed system, were obtained from all the students.

KEYWORDS

Technology education, electronic circuit, experiments involving circuit construction, mixed reality

1. INTRODUCTION

Teaching and learning electronic circuit construction is an important element in the field of technology education. Recently, several education systems have been developed to improve students' understanding of the concepts of electrical and electronic circuits. These so-called learning tools for circuit analysis (Becker et al., 2014; Holmes et al., 2014; Johnson et al., 2014) facilitate an understanding of the basic theories of electrical circuits. A learning kit to help beginners understand the functioning of fundamental components in a simple electric circuit was developed (Reisslein et al., 2013). However, these learning tools can cope with only elementary electric circuits; therefore, they are not sufficient for higher education or experiments involving the construction of practical circuits. To overcome the disadvantages of these conventional tools, several education support systems have been developed to improve students' understanding and circuit-making abilities. Stand-alone simulation systems (Abramovitz, 2011; Fitch, 2011) and a virtual circuit-making and measurement system (Takemura, 2013) are useful for students lacking physical circuit components, measurement instruments, or facilities (e.g., laboratories). However, these systems can provide learners with only the specific characteristics (e.g., current and voltage signals) of designed and constructed circuits. In addition to the specific characteristics, providing learners with a simulation of a circuit's behavior (e.g., illumination and motor rotation) is expected to be effective for understanding the construction of practical circuits and applicability to various experiments in the educational field (e.g., sensing and robotics). To this end, this paper proposes a novel e-Learning system for experiments involving circuit construction that is capable of the simulations of illuminating light-emitting diodes (LEDs) and motor rotation using the mixed reality (MR) technique, which comprises virtual reality (VR) and augmented reality (AR). The proposed system's technological novelty is that it can perform image processing on a circuit image and supply segmentation-based MR simulation to enable learners.

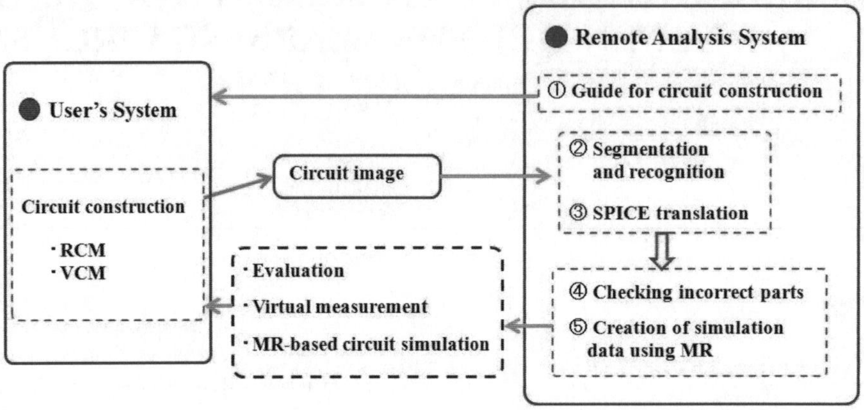

Figure 1. Schematic of the proposed e-Learning system for experiments involving circuit construction

2. METHODOLOGY

Figure 1 illustrates all necessary technological functions of the proposed e-Learning system. The system comprises individual learners' computers and a remote analysis system. All functions and technological features are described in Sections 2.1–2.3. To evaluate the proposed e-Learning system, experiments involving the construction of practical circuits to control the illumination of LEDs and rotation of motors are conducted.

2.1 Function for Supporting Circuit Construction

As shown in Figure 1, the proposed e-Learning system provides users with the necessary guides to design and construct circuits (e.g., circuit diagrams and specifications). This proposed system enables users to choose between two learning modes (real circuit-making mode, RCM; virtual circuit-making mode, VCM) depending on the required purpose or environment (described in A and B). This paper has improved on the previous circuit-making system (Takemura, 2013) to integrate the segmentation-based MR technique (described in 2.2 and 2.3).

A) The RCM is to be used by learners who have the physical components necessary for circuit making but do not have the instruments for operation and measurement of the circuit. The RCM allows learners to observe and measure the characteristics of the constructed circuit using the system's virtual measurement function.

B) The VCM is useful because users do not need to work with physical circuit components to learn electronic circuit design and construction. The VCM enables individual learners to use their preferred graphics editor to indicate connections between virtual circuit components that are downloaded via a computer network and connected on a virtual circuit (Figure 2). The experimenters indicate the virtual circuit connections by drawing colored lines on the circuit board image using a graphical user interface. The VCM allows learners to observe and measure the characteristics of the constructed circuit using the system's virtual measurement function.

2.2 Segmentation and Recognition of Circuit Images

The experimenter transmits the image of the constructed circuit to the analysis system. To automatically recognize circuit construction, the analysis system performs image processing as described in (1) and (2).

(1) The remote analysis system binarizes the circuit image and detects the connecting terminals. Based on the array of the detected connecting terminals, the inclination of the circuit image is corrected and the circuit size is measured.

(2) The analysis system differentiates between circuit components nodes from the connecting-terminals detected in the first part of the process, and circuit components connected at the nodes are identified by pattern matching between the circuit image and the circuit components available in the analysis system's database.

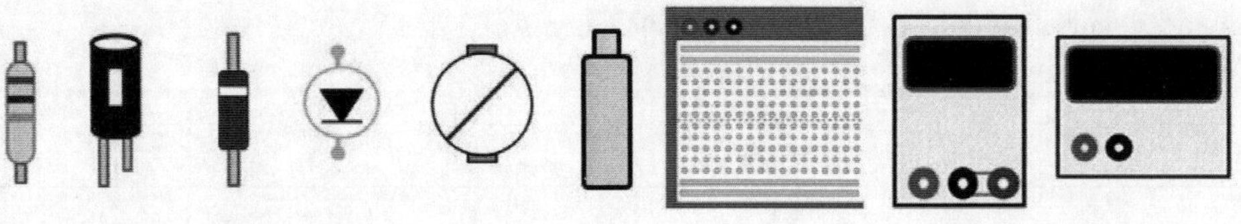

(a) (b) (c) (d) (e) (f) (g) (h) (i)

Figure 2. Examples of virtual circuit components and virtual instruments: (a) resistor, (b) capacitor, (c) diode, (d) LED, (e) DC motor, (f) 1.5V battery, (g) breadboard, (h) DC power supply, (i) synthesized function generator

2.3 Circuit Simulation based on SPICE and MR

Based on the result of the circuit recognition (described in 2.2), the analysis system performs an automated translation of the circuit into a general circuit-description language (simulation program integrated circuit emphasis, SPICE) (Rabaey). The SPICE information obtained from this automated translation process enables the simulation of the circuit operation, and individual users can observe circuit characteristics without the instruments for operation and measurement of their circuits. The analysis system can indicate the presence and location of incorrect parts in a learner's circuit by checking any differences that exist between the SPICE information for correct circuits and those constructed by a learner. This SPICE translation technique can cope with the various structures (circuit component layouts and wirings) of circuits made by individual learners. In addition, this paper proposes a novel circuit simulation function using the MR technique based on circuit information obtained from the segmentation process (described in 2.2(2)). The MR is a view that comprises VR and AR. VR is a computer-generated view that is similar to a real environment. AR is an augmented view comprising physical contents and additional computer-generated information such as computer graphics or moving image data. The proposed MR technique generates a moving image that simulates the motion of a circuit component (e.g., rotation of a DC motor) and supplies learners with simulated moving images at the accurate size and position in the circuit image based on the segmentation result.

To improve the usability of the proposed technique, the proposed e-Learning system sends messages to individual learners during experiments and instructs them to check their results as follows.

1) When incorrect components or faulty wiring is detected from a circuit image, the analysis system indicates the errors and instructs the learner to check and correct them.
2) When the analysis system detects a serious error (e.g., short circuit), the system sends the learner a critical warning to correct the incorrect part.
3) The analysis system requests the learner to check whether simulated behavior of the constructed circuit corresponds to their specification.

3. RESULTS AND DISCUSSION

The proposed system was evaluated using circuits constructed by 42 undergraduate students in a class at Tokyo University of Agriculture and Technology. Figure 3 shows the circuit diagrams used for evaluation. The circuit in Figure 3(a) is a square pulse generator, namely, multivibrator. This circuit alternately turns two LEDs on and off. Figure 3(b) shows a circuit to control DC voltage. Individual students constructed the circuits using the VCM and RCM. The students were allowed to use both virtual and physical circuit components as necessary but the DC battery and instruments for operation and measurement (DC power supply and the function generator) were not provided. Therefore, the students used the proposed MR simulation function to measure the characteristics of the constructed circuits and evaluate the circuit behavior (illumination of LEDs and motor rotation).

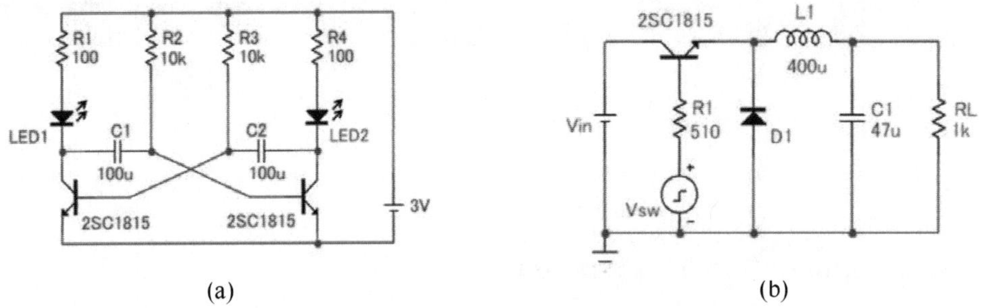

Figure 3. Circuit diagrams for circuit-making experiments: (a) multivibrator (square pulse generator) and (b) DC voltage controller (step-down chopper)

Figure 4 shows examples of the circuit (multivibrator) that was constructed by a student using the two modes (VCM and RCM) of the proposed system. Figure 4(a) shows the circuit constructed using the VCM. Figure 4(b) shows the virtual DC battery that was connected using VCM at the correct position and the MR simulation of illuminating LEDs was performed by the proposed segmentation-based MR technique; here the placement of the virtual LEDs was set using image segmentation. Figures 4(c) and 4(d) show the circuit constructed using RCM and the MR simulation of illuminating LEDs, respectively; here the placement of the virtual LEDs was set using image segmentation.

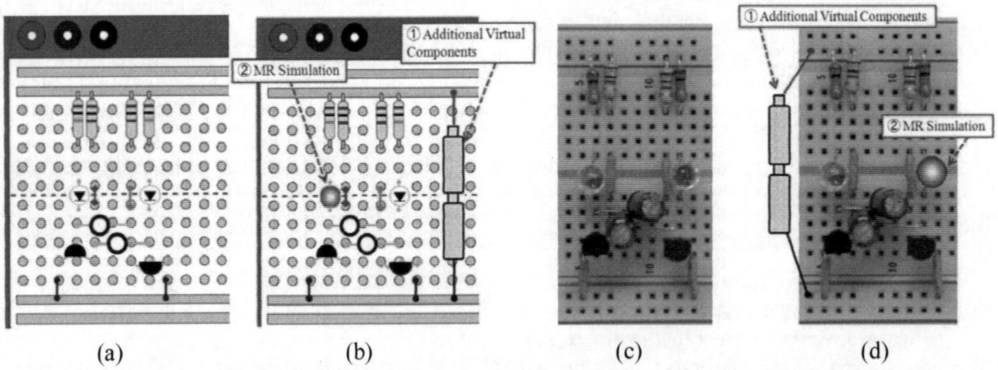

Figure 4. Circuit construction and MR simulation of multivibrator: (a) virtual circuit constructed using the VCM, (b) simulation of illuminating LEDs on the virtual circuit created using the proposed MR technique, (c) constructed physical circuit, and (d) MR simulation illuminating LEDs of the circuit constructed using the RCM

Figure 5 shows examples of the circuits (DC voltage controller) that were constructed by a student using the proposed system. Figure 5(a) shows the circuit constructed using the VCM. Figure 5(b) shows the result of a simulation created using the proposed segmentation-based MR technique. The analysis system located the region of the virtual DC motor in the circuit image (Figure 5(a)) and changed this virtual component with the corresponding MR components (rotating motor). The rotation speed of the motor is controlled based on the output voltage obtained from SPICE simulation. Figure 5(c) shows a constructed physical circuit. After connecting the virtual instruments (DC power supply and function generator) correctly in the image of the constructed circuit, created using the RCM, the simulation of a rotating motor was obtained using the proposed MR technique (Figure 5(d)).

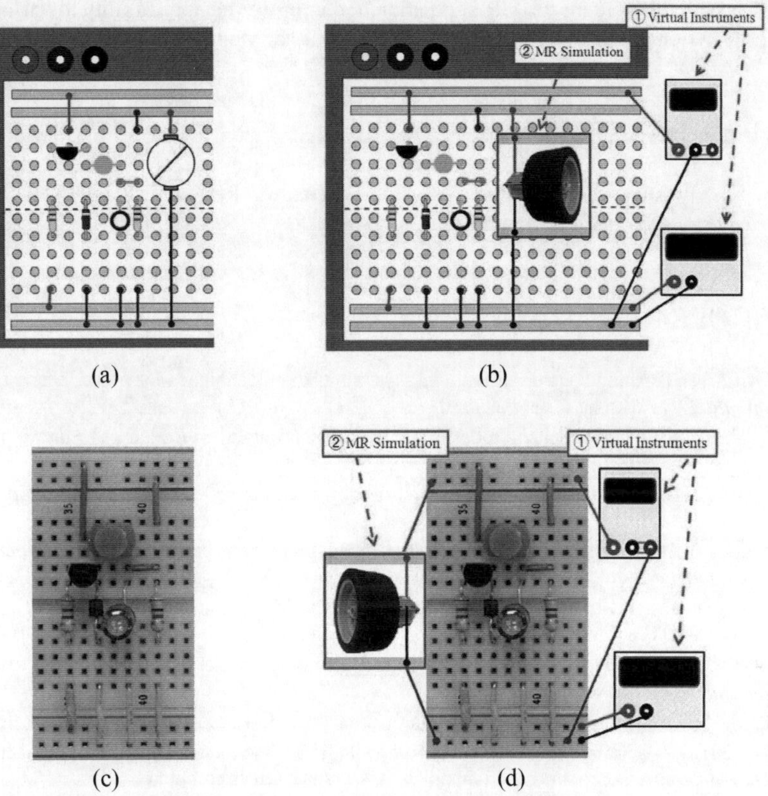

Figure 5. Circuit construction and MR simulation of the DC voltage controller: (a) virtual circuit constructed using the VCM, (b) simulation of motor rotation of the virtual circuit obtained using the MR technique, (c) constructed physical circuit, and (d) MR simulation (motor rotation) of the circuit constructed using the RCM

The proposed system coped with various structures (layouts of circuit components and wirings) of the circuits constructed by students and supplied each student with the correct circuit behaviors. Positive responses, which indicate the usefulness of the proposed system, were obtained from all students during the evaluation; the responses are as follows.

- The e-Learning system was useful for learning the construction and behavior of practical circuits without expensive instruments and facilities (e.g., a laboratory).
- The e-Learning system improved safety because learners were able to check a circuit's behavior using the virtual instruments and MR simulation, thus avoiding serious accidents (e.g., electric shock and fire).
- The e-Learning system was convenient and flexible because no special software was required to be used exclusively on users' computers.

However, there were also a few technical suggestions for improvement, e.g., to improve the usability to various circuits studied in university lectures (e.g., logic circuits and robotics).

4. CONCLUSION

This paper proposes a novel e-Learning system for the construction of electronic circuits using a segmentation-based MR technique. The usefulness and effectiveness of the system was verified by 42 undergraduate students in a university class. The analysis system of the proposed system performed accurate circuit image processing and translation into SPICE. This SPICE information and the proposed segmentation-based MR succeeded in providing learners with virtual measurement and simulated behaviors of the constructed circuits. Positive responses, which pertain to the usefulness and efficiency of the proposed system, were obtained from all students. The steps that are necessary to practically implement the proposed system are as follows.

- Increase available content for MR simulation and improve the applicability to various circuits.
- Make the system more user-friendly (e.g., availability of mobile tools).

ACKNOWLEDGMENT

This study was partly supported by a Grant-in-Aid for Scientific Research (KAKENHI) 16K01060 from the Japan Society for the Promotion of Science (JSPS).

REFERENCES

Abramovitz, A., 2011. Teaching behavioral modeling and simulation techniques for power electronics courses, *In IEEE Trans. Education*, Vol. 54, No. 4, pp. 523–530.

Becker J. P. et al., 2014. Project circuits in a basic electric circuits course, *In IEEE Trans Education*, Vol. 57, No. 2, pp. 75–82.

Fitch, A. L. et al., 2011. An analog computer for electronic engineering, *In IEEE Trans. Education*, Vol. 54, No. 4, pp. 550–557.

Holmes A. F. et al., 2014. The effect of reworking exam problems on problem-solving performance in a circuit analysis course: An exploratory study, *In IEEE Trans Education*, Vol. 57, No. 2, pp. 107–112.

Johnson, A. M. et al., 2014. Introductory circuit analysis learning from abstract and contextualized circuit representations: Effects of diagram labels, *In IEEE Trans Education*, Vol. 57, No. 3, pp. 160–168.

Reisslein, J. et al., 2013, Circuits kit K–12 outreach: impact of circuit element representation and student gender, *In IEEE Trans. Education*, Vol. 56, No. 3, pp. 316–322.

Rabaey, J. M., The Spice Page, <URL: http://bwrc.eecs.berkeley.edu/Classes/IcBook/SPICE/> (accessed July 26 2016).

Takemura, A., 2013. e-Learning system for experiments involving construction of practical electronic circuits, *Proc. IADIS Conference e-Learning 2013*, pp. 403–407, Prague, Czech Republic.

STUDENTS' GOOGLE DRIVE INTENDED USAGE: A CASE STUDY OF MATHEMATICS COURSES IN BANGKOK UNIVERSITY

Asst. Prof. Krisawan Prasertsith[1], Penjira Kanthawongs, Ph.D.[2] and Tan Limpachote[3]
[1]*Information Technology Department, School of Science and Technology, Bangkok University*
Rama IV Rd., Klong-Toey, Bangkok 10110, Thailand
[2]*Business Computer Department, School of Business Administration, Bangkok University*
Phahonyothin Rd., Pathum Thani 12120 Thailand
[3]*School of Business Administration (International Program), Kasem Bundit University*
Kasem Bundit University, 1761 Phatthanakan Rd., Bangkok 10250 Thailand

ABSTRACT

Many technologies have changed the way individuals live and learn. Google Inc. has played significant roles in business and academic worlds. Google Apps for Education and Google Classroom have been offered to higher institutions around the globe. Although large cloud service provider such as Google do not encrypt all their stored electronic data and correlate identifiable data across accounts, Google Drive has been a popular feature of Google for teachers and students in Thai higher educational institutions. The purpose of this research is to explore the impact of message quality and digital literacy in terms of technological dimensions toward intention to use of Google Drive of Bangkok University's students. However, the four dimensions were extracted from fourteen statements. The factors were message quality, digital literacy in terms of learning new technology, digital literacy in terms of technical and IT skills, and intention to use. Furthermore, message quality, digital literacy in terms of learning new technology, and digital literacy in terms of technical and IT skills positively affected intended usage of the system.

KEYWORDS

Google Drive, message quality, digital literacy, intention to use, Thailand

1. INTRODUCTION

Google has official platforms for email and collaboration services customized for educational institutions' use. Starting in 2014, Google combined the power of Google Docs, Slides, or Forms into Google Classroom (classroom.google.com), a simplified learning management system for users of Google Apps for Education (Amanda and Katie, 2015). Teachers or students who sign up to use Google Classroom can connect to Google's other products. When a teacher or student starts a new class to his or her Classroom site, the process creates a folder within Google Drive with features that work specially with Google Classroom. On one side, instructors can get a folder that holds assignment and exercise templates as well as folder that holds copies of student materials. On the other side, students get a folder that stores their copies of documents submitted as assignments. Instructors can post announcements and assignments. Discussion forums can be used in the form of comments directly on the interaction pages without students having to go to separate forums or discussion tools. The most useful delivery method provided by this tool is that instructors can make a copy for each student which automatically adds a copy of the assignment to the student's Google Drive (Amanda and Katie, 2015). However, in 2015 the grading system provided by Classroom was not as sophisticated as other learning management systems like Blackboard or Moodle (Shiohara et al., 2014). Moreover, there were no comprehensive gradebook, test, or quiz features. Additionally, there are some privacy concerns since the actual applications of Drive, Docs, or Slides work the same way as those bundled with public accounts (Amanda and Katie, 2015). Misuse, sale of personal user data by vendors, lack of protection against hacking, and identity theft are additional concerns since large cloud vendors such as Google do not encrypt all of their stored electronic data and correlate identifiable data across accounts. Last but not least, "loss of management control or intellectual property rights of materials uploaded to free cloud services is a potential barrier for creators of learning objects" (Weber, 2011).

However, Bangkok University, the first private university in Thailand, has implemented many learning management tools including Google Apps for Education. Teachers and students would receive Google's official platform for emails such as "krisawan.p@bu.ac.th" for a teacher and "vichaiyut.sara@bumail.net" for a student. Then, the collaboration customized tools for use at the university such as Google Docs, Slides, Forms, Sites, Classroom, as well as Drive are set up for teachers to use with their course materials.

Google Drive, is a file storage and synchronization service created by Google. It allows users to store files in the cloud, share files, and edit documents, spreadsheets, and presentations with collaborators. Google Drive encompasses Google Docs, Sheets, and Slides, an office suite that permits collaborative editing of documents, spreadsheets, presentations, drawings, forms, and more (Wikipedia, 2016).

The students can access the teachers' course materials through the use of Google Drive at any time with multiple devices like smartphones, computers, or tablets (Google Drive, 2016). Teachers can get a drive that stores their course materials and choose to share with specific student email addresses generating from the student email list creating by the university. Teachers can choose specific student email addresses to access the course materials as "CAN VIEW" option or "CAN EDIT" option. With "CAN VIEW" option, the students can only view the course materials. With "CAN EDIT" option, the students would be able to upload, submit, or share files in the drive.

Amanda and Katie (2015) suggested that students generally responded favorably to the Google tools. They are likely to have no worry about saving documents on the classroom computers due to the autosave feature and the use of Google Drive have made collaborating on assignments easier due to the sharing capabilities. Nevertheless, limited studies have investigated the learners' learning competencies. Therefore, this research's aim is to explore message quality and digital literacy in terms of technical dimensions affecting intention to use Google Drive of the students in Bangkok University. If learners' learning competencies are enhanced, it is likely to enable effective utilization of the cloud technologies in higher education.

2. RESEARCH METHOD

The researchers planned, created, and utilized Google Drive features throughout the third semester of 2015 (June - July 2016) for all the courses to share course materials such as lecture files, assignment details, pictures, and videos with specific student email addresses generated from Bangkok University's Student Email List system. Students could only have "CAN VIEW" option in some classes if there were no requirements for students to submit assignments back to the instructor. In other classes, students would have "CAN EDIT" option in order to be able to upload assignments back to the instructors as well as share files with their classmates. Survey and observations were used to collect data. The authors observed student behaviors in class as well as online. Before collecting data, the researchers met with participants at the end of the second semester of 2015 to explain the purpose of the study and acquaint them with the type of the questions they will be answering. The researchers collected the paper-based survey questionnaires from the students in their classrooms. Students spent approximately 15-20 minutes answering the questions. The samples in this study consisted of 151 students, who registered in Mathematics courses. The variables in this research are as follows: the independent variables are Digital Literacy: Technical Dimension (DLTD) and Message quality (MQ). The dependent variable is Intention to use (IEU). Concerning the reliability of the questionnaires, Cronbach's alpha coefficient values were in the following: Digital Literacy: Technical Dimension (DLTD) = 0.817, Message Quality (MQ) = 0.781 and Intention to Use (IEU) = 0.766. Then, all alpha coefficients passed the 0.65 (Nunnally, 1978) recommended level and had proven to be reliable. Descriptive statistics was used initially including frequency, mean, standard deviation for description of sample group demographics. The questions were grouped for Google Drive usage using the Exploratory Factor Analysis. Then, multiple regression analysis

3. RESEARCH RESULTS

The fourteen statements concerning the students' Google Drive usage were analyzed using principle components analysis with varimax rotation method to determine the underlying dimensions. In this process, the minimum Eigenvalue of 1.0 was used as cut-off. Only the constituent statements with factor loading of more than 0.5 were retained. The Kaiser-Meyer-Olkin (KMO) measure of sampling adequacy and the Bartlett's test of sphericity were used to test the fitness of the data (Wilailuk Sereetrakul, 2013). The result of KMO was 0.856 and the Bartlett's test of sphericity was found at the significant level of 0.000. These figures suggested that the use of factor analysis was appropriate (Hair, Anderson, Taham, & Black, 1998). This technique allowed the researchers to answer questions about which measures varied in explaining the highest percentage of the variance in the dataset. This factorial validity helped to confirm that a certain set of measures did or did not reflect latent constructs (Straub, 1989). However, the four dimensions were extracted from fourteen statements. The factors were message quality, digital literacy in terms of learning new technology, digital literacy in terms of technical and IT skills, and intention to use. The cumulative percentage of explained variance was 64.369% which mean that four factors could explain 64.369% of variation of students' Google Drive usage.

Then, multiple regression analysis by enter method determined the contribution of dependent variable to predict intention to use (IEU). The three predictors identified by factor analysis which were message quality (MQ), digital literacy: learning new technology (DLTD1-4) and digital literacy: technical and it skills (DLTD5-6). Factors affecting on intention to use (IEU) of Bangkok University's students with the level of statistical significance at 0.05, arranged in respective sequences of the high-level to low-level affecting factor, were message quality (MQ) (standardized beta coefficient of 0.287), digital literacy in terms of learning new technology (standardized beta coefficient of 0.273) (DLTD1-4), and digital literacy in terms of technical and IT skills (standardized beta coefficient of 0.194) (DLTD5-6). All those factors could explain the intention to use the Google Drive of Bangkok University's students at the 37.80 percent of variance.

4. CONCLUSION

Google Inc. had played major roles in business as well as academic worlds. Google Apps for Education has been offered to universities around the world. Although large cloud service providers like Google do not encrypt all their stored electronic data and correlate identifiable data across accounts, Google Drive has been one of a key feature of Google for teachers and students in higher educational institutions. This study revealed that the overall view of the total mean scores of the variables showed that the users were likely to have moderate agreement for message quality, digital literacy in terms of technical dimension, and intention to use the system. Moreover, the four dimensions (instead of the original three dimensions) were extracted from fourteen statements, which slightly differed from past researches (Handa, 2001; Ng, 2012). Therefore, the four factors were message quality, digital literacy in terms of learning new technology, digital literacy in terms of technical and IT skills, and intention to use. Furthermore, message quality, digital literacy in terms of learning new technology, and digital literacy in terms of technical and IT skills respectively affect intent to use of Google Drive of Bangkok University's students. These results are supported by past literature (Handa, 2001; Huang et al., 2009; Lee et al., 2016; Ng, 2012). It is recommended that university administrators and teachers should emphasize message quality, digital literacy in terms of learning new technology, and digital literacy in terms of technical and IT skills to optimize the benefits of using Google Drive in their universities. The limitation of this study was that the data was collected from students coming from one university only; therefore, data collection from more universities should provide clearer view of the results. Also, longitudinal survey of this study may improve the generalizability of the results for higher institution education. Further studies should also include cultural dimensions to the conceptual model to explore different perspectives of the students.

REFERENCES

Amanda, I. and Katie, L. L., 2015. Google classroom for librarians: features and opportunities. *Library Hi Tech News*, Vol. 32, pp. 1-3.

Google drive, 2016. A Safe Place for All Your Files [Online]. Retrieved July 1, 2016, from Web site: https://www.google.com/intl/en/drive/.

Hair, J. F. et al, 1998. *Multivariate data analysis with readings*, (5thed). Prentics-Hall International, Englewood Cliffs, NJ.

Handa, C., 2001. Digital Literacy and Rhetoric: A Selected Bibliography. *Computers and Composition*, Vol. 18, pp. 195-202.

Huang, C.-C. et al, 2009. Factors Affecting Pass-Along Email Intentions (Paris): Integrating the Social Capital and Social Cognition Theories. *Electronic Commerce Research and Applications*, Vol. 8, pp. 160-169.

Lee, C. J. et al, 2016. Intentions and Willingness to Drive While Drowsy Among University Students: An Application of an Extended Theory of Planned Behavior Model. *Accident Analysis & Prevention*, Vol. 93, pp. 113-123.

Ng, W., 2012. Can We Teach Digital Natives Digital Literacy? *Computers & Education*, Vol. 59, pp. 1065-1078.

Nunnally, J. C., 1978. *Psychometric Theory*. Mcgraw–Hill, New York, USA.

Shiohara, K. et al, 2014. Using Cloud Computing Platforms for Developing Software Applications in Low Cost. *Proceeding of IADIS: International Conference Applied Computing 2014.* Porto, Portogal, pp. 3-10.

Straub, D. W., 1989. Validating Instruments in Mis Research. *Mis Quarterly*, Vol. 13, pp. 146-169.

Weber, A. S., 2011. Dark Clouds on the Horizon? Unresolved Issues in Cloud Computing In Education. *Proceeding of Iadis: International Conference Cognition and Exploratory Learning in Digital Age 2011.* Rio de Janeiro, Brazil, pp. 203-210.

Wikipedia, 2016. Google Drive [Online]. Retrieved July 1, 2016, from Web site: https://En.Wikipedia.Org/Wiki/Google_Drive.

Wilailuk Sereetrakul, 2013. Students' Facebook Usage and Academic Achievement: A Case Study of Private University in Thailand. *Proceedings of the IADIS International Conference on Cognition and Exploratory Learning in the Digital Age*. Texas, USA, pp. 40-46.

AN EMPIRICAL STUDY ON THE IMPACT OF SELF-REGULATION AND COMPULSIVITY TOWARDS SMARTPHONE ADDICTION OF UNIVERSITY STUDENTS

Penjira Kanthawongs, Ph.D.[1], Felicito Angeles Jabutay[2], Ruangrit Upalanala, DBA.[2] and Penjuree Kanthawongs[2]
[1]Business Computer Department, School of Business Administration
Bangkok University, Phahonyothin Rd., Pathum Thani 12120 Thailand
[2]School of Business Administration (International Program)
Kasem Bundit University, 1761 Phatthanakan Rd., Bangkok 10250 Thailand

ABSTRACT

Apart from Internet addiction, smartphone addiction has played important roles in students' lives as observed in recent studies. There are positive and negative aspects in using smartphones especially in higher education. University administrators or instructors should take into account what factors are affecting students' smartphone addiction in order to limit its negative effect and introduce more innovative measures such as developing ways of teaching and learning in digital age using smartphones. The aim of this study is to investigate the impact of self-regulation and compulsivity towards smartphone addiction of university students in two private universities in Thailand. 157 survey questionnaires were collected during April to May 2016 and analyzed with multiple regression analysis. Although the conceptual model explains 60.40% of the variance in smartphone addiction, only compulsivity is found to have significant determinant of smartphone addiction. Self-regulation has no significant effect on smartphone addiction.

KEYWORDS

Smartphone, Addiction, Self-Regulation, Compulsivity, Thailand

1. INTRODUCTION

A smart phone refers to a cellular telephone with built-in applications and an Internet connection. The terms "smart phone" and "smartphone" have been used interchangeably (Hsiao and Chen, 2015; Hawi and Samaha, 2016). The device has transformed into a tool in which individuals cannot live without. People seek friends, relatives, enjoyment, shopping, or finances through the device. By the end of 2017, approximately 2.6 billion people, over a third of the world population, in the world are expected to own and use smartphones (statista.com, 2016).

On the positive side, smartphone users tend to have more friends online and more "online-only" friends than non-users (Eun and Sangwon, 2015). In difficult times, smartphones can also be helpful as demonstrated by the finding that mobile technologies improved mental health before, during, and after disasters in Asia (Sobowale and Torous, 2016).

On the negative side, smartphones may sometimes distract, rather than complement, social interactions. The term "phubbing" refers to the act of snubbing someone in a social setting by concentrating on one's phone instead of talking to the person directly. Several researchers found the Internet addiction, fear of missing out, and self-control predicted smartphone addiction (Chotpitayasunondh and Douglas, 2016). Moreover, taking a break with a smartphone such as browsing the Internet or using social network services would increase the average level of emotional exhaustion than conventional breaks such as walking or chatting face to face with friends (Rhee and Kim, 2016).

Smartphones have emerged to the extent where they have become an integral part of university students' lives. The smart options of the phones allow thousands of photos, songs, apps, games, and videos to be shared, communicated, produced, entertained, and utilized (Hawi and Samaha, 2016). However, with virtually all of the students owning mobile phones, with 85% smartphone ownership (64% iPhone and 21%

Android); it is rather strange to learn that the majority of students considered themselves "digital natives". Their mobile social media activity mainly limited to Facebook (100%), text messaging (93%), Web browsing (93%), Calendar (86%), YouTube viewing (86%), Google Maps (72%), and Instagram (64%) usage; with limited use of mobile social media within educational contexts. Many researchers around the world have shown concern about smartphone addiction among university students (Aljomaa et al., 2016; Hawi and Samaha, 2016; Gökçearslan et al., 2016). Therefore, to help address the issue, the objective of this study is to find the impact of self-regulation and compulsivity towards smartphone addiction of university students in two private universities in Thailand.

2. RELATED WORK

Concept of smartphone addiction means excessive use of smartphones in a way that is difficult to control and its influence extends to other areas of life in a negative way (Park and Lee, 2011). Apart from providing access to the Internet, smartphones open the opportunities to share media files, produce new materials, connect social interaction, play games, or use various applications. Even though they are beneficial devices which facilitate countless social and individual activities, the use of smartphones also bring numerous problems in the domestic, academic, occupational, and social aspects (Gökçearslan et al., 2016). Smartphone addiction differs from drug-based physiological addictions (e.g., addictions to alcohol or heroin) and it is behavior-based (van Deursen et al., 2015). Overuse of smartphones may cause sleeping problems, stress, as well as various health disorders (Thomée et al., 2011). Smartphone addiction can be considered a disorder. Individuals with disorder have difficulty controlling their smartphone use and are likely to encounter social, psychological, and health problems (Aljomaa et al., 2016). Smartphone overuse by students may have negative effects on their academic performance as well. For example, they are likely to have shorter periods of studying or suffer from mental health (Aljomaa et al., 2016). In the US, 480 students who spent more time engaged in technology would spend less time studying; as a result, they tended to have lower grade point averages (GPAs) (Hawi and Samaha, 2016).

Social cognitive learning theory (Bandura, 1993) suggests that individual's self-regulatory mechanism influence individual's level of self-control. Self-regulation is also defined as the one's ability to focus on predetermined goals without distraction (Gökçearslan et al., 2016). People's failure to self-regulate might cause their media usage to increase. Consequently, this situation is likely to turn into an addiction to media. Students having higher self-regulation skills would show lower addictive smartphone behaviors (Gökçearslan et al., 2016).

In this research, compulsivity means the negative consequences such as discomfort, emotional distress (e.g., anxiety, irritation and tension) and live psychological feelings of not being able to use the smartphones by individuals (Lin et al. 2014; Park, 2005). Compulsivity is a factor showing good convergent validity with smartphone overuse of young European people. Compulsive behavior can negatively affect interpersonal relationships and the amount of time spent on the smartphone (Pavia et al., 2016). In parallel with the above studies, the hypothesis is suggested that self-regulation and compulsivity affect smartphone addiction of university students.

3. RESEARCH METHODOLOGY AND FINDINGS

A total of 157 questionnaires were collected from students studying in different schools at two private universities in Thailand during April to May of 2016, and they are analyzed with multiple regression analysis. The research was conducted using convenience sampling method. All measurement items for this study were adapted and modified from previous research. All items were measured using 5-point Likert scales (1-strongly disagree and 5-strongly disagree). The questionnaire was approved from experts in research method and ICT. The alpha coefficients of the reliability analysis of were 0.793 for smartphone addiction, 0.780 for self-regulation, and 0.842 for compulsivity. These alpha coefficients were acceptable because all the values were greater than 0.7 (Nunnally, 1978).

The results showed that the respondents mostly were males (57.3%) at the age of 19-year-old (31.2%) and undergraduate students studying in two private universities in Thailand. The majority of students had the grade point averages of 2-2.99 (51%) and mostly studying in School of Business Administration (58.6%). The hypothesis testing results revealed that only compulsivity with standardized beta coefficient of 0.778 showed the positive effect on smartphone addiction at .01 level of significance. All results and multiple regression analysis are reported in the Table 1.

Table 1. Multiple Regression Analysis' Results

Dependent Variable: Smartphone addiction (mean = 3.2930, S.D. = 0.8368, "moderate level", C.A. = 0.793, r = 0.777, R^2 = 0.604)			
Independent Variables	β	Sig.	VIF
Self-regulation	-0.002	0.966	1.120
Compulsivity	0.778**	0.000	1.120

**Significance Level .01, N = 157

Referring to Table 1 in analyzing the multicollinearity problem, Variance Inflation Factor (VIF) was examined. It was seen in the data set that VIF values were lower than 10; therefore, there was no problem of multicollinearity (Hair et al., 1984). Hence, the hypothesis was supported, but only compulsivity was found to be significant determinant of smartphone addiction, explaining 60.40% of the total variance.

4. DISCUSSION

The objective of this study is to investigate the impact of self-regulation and compulsivity towards smartphone addiction of university students in two private universities in Thailand. The hypothesis was supported, but only compulsivity was found to be significant and positive determinant of smartphone addiction. The result shows that smartphone addiction is significantly determined by individual's compulsivity because compulsivity is the only independent variable with the strongest effect on smartphone addiction (β = 0.778). This is supported by previous studies that also examined similar relationships within the smartphone context (Pavia et al., 2016, Lin et al., 2014, Park, 2005). However, self-regulation of the respondents, though showing negative impact, does not have significant effect on smartphone addiction as supported by previous studies that also examined the relationships between self-regulation and smartphone addiction (Gökçearslan et al., 2016, van Deursen et al., 2015). This finding may be explained that self-regulation may not be determinant of smartphone addictions for Thai students.

5. IMPLICATIONS, LIMITATIONS, AND FURTHER STUDIES

This study presents several implications from the theoretical perspective. First, it analyzes the effect of self-regulation and compulsivity towards smartphone addiction. Apart from Internet addiction, smartphone addiction has also gained interest in recent researches (Pavia et al., 2016, Aljomaa et al., 2016, Gökçearslan et al., 2016). Second, the result of this research is inconsistent with previous studies (Gökçearslan et al., 2016, van Deursen et al., 2015) since self-regulation has no effect on smartphone addiction among university students in Thailand. Thus, this study has made contribution to enhance theoretical foundations of smartphone addiction, self-regulation, and compulsivity in the context of smartphones in particular. Third, university administrators or instructors should know what factors are affecting students' smartphone addiction. University administrators or instructors may utilize the findings of this study to introduce innovative ways of teaching in the digital age.

This study has several limitations which provide opportunities for future researches. First, it focuses on the Thai students' smartphone market and uses survey sample from the Thai population. In order to generalize the findings, comparative studies in different context should be accomplished. The determinants of smartphone addiction may differ by universities, provinces, or countries. More results from future comparative studies could be generalized to strengthen research theories. Cultural differences can be independent factors for future studies. Comparative researches between USA, European, Asia countries, between developed and developing countries, or between smartphones and tablets would be example for future researches.

REFERENCES

Aljomaa, S. S., Al.Qudah, M. F., Albursan, I. S., Bakhiet, S. F. and Abduljabbar, A. S. (2016) 'Smartphone addiction among university students in the light of some variables', *Computers in Human Behavior,* Vol.61, pp. 155-164.

Bandura, A. (1993) 'Perceived self-efficacy in cognitive development and functioning', *Educational Psychologist,* Vol.28, No.1, pp. 117-148.

Chotpitayasunondh, V. and Douglas, K. M. (2016) 'How "phubbing" becomes the norm: The antecedents and consequences of snubbing via smartphone', *Computers in Human Behavior,* Vol.63, pp. 9-18.

Eun, A. P. and Sangwon, L. (2015) 'Multidimensionality: redefining the digital divide in the smartphone era', *info,* Vol.17, No.2, pp. 80-96.

Gökçearslan, Ş., Mumcu, F. K., Haşlaman, T. and Çevik, Y. D. (2016) 'Modelling smartphone addiction: The role of smartphone usage, self-regulation, general self-efficacy and cyberloafing in university students', *Computers in Human Behavior,* Vol.63, pp. 639-649.

Hair, J. F., Anderson, R. E., Tatham, R. and Black, W. C. (1984) *Multivar data analysis with readings.* Macmillan Pub. ISO 690.

Hawi, N. S. and Samaha, M. (2016) 'To excel or not to excel: Strong evidence on the adverse effect of smartphone addiction on academic performance', *Computers & Education,* Vol.98, pp. 81-89.

Hsiao, M.-H. and Chen, L.-C. (2015) 'Smart phone demand: An empirical study on the relationships between phone handset, Internet access and mobile services', *Telematics and Informatics,* Vol.32, No.1, pp. 158-168.

Lin, Y.-H., Chang, L.-R., Lee, Y.-H., Tseng, H.-W., Kuo, T. B. J. and Chen, S.-H. (2014) 'Development and Validation of the Smartphone Addiction Inventory (SPAI)', *PLoS ONE,* Vol.9, No.6, pp. e98312.

Nunnally, J. C. (1978) *Psychometric theory.* New York McGraw–Hill.

Park, B.-W. and Lee, K. C. (2011) 'The Effect of Users' Characteristics and Experiential Factors on the Compulsive Usage of the Smartphone', in Kim, T.-h., Adeli, H., Robles, R.J. & Balitanas, M. (eds.) *Ubiquitous Computing and Multimedia Applications: Second International Conference, UCMA 2011, Daejeon, Korea, April 13-15, 2011. Proceedings, Part II.* Berlin, Heidelberg: Springer Berlin Heidelberg, pp. 438-446.

Park, W. K. (2005) 'Mobile Phone Addiction', *Mobile Communications: Re-negotiation of the Social Sphere.* London: Springer London, pp. 253-272.

Pavia, L., Cavani, P., Di Blasi, M. and Giordano, C. (2016) 'Smartphone Addiction Inventory (SPAI): Psychometric properties and confirmatory factor analysis', *Computers in Human Behavior,* Vol.63, pp. 170-178.

Rhee, H. and Kim, S. (2016) 'Effects of breaks on regaining vitality at work: An empirical comparison of 'conventional' and 'smart phone' breaks', *Computers in Human Behavior,* Vol.57, pp. 160-167.

Sobowale, K. and Torous, J. (2016) 'Disaster psychiatry in Asia: The potential of smartphones, mobile, and connected technologies', *Asian Journal of Psychiatry,* Vol.22, pp. 1-5.

statista.com (2016) *Statistics and facts about Smartphones.* Available at: http://www.statista.com/topics/840/smartphones/ (Accessed: 13 July 2016).

Thomée, S., Härenstam, A. and Hagberg, M. (2011) 'Mobile phone use and stress, sleep disturbances, and symptoms of depression among young adults - a prospective cohort study', *BMC Public Health,* Vol.11, No.1, pp. 1-11.

van Deursen, A. J. A. M., Bolle, C. L., Hegner, S. M. and Kommers, P. A. M. (2015) 'Modeling habitual and addictive smartphone behavior: The role of smartphone usage types, emotional intelligence, social stress, self-regulation, age, and gender', *Computers in Human Behavior,* Vol.45, pp. 411-420.

ADAPTIVE GAME BASED LEARNING USING BRAIN MEASURES FOR ATTENTION – SOME EXPLORATIONS

Jelke van der Pal, Christopher Roos, Ghanshaam Sewnath and Christian Rosheuvel
Netherlands Aerospace Centre NLR
Anthony Fokkerweg 2, 1059CM, Amsterdam, The Netherlands

ABSTRACT

The prospective use of low fidelity simulation and gaming in aviation training is high, and may facilitate individual, personal training needs in usually asynchronous training setting. Without direct feedback from, or intervention by, an instructor, adaptivity of the training environment is in high demand to ensure training sessions maintain an optimal training value to the trainee. In game design theory, the flow principle is used to provide an optimally engaging experience, whereas its equivalent in instructional design theory is maintaining the optimal cognitive load by adjusting the task complexity or by scaffolding. The control of these principles can be based on user activity or performance. Alternatively, brain measures may be used to control the learning experience of professionals. This paper explores the options for using brain measures for professional gaming and provides results of a pilot study. Based on the pilot study, it is concluded that brain measures may be a viable but demanding mechanism for optimizing the learning process.

KEYWORDS

Adaptive training, Brain Computer Interfacing, EEG

1. INTRODUCTION

Aviation has a long history of using simulation for training purposes. In particular the yearly recurrent and compulsory training for pilots is provided in mostly high-end simulators. There is growing insight that the standard curriculum is in need of revision. A wider use of training media may be required to ensure more training goals are covered in a better way while addressing more personal needs. PC based simulation and game based learning are considered candidates that partly replace and partly extend training on high end simulators. As training time is very expensive and personal needs require flexible solutions, a considerable part of new training options will require unscheduled and mobile activity, in which the pilot is more in control of what, how and when to train. This may lead to new organizational and regulatory mechanisms to register and accredit training as well as new instructional techniques to support the personal training needs without immediate availability of an instructor. Without direct feedback from, or intervention by, an instructor, adaptivity of the training environment is in high demand to ensure training sessions maintain an optimal value to the trainee.

In game design theory, the flow principle is used to provide an optimally engaging experience, whereas its equivalent in instructional design theory is maintaining the optimal cognitive load (Paas, Tuovinen, Tabbers, & Van Gerven, 2003). Good game experience requires the player to be in a 'flow' state of mind (Csíkszentmihályi, 1991) which is feeling competent but challenged while being immersed in the game. This requires game designers to build up game events and levels that are neither too easy (boring) nor too difficult (frustrating) while ensuring that challenging periods are balanced with more relaxing periods without losing the players' attention. Instructional design sequencing principles have similar goals which are achieved by increasing the task difficulty and by scaffolding principles (supporting or automating part of the tasks, such as the trainer wheels for learning to ride a bicycle), see Van Merriënboer & Kirschner, 2007. Adaptive training regulated by combining measures of performance and mental effort has shown to accelerate the learning curve for Air Traffic Control (Salden, Paas, Broers, & Van Merriënboer, 2004) and Flight Management System training (Salden, Paas, van der Pal, & Van Merriënboer, 2004). The learner's cognitive load needs to be in an optimal band to ensure efficient learning. Over- or understimulation leads to frustration or boredom and results in inefficient or even ineffective training. The principles of flow and the optimization of cognitive load both aim to control a learning curve, although they differ in which technique is applied. In gaming, the focus is centered on experience, whereas the focus in training is on performance.

In training, cognitive load is usually controlled by measuring the load and performance after completion of a learning task. For aviation training to be fully effective, the events need to adapt to the cognitive load of events *within* a training session. Performance measured *during* the simulation or game is labeled as in-game measurement or stealth assessment (Shute, Ventura, Bauer, & Zapata-Rivera, 2009), techniques that require a coherent assessment framework, a user model and considerable further research and development (Baalsrud Hauge et. al. 2015) before well-grounded and practical use for automated adaptive training is achieved. Real time measures of mental states that reflect the experience of cognitive load (such as attention, engagement, situation awareness and boredom) should be part of such a framework. In this paper, brain measures are explored as a potential instrument for controlling the learning activity by automatically adjusting events in the learning scenario to ensure an optimal learning experience. Brain measures for attention and cognitive load are of particular interest.

2. USING BCI FOR ADAPTIVE TRAINING

Brain Computer Interface (BCI) stands for a range of techniques that support the brain to control a device without using muscles. For adaptive training, the trainee does not control the training tasks, events, setting or feedback by active thought or sheer will power (which is known as active BCI), but in a more indirect and involuntary way (also known as passive BCI), based on the measured amount of attention or relaxation, engagement or drowsiness, or other relevant mental states. BCI techniques for real, daily training will require a non-invasive, easy to use device. Wireless EEG devices with dry sensors may be candidates for practical BCI. There are several commercial EEG devices on the market that seem to be suitable. A range of validation studies have revealed some application areas as well as the limitations of these 'simple' devices.

EEG (electroencephalography) is a well-known technique to measure the electric activity of the brain (groups of neurons firing simultaneously) on the scalp. After removal of e.g., muscle generated artifacts, EEG contains oscillations of various frequencies (from 0.1-100Hz) and amplitudes (up to 200 microvolts). These vary as a result of processing sensory input and internal mental activity. As a result, EEG is different on the various parts of the brain, although precise location is not a strong feature of EEG. The different frequencies have been found to indicate certain mental states and emotions. For example, a low amplitude in the region of 8-12 Hz indicates attention, especially in combination with a high amplitude in the 13-30 Hz range. The frequency bands have been labeled by Greek letters (alpha to gamma), and include sub-bands like low and high beta. The (sub-)bands and certain composite measures indicate a variety of mental states and functions. An example of a composite measure is the Task Engagement Index, calculated by beta / (alpha + theta), which has been constructed for adaptive automated flight control (Pope et al , 1995) and has for instance been applied in measuring immersion during game play (McMahan, Parberry, & Parsons, 2015).

Raw EEG data is normally recorded for later analysis, which requires powerful computers, complex algorithms and time. BCI cannot work this way, as specific EEG frequencies or indexes need to be calculated and corrected for muscle activity in real time. This requires a highly dedicated algorithm tuned to the specific sensors and locations, hardwired into a small chip in the device itself. This in turn demands considerable research and development, and the companies consequently consider the results as proprietary, including basic information on the frequency bands or composite measures used. A number of currently available BCI measures are presented in Table 1.

Table 1. Preprocessed EEG measures in commercial EEG devices

Neurosky Mindwave	Emotive Insight
Meditation	Relaxation
	Interest/ Affinity
Attention	Focus
	Engagement
	Instantaneous excitement
	Long term excitement

For the concepts of flow and optimal cognitive load, EEG indicators for cognitive load/task difficulty, attention, and task engagement are relevant. Task difficulty is associated with theta and alpha oscillations. Theta (which is most prominent in the frontal midline) is increased in high difficulty tasks in flight simulators (Smith & Gevins 2005), Alpha indicates the cognitive load of visual/auditory tasks (Gerlic 1999). For military pilots, alpha is found to decrease during demanding air refueling and landing exercises (Sterman et al, 1994). There are indications that the high alpha band is more related to (verbal) long term memory activities and theta to working memory (Antonenko, Paas, Grubner, & van Gog, 2010). Theta is therefore a candidate trigger to control overstimulation and high alpha is a candidate trigger to control understimulation in a scenario.

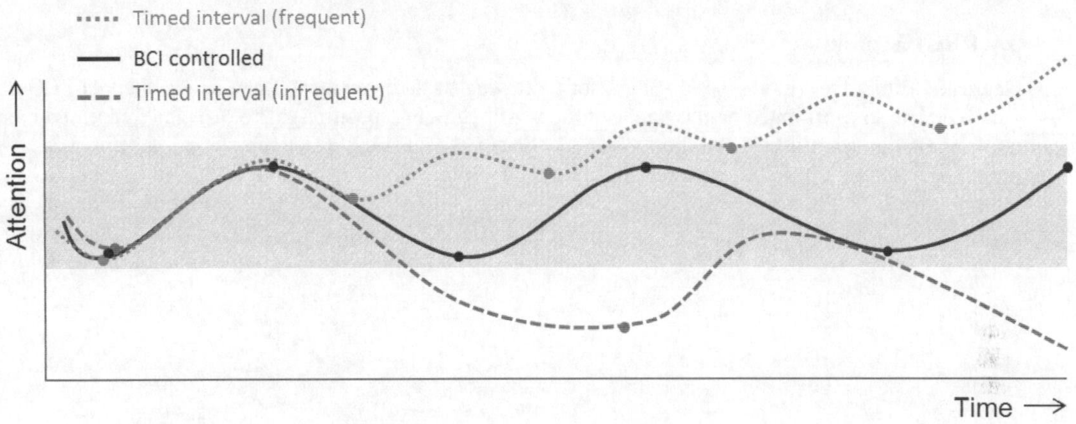

Figure 1. Expected progress of attention level based on different methods for triggering simulator events; timed interval (frequent as well as infrequent intervals) and BCI controlled (set to target attention optimal values)

3. METHOD

To determine if BCI devices can be used to more effectively trigger scenario events, a pilot experiment is set up. The between subjects design compares two conditions – time interval triggered vs mental state triggered simulator events. Participants are asked to perform a short training by flying a helicopter around an urban area in a low fidelity (gaming) simulated environment. The objective of the training is to familiarise with basic helicopter control mechanisms (pitch, role and yaw). The training task consists of flying through consecutive augmented cues, a kind of 'virtual checkpoints' in the sky. These hoop-shaped checkpoints are placed in a track configuration, and are located on different heights.

Eight participants (7 male, 1 female; age ranges from 21 to 36 years with an average of 27) are randomly assigned to either one condition. The test starts with a 1 minute familiarisation of the task, where the task is explained. Once the participants understand the task, the helicopter control training commences.

The training task is identical for all participants: to learn to control the helicopter by flying through a set of consecutive digital 'checkpoints'. This training takes # minutes to complete. Depending on the assigned condition, the task either automatically increases in difficulty (time based interval condition, 'A') or varies in difficulty depending on the participant's attention level (mental state based condition, 'B').

In the time based interval condition (A), to increase difficulty the checkpoint diameter decreases gradually over 5 minutes. This reduction triggers regardless of how well the trainee performs. In the mental state based (B) condition, the task complexity changes on the basis of the level of attention of the trainee. When strained by the task, trainee attention will increase, thus increasing the diameter of the checkpoints. When the task no longer requires high attention (through increased mastery of the controls), the checkpoint diameter will remain constant. When the attention level becomes too low, the checkpoint diameter will dynamically decrease, thus increasing the task complexity. During training, the checkpoint diameter decreases when the participant's attention level is higher than 70, and increases when attention level is lower than 30 on a scale from 0 to 100. An optimal level of attention is achieved between 30 and 70. The checkpoint diameter does not change between these levels. The total checkpoint diameter size reduction over 5 minutes in condition B is therefore not known beforehand, and depends on the participants' efficiency in mastering the task.

After completing the helicopter control training, all participants receive the same exam, where they are required to fly one track with the smallest checkpoints used during the training. Trainee performance is determined by the number of checkpoints correctly flown through and the time needed to finish the track. A post-experiment questionnaire measured subjective ratings on the amount of challenge experienced.

3.1 Apparatus

3.1.1 BCI Tooling

Neurosky Mindwave Mobile (see Figure 1 for a drawing of its components) is a single channel EEG device with a dry sensor positioned on the forehead (approximately Fp1 position). The real-time processed measure used for BCI in this study is attention. Neurosky does not reveal the exact composition of this measure, but indicates that the attention is based primarily on beta waves. Attention is scaled from 1-100, with interpretations: 1-20 strongly lowered, 20-40 reduced, 40-60 neutral, 60-80 slightly elevated, 80-100 elevated.

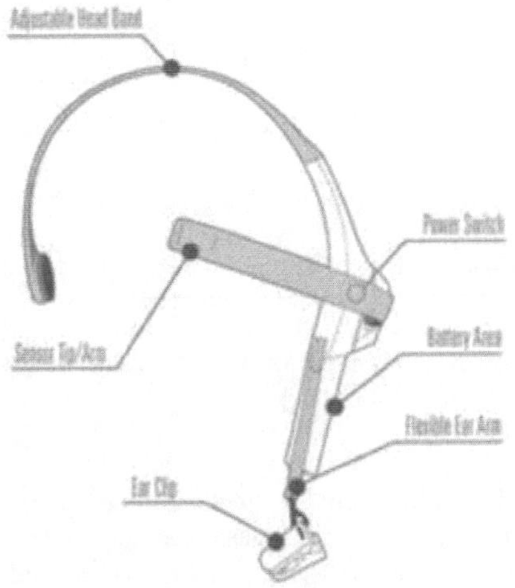

Figure 2. Mindwave Mobile

Figure 3. Screenshot of Helicopter Control Training Game

3.1.2 Helicopter Control Training Game

The Helicopter Control Training Game (see Fig. 2) is a low fidelity simulation environment developed using the Unity engine in the XLab at the Netherlands Aerospace Centre - NLR. The game is used to familiarise participants with basic principles of helicopter controls such as pitch, roll and yaw. The simulation features highly simplified helicopter flight models and controls, allowing for relatively easy mastery of basic flight control. The task is to fly through 'augmented hoops' in the sky. The hoops change from large to small in the time based condition, while in the mental state based condition the hoops vary as a function of attention level.

4. RESULTS

All participants completed the experiment successfully. Unexpectedly, participants in the BCI controlled condition did not perform better on the exam than participants in the time interval controlled condition (see Table 2 for results).

Table 2. Means and standard deviations (in brackets) of the results on the Helicopter Control Training Game for the conditions time based and mental state based control of task difficulty. Exam score indicates the average number of correctly flown checkpoints; experienced challenge indicates the average subjective rating from 1 to 10 (1 = easy, 10 = hard)

Condition	Total sum deviation from optimal attention range during training	Total time deviation from optimal attention range during training (seconds)	Total training time (seconds)	Exam score	Experienced challenge
A Time based	839 (323)	84 (24)	335 (13)	4.0 (0.7)	7.25 (1.3)
B Mental state based	611 (255)	58 (16)	355 (34)	2.0 (1.9)	8.0 (1.4)

Participants in the time based condition spent an average of 26 seconds more outside of the optimal attention range (25% of total training time) compared to participants in the BCI controlled condition (16% of total training time). For some participants, the attention level graphs showed clearly that whenever a participant's attention level surpassed the threshold, the task difficulty would change, causing the participant's attention level to normalize in turn. For other participants, BCI triggers are less clearly or not always associated to excess of the optimal attention range. For example, Figure 4 illustrates five correct BCI triggers, but the triggers at 135 and 210 seconds seem to be influenced by EEG spikes and lead to incorrect events. Later attention levels (at 250, 280 and 290 seconds) should have been detected and events should have been triggered. One participant (mental state based condition) remained in the optimal attention range, but kept performing poorly and ended up with zero correct checkpoints in the exam.

Participants in the time based condition varied considerably in overall attention level (either very high or very low), but did not differ much in exam scores. For two participants in the time based condition the subjective ratings were inconsistent to the measured attention levels: intermediate challenging (5) versus high attention levels, and rather challenging (8) versus low attention levels.

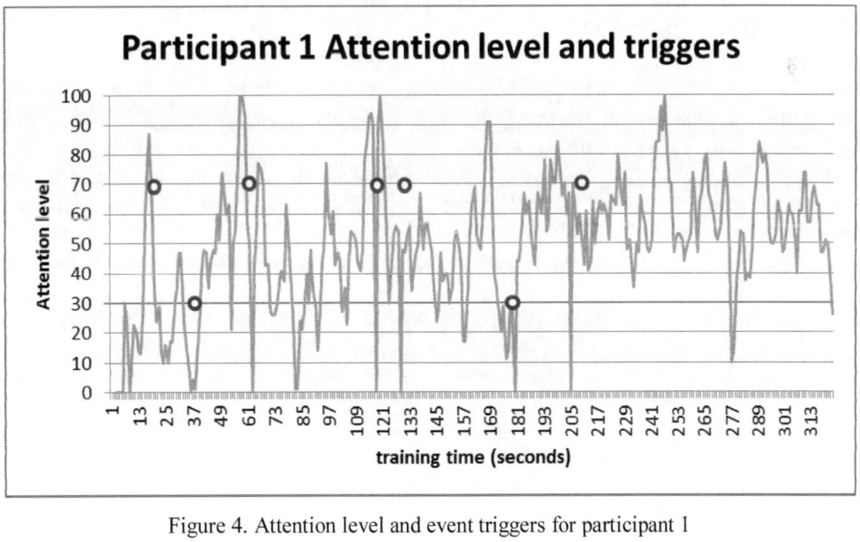

Figure 4. Attention level and event triggers for participant 1

5. DISCUSSION

This study was set up to determine whether BCI devices can be used to more effectively trigger scenario events in realistic training settings (as opposed to EEG laboratory conditions). The pilot study revealed the potential of BCI for training as well as some improvements to make. BCI using the Mindwave attention level functions reasonably well to adjust the task difficulty by increasing or decreasing the diameter of an augmented hoop in the sky. Some technical adjustments in the attention level criteria (such as dealing with EEG spikes) may increase reliability, while an adjusted size and timings of the hoops may improve the effect on the learning progress. Also, the allotted training time (five minutes) might not have been sufficient to significantly increase the performance of participants with poor initial skill level. For fair comparison of the conditions, the time intervals should be based on the average learning curve of the intended training audience. Ensuring sufficient statistical power of the test will require a larger sample of trainees who are more homogeneous with respect to game experience in general and experience with flight simulators in particular.

The mindwave attention level may be used as a rough motivational indicator the trainees have to the task, but other EEG indicators may be more clearly linked to task difficulty (increased theta band) or cognitive load (reduced high alpha band). Using these measures will require some additional real time algorithms to be developed. BCI controlled training using EEG devices that are easy to apply in real training settings appears to be viable, although considerable effort is needed to ensure the measurements and the trigger events are well tuned to the training audience characteristics such as the learning curve. Based on the potential demonstrated in the current pilot experiment, the full experiment is intended to be performed after implementing the aforementioned improvements.

Modern consumable EEG devices are promising in achieving adaptive training in real training organisations through maintaining optimal cognitive load for the trainee. This may enhance the training effectiveness of the training session while achieving personalized training trajectories. Fully automated training however will require improved modeling and measuring of learning and performance which can be very complex in professional settings. This effort is likely to pay off as the potential of reducing the average (formal) training time, personalize training schedules, and reducing trainee attrition has significant economic effects.

REFERENCES

Csíkszentmihályi, M., 1991, *Flow: The Psychology of Optimal Experience.* New York: Harper Perennial.

Antonenko. P., Paas, F., Grubner, R. Van Gog, T., 2010, Using Electroencephalography to Measure Cognitive Load. Educational Psychology Review 22(4), pp 425-438.

Baalsrud Hauge, J., Stanescu , I. A., Moreno-Ger, P., Arnab, S., Lim, T., Serrano-Laguna, A., ... Degano, C. 2015. Learning analytics architecture to scaffold learning experience through technology-based methods. *International Journal of Serious Games, 2*(1), 29-44.

Smith, M. E., & Gevins, A. (2005, May). Neurophysiologic monitoring of mental workload and fatigue during operation of a flight simulator. In Defense and Security (pp. 116-126).

Sterman, M. B., Mann, C. A., Kaiser, D. A., & Suyenobu, B. Y. (1994). Multiband topographic EEG analysis of a simulated visuomotor aviation task. *International Journal of Psychophysiology, 16*, 49–56

Shute, V., Ventura, M., Bauer, M., & Zapata-Rivera, D. 2009. Melding the Power of Serious Games and Embedded Assessment to Monitor and Foster Learning. In: U. Ritterfield, M. Cody, & P. Vorderer (Eds). *Serious Games: Mechanisms and Effects.* New York: Routlegde, pp295-321

MacMahan, T., Parberry, I, & Parsons, T.D., 2015, Evaluating Player Task Engagement and Arousal using Electroencephalography. Procedia Manufacturing 3, 2303-2310.

Pope, A.T., Bogart, E.H., & Bartolome, D.S. 1995, Biocybernetic system evaluates indices of operator engagement in automated task. *Biological Psychology, 40* (1–2), Pages 187-195

Van Merriënboer, J.J.G. & Kirschner, P.A., 2007, Ten Steps to Complex Learning. Mahwah, NJ: Lawrence Erlbaum Associates.

EVALUATION OF THE COURSE OF THE FLIGHT SIMULATORS FROM THE PERSPECTIVE OF STUDENTS AND UNIVERSITY TEACHERS

Feyzi Kaysi[1], Bünyamin Bavlı[2] and Aysun Gürol[2]
[1]İstanbul University, Technical Vocational School, Department of Electronics and Automation,
[2]Yıldız Teknik University School of Education,
Istanbul-Turkey

ABSTRACT

The study evaluates the flight simulators course which was opened to fulfill the intermediate staff need of the sector. To collect data, Qualitative techniques were applied. Within this scope, the case study method was employed in the study. The study group consisted of students and instructors. In-depth and focus group interviews were conducted with the participants by using semi-structured interview forms. To analyze data and obtain findings, content analysis technique was used. Findings explored that, participants were satisfied with the course, the staff need of the sector was fulfilled, the learners gained sector knowledge, and the aim of the teaching process included a practice opportunity in the sector. Additionally, participants expected to the significance of the cooperation between the sector and the university.

KEYWORDS

Flight Simulators Course, Program Evaluation, Sector

1. INTRODUCTION

It is clear that there is a need of cooperation between the sector and the vocational schools of higher education to fulfill the needs desired human source. For a qualified human source of the sector, education and the programs should be of high quality to fulfil the needs of the sector (Akyurt, 2009). Hence, it is necessary to check the existing state of the program from the insiders' point of view. In this study, the course "Flight Simulator I" which was started in accordance with the demands of the sector was evaluated students and instructors point of view. For this purpose, Educational Criticism model which was called the "educational expertise" suggested by Elliot Eisner for qualitative and interpretative date was employed (Alkin, 2003).

By this means, it is believed that an important model will be provided for the courses which will be established later through the evaluations of the views of students, instructors and head of the program. Educational Criticism model which was called the "educational expertise" by Elliot Eisner in the beginning appeared as a result of the objection to the experimental and quasi-experimental studies. Eisner indicated that problems cannot be solved by using quantitative data and the activity of evaluation is a sophisticated and interpretive study (Alkin, 2003). To that end, educational criticism model was utilized in this study, which is frequently used to evaluate "value" and "judgement" dimensions in social studies and also considered as suitable in this design.

2. BODY OF PAPER

2.1 Research Questions

The study reported in this paper aims to investigate the following questions:

1- What are the expectations of the participants about the opened course?
2- What are the benefits of the course to the participants?

3. METHODOLOGY

Design

To inquire a phenomenon through the views of the persons who took part in the activity, qualitative research method is applied. (Merriam, 2009). Hence, qualitative case study method, sample case study, was employed for the evaluation of the course.

Participants

The participant of the current study consists of the students and instructors of the program. Students consisted of 9 male, 4 female participants, instructors consisted of 3 males. Notices and announcements including verbal and written information about the study referred to define convenient and volunteer participants. At the end, 12 male, 4 female participants accepted to take part in the study in the academic year of 2013-2014. In the study, as the data unit was close to and easily accessible to the researcher convenience sampling technique was employed (Yin, 2011). To collect data, focus group interviews with students and semi-structured in-depth interviews with other participants were conducted to get into the inner world of a person and to understand and grasp the events from his/her perspective Patton (1987).

Data collection

The researcher has been a staff at the department for five years. Hence, it was an opportunity to organize the interviews and collect data. At first, interview questions prepared as a draft by the researcher. After the review of the experts on the field, the final interview questions, the validity of the questions was ensured. Structured interviews with instructors and with the students, semi-structured face to face focus group interviews were employed. Before the interviews, it was stated that the participation was voluntary based and withdrawal was possible any time during the interviews. For the interviews, the places and time convenient for the participants preferred. The interviews were audio recorded with the permission of the participants.

Data Analyses

To analyze data, content analysis technique was employed. The objective of the content analysis is to reduce the words in a research text to a fewer number of content categories (Creswell, 2013). Audio recorded interviews transcribed by the researcher send to each participant to verify. Furthermore, each participant's transcription was analyzed by other experts to compare and verify the results. To provide anonymity, each participant was coded with a pseudonym. For the students, O, for the instructors OE pseudonym was applied during coding. 'In Vıvo' coding technique allowing to code each participant's expressions directly was practiced (Chenail, 2012).

4. RESULTS

Themes

1. The Expectations of the Participants from the Course

To define participants' expectations from the course, following results were obtained at figure 1.

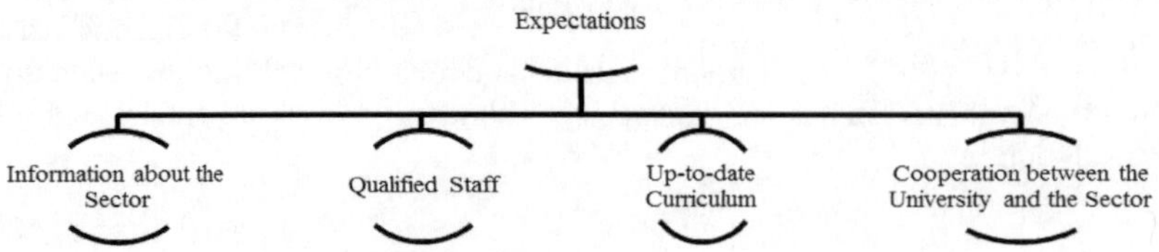

Figure 1. The Expectations about the Opening of this Course

The participants expressed that the program should accomplish the needs of the sector with qualified staff. The program should be up-to-date and also equip students with the basic knowledge of the sector, provide cooperation between the sector and the university.

PB: The companies want to minimize their external dependency by improving their technical staff capacities. Besides, our major objective as the head of the program is to update our teaching curriculum by cooperating with the companies operating in the field of industry. For this reason, a protocol was signed between our program and a leading company operating in flight simulators and giving importance to cooperation with the university. Within the framework of this protocol, thanks to courses which are offered to be opened, our students can graduate as experts in flight simulators as their teaching is still in progress. Thanks to these courses, students will have opportunities to find a job including their internships first by providing education which is parallel with the needs of the industrial sector through realizing the cooperation between the university and industry.

OE-3: We demanded the opening of this course as there has not been an education for training flight simulator technical staff in the aviation sector so far and the background of the staff who applied to our company for a job or internship is insufficient. The main purpose of this course is to provide information about aviation and flight simulators to the staff who will apply to our company for internship and to make their internship period effective.

2. The Benefits of the Course to the Participants

Themes occurred related to benefits of the course to the participants figured out in Figure 2.

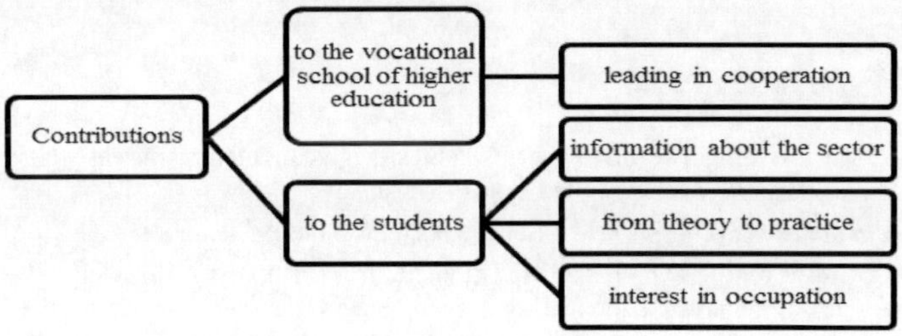

Figure 2. Contribution of the Course to the Students and Vocational Schools of Higher

The participants underlined that the program provided practice opportunity for them. Through the internships, students had the opportunity to know the sector better. Consequently, the motivation of the students to learn increased as well. Some of the transcriptions of the participants are as in the following:

O1-K3: Also it is something that we have known before. In fact, there is a servo-system and a hydro pneumatic system in the plane. We knew this before. And there is a complicated system for everything on the plane. When somebody sees this, he/she becomes more curious and gets more interested in his/her job.

PB: There will be a two-stage benefit from this course. First of all, our students can graduate as experts in Flight Simulators thanks to these courses when they receive their education. In this way, they can use directly their own professional knowledge and skills in the Flight simulators topic. Thus, the current need for qualified technical staff in the fields of aviation and flight simulators will be fulfilled continuously. Another, more important benefit is as following: There is a wide gap between universities which have been providing technical education and industrial companies. Thanks to this course, there will be cooperation between the private sector company and the university. Solutions will be sought to overcome problematic situations, there will be background for other partnerships and we will gain experiences of cooperation with private companies. In conclusion, a model can be created for the cooperation between the university and the industry.

5. DISCUSSION

The issue of cooperation between the university and the sector is among the problems of the sector in Turkey (Çağlayan & Bener, 2006). In addition to that, very few lines of communication and cooperation exist between universities and the sector (Bulgan & Dolmacı, 2015). Whereas the sector tends to collaborate more with universities (Beyhan & Fındık, 2014: 91). It is easier to develop cooperation with the help of qualified instructors (Kyvikand Aksnes, 2015). Keeping university curriculums up-to-date in a parallel manner to the sector and being comfortable about adapting students to the sector after their graduation are among the expected outputs. It is a well-known fact that vocational schools are insufficient (Çağlayan & Bener, 2006)

Because, among known problems, there has been a wide gap between the competencies acquired by the students studying in vocational schools of higher education and the needs of the sector (Gül Koçak, 2006). In the process of filling the gap, the contribution of the qualified staff will be upmost important. The program provided opportunity the theory into practice by practicing learned knowledge during the course (Becit, Kurt & Kabakçı, 2009;Postareff & Linndblom-Ylanneand Nevgi, 2004; Wagler, 2007). In a study carried out by Çağıltay and others (2007) enriching the courses with simulators was highlighted among the expectations of students attending the courses. Besides, having good content knowledge, following current developments and improvements are among the most important expectations of the learners from the instructors (Ekinci & Burgaz, 2007; Aydın, Görmüs & Altıntop, 2014).

6. CONCLUSION

Flight Simulators I-II courses opened for the first time in Turkey at a state school was appreciated by the instructors and the students. The program provided the learners to put the knowledge into the practice. The program included competent instructors and also obtained positive contributions from the sector which supported learners' future carrier.

REFERENCES

Akyurt, N.,2009. Meslek yüksekokulları ve marmara üniversitesi sağlık hizmetleri meslek yüksekokulu öğrencilerinin genel profili. *Fırat Sağlık Hizmetleri Dergisi*, 4(11), pp.175-189.

Alkin, C. M., 2013. *Evaluation roots (2nd ed.).* Thousand Oaks, CA: Sage Publications.

Aydın, S., Görmüş, A. Ş., & Altıntop, M. Y., 2014. Öğrencilerin memnuniyet düzeyleri ile demografik özellikleri arasındaki ilişkinin doğrusal olmayan kanonik korelasyon analizi ile incelenmesi: meslek yüksekokulu'nda bir uygulama. *Abant İzzet Baysal Üniversitesi Sosyal Bilimler Enstitüsü Dergisi,* 14(1), pp. 35-58.

Becit, G., Kurt, A. A., & Kabakçı, I., 2009. Bilgisayar öğretmen adaylarının okul uygulama derslerinin yararlarına ilişkin görüşleri. *Anadolu Üniversitesi Sosyal Bilimler Dergisi,* 9(1), pp. 169–184

Beyhan, B. &Fındık D. ,2014. Firma yenilik stratejisi ve üniversite-sanayi işbirliği: Türkiye üzerine bir çalişma. *İktisat İşletme ve Finans*, *29* (242),pp. 71-102.

Bulgan, G. & Dolmacı, N., 2015. Önlisans eğitiminde öğrenci gözüyle sorunlar fırsatlar; Isparta myo örneği. *I. Ulusal Şişli Sempozyumu.* Istanbul, Turkey, pp. 1-21.

Chanail, R. J. ,2012. Conducting qualitative data analysis: qualitative data analysis as a metaphoric process. *Qualitative Report*, (17), pp. 248-253.

Çağıltay, K., et al, 2007. Öğretim teknolojilerinin üniversitede kullanımına yönelik alışkanlıklar ve beklentiler: Betimleyici bir çalışma. *Akademik Bilişim Konferansı Bildirileri.* Kütahya, Türkiye, pp.209-216.

Çağlayan, U & Bener, A 2006, *Avrupa birliği sürecinde Türkiye'de bilişim ve telekomünikasyon teknolojileri sektörü üzerine görüş ve öneriler*. Available from: http://goo.gl/pxhHeU [13 October 2015]

Ekinci, C. E., & Burgaz, B., 2007. Hacettepe üniversitesi öğrencilerinin bazı akademik hizmetlere ilişkin beklenti ve memnuniyet düzeyleri. *Hacettepe Üniversitesi Eğitim Fakültesi Dergisi*, 33(33), pp. 120-134.

Koçak, H., G., 2006. Bilgisayar teknolojisi ve programlama eğitim programının sorunları, master thesis, Çukurova Üniversitesi, Sosyal Bilimler Enstitüsü, Adana, viewed 28 April 2016, http://library.cu.edu.tr/tezler/5998.pdf

Kyvik, S. & Aksnes, D.W., 2015. Explaining the increase in publication productivity among academic staff: a generational perspective. *Studies in Higher Education*, 40(8), pp.1438–1453.

Merriam, S. B., 2009. *Qualitative research: a guide to design and implementation*, San Francisco, CA: John Wiley and Sons.

Patton, M.Q., 1987. *How to use qualitative methods in evaluation*, Newbury Park, CA: Sage Publications.

Postareff, L., Lindblom-Ylänne, S. & Nevgi, A., 2004. The effect of pedagogical training on teaching in higher education. *European Association for Research on Learning and Instruction (EARLI) Higher Education Special Interest Group Conference.* Stockholm, Sweden, pp. 557-571.

Wagler, R.R 2007. Assessing the impact of vicarious experiences on preservice elementary science teacher efficacy and preservice elementary teacher efficacy, master thesis, Oklahoma State University, Oklahoma, viewed 15 May 2016, http://digital.library.okstate.edu/etd/umi-okstate-2529.pdf

Yin, R.K., 2011. *Qualitative Research from Start to Finish*, Guilford Press: New York.

DEVELOPMENT OF CRITICAL THINKING WITH METACOGNITIVE REGULATION

Yasushi Gotoh
Niigata University
8050,Ikarashi 2no cho, Nishi ku, Niigata City, Niigata, Japan

ABSTRACT

In this research the author defines critical thinking as the set of skills and dispositions which enable one to solve problems logically and to attempt to reflect autonomously by means of Metacognitive regulation on one's own problem-solving processes. In order to develop their critical thinking, it is important for students to be able to use this rubric and assess themselves. The author focuses on providing Metacognitive regulation to help with self-assessment. Metacognitive regulation consist of two aspects: a critical thinking rubric as criterion and evidence of the problem-solving process. Comparison of achievement levels in the above critical thinking rubric, and content analysis of the reasons for a particular level of achievement in critical thinking, suggest that Metacognitive regulation with this critical thinking rubric as the criterion, and evidence of the problem-solving process, could enhance students' critical thinking ability.

KEYWORDS

Critical Thinking, Metacognitive regulation, Self-assessment, Critical thinking rubric, evidence of the problem-solving process

1. INTRODUCTION

The development of students' ability to work together to solve problems is an important factor in education. The ATCS21 (Assessing and Teaching 21st Century Skills) Project proposes ways of thinking; tools for working; ways of working; and ways of living in the world as the skills needed for the 21st century. According to ATCS21, critical thinking is one aspect of ways of thinking. A number of researchers such as Dewey (1910), Glaser (1941), and Ennis (1985) define critical thinking as reflective and logical thinking. The Association of American Colleges and Universities (AACU) defines critical thinking as a habit of mind characterized by the comprehensive exploration of issues, ideas, artifacts, and events before accepting or formulating an opinion or conclusion.

In this research the author defines critical thinking as the set of skills and dispositions which enable one to solve problems logically and to attempt to reflect autonomously by means of Metacognitive regulation on one's own problem-solving processes. Metacognitive regulation is the regulation of cognition and learning experiences through a set of activities that help people control their learning (Flavell, 1979). AACU also provides a rubric known as a value rubric as a critical thinking assessment tool. In order to develop their critical thinking, it is important for students to be able to use this rubric and assess themselves.

The author focuses on providing Metacognitive regulation to help with self-assessment. The important thing is reflection based on evidence of the problem-solving process. The critical thinking rubric, while a useful criterion, is not in itself enough. Metacognitive regulation consist of two aspects: a critical thinking rubric as criterion and evidence of the problem-solving process. Metacognitive regulation with a critical thinking rubric as criterion and evidence of the problem-solving process would enhance students' critical thinking. The purpose of this study is to identify the effectiveness of such Metacognitive regulation.

2. METHOD

24 university students took part in the study. Cooperative problem-solving methods such as the knowledge-constructive jigsaw method were selected as materials. The research project consisted of the knowledge-constructive jigsaw method and Metacognitive regulation. In order to evaluate the results, the lesson was carried out twice.

2.1 Knowledge-Constructive Jigsaw Method

In the first term, students held a discussion on the subject of introducing non-Japanese workers into Japan. Four types of different information were provided separately: depopulation in Japanese society; disadvantages and difficulties of employing non-Japanese workers; an overseas case study; and trends among non-Japanese workers in selecting an employment destination. After reading these different types of information individually, the students discussed the following topic: "Should Japan bring in more foreign workers?"

2.2 Metacognitive Regulation

The entire discussion was audio- recorded and a lesson protocol was developed to be used in subsequent Metacognitive regulation and reflection. Several studies exist on critical thinking rubrics (Griffin, et.al 2012, Beyer 1985, Miyake 2014, VALUE project). On the basis of these studies, students were asked to carry out self-assessment using the following critical thinking rubric(Gotoh2006;2011)

- I pay attention to the information source (who wrote it).
- I pay attention to the information destination (who reads it).
- I pay attention to the information purpose (agenda).
- I assume information from an opposing point of view.
- I pay attention to information period (when it was produced).
- I pay attention to inconsistencies and missing information.
- I pay attention to gaps in the argument.
- If necessary, I reserve judgment.
- If necessary, I make a conditional judgment.

Self-assessment was carried out while listening to the audio recording of the discussion and reading the lesson protocol. Students were asked to self-assess their critical thinking ability on three levels: achieved, partly achieved, failed. They were also asked to note their reasons for assigning these levels.

In the second term, students discussed the introduction of English lessons in Japanese elementary schools. Four types of different information were provided: trends in elementary school English education overseas; parents' opinion; case study of an English learner; and relationship between language and culture.

Self-assessment was carried out using the above critical thinking rubric.

3. RESULT

3.1 Comparison of Achievement Levels in Critical Thinking Rubric

In order to compare achievement levels in the critical thinking rubric during the first and second terms, the following scores were awarded: achieved (3points), partly achieved (2points), failed (1point).

Figure 1 shows a comparison of achievement levels in the critical thinking rubric.

T-test (paired) results show a significant difference in eight items between the first and second terms. I pay attention to the information source (who wrote it), I pay attention to the information destination (who reads it), I pay attention to the information purpose (agenda), I assume information from an opposing point of view, I pay attention to information period (when it was produced), I pay attention to inconsistencies and missing information and I pay attention to gaps in the argument.

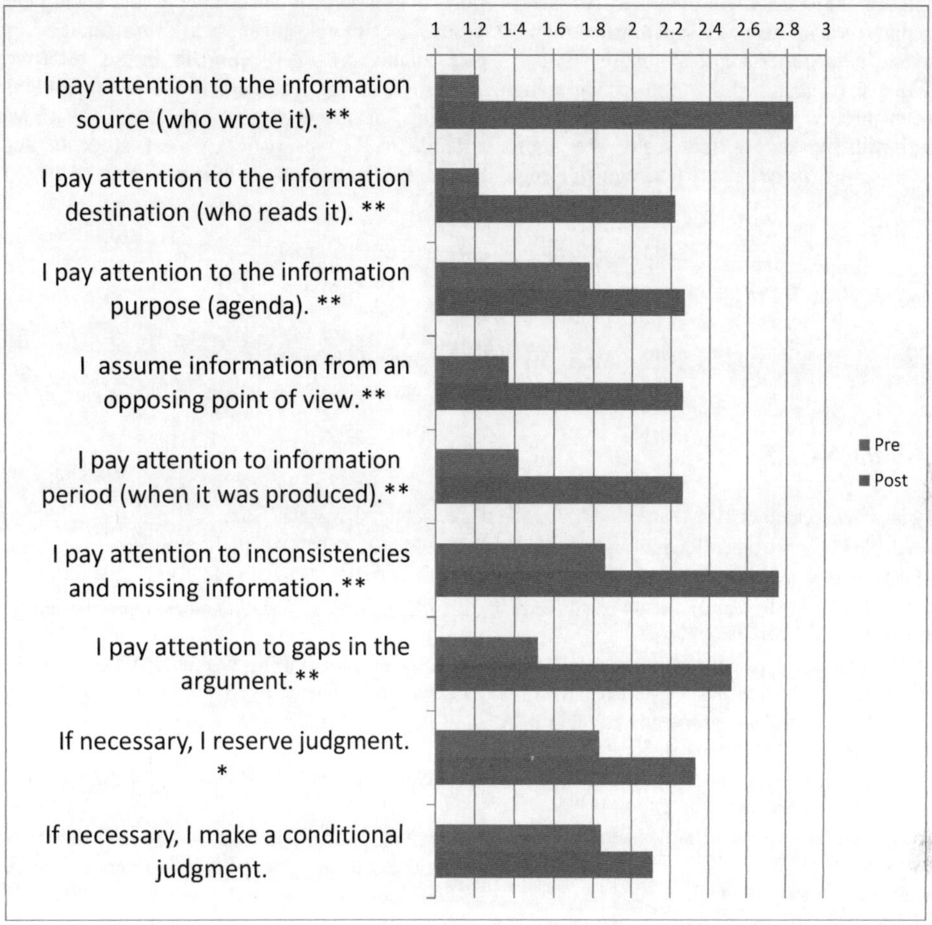

*p<.05, ** p<.01

Figure 1. Comparison of Achievement Levels In Critical Thinking Rubric

3.2 Contents Analysis of Reasons for Different Levels of Achievement in Critical Thinking

In the first term, the reasons mentioned in self-assessment concerned a lack of awareness of critical thinking. Thanks to Metacognitive regulation, students realized that they do not pay attention to the reliability of information. Some students wrote "I trusted the information completely and was not suspicious about it." I tried to make a judgment based only on the given information, and did not consider the information agenda."

In the second term, the reasons for self-assessment concerned the fact that students had acquired critical thinking ability. Some students wrote "I paid attention to whether or not there was information other than the information I had obtained, and also to the agenda of the information." "If necessary, I was able to reserve judgment."

4. CONCLUSION

Comparison of achievement levels in the above critical thinking rubric, and content analysis of the reasons for a particular level of achievement in critical thinking, suggest that Metacognitive regulation with this critical thinking rubric as the criterion, and evidence of the problem-solving process, could enhance students' critical thinking ability. On the other hand, self-report isn't an objective assessment, and it's not clear whether the reporting is an accurate self-improvement assessment, or mere awareness with no change in meaningful behavior. It is important to compare students' performance with self-report.In future, differences among individuals will also be taken into consideration. In particular, the difference in the problem-solving process between those who have an aptitude for critical thinking and those who do not, is not yet known. Using a critical thinking disposition scale, the author intends to extract two types of students and compare problem-solving processes, Metacognitive regulation and reflection, and self-assessment, between these two types.

ACKNOWLEDGEMENT

This work was supported by JSPS KAKENHI Grant Number 15K01020.

REFERENCES

Assessment & teaching of 21st century skills 2015 21st skills. http://www.atc21s.org/

Dewey,J.1933.How we think (Revised and expanded edition). MA: Houghton Mifflin Company.

Ennis,R.H. 1985 A logical basis for measuring critical thinking skills. Educational Leadership, 43, 44-48

Flavell, J.H. 1979. "Metacognition and cognitive monitoring. A new area of cognitive-development inquiry". American Psychologist 34 (10): 906–911.

Gotoh,Y. 2015 Development of Critical Thinking Self-Assessment System using Wearable Device. Proceedings of 12th international Conference on Cognition and Exploratory Learning in Digital Age(CELDA2015), 387- 389

Gotoh,Y. 2013 Visualization of Understanding of Media Characteristics Using Analytic Hierarchy Process. Computer Technology and Application, 4, 563-567

Gotoh,Y. 2011 Development of Simple Critical Viewing Skills Scale on Web Browsing. Proceedings of International Conference for Media in Education,1-4

Gotoh,Y. 2006 Structure and Development of Media Literacy. Niigata, Japan: Niigata University,Doctoral Thesis

Graser, E.M. 1941 An experiment in the development of critical thinking. New York: Teachers College of Columbia University, Bureau of Publications.

Ministry of education, culture, sports science and technology Japan 2015 Result of National Assessment of Information Utilization Ability in Japan. http://www.mext.go.jp/a_menu/shotou/zyouhou/1356188.htm

The Association of American Colleges and Universities 2015 Critical thinking value rubric https://www.aacu.org/value/rubrics/critical-thinking

ENACTING STEM EDUCATION FOR DIGITAL AGE LEARNERS: THE *MAKER* MOVEMENT GOES TO SCHOOL

Dale S. Niederhauser[1] and Lynne Schrum[2]
[1]*West Virginia University, USA*
[2]*Nova Southeastern University, USA*

ABSTRACT

The importance of STEM Education has become central to discussions about the future of schooling over the past 20 years. Predicated on the idea that a primary purpose of schooling is to prepare skilled and knowledgeable workers, these discussions have been grounded, in part, in cold-war era concerns about rapid advancements in STEM fields driven by more efficient and effective application of the systematic and structured ways of thinking that are common to these disciplines. However, curricula and pedagogical routines in these fields are fully established, and changing curricula, and reforming instructional practice, has been a daunting process. In this paper we examine the idea that educators can draw on the kinds of learning experiences that occur in informal educational settings, like *Makerspaces,* to shape in-school activities in ways that make learning STEM content more contextualized, authentic, and meaningful for students.

KEYWORDS

STEM Education, Problem-solving, Makerspaces, Project-based Learning

1. INTRODUCTION

The STEM acronym was coined by the national science foundation in the late 1990's: to refer to the four separate and distinct fields we know as science, technology engineering, and/or mathematics (Sanders, 2009). More recently a cohesive conceptualization of STEM Education has emerged. *Integrative STEM Education* draws on the interrelationships among the four distinct disciplines, and focuses on constructing curricular and pedagogical approaches that help students develop ways of thinking and solving problems that are grounded in *purposeful design and inquiry*. This marks a distinct change in the ways educators think about teaching.

Developed at Virginia Tech, Integrative STEM Education is grounded in constructivism and draws on the findings of three decades of cognitive science research (Sanders, 2009). Integrative STEM Education principles include the idea that learning is a constructive, not a receptive, process; that motivation and beliefs are integral to cognition; that social interaction is fundamental to cognitive development, and that knowledge, strategies, and expertise are contextual (see Bruning, Schraw, Norby, & Ronning, 2004). When enacted, these principles draw on purposeful design and inquiry to ". . . provide a context and framework for organizing abstract understandings of science and mathematics, and encourage students to actively construct contextualized knowledge of science and mathematics, thereby promoting recall and learning transfer" (Sanders, 2009, p. 23). Central to this approach is the use of authentic, situated problems to drive the educational process. In this paper we examine the nature of STEM Education, the relationship between STEM Education and problem-solving, and describe some recent efforts to incorporate some of the principles that underlie the *Maker Movement* into K-12 education systems.

2. PROBLEM-SOLVING, STEM ED AND THE MAKER MOVEMENT

Solving problems is a routine part of the U.S. schoolchild's day—although the kinds of problem-solving activities students typically engage in leave much to be desired. For example, school-based problem-solving in mathematics typically involves the explanation of a mathematical concept by the teacher (reinforced with information from a textbook), worked examples to model solution procedures, guided practice with a problem set, and independent practice with additional problem sets (homework). Problem-solving in science also tends to be procedural, with students working through problems on Punnett squares, acceleration of mass, or some other scientific conception, with occasional scripted verification labs that require students to follow the steps to arrive at the "right answer." In a technology class, assignments often include designing and creating a product (PowerPoint presentation, word processed document, spreadsheet, etc.), with problem-solving in this context involving figuring out how to create a product that meets the criteria established by the teacher. Engineering education, although largely absent in the k-12 environment, often draws on the problem set-activity that is prevalent in the kinds of mathematics and science problem-solving activities students engage in—especially in introductory engineering courses. These types of pedagogical practices continue to persist despite significant pedagogical and curricular reform efforts across all of the STEM content areas over the past 25+ years (e.g., AAAS, 1993; ABET, 1997; ITEA, 1996; NCTM, 1989, 2000)

It is, perhaps, not surprising that traditional pedagogy continues to endure in schools. Pedagogical reform is notoriously difficult (Richardson, Anders, Tidwell, & Lloyd, 1991), with entrenched teachers tending to teach in ways they were taught (Lortie, 1975) as they work within traditional administrative structures and employ the same didactic teaching methods that their teachers had used when they were students (Cohen, 1990). The emphasis is on transmitting discrete, inert knowledge that can be assessed using standardized tests; the school day is fragmented with separate periods for each subject—especially at the secondary level; teachers often lack deep and coherent understanding of content expertise; and there is a general lack of pedagogical sophistication and imagination. However, the post-schooling world increasingly requires individuals who can develop creative, sophisticated and elegant solutions to the myriad of social, political, economic, environmental, and security challenges facing our interconnected and interdependent world. Unfortunately, the isolated and oversimplified problem-solving activities that are so pervasive in schoolchildren's classroom-based learning experiences are not likely to promote the kinds of sophisticated problem-solving strategies necessary for addressing complex real-world problems facing our modern society.

2.1 Problem-solving and Integrative STEM Education

Jonassen (2011) proposed a taxonomy of problem types that include school-based activities like algorithms, story problems, and rule-using/induction problems, as well as more complex real-world problems like diagnosis-solution problems, policy-analysis problems, and design problems. His taxonomy is based on five external characteristics of problems: structuredness, context, complexity, dynamicity, and domain specificity. He claims the kinds of problems typically worked in schools tend to be more structured, contextualized, simple, static and domain specific—while real-world problems tend to be unstructured, context independent, complex, dynamic and domain neutral. Real-world problem solutions are hallmarks of "purposeful design and inquiry," fundamental principles of Integrative STEM Education pedagogy proposed by Sanders (2009).

As Butler, et al. (2014) said, "The integration of simple, yet powerful principles of learning into advanced technologies creates the potential to apply effective practices to education systems worldwide" (p. 332). The most exciting result is that as schools react to changes in our students' needs, they are beginning to incorporate ideas and strategies from informal learning environments that have not traditionally intermingled with formal educational institutions. To that end, the *Makerspace* movement has become a cultural phenomenon that is beginning to capture the imagination of educators.

2.2 Informal Education

Across the US, informal education has rapidly emerged as a way to provide opportunities for students to engage in meaningful learning outside of school. Lai, Khaddage, and Knezek (2013) suggested educators consider the "importance of recognizing students' technology-enhanced informal learning experiences and develop pedagogies to connect students' formal and informal learning experiences, in order to meet the demands of the knowledge society" (p. 414). Further, they consider a new way of thinking about learning within the concept of a learning ecology, which proposes "While students learn differently in school and out-of-school settings, learning can take place across boundaries, and what has been learned out of school can help shape what is learned in school" (p. 415). Cox (2013) reminded us that "research into students' use of technologies outside formal settings has shown that many students use it outside school even more than in school, and learning outside school is equally important in young peoples' development" (p. 15).

In a number of locations, informal education has rapidly developed in an effort to provide opportunities to students outside of school. Hung, Lee, and Lim (2012) define formal education as "school curriculum in which learning might be characterized as focusing on structured content, extrinsic motivation, and strict assessments" (p. 1072) and informal education as less structured activities, in which learning outcomes might not be explicitly foregrounded. Time and space is given for exploration, experimentation, developing interests, and intrinsic motivations. Assessments are less formal and might take the form of peer-recognition and critique to co-inform like-minded peers in their pursuits (p. 1072).

2.3 Bridging the Formal and Informal

Barron (2006) submitted that the literature on the importance of authenticity to learning is focused on either the formal or informal curriculum; therefore, it is important to look more closely at the interaction between the two. Literature on informal learning suggests that participants are "inclined to tinker, experiment, and 'mess around' with things as settings are relaxed and the stakes are low" (Hung et al., 2012, pp. 1077–78). More importantly, we agree with scholars who believe that it is important to find ways to blend the two (Shimic & Jevremovic, 2012). Erstad (2012) encouraged a view of "learning lives" as a way to examine all aspects of the ways learning occurs throughout one's life experiences. She reported that youths' time is consumed by formal school and media use, and suggested that "young people as learners move between different contexts of learning, both offline and online, in a constant flow of activity" (p. 26).

2.4 Makerspaces

Makerspaces, sometimes also referred to as hackerspaces, or fablabs, are creative, do-it-yourself spaces where people can gather to create, invent, and learn. Makerspaces are "places where learners have the opportunity to explore their own interests, to tinker, create, invent, and build…" (Fleming, 2015, p. 2) using a wide variety of physical and digital tools and materials. In libraries, they often have 3-D printers, software, electronics, craft and hardware supplies and tools, and more. While these began as community resources and in nonacademic settings, educational entities have quickly adopted the model; at first, only universities were developing them. Makerspaces were originally community-operated workspaces where people with common interests in computers, cooking, machining, fabrication, robotics, technology, science, digital art, or electronic art could meet, socialize, and collaborate. Although the topics may be disparate, they share "commitment to open exploration, intrinsic interest and creative ideas" (Peppler & Bender, 2013, p. 23). Makerspaces are located in community centers, libraries, museums, schools, and other formal and informal settings; while these began as community resources in nonacademic landscapes, educational entities have quickly adopted the model. Now we are seeing them begin to proliferate in K–12 too.

There is also a relationship between the maker movement and the effort to increase STEM-related curriculum and interest in STEM careers and to move beyond current careers to "make their own jobs and industries" (Peppler & Bender, 2013, p. 23). Hatch (2014) suggests the maker movement is actually an "internet of physical things" (p. 3) with physical objects connected via sensors to the internet. Martinez and Stager (2013) suggest that "making" is a pedagogical orientation; its strength is integrating creativity and imagination with design and encourages problem-finding in addition to problem solving. Further, making appears to stimulate creativity (Mitra, Dangwal, Chatterjee, Jha, Bisht, & Kapur, 2014).

New Milford, NJ high school, established a Makerspace in its media center and allows students to visit and work there whenever they have free time. Library media specialist, Laura Fleming, reported that it cost about $1,500 to get started since many items were donated. She says the students often start projects, but when they go home, they investigate further. In a school near Pittsburgh, PA, learners have the opportunity to build robots. The librarian/English teacher in the Cornell school district is using robotics kits in the classroom to build characters from stories students read. Using cardboard, pipe cleaners, and whatever else they come up with, along with the equipment in the kits created by Carnegie Mellon's create lab (motors, led lights, digital sensors), learners bring their characters to life. These represent just a few of the educators who are turning to hands-on projects that are part of the maker movement, including a growing network of do-it-yourself (DIY) enthusiasts. These teachers are leveraging learners' natural inclination to tinker and encouraging them to create projects from marshmallow cannons to hovercrafts that provide excellent learning opportunities.

3. CONCLUSION

Schools and schooling must adapt over time to meet the ever-changing needs of society, and the learners they serve. Informal learning contexts can motivate and engage learners by drawing on their interests and providing flexible social learning environments that promote active participation and meaningful learning through authentic activity. Conceptualizing, designing and creating products that meet real needs to address real problems provide excellent opportunities for learners to engage in the work of scientists, engineers, technologists and mathematicians and explore the relationships among them.

REFERENCES

ABET Engineering Accreditation Commission. (1997). *Engineering Criteria 2000 (EC2000).* ABET Engineering Accreditation Commission, Baltimore, USA.

American Association for the Advancement of Science. (1993). *Benchmarks for science literacy, Project 2061.* American Association for the Advancement of Science, Washington, DC, USA.

Barron, B. (2006). Interest and self-sustained learning as catalysts of development: A learning ecology perspective. *Human Development*, Vol. 49, pp. 193-224.

Bruning, R. H., Schraw, J. G., Norby, M. M., & Ronning, R. R. (2004). *Cognitive psychology and instruction.* Pearson, Columbus, OH, USA.

Butler, A. C., Marsh, E. J., Slavinsky, J. P., & Baraniuk, R. G. (2014). Integrating cognitive science and technology improves learning in a STEM classroom. *Educational Psychology Review,* Vol. 26, No. 2, pp. 331–340.

Cohen, D. K. (1990). Teaching practice: Plus ca change. In P. W. Jackson (Ed.), *Contributing to educational change: Perspectives on research and practice* (pp. 27-84). McCutcheon, Berkley, USA.

Cox, M. (2013). Formal to informal learning with IT: Research challenges and issues for e-learning. *Journal of Computer Assisted Learning,* Vol. 28, No. 1, pp. 85-105.

Erstad, O. (2012). The learning lives of digital youth: Beyond the formal and informal. *Oxford Review of Education,* Vol. 38, No. 1, pp. 25-43.

Fleming, L. (2015). *Worlds of making: Best practice for establishing a MakerSpace in your school.* Corwin, Thousand Oaks, CA, USA.

Hatch, M. (2014). *The maker movement manifesto: Rules for innovation in the new world of crafters, hackers, and tinkerers.* McGraw-Hill, New York, USA.

Hung, D., Lee, S.-S., & Lim, K. Y. T. (2012). Authenticity in learning for the twenty-first century: Bridging the formal and the informal. *Educational Technology Research and Development,* Vol. 60, pp. 1071-1091.

International Technology Education Association. (1996). *Technology for all Americans: A rationale and structure for the study of technology.* International Technology Education Association, Reston, VA, USA.

Jonassen, D. H. (2011). *Learning to Solve Problems: A Handbook for Designing Problem-Solving Learning Environments.* Taylor and Francis, New York, USA.

Lai, K.-W., Khaddage, F., & Knezek, G. (2013). Blending student technology experiences in formal and informal learning. *Journal of Computer Assisted Learning,* Vol. 29, pp. 414-425.

Lortie, D. C. (1975) *Schoolteacher: A Sociological Study.* The University of Chicago, Chicago, USA.

Martinez, S. L., & Stager, G. S. (2013). *Invent to learn: Making, tinkering, and engineering in the classroom.* Constructing Modern Knowledge Press, Torrance, CA, USA.

Mitra, S., Dangwal, R., Chatterjee, S., Jha, S., Bisht, R., & Kapur, P. (2014). Acquisition of computing literacy on shared public computers: Children and the "hole in the wall." *Australasian Journal of Educational Technology,* Vol. 21, pp. 407-426.

National Council of Teachers of Mathematics. (1989). *Curriculum and evaluation standards for school mathematics.* National Council of Teachers of Mathematics, Reston, VA, USA.

National Council of Teachers of Mathematics. (2000). *Principles and standards for school mathematics.* National Council of Teachers of Mathematics, Reston, VA, USA.

Peppler, K., & Bender, S. (2013). Maker movement spreads innovation one project at a time. *Kappan,* Vol. 95, No. 3, pp. 22-27.

Richardson, V., Anders, P., Tidwell, D., & Lloyd, C. (1991). The relationship between teachers' beliefs and practices in reading comprehension. *American Educational Research Journal*, Vol. 28, No. 3, pp. 559-586.

Sanders, M. (2009). STEM, STEM education, STEM mania. *Technology Teacher*, Vol. 68, No. 4, pp. 20–26.

Shimic, G., & Jevremovic, A. (2012). Problem-based learning in formal and informal learning environments. *Interactive Learning Environments,* Vol. 20, pp. 351-367.

NEW SCENARIOS FOR AUDIENCE RESPONSE SYSTEMS IN UNIVERSITY LECTURES

Daniel Schön, Stephan Kopf, Melanie Klinger and Benjamin Guthier
University of Mannheim, Germany

ABSTRACT

Mobile devices like smartphones and tablet PCs are widely used among university students and can be used for audience response systems (clicker systems) to improve teaching. Modern implementations of these systems are no longer limited to plain multiple-choice questions, but enable the lecturers to perform a variety of teaching scenarios. We present and discuss two novel extensions for audience response systems, namely *message boards* and *teacher controlled self-learning tasks*. In the former, students can use their mobile device to make comments and ask questions related to a lecture, which are then discussed directly during class. The second extension can be used to build multi-stage learning and exercise scenarios that accompany the lecture. These two techniques bring new pedagogical and technical questions with them. We discuss their large potential and point out some pitfalls we have encountered in our experiments.

KEYWORDS

Audience Response Systems, Audience Feedback, Mobile Devices, Self-Learning

1. INTRODUCTION

Smartphones and tablet PCs are in widespread use among today's students. These devices are permanently used for communication and socializing, and students will swiftly shift their focus to them, as soon as their interest in the lecturer's presentation diminishes. Even though such usage may be undesirable during a lecture, the overwhelming availability of mobile devices can be used successfully in audience response systems (ARS) to overcome the students' fading attention and to enrich teaching. The functionality of these systems has been improving constantly in recent years, and they are no longer limited to plain multiple-choice questions. Message boards and collaborative applications can be used in classrooms nowadays, which raise novel pedagogical and technical questions. When we developed our novel quiz application, the *MQ2* (Schön, 2016) with the capability to support advanced teaching scenarios, we experienced large potential as well as some shortcomings. Out of our developed enhancements, *message board* scenarios and *teacher controlled self-learning tasks* seem particularly promising. In this paper, we present these two extensions of our audience response system and discuss the feedback we got from students and lecturers during the past four semesters.

2. RELATED WORK

With almost every new evolving technology, approaches are made to use it for teaching and learning; mobile devices are no exception. The first available smart pocket PCs brought up the idea to implement device-independent applications to perform quizzes within university lectures. As one of the first systems, Scheele et al. presented the Wireless Interactive Learning (WIL/MA) system to support interactive lectures (Scheele, 2005). It consists of a central server and client software for pocket PCs. A quiz, a chat, a feedback tool, and a call-in module are supported by the system. Major disadvantages are the requirements of a Java compatible hand-held device and the effort to manually install the client software.

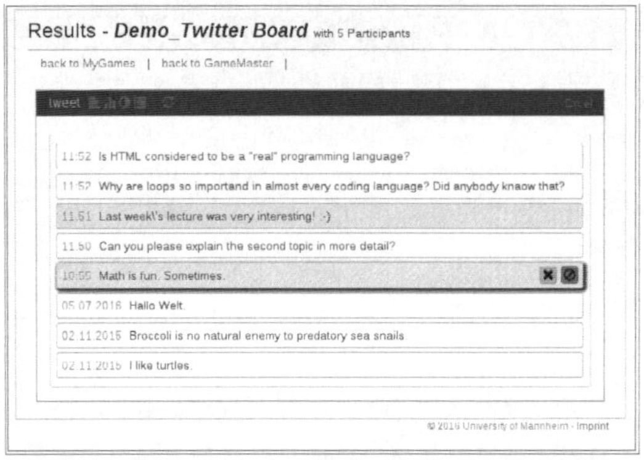

Figure 1. Example of a Message Board with students' comments about live programming in an exercise lecture

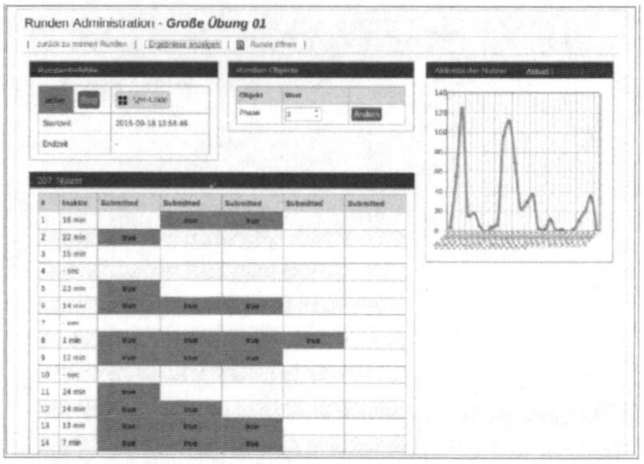

Figure 2. The overview page while running a quiz with five phases. The lecturer can see how many students already submitted the right answers as green colored fields

With the advancement of mobile technologies and hand-held electronic devices, more and more applications have been developed and deployed which run directly on the students' mobile devices (e.g. Abramson, 2013 and Adam, 2014). Most systems use a similar architectural structure: a dedicated interface to create the content and an application for the students' devices that enables the answering and response to the central interface.

Applications like *Clicker* (Rajavel, 2014) or *QuizIt* (Adam, 2014) are only a few examples of the bring-your-own-device era. Abramson et al. showed in 2013 that 86% of undergraduate students at American colleges and universities use laptop computers, while 62% of those students use a smartphone. Buchholz revealed in 2016, that already more than 90% of the questioned students owned smartphones. Therefore, making use of all these mobile devices is an obvious and economic step. By now, the mobile devices evolved in technical functionality and propagation. They not only allow an easy interaction with the device, but also support the visualization and playback of multimedia content like audio, text, images, or videos (e.g. Schön, 2012). This new generation of lightweight ARS can also be used more easily in combination with different learning materials like lecture recordings and e-books (Vinaja, 2014). As students now carry their voting devices anyway and modern ARS usually communicate via the Internet, it became easy to virtually enlarge the classroom and decouple feedback from time and location. Students can participate remotely in virtual lectures or repeat quizzes for themselves when watching a video recording of the lecture.

With the ease of developing Web-based ARS, dozens of new clicker systems appeared. Some systems only require a Web-server where the new applications are hosted, so that they are fast to create and cheap to maintain. In their survey of Web-based ARSs, Kundisch et al. presented as many commercial products like *ActiVote*, *eClicker*, or *i>clicker*, as free software like *PINGO*, *Socrative*, *Kahoot!*, or *inVote* (Kundisch, 2013).

All these systems have in common that they can enrich learning by activating students, by giving the lecturer feedback on the learning progress, and by providing variety in teaching and thereby reducing boredom. But they are very limited in the variety of supported scenarios as they are mostly focused on plain question scenarios. However, the more flexible the systems are, the more useful they can be for teaching as they can be adapted to the lecturer's needs.

3. ADVANCED AND CUSTOMIZED AUDIENCE RESPONSES

In contrast to the applications mentioned above, our novel ARS, the *MobileQuiz2* is capable of performing a large variety of different quiz scenarios on the students' mobile devices. Besides standard single and multiple-choice questions, it supports individual customized quizzes that are defined by a set of rules. Therefore, it enables lecturers to individually customize their quiz scenarios or to create new ones. Among the already created ones are survey scenarios using a Likert-scale, presentation evaluations, and dynamic game-theory experiments. The two most interesting scenarios that we created so far are the *message board* and the *teacher controlled self-learning tasks*.

3.1 Message Board

The *Message Board* is a scenario that supports real-time commentaries from students. The Web-based client provides a short textual description, a text input field, and a submit button. Students enter a comment into the text input field and submit it to the server. The comments are visualized on a Twitter-like message board, where the latest post is shown on top of the list. Figure 1 shows the message board with two highlighted comments that was used in a large computer science exercise in the Fall semester of 2015. About eighty students participated in the lecture. The lecturer explained the exercises while doing live programming of the solutions. The students had the possibility to give feedback to the lecturer and to ask questions by using the message board. After the teacher developed an example code snippet, he evaluated the comments and displayed them in front of the classroom. Within the first ten minutes of one lecture, thirty comments were received and the feedback was discussed immediately. This form of interaction with the lecturer allows students to ask questions, which they are too shy to ask in a large classroom, or to give a dynamic input to the current topic. The teacher can incorporate the questions and comments into the lecture and adapt it to the current needs of the students.

Unfortunately, the perceived anonymity can also lead to annoying behavior, if the messages are not controlled. In our experiment, some students got bored halfway through the lecture and started submitting disruptive messages to the board. Seeing this content on the classroom projection motivated other students to send similar unwanted comments. To prevent the misuse of the system, the lecturer's ability to block inappropriate comments, to highlight noteworthy ones, and to ban students from participation was added. Filtering through the messages in addition to the regular teaching causes an additional cognitive load on the lecturer, especially in large courses.

3.2 Teacher Controlled Self-Learning Tasks

The second scenario enables lecturers to switch through several quiz phases with different tasks that build upon one another. Each phase is started separately. In the scenario of our experiment, the lecturer of the computer science exercise explains the process of converting binary numbers into the decimal and hexadecimal system. The students open the quiz and are presented with the task of converting a given decimal number into the binary system. The answer is entered into a text-field and submitted to the server. The results are evaluated automatically and the students get direct feedback. In the case of an incorrect answer, a second attempt can be made. By using this quiz, students are able to practice the conversion by themselves. The lecturer can watch a list of submitted results as seen in Figure 2 and obtains immediate feedback about the students' level of skill at number conversion. After a discussion of the calculations and the correct results, the lecturer introduces a more complex conversion problem and starts the next quiz phase. The tasks shown on the students' devices change automatically and the students are challenged with a more difficult conversion problem. By continuously being guided through multiple phases of exercises with increasing difficulty, the students are able to practice the learning content and difficulties can be identified and discussed immediately as they arise. Additionally, the tracking of ones student's answers in the course of the phases enables the teacher to identify correlations in the answering behavior. These can reveal causes of students' problems with the contents and needs for additional explanations. So if, for example, many students are not able to answer phase 2 and 5 correctly, there could be a need to go once again back to the more basic contents needed in phase 2.

3.3 Discussion

We performed a separate feedback scenario at the end of the semester, where the students evaluated the steady variety of the mobile teaching scenarios. The lecturer's opinion was collected continually after every scenario usage. Lecturer and students state, that the new scenarios for audience response systems enhance the existing e-learning activities greatly. The participants report seeing the benefit and would like to use more of such scenarios. Nevertheless, several technical limitations of the developed system were recognized. Compared to our basic audience response system, the advanced applications do not scale well and there were complaints about the performance of the system. We observed this problem when more than about 50 students used a complex scenario. Regardless of the scalability issue, the potential of the novel audience response systems is high. Even after experiencing significant performance problems, some lecturers kept using novel audience response scenarios and created new tasks for their future courses. So the interest in and the need for new teaching methods are obviously high, especially when they enable lecturers to customize the teaching on learners' needs by easily accessible means as students' mobile devices.

4. CONCLUSION

We presented two novel scenarios for audience response systems that we developed and tested in different lectures. The message board allows students in large lectures to interact with the teacher and to ask questions and provide feedback. The lecturer can incorporate the feedback into the lecture and adapt the teaching to students' needs. But our experience shows that the messages should be filtered, so that only the appropriate ones are presented in the classroom.

The teacher controlled self-learning tasks are multi-stage learning and exercise scenarios that students use in class. They give students the ability to test their own understanding of the presented material, and allow the lecturer to adapt the pace of the lecture based on students' performance. Unfortunately, they also demand higher requirements on the technical implementation. But they allow a more direct and better-monitored guidance through a set of tasks than usual single phased quizzes.

REFERENCES

Abramson D. et al, 2013. Classroom response systems in higher education: Meeting user needs with NetClick. In *2013 IEEE Global Engineering Education Conference (EDUCON)*, Berlin, Germany, pp. 840-846.

Adam D. et al, 2014. Do Your Students Get It? Quiz It! The Android Classroom Response System. In *2014 IEEE 14th International Conference on Advanced Learning Technologies*, Athens, Greek, pp. 168-170.

Buchholz, A. et al, 2016. Smartphone use and perceptions among medical students and practicing physicians. In *Journal of Mobile Technology in Medicine*, Vol. 5, Issue 1, pp. 27-32.

Kundisch D. et al, 2013, Classroom Response Systems. In *Informatik-Spektrum*, Vol. 36, No. 4, pp. 389-393.

Llamas-Nistal M. et al, 2012, Web-based Audience Response System using the educational platform called BeA. In *2012 International Symposium on Computers in Education (SIIE)*, Andorra la Vella, Andorra, pp. 1-6.

Jagar M. et al, 2012. AuResS: The audience response system. In *ELMAR, 2012 Proceedings*, Zadar, Croatia, pp. 171-174.

Rajavel D. and Kushalkar R., 2014. Clicker: Device Independent Student Response System, Developed for Classroom and Remote Learning to Provide Instant Response and Feedback. In *2014 IEEE Sixth International Conference on Technology for Education*, Clappana, India, pp. 62-65.

Scheele N. et al, 2005. Experiences with Interactive Lectures: Considerations from the Perspective of Educational Psychology and Computer Science. In *Proceedings of the 2005 Conference on Computer Support for Collaborative Learning: Learning 2005: The Next 10 Years!*, CSCL '05, pp. 547-556.

Schön D. et al, 2012. A lightweight mobile quiz application with support for multimedia content. *e-Learning and e-Technologies in Education (ICEEE), 2012 International Conference on*, Lodz, 2012, pp. 134-139.

Schön D. et al, 2016. Customizable Learning Scenarios for Students' Mobile Devices in Large University Lectures: A Next Generation Audience Response System. In *Computer Supported Education: 7th International Conference, CSEDU 2015, Lisbon, Portugal, May 23-25, 2015, Revised Selected Papers,* Springer International Publishing, Cham, pp. 189-207.

Vinaja R., 2014. The Use of Lecture Videos, eBooks, and Clickers in Computer Courses. *Journal of Computing Sciences in Colleges*, Vol. 30, No. 2, pp. 23-32.

ACADEMIC RETENTION: RESULTS FROM A STUDY IN AN ITALIAN UNIVERSITY COURSE

Maria Lidia Mascia[1], Mirian Agus[1], Maria Assunta Zanetti[2], Eliano Pessa[2],
and Maria Pietronilla Penna[1]
[1]Department of Pedagogy, Psychology, Philosophy, University of Cagliari, Italy
[2]Department of Brain and Behavioural Sciences, University of Pavia, Italy

ABSTRACT

This study analyzes the possible influences of some individual variables related with the attendance of specific online laboratory activities on the academic retention and achievement of a group of freshmen attending the first year of the Bachelor of Education. Online platforms allowed students both to use a supporting network and autonomously taking advantage of suitable materials to achieve their learning goals and to bridge an orientation gap that often, in Italy, is present in the transition between high school and University. In general, we can say that the experience of the online laboratory was positive and represented a supporting element for these students.

KEYWORDS

Drop-out; Online laboratory; Freshmen; Self-regulation; Academic retention.

1. INTRODUCTION

Frequently, the so-called drop-out phenomenon among early University leavers coincides with a lack of adaptation to the new context (Allen & Seaman 2011). An in-depth review and analysis of the academic system in the Italian and the European scenario evidenced the role of the student within a new reality and which can be the advantages that a student can have from these constant changes (Afonso et al. 2007; Braga et al. 2013). In this regard we remember that in Italy the high school-University transition is particularly deficient with respect to the international context (Malaspina & Rimm-Kaufman 2015). One of the weakness point in the Italian University system is that there is not an educational continuum from the upper secondary school to University. The educational goal of both systems is the same; however, they differ in the degree of organizational complexity. Indeed, the university attendance requires students to take a more active and self-regulating role with respect to secondary school. In this regard, many theories focus on the analysis of sociological and organizational factors, while others take into greater account the individual aspects. Anyway, we lack the individuation of a single variable that can explain retention process, since we need to take into consideration most variables reciprocally interacting: What appears evident is a lack of a model accounting for these interactions. Besides, we remark that, actually, the models that attempt to account for the maintenance of choice and achievement of academic success have been mainly introduced in an Anglo-Saxon context (Harvey et al. 2006).

In this contribution, the principal aim is to investigate some psychological and individual dimensions related to the academic success or failure. Among the variables present in the literature, we take into account the role of motivation, self-concept, perception of the time perspective and self-regulation (Ryan & Deci 2004; Moliterni et al. 2011; de Bilde et al. 2011; Di Benedetto & Zimmerman 2010; Lehmann et al. 2014). As international and national literature states that it is necessary (above all in the first year) to support students in order to promote retention and to enhance students engagement (Box et al. 2012) we also took into account the influence of some university educational supports, with particular reference to e-learning (Mohamad et al. 2013), which can be a motivational stimulus if backed up by frontal lectures (Penna & Stara 2009). In particular, we made reference to a online laboratory of the Cagliari University. Within our study, two specific hypotheses have been formulated. Hypothesis 1: is it present a positive correlation between academic self-concept, motivation, self-regulation, time perspective, frequency at the online laboratory and the academic success? Hypothesis 2: is it possible to assess the validity of a retention model based on the association between the observed variables?

2. METHOD

2.1 Participants

One hundred and eighty five freshmen, enrolled in the first year of the degree course in Education Science (University of Cagliari), took part in the study. The sample consisted of 174 females and 11 males aged between 19 and 54 years (M = 24.37; SD = 6.32). Students came from different high schools, with percentages of 37.3% from high schools, 18.9% from technical schools, 43.2% from secondary school diploma with specialization in teacher training. In the current study 28% were from the municipality (Cagliari), 52% from the province and 20% from outside the province of Cagliari. Finally, 71% of the sample had a low average high school diploma grade, while 29% of the sample had a high average high school diploma grade.

2.2 Materials

Students were presented a standardized multidimensional questionnaire, constituted by: *Academic Motivation Scale* (Alivernini & Lucidi 2008); *Self-Description Questionnarie III* (Marsh & O'Neill 1984); *Self-regulation questionnaire* (Moè & De Beni, 2000); *Stanford Time Perspective Inventory – short form* (D'Alessio et al. 2003).

The online laboratory was supporting the General Psychology class.. The proposed activities supported students in their studies and provided guidance during their first academic year. The laboratory provides for the presence of the online tutor as manager and supervisor of contents and interactions (Rotta & Ranieri 2005; Michinov et al. 2011; Mattana 2014). The class was entirely available on the University Moodle platform (moodle.unica.it). The activities were those allowed by the platform, namely forum, documents, chat, and learning objects on topics already covered. The tutor also answered orientation questions. In this study, academic success was measured through the number of credits reached by the student at the end of the first academic year.

2.3 Procedure

The questionnaire was given in a single administration, in paper format and the distribution has been collective. Students were tested in one session during the first semester, and were divided in two groups: participants only to frontal lectures and participants both to frontal lectures and to Moodle online laboratory.

3. RESULTS

The observed variables were represented by the values of nine indicators: Lab (attendance to the laboratory), Academic Success (number of obtained credits), Academic Self (assessment of academic self-concept), Amotivation (degree of amotivation in Academic Motivation Scale), Intrinsic Motivation (degree of intrinsic motivation in Academic Motivation Scale), Autoregulation (assessment of self-regulation ability), Hedonistic Present (assessment of tendency towards Hedonistic Present attitude in Stanford Time Perspective Inventory), Fatalistic Present (assessment of tendency towards Fatalistic Present attitude in Stanford Time Perspective Inventory), Future (assessment of tendency towards Future attitude in Stanford Time Perspective Inventory). In relation to the *hypothesis 1* the analysis of the matrix of correlations between variables shown below (see Table 1) evidences the emergence of positive associations between high levels of self-regulation and future time perspective. This characterizes a behavior dominated by an effort to achieve goals and future rewards, participation in the laboratory, intrinsic motivation, academic success and good academic self-concept. We also observe a positive correlation between intrinsic motivation, academic self-concept and participation to the online laboratory activities, as well as with self-regulation and self-concept, and between the latter and the academic success. The data highlight the negative correlations between levels of "amotivation" and intrinsic motivation and future time perspective.

Table 1. Correlation among variables observed (*p<.05 - *p<.01)

	1	2	3	4	5	6	7	8
1 Lab	*1*							
2 Academic success	*,199***	*1*						
3 Academic self	*0,002*	*0,075*	*1*					
4 Amotivation	*0,048*	*-0,045*	*-0,027*	*1*				
5 Intrinsic Motivation	*0,052*	*0,14*	*,220***	*-,461***	*1*			
6 Autoregulation	*0,105*	*,216***	*0,075*	*-,165**	*,389***	*1*		
7 Hedonistic present	*0,125*	*-0,058*	*-0,06*	*0,063*	*-0,124*	*-0,089*	*1*	
8 Fatalistic present	*-,227***	*-0,072*	*-0,056*	*0,022*	*-0,079*	*-0,083*	*,679***	*1*
9 Futur	*-0,036*	*,164**	*,188**	*-0,116*	*,706***	*,438***	*-,213***	*-,195***

The values present in the correlation table and the use of a Path Analysis allow proposing a retention model, whose logical structure is depicted below (see *Figure 1*).

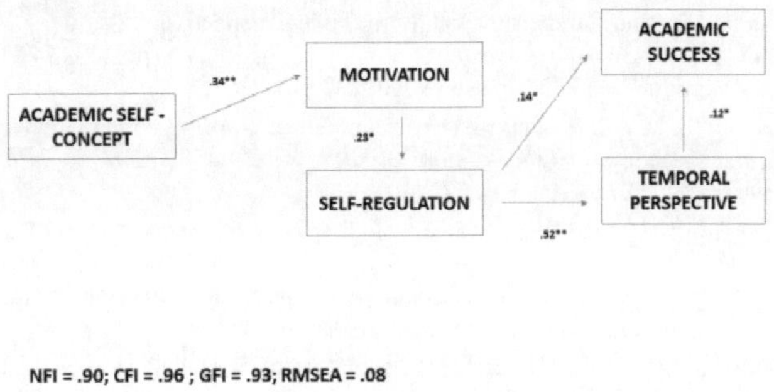

Figure 1. Path Analysis Model

The model shows a causal relationship between high self-concept and self-determined motivation. The high self-concept influences positively the ability to self-regulate in studies, which, in turn, affects both the success in studies and future time perspective of the student. The latter finally has a positive weight on academic achievement. This path analysis is interesting because it shows the influences among variables in order to create an interrelation system and a set of tools in order to support academic success and retention.

4. DISCUSSION AND CONCLUSIONS

The maim results confirm the evaluations carried out during the previous years of experience of the online laboratory, highlighting the benefits perceived by the involved students, useful in promoting an approach towards a more self-regulated study and an academic achievement

Data on laboratory attendance show that students had benefits in terms of strengthening and growth of all variables considered as crucial for the development of academic success and retention in the university system. Today, both through the activity of the online laboratory and its data collection work (in more University courses), we are allowed to pursue the goal of finding a model that can support the academic success in the Italian context and can be the base to create a solid bridge between high school and University.

REFERENCES

Afonso, M.C.G. et al., 2007. El abandono de los estudios universitarios: factores determinantes y medidas preventivas. *Dropout in university studies: determinant factors and preventives measures.*, (236), pp.71–85.

Alivernini, F. & Lucidi, F., 2008. The Academic Motivation Scale (AMS): Factorial structure, invariance and validity in the Italian context. *TPM*, 15(4), pp.211–220.

Allen, I.E. & Seaman, J., 2011. Going the Distance: Online Education in the United States, 2011. *Sloan Consortium (NJ1).*

Belloc, F., Maruotti, A., & Petrella, L., 2010. University drop-out: an Italian experience. *Higher Education*, 60(2), pp.127-138.

Di Benedetto, M. & Zimmerman, B., 2010. The International Journal of Educational and Psychological Assessment Special Issue on Assessing Learning Context and leanring Strategies Time Taylor Academic Journals International. *The International Journal of Educational and Psychological Assessment*, 5.

de Bilde, J., Vansteenkiste, M. & Lens, W., 2011. Understanding the association between future time perspective and self-regulated learning through the lens of self-determination theory. *Learning and Instruction*, 21(3), pp.332–344.

Box, G. et al., 2012. University First Year Advisors: A network approach for first year student transition and retention. A Practice Report. *The International Journal of the First Year in Higher Education ISSN The International Journal of the First Year in Higher Education*, 3(31), pp.1838–2959.

Braga, M. et al., 2013. Educational policies in a long-run perspective. *Economic Policy*, 28(73), pp.45–100.

D'Alessio, M. et al., 2003. Testing Zimbardo's Stanford Time Perspective Inventory (STPI) -Short Form: An Italian Study. *Time & Society*, 12(2), pp.333–347. Available at: http://tas.sagepub.com/cgi/doi/10.1177/0961463X030122010.

Harvey, L., Drew, S. & Smith, M., 2006. The first-year experience: briefing paper, overview for higher education policy makers and practitioners. *Higher Education Academy, York. http://www. heacademy. ac. uk/assets/York/documents/ourwork/research/FYE/w eb0577_the_first_year_experience_overview_for_higher_education_policy_m akers_and_practitioners. pdf(Last accessed March 2009).*

Lehmann, T., Hähnlein, I., & Ifenthaler, D., 2014. Cognitive, metacognitive and motivational perspectives on preflection in self-regulated online learning. *Computers in human behavior*, 32, pp. 313-323.

Malaspina, D. & Rimm-Kaufman, S.E., 2015. Early Predictors of School Performance Declines at School Transition Points. *http://dx.doi.org/10.1080/19404476.2008.11462052.*

Marsh, H. & O'Neill, R., 1984. Self description questionnaire III: the construct validity of multidimensional self - concept ratings by late adolescents. *Journal of Educational Measurement*, 21(2), pp.153–174. Available at: http://doi.wiley.com/10.1111/j.1745-3984.1984.tb00227.x.

Mattana, V., 2014. L'e-tutor in Italia: una rassegna della letteratura scientifica. *Form@re, Open Journal per la formazione in rete*, 14, pp.38–48. Available at: http://www.fupress.com/formare.

Meggiolaro, S., Giraldo, A., & Clerici, R., 2015. A multilevel competing risks model for analysis of university students' careers in Italy. *Studies in Higher Education*, pp. 1-16.

Michinov, N. et al., 2011. Procrastination, participation, and performance in online learning environments. *Computers & Education*, 56(1), pp.243–252.

Moè, A., & De Beni, R., 2000. Strategie di autoregolazione e successo scolastico: Uno studio con ragazzi di scuola superiore e universitari. *Psicologia dell'Educazione e della Formazione*, 2(1), pp. 31-44.

Mohamad, S.K. et al., 2013. Pattern of reflection in learning Authoring System through blogging. *Computers & Education*, 69, pp.356–368.

Ofori, R. & Charlton, J.P., 2002. A path model of factors influencing the academic performance of nursing students. *Journal of Advanced Nursing*, 38(5), pp.507–515. Available at: http://doi.wiley.com/10.1046/j.1365-2648.2002.02212.x.

Penna, M.P. & Stara, V., 2009. Opinions on computers, and efficacy of a computer-based learning: A pilot study. *Education and Information Technologies*, 15(3), pp.181–204. Available at: http://www.scopus.com/inward/record.url?eid=2-s2.0-77954144394&partnerID=tZOtx3y1.

Porter, S. R., & Swing, R. L., 2006. Understanding how first-year seminars affect persistence. *Research in Higher Education*, 47(1), pp.89-109.

Rotta, M. & Ranieri, M., 2005. *E-tutor: identità e competenze. Un profilo professionale per l'e-learning*, Edizioni Erickson.

Ryan, R.M. & Deci, E.L., 2004. Autonomy is no illusion. *Handbook of experimental existential psychology*, pp.449–479.

LEARNING HOW TO WRITE AN ACADEMIC TEXT: THE EFFECT OF INSTRUCTIONAL METHOD AND REFLECTION ON TEXT QUALITY

Janneke van der Loo, Emiel Krahmer and Marije van Amelsvoort
Tilburg center for Cognition and Communication, Tilburg University, The Netherlands

ABSTRACT

In this paper we present preliminary results on a study on the effect of instructional method (observational learning and learning by doing) and reflection (yes or no) on academic text quality and self-efficacy beliefs. 56 undergraduate students were assigned to either an observational learning or learning-by-doing condition, with or without reflection. The participants were tested on academic text quality, self-efficacy beliefs and satisfaction with the instructional method. Our preliminary results suggest that there is no main effect of instructional method on academic text quality and self-efficacy beliefs. Observational learning and learning by doing seem equally effective for learning how to write a large and complex writing assignment, even though participants who learned by doing were more satisfied with the method than participants who learned by observing models. We found no effect of reflection. However, there appears to be an interaction between instructional method and reflection: in observational learning reflection seems to have a negative effect on academic text quality while in learning by doing it appears to have a positive effect. We will repeat the experiment in September 2016.

KEYWORDS

Observational learning, Reflection, Academic Text Quality

1. INTRODUCTION

Writing a coherent and effective text is a complex and demanding task. A writer has to plan ideas, translate these ideas into sentences, and type the sentences on a word processor while monitoring these activities at the same time (Kellogg, 2008). This implies that writers have to carry out different processes, and pay attention to many textual characteristics simultaneously and therefore may lose track of their own thoughts during the process. This applies especially to those who are learning to write: the learner becomes so closely involved in the writing process that hardly any cognitive energy is left for learning from that process. A method that allows for a distinction between writing and learning to write is observational learning (Braaksma, et al., 2004). Observational learning is the process of learning a new task by watching and/or listening how someone else performs this task. Learners should be able to infer others' intentions from action observation, process others' action outcomes and combine these sources of information in order to select behaviors leading to desired outcomes later on (e.g. Monfardini, et al., 2013; Rak, et al., 2013). Various studies have shown the effectiveness of observational learning in the writing domain (e.g. De Wachter, et al., 2015; Rijlaarsdam et al., 2008; Raedts, et al., 2007). Braaksma, et al. (2004) suggest that the effectiveness of observational learning in learning to write is a result from the observers' strong engagement in metacognitive activities. Observers internalize, apply, and develop criteria for effective writing by observing the models' writing, identifying and conceptualizing the writing strategies, evaluating the performance of the models and reflecting on the observed performances.

In the current study we want to investigate whether observational learning would be a suitable method for university students to learn how to write an academic text. Only a handful of studies, all by Raedts and colleagues, have asked this question (e.g., Raedts, et al., 2007). These studies investigated the effects of observational learning with undergraduate students on self-efficacy beliefs and text quality by comparing observational learning with learning without a model (learning by doing). The studies showed that observational learning helped students to bring their self-efficacy beliefs regarding a new writing task to an accurate level. With regards to text quality, the studies showed that students in the observational learning condition outperformed those in the learning-by-doing condition: they linked the source material more often, and wrote better organized literature reviews compared to the students in the learning-by-doing condition (Raedts, et al., 2007). In Raedts, et al. (2007) and most other studies on observational learning, learning through modeling, is compared with learning by doing. In learning by doing, learners put their own knowledge and beliefs on how a certain task should be done into practice, without observing someone else performing the task (Bandura, 1977). The main difference between observational learning and learning by doing is the absence of a model in the latter. However, closer inspection of the methods suggests that there might be a confounding factor; reflection. In observational learning, reflection is often encouraged by asking participants questions about the model's performance. In learning by doing, reflection is not an intrinsic part of the process. Adding reflection to learning-by-doing could therefore make these two types of learning more comparable. Could reflection account for the differences found between observational learning and learning by doing? Reflection within observational learning in the writing domain has been studied by Braaksma, et al. (2002). In their experiment participants observed two models performing a writing task. One group started with the writing task immediately after the observation, whereas two other groups reflected upon the models. Both reflection groups outperformed the no reflection group on the writing tasks. However, this was not compared to learning-by-doing. Additionally, the influence of reflection on learning in general has been studied. Reflection is found to be beneficial under certain circumstances (see i.e. Bulman and Schutz, 2013). Asking learners to monitor or record their performances during their learning process enables them to detect, attribute and correct their errors (Zimmerman and Kitsantas, 2002).

The common belief in educational research seems to be that both observational learning and reflection have a positive effect on learning. However, how reflection interacts with observational learning and learning by doing is not clear yet. This raises the question whether reflection causes the differences between observational learning and learning by doing. In the current study we investigate the effect of instructional method (observational learning, learning by doing) and reflection on academic text quality and writing self-efficacy beliefs. We hypothesize that observational learning positively influences academic text quality and self-efficacy beliefs compared to learning by doing. Secondly, we expect reflection to lead to higher academic text quality and self-efficacy beliefs than no reflection. Thirdly, we hypothesize that reflection reduces the effect of instructional method on academic text quality and self-efficacy. If observational learning proves to be at least as effective as learning by doing, educators could consider this method as part of a flipped classroom environment in which students gather information largely outside of class (Berrett, 2012).

2. METHOD

2.1 Design

A 2 x 2 design was used in this experiment, with instructional method (observational learning, learning by doing) and reflection (yes or no) as the independent variables. In the posttest the effect of instructional method and reflection on academic writing performance, self-efficacy and satisfaction were measured. In this paper we only report preliminary results. Due to the small sample size, we will repeat the experiment in September 2016.

2.2 Participants

The participants were recruited from an obligatory introductory course on academic writing for undergraduate students at a Dutch University. The sample consisted of 56 participants (male = 13, female = 43). The average age was 18,6 years (SD = 1.41). The participants were divided into four tutorial groups. Each group was assigned to one of four conditions: observational learning with reflection (n = 9), observational learning without reflection (n = 10), learning by doing with reflection (n = 19) and learning by doing without reflection (n = 18).

2.3 Materials and Procedures

The interventions took place during the first two tutorials of the academic writing course. All four conditions consisted of two interventions. In the observational learning conditions five videos were shown: two during the first intervention and three in the second intervention. The participants received a handout that contained the introduction to the videos and three index cards that were used in the videos by the actors. The index cards contained a summary of a scientific article, which consisted of the full reference of the article; the research question, the type of research and data; and a summary of the most important findings of the study. The first and third index card represented a similar viewpoint. The second index card contained an opposing view point.

In each video the participants saw two peer models writing an introduction to an academic paper based on these three index cards. Each video focused on a certain aspect of writing an introduction to an academic research paper. See Table 1 for the content of the videos.

Table 1. Content of the Videos and Exercises

Intervention (duration)	Video / Exercise	Content
1 (45 minutes)	1	Reading, selecting, organizing and paraphrasing the information on the index cards
	2	Planning the content and main structure
2 (45 minutes)	3	Writing the body of the introduction
	4	Adding an opening and scientific / social relevance
	5	Revising the text at text, sentence and word level

The models in the videos were student actors who had received a script for each exercise and had been instructed to think aloud during the exercise. One of the models used effective writing strategies to complete the assignments (strong model), the other model used counterproductive strategies (weak model). Each fragment contained a recording of the model working on the computer, the model's voice and the computer screen the model was working on. In the observational learning with reflection condition participants were asked after each video to reflect on what they had seen. They answered questions as: which differences between the two writers did you observe and who do you think was the better writer and why? In the observational learning without reflection condition the instructor started the next video immediately after the previous one. The learning-by-doing condition took place in a computer room. Each participant had access to a computer. The instructor told the participants that they would be writing an introduction to an academic paper based on three index cards by executing five pre-structured exercises: two during intervention 1 and three during intervention 2. The exercises the participants executed were the same as the tasks the student actors performed in the videos. The participants received a handout with the introduction to the exercises and the three index cards they had to use during the exercises. These index cards were identical to the ones the student actors in the videos used. The five exercises were displayed one by one on a screen. In the learning-by-doing condition with reflection participants were asked to reflect on their activities after each exercise. They answered questions such as: How did you handle the last exercise? What would you do differently next time? In the learning-by-doing condition without reflection each exercise was followed immediately by the next one.

2.4 Measures

To measure the participants' academic writing performance after the interventions the first author scored the introduction section of the first paper the participants had to write for the academic writing course. The participants were provided with three index cards similar to the ones used in the interventions. The studies on index card 1 and 3 showed similarities in their results, while the study on index card 2 displayed an opposing viewpoint. The participants were instructed to write an opening for their introduction, to include all three index cards in the body of the introduction and to make sure that the introduction would lead to the research question and hypotheses. The texts were scored on (1) opening paragraph (2) similarity between index card 1 and index card 3 (3) contradiction between index card 1/3 and index card 2 (4) mentioning of scientific relevance (5) mentioning of social relevance and (6) structure in general. For each item two or three points could be appointed which resulted in a possible maximal score of fifteen points. Self-efficacy was measured with ten items of which the participants had to indicate on a scale from 0 (not confident at all) to 100 (very confident) how confident they felt that they were able to perform a certain task. An example of an item is: "I am able to paraphrase information from index cards." The average score (Cronbach's Alpha .88) was used as the participants' self-efficacy score. We also measured the participants' satisfaction with the instructional method with five items of which they had to indicate on a scale from 1 to 5 to what extent they agreed (1 = not at all, 5 = very much). The average score (Cronbach's Alpha .76) was used as the participants' satisfaction score.

3. PRELIMINARY RESULTS AND CONCLUSION

The score on the posttest has been evaluated with an analysis of covariance (ANCOVA) with Instructional Method (learning by doing), observational learning) and Reflection (yes, no) as the independent factors. Due to the small sample size, we only report mean scores here. First, we investigated the effect of instructional method and reflection on academic writing quality. The preliminary results indicate that there are no main effects for instructional method (M_observational learning = 8.17, M_learning by doing = 7.88) and reflection (M_reflection = 8.08, M_no reflection = 7.89) on academic text quality. However, there seems to be an interaction between instructional method and reflection. In observational learning reflection appears to have a negative effect (M = 7.13) compared to no reflection (M = 9.00). In learning by doing the opposite seems to be the case. Reflection appears to have a positive effect (M = 8.56) compared to no reflection (M = 7.24). Secondly, we investigated the effect of instructional method and reflection on self-efficacy beliefs. The preliminary results indicate that there are no main effects of instructional method (M_observational learning = 71.86, M_learning by doing = 70.07) and reflection (M_reflection = 70.05, M_no reflection = 71.36). Also, there seem to be no interactions. Thirdly, we looked at the satisfaction scores. The preliminary results suggest that participants who learn by doing (M = 3.94) are more satisfied with the instructional method than participants who learn by observation (M = 3.35). Reflections seems to have no effect on satisfaction (M_reflection = 3.75, M_no reflection = 3.73). Our preliminary results appear not to support our first two hypotheses. Observational learning does not lead to higher academic text quality or higher self-efficacy beliefs than learning by doing, and neither does reflection compared to no reflection. We have found some evidence for the third hypothesis. There appears to be an interaction between instructional method and reflection. In observational learning reflection seems to have a negative effect on text quality. This is not in line with Braaksma, et al. (2002). In learning by doing however reflection appears to have a positive effect on academic text quality. We hope to be able to draw more founded conclusion after we repeat the experiment.

REFERENCES

Bandura, A., 1977. Self-efficacy: toward a unifying theory of behavioral change. *Psychological Review*, 84(2), p.191.

Berrett, D., 2012. How 'flipping' the classroom can improve the traditional lecture. *The chronicle of higher education*, 12, pp.1-14.

Braaksma, M. A. et al., 2002. Observational learning and the effects of model-observer similarity. *Journal of Educational Psychology*, 94(2), p.405.

Braaksma, M. A. et al., 2004. Observational learning and its effects on the orchestration of writing processes. *Cognition and Instruction*, 22(1), pp.1-36.

Bulman, C. and Schutz, S. ed., 2013. *Reflective Practice In Nursing*. West-Sussex: John Wiley & Sons.

De Wachter, L. et al., 2015. Meaningful and enjoyable writing tasks in an academic writing workshop through observation of peers. *Proceedings of the International CALL Research Conference*. Tarragona, Spain, pp. 223-225

Kellogg, R.T., 2008. Training writing skills: A cognitive developmental perspective. *Journal of Writing Research*, 1(1), pp.1-26

Monfardini, E. et al., 2013. Vicarious neural processing of outcomes during observational learning. *PloS one*, 8(9), e73879.

Rak, N. et al., 2013. Empathy and feedback processing in active and observational learning. *Cognitive, Affective, and Behavioral Neuroscience*, 13(4), pp.869-884.

Raedts, M., et al., 2007. Observational learning through video-based models: impact on student's accuracy of self-efficacy beliefs, task knowledge and writing performances In: G. Rijlaarsdam, Series Ed. and P. Boscolo and S. Hidi, Volume Eds. 2007. *Studies in Writing, Volume 19, Writing and Motivation*. Oxford: Elsevier. pp.219-238.

Rijlaarsdam, et al., 2008. Observation of peers in learning to write, Practice and Research. *Journal of Writing Research*, 1(1), pp.53-83

Zimmerman, B. J., and Kitsantas, A., 2002. Acquiring writing revision and self-regulatory skill through observation and emulation. *Journal of Educational Psychology*, 94(4), p.660.

Reflection Papers

TEACHERS' ATTITUDE TOWARDS ICT USE IN SECONDARY SCHOOLS: A SCALE DEVELOPMENT STUDY

Mehmet Kemal Aydin[1], Ali Semerci[2] and Mehmet Gürol[1]
[1]*Yildiz Technical University,* 34349 Beşiktaş/İstanbul, Turkey
[2]*Ankara University, Dögol Cd., 06560 Tandoğan/Ankara, Turkey*

ABSTRACT

The current study aims to develop a valid and reliable instrument that measures secondary school teachers' attitudes towards ICT use in teaching and learning process. A cross-sectional survey design was employed with a group of 173 teachers. Based on the literature review, a pool of 21 items was proposed and reviewed by a board of experts. As to psychometric quality of the scale, the Cronbach's Alpha coefficient, item total variance and item distinctiveness indices were estimated. The results illustrated that Teachers' ICT Attitudes Scale (TICTAS) has a high level reliability standard ($\alpha = .898$) and also Exploratory and Confirmatory Factor Analyses indicated good goodness of fit estimates. As a result, a reliable and valid scale comprising of 16 items loaded in two factors (ICT willingness and ICT anxiety) was developed.

KEYWORDS

Teachers' ICT attitude, scale development, ICT in education

1. INTRODUCTION

For the last two decades, the integration of ICT in education has been of increasing concern in both developed and developing countries. For example, in the Education and Training 2020 strategy framework, the European Commission strongly emphasized the innovative use of ICT and identified it as a priority and catalyst for achieving transformation in education (Vanderlinde & van Braak, 2010). More recently, with the announcement of large-scale ICT roll outs, not only educational goals of a country, but also many interrelated political, social and economic outcomes have gained currency. In line with this, effective use of ICT in educational context has become closely associated with achieving these interrelated strategic outcomes. In this vein, many countries have been allocating huge budgets on improving ICT infrastructure in schools.

Despite this increasing public spending on ICT tools and ICT infrastructure, Afshari, Bakar, Luan, Samah, & Fooi (2009) argued that "most teachers neither use technology as an instructional delivery system nor integrate technology into their curriculum" (p. 77). Likewise, Yildirim (2007) noted that "most teachers do not use ICT to promote pupils attainment in areas across the curriculum, but they use computers frequently for preparing handouts and tests" (p. 171). In a similar vein, a significant number of research studies illustrate that teachers do not use ICT in teaching and learning process as a mediator of achieving educational outcomes. This leads to a gap between current use of ICT in class and its potential, which signals the teachers' central role in effective use of ICT in teaching and learning. Thus, the teachers ICT attitudes, pedagogical beliefs, ICT skills and training have gained currency and under scrutiny in today's educational settings. As part of this kind research initiative, the current study aimed to measure teachers' attitudes towards ICT use in teaching and learning process.

2. METHODS

2.1 Study Group and Procedure

The current study employed a cross-sectional design to measure teachers' attitudes towards ICT use in class. The Instrument development procedure has been framed by the 8 step scale development procedure proposed by Anderson (1981). In the first step, 18 positive and 18 negative scale items have been formed based on the literature review. Secondly, this pool of 36 items have been reviewed by a board of experts comprising of 2 language expert, 2 ICT in education expert, and 2 scale development and measurement expert. Then, 21-item draft scale has been agreed up on the expert revision. The co-agreed 21-item form was administered to 200 secondary school teachers selected by employing a convenience sampling technique (Creswell, 2012). After eliminating incomplete and faulty responses, the final participating group comprised of 173 teachers, 53% males, 61% younger than 40 years, 60% with less than 15 years of teaching experience.

Prior to statistical analyses, Kaiser-Meyer Olkin (KMO) measure and Barlett Sphericity test have been administered in order to test if the data set is suitable for Factor Analysis. Results illustrated that the data well suits for Factor Analysis (KMO= 0.911, Barlett= [X^2=1245,293, $p< .05$]).

3. FINDINGS

3.1 Exploratory Factor Analysis

As a preliminary analysis, the draft Likert type scale with 21 items has been administered to 105 participating teachers from the target sample. Prior to Principal Components Analaysis (PCA), factor loads with a higher eigenvalues than 1.00 have been explored as well as examining scree plot and explained variance by each factor. The results illustrated that the items have loaded in three factors and total variance explained by these factors are 58,41%. Yet, the Varimax rotated PCA results showed that 5 items have been loaded more than one factor. These 5 items have been omitted and the analysis re-run. The re-run PCA results proposed a two factor solution and total variance explained by these two factors is 53,54%. These two factors are labeled as ICT willingness (11 item) and ICT anxiety (5 item).

3.2 Confirmatory Factor Analysis

The two factor model proposed by the EFA results have been tested employing Confirmatory Factor Analysis along with examining RMSEA, NFI, CFI, IFI indices.

Table 1. Model Fitness Indices

Model	X^2	*df*	*p*	X^2/df	RMSEA	CFI	IFI	NFI
Two Factor Model	186.676	103	.00	1.812	.069	.929	.930	.855
Modified Model	146.880	101	.00	1.454	.051	.961	.961	.886

* $p< .05$

The CFA results illustrated that two factor modified model have better fitness values with modifications. The modifications included correlating the residual error values of items 1 and 19; 5 and 7. Considering that those items are signaling the importance of ICT use in teaching and learning, these modifications have been theoretically confirmed. Table 2 below illustrates the t and R^2 values of the items after CFA.

Table 2. CFA Results and t and R^2 Values for items

Items (ICT willingness)	*t*	*R2*	*Items (ICT anxiety)*	*t*	*R2*
1	4.27	.63	2	4.14	.75
5	4.17	.63	4	4.16	.73
7	4.33	.59	20	4.12	.63
11	4.32	.67	22	4.33	.56
19	4.08	.83	30	3.77	.56
21	4.05	.67			
23	4.08	.83			
27	4.06	.67			
29	3.76	.64			
31	3.05	.42			
35	3.76	.81			

Table 2 illustrates that items 19 and 23 in factor 1, 2 and 4 in factor 2 have made the strongest contribution in measurement of teachers ICT attitude, conversely item 31 in factor 1 and items 22 and 30 in factor 2 have made the weakest contribution in the same endeavor. These results strongly concurred with the EFA and illustrated a high level construct validity of the scale.

As to the psychometric quality of TICTAS, the Cronbach's Alpha coefficient has been estimated for the scale total and factors separately. In line with this, for ICT willingness (11 item) estimated $\alpha = .903$, and for ICT anxiety (5 items) $\alpha = .781$, and for the scale total (16 items) $\alpha = .898$. As a result, TICTAS has showed a high level of reliability standard.

4. CONCLUSION AND IMPLICATIONS

The current study aimed to develop a valid and reliable scale that measures teachers' attitudes towards ICT use in teaching and learning. In this regard, a valid and reliable scale, TICTAS, which measures teachers' attitudes towards ICT use have been developed after administering EFA, CFA and Reliability analysis. The results illustrated that TICTAS have two factors namely ICT willingness and ICT anxiety. TICTAS can be effectively used by researchers who would like to explore the determinants of teachers' ICT use in class.

REFERENCES

Afshari, M., Bakar, K. A., Luan, W. S., Samah, B. A., & Fooi, F. S. (2009). Factors affecting teachers' use of information and communication technology. *International Journal of Instruction*, *2*(1), 77–104.

Anderson, L.W. (1981). *Assessing Affective Characteristics in the Schools*, Boston: Allyn and Bacon.

Buyukozturk, Ş. (2010). *Sosyal Bilimler İçin Veri Analizi El Kitabı: İstatistik, Araştırma Deseni, SPSS Uygulamaları ve Yorum*, 12nd. Edition. Ankara: PEGEM A Yayıncılık.

Vanderlinde, R., & Van Braak, J. (2010). The e-capacity of primary schools: development of a conceptual model and scale construction from a school improvement perspective. *Computers & Education*, *55*(2), 541–553. doi:10.1016/j.compedu.2010.02.016

Yildirim, S. (2007). Current utilization of ICT in Turkish basic education schools: A review of teacher's ICT use and barriers to integration. *International Journal of Instructional Media*, *34*(2), 171–186.

INVENTING THE INVENTED FOR STEM UNDERSTANDING

Alicia Stansell[1], Tandra Tyler-Wood[1] and Christina Stansell[2]
[1]*University of North Texas, Denton TX, United States of America*
[2]*Hasso Plattner Institute Academy, Postdam, Germany*

ABSTRACT

The reverse engineering of simple inventions that were of historic significance is now possible in a classroom by using digital models provided by places like the Smithsonian. The digital models can facilitate the mastery of students' STEM learning by utilizing digital fabrication in maker spaces to provide an opportunity for reverse engineer and the creation of working models of the inventions. Students can start with understanding the original design, and then modify it to create working replicas and proximities showing the understanding of the underlying STEM concepts.

KEYWORDS

Maker space, 3D-printing, digital fabrication, Smithsonian

1. INTRODUCTION

Maker spaces with digital fabrication allow students to make creations that rely on digital technologies to design and help create physical models. Maker spaces vary from location to location, but tend to focus on things such as collaboration for people to share ideas, explore concepts, and craft or create (Moorefield-Lang, 2014). Students can imagine an object, design it digitally, then print, or cut, custom objects to construct, giving physical shape to an idea. In essence, students have the power to act as inventors in these maker spaces. Invention by definition is, "A new device, method, or process developed from study and experimentation." (American Heritage, 1994, p. 441). While students may not always be original inventors in maker spaces, they now have the opportunity to experience a process that parallels original inventors while applying science, technology, math, and engineering (STEM) to their inventions.

The process of inventing what has already been invented is called reverse engineering. The process involves taking apart another object to discover and understand how that object works (Badraslioglu, 2016). The fundamentals of the original object can then be applied to a different, similar product, to save time and energy on making the second, new object (Badraslioglu, 2016). In education, classes strive to teach concepts quickly, effectively, and in a way that transfers knowledge to situations and contexts outside the direct learning environment. Reverse engineering allows for these teaching goals to be met, but does not sacrifice the learning objectives for the students, as they are learning through the act of doing.

Students learn the STEM concepts through their actions of actually applying and doing STEM. Learning by doing is a process that has foundations in Dewey's educational view, and still shows positive learning results in studies today, including: encouraging student engagement, involving critical thinking, problem solving, and collaboration (Dewey, et al., 1915,; Schamk, 1995,; Yazici, et. al 2014). As students are actually building, designing, and creating there is no disconnect between what their hands are accomplishing and the digital version on the screen. Students have a concrete connection to abstract concepts that cannot be easily dismissed from a digital disconnect. Rather, the end object either functions or does not function as a result of how the project was reversed engineered. The act of learning by doing through reverse engineering and product creation with digital fabrication provides a valuable tool base for reaching the educational goals of teaching STEM concepts in a transferable and real life way.

2. REMAKING INVENTIONS

Learning in the digital age provides access to ideas, concepts, and resources that would otherwise be out of reach to the general populace. Some items of historic significance must be carefully preserved through special lighting, limited air exposure, or other means in a singular historical preservation location. These items may now be scanned with a digitizer and be accessible to people all over the world. The access to these items is possible as a 3-dimensional (3D) digital model that may be turned, rotated, broken apart and put back together. Instead of taking a field trip, where educators need to collect permission forms, entrance fees, and transportation to take students to look at objects behind a piece of glass for a few hours, teachers can now use technology to bring those objects into the classroom, allowing students to interact with the objects on a computer screen. Given the time and resources of maker spaces, that are gaining support as a learning tool (Chu, 2016), students and teachers can now re-create historical museum objects, make similar objects, and produce objects that they can physically hold, manipulate, and use in experiments.

2.1 Specific Invention Application

An example of this process is, "the Smithsonian and American Innovations in an Age of Discovery: Teaching Science and Engineering through Historical Reconstruction, (which) uses transformational inventions such as the telegraph, the telephone, and early electric motors as a context for reverse engineering." (Bull, et. al., 2016, p. 490). In this type of project, students manipulate 3D versions of the original inventions and apply science and math concepts to reconstruct these devices in a physical form. The way in which things are made will determine how, and if, the physically printed artifact will work to accomplish the task for which it was designed. Having the 3D model of an invention is not enough to make a printed model work. Students must think through the science and apply what they know to reverse engineer from the given digital 3D model to create their own similar working model.

The early electric motor is an example of an invention that applies many physics concepts in a straightforward way. Constructing a simple working motor requires students to, "investigate and describe the relationship between electric and magnetic fields in applications..." (Texas Education Agency, 2010, 5G) which is a state standard in Texas physics classrooms. To understand how the motor works, critical learning connections must be made. Some of the fundamental concepts to make a working motor have been scaffolded for starting in elementary school science classes. For example, understanding the concept of what materials will conduct electricity and heat versus those that will insulate. Students must understand the differences between conductors and insulators in order to deduce which parts of a motor need to conduct electricity to work, versus the parts of a motor that need to act as an insulator. If students simply print the model with plastic, or cut it out of wooden pieces, the motor will not be able to produce movement. In order to create a design that produces movement, key pieces of the motor need to be conductors to produce an electromagnetic field, and other parts of the design need to be insulators like plastics and woods.

More advanced science concepts that must be understood include magnetic attraction and repulsion and how an electric current produces a magnetic field. Once these concepts are understood, students must take the next step to be able to apply these concepts to create a design that will produce movement. Key pieces of the motor must be able to produce an electromagnetic field and interact with other magnetic fields, including fixed magnets. Students start with reverse engineering the design of the original patented motor at the Smithsonian through the 3D version, to begin considering why the motorwas designed the way it was. Students can refer to the design elements in the 3D version to understand the placement of the various parts of the motor in regards to science principles. As students begin connecting design elements and design choices of the existing model, understanding will develop that indicates that parts of these original inventions were not a decorative or aesthetic choice of the creator, but rather a fundamental and essential part of the invention. The coils in a motor allow the electrical circuit necessary for powering the movement of a motor, but may be otherwise thought as an aesthetically drawing feature. Students do not need to figure out how to apply all these science concepts to an open-ended project, but rather how to reconstruct a motor by going through the process of connecting the science concepts, examining the model design, and hands-on inquiry to see science in action.

Although the basic scientific understandings are fundamental in many complex inventions today, the original inventions have a simplicity that is easy to grasp without having to chunk multiple complex understandings to see results. Looking at the complex applications used today for these same concepts, may seem overwhelming to students who are just beginning to develop such conceptual understandings. Examining some of the original inventions allows students to focus on the basic concepts that allowed for a simple design and a basic application of the underlying STEM concepts. Through reverse engineering these machines and creating similar features through digital fabrication and maker spaces, students apply what they are learning and receive immediate feedback regarding their level of understanding of the concepts at work by seeing the invention work the way it was designed.

3. CONCLUSION

Allowing students to digitally and physically explore some of history's inventions provides insights into fundamental concepts of STEM. Students know they are successfully applying the principals of STEM subjects when they have recreated versions of the original invention. Students may also feel ownership as their inventions draw on the same principles to work, but will not be an identical mechanism, thus providing student ownership of both the invention and furthering their learning. The end result may include student engagement, greater understanding of the content, and appreciation for science and history.

ACKNOWLEDGEMENT

The research was made possible in part by the collaborative NSF grant #1510289.

REFERENCES

American Heritage Dictionary. (3rd ed.). (1994). New York, New York.

Bull, G., Standish, N., Tyler-Wood, T. 2016, Teaching science and engineering through reconstruction of historic events. IEEE 16th International Conference on Advanced Learning Technologies. Austin, TX, United States of America, p. 489 – 492.

Badrasliogl, D. (2016). "Reverse engineering" in introductory physics education. The Physics Teacher, 54, p 314-314. DOI:http://dx.doi.org/10.1119/1.4947166

Chu, S. L., Angello, G., Quek, F., & Suarez, M. (2016). A systemic analysis of making in elementary schools. IEEE 16th International Conference on Advanced Learning Technologies. Austin, TX, United States of America, p. 478 – 482.

Dewey, J. Dewey, E. (1915). Schools of to-morrow. New York, New York. http://www.gutenberg.org/files/48906/48906-h/48906-h.htm

Moorefield-Lang, H. M. (2014). Makers in the library: case studies of 3D printers and maker spaces in library settings. Library Hi Tech, 32(4), 583–593. doi:10.1108/LHT-06-2014-0056

Schank, R.C., 1995. What we learn when we learn by doing.

Texas Education Agency, 2010, Chapter 112. Texas Essential Knowledge and Skills for Science Subchapter C. High School. Retrieved from http://ritter.tea.state.tx.us/rules/tac/chapter112/ch112c.html

Yazici, Y.E. and Töre, E., 2014. Learning by Doing in Architectural Education: From Urban Design to Architectural Design, Yenikapi-Inebey Case Study. *Egitim ve Bilim*, *39*(175).

AUTHOR INDEX